Introduction to Communication

Third Edition

Alexandre Sévigny
McMaster University

Kendall Hunt
publishing company

Kendall Hunt
publishing company

www.kendallhunt.com
Send all inquiries to:
4050 Westmark Drive
Dubuque, IA 52004-1840

Copyright © 2005, 2010, 2013 by Kendall Hunt Publishing Company

ISBN 978-1-4652-2343-2

Printed in Canada
10 9 8 7 6 5 4 3 2 1

Contents

Introduction

Dr. Alexandre Sévigny

McMaster University, Hamilton, Ontario

I began teaching communication studies in 2001, when I was hired out of my post-doctoral fellowship to be the first professor in the new communication studies program at McMaster University in Hamilton, Ontario. My first week was marked by the first great tragedy of the twenty-first century, when the World Trade Center was bombed and everything changed. Suddenly, the world seemed smaller and more interconnected. Cable news networks, cell phones, and e-mail gave us a sense of being there and participating in the events as they unfolded in New York City—a feeling that was only intensified by the advent of social media and ubiquitous mobile computing. Since that fateful September tragedy, change not only has accelerated, but the world that is emerging somehow feels more human and more comfortable than the world that is rapidly fading away.

The technologies of communication have always had a big impact on our society, culture, and business. The printing press ushered in a new age of knowledge sharing and standardization that culminated in the industrial revolution. Now social media, smartphones, and tablet technologies are binding us into a tightly knit network that doesn't so much resemble an orderly grid, as it does the heaving surges and flows of communication in a town square packed with people, awaiting an event. If anything, social media have turned everyday life into a series of transparent events, which capture the poetry of the everyday.

We have all heard the complaint that "no one wants to know what you had for lunch" and yet we share this information on Twitter and Facebook and we are inspired by it, wanting to meet the challenge posed by knowledge of what another has done. Indeed, social media have begun to transform our culture, politics, and economics. Our world is no longer as it was. Our world is no longer as even I—with my thirty-nine short years on this Earth—remember it to be.

My father often speaks wistfully of a rural Northern Ontario world that is long gone and mostly forgotten. I always thought that I would not be in his position: that the world I lived in was always vital and real and true, that it would persist and exist forever. It has not. The world I grew up in during the 1970s and 1980s is as remote to the digital natives of today as the world of my father's youth in the Northern bush camps was to me. Truthfully, we are in the beginnings of a move from the print and broadcast model of newspapers, book publishers, terrestrial radio stations, and broadcast television networks to an age of self-publishing and interpersonal sharing via social media. This change is a shift from a culture of gatekeepers, editors, and experts to a culture of storytellers, rhetoric, and persuasion. This means a move from understanding culture and business through the lens of mass communication theory toward thinking of mediated communication as a primarily interpersonal phenomenon.

While this might seem to many to be a largely academic distinction, having little bearing on the world of motion and action outside the university, in fact it is a phenomenally important distinction to begin to fathom. Mass communication privileged experts and gatekeepers. It had very high production values that demanded significant investment on the part of media companies to create content that was fit to print or broadcast. It was a world of hierarchy, rules, and constraint. That world is rapidly disappearing and being replaced by a place where the human voice, the story, and the village are of primary importance.

We are morphing into a society shaped and organized by the tenets of oral culture—fluid, chatty, emotional, and mistrustful of expertise and authority. Its rhythms are in tune with the flow of conversation, rather than segregated by the categories and boxes of print and broadcast culture. The operative skill, identified half a century ago by Marshall McLuhan, is pattern matching and fit. Statistics and probability reign in this world, while rigid logic fades. It is a world of relative and local understanding, not universalism. It is a world where people are motivated by principles rather than constrained by unenforceable rules.

I have refreshed this anthology to reflect this transformation. You will find more articles related to digital communication and how it is transforming the way we work and play. Moreover, digital communication has completely revolutionized the way we build and manage our relationships—in our intimate, business, and social lives.

Communication media changes very quickly and when it changes, it sends ripples through our society and culture, subtly changing the way we do business, the way we relate to one another, and the ways in which we reflect on our identities and sense of ourselves. These wide-ranging effects mean that the field of communication studies requires an interdisciplinary approach. Constructing theories of communication requires an understanding, not only of social and cultural theory, but also a background in sociolinguistics and psychology. As well, an up-to-date education in communication studies is not complete without exposure to new media, artificial intelligence, social media, and mobile computing. For example, when a communication researcher is looking at possible interpretations of an element of popular culture, it is necessary to examine how the cultural object was created, for whom, by whom, and by what means. Finding answers to these questions means studying the language used, asking questions about identity and behaviour, as well as how the viewer represents the network of associations triggered by the cultural object in his mind. As such, it can be argued that communication technologies and the messages they contain and send have a big role to play in shaping and colouring our perceptions of reality. Some questions that an interdisciplinary approach leads us to ask are:

- How do people interact with one another through social media? What does it do to their sense of self?
- Why is a cultural object produced at a particular time in history?
- How are print, television, and radio being transformed by the digital communication revolution?
- How is professional communication changing as a result of social media and mobile computing?
- What ideas and concepts are the viewing public being persuaded to believe? How do these ideas determine the potential happiness and prosperity of the citizen?

Communication researchers also examine how people communicate amongst themselves. This leads to questions such as the following:

- How do we understand the messages that others are sending us?
- How do humans operate in groups, in dyads (pairs of two), and in public speaking?
- That is, how do we perform in different settings?

Finally, communication researchers study the media: their economics, politics, institutions, and systems. Questions they might ask include:

- What are the political economics of the mainstream and social media and what are the deciding factors underlying them?
- Which institutions control distribution of messages transmitted over mass and social media and why do they have such power?
- How does government regulate the market for communication in Canada and the United States?
- How is access to information changing the lives of Canada's Native people?
- How is the information and communication technology revolution changing workplace conditions?
- How are Canada's politics being transformed by new waves of information and communication technologies as well as by advances in public affairs strategy?

This diverse set of questions requires knowledge from many different fields. To apprehend their meaning, it is useful to consider perspectives from history, linguistics, sociology, cultural studies, mass communication, cognitive psychology, anthropology, rhetoric, public relations, communications management, amongst many others.

This anthology is meant to provide the student with a bird's-eye view of the field of communication phenomena, from a strongly interdisciplinary perspective. It is a collection of original pieces from seminal and often controversial thinkers, whose work illustrates how various disciplines from the humanities as well as the social, cognitive, and commercial sciences have contributed to the formation and investigation of research questions about communication.

There is a long-standing debate regarding the relationship between socialization and nature. Underlying the approach taken in this anthology is the belief that a basic knowledge of how the mind works can help to shed light on questions of identity, politics, and the effects of discourse on our value systems. Society, culture, language, and cognition form a fruitful and fascinating continuum that can help us better understand ourselves, our society, and its politics as well as our diverse, interculturally-blended, and hybridized population. In fact, one of the guiding principles to bear in mind when reading these texts is that they take you on a journey inside and outside the body. Some of the articles address cognitive aspects of communication such as language, the mind, and perception. Others examine social and cultural facets of the phenomenon, focusing on identity, audience effects, labour conditions, and how our society is being transformed. The reason for this journey inside and outside the body is simple: communication is one of the most fundamental parts of being human and being human means having a body, a mind, and living in some sort of society. It would be wrong to neglect the body and its yearnings, pains, or limitations; the mind and its capacity to envision and represent whole new worlds; and society and its impact on the individual. I have tried to give students a set of readings in this book that weave together those threads into a tapestry that represents the richness of communication as an object of study. The following paragraphs provide a short journey through some of the research questions and controversies proposed to the reader of this book.

Minerva's Owl, by Harold Innis, a Canadian political economist and a foundational thinker in Communication Studies presents his theory of the interplay between communication technologies and the social, economic, and political development of nations. Innis's theory of media proposes that societies and technologies can be grouped into two categories: *time binding technologies* and *space binding technologies*. *Time-binding societies* are pre-literate, oral, and tribal. They emphasize continuity and rely on oral traditions to conserve practical, religious, or magical knowledge. As such, time-binding media are oral or handwritten, less transportable, harder to work with, and quite durable (e.g., stone tablets, papyrus). The flow of time in time-binding societies is circular and features a recurrent present. *Space-binding societies* are secular, materialistic, militarized, monetarized, and socially impersonal. Information is quantified and valued in these societies leading to space-binding media that are easy to work with, contain great quantities of information, are easy to transport but are less durable than time-binding media (e.g., newsprint, electronic media).

The next set of articles is by Marshall McLuhan, the Canadian father of communication theory who essentially described the effects and power of digital communications and social media fifty years before it existed. Although his philosophy is difficult to summarize, it can be said that he was more concerned with the effects that media have than on the specific programs or messages that they carry. McLuhan was greatly celebrated during the 1970s before fading into relative obscurity during the 1980s and early 1990s when the rising Marxist tide in cultural analysis perceived McLuhan as a wild-eyed prognosticator. The advent of the Internet and the explosion in electronic communication saw many of McLuhan's prophecies come true and soon he was once again a sober and clear-eyed analyst. McLuhan, like Innis, thought that the content of objects is less important than the fact that they exist in culture and society. He theorized that media can be classified into two types: *hot* and *cool media*. *Hot media* extend our senses in a high-definition fashion; they paint an explicit sensory picture for the recipient, thus not obliging us to tax our imaginations (e.g., unillus-trated printed copy). *Cool media* provide very little information, requiring the recipient to fill in the details by using imagination (e.g., comic books, impressionist paintings).

Steven Pinker's chapters introduce the ideas underlying Noam Chomsky's theory of universal grammar. Pinker explains and illustrates Chomsky's discovery that human languages have much more in common with one another than anyone had ever sus-pected before. In fact, he and other cognitive scien-tists noticed that children acquire human languages in much the same stages in every culture of the world. This observation, supported by many others, led Chomsky to propose that human beings are born with a universal grammar: a set of principles and parameters that constrain the type of human lan-guage that the child might eventually acquire. According to Pinker, language is complex and intri-cate and yet uniform across *all* of the Earth's human populations. Pinker's main point is his critique of the idea that language determines thought, that is to say that human beings cannot conceive of anything before they have expressed the concept or at least experienced it linguistically. Chiefly, he attacks the validity of the Sapir-Whorf Hypothesis that states that language and culture determine the human ability to conceive of reality.

While it may seem slightly idiosyncratic to include Alan Turing's article, *Computing Machinery and Intelligence*, in a communications anthology, there are very good reasons for doing so. While Turing is best known for having essentially initiated the field of computer science and for having cracked the Enigma code for the Allies during World War II, there is another, more subtle reason for students of communication to be interested in his work: his def-inition of intelligence. For Turing, intelligence was an interface condition—something that had to be present for actors to be able to communicate.

Turing's definition of intelligence is highly con-troversial, given that it rests upon the idea that the only way by which humans are convinced of the intelligence of an entity is if it convincingly approx-imates behaviours that we consider intelligent. This behaviourist and simulationist definition is limiting of human consciousness because it eliminates the need for an individual mind—rather, it moves the mind of the individual to a social level by saying that the necessary condition for intelligence is just to simulate intelligence enough to persuade the person you are talking to that you are intelligent.

All of the other readings in this book discuss in different ways how the tools that we use to commu-nicate shape the way we communicate and the way in which we frame our communication. Once this perceptual adjustment is made to a new technology, our entire sensory and cognitive perception of the world is altered slightly—shaped and coloured—by the means of communication. Thus our tools shape our thoughts, our culture, and our society. Should we allow an unexamined and reductionist definition of "intelligence as successful simulation," as Turing proposes, we may end up with machines that ape the lowest common denominator of human behaviour to "convince" us of their intelligence. This aping of the most simplified versions of human emotion, aes-thetics, sensory nuance, and psychological beliefs and desires can only lead to a reduction in the range and subtlety of what our society deems "intelligent" behaviours.

In *The Vital Paths*, Nicholas Carr illustrates the power of thinking and experience to rewire our brains. He details, in an accessible and fascinating fashion, how the concept of neuroplasticity explains the fact that our brain's very neurology is reshaped by what we think about. The idea of neuroplasticity supports the idea brought forward by Marshall McLuhan that new communication technologies amplify or deaden parts of our bodies. This means that media are actually affecting the biological makeup of our brains and bodies.

George Lakoff is a cognitive scientist and American liberal political consultant and analyst at the University of California at Berkeley. He was the founder of the Rockridge Institute, a now defunct liberal think tank. He began as a linguist but quickly discovered that underlying human communication and culture is a complex metaphorical system. For Lakoff, metaphor is a cognitive tool used by humans for thinking and perceiving; metaphors pervade our talk about our lives, bodies, and conception of space. As such, metaphor is not a purely linguistic human characteristic. Rather, metaphor governs the func-tioning of *most* of our everyday functions. Lakoff's theory of communication and cognition is based on a concept of an embodied mind, which means that the conceptual structure and mechanisms of rea-soning are shaped by input from the sensorimotor systems. As such, Lakoff argues that no metaphor can ever be comprehended or even adequately represented independently of its experiential basis. Lakoff has extended his theory of metaphor to enable us to engage in the scientific study of culture. He argues that the metaphors we live by don't necessarily hold in other cultures. Thus, if we study the set of metaphors used by people who belong to a certain culture, we will gain a very deep and useful understanding of the thoughts, beliefs, and desires underlying that culture.

Gustav Le Bon was a French social psychologist who put forward the first theory of crowd psychology. His work is important to examine from the point of view of communication theory because of the importance it has enjoyed in the development of the public relations and advertising industry. Central to Le Bon's theory of crowd psychology is the idea that when people join a crowd or mob, they give up a large part of their will and personality and accept the ideas of the crowd/mob as their own. According to Le Bon, people feel invincible in crowds, because of the feeling that they are a small, anonymous part of a larger entity. Many contemporary leftist researchers find Le Bon's work problematic, given the fact that he was a conservative who theorised largely in reaction to what he perceived as the threat posed by the potential of socialist revolution. A typical critique is that Le Bon never lists any of the good things that can be achieved by crowds and that he characterises any collective behaviour as a regressive step toward brutishness and the decline of civilisation. Another critique has to do with Le Bon's definition of the unconscious mind as primal and emotional versus the conscious mind which is intelligent, reasonable, and civilized. Many modern theorists find this definition reductive, driven by a Freudian model of how the human mind works.

Alia presents an analysis of the impact that communications technologies are having on the Canadian North, with a particular emphasis on their effects on aboriginal cultures and societies. She notes that northerners have always been early adopters of communications technologies but that the effects of this adoption have been a mixed blessing. Government investment has been sporadic, with periods of heavy subsidy and then periods of severe cutbacks and privatisations that jeopardize any gains made through past investment. Alia narrates the development of several important and successful aboriginal communications initiatives, such as Television Nothern Canada, Aboriginal People's Television Network, and Project Inukshuk. She also discusses how the Internet may or may not be a medium that helps reinforce aboriginal cultures and consensus-based forms of governing. The generally hopeful tone of her article is mitigated by the observation that Aboriginal Elders appear to have mixed opinions about the effects of the Internet: they specifically worry that it will, like television, become an assimilationist medium and thus accelerate the migration of technology-savvy aboriginal youth to southern Canada where they can find highly paid jobs using their newfound skills.

In *Cool Bodies: TV Ad Talk*, Gillespie presents us with a picture of the social life of South Asian youth in Southall, England. She claims that they are very sophisticated consumers of marketing messages delivered by American media for iconic products such as Coca Cola. Rather than being passive victims of imperialist American messages, these youths are savvy to the fact that the world painted in the American ads is not an accurate reflection of American life, but rather a palette of idealized images and scenarios of racial harmony, upward social mobility, affluence, empowered youth, freedom, and self-determination from which they can pick and choose ideas to construct their own identity. They consume and appropriate images and ideas from American culture to carve out an identity for themselves which would be: (a) separate from their parents' South Asian perspective, which they find oppressive; (b) separate from that of mainstream British culture that excludes and alienates them because of their ethnicity and lower socioeconomic status. Gillespie notes that "being cool" among South Asian youth in Southall means being open to new ideas, being cosmopolitan, and *individualistic*, i.e., being willing to engage with others, open toward divergent cultural experience, and searching for contrasts rather than uniformity. They are attracted by the utopian, mythical America presented in the ads, because they see it as a haven where they would not be constrained by automatic ethnic identification.

Convergence of ownership in media is a serious concern for those who believe that the free flow of information and opinion is necessary for the public to remain educated and aware about current affairs. Without this awareness, voters cannot make educated decisions when choosing who to vote for or which policy initiatives to support with their signatures or their donations. In *Printed Matter: Canadian Newspapers*, Christopher Dornan describes the evolution of convergence and corporate ownership in the Canadian newspaper industry, with the exception of the *National Post, Le Devoir,* and the *Globe and Mail,* Canada's newspapers are fundamentally local monopolies. He discusses the history and effects of corporate ownership on this unique industry and how it has had an impact on how Canadians are informed about the topics vital for maintaining a healthy democracy and an honest polity. He discusses the effect of advertising and examines a specific case of censorship that occurred within the CanWest Global family of newspapers that led to the resignation of Russell Mills, publisher of the *Ottawa Citizen*.

Christopher Lasch presents us with a populist critique of the media in *The Lost Art of Argument* and in *The Revolt of the Elites*. In the first article, he claims that the corporatization of media has destroyed genuine political debate. Lasch points out that the homogenizing influence of corporate media has led to the fact that the real agendas of politicians and political parties are not put to the test of public controversy. Rather, they are constructed in easy-to-follow, snappy slogans, designed by public relations experts to shape opinion in an insidious and almost sub-conscious fashion. In *The Revolt of the Elites*, Lasch examines a group that we are rarely asked to question: ourselves. He makes the point that since our economy has moved from industry to information, a new breed of elite has arisen: the symbolic analyst. Symbolic analysts are generally university-educated, highly mobile, and transient. Their jobs involve manipulating symbols (e.g., financial, academic, legal, or technology workers). They don't feel a strong connection to their country or city of residence and have almost nothing to do with the working-class people by whom they are surrounded; they feel more at home with symbolic analysts from other world capitals. Lasch observes that this disconnection between the classes of symbolic analysts and other workers is a serious problem for our democracy because the class of symbolic analysts looks down upon the remaining 70–80% of the population—thinking of them as nasty, brutish, and backward. What disturbs Lasch most is that the class of symbolic analysts holds almost all the keys to our political system and culture: they dominate science and technology, the financial industry as well as

government and communications. Lasch's argument is of particular importance to university students because they will form the next cohort of symbolic analysts for our society.

In *The Story Behind the Story,* Mark Bowden examines what happens when journalists are laid off in great numbers and there is a vacuum of commentary about current affairs, politics, and public life. He makes the case that the vacuum is filled by ideologues from both the Left and the Right who replace opinion with key message-driven pontification that aims only to garner ammunition for political, social, or commercial movements to advance their causes with an increasingly uninformed public. He laments the loss of great newspaper organizations and the decline of television news. He argues that "[t]he honest, disinterested voice of a true journalist carries an authority that no self-branded liberal or conservative can have," and makes the claim that journalism should not seek power but, rather, seek to uncover truth.

In *Are You Smarter than a Television Pundit*, Nate Silver, the expert statistician of "sabermetrics" fame, complements the Issenberg chapter by providing a guided tour of the world of television punditry and the statistics that pundits use to sound intelligent on television. He talks about the difference between two types of experts: *foxes*, who are adaptable generalists and *hedgehogs*, who are stalwart specialists. He also discusses the important distinction to be made between qualitative and quantitative data—making the important point that quantitative doesn't necessarily equal objective. This chapter demonstrates the importance of having a solid level of statistical literacy to work in the modern media and professional communications industries.

In *From the "Electronic Cottage" to the "Silicon Sweatshop": Social Implications of Telemediated Work in Canada*, Barbara Crow and Graham Longford describe how while information and communication technologies (ICTs) have generated enormous wealth for the happy few who invent, maintain, and market them, they have created a new class of distributed sweatshop where poorly educated people work in isolation at repetitive tasks, while sitting at their terminals in their basements, waiting for the next batch of jobs to be wired to them via e-mail. Crow and Longford claim that dystopic state-of-affairs has terrible effects on workers' emotional well-being, the suburban environment, as well as the potential for social mobility. They conclude by saying that governments must move to regulate the ICT industries and create standards and that the only reason this hasn't happened yet is that technology has completely revolutionized the workplace over the last fifteen years and that social scientific and government studies are only now catching up.

Dwight Conquergood, in *Performance Studies: Interventions and Radical Research,* makes the case for radical, engaged research into creative endeavours as evidence of different sorts of knowledge. He claims that the post-colonial world is criss-crossed by transnational narratives, diaspora affiliations, and the movements and migrations of people, either economically motivated or politically coerced. Migrant people have constructed narratives of identity that have defined them and their position within the larger social hierarchy. Conquergood makes the point that, to understand the cultures and societies of subjugated peoples, the researcher must travel between two different domains of knowledge:

- the official, objective, and abstract one—the map of knowledge—*knowing what*;
- the practical, embodied, and popular one—the story—*knowing who, when,* and *how*.

The academic world has traditionally privileged empirical analysis and scholarly critical analysis that leads to *knowing what*, a disembodied way of knowing that disqualifies other ways of knowing such as embodied experience and oral culture. These dominant forms of knowledge are not attuned to finding meanings that are masked, camouflaged, indirect, embedded, or hidden in context. Performance researchers observe these sorts of knowledge by *being engaged* with the people they are studying. *Being in solidarity* with them makes *proximity* an important feature of the research. Conquergood puts forward the idea that performance studies bring a rare hybridity into the academic world: the study of works of imagination using a rigourous and practical method while intervening to help improve conditions for one's research subjects.

Finally, Ted Sorensen takes on a nostalgic journey through his memories of his time as the closest advisor to John F. Kennedy. He discusses the role of a senior communications and policy counselor, demonstrating the power of the communicator as the conscience and relationship builder for an organization. He discusses the power that a communications advisor can have in the upper reaches of government, but what Sorensen describes is easily applied to the world of corporate communications or the not-for-profit world. What we see through Sorensen's work is that being a professional communicator is a role that often goes uncelebrated, but which is crucial to the success of an organization.

Thus ends our whirlwind tour of the articles contained in this anthology. They present a uniquely interdisciplinary set of perspectives on media and communication, and their effect on language, society, culture, politics, and mind. The world of communication is large and expanding very quickly. Studying its social, cultural, cognitive, and political impact is probably one of the most exciting and useful academic pursuits for the student who wishes to understand why our interpersonal relationships, society, culture, and politics are the way they are today.

A final note. Since I have finished writing this introduction on my father, Georges Sévigny's birthday, I would like to dedicate this book to him. A visionary intellect, teacher, and profoundly religious and principled man, he is the reason that I have chosen this profession and have the wide-ranging set of interests that have helped me bring these diverse readings to you. I aspire to one day reach the bar he has set for being ethical, helping others, thinking through complex problems, and really just being human.

Alex Sévigny
Ancaster, Ontario
May 12, 2013

A Reflection on the Evolution of the Field of Professional Communication

Alex Sévigny* and Terence (Terry) Flynn

Key Words

Professional Communication
Public Relations
Promotionalism
Communication Metrics
Journalism

Abstract

This editorial describes the birth of the Journal of Professional Communication (JPC). It discusses how four fields—public relations, promotionalism (including advertising and advocacy), communication metrics and journalism—appear to be converging into a blended profession, which requires an increasingly similar set of skills and faces many common ethical questions. The authors describe how the advent of social media and a return to oral culture, predicted by Marshall McLuhan, has heralded this convergence. JPC's conception is also discussed: an interdisciplinary venue for practitioners, academics, artists, professional researchers, journalists and policy makers to explore this emerging convergence, exchange ideas and debate current and historic issues in and across their diverse fields.

This journal was born of a conversation between two professional communicators—one who had spent the greater part of his working life as a public relations consultant and the other who had devoted most of his life to research and teaching. The conversation ranged from politics and journalism to public relations and advertising, from education to evaluation. As the hours passed, one point recurred consistently: the interests of professional communicators who practice and teach those disciplines are converging rapidly. We discussed the challenges of communicating in the complex, frenetic environment we now live and work in, where new technologies stimulate all our senses, imbuing much of what we hear, see, smell, taste and touch with communicative intent. We debated whether the radical changes in our information-overloaded society were causing the divided fields of communications to converge or simply collaborate. In the end, we agreed that this discussion required further dialogue and deliberation with others, in Academe, policy circles and in the communications industries.

Thus was born the concept of a hybrid, peer-reviewed journal where professional communicators, academics, artists, students and policy makers could have an open and ongoing discussion about the evolving interests of the many fields that fall

*Corresponding author. (Alex Sévigny)
From *Journal of Professional Communication, Volume 1, Issue 1* by Alex Sevigny, Terence Flynn. Copyright © 2011 by Journal of Professional Communication. Reprinted by permission.

under the umbrella of professional communication. Whether you work in corporate communications, not-for-profits, a political office, government relations, the media, communications management, publishing, journalism, advertising, communication and opinion measurement, or any other area where professional communication is practiced, you may have felt that change is in the air.

During the last two decades, we have witnessed and experienced the blurring of lines between public relations, promotionalism and advocacy (including advertising or marketing communications), traditional and citizen journalism, and communication, audience and opinion measurement. This change goes beyond simple integration of tactics, strategies and platforms. It eclipses who manages and controls communications within organizations. In essence it is a fundamental shift away from a traditional form of controlled communications to an era of self-determined, on-demand, user-centric content co-creation.

The culture and context of professional communication is changing at both an alarming and exhilarating rate. Traditional forms of communication have been supplemented by the speed and reach of new social media outlets. Communicating in this turbulent environment has never been easier and yet never presented more complex problems for the management of reputation and the resolution of crises. The processes of creation, distribution and re-distribution of content are becoming effortless, as the traditional walls and gates of control have begun to fall. Some might argue that this new era has seen communicative power wrestled out of the hands of the media and organizational elites, to rest in keyboards at the fingertips of individuals and community groups. Others will argue that while we have witnessed an increasing level of influence through individual action, powerful media and corporate elites still have the ability and resources to control the channels and technology of communication, which shape collective and individual imagination and consciousness.

Professional communicators, policy makers and scholars are trying to make sense of this new media-saturated era with its rapidly multiplying media and technologies. From the "old" technologies of email and websites to the new realms of social media, geolocation and participatory culture, communicators are searching for more meaningful forums of en-gagement with their publics. At the same time, newer technologies and platforms are being launched and adopted by evangelists of information and communication technology, creating uncertainty, anxiety and imbalance. In fact, each revolutionary new communication technology causes a change in who controls the flow of information through communication.

Recipients and consumers of communication are also finding it difficult to cope with the ocean of information in which their minds and senses are bathed. Indeed, an important question to ask is how this growing list of technologies and tools is reshaping the human condition itself. How is society making sense of the concepts of self, culture and social life within these new conditions? How are people receiving and processing this tidal wave of information and what impact will it have on how professional communicators engage with them in the future? How are artists, designers and video game makers responding to this new reality? How is the world of sound and music, made so pervasive by the iPod, creating meaningful experiences and helping to interpret the deluge of information that is upon us? These questions are fundamental to the future of communication in Canada and around the world. This journal was founded to explore these questions from the point of view of professional communication.

Our Culture is Shifting from Text to Talk

Marshall McLuhan, the great Canadian theorist of communication and culture, spent much of his prolific career developing the theory that electronic technology is moving our culture away from the linear strictures of print toward the open and multifaceted world of oral culture. What this means is a fundamental shift in the way that messages are communicated, truths are established, and our perceptions of the world are organized.

Linear culture was strongly rule-bound and constrained by the requirements of the printed word. Once a word is printed on paper, there is a long-term record of that word. The opinions the word expresses are locked in perpetuity. Most of our communications to one another, up to the advent of the World Wide Web and social media, were done in print. With the arrival of these digital communication technologies, however, our culture started to undergo a radical shift. It lurched away from the order and structure of print, toward the shifting sands of oral communication.

The first shift, from paper to digital, meant that our communication could be changed and altered at will. No longer was it so terribly onerous to revise a news story or an essay once it was produced. Rather, we faced writing that behaved more like conversation. The story would change as events unfolded, as though spoken by a town crier instead of a scribe. As Google News creator, Krishna Bharat has stated:

> Why is it that a thousand people come up with approximately the same reading of matters? Why couldn't there be five readings? And meanwhile use that energy to observe something else, equally important, that is currently being neglected (Fallows, 2010).

This comment suggests that how the news is produced, consumed and interpreted has changed in a digital world. Rather than being a cumulative compendium of solid ideas, where one news article builds upon another, news becomes a cacophonous and conformist space. Now, while the effects of this are having a powerful impact on how the news is created and written up, it is also indicative of a larger tendency in the culture.

The movement from print to oral culture means that rhetoric and influence are regaining some of the power they lost with the shift to print. In fact, the concept of persuasion through strategic, well-crafted and pleasing expression appears to be becoming more important for gaining power and influence in society. This means that the professional communicator is becoming a key part of any common effort in business, social life, politics and popular culture. The profession must reconsider how it defines itself, and in particular how it defines its boundaries and relationships to neighbouring professions. As well, it must define its relationship to the concept of influence, which seems to be rapidly becoming a serious currency in the oral culture that we are developing.

Another great thinker—also a Canadian—Harold Innis, made a powerful point, developing the idea through his life's work that new communication technologies create struggles not only between groups of people, but also between different types of ideas. What types of ideas will be central to the oral culture currently emerging?

Following the initial communications revolution introduced by the World Wide Web, we have seen the evolution of social media, which has in turn created a suite of new information appliances such as tablet computers with audio and video capabilities built-in. At first, social media technologies were largely print-based, with the prevalence of easily manipulated blogging systems such as Wordpress and Blogger, and microblogging services such as Twitter, but this appears to be a transitional moment.

It appears, however, that this reliance on print is just a way station in the social media journey that lies before us. The transformation of social media from print to oral culture is gathering speed, with the evolution of social video and audio. In a few short years, the trend toward social video sharing via Twitter and other such services will grow, and the balance of content shared via social media will hit a tipping point, shifting from text to talk. Next generation blogging platforms such as Tumblr presage this turning of the tide, as do the efforts to promote a more organized and structured means of video sharing by Apple Inc. and Google through their respective social media commerce platforms and information appliances, such as the iPad or the Android tablet. Social networking technologies are quickly moving from privileging the linear word and the still image to favouring video and audio. The video hangouts that Google+ offers, which accommodate up to 10 participants at once, are an example of this trend. This emerging state of affairs announces a new world of conversational media, in which spoken culture and the moving image replace print and paper as the predominant media for exchanging our stories. The emphasis in this developing world of social media will be on mobility, cloud computing, the developing HTML5 standard, and device-specific internet applications. Being able to understand, criticize and strategically deploy all of these emerging phenomena will soon be at the core of professional communication practice.

The Pillars of Professional Communication: Four Professions in Evolution

The emergent massively networked society is creating a heaving sea for those professions that have traditionally been the guardians of image, message and opinion. Many fear being swept under by the waves of change and seek to navigate to calmer waters and eventually to safe harbour. To ensure the success of that journey, practitioners, policy makers and academics need to explore how the component fields of professional communication might evolve or converge to better understand and anticipate their interconnected future. What is this new and emerging field of professional communication and who falls under this umbrella?

The individual fields of communication are being transformed by changes in technology and in our culture. As social media draws us away from print and more deeply into conversation, the walls between the professions of communication have been crumbling. Journalism, promotionalism, communication measurement and public relations/public affairs are converging, forcing the modern practitioner to understand the emergent rules and norms that bridge the four fields. This demands common theoretical reasoning and ethical frameworks that pose the best practices as well as the moral hazards that exist in the grey areas between the fields.

It is at this nexus that the interdisciplinary field of professional communication exists. Recognizing common theoretical underpinnings and skill sets that stem from an understanding of: how people relate to one another, how governments communicate, how persuasion, influence and rhetoric operate, how communicative effects and impacts can be measured, and how relationships between journalists and other communicators are being renegotiated in this emerging new professional context. The question that unites these ideas is how, within a critical perspective, the practice of professional communication affects society, commerce, culture and the individual.

First, let us consider the field of communication, opinion, media and audience measurement. As our society moves from paper to digital and from print to oral culture, measurement will be more readily available and in demand. Evolving computational linguistic models of semantic and natural language understanding will provide the tools to parse and study online content, in text, video or audio forms. Communication measurement experts will provide more and more spectacular, real-time interactive visualizations of the evolving landscape—contemporary and historical—of public opinion, attitudes

and beliefs. The centrality of metrics and data visualization to public relations, advertising, advocacy and journalism in a digital world will mean that professional communicators will have to have a certain level of numeracy and critical awareness of research methods to be successful. This also means that the field of measurement and data visualization will be an integral part of the larger ethical, theoretical and practical discussions emerging to form the field of professional communication.

Next, let us reflect on the field of public relations and its many sibling fields such as public affairs, communications management and strategic communications, whose theory is shaped and guided by the research conducted in the measurement industry. Traditionally, these interconnected fields define the function of how organizations communicate with their publics. Today, due to emerging and rapidly mutating social media, the questions of how organizations communicate internally and how they relate to the world have become much more complex. This complexity means that communication is rapidly becoming centrally important within organizations, as success in the court of public opinion is becoming a core requirement for the achievement of other strategic objectives. In short, communicators are finding themselves at the decision-making table. Academically, these fields will be integrated into the interdisciplinary field of professional communication, the study of which will be similar to what legal education is to the practice of law—a training ground that produces experts in techniques of establishing, building and maintaining relationships through a rapidly moving kaleidoscope of interconnected media.

Third, let us discuss the field of promotionalism, that is to say the area that encompasses advertising, advocacy and marketing communication, which will find itself integrated into the realm of professional communication, as its role in creating tools and products that aid in persuasion and relationship-building becomes more pronounced, and its new media tools become more ubiquitous, accessible and easily used to produce professional-looking communication products. Knowledge of the theory and practice of promotionalism will be a core competency of the professional communicator. As such, it must be part of the critical, theoretical and ethical conversation within an integrated field of professional communication.

Finally, it is impossible to ignore how journalism is being transformed, as an always-on mediascape pushes the limits of how much content can be created and made available to audiences. The lines between journalism and public relations are blurring more and more. This is an unavoidable consequence of the mashing together of communication channels and the democratization of publishing through electronic media. In a world where the average citizen trusts opinions from "people like me" more than those of experts, the role of the journalist is being transformed. Increasingly, journalism is being produced "inhouse," a trend which is drawing the practice of journalism closer to the other practices of professional communication. The example of the *News of the World* telephone hacking scandal that led to the demise of the United Kingdom's largest-selling daily demonstrates how moving the line between journalism and public relations will necessitate a larger ethical and definitional discussion. This discussion should happen under the aegis of the emerging interdisciplinary field of professional communication.

The future of the field is definitely interdisciplinary. The questions that must be answered require education, training and accreditation, perhaps even licensing and regulation, much as law societies impose the bar exam and an articling period. In fact, this is not a new debate for professional communicators. Edward L. Bernays spent the latter part of his life struggling to have the field of public relations regulated in much the same way as law or accounting is regulated in the United States. In the United Kingdom, the field of public relations has become a chartered profession, governed by the Chartered Institute for Public Relations, which has recently decided to extend membership to professionals practicing the other fields of professional communication. The need to have this debate is growing more pressing as the convergence among the fields comprising professional communications accelerates and the organizational importance of professional communication practitioners grows. Another pressing reason concerns social media: the social media profile of an organization is a function that affects the whole organization, including the highest levels of decision-making. This emerging state of affairs necessitates an integrated perspective on professional communication, which transcends the boundaries of the individual disciplines.

Emergence of Academic Programs

The field of professional communication has evolved slowly and incrementally in Canada over the last sixty years. The emergence and growth of mass communication courses and programs, including journalism, public relations and promotion, at Carleton, Ryerson, University of Western Ontario and Laval universities in the 1950s and 1960s foreshadowed the beginning of professional, university-based study and training at post-secondary institutions across Canada. The development of these programs has historically been measured, however, today students at almost all colleges and universities have the ability to enroll in communication courses in a diverse range of disciplinary programs at both the undergraduate and graduate levels. While universities and colleges are struggling to cope with the growing demand for post-secondary education, scholars and academic administrators are reporting a rapidly growing interest in the fields of professional communication. For example, to meet this demand, in the last year alone, three new Bachelor of Public Relations programs have been approved and introduced in Ontario at both Conestoga College and Humber College, and at the University of Ottawa. This is in addition to the forty-four collegiate and university programs that teach public relations in Canada. At the same time, new undergraduate programs in journalism have been launched across Canada increasing the number of college and university or joint programs to nearly fifty.

At the same time, new professionally focused graduate programs have been launched to meet the increasing needs of working professionals whose workplace demands require further instruction, training and research on new communication methodologies, skills and theories. Programs such as the Master of Communications Management at McMaster University, the Master of Public Relations at Mount St. Vincent University and the Master of Professional Communication at Royal Roads University all provide professional communicators with an opportunity to obtain advanced degrees while continuing their careers. One of the intended outcomes of these new graduate programs is an increase in high-quality empirical research, conducted by these students as part of their programs. This new research will expand our understanding and knowledge of these fields from both theoretical and practical perspectives.

The challenge for most of these graduate students and their professors is to find appropriate professional and academic venues in Canada to present and publish their research. The annual conferences of the Canadian Communication Association and the Canadian Public Relations Society only recently engaged the professional communication academic community by highlighting professional and academic research tracks in their conferences. The same applies to the *Canadian Journal of Communication*, which has very successfully focused on critical and theoretical approaches to communication research. It cannot be debated that presenting scholarly research is an important component of knowledge dissemination and fundamental to the growth and development of an emerging field. Currently, there exists a void in Canadian communications research for an interdisciplinary, peer-reviewed, scholarly journal that encourages both critical and administrative discussion, deliberation and debate about the converging issues in professional communication theory, policy and practice.

Where Does JPC Fit In?

The *Journal of Professional Communication* was created to start this dialogue. As its diverse editorial advisory board demonstrates, JPC aims to provide a forum for the varied fields of communications to meet, share ideas and exchange opinions. JPC's contents will be varied and eclectic, reflecting the interdisciplinary nature of both the study and practice of professional communication. JPC will publish op-eds, scholarly articles, policy documents, white papers, provocations and book reviews, all of which are represented in this inaugural issue.

It is also the wish to emphasize that the JPC is not exclusively a scholarly journal, but rather one that aims to put academics in fruitful dialogue with practitioners and policy makers. The make-up of this first issue, we think, reflects that aim, including contributions from practitioners, seasoned academics and students. We also feature a policy document, "Pathways to the Profession," which was produced by the National Council on Education of the Canadian Public Relations Society (CPRS) and is reproduced here by permission of CPRS, on a one-time

license of content. This issue of the JPC is inclusive. We hope that this encourages practitioners, creative professionals, journalists, policy makers, academics and any other invested parties to contribute in the future, so that the emerging field of professional communication has an evolving venue within which to try out new ideas, report on successes and debate pitfalls as we all face an uncharted future of convergence and interdisciplinarity.

Overview of the Articles In This Issue

Putting this first issue of the JPC together has been a voyage of discovery. We started by making a general call at the Canadian Public Relations Society meeting in Regina in June of 2010, and also through word-of-mouth. We received thirty submissions of scholarly manuscripts, case studies and book reviews. Of these we have published five scholarly articles, one case study and five book reviews. In addition, we include one guest lecture by James and Larissa Grunig, five op-eds from practitioners in the various fields of professional communication, and an historic education policy document from the Canadian Public Relations Society.

We have a range of op-eds in this issue, covering topics of interest to all professional communicators. In "Open Data: 'There's an App for That'," Joey Coleman discusses how the open data movement is transforming how governments communicate information about how they work. He makes the provocative claim that open data will challenge how journalists and other professional communicators do their work. David Estok, in "Paywalls," discusses how the paywall may be a necessary part of the future financial viability of the news media. In "Polling in Election 2011," Nik Nanos discusses the effects and value of polling in elections, using the case of how his firm, Nanos Research, tracked voter attitudes and opinion as an example. Rikia Saddy brings a critical perspective on the social and political impact of social media communications in "Social Media Revolutions." She explains how power and fear should be replaced by more altruistic principles in marketing and public relations, to activate people's hopeful imaginations rather than scaring them into action. Finally, David Scholz, in "The Several Premature Autopsies of AVE," explains, through his own professional experiences, that it is time for him to stop using advertising value equivalence as a metric for measuring campaign success.

We are very pleased to present a lecture by those eminent and foundational scholars of public relations, James and Larissa Grunig. We publish in this issue the text of "The Third Annual Grunig Lecture Series: Public Relations Excellence 2010," which they delivered in New York City. The lecture is a reflection on the growing influence and importance of the study of relationships within the public relations profession.

This issue of the JPC offers five fully peer-reviewed scholarly articles, all of which have undergone strict double-blind peer review. Jeremy Berry discusses the importance of writing to the practice of professional communication in "US-Canada Study of PR Writing By Entry-Level Practitioners Reveals Significant Supervisor Dissatisfaction." He forcefully makes the case that there is not enough of a focus on writing in professional communication college and university programs. Denise Brunsdon, in "The Gendered Engagement of Canada's National Affairs & Legislative Elite, Online," discusses how women in politics and national affairs blog and use Twitter differently from men. Her data suggest that there still exists a gender divide in the emerging arena of online communications. In a French-language article, « L'utilisation du Marketing Politique par les Groupes D'intérêt: Proposition d'un Modèle Théorique, » Émilie Foster presents a model for political marketing that recognizes the important and unique role of special interest groups. Andrew Laing takes us into the realm of media measurement and crisis communication in his article, "The H1N1 Crisis: Roles Played by Government Communicators, Media and the Public." He presents a content analysis suggesting that the public, the media and government communicators all bore a share of the responsibility for the response to the SARS vaccination crisis. Finally, Philip Savage & Sarah Marinelli explore the gendered nature of the op-ed page in Canadian newspapers in "Sticking to Their Knitting? A Content Analysis of Gender in Canadian Newspaper Op-Eds." They present evidence of a significant gender divide that exists in Canada's op-ed pages, demonstrating that this divide between men and women transcends editorial choice, extending into the arena of perceived credibility and the level of willingness to take risks. We also feature one full-length, peer-reviewed case study by Heather Pullen, in the vital and developing area of health communications: "Eastern Health: A Case Study on the Need for Public Trust in Health Care Communications."

This issue presents five reviews of books. Alan Chumley reviews *Measure What Matters: Online Tools for Understanding Customers, Social Media, Engagement and Key Relationships* by Katie Delahaye Paine, while Rebecca Edgar presents a critical perspective on *Putting the Public Back in Public Relations* by Brian Solis & Deirdre Breakenridge, and Laurence Mussio presents a very thoughtful perspective on how information and communication technologies are changing our cognitive capacities in his review of *The Shallows* by Nicholas Carr. Lars Wessman presents a provocative review of three works discussing the impact of the internet and digital communication on our culture in a comparative review of: *The Net Delusion: The Dark Side of Internet Freedom* by Evgeny Morozov, *You Are Not a Gadget: A Manifesto* by Jaron Lanier and *Digital Barbarism* by Mark Helprin. Finally, Lauren Yaksich discusses how globalization is affecting professional communication in her review of *The Global Brand* by Nigel Hollis.

To round out this issue, we publish, under special permission of the Canadian Public Relations Society, "Pathways to the Profession," the first thorough characterization of education and training leading to the practice of public relations in Canada.

Our Invitation to You

This issue is large for a reason: it presents a multiplicity of perspectives on the professions of communication. Featured are op-eds, book reviews, scholarly articles, a case study, a policy document, and a guest lecture by two foundational communications scholars. For future editions we encourage you to submit interviews with communication professionals, short informal case studies, squibs, and professional profiles.

It is an important and exciting time to create this new forum for deliberation, and debate among communicators, researchers and teachers in order to advance our knowledge and understanding of the challenges and opportunities that face our unique disciplines.

As such, this journal is meant, certainly, to be a repository of peer-reviewed analysis, knowledge and critique. However, it is also meant to be an arena for opinion, debate, policy discussion, provocation and perhaps even a little storytelling of personal narratives and the histories of those who may have marked us. It is our collective journal, shared among our diverse communities of academics, practitioners, policy makers and artists. You are warmly invited and encouraged to contribute and be heard.

A Note of Thanks

This journal could not have been founded without the support and encouragement of several important friends and colleagues. First and foremost, we would like to thank our generous Dean of Humanities, Suzanne Crosta, who has supported this endeavour since its conception, both materially and through her constant mentorship and encouragement. Great thanks to Jeff Trzeciak, McMaster's chief librarian, whose investment in the BePress digital journal publishing technology made possible the creation of a freely available, open access journal. We would also like to recognize research assistants Morgan Harper and Natalie St. Clair, who both contributed to JPC in its earliest days. A tip of the hat is due to our two proofreaders, Christine Larabie and Dwayne Ali, who kept a watchful eye on the formatting and page layout, catching errors and suggesting improvements. Thanks also to Parker David Martin, who designed JPC's cover layout and art, and to Jonathan Cadle of BePress who provided patient advice on how to use our digital commons electronic publishing engine. Of course, we would be remiss if we did not thank our team of associate editors and our editorial advisory board, whose support is invaluable to JPC's success. A huge thank you to Shelagh Hartford, our tireless assistant editor, whose dedication and passion for detail in reading, editing and APA formatting has made this issue both elegant and readable. Finally, a note of special appreciation for all of our anonymous peer reviewers: without your volunteer support it would be impossible for the machinery of open academic publishing to function on a lean budget.

References

Fallows, J. (2010, June). *How to save the news.* The Atlantic. Retrieved from http://www.theatlantic.com/magazine

Minerva's Owl[1]

Harold Innis

"Minerva's OWL begins its flight only in the gathering dusk . . ." Hegel wrote in reference to the crystallization of culture achieved in major classical writings in the period that saw the decline and fall of Grecian civilization. The richness of that culture, its uniqueness, and its influence on the history of the West suggest that the flight began not only for the dusk of Grecian civilization but also for the civilization of the West.

I have attempted to suggest that Western civilization has been profoundly influenced by communication and that marked changes in communications have had important implications. Briefly this address is divided into the following periods in relation to media of communication: clay, the stylus, and cuneiform script from the beginnings of civilization in Mesopotamia; papyrus, the brush, and hieroglyphics and hieratic to the Graeco-Roman period, and the reed pen and the alphabet to the retreat of the Empire from the west; parchment and the pen to the tenth century or the dark ages; and overlapping with paper, the latter becoming more important with the invention of printing; paper and the brush in China, and paper and the pen in Europe before the invention of printing or the Renaissance; paper and the printing press under handicraft methods to the beginning of the nineteenth century, or from the Reformation to the French Revolution; paper produced by machinery and the application of power to the printing press since the beginning of the nineteenth century to paper manufactured from wood in the second half of the century; celluloid in the growth of the cinema; and finally the radio in the second quarter of the present century. In each period I have attempted to trace the implications of the media of communication for the character of knowledge and to suggest that a monopoly or an oligopoly of knowledge is built up to the point that equilibrium is disturbed.

An oral tradition[2] implies freshness and elasticity but students of anthropology have pointed to the binding character of custom in primitive cultures. A complex system of writing becomes the possession of a special class and tends to support aristocracies. A simple flexible system of writing admits of adaptation to the vernacular but slowness of adaptation facilitates monopolies of knowledge and hierarchies. Reading in contrast with writing implies a passive recognition of the power of writing. Inventions in communication compel realignments in the monopoly or the oligopoly of knowledge. A

---

[1]Presidential Address to the Royal Society of Canada, 1947.

[2]"Communications and Archaeology," *Canadian Journal of Economics and Political Science,* XVII, May, 1951, 237–40.

---

monopoly of knowledge incidental to specialized skill in writing which weakens contact with the vernacular will eventually be broken down by force. In the words of Hume: "As force is always on the side of the governed, the governors have nothing to support them but opinion. It is, therefore, on opinion that government is founded; and this maxim extends to the most despotic and the most military governments as well as to the most free and most popular." The relation of monopolies of knowledge to organized force is evident in the political and military histories of civilization. An interest in learning assumes a stable society in which organized force is sufficiently powerful to provide sustained protection. Concentration on learning implies a written tradition and introduces monopolistic elements in culture which are followed by rigidities and involve lack of contact with the oral tradition and the vernacular. "Perhaps in a very real sense, a great institution is the tomb of the founder." "Most organizations appear as bodies founded for the painless extinction of ideas of the founders." "To the founder of a school, everything may be forgiven, except his school."[3] This change is accompanied by a weakening of the relations between organized force and the vernacular and collapse in the face of technological change which has taken place in marginal regions which have escaped the influence of a monopoly of knowledge. On the capture of Athens by the Goths in 267 A.D. they are reported to have said, "Let us leave the Greeks these books for they make them so effeminate and unwarlike."

With a weakening of protection of organized force, scholars put forth greater efforts and in a sense the flowering of the culture comes before its collapse. Minerva's owl begins its flight in the gathering dusk not only from classical Greece but in turn from Alexandria, from Rome, from Constantinople, from the republican cities of Italy, from France, from Holland, and from Germany. It has been said of the Byzantine Empire that "on the eve of her definite ruin, all Hellas was reassembling her intellectual energy to throw a last splendid glow."[4] ". . . the perishing Empire of the fourteenth and fifteenth centuries,

especially the city of Constantinople, was a centre of ardent culture, both intellectual and artistic."[5] In the regions to which Minerva's owl takes flight the success of organized force may permit a new enthusiasm and an intense flowering of culture incidental to the migration of scholars engaged in Herculean efforts in a declining civilization to a new area with possibilities of protection. The success of organized force is dependent on an effective combination of the oral tradition and the vernacular in public opinion with technology and science. An organized public opinion following the success of force becomes receptive to cultural importation.

Burckhardt has stated: "It may be, too, that those great works of art had to perish in order that later art might create in freedom. For instance, if, in the fifteenth century, vast numbers of well-preserved Greek sculptures and paintings had been discovered, Leonardo, Raphael, Titian and Correggio would not have done their work, while they could, in their own way, sustain the comparison with what had been inherited from Rome. And if, after the middle of the eighteenth century, in the enthusiastic revival of philological and antiquarian studies, the lost Greek lyric poets had suddenly been rediscovered, they might well have blighted the full flowering of German poetry. It is true that, after some decades, the mass of rediscovered ancient poetry would have become assimilated with it, but the decisive moment of bloom, which never returns in its full prime, would have been irretrievably past. But enough had survived in the fifteenth century for art, and in the eighteenth for poetry, to be stimulated and not stifled."[6] David Hume wrote that "when the arts and sciences come to perfection in any state, from that moment they naturally, or rather necessarily decline, and seldom or never revive in that nation, where they formerly flourished. . . . Perhaps it may not be for the advantage of any nation to have the arts imported from their neighbours in too great perfection. This extinguishes emulation and sinks the ardour of the generous youth."[7]

Dependence on clay in the valleys of the Euphrates and the Tigris involved a special technique in writing and a special type of instrument, the reed

---

[3]Albert Guérard, *Literature and Society* (Boston, 1935), p. 286.

[4]Cited by A. A. Vasiliev, *History of the Byzantine Empire,* II, "University of Wisconsin Studies in the Social Sciences and History," no. 14 (Madison, 1929), p. 401.

[5]Ibid, p. 400.

[6]Jacob Burckhardt, *Force and Freedom* (New York, 1943), pp. 368–9.

[7]David Hume, *Essays, Moral, Political and Literary,* ed. T. H. Green and T. H. Grose (London, 1875), I, 195–6.

stylus. Cuneiform writing on clay involved an elaborate skill, intensive training, and concentration of durable records. The temples with their priesthoods became the centres of cities. Invasions of force based on new techniques chiefly centring around the horse, first in the chariot and later in cavalry, brought the union of city states, but a culture based on intensive training in writing rendered centralized control unstable and gave organized religion an enormous influence. Law emerged to restrain the influence of force and of religion. The influence of religion in the Babylonian and Assyrian empires was evident also in the development of astronomy, astrology, and a belief in fate, in the seven-day week, and in our sexagesimal time system. Successful imperial organization came with the dominance of force represented by the Pharaoh in Egypt though the Egyptian Empire depended on cuneiform for its communications. It was followed by the Assyrian, the Persian, the Alexandrian, and the Roman empires.

While political organization of oriental empires followed the Egyptian model, religious organization was powerfully influenced by Babylonia as was evident in the traditions of the Hebrews in the marginal territory of Palestine. With access to more convenient media such as parchment and papyrus and to a more efficient alphabet the Hebrew prophets gave a stimulus to the oral and the written tradition which persisted in the scriptures, the Jewish, Christian, and Mohammedan religions. Written scriptures assumed greater accessibility and escaped from the burdens of the temples of Babylonian and Assyrian empires.

The Egyptians with an abundance of papyrus and the use of the brush had worked out an elaborate system of writing and the Babylonians with dependence on clay and the stylus had developed an economical system of writing. Semitic peoples borrowed the Sumerian system of writing but retained their language and in turn improved the system of writing through contacts with the Egyptians. The Phoenicians as a marginal Semitic people with an interest in communication and trade on the Mediterranean improved the alphabet to the point that separate consonants were isolated in relation to sounds. The Greeks took over the alphabet and made it a flexible instrument suited to the demands of a flexible oral tradition by the creation of words. The flowering of the oral tradition was seen in provision for public recitations in the Panathenaea of the *Iliad* and the *Odyssey* and in the birth of tragedy after 500 B.C.

An intense and sustained interest in Greek civilization by a wide range of scholars has pointed to numerous factors leading to its cultural flowering. Ionian culture reflected the contact of a vigorous race with the earlier rich Minoan civilization and the emergence of a potent oral tradition. This tradition absorbed and improved the instruments of a written tradition built up on the opposite side of the Mediterranean. Toynbee has emphasized the limitations of migration across bodies of water and the significance of those limitations to cultural borrowing.

In the written tradition the improved alphabet made possible the expression of fine distinctions and light shades of meaning. Opening of Egyptian ports to the Greeks in 670 B.C. and establishment of Naucratis about 650 B.C. made papyrus more accessible. The burst of Greek lyric poetry in the seventh century has been attributed to the spread of cheap papyrus. Werner Jaeger has shown the significance of prose to law and the city state. The flexibility of law shown in the major reforms centring around the names of Draco, Solon, and Cleisthenes was possible before a written tradition had become firmly entrenched. Written codes not only implied uniformity, justice, and a belief in laws but also an element of rigidity and necessity for revolution and drastic change. No effective device was developed to facilitate the constant shifting power and as in present-day Russia ostracism was essential. Laws weakened the interest in punishment in another world for those who escaped justice in this. Solon reflected the demands of an oral tradition for flexibility by providing for the constitution of judicial courts from the people, and Cleisthenes gave the whole body of citizens a decisive part in the conduct of human affairs. Political science became the highest of the practical sciences. Political freedom was accompanied by economical freedom particularly with the spread in the use of coins after 700 B.C. To quote Mirabeau: "The two greatest inventions of the human mind are writing and money—the common language of intelligence and the common language of self-interest."

Encroachment from the centralized empires of the east through the Persians led to the flight of Ionians, who had inherited to the fullest degree the legacies of earlier civilizations, from Miletus, and to an interest in science and philosophy in Athens. Ionians developed the great idea of the universal rule of law, separated science from theology, and rescued Greece from the tyranny of religion. The self was detached from the external object. With this came limitations reinforced by an interest in music and geometry which implied concern with form and measure, proportion and number in which relations between things in themselves were neglected. But in spite of this neglect an appeal to atomism and science had been made and through this Europeans worked themselves out of the formal patterns of the Orient. The Ionian alphabet was adopted in Athens in 404–3 B.C. suggesting the demands of the city for greater standardization in writing. Prose was brought to perfection by the middle of the fourth century and Plato sponsored its supremacy by ruling out the poets and by his own writing. When Athens became the centre of the federation in 454 B.C. the way was opened to greater flexibility in law notably through the contributions of orators to the improvement of prose from 420 to 320 B.C. By 430 a reading public had emerged in Athens and Herodotus turned his recitations into book form. The spread of writing checked the growth of myth and made the Greeks sceptical of their gods. Hecataeus of Miletus could say, "I write as I deem true, for the traditions of the Greeks seem to me manifold and laughable" and Xenophanes that "if horses or oxen had heads and could draw or make statues, horses would represent forms of the gods like horses, oxen like oxen." Rapid expansion in the variety and volume of secular literature became a check to organized priesthood and ritual.

Socrates protested against the materialistic drift of physical science and shifted from a search for beginnings to a search for ends. Concentrating on human life he discovered the soul. Absolute autocracy of the soul implied self-rule. Virtue is knowledge. "No one errs willingly." After the fall of Athens and the death of Socrates, Plato turned from the state. Socrates had been profoundly influenced by the advance of medical science but Plato gave little attention to experimental science. Collapse of the city state and of religion attached to the city state was followed by conscious individualism. The results were evident in complexity, diversity, and perfection in a wide range of cultural achievements. The significance of the oral tradition was shown in the position of the assembly, the rise of democracy, the drama, the dialogues of Plato, and the speeches including the funeral speech of Pericles in the writings of Thucydides. Hegel wrote regarding Pericles: "Of all that is great for humanity the greatest thing is to dominate the wills of men who have wills of their own." The Greeks produced the one entirely original literature of Europe. The epic and the lyric supported the drama. Democracy brought the comedy of Aristophanes. Poetics and the drama had a collective purgative effect on society but with decline of the stage, oratory and rhetoric reflected the influence of an individual.

The oral tradition emphasized memory and training. We have no history of conversation or of the oral tradition except as they are revealed darkly through the written or the printed word. The drama reflected the power of the oral tradition but its flowering for only a short period in Greece and in England illustrates its difficulties. A simplified and flexible alphabet and the spread of writing and reading emphasized logic and consequently general agreement. The spread of writing widened the base by which the screening of ability could take place. The feudal hierarchy of Greece was weakened by an emphasis on writing which became a type of intelligence test. A writing age was essentially an egoistic age. Absorption of energies in mastering the technique of writing left little possibility for considering implications of the technique.

Richness of the oral tradition made for a flexible civilization but not a civilization which could be disciplined to the point of effective political unity. The city state proved inadequate in the field of international affairs. Consequently it yielded to force in the hands of the Macedonians though the genius of Greek civilization was again evident in the masterly conquests of Alexander. The heavy infantry of Greece and the navy were no match for the light infantry and cavalry which struck from the rear. The first of the great sledge-hammer blows of technology in which force and the vernacular hammered monopolies of knowledge into malleable form had been delivered. The Alexandrian Empire and the Hellenistic kingdoms favoured the organization of Alexandria as the cultural centre of the Mediterranean.

Aristotle bridged the gap between the city state and the Alexandrian Empire. He rejected the dualism of Plato and affirmed the absolute monarchy of the mind. He marked the change "from the oral instruction to the habit of reading." The immortal inconclusiveness of Plato was no longer possible with the emphasis on writing. It has been said that taught law is tough law; so taught philosophy is tough philosophy. The mixture of the oral and the written traditions in the writings of Plato enabled him to dominate the history of the West. Aristotle's interest in aesthetics reflected a change which brought the dilettante, taste, respectability, collectomania, and large libraries. As an imperial centre Alexandria emphasized the written tradition in libraries and museums. The scholar became concerned with the conservation and clarification of the treasures of a civilization which had passed. Minerva's owl was in full flight. Other imperial centres such as Pergamum (197–159 B.C.) became rivals in the development of libraries and in the use of parchment rather than papyrus. The period had arrived when a great book was regarded as a great evil. Books were written for those who had read all existing books and were scarcely intelligible to those who had not. Literature was divorced from life. In the words of Gilbert Murray, Homer in the Alexandrian period came under "the fatal glamour of false knowledge diffused by the printed text." Alexandria broke the link between science and philosophy. The library was an imperial instrument to offset the influence of Egyptian priesthood. Greek advances in mathematics were consolidated and the work of Aristotle as the great biologist extended.

Writing with a simplified alphabet checked the power of custom of an oral tradition but implied a decline in the power of expression and the creation of grooves which determined the channels of thought of readers and later writers. The cumbersome character of the papyrus roll and its lack of durability facilitated revision and restricted the influence of writing at least until libraries were organized under an imperial system. Greece had the advantage of a strong oral tradition and concentration on a single language. With the strong patriarchal structure of European peoples she resisted the power on the one hand of the Babylonian priesthood and goddesses and on the other of the Egyptian monarchy as reflected in the pyramids.

As the Greeks had absorbed an earlier culture and adapted it to their language so the Latins absorbed Etruscan culture. The absorptive capacity of language was significant in the history of Greece, Rome, and England. The contact of language with an earlier developed culture without its complete submergence implied an escape from the more subtle aspects of that culture. It facilitated the rise of philosophy and science in Greece in contrast with religion. The civilization of Greece emphasized unity of approach but Rome absorbed rhetoric and excluded science. In the East, Persian and Arabic literature excluded the influence of Greek literature but absorbed science. Pervasiveness of language becomes a powerful factor in the mobilization of force particularly as a vehicle for the diffusion of opinion among all classes. Language exposed to major incursions became more flexible, facilitated movement between classes, favoured the diffusion of technology, and made for rapid adjustment.

Roman force supported the extension of the Republic to Carthage and Corinth in 146 B.C. and was followed in turn by the Hellenistic cultural invasion of Rome. Inclusion of Egypt in her possessions widened the gap by which Eastern influences penetrated Rome. Greek literature collected and edited in Alexandria had its impact on Rome. Roman literature was "over-powered by the extremely isolated and internally perfect Greek literature." Greek became a learned language and smothered the possibilities of Latin. Access to supplies of papyrus brought the growth of libraries, and of offices of administration. Hellenistic civilization warped the development of Rome toward an emphasis on force, administration, and law. While Cicero contributed to the perfection of Latin prose he followed the model set up by Isocrates. As the Empire followed the Republic, restrictions were imposed on the senate and on the oral tradition. Disappearance of political activity through censorship meant the increased importance of law and rhetoric. The literature of knowledge was divorced from the literature of form which eventually became panegyric. Oratory and history were subordinated to the state, the theatre was displaced by gladiatorial games. "It was jurisprudence, and jurisprudence only which stood in the place of poetry and history, of philosophy and science."[8] Interest in Greek in Rome halted literature and accentuated the interest in the codification of law.

The spread of militarism implied an emphasis on territorial rather than personal interests. It meant individual self-assertion and the temporary overthrow of customary restraints. Blood relationship and the dominance of the group over the individual were not suited to the military efficiency of the Roman legion. The extent of the Roman Empire in contrast with the city state necessitated written law as a means of restraining the demands of force. The rise of a professional legal class particularly with the decline of the

---

[8]H. S. Maine, *Ancient Law* (London, 1906), p. 352.

Republic and the senate, and the separation of judicial power from legislative and executive powers, were marked by systematic development of law which weakened the power of *patria potestas*. Force and law weakened the patriarchal system. Family relations were created artificially, a development concerning which Maine wrote that there was "none to which I conceive mankind to be more deeply indebted." Legal obligation was separated from religious duty. The contract was developed from the conveyance and as a pact plus an obligation was, again in the words of Maine, "the most beautiful monument to the sagacity of Roman jurisconsults." Written testimony and written instruments displaced the cumbersome ceremonies of the oral tradition. It has been said of Roman law that the indestructibility of matter is as nothing compared to the indestructibility of mind. While Roman law was flexible in relation to the demands of Mediterranean trade and in the hands of the bar and the lecturers rather than the bench it began to harden under the influence of Greek scholars and commentators and eventually was subjected to elaborate codes. "It is only when people begin to want water that they think of making reservoirs, and it was observed that the laws of Rome were never reduced into a system till its virtue and taste had perished."[9] Papyrus and the roll limited the possibilities of codification of Roman law.

The increasing rigidity of law and the increasing influence of the East shown in the emergence of the absolute emperor opened the way to the penetration of Eastern religions. The political animal of Aristotle became the individual of Alexander. Roman architecture, Roman roads, and Roman law enhanced the attraction, accessibility, and prestige of Rome. The Alexandrian tradition of science and learning implied not only a study of the classics of Greece but also a study and translation of the Hebrew scriptures. Hebraic literature had arisen among a people who had been trampled over by the armies of oriental empires and exposed during periods of captivity to the influence notably of Persian religion with its conceptions of immortality and of the devil. The law and the prophets had been incorporated in holy scriptures. Under the influence of monotheism writings had become sacred. The written bible assumed monotheism, doctrine, and priesthood. "No book, no doctrine, no doctrine, no book" (De Quincey). Pagan cultures lacked the act of thanksgiving and the act of confession. Greece and Rome as polytheistic cultures had supported an empire. Bibles were not suited to empires. Greek philosophy was represented by the teacher and Eastern religions by the priests and the prophets. "Thus saith the Lord." Zeno the Stoic had introduced the latter note into Greek philosophy and its influence was evident in the absorption of Stoicism in Roman law. "The exile of the Jews and the defeat of Greece brought Christianity and Stoicism. All great idealisms appear to spring from the soil of materialistic defeat."[10]

The development of the Empire and Roman law reflected the need for institutions to meet the rise of individualism and cosmopolitanism which followed the breakdown of the polis and the city state. The Roman Empire opened the way to a rich growth of associations and the spread of religious cults. Organized religion emerged to prevent the sense of unity implied in Greek civilization. A relatively inflexible alphabet such as Hebrew and limited facilities for communication narrowed the problem of education to a small highly-trained group or special class. Its capacities were evident in the literary achievements of the Old Testament. The dangers became apparent in the difficulty of maintaining contact with changes in the oral language. The people spoke Aramaic and Hebrew became a learned language. Christianity was saved from being a Jewish sect by the necessity of appealing to the spoken Greek language. "It is written . . . , but I say unto you." The New Testament was written in colloquial Greek.

Christianity exploited the advantages of a new technique and the use of a new material. Parchment in the codex replaced papyrus in the roll. The parchment codex was more durable, more compact, and more easily consulted for reference. The four Gospels and the Acts could be placed in four distinct rolls or a single codex. Convenience for reference strengthened the position of the codex in the use of the scriptures or of codes of law. The codex with durability of parchment and ease of consultation emphasized size and authority in the book. Verse and prose which had been read aloud and in company to the third and fourth centuries declined. Reading without moving of the lips introduced a taste and

---

[9]Thomas Constable, *Archibald Constable and His Literary Correspondents* (Edinburgh, 1823), I, 261.

[10]R. T. Flewelling, *The Survival of Western Culture* (New York, 1943), p. 26.

style of its own. The ancient world troubled about sounds, the modern world about thoughts. Egoism replaced an interest in the group. A gospel corpus of powerful coherent pamphlets written in the Greek vernacular had emerged as the basis of the New Testament by 125 A.D. and with the Old Testament constituted a large volume which became a dominant centre of interest in learning.

Pressure from the barbarians to the north led to a search for a more secure capital than Rome, to the selection of Constantinople in 330 A.D., and to the fall of Rome in 410 A.D. The court had cut itself off from the centre of legal development and turned to organized religion as a new basis of support. Christianity based on the book, the Old and New Testaments, absorbed or drove out other religions such as Mithraism and lent itself to cooperation with the state. In the East the oriental concept of empire developed in Egypt, Babylonia, Assyria, and Persia was restored. In the West law tempered the influence of Christianity and in the East particularly after the Justinian codes the influence of the absolute emperor. To quote Maine again: "It is precisely because the influence of jurisprudence begins to be powerful that the foundation of Constantinople and the subsequent separation of the western empire from the eastern are epochs in philosophical history." "Of the subjects which have whetted the intellectual appetite of the moderns, there is scarcely one, except physics, which has not been filtered through Roman jurisprudence."[11] Unequal to Greek metaphysical literature the Latin language took it over with little question. The problem of free will and necessity emerged with Roman law.

The Roman Empire failed to master the divisive effects of the Greek and Latin languages. Inability to absorb Greek culture was evident in movement of the capital to Constantinople and the tenacity of Greek language and culture supported the Byzantine Empire to 1453. Greek disappeared in Rome under pressure from the vernacular as did Latin in Constantinople. The alphabet had proved too flexible and too adaptable to language. Language proved tougher than force and the history of the West was in part an adaptation of force to language. The richness of Greek civilization, the balance between religion, law, and emperor which characterized the Byzantine

Empire, enabled it to withstand the effects of new developments in the application of force.

William Ridgeway has shown the significance of the crossing of the light Libyan horse with the stocky Asiatic horse in the development of an animal sufficiently strong to carry armed men, and in turn, of the cavalry. Charles Oman has described the defeat of the Emperor Valens at Adrianople in 378 A.D. by heavy Gothic cavalry, the reorganization of the armies of the Byzantine Empire, the defeat of the barbarians following that reorganization, and the movement of the barbarians, successfully resisted in the East, to the conquest of the West. Dependence on roads in the Roman Empire, as in the Persian Empire, facilitated administration and invasion. In the West in the face of barbarian encroachment the hierarchy of the Roman Empire became to an important extent the hierarchy of the church. Monarchy in the Eastern empire was paralleled by monarchy in the Western papacy. In the East the position of the emperor and his control over the state were followed by religious division and heresy whereas in the West the position of the papacy was followed by political division.

Ecclesiastical division in the East weakened political power in that heresies reinforced by regionalism brought the loss of Egypt and other parts of the Byzantine Empire to the Mohammedans. With the fanaticism of a new religion based on a book, the Koran, with polygamy, with the opening of new territory to crowded peoples, and with the division of Christendom, Mohammedanism spread to the east and to the west. Defeated at Constantinople in 677 its followers concentrated on the West until they were halted by Charles Martel in 732. Again following Ridgeway, the heavier cross-bred horses of the Franks defeated the lighter cavalry of the Mohammedans. Military pressure from Spain brought the growth of centralization which culminated in Charlemagne and the rise of the German emperors. "Without Islam the Frankish Empire would probably never have existed and Charlemagne, without Mahomet, would be inconceivable" (Pirenne). In 800 the Byzantine Empire was ruled by an empress, Irene, and the emphasis on the male line in the West strengthened the position of Charlemagne, crowned by the papacy. A new empire in the West was followed by the Carolingian renaissance.

The position of the emperor in the East led to a clash with monasticism, the iconoclastic controversy,

---

[11]Maine, *Ancient Law,* pp. 351-2.

and separation of the Eastern from the Western church. In the West monasticism with little check accentuated the influence of celibacy and of Latin in the church. In the East monasticism was brought under control but in the West it strengthened its position to the point that political history has been powerfully influenced by the struggle between church and state to the present century. The power of monasticism in the West was enhanced by the monopoly of knowledge which followed the cutting-off of supplies of papyrus from Egypt by the Mohammedans. "The Mediterranean had been a Roman Iake; it now became, for the most part, a Muslim lake" (Pirenne). In the East the last of the schools of Athens were closed by Justinian in 529 and new centres of learning were established in Constantinople, but in the West an interest in classical studies was discouraged by the monastic tradition of learning which began in Italy. Monasteries concentrated on the scriptures and the writings of the Fathers. The classics were superseded by the scriptures. The blotting-out of the learning of Spain by the Mohammedans and restricted interest in learning in Europe meant that the most distant area of Europe, namely Ireland, alone remained enthusiastic for knowledge and from here an interest in learning spread backwards to Scotland and England and to Europe. Alcuin was brought from the north of England to strengthen the position of learning under Charlemagne. A renewed interest in learning brought an improvement of writing in the appearance of the Carolingian minuscule. Its efficiency was evident in a spread throughout Europe, in ultimate supremacy over the Beneventan script in the south of Italy, and a supply of models for the modern alphabet.

The spread of learning from the British Isles to the Continent preceded the invasions of the Scandinavians to the north. Pressure from this direction was evident in the emergence of the duchy of Normandy in 911 and the reorganization of European defence. By the eleventh century the invasions of the Vikings and the Magyars had left cavalry and the feudal knights in supremacy. The cultural tenacity of language was shown in the conquest of the conquered, the adoption of the French language in Normandy and eventually of the English language in England by the Normans. Military reorganization in Europe, the ascendancy of the papacy, and the break between the Eastern and the Western church in 1054 were followed by the Crusades, the Norman conquest of Apulia and Sicily after 1061, and of England in 1066, and the driving of the Moors out of Spain. The energies of the West were turned against the Mohammedans in the Holy Land and against the schismatic church of the Byzantine Empire. The capture of Constantinople in 1204 was the beginning of the end of the eastern Roman Empire.

Decline in the use of papyrus particularly after the spread of Mohammedanism necessitated the use of parchment. The codex was suited to the large book whether it was the Roman law or the Hebrew scriptures. In the Byzantine Empire successive codifications of Roman law were undertaken. Caesaropapism and the iconoclastic controversy assumed control over the church by the emperor. In the West the law of the barbarians was personal and the church emphasized the scriptures and the writings of the Fathers. With the Greeks virtue is knowledge, particularly the knowledge that we know nothing, and with the Hebrew prophets, perhaps in protest against the monopoly of knowledge held by the scribes of Egypt and Babylonia, knowledge is evil. The emphasis on the authority of the scriptures and the writings of the Fathers in the West was supplemented by ceremonial and by allegorical writings. The metre of classical poetry was replaced by accent and rhyme. Reading assumed submission to authority.

But long before the influence of Grecian culture was being filtered through Persian and Arabian civilization in the south to Spain, Sicily, and Europe. The process was hastened by a new medium, namely paper, from China. The invention of the manufacture of paper from textiles in China in the early part of the second century A.D., the adaptation of the brush used in painting to writing, and the manufacture of ink from lamp black marked the beginnings of a written tradition and a learned class. In the Chinese language the pictograph survived though most of the characters were phonetic. With a limited number of words, about 1,500, it was used with extraordinary skill to serve as a medium for a great diversity of spoken languages. But its complexity emphasized the importance of a learned class, the limited influence of public opinion, and the persistence of political and religious institutions. The importance of Confucianism and the classics and worship of the written word led to the invention of devices for accurate reproduction. Neglect of the masses hastened the spread of Buddhism and the development of a system for rapid reduplication, particularly of charms. Buddhism spread from India where the oral tradition of the Brahmins flourished at the expense of the written tradition and proved singularly adaptable to the demands of an illiterate population. Printing emerged from the demands of Buddhism in its appeal to the masses and of Confucianism with its interest in the classics, the literature of the learned. Complexity of the characters necessitated the development of block printing and reproduction of the classics depended on large-scale state support. The first printed book has been dated 868 A.D. Severe limitations on public opinion involved a long series of disturbances in the overthrow of dynasties and in conquest by the Mongols but the tenacity of an oral tradition gave enormous strength to Chinese institutions and to scholars.

Expansion of Mohammedanism and the capture of Turkestan by the Arabs in 751 were followed by the introduction of paper to the West. It was manufactured in Baghdad and its introduction corresponded with the literary splendour of the reign of Haroun-al-Raschid (786–809). It was used in Egypt by the middle of the ninth century, spread rapidly in the tenth century, declined sharply in the eleventh century, and was produced in Spain in the twelfth century, and in Italy in the thirteenth century. By the end of the fourteenth century the price of paper in Italy had declined to one-sixth the price of parchment. Linen rags were its chief cheap raw material. In the words of Henry Hallam, paper introduced "a revolution . . . of high importance, without which the art of writing would have been much less practised, and the invention of printing less serviceable to mankind. . . ." It "permitted the old costly material by which thought was transmitted to be superseded by a universal substance which was to facilitate the diffusion of the works of human intelligence." With a monopoly of papyrus and paper the Mohammedans supported an interest in libraries and in the transmission of Greek classics, particularly Aristotle and science. Prohibition of images in the Mohammedan religion facilitated an emphasis on learning. From libraries in Spain a knowledge of Aristotle spread to Europe and became important to the works of Albertus Magnus and St. Thomas Aquinas. Arabic numerals, and a knowledge of mathematics and astronomy, of science and medicine found their way through Sicily and Spain to Europe. Writing developed beyond monastic walls and in the twelfth century numerous attacks were made on ecclesiastical corruption. Werner Sombart has empha-

sized the importance of Arabic numerals to the spread of exact calculations, the growth of business, and the commercial revolution from 1275 to 1325. Cursive handwriting emerged in the thirteenth century. Expansion of commerce favoured the growth of lay schools and closing of the monasteries to secular students increased the importance of cathedral schools and universities. The rural interest of the monasteries was succeeded by the urban interest of the university. Knowledge of architecture imported from Constantinople and adaptation of buildings to northern conditions led to the wave of construction of Gothic cathedrals from 1150 to 1250. With the cathedral came an improvement in various arts such as stained glass and counterpoint music. The University of Paris was started about 1170 and as a master's university its model was followed in later institutions.

The spread of paper from China hastened the growth of commerce in Italy and northern Europe. It supported an increase in writing beyond the bounds of the monasteries. It was a medium for the spread of Greek science through Mohammedan territory and of Arabic numerals and more efficient calculation into Europe. Aristotle became accessible through Arabic and attempts to reconcile his writings with the scriptures were evident in the work of Maimonides and St. Thomas Aquinas. Universities emerged in cathedral centres and supported an interest in the oral tradition, dialectic, and scholasticism. The Byzantine Empire disappeared as a balance between papacy and empire and left them to destroy each other. The papacy became more involved in problems of territorial rights. As a result of the Babylonian captivity in Avignon it incurred the antagonism of England. The papacy was no longer able to check the spread of translations of the scriptures in the vernacular, and the spread of Roman law from the Byzantine Empire strengthened the new monarchies in France and England. Concentration on the vernacular produced a new and powerful literature.

Commercial activity in Italy assumed a renewed interest in law. The barbarian invasions had meant an emphasis on personal law and through this Roman law persisted in a modified form. At the beginning of the twelfth century there emerged at Bologna an intensified interest in the study of Roman law and the student type of university. Weakening of the Byzantine Empire was followed by the struggle between church and empire in the West and the latter seized upon Roman law as a powerful instrument with which to reinforce the position of the emperor. Its influence spread in Italy and in southern France and was evident in the development of canon law in the church. "The worst corruption of the middle ages lay in the transformation of the sacerdotal hierarchy into a hierarchy of lawyers" (Hastings Rashdall). In the words of Frederic Harrison: "The peculiar, indispensable service of Byzantine literature was the preservation of the language, philology, and archaeology of Greece." But it had perhaps no influence in any field greater than in that of Roman law.

The strength of the church in the north where the traditions of Roman municipalities and Roman law were weak was shown in the University of Paris. In France and particularly in England the weakness of the written tradition favoured the position of custom and the common law. Law was found, not made, and the implications were evident in the jury system, the King's Court, common law, and parliament. In England, law and religion were not fortified by universities since these were not located at the capital or in cathedral cities. Law and religion were responsive to the demands of an oral tradition. The flexibility of the English language as a result of the invasion of successive languages from Europe made for common law, parliamentary institutions, and trade. In Scotland the universities were typically urban and, located in large cities, became the basis for the rich development in philosophy in the eighteenth century. The variety of types of university and geographical isolation provided the background for the diversity of interest which characterized the intellectual activity of Europe. The increasing strength of the vernaculars weakened the position of the University of Paris. The Franciscans in Oxford revived an interest in Plato in contrast with the Dominican interest in Aristotle in Paris. The councils of the church became ineffectual and the monarchy of the papacy became more absolute. The supremacy of celibacy favoured the concentration of power in Rome, prevented the establishment of ecclesiastical dynasties, and facilitated constant appeal to intellectual capacity. Concentration of power in Rome hastened the development of the Gallican church.

In Europe the rise of commerce, of cities, and of universities brought conflict between monasticism and the secular clergy, and between the church and the state particularly in the control over education.

Introduction of paper and the spread of writing hastened the growth of the vernacular and the decline of Latin. Control of the church was inadequate to check the oral tradition, and the spread of heresies which followed the growth of trade and the weakening of the Byzantine Empire. But the church undertook its first counter-reformation. In a letter of 1199 Innocent III frowned on translations of the scriptures, writing that "the secret mysteries of the faith ought not therefore to be explained to all men in all places." Translation and lay reading of the New Testament by the Waldensians, and the rise of romantic poetry in Provence probably under the influence of the Mohammedans and the Byzantine Empire, were ruthlessly stamped out. Establishment of new orders, the Dominicans and the Franciscans, and of the Inquisition was designed to check the spread of heresy incidental to the emergence of translations in the vernacular and of oral discussions in universities. The new courts of Europe were strengthened by the lawyers and writers in the vernacular. Dante wrote that "a man's proper vernacular is nearest unto him as much as it is more closely united to him, for it is singly and alone in his mind before any other." "Since we do not find that anyone before us has treated of the science of the Vulgar Tongue, while, in fact, we see that this tongue is highly necessary for all, inasmuch as not only men, but even women and children strive, in so far as Nature allows them, to acquire it . . . we will endeavour by the aid of the Wisdom which breathes from Heaven to be of service to the speech of the common people."[12] The power of the vernacular was evident in the growth of nationalism and the rise of universities particularly in Germany. Wycliffe's translation of the Lollard Bible and his influence on Huss in Bohemia pointed to the breaking of the power of the church on the outer fringes of Europe. Opposed to the influence of the University of Paris and its interest in councils the papacy favoured the establishment of universities in Germany and in Spain. The republican cities of Italy, particularly Venice and Florence, prospered with the decline of Byzantine commerce and the Hohenstaufen court. The migration of Greek scholars from the East con-

---

[12]Dante in *De vulgari eloquentia;* cited in Vernon Hall, Jr., *Renaissance Literary Criticism* (New York, 1945), pp. 16–17.

tributed to an intense interest in classical civilization. Florence became a second Athens in its concern for letters and the arts. Learning had been banked down in the Byzantine Empire and broke out into new flames in the Italian Renaissance. The vitality of the classics of Greece which reflected the power of civilization based on an oral tradition gradually weakened the monopoly of knowledge held by the church. "Nothing moves in the modern world that is not Greek in its origin" (Maine).

As the prejudice against paper as a product of Jews and Arabs had been broken down with the spread of commerce the position of parchment as a medium for the scriptures and the classics was enhanced. The product of the copyist and the miniaturist increased in value. The monopoly of the manuscript and its high value intensified an interest in the development of a technique of reproduction in areas in which the copyist had limited control, namely in Germany. The use of oil in painting and its extension to ink, the development of an alloy which could be melted at low temperatures and remained consistent in size with changes in temperature, the growth of skill in cutting punches, the invention of an adjustable type mould, and the adaptation of the press were brought into a unified system as a basis for printing. Production of a large volume such as the Bible assumed concentration of capital on a substantial scale and a continued output of books. Limited transportation facilities and a limited market for books hastened the migration of printers particularly to Italy, a region with abundant supplies of paper, a commodity adapted to the printing press. Migration to new markets compelled the adoption of new types. The Gothic black-letter type which characterized German printing was replaced by the Roman type in Italy. Resistance of copyists delayed the spread of printing in France, but the delay possibly facilitated artistic development in French type. The demands of the press for manuscripts and the necessity of creating new markets favoured extension to the production of the classics in Greek, the use of more compact type for smaller portable volumes in italic, and the emphasis on the vernacular. The technique of printing crossed the water of the English Channel and Caxton with a concern for the market concentrated on English and avoided the depressed market for books in the classical languages.

An enormous increase in production and variety of books and incessant search for markets hastened the rise of the publisher, an emphasis on commerce at the expense of the printer, and a neglect of craftsmanship. As the supply of manuscripts in parchment which had been built up over centuries had been made available by printing, writers in the vernacular were gradually trained to produce material. But they were scarcely competent to produce large books and were compelled to write controversial pamphlets which could be produced quickly and carried over wide areas, and had a rapid turnover. The publisher was concerned with profits. The flexibility of the European alphabet and the limited number of distinct characters, capable of innumerable combinations, facilitated the development of numerous printing plants and the mobilization of a market for a commodity which could be adapted to a variety of consumers. Knowledge was not only diversified, it was designed by the publisher to widen its own market notably in the use of advertising.

The monopoly position of the Bible and the Latin language in the church was destroyed by the press and in its place there developed a widespread market for the Bible in the vernacular and a concern with its literal interpretation. To quote Jefferson, "The printers can never leave us in a state of perfect rest and union of opinion." In the words of Victor Hugo the book destroyed the "ancient Gothic genius, that sun which sets behind the gigantic press of Mayence." Architecture which for six thousand years had been "the great handwriting of the human race" was no longer supreme. It was significant that printing spread most rapidly in those regions in Europe in which the cathedral was not dominant and in which political division was most conspicuous—in Italy and in Germany. In Italy, with its access to Constantinople, emphasis had been given to the classics; in Germany emphasis was given first to bulky theological volumes and in turn, with the shift of the industry to Leipzig, to the small polemical publications which characterized the writings of Luther and his successors of the Reformation and to the Bible in High German dialect. "The growth and surprising progress of this bold sect [Lutherans] may justly in part be ascribed to the late invention of printing and revival of learning." "The books of Luther and his sectaries, full of vehemence, declamation and rude eloquence were propagated more quickly and in greater numbers." (Hume.) "One of the first effects of printing was to make proud men look upon learning as disgraced by being brought within reach of the common people" (Southey).

As in the paper revolution the church was compelled to mobilize its resources in counter-attack, notably in the Council of Trent and the establishment of the Jesuit order. In Italy the power of law and of the church and division among the republics checked the spread of the Reformation and produced Machiavelli. He wrote: "We Italians then owe to the church of Rome and to her priests our having become irreligious and bad; but we owe her a still greater debt, and that will be the cause of our ruin namely, that the church has kept and still keeps our country divided." In France the restricted influence of Greek and the supremacy of Latin favoured an outburst of literary activity in the vernacular in Montaigne and Rabelais. With the suppression of Protestantism Estienne and Calvin fled to Geneva and by the end of the sixteenth century the great scholars of France left for Holland. In Germany political division laid the basis for the bitter religious wars of the seventeenth century. The arguments of William of Occam and of Wycliffe had gained in England with the decline of Italian financiers. Weakness of the church, of monasticism, and of the universities enabled the crown to break with the papacy. The rise of the printing industry had its implication in technological unemployment shown in part in the decline of monasticism.

The failure of the Counter-Reformation reflected the influence of force. The growth of industrialism, the interest in science and mathematics, and the rise of cities had their effects in the use of gunpowder and artillery. The application of artillery in destroying the defences of Constantinople in 1453 was spectacular evidence of the decline of cavalry and systems of defence which had characterized feudalism. The instruments of attack became more powerful than those of defence and decentralization began to give way to centralization. The limitations of cavalry had been evident in the mountainous region of Switzerland and the low country of the Netherlands and in the success of movements toward independence in those regions. The military genius of Cromwell and of Gustavus Adolphus in using new instruments of warfare guaranteed the position of Protestantism in England and Germany.

A revolution in finance accompanied change in the character of force. In Italy independent republics had continued the traditions of Rome in the emphasis on municipal institutions. The importance of defence in construction of city walls necessitated development of municipal credit and responsibility of citizens for the debt of a corporate entity. In the struggle of the Netherlands against Spain the principle was extended and the republic became an instrument of credit. In England the ultimate supremacy of parliament in 1689 meant further elaboration, and recognition of the role of public debts was shown in the establishment of the Bank of England in 1694. Extension of the principle of corporate entity from Roman law eventually clashed with the traditions of common law in the revolt of the American colonies in the eighteenth century. The growth of public credit increased the importance of information, of organized news services, and of opinion. Organized exchanges emerged in Antwerp, in Amsterdam, and in London. The importance of opinion in relation to finance accentuated the significance of the vernacular.

The effects of the Counter-Reformation in France were shown in the suppression of printing, the massacre of St. Bartholomew in 1572, and finally in the revocation of the Edict of Nantes in 1685. Suppression of printing in response to ecclesiastical demands was accompanied by an interest in the increased production and export of paper by the state. As a result of this conflict between restriction of consumption and increase of production and exports, cheaper supplies were available in the Netherlands, Geneva, and countries in which printing remained free. From these marginal areas printed material was smuggled back into France. Freedom of the press in marginal free countries was supported by repression in France. In the eighteenth century evasion of censorship was shown in the preparation and printing of the *Encyclopaedia*, and the writings of Voltaire and Rousseau.

Abolition of the monasteries and celibacy in the Church of England, the reform of education in the first half of the sixteenth century, and censorship of the press in the second half of the century had their effects in the flowering of the drama in the plays of Shakespeare. Weakening of the monarchy under the Stuarts was accompanied by the publication of the King James version of the Bible and the prose of Milton and the sharp decline of the theatre. The impact of the Bible was shown in the separation of church and state as enunciated by the Puritans. It recognized the clash between the written and the oral tradition, the latter persisting in parliament and the common law, and the former in the scriptures. In the Restoration Dryden supported the interest of the court and after the revolution of 1689 and the lapse of the Licensing Act in 1694 the demands of political parties were met by the writings of Addison, Steele, Swift, Defoe, and others. Suspension of printing had brought newsletters and discussion in the coffee-houses. Revival of the classics by Dryden and Pope was the prelude to financial independence of Pope, Johnson, and Goldsmith. The restrictive measures of Walpole and the increasing importance of advertising as a source of revenue for newspapers directed the interest of writers to compilations, children's books, and novels, and the interest of readers to the circulating library. The position of the church with the supremacy of parliament and constitutional monarchy favoured the growth of deism on the one hand and of Methodism on the other.

In the colonies books were imported on a large scale from England and Europe by booksellers and the colonial printer turned his attention to newspapers. In the eighteenth century the energetic writing in London papers before their suppression by Walpole and after the success of Wilkes and others in securing the right to publish parliamentary debates served as an example to colonial journalists. The printing industry crossed the water of the Atlantic Ocean and changed its character. The prominent role of the newspaper in the American Revolution was recognized in the first article of the Bill of Rights. The movement towards restriction of the press by taxes in the latter part of the eighteenth century and the early part of the nineteenth century in England was paralleled by an insistence on freedom of the press in the United States. The results were shown in the rapid expansion in exports of rags from Italy to the United States.

From the invention of printing to the beginning of the nineteenth century the manufacture of paper and the production of the printed word were handicraft processes. The invention of the paper machine and the introduction of the mechanical press involved a revolution in the extension of communication facilities. In England taxes on paper and advertising favoured the monopoly of *The Times* to the middle of the century and removal of these taxes by 1861 was followed by a rapid increase in the number of newspapers and in their circulation and in the demand for raw material. In the United States the demands of large numbers of newspapers hastened the introduction of the fast press, the spread of advertising, inventions such as the telegraph and the cable and the linotype, and a rapid shift from rags to wood as a source of raw material. English authors such as Dickens emphasized the importance of sentimentalism and sensationalism in part through the demands of a new reading class and of an American market. "Dickens introduces children into his stories that he may kill them to slow music" (J. M. Barrie). American authors with lack of copyright protection turned to journalism. Artemus Ward stated that "Shakespeare wrote good plays but he wouldn't have succeeded as the Washington correspondent of a New York daily newspaper. He lacked the reckisit fancy and imagination." Extension of the newspaper in the United States had its implications for Great Britain in the rise of the new journalism particularly after the South African War. Hearst, Pulitzer, Scripps, Northcliffe, and Beaverbrook became dominant figures. In the United States the political ambitions of journalists were checked by competition, in England by nomination to the House of Lords, in Canada by an LL.D. In the twentieth century the power of English journalists was evident in restrictions imposed on the radio through government ownership while limitations of the power of American journalists in the United States were indicated by the effective use of radio by Franklin Delano Roosevelt.

In Anglo-Saxon countries the impact of technological advances on the frontier in the course of which Hearst and Pulitzer from San Francisco and St. Louis introduced revolutionary changes in New York and J. G. Bennett, Jr. and Whitelaw Reid hastened revolutionary changes in Great Britain and Europe, involved an irregular interest on the part of governments in communication and education. Extension of the franchise and the problems of military organization with its demands for technical knowledge and trained men contributed to the improvement of postal facilities and the extension of compulsory education. In Europe the dominance of the book meant less rapid extension of newspapers and restriction in such countries as Germany, Italy, and Russia, and personal and political journalism in France. The varied rate of development of communication facilities has accentuated difficulties of understanding. Improvements in communication, like the Irish bull of the bridge which separated the two countries, make for increased difficulties of understanding. The cable compelled contraction of language and facilitated a rapid widening between the English and American languages. In the vast realm of fiction in the Anglo-Saxon world, the influence of the newspaper and such recent developments as the cinema and the radio has been evident in the best seller and the creation of special classes of readers with little prospect of communication between them. Publishers demand great names and great books particularly if no copyright is involved. The large-scale mechanization of knowledge is characterized by imperfect competition and the active creation of monopolies in language which prevent understanding and hasten appeals to force.

I have tried to show that, in the words of Mark Pattison, "Writers are apt to flatter themselves that they are not, like the men of action, the slaves of circumstance. They think they can write what and when they choose. But it is not so. Whatever we may think and scheme, as soon as we seek to produce our thoughts or schemes to our fellow-men, we are involved in the same necessities of compromise, the same grooves of motion, the same liabilities to failure or half-measures, as we are in life and action."[13] The effect of the discovery of printing was evident in the savage religious wars of the sixteenth and seventeenth centuries. Application of power to communication industries hastened the consolidation of vernaculars, the rise of nationalism, revolution, and new outbreaks of savagery in the twentieth century. Previous to the invention of printing the importance of Latin and the drain on intellectual energies of a dual language had been evident in the problems of scholastic philosophy. After the invention of printing, interest in the classics in Italy and France and in the Bible in Protestant countries divided the Western world. Hebraism and Hellenism proved difficult to reconcile as did Aristotle and Plato. Roman law and the classics in Italy and the cathedrals in France checked the influence of the Bible and in France emphasized an interest in literature. In Germany the influence of the Bible strengthened the power of the state and favoured the growth of music and letters independent of political life. In England division between the crown, parliament, law, the universities,

and trade checked the dominance of single interests, but favoured mediocrity except in finance and trade. In England monasticism contributed to the delay in education and printing which strengthened the position of the vernacular to the point that violence broke out in destruction of the monasteries in the sixteenth century, civil war in the seventeenth century, and the American Revolution in the eighteenth century.

In the free countries of Europe revival of the classics and the demands of printing on logic had their effects in the powerful impact of mathematics on philosophy in Descartes and on political science in Hobbes. The application of power to the communication industries after 1800 hastened the spread of compulsory education and the rise of the newspaper, and intensified interest in vernaculars, in nationalism, and in romanticism. Mechanized communication divided reason and emotion and emphasized the latter. Printing marked the first stage in the spread of the Industrial Revolution. "The influence of passion over any assembly of men increases in proportion to their numbers more than the influence of reason" (J. Scarlett). It became concerned increasingly with the problem of distribution of goods, and with advertising. Its limitations became evident in the decline of the book to the level of prestige advertising, in the substitution of architecture in the skyscraper, the cathedral of commerce, and in simplified spelling and semantics. Ernst Cassirer, a German refugee scholar, has described the word-coiners as masters of the art of political propaganda. *Nazi-Deutsch,* a glossary of contemporary German usage, included a long list of words which he found it impossible to render adequately into English. As a result of the new words coined to support the Hitler-fascist myth he no longer understood the German language.

Since its flight from Constantinople Minerva's owl has found a resting-place only at brief intervals in the West. It has flown from Italy to France, the Netherlands, Germany and after the French Revolution back to France and England and finally to the United States. These hurried and uncertain flights have left it little energy and have left it open to attack from numerous enemies. In the words of the Parnassus Plays:

Let schollers bee as thriftie as they maye
They will be poore ere their last dying daye;
Learning and povertie will ever kisse.

[13]"Mark Pattison," *Isaac Casaubon (1559–1614)* (London, 1875), p. 383.

Or, as Johnson put it:

> There mark what ills the scholar's life assail,—
> Toil, envy, want, the patron, and the jail.

The Industrial Revolution and mechanized knowledge have all but destroyed the scholar's influence. Force is no longer concerned with his protection and is actively engaged in schemes for his destruction. Enormous improvements in communication have made understanding more difficult. Even science, mathematics, and music as the last refuge of the Western mind have come under the spell of the mechanized vernacular. Commercialism has required the creation of new monopolies in language and new difficulties in understanding. Even the class struggle, the struggle between language groups, has been made a monopoly of language. When the Communist Manifesto proclaimed, "Workers of the world unite, you have nothing to lose but your chains!" in those words it forged new chains.

I have attempted to show that sudden extensions of communication are reflected in cultural disturbances. The use of clay favoured a dominant role for the temples with an emphasis on priesthood and religion. Libraries were built up in Babylon and Nineveh to strengthen the power of monarchy. Papyrus favoured the development of political organization in Egypt. Papyrus and a simplified form of writing in the alphabet supported the growth of democratic organization, literature, and philosophy in Greece. Following Alexander empires returned with centres at Alexandria and elsewhere and libraries continued as sources of strength to monarchies. Rome extended the political organization of Greece in its emphasis on law and eventually on empire. Establishment of a new capital at Constantinople was followed by imperial organization on the oriental model particularly after official recognition of Christianity. Improvement of scripts and wider dissemination of knowledge enabled the Jews to survive by emphasis on the scriptures and the book. In turn Christianity exploited the advantages of parchment and the codex in the Bible. With access to paper the Mohammedans at Baghdad and later in Spain and Sicily provided a medium for the transmission of Greek science to the Western world. Greek science and paper with encouragement of writing in the vernacular provided the wedge between the temporal and the spiritual power and destroyed the Holy Roman Empire. The decline of Constantinople meant a stimulus to Greek literature and philosophy as the decline of Mohammedanism had meant a stimulus to science. Printing brought renewed emphasis on the book and the rise of the Reformation. In turn new methods of communication weakened the worship of the book and opened the way for new ideologies. Monopolies or oligopolies of knowledge have been built up in relation to the demands of force chiefly on the defensive, but improved technology has strengthened the position of force on the offensive and compelled realignments favouring the vernacular. Cultural disturbances are accompanied by periods in which force occupies an important place and are followed by periods of quiescence in which law establishes order. The disturbances of the Macedonian and Roman wars were followed by the growth of Roman law, the end of the barbarian invasions by the revival of Roman law, the end of the religious wars by the development of international law under Grotius, and the end of the present wars of ideology by a search for a new basis of international law.

Perhaps we might end by a plea for consideration of the role of the oral tradition as a basis for a revival of effective vital discussion and in this for an appreciation on the part of universities of the fact that teachers and students are still living and human. In the words of Justice Holmes, "To have doubted one's own first principles is the mark of a civilized man," but the same wise man in *Abrams v. United States* stated that "the best test of truth is the power of thought to get itself accepted in the competition of the market" without appreciating that monopoly and oligopoly appear in this as in other markets.

Playboy Interview

Eric McLuhan and Frank Zingrone

A candid conversation with the high priest of popcult and metaphysician of media.

In 1961, the name of Marshall McLuhan was unknown to everyone but his English students at the University of Toronto — and a coterie of academic admirers who followed his abstruse articles in small-circulation quarterlies. But then came two remark-able books — *The Gutenberg Galaxy* (1962) and *Understanding Media* (1964) — and the graying professor from Canada's western hinterlands soon found himself characterized by the *San Francisco Chronicle* as "the hottest academic property around." He has since won a world-wide following for his brilliant — and frequently baffling — theories about the impact of the media on man; and his name has entered the French language as *mcluhanisme*, a synonym for the world of pop culture.

Though his books are written in a difficult style — at once enigmatic, epigrammatic and overgrown with arcane literary and historic allusions — the revolutionary ideas lurking in them have made McLuhan a best-selling author. Despite protests from a legion of outraged scholastics and old-guard humanists who claim that McLuhan's ideas range from demented to dangerous, his free-for-all theorizing has attracted the attention of top executives at General Motors (who paid him a handsome fee to inform them that automobiles were a thing of the past), Bell Telephone (to whom he explained that they didn't really understand the function of the telephone) and a leading package-design house (which was told that packages will soon be obsolete). Anteing up $5000, another huge corporation asked him to predict — via closed-circuit television — what their own products will be used for in the future; and Canada's turned-on Prime Minister Pierre Trudeau engages him in monthly bull sessions designed to improve his television image.

McLuhan's observations — "probes," he prefers to call them — are riddled with such flamboyantly undecipherable aphorisms as "The electric light is pure information" and "People don't actually read newspapers — they get into them every morning like a hot bath." Of his own work, McLuhan has remarked: "I don't pretend to understand it. After all, my stuff is very difficult." Despite his convoluted syntax, flashy metaphors and word-playful one-liners, however, McLuhan's basic thesis is relatively simple.

McLuhan contends that all media — in and of themselves and regardless of the messages they communicate — exert a compelling influence on man and society. Prehistoric, or tribal, man existed in a harmonious balance of the senses, perceiving the world equally through hearing, smell, touch, sight and taste. But technological innovations are extensions of

---

human abilities and senses that alter this sensory balance — an alteration that, in turn, inexorably reshapes the society that created the technology. According to McLuhan, there have been three basic technological innovations: the invention of the phonetic alphabet, which jolted tribal man out of his sensory balance and gave dominance to the eye; the introduction of movable type in the 16th Century, which accelerated this process; and the invention of the telegraph in 1844, which heralded an electronics revolution that will ultimately retribalize man by restoring his sensory balance. McLuhan has made it his business to explain and extrapolate the repercussions of this electronic revolution.

For his efforts, critics have dubbed him "the Dr. Spock of pop culture," "the guru of the boob tube," a "Canadian Nkrumah who has joined the assault on reason," a "metaphysical wizard possessed by a spatial sense of madness," and "the high priest of pop-think who conducts a Black Mass for dilettantes before the altar of historical determinism." Amherst professor Benjamin DeMott observed: "He's swinging, switched on, with it and NOW. And wrong."

But as Tom Wolfe has aptly inquired, "What if he is *right*? Suppose he *is* what he sounds like — the most important thinker since Newton, Darwin, Freud, Einstein and Pavlov?" Social historian Richard Kostelanetz contends that "the most extraordinary quality of McLuhan's mind is that it discerns significance where others see only data, or nothing; he tells us how to measure phenomena previously unmeasurable."

The unperturbed subject of this controversy was born in Edmonton, Alberta, on July 21, 1911. The son of a former actress and a real-estate salesman, McLuhan entered the University of Manitoba intending to become an engineer, but matriculated in 1934 with an M.A. in English literature. Next came a stint as an oarsman and graduate student at Cambridge, followed by McLuhan's first teaching job — at the University of Wisconsin. It was a pivotal experience. "I was confronted with young Americans I was incapable of understanding," he has since remarked. "I felt an urgent need to study their popular culture in order to get through." With the seeds sown, McLuhan let them germinate while earning a Ph.D., then taught at Catholic universities. (He is a devout Roman Catholic convert.)

His publishing career began with a number of articles on standard academic fare; but by the mid-

Forties, his interest in popular culture surfaced, and true McLuhan efforts such as "The Psychopathology of *Time* and *Life*" began to appear. They hit book length for the first time in 1951 with the publication of *The Mechanical Bride* — an analysis of the social and psychological pressures generated by the press, radio, movies and advertising — and McLuhan was on his way. Though the book attracted little public notice, it won him the chairmanship of a Ford Foundation seminar on culture and communications and a $40,000 grant, with part of which he started *Explorations,* a small periodical outlet for the seminar's findings. By the late Fifties, his reputation had trickled down to Washington: In 1959, he became director of the Media Project of the National Association of Educational Broadcasters and the United States Office of Education, and the report resulting from this post became the first draft of *Understanding Media.* Since 1963, McLuhan has headed the University of Toronto's Center for Culture and Technology, which until recently consisted entirely of McLuhan's office, but now includes a six-room campus building.

Apart from his teaching, lecturing and administrative duties, McLuhan has become a sort of minor communication industry unto himself. Each month he issues to subscribers a mixed-media report called *The McLuhan Dew-Line*; and, punning on that title, he has also originated a series of recordings called "The Marshall McLuhan Dew-Line Plattertudes." McLuhan contributed a characteristically mind-expanding essay about the media — "The Reversal of the Overheated Image" — to our December 1968 issue. Also a compulsive collaborator, his literary efforts in tandem with colleagues have included a high school textbook and an analysis of the function of space in poetry and painting. *Counterblast,* his next book, is a manically graphic trip through the land of his theories.

In order to provide our readers with a map of this labyrinthine terra incognita, *Playboy* assigned interviewer Eric Norden to visit McLuhan at his spacious new home in the wealthy Toronto suburb of Wychwood Park, where he lives with his wife, Corinne, and five of his six children. (His eldest son lives in New York, where he is completing a book on James Joyce, one of his father's heroes.) Norden reports: "Tall, gray and gangly, with a thin but mobile mouth and an otherwise eminently forgettable face, McLuhan was dressed in an ill-fitting brown tweed suit, black shoes, and a clip-on necktie. As we talked on into the night before a crackling fire, McLuhan expressed his reservations about the interview — indeed, about the printed word itself — as a means of communication, suggesting that the question-and-answer format might impede the in-depth flow of his ideas. I assured him that he would have as much time — and space — as he wished to develop his thoughts."

The result has considerably more lucidity and clarity than McLuhan's readers are accustomed to — perhaps because the Q. and A. format serves to pin him down by counteracting his habit of mercurially changing the subject in mid-stream of consciousness. It is also, we think, a protean and provocative distillation not only of McLuhan's original theories about human progress and social institutions but of his almost immobilizingly intricate style — described by novelist George P. Elliott as "deliberately anti-logical, circular, repetitious, unqualified, gnomic, outrageous" and, even less charitably, by critic Christopher Ricks as "a viscous fog through which loom stumbling metaphors." But other authorities contend that McLuhan's stylistic medium is part and parcel of his message — that the tightly structured "linear" modes of traditional thought and discourse are obsolescent in the new "postliterate" age of the electric media. Norden began the interview with an allusion to McLuhan's favorite electric, medium: television.

Computing Machinery and Intelligence

A.M. Turing

The Imitation Game

I propose to consider the question "Can machines think?" This should begin with definitions of the meaning of the terms "machine" and "think." The definitions might be framed so as to reflect so far as possible the normal use of the words, but this attitude is dangerous. If the meaning of the words "machine" and "think" are to be found by examining how they are commonly used it is difficult to escape the conclusion that the meaning and the answer to the question, "Can machines think?" is to be sought in a statistical survey such as a Gallup poll. But this is absurd. Instead of attempting such a definition I shall replace the question by another, which is closely related to it and is expressed in relatively unambiguous words.

The new form of the problem can be described in terms of a game which we call the "imitation game." It is played with three people, a man (A), a woman (B), and an interrogator (C) who may be of either sex. The interrogator stays in a room apart from the other two. The object of the game for the interrogator is to determine which of the other two is the man and which is the woman. He knows them by labels X and Y, and at the end of the game he says either "X is A and Y is B" or "X is B and Y is A." The interrogator is allowed to put questions to A and B thus:

> c: Will X please tell me the length of his or her hair?

Now suppose X is actually A, then A must answer. It is A's object in the game to try to cause C to make the wrong identification. His answer might therefore be

"My hair is shingled, and the longest strands are about nine inches long."

In order that tones of voice may not help the interrogator the answers should be written, or better still, typewritten. The ideal arrangement is to have a teleprinter communicating between the two rooms. Alternatively the question and answers can be repeated by an intermediary. The object of the game for the third player (B) is to help the interrogator. The best strategy for her is probably to give truthful answers. She can add such things as "I am the woman, don't listen to him!" to her answers, but it will avail nothing as the man can make similar remarks.

We now ask the question, "What will happen when a machine takes the part of A in this game?" Will the interrogator decide wrongly as often when the game is played like this as tie does when the game

A.M. Turing, "Computing Machinery and Intelligence," Mind, 1950, vol. 59, issue 236, pp. 433–460, by permission of Oxford University Press.

is played between a man and a woman? These questions replace our original, "Can machines think?"

Critique of the New Problem

As well as asking "What is the answer to this new form of the question," one may ask, "Is this new question a worthy one to investigate?" This latter question we investigate without further ado, thereby cutting short an infinite regress.

The new problem has the advantage of drawing a fairly sharp line between the physical and the intellectual capacities of a man. No engineer or chemist claims to be able to produce a material which is indistinguishable from the human skin. It is possible that at some time this might be done, but even supposing this invention available we should feel there was little point in trying to make a "thinking machine" more human by dressing it up in such artificial flesh. The form in which we have set the problem reflects this fact in the condition which prevents the interrogator from seeing or touching the other competitors, or hearing their voices. Some other advantages of the proposed criterion may be shown up by specimen questions and answers. Thus:

Q: Please write me a sonnet on the subject of the Forth Bridge.

A: Count me out on this one. I never could write poetry.

Q: Add 34957 to 70764.

A: (Pause about 30 seconds and then give as answer) 105621.

Q: Do you play chess?

A: Yes.

Q: I have K at my K1, and no other pieces. You have only K at K6 and R at R1. It is your move. What do you play?

A: (After a pause of 15 seconds) R-R8 mate.

The question and answer method seems to be suitable for introducing almost any one of the fields of human endeavor that we wish to include. We do not wish to penalize the machine for its inability to shine in beauty competitions, nor to penalize a man for losing in a race against an airplane. The conditions of our game make these disabilities irrelevant. The "witnesses" can brag, if they consider it advisable, as much as they please about their charms, strength or heroism, but the interrogator cannot demand practical demonstrations.

The game may perhaps be criticized on the ground that the odds are weighted too heavily against the machine. If the man were to try and pretend to be the machine he would clearly make a very poor showing. He would be given away at once by slowness and inaccuracy in arithmetic. May not machines carry out something which ought to be described as thinking but which is very different from what a man does? This objection is a very strong one, but at least we can say that if, nevertheless, a machine can be constructed to play the imitation game satisfactorily, we need not be troubled by this objection.

It might be urged that when playing the "imitation game" the best strategy for the machine may possibly be something other than imitation of the behavior of a man. This may be, but I think it is unlikely that there is any great effect of this kind. In any case there is no intention to investigate here the theory of the game, and it will be assumed that the best strategy is to try to provide answers that would naturally be given by a man.

The Machines Concerned in the Game

The question which we put earlier will not be quite definite until we have specified what we mean by the word "machine." It is natural that we should wish to permit every kind of engineering technique to be used in our machines. We also wish to allow the possibility that an engineer or team of engineers may construct a machine which works, but whose manner of operation cannot be satisfactorily described by its constructors because they have applied a method which is largely experimental. Finally, we wish to exclude from the machines men born in the usual manner. It is difficult to frame the definitions so as to satisfy these three conditions. One might for instance insist that the team of engineers should be all of one sex, but this would not really be satisfactory, for it is probably possible to rear a complete individual from a single cell of the skin (say) of a man. To do so would be a feat of biological technique deserving of the very highest praise, but we would not be inclined to regard it as a case of "constructing a thinking machine." This prompts us to abandon the requirement that every kind of technique should be permitted. We are the more ready to do so in view of the fact that the present interest in "thinking machines" has been aroused by a particular kind of machine, usually called an "electronic computer" or "digital computer." Following this suggestion we only permit digital computers to take part in our game. . . .

This special property of digital computers, that they can mimic any discrete machine, is described by saying that they are *universal* machines. The existence of machines with this property has the important consequence that, considerations of speed apart, it is unnecessary to design various new machines to do various computing processes. They can all be done with one digital computer, suitably programmed for each case. It will be seen that as a consequence of this all digital computers are in a sense equivalent.

Contrary Views on the Main Question

We may now consider the ground to have been cleared and we are ready to proceed to the debate on our question "Can machines think?" . . . We cannot altogether abandon the original form of the problem, for opinions will differ as to the appropriateness of the substitution and we must at least listen to what has to be said in this connection.

It will simplify matters for the reader if I explain first my own beliefs in the matter. Consider first the more accurate form of the question. I believe that in about fifty years' time it will be possible to program computers, with a storage capacity of about 10^9, to make them play the imitation game so well that an average interrogator will not have more than 70 percent chance of making the right identification after five minutes of questioning. The original question, "Can machines think?" I believe to be too meaningless to deserve discussion. Nevertheless I believe that at the end of the century the use of words and general educated opinion will have altered so much that one will be able to speak of machines thinking without expecting to be contradicted. I believe further that no useful purpose is served by concealing these beliefs. The popular view that scientists proceed inexorably from well-established fact to well-established fact, never being influenced by any unproved conjecture, is quite mistaken. Provided it is made clear which are proved facts and which are conjectures, no harm can

result. Conjectures are of great importance since they suggest useful lines of research.

I now proceed to consider opinions opposed to my own.

1. *The Theological Objection.* Thinking is a function of main's immortal soul. God has given an immortal soul to every man and woman, but not to any other animal or to machines. Hence no animal or machine can think.[1]

I am unable to accept any part of this, but will attempt to reply in theological terms. I should find the argument more convincing if animals were classed with men, for there is a greater difference, to my mind, between the typical animate and the inanimate than there is between man and the other animals. The arbitrary character of the orthodox view becomes clearer if we consider how it might appear to a member of some other religious community. How do Christians regard the Moslem view that women have no souls? But let us leave this point aside and return to the main argument. It appears to me that the argument quoted above implies a serious restriction of the omnipotence of the Almighty. It is admitted that there are certain things that He cannot do such as making one equal to two, but should we not believe that He has freedom to confer a soul on an elephant if He sees fit? We might expect that He would only exercise this power in conjunction with a mutation which provided the elephant with an appropriately improved brain to minister to the needs of this soul. An argument of exactly similar form may be made for the case of machines. It may seem different because it is more difficult to "swallow." But this really only means that we think it would be less likely that He would consider the circumstances suitable for conferring a soul. The circumstances in question are discussed in the rest of this paper. In attempting to construct such machines we should not be irreverently usurping His power of creating souls, any more than we are in the procreation of children: rather we are,

---

[1]Possibly this view is heretical. St. Thomas Aquinas (*Summa Theologica*, quoted by Bertrand Russell, *A History of Western Philosophy* [New York: Simon and Schuster, 1945, p. 458) states that God cannot make a man to have no soul. But this may not be a real restriction on his powers, but only a result of the fact that men's souls are immortal, and therefore indestructible.

in either case, instruments of His will providing mansions for the souls that He creates.

However, this is mere speculation. I am not very impressed with theological arguments whatever they may be used to support. Such arguments have often been found unsatisfactory in the past. In the time of Galileo it was argued that the texts, "And the sun stood still . . . and hasted not to go down about a whole day" (Joshua x. 13) and "He laid the foundations of the earth, that it should not move at any time" (Psalm cv. 5) were an adequate refutation of the Copernican theory. With our present knowledge such an argument appears futile. When that knowledge was not available it made a quite different impression.

2. *The "Heads in the Sand" Objection.* "The consequences of machines thinking would be too dreadful. Let us hope and believe that they cannot do so."

This argument is seldom expressed quite so openly as in the form above. But it affects most of us who think about it at all. We like to believe that Man is in some subtle way superior to the rest of creation. It is best if he can be shown to be *necessarily* superior, for then there is no danger of him losing his commanding position. The popularity of the theological argument is clearly connected with this feeling. It is likely to be quite strong in intellectual people, since they value the power of thinking more highly than others, and are more inclined to base their belief in the superiority of Man on this power.

I do not think that this argument is sufficiently substantial to require refutation. Consolation would be more appropriate: perhaps this should be sought in the transmigration of souls.

3. *The Mathematical Objection.* There are a number of results of mathematical logic which can be used to show that there are limitations to the powers of discrete state machines. The best known of these results is known as Gödel's theorem, and shows that in any sufficiently powerful logical system statements can be formulated which can neither be proved nor disproved within the system, unless possibly the system itself is inconsistent. There are other, in some respects similar, results due to Church, Kleene, Rosser, and Turing. The latter result is the most convenient to consider, since it refers directly to machines, whereas the others can only be used in a comparatively indirect argument:

for instance if Gödel's theorem is to be used we need in addition to have some means of describing logical systems in terms of machines, and machines in terms of logical systems. The result in question refers to a type of machine which is essentially a digital computer with an infinite capacity. It states that there are certain things that such a machine cannot do. If it is rigged up to give answers to questions as in the imitation game, there will be some questions to which it will either give a wrong answer, or fail to give an answer at all however much time is allowed for a reply. There may, of course, be many such questions, and questions which cannot be answered by one machine may be satisfactorily answered by another. We are of course supposing for the present that the questions are of the kind to which an answer "Yes" or "No" is appropriate, rather than questions such as "What do you think of Picasso?" The questions that we know the machines must fail on are of this type, "Consider the machine specified as follows. . . . Will this machine ever answer 'Yes' to any question?" The dots are to be replaced by a description of some machine in a standard form. . . . When the machine described bears a certain comparatively simple relation to the machine which is under interrogation, it can be shown that the answer is either wrong or not forthcoming. This is the mathematical result: it is argued that it proves a disability of machines to which the human intellect is not subject.

The short answer to this argument is that although it is established that there are limitations to the powers of any particular machine, it has only been stated, without any sort of proof, that no such limitations apply to the human intellect. But I do not think this view can be dismissed quite so lightly. Whenever one of these machines is asked the appropriate critical question, and gives a definite answer, we know that this answer must be wrong, and this gives us a certain feeling of superiority. Is this feeling illusory? It is no doubt quite genuine, but I do not think too much importance should be attached to it. We too often give wrong answers to questions ourselves to be justified in being very pleased at such evidence of fallibility on the part of the machines. Further, our superiority can only be felt on such an occasion in relation to the one machine over which we have scored our petty triumph. There would be no question of triumphing simultaneously over *all* machines. In short, then, there might be men cleverer than any given machine, but then again there might be other machines cleverer again, and so on.

Those who hold to the mathematical argument would, I think, mostly be willing to accept the imitation game as a basis for discussion. Those who believe in the two previous objections would probably not be interested in any criteria.

4. *The Argument from Consciousness*. This argument is very well expressed in Professor Jefferson's Lister Oration for 1949, from which I quote. "Not until a machine can write a sonnet or compose a concerto because of thoughts and emotions felt, and not by the chance fall of symbols, could we agree that machine equals brain—that is, not only write it but know that it had written it. No mechanism could feel (and not merely artificially signal, an easy contrivance) pleasure at its successes, grief when its valves fuse, be warmed by flattery, be made miserable by its mistakes, be charmed by sex, be angry or depressed when it cannot get what it wants."

This argument appears to be a denial of the validity of our test. According to the most extreme form of this view the only way by which one could be sure that a machine thinks is to *be* the machine and to feel oneself thinking. One could then describe these feelings to the world, but of course no one would be justified in taking any notice. Likewise according to this view the only way to know that a *man* thinks is to be that particular man. It is in fact the solipsist point of view. It may be the most logical view to hold but it makes communication of ideas difficult. A is liable to believe "A thinks but B does not" while B believes "B thinks but A does not." Instead of arguing continually over this point it is usual to have the polite convention that everyone thinks.

I am sure that Professor Jefferson does not wish to adopt the extreme and solipsist point of view. Probably he would be quite willing to accept the imitation game as a test. The game (with the player B omitted) is frequently used in practice under the name of *viva voce* to discover whether someone really understands something or has "learned it parrot fashion." Let us listen in to a part of such a *viva voce*:

INTERROGATOR: In the first line of your sonnet which reads "Shall I compare thee to a summer's day," would not "a spring day" do as well or better?

WITNESS: It wouldn't scan.

INTERROGATOR: How about "a winter's day"? That would scan all right.

WITNESS: Yes, but nobody wants to be compared to a winter's day.

INTERROGATOR: Would you say Mr. Pickwick reminded you of Christmas?

WITNESS: In a way.

INTERROGATOR: Yet Christmas is a winter's day, and I do not think Mr. Pickwick would mind the comparison.

WITNESS: I don't think you're serious. By a winter's day one means a typical winter's day, rather than a special one like Christmas.

And so on. What would Professor Jefferson say if the sonnet-writing machine was able to answer like this in the *viva voce*? I do not know whether he would regard the machine as "merely artificially signaling" these answers, but if the answers were as satisfactory and sustained as in the above passage I do not think he would describe it as "an easy contrivance." This phrase is, I think, intended to cover such devices as the inclusion in the machine of a record of someone reading a sonnet, with appropriate switching to turn it on from time to time.

In short, then, I think that most of those who support the argument from consciousness could be persuaded to abandon it rather than be forced into the solipsist position. They will then probably be willing to accept our test.

I do not wish to give the impression that I think there is no mystery about consciousness. There is, for instance, something of a paradox connected with any attempt to localize it. But I do not think these mysteries necessarily need to be solved before we can answer the question with which we are concerned in this paper.

5. *Arguments from Various Disabilities*. These arguments take the form "I grant you that you can make machines do all the thinks you have mentioned but you will never be able to make one to do X." Numerous features X are suggested in this connection. I offer a selection:

Be kind, resourceful, beautiful, friendly . . . have initiative, have a sense of humor, tell right from wrong, make mistakes . . . fall in love, enjoy strawberries and cream . . . make someone fall in love with it, learn from experience . . . use words properly, be the subject of its own thought . . . have as much diversity of behavior as a man, do something really new . . . .

No support is usually offered for these statements. I believe they are mostly founded on the principle of scientific induction. A man has seen thousands of machines in his lifetime. From what he sees of them he draws a number of general conclusions. They are ugly, each is designed for a very limited purpose, when required for a minutely different purpose they are useless, the variety of behavior of any one of them is very small, etc., etc. Naturally he concludes that these are necessary properties of machines in general. Many of these limitations are associated with the very small storage capacity of most machines. (I am assuming that the idea of storage capacity is extended in some way to cover machines other than discrete state machines. The exact definition does not matter as no mathematical accuracy is claimed in the present discussion.) A few years ago, when very little had been heard of digital computers, it was possible to elicit much incredulity concerning them, if one mentioned their properties without describing their construction. That was presumably due to a similar application of the principle of scientific induction. These applications of the principle are of course largely unconscious. When a burned child fears the fire and shows that he fears it by avoiding it, I should say that he was applying scientific induction. (I could of course also describe his behavior in many other ways.) The works and customs of mankind do not seem to be very suitable material to which to apply scientific induction. A very large part of space-time must be investigated if reliable results are to be obtained. Otherwise we may (as most English children do) decide that everybody speaks English, and that it is silly to learn French.

There are, however, special remarks to be made about many of the disabilities that have been mentioned. The inability to enjoy strawberries and cream may have struck the reader as frivolous. Possibly a machine might be made to enjoy this delicious dish, but any attempt to make one do so would be idiotic. What is important about this disability is that it contributes to some of the other disabilities, e.g., to the difficulty of the same kind of friendliness occurring between man and machine as between white man and white man, or between black man and black man.

The claim that "machines cannot make mistakes" seems a curious one. One is tempted to retort, "Are they any the worse for that?" But let us adopt a more sympathetic attitude, and try to see what is really meant. I think this criticism can be explained in terms of the imitation game. It is claimed that the interrogator could distinguish the machine from the man simply by setting them a number of problems in arithmetic. The machine would be unmasked because of its deadly accuracy. The reply to this is simple. The machine (programmed for playing the game) would not attempt to give the *right* answers to the arithmetic problems. It would deliberately introduce mistakes in a manner calculated to confuse the interrogator. A mechanical fault would probably show itself through an unsuitable decision as to what sort of a mistake to make in the arithmetic. Even this interpretation of the criticism is not sufficiently sympathetic. But we cannot afford the space to go into it much further. It seems to me that this criticism depends on a confusion between two kinds of mistakes. We may call them "errors of functioning" and "errors of conclusion." Errors of functioning are due to some mechanical or electrical fault which causes the machine to behave otherwise than it was designed to do. In philosophical discussions one likes to ignore the possibility of such errors; one is therefore discussing "abstract machines." These abstract machines are mathematical fictions rather than physical objects. By definition they are incapable of errors of functioning. In this sense we can truly say that "machines can never make mistakes." Errors of conclusion can only arise when some meaning is attached to the output signals from the machine. The machine might, for instance, type out mathematical equations, or sentences in English. When a false proposition is typed we say that the machine has committed an error of conclusion. There is clearly no reason at all for saying that a machine cannot make this kind of mistake. It might do nothing but type out repeatedly "0=1." To take a less perverse example, it might have some method for drawing conclusions by scientific induction. We must expect such a method to lead occasionally to erroneous results.

The claim that a machine cannot be the subject of its own thought can of course only be answered if it can be shown that the machine has *some* thought with *some* subject matter. Nevertheless, "the subject matter of a machine's operations" does seem to mean something, at least to the people who deal with it. If, for instance, the machine was trying to find a solution of the equation $x^2 - 40x - 11 = 0$, one would be tempted to describe this equation as part of the machine's subject matter at that moment. In this sort of sense a machine undoubtedly can be its own subject matter. It may be used to help in making up its own programs, or to predict the effect of alterations in its own structure. By observing the results of its own behavior it can modify its own programs so as to achieve some purpose more effectively. These are possibilities of the near future, rather than Utopian dreams.

The criticism that a machine cannot have much diversity of behavior is just a way of saying that it cannot have much storage capacity. Until fairly recently a storage capacity of even a thousand digits was very rare.

The criticisms that we are considering here are often disguised forms of the argument from consciousness. Usually if one maintains that a machine *can* do one of these things, and describes the kind of method that the machine could use, one will not make much of an impression. It is thought that the method (whatever it may be, for it must be mechanical) is really rather base. Compare the parenthesis in Jefferson's statement quoted above.

6. *Lady Lovelace's Objection*. Our most detailed information of Bahbage's Analytical Engine comes from a memoir by Lady Lovelace. In it she states, "The Analytical Engine has no pretensions to *originate* anything. It can do *whatever we know how to order it* to perform" (her italics). This statement is quoted by Hartree who adds: "This does not imply that it may not be possible to construct electronic equipment which will 'think for itself,' or in which, in biological terms, one could set up a conditioned reflex, which would serve as a basis for 'learning.' Whether this is possible in principle or not is a stimulating and exciting question, suggested by some of these recent developments. But it did not seem that the machines constructed or projected at the time had this property."

I am in thorough agreement with Hartree over this. It will be noticed that he does not assert that the machines in question had not got the property, but rather that the evidence available to Lady Lovelace did not encourage her to believe that they had it. It is quite possible that the machines in question had in a sense got this property. For suppose that some discrete state machine has the property. The Analytical Engine was a universal digital computer, so that, if its storage capacity and speed were adequate, it could by suitable programming be made to mimic the machine in question. Probably this argument did not occur to the Countess or to Babbage. In any case

there was no obligation on them to claim all that could be claimed.

A variant of Lady Lovelace's objection states that a machine can "never do anything really new." This may be parried for a moment with the saw, "There is nothing new under the sun." Who can be certain that "original work" that he has done was not simply the growth of the seed planted in him by teaching, or the effect of following well-known general principles? A better variant of the objection says that a machine can never "take us by surprise." This statement is a more direct challenge and can be met directly. Machines take me by surprise with great frequency. This is largely because I do not do sufficient calculation to decide what to expect them to do, or rather because, although I do a calculation, I do it in a hurried, slipshod fashion, taking risks. Perhaps I say to myself, "I suppose the voltage here ought to be the same as there; anyway let's assume it is." Naturally I am often wrong, and the result is a surprise for me, for by the time the experiment is done these assumptions have been forgotten. These admissions lay me open to lectures on the subject of my vicious ways, but do not throw any doubt on my credibility when I testify to the surprises I experience.

I do not expect this reply to silence my critic. He will probably say that such surprises are due to some creative mental act on my part, and reflect no credit on the machine. This leads us back to the argument from consciousness, and far from the idea of surprise. It is a line of argument we must consider closed, but it is perhaps worth remarking that the appreciation of something as surprising requires as much of a "creative mental act" whether the surprising event originates from a man, a book, a machine or anything else.

The view that machines cannot give rise to surprises is due, I believe, to a fallacy to which philosophers and mathematicians are particularly subject. This is the assumption that as soon as a fact is presented to a mind all consequences of that fact spring into the mind simultaneously with it. It is a very useful assumption under many circumstances, but one too easily forgets that it is false. A natural consequence of doing so is that one then assumes that there is no virtue in the mere working out of consequences from data and general principles.

7. *Argument from Continuity in the Nervous System*. The nervous system is certainly not a discrete state machine. A small error in the information

about the size of a nervous impulse impinging on a neuron may make a large difference to the size of the outgoing impulse. It may be argued that, this being so, one cannot expect to be able to mimic the behavior of the nervous system with a discrete state system.

It is true that a discrete state machine must be different from a continuous machine. But if we adhere to the conditions of the imitation game, the interrogator will not be able to take any advantage of this difference. The situation can be made clearer if we consider some other simpler continuous machine. A differential analyzer will do very well. (A differential analyzer is a certain kind of machine not of the discrete state type used for some kinds of calculation.) Some of these provide their answers in a typed form, and so are suitable for taking part in the game. It would not be possible for a digital computer to predict exactly what answers the differential analyzer would give to a problem, but it would be quite capable of giving the right sort of answer. For instance, if asked to give the value of π (actually about 3.1416) it would be reasonable to choose at random between the values 3.12, 3.13, 3.14, 3.15, 3.16 with the probabilities of 0.05, 0.15, 0.55, 0.19, 0.06 (say). Under these circumstances it would be very difficult for the interrogator to distinguish the differential analyzer from the digital computer.

8. *The Argument from Informality of Behavior.* It is not possible to produce a set of rules purporting to describe what a man should do in every conceivable set of circumstances. One might for instance have a rule that one is to stop when one sees a red traffic light, and to go if one sees a green one, but what if by some fault both appear together? One may perhaps decide that it is safest to stop. But some further difficulty may well arise from this decision later. To attempt to provide rules of conduct to cover every eventuality, even those arising from traffic lights, appears to be impossible. With all this I agree.

From this it is argued that we cannot be machines. I shall try to reproduce the argument, but I fear I shall hardly do it justice. It seems to run something like this. "If each man had a definite set of rules of conduct by which he regulated his life he would be no better than a machine. But there are no such rules, so men cannot be machines." The undis-

tributed middle is glaring. I do not think the argument is ever put quite like this, but I believe this is the argument used nevertheless. There may however be a certain confusion between "rules of conduct" and "laws of behavior" to cloud the issue. By "rules of conduct" I mean precepts such as "Stop if you see red lights," on which one can act, and of which one can be conscious. By "laws of behavior" I mean laws of nature as applied to a man's body such as "if you pinch him he will squeak." If we substitute "laws of behavior which regulate his life" for "laws of conduct by which he regulates his life" in the argument quoted the undistributed middle is no longer insuperable. For we believe that it is not only true that being regulated by laws of behavior implies being some sort of machine (though not necessarily a discrete state machine), but that conversely being such a machine implies being regulated by such laws. However, we cannot so easily convince ourselves of the absence of complete laws of behavior as of complete rules of conduct. The only way we know of for finding such laws is scientific observation, and we certainly know of no circumstances under which we could say, "We have searched enough. There are no such laws."

We can demonstrate more forcibly that any such statement would be unjustified. For suppose we could be sure of finding such laws if they existed. Then given a discrete state machine it should certainly be possible to discover by observation sufficient about it to predict its future behavior, and this within a reasonable time, say a thousand years. But this does not seem to be the case. I have set up on the Manchester computer a small program using only 1000 units of storage, whereby the machine supplied with one sixteen-figure number replies with another within two seconds. I would defy anyone to learn from these replies sufficient about the program to be able to predict any replies to untried values.

9. *The Argument from Extrasensory Perception.* I assume that the reader is familiar with the idea of extrasensory perception, and the meaning of the four items of it, viz., telepathy, clairvoyance, precognition, and psychokinesis. These disturbing phenomena seem to deny all our usual scientific ideas. How we should like to discredit them! Unfortunately the statistical evidence, at least for telepathy, is over-

whelming. It is very difficult to rearrange one's ideas so as to fit these new facts in. Once one has accepted them it does not seem a very big step to believe in ghosts and bogies. The idea that our bodies move simply according to the known laws of physics, together with some others not yet discovered but some-what similar, would be one of the first to go.

This argument is to my mind quite a strong one. One can say in reply that many scientific theories seem to remain workable in practice, in spite of clashing with E.S.P.; that in fact one can get along very nicely if one forgets about it. This is rather cold comfort, and one fears that thinking is just the kind of phenomenon where E.S.P. may be especially relevant.

A more specific argument based on E.S.P. might run as follows: "Let us play the imitation game, using as witnesses a man who is good as a telepathic receiver, and a digital computer. The interrogator can ask such questions as 'What suit does the card in my right hand belong to?' The man by telepathy or clairvoyance gives the right answer 130 times out of 400 cards. The machine can only guess at random, and perhaps get 104 right, so the interrogator makes the right identification." There is an interesting possibility which opens here. Suppose the digital computer contains a random number generator. Then it will be natural to use this to decide what answer to give. But then the random number generator will be subject to the psychokinetic powers of the interrogator. Perhaps this psychokinesis might cause the machine to guess right more often than would be expected on a probability calculation, so that the interrogator might still be unable to make the right identification. On the other hand, he might be able to guess right without any questioning, by clairvoyance. With E.S.P. anything may happen.

If telepathy is admitted it will be necessary to tighten our test. The situation could be regarded as analogous to that which would occur if the interrogator were talking to himself and one of the competitors was listening with his ear to the wall. To put the competitors into a "telepathy-proof room" would satisfy all requirements.

Reflections

Most of our response to this remarkable and lucid article is contained in the following dialogue. However, we wish to make a short comment about Turing's apparent willingness to believe that extrasensory perception might turn out to be the ultimate difference between humans and the machines they create. If this comment is taken at face value (and not as some sort of discreet joke), one has to wonder what motivated it. Apparently Turing was convinced that the evidence for telepathy was quite strong. However, if it was strong in 1950, it is no stronger now, thirty years later—in fact, it is probably weaker. Since 1950 there have been many notorious cases of claims of psychic ability of one sort or another, often vouched for by physicists of some renown. Some of those physicists have later felt they had been made fools of and have taken hack their public pro-ESP pronouncements, only to jump on some new paranormal bandwagon the next month. But it is safe to say that the majority of physicists— and certainly the majority of psychologists, who specialize in understanding the mind—doubt the existence of extrasensory perception in any form.

Turing took "cold comfort" in the idea that paranormal phenomena might be reconcilable in some way with well-established scientific theories. We differ with him. We suspect that if such phenomena as telepathy, precognition, and telekinesis turned out to exist (and turned out to have the remarkable properties typically claimed for them), the laws of physics would not be simply *amendable* to accommodate them; only a major revolution in our scientific world view could do them justice. One might look forward to such a revolution with eager excitement—but it should be tinged with sadness and perplexity. How could the science that had worked so well for so many things turn out to be so wrong? The challenge of rethinking all of science from its most basic assumptions on up would be a great intellectual adventure, but the evidence that we will need to do this has simply failed to accumulate over the years.

Metaphors We Live By

George Lakoff and Mark Johnson

Concepts We Live By

Metaphor is for most people a device of the poetic imagination and the rhetorical flourish—a matter of extraordinary rather than ordinary language. Moreover, metaphor is typically viewed as characteristic of language alone, a matter of words rather than thought or action. For this reason, most people think they can get along perfectly well without metaphor. We have found, on the contrary, that metaphor is pervasive in everyday life, not just in language but in thought and action. Our ordinary conceptual system, in terms of which we both think and act, is fundamentally metaphorical in nature.

The concepts that govern our thought are not just matters of the intellect. They also govern our everyday functioning, down to the most mundane details. Our concepts structure what we perceive, how we get around in the world, and how we relate to other people. Our conceptual system thus plays a central role in defining our everyday realities. If we are right in suggesting that our conceptual system is largely metaphorical, then the way we think, what we experience, and what we do every day is very much a matter of metaphor.

But our conceptual system is not something we are normally aware of. In most of the little things we do every day, we simply think and act more or less automatically along certain lines. Just what these lines are is by no means obvious. One way to find out is by looking at language. Since communication is based on the same conceptual system that we use in thinking and acting, language is an important source of evidence for what that system is like.

Primarily on the basis of linguistic evidence, we have found that most of our ordinary conceptual system is metaphorical in nature. And we have found a way to begin to identify in detail just what the metaphors are that structure how we perceive, how we think, and what we do.

To give some idea of what it could mean for a concept to be metaphorical and for such a concept to structure an everyday activity, let us start with the concept ARGUMENT and the conceptual metaphor ARGUMENT IS WAR. This metaphor is reflected in our everyday language by a wide variety of expressions:

ARGUMENT IS WAR

Your claims are *indefensible*.
He *attacked every weak point* in my argument.
His criticisms were *right on target*.
I *demolished* his argument.
I've never *won* an argument with him.
You disagree? Okay, *shoot!*
If you use that *strategy*, he'll *wipe you out*.
He *shot down* all of my arguments.

It is important to see that we don't just *talk* about arguments in terms of war. We can actually win or lose arguments. We see the person we are arguing with as an opponent. We attack his positions and we defend our own. We gain and lose ground. We plan and use strategies. If we find a position indefensible, we can abandon it and take a new line of attack. Many of the things we *do* in arguing are partially structured by the concept of war. Though there is no physical battle, there is a verbal battle, and the structure of an argument—attack, defense, counterattack, etc.—reflects this. It is in this sense that the ARGUMENT IS WAR metaphor is one that we live by in this culture; it structures the actions we perform in arguing.

Try to imagine a culture where arguments are not viewed in terms of war, where no one wins or loses, where there is no sense of attacking or defending, gaining or losing ground. Imagine a culture where an argument is viewed as a dance, the participants are seen as performers, and the goal is to perform in a balanced and aesthetically pleasing way. In such a culture, people would view arguments differently, experience them differently, carry them out differently, and talk about them differently. But *we* would probably not view them as arguing at all: they would simply be doing something different. It would seem strange even to call what they were doing "arguing." Perhaps the most neutral way of describing this difference between their culture and ours would be to say that we have a discourse form structured in terms of battle and they have one structured in terms of dance.

This is an example of what it means for a metaphorical concept, namely, ARGUMENT IS WAR, to structure (at least in part) what we do and how we understand what we are doing when we argue. *The essence of metaphor is understanding and experiencing one kind of thing in terms of another*. It is not that arguments are a subspecies of war. Arguments and wars are different kinds of things—verbal discourse and armed conflict—and the actions performed are different kinds of actions. But ARGUMENT is partially structured, understood, performed, and talked about in terms of WAR. The concept is metaphorically structured, the activity is metaphorically structured, and, consequently, the language is metaphorically structured.

Moreover, this is the *ordinary* way of having an argument and talking about one. The normal way for us to talk about attacking a position is to use the words "attack a position." Our conventional ways of talking about arguments presuppose a metaphor we are hardly ever conscious of. The metaphor is not merely in the words we use—it is in our very concept of an argument. The language of argument is not poetic, fanciful, or rhetorical; it is literal. We talk about arguments that way because we conceive of them that way—and we act according to the way we conceive of things.

The most important claim we have made so far is that metaphor is not just a matter of language, that is, of mere words. We shall argue that, on the contrary, human *thought processes* are largely metaphorical. This is what we mean when we say that the human conceptual system is metaphorically structured and defined. Metaphors as linguistic expressions are possible precisely because there are metaphors in a person's conceptual system. Therefore, whenever in this book we speak of metaphors, such as ARGUMENT IS WAR, it should be understood that *metaphor* means *metaphorical concept*.

The Systematicity of Metaphorical Concepts

Arguments usually follow patterns; that is, there are certain things we typically do and do not do in arguing. The fact that we in part conceptualize arguments in terms of battle systematically influences the shape arguments take and the way we talk about what we do in arguing. Because the metaphorical concept is systematic, the language we use to talk about that aspect of the concept is systematic.

We saw in the ARGUMENT IS WAR metaphor that expressions from the vocabulary of war, e.g., *attack a position, indefensible, strategy, new line of attack, win, gain ground*, etc., form a systematic way of talking about the battling aspects of arguing. It is no accident that these expressions mean what they mean when we use them to talk about arguments. A portion of the conceptual network of battle partially characterizes the concept of an argument, and the language follows suit. Since metaphorical expressions in our language are tied to metaphorical concepts in a systematic way, we can use metaphorical linguistic expressions to study the nature of metaphorical concepts and to gain an understanding of the metaphorical nature of our activities.

To get an idea of how metaphorical expressions in everyday language can give us insight into the metaphorical nature of the concepts that structure our everyday activities, let us consider the metaphorical concept TIME IS MONEY as it is reflected in contemporary English.

TIME IS MONEY

You're *wasting* my time.
This gadget will *save* you hours.
I don't *have* the time to *give* you.
How do you *spend* your time these days?
That flat tire *cost* me an hour.
I've *invested* a lot of time in her.
I don't *have enough* time to *spare* for that.
You're *running out* of time.
You need to *budget* your time.
Put aside some time for ping pong.
Is that *worth your while*?
Do you *have* much time *left*?
He's living on *borrowed* time.
You don't *use* your time *profitably*.
I *lost* a lot of time when I got sick.
Thank you for your time.

Time in our culture is a valuable commodity. It is a limited resource that we use to accomplish our goals. Because of the way that the concept of work has developed in modern Western culture, where work is typically associated with the time it takes and time is precisely quantified, it has become customary to pay people by the hour, week, or year. In our culture TIME IS MONEY in many ways: telephone message units, hourly wages, hotel room rates, yearly budgets, interest on loans, and paying your debt to society by "serving time." These practices are relatively new in the history of the human race, and by no means do they exist in all cultures. They have arisen in modern industrialized societies and structure our basic everyday activities in a very profound way. Corresponding to the fact that we *act* as if time is a valuable commodity—a limited resource, even money—we *conceive of* time that way. Thus we understand and experience time as the kind of thing that can be spent, wasted, budgeted, invested wisely or poorly, saved, or squandered.

TIME IS MONEY, TIME IS A LIMITED RESOURCE, and TIME IS A VALUABLE COMMODITY are all metaphorical concepts. They are metaphorical since we are using our everyday experiences with money, limited resources, and valuable commodities to conceptualize time. This isn't a nec-essary way for human beings to conceptualize time; it is tied to our culture. There are cultures where time is none of these things.

The metaphorical concepts TIME IS MONEY, TIME IS A RESOURCE, and TIME IS A VALUABLE COMMODITY form a single system based on subcategorization, since in our society money is a limited resource and limited resources are valuable commodities. These subcategorization relationships characterize entailment relationships between the metaphors. TIME IS MONEY entails that TIME IS A LIMITED RESOURCE, which entails that TIME IS A VALUABLE COMMODITY.

We are adopting the practice of using the most specific metaphorical concept, in this case TIME IS MONEY, to characterize the entire system. Of the expressions listed under the TIME IS MONEY metaphor, some refer specifically to money (*spend, invest, budget, profitably, cost*), others to limited resources (*use, use up, have enough of, run out of*), and still others to valuable commodities (*have, give, lose, thank you for*). This is an example of the way in which metaphorical entailments can characterize a coherent system of metaphorical concepts and a corresponding coherent system of metaphorical expressions for those concepts.

Metaphorical Systematicity: Highlighting and Hiding

The very systematicity that allows us to comprehend one aspect of a concept in terms of another (e.g., comprehending an aspect of arguing in terms of battle) will necessarily hide other aspects of the concept. In allowing us to focus on one aspect of a concept (e.g., the battling aspects of arguing), a metaphorical concept can keep us from focusing on other aspects of the concept that are inconsistent with that metaphor. For example, in the midst of a heated argument, when we are intent on attacking our opponent's position and defending our own, we may lose sight of the cooperative aspects of arguing. Someone who is arguing with you can be viewed as giving you his time, a valuable commodity, in an effort at mutual understanding. But when we are preoccupied with the battle aspects, we often lose sight of the cooperative aspects.

A far more subtle case of how a metaphorical concept can hide an aspect of our experience can be seen in what Michael Reddy has called the "conduit metaphor." Reddy observes that our language about language is structured roughly by the following complex metaphor:

IDEAS (or MEANINGS) ARE OBJECTS.
LINGUISTIC EXPRESSIONS ARE CONTAINERS.
COMMUNICATION IS SENDING.

The speaker puts ideas (objects) into words (containers) and sends them (along a conduit) to a hearer who takes the idea/objects out of the word/containers. Reddy documents this with more than a hundred types of expressions in English, which he estimates account for at least 70 percent of the expressions we use for talking about language. Here are some examples:

The CONDUIT Metaphor

It's hard to *get* that idea *across* to him.
I *gave* you that idea.
Your reasons *came through* to us.
It's difficult to *put* my ideas *into* words.
When you *have* a good idea, try to *capture* it immediately *in* words.
Try to *pack* more thought *into* fewer words.
You can't simply *stuff* ideas *into* a sentence any old way.
The meaning is right there *in* the words.
Don't *force* your meanings *into* the wrong words.
His words *carry* little meaning.
The introduction *has* a great deal of thought *content*.
Your words seem *hollow*.
The sentence is *without* meaning.
The idea is *buried in* terribly dense paragraphs.

In examples like these it is far more difficult to see that there is anything hidden by the metaphor or even to see that there is a metaphor here at all. This is so much the conventional way of thinking about language that it is sometimes hard to imagine that it might not fit reality. But if we look at what the CONDUIT metaphor entails, we can see some of the ways in which it masks aspects of the communicative process.

First, the LINGUISTIC EXPRESSIONS ARE CONTAINERS FOR MEANINGS aspect of the CONDUIT metaphor entails that words and sentences have meanings in themselves, independent of any context or speaker. The MEANINGS ARE OBJECTS part of the metaphor, for example, entails that meanings have an existence independent of people and con-

texts. The part of the metaphor that says LINGUISTIC EXPRESSIONS ARE CONTAINERS FOR MEANING entails that words (and sentences) have meanings, again independent of contexts and speakers. These metaphors are appropriate in many situations—those where context differences don't matter and where all the participants in the conversation understand the sentences in the same way. These two entailments are exemplified by sentences like

The meaning is *right there in* the words,

which, according to the CONDUIT metaphor, can correctly be said of any sentence. But there are many cases where context does matter. Here is a celebrated one recorded in actual conversation by Pamela Downing:

Please sit in the apple-juice seat.

In isolation this sentence has no meaning at all, since the expression "apple-juice seat" is not a conventional way of referring to any kind of object. But the sentence makes perfect sense in the context in which it was uttered. An overnight guest came down to breakfast. There were four place settings, three with orange juice and one with apple juice. It was clear what the apple-juice seat was. And even the next morning, when there was no apple juice, it was still clear which seat was the apple-juice seat.

In addition to sentences that have no meaning without context, there are cases where a single sentence will mean different things to different people. Consider:

We need new alternative sources of energy.

This means something very different to the president of Mobil Oil from what it means to the president of Friends of the Earth. The meaning is not right there in the sentence—it matters a lot who is saying or listening to the sentence and what his social and political attitudes are. The CONDUIT metaphor does not fit cases where context is required to determine whether the sentence has any meaning at all and, if so, what meaning it has.

These examples show that the metaphorical concepts we have looked at provide us with a partial understanding of what communication, argument, and time are and that, in doing this, they hide other aspects of these concepts. It is important to see that the metaphorical structuring involved here is partial, not total. If it were total, one concept would actually *be* the other, not merely be understood in terms of it. For example, time isn't really money. If you *spend your time* trying to do something and it doesn't work, you can't get your time back. There are no time banks. I can *give you a lot of time*, but you can't give me back the same time, though you can *give me back the same amount of time*. And so on. Thus, part of a metaphorical concept does not and cannot fit.

On the other hand, metaphorical concepts can be extended beyond the range of ordinary literal ways of thinking and talking into the range of what is called figurative, poetic, colorful, or fanciful thought and language. Thus, if ideas are objects, we can *dress them up in fancy clothes, juggle them, line them up nice and neat*, etc. So when we say that a concept is structured by a metaphor, we mean that it is partially structured and that it can be extended in some ways but not others.

Orientational Metaphors

So far we have examined what we will call *structural metaphors*, cases where one concept is metaphorically structured in terms of another. But there is another kind of metaphorical concept, one that does not structure one concept in terms of another but instead organizes a whole system of concepts with respect to one another. We will call these *orientational metaphors*, since most of them have to do with spatial orientation: up-down, in-out, front-back, on-off, deep-shallow, central-peripheral. These spatial orientations arise from the fact that we have bodies of the sort we have and that they function as they do in our physical environment. Orientational metaphors give a concept a spatial orientation; for example, HAPPY IS UP. The fact that the concept HAPPY IS oriented UP leads to English expressions like "I'm feeling *up* today."

Such metaphorical orientations are not arbitrary. They have a basis in our physical and cultural experience. Though the polar oppositions up-down, in-out, etc., are physical in nature, the orientational metaphors based on them can vary from culture to culture. For example, in some cultures the future is in front of us, whereas in others it is in back. We will be looking at up-down spatialization metaphors, which have been studied intensively by William Nagy (1974), as an illustration. In each case, we will give a brief hint about how each metaphorical con-

cept might have arisen from our physical and cultural experience. These accounts are meant to be suggestive and plausible, not definitive.

> HAPPY IS UP; SAD IS DOWN
> I'm feeling *up*. That *boosted* my spirits. My spirits *rose*. You're in *high* spirits. Thinking about her always gives me a *lift*. I'm feeling *down*. I'm *depressed*. He's really *low* these days. I *fell* into a depression. My spirits *sank*.

Physical basis: Drooping posture typically goes along with sadness and depression, erect posture with a positive emotional state.

> CONSCIOUS IS UP; UNCONSCIOUS IS DOWN
> Get *up*. Wake *up*. I'm *up* already. He *rises* early in the morning. He *fell* asleep. He *dropped* off to sleep. He's *under* hypnosis. He *sank* into a coma.

Physical basis: Humans and most other mammals sleep lying down and stand up when they awaken.

> HEALTH AND LIFE ARE UP; SICKNESS AND DEATH ARE DOWN
> He's at the *peak* of health. Lazarus *rose* from the dead. He's in *top* shape. As to his health, he's way *up* there. He *fell* ill. He's *sinking* fast. He came *down* with the flu. His health is *declining*. He *dropped* dead.

Physical basis: Serious illness forces us to lie down physically. When you're dead, you are physically down.

> HAVING CONTROL or FORCE IS UP; BEING SUBJECT TO CONTROL or FORCE IS DOWN
> I have control *over* her. I am *on top* of the situation. He's in a *superior* position. He's at the *height* of his power. He's in the *high* command. He's in the *upper* echelon. His power *rose*. He ranks *above* me in strength. He is *under* my control. He *fell* from power. His power is on the *decline*. He is my social *inferior*. He is *low man* on the totem pole.

Physical basis: Physical size typically correlates with physical strength, and the victor in a fight is typically on top.

> MORE IS UP; LESS IS DOWN
> The number of books printed each year keeps going *up*. His draft number is *high*. My income *rose* last year. The amount of artistic activity in this state has gone *down* in the past year. The number of errors he made is incredibly *low*. His

income *fell* last year. He is *underage*. If you're too hot, turn the heat *down*.

Physical basis: If you add more of a substance or of physical objects to a container or pile, the level goes up.

FORESEEABLE FUTURE EVENTS ARE UP (and AHEAD)
All *up* coming events are listed in the paper. What's coming *up* this week? I'm afraid of what's *up ahead* of us. What's *up*?

Physical basis: Normally our eyes look in the direction in which we typically move (ahead, forward). As an object approaches a person (or the person approaches the object), the object appears larger. Since the ground is perceived as being fixed, the top of the object appears to be moving upward in the person's field of vision.

HIGH STATUS IS UP; LOW STATUS IS DOWN
He has a *lofty* position. She'll *rise* to the top. He's at the *peak* of his career. He's *climbing* the ladder. He has little *upward* mobility. He's at the *bottom* of the social hierarchy. She *fell* in status.

Social and physical basis: Status is correlated with (social) power and (physical) power is UP.

GOOD IS UP; BAD IS DOWN
Things are looking *up*. We hit a *peak* last year, but it's been *downhill* ever since. Things are at an all-time *low*. He does *high*-quality work.

Physical basis for personal well-being: Happiness, health, life, and control—the things that principally characterize what is good for a person—are all UP.

VIRTUE IS UP; DEPRAVITY IS DOWN
He is *high*-minded. She has *high* standards. She is *upright*. She is an *upstanding* citizen. That was a *low* trick. Don't be *underhanded*. I wouldn't *stoop* to that. That would be *beneath* me. He *fell* into the *abyss* of depravity. That was a *low-down* thing to do.

Physical and social basis: GOOD Is UP for a person (physical basis), together with a metaphor that we will discuss below, SOCIETY IS A PERSON (in the version where you are *not* identifying with your society). To be virtuous is to act in accordance with the standards set by the society/person to maintain its well-being. VIRTUE IS UP because virtuous actions correlate with social well-being from the society/person's point of view. Since socially based

metaphors are part of the culture, it's the society/person's point of view that counts.

RATIONAL IS UP; EMOTIONAL IS DOWN
The discussion *fell to the emotional* level, but I *raised* it back *up to the rational* plane. We put our *feelings* aside and had a *high-level intellectual* discussion of the matter. He couldn't *rise above* his *emotions*.

Physical and cultural basis: In our culture people view themselves as being in control over animals, plants, and their physical environment, and it is their unique ability to reason that places human beings above other animals and gives them this control. CONTROL IS UP thus provides a basis for MAN IS UP and therefore for RATIONAL IS UP.

Conclusions

On the basis of these examples, we suggest the following conclusions about the experiential grounding, the coherence, and the systematicity of metaphorical concepts:

—Most of our fundamental concepts are organized in terms of one or more spatialization metaphors.
—There is an internal systematicity to each spatialization metaphor. For example, HAPPY IS UP defines a coherent system rather than a number of isolated and random cases. (An example of an incoherent system would be one where, say, "I'm feeling up" meant "I'm feeling happy," but "My spirits rose" meant "I became sadder.")
—There is an overall external systematicity among the various spatialization metaphors, which defines coherence among them. Thus, GOOD IS UP gives an UP orientation to general well-being, and this orientation is coherent with special cases like HAPPY IS UP, HEALTH IS UP, ALIVE IS UP, CONTROL IS UP. STATUS IS UP is coherent with CONTROL IS UP.
—Spatialization metaphors are rooted in physical and cultural experience; they are not randomly assigned. A metaphor can serve as a vehicle for understanding a concept only by virtue of its experiential basis. (Some of the complexities of the experiential basis of metaphor are discussed in the following section.)

—There are many possible physical and social bases for metaphor. Coherence within the overall system seems to be part of the reason why one is chosen and not another. For example, happiness also tends to correlate physically with a smile and a general feeling of expansiveness. This could in principle form the basis for a metaphor HAPPY IS WIDE; SAD IS NARROW. And in fact there are minor metaphorical expressions, like "I'm feeling *expansive*," that pick out a different aspect of happiness than "I'm feeling *up*" does. But the major metaphor in our culture is HAPPY IS UP; there is a reason why we speak of the height of ecstasy rather than the breadth of ecstasy. HAPPY IS UP is maximally coherent with GOOD IS UP, HEALTHY IS UP, etc.

—In some cases spatialization is so essential a part of a concept that it is difficult for us to imagine any alternative metaphor that might structure the concept. In our society "high status" is such a concept. Other cases, like happiness, are less clear. Is the concept of happiness independent of the HAPPY IS UP metaphor, or is the up-down spatialization of happiness a part of the concept? We believe that it is a part of the concept within a given conceptual system. The HAPPY IS UP metaphor places happiness within a coherent metaphorical system, and part of its meaning comes from its role in that system.

—So-called purely intellectual concepts, e.g., the concepts in a scientific theory, are often—perhaps always—based on metaphors that have a physical and/or cultural basis. The *high* in "high-energy particles" is based on MORE IS UP. The *high* in "high-level functions," as in physiological psychology, is based on RATIONAL IS UP. The *low* in "low-level phonology" (which refers to detailed phonetic aspects of the sound systems of languages) is based on MUNDANE REALITY IS DOWN (as in "down to earth"). The intuitive appeal of a scientific theory has to do with how well its metaphors fit one's experience.

—Our physical and cultural experience provides many possible bases for spatialization metaphors. Which ones are chosen, and which ones are major, may vary from culture to culture.

—It is hard to distinguish the physical from the cultural basis of a metaphor, since the choice of one physical basis from among many possible ones has to do with cultural coherence.

Experiential Bases of Metaphors

We do not know very much about the experiential bases of metaphors. Because of our ignorance in this matter, we have described the metaphors separately, only later adding speculative notes on their possible experiential bases. We are adopting this practice out of ignorance, not out of principle. *In actuality we feel that no metaphor can ever be comprehended or even adequately represented independently of its experiential basis.* For example, MORE IS UP has a very different kind of experiential basis than HAPPY IS UP or RATIONAL IS UP. Though the concept UP is the same in all these metaphors, the experiences on which these UP metaphors are based are very different. It is not that there are many different UPS; rather, verticality enters our experience in many different ways and so gives rise to many different metaphors.

One way of emphasizing the inseparability of metaphors from their experiential bases would be to build the experiential basis into the representations themselves. Thus, instead of writing MORE IS UP and RATIONAL IS UP, we might have the more complex relationship shown in the diagram.

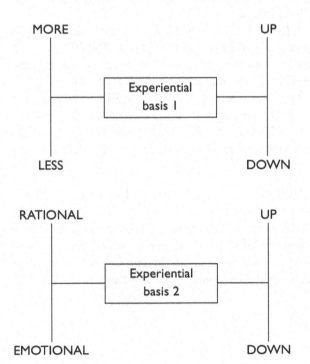

Such a representation would emphasize that the two parts of each metaphor are linked only via an experiential basis and that it is only by means of these experiential bases that the metaphor can serve the purpose of understanding.

We will not use such representations, but only because we know so little about experiential bases of metaphors. We will continue to use the word "is" in stating metaphors like MORE IS UP, but the IS should be viewed as a shorthand for some set of experiences on which the metaphor is based and in terms of which we understand it.

The role of the experiential basis is important in understanding the workings of metaphors that do not fit together because they are based on different kinds of experience. Take, for example, a metaphor like UNKNOWN IS UP; KNOWN IS DOWN. Examples are "That's *up in the air*" and "The matter is *settled*." This metaphor has an experiential basis very much like that of UNDERSTANDING IS GRASPING, as in "I couldn't *grasp* his explanation." With physical objects, if you can grasp something and hold it in your hands, you can look it over carefully and get a reasonably good understanding of it. It's easier to grasp something and look at it carefully if it's on the ground in a fixed location than if it's floating through the air (like a leaf or a piece of paper). Thus UNKNOWN IS UP; KNOWN IS DOWN is coherent with UNDERSTANDING IS GRASPING.

But UNKNOWN IS UP is not coherent with metaphors like GOOD IS UP and FINISHED IS UP (as in "I'm finishing *up*"). One would expect FINISHED to be paired with KNOWN and UNFINISHED to be paired with UNKNOWN. But, so far as verticality metaphors are concerned, this is not the case. The reason that UNKNOWN IS UP has a very different experiential basis than FINISHED IS UP.

Metaphor and Cultural Coherence

The most fundamental values in a culture will be coherent with the metaphorical structure of the most fundamental concepts in the culture. As an example, let us consider some cultural values in our society that are coherent with our UP-DOWN spatialization metaphors and whose opposites would not be.

"More is better" is coherent with MORE IS UP and GOOD IS UP. "Less is better" is not coherent with them.

"Bigger is better" is coherent with MORE IS UP and GOOD IS UP. "Smaller is better" is not coherent with them.

"The future will be better" is coherent with THE FUTURE IS UP and GOOD IS UP. "The future will be worse" is not.

"There will be more in the future" is coherent with MORE IS UP and THE FUTURE IS UP.

"Your status should be higher in the future" is coherent with HIGH STATUS IS UP and THE FUTURE IS UP.

These are values deeply embedded in our culture. "The future will be better" is a statement of the concept of progress. "There will be more in the future" has as special cases the accumulation of goods and wage inflation. "Your status should be higher in the future" is a statement of careerism. These are coherent with our present spatialization metaphors; their opposites would not be. So it seems that our values are not independent but must form a coherent system with the metaphorical concepts we live by. We are not claiming that all cultural values coherent with a metaphorical system actually exist, only that those that do exist and are deeply entrenched are consistent with the metaphorical system.

The values listed above hold in our culture generally—all things being equal. But because things are usually not equal, there are often conflicts among these values and hence conflicts among the metaphors associated with them. To explain such conflicts among values (and their metaphors), we must find the different priorities given to these values and metaphors by the subculture that uses them. For instance, MORE IS UP seems always to have the highest priority since it has the clearest physical basis. The priority of MORE IS UP over GOOD IS UP can be seen in examples like "Inflation is rising" and "The crime rate is going up." Assuming that inflation and the crime rate are bad, these sentences mean what they do because MORE IS UP always has top priority.

In general, which values are given priority is partly a matter of the subculture one lives in and partly a matter of personal values. The various subcultures of a mainstream culture share basic values but give them different priorities. For example, BIGGER IS BETTER may be in conflict with THERE WILL BE MORE IN THE FUTURE when it comes to the question of whether to buy a big car now, with large time payments that will eat up future salary, or whether to buy a smaller, cheaper car. There are American subcultures where you buy the big car and don't worry about the future, and there are others where the future comes first and you buy the small car. There was a time (before inflation and the energy crisis) when owning a small car had a high status within the subculture where VIRTUE IS UP and SAVING RESOURCES IS VIRTUOUS took priority over BIGGER IS BETTER. Nowadays the number of small-car owners has gone up drastically because there is a large subculture where SAVING MONEY IS BETTER has priority over BIGGER IS BETTER.

In addition to subcultures, there are groups whose defining characteristic is that they share certain important values that conflict with those of the mainstream culture. But in less obvious ways they preserve other mainstream values. Take monastic orders like the Trappists. There LESS IS BETTER and SMALLER IS BETTER are true with respect to material possessions, which are viewed as hindering what is important, namely, serving God. The Trappists share the mainstream value VIRTUE IS UP, though they give it the highest priority and a very different definition. MORE is still BETTER, though it applies to virtue; and status is still UP, though it is not of this world but of a higher one, the Kingdom of God. Moreover, THE FUTURE WILL BE BETTER is true in terms of spiritual growth (UP) and, ultimately, salvation (really UP). This is typical of groups that are out of the mainstream culture. Virtue, goodness, and status may be radically redefined, but they are still UP. It is still better to have more of what is important, THE FUTURE WILL BE BETTER with respect to what is important, and so on. Relative to what is important for a monastic group, the value system is both internally coherent and, with respect to what is important for the group, coherent with the major orientational metaphors of the mainstream culture.

Individuals, like groups, vary in their priorities and in the ways they define what is good or virtuous to them. In this sense, they are subgroups of one. Relative to what is important for them, their individual value systems are coherent with the major orientational metaphors of the mainstream culture.

Not all cultures give the priorities we do to up-down orientation. There are cultures where balance or centrality plays a much more important role than it does in our culture. Or consider the nonspatial orientation active-passive. For us ACTIVE IS UP and PASSIVE IS DOWN in most matters. But there are cultures where passivity is valued more than activity. In general the major orientations up-down, in-out, central-peripheral, active-passive, etc., seem to cut across all cultures, but which concepts are oriented which way and which orientations are most important vary from culture to culture.

General Characteristics of Crowds— Psychological Law of Their Mental Utility

Gustav LeBon

What constitutes a crowd from the psychological point of view—A numerically strong agglomeration of individuals does not suffice to form a crowd—Special characteristics of psychological crowds—The turning in a fixed direction of the ideas and sentiments of individuals composing such a crowd, and the disappearance of their personality—The crowd is always dominated by considerations of which it is unconscious—The disappearance of brain activity and the predominance of medullar activity—The lowering of the intelligence and the complete transformation of the sentiments—The transformed sentiments may be better or worse than those of the individuals of which the crowd is composed—A crowd is as easily heroic as criminal.

In its ordinary sense the word "crowd" means a gathering of individuals of whatever nationality, profession, or sex, and whatever be the chances that have brought them together. From the psychological point of view the expression "crowd" assumes quite a different signification. Under certain given circumstances, and only under those circumstances, an agglomeration of men presents new characteristics very different from those of the individuals composing it. The sentiments and ideas of all the persons in the gathering take one and the same direction, and their conscious personality vanishes. A collective mind is formed, doubtless transitory, but presenting very clearly defined characteristics. The gathering has thus become what, in the absence of a better expression, I will call an organised crowd, or, if the term is considered preferable, a psychological crowd. It forms a single being, and is subjected to the *law of the mental unity of crowds*.

It is evident that it is not by the mere fact of a number of individuals finding themselves accidentally side by side that they acquire the character of an organised crowd. A thousand individuals accidentally gathered in a public place without any determined object in no way constitute a crowd from the psychological point of view. To acquire the special characteristics of such a crowd, the influence is necessary of certain predisposing causes of which we shall have to determine the nature.

The disappearance of conscious personality and the turning of feelings and thoughts in a definite direction, which are the primary characteristics of a crowd about to become organised, do not always involve the simultaneous presence of a number of individuals on one spot. Thousands of isolated individuals may acquire at certain moments, and under the influence of certain violent emotions—such, for example, as a great national event—the characteristics of a psychological crowd. It will be sufficient in that case that a mere chance should bring them together for their acts to at once assume the characteristics peculiar to the acts of a crowd. At certain moments half a dozen men might constitute a psychological crowd, which may not happen in the case of hundreds of men gathered together by accident. On the other hand, an entire nation, though there may be no visible agglomeration, may become a crowd under the action of certain influences.

A psychological crowd once constituted, it acquires certain provisional but determinable general characteristics. To these general characteristics there are adjoined particular characteristics which vary according to the elements of which the crowd is composed, and may modify its mental constitution. Psychological crowds, then, are susceptible of classification; and when we come to occupy ourselves with this matter, we shall see that a heterogeneous crowd—that is, a crowd composed of dissimilar elements—presents certain characteristics in common with homogeneous crowds—that is, with crowds composed of elements more or less akin (sects, castes, and classes)—and side by side with these common characteristics particularities which permit of the two kinds of crowds being differentiated.

But before occupying ourselves with the different categories of crowds, we must first of all examine the characteristics common to them all. We shall set to work like the naturalist, who begins by describing the general characteristics common to all the members of a family before concerning himself with the particular characteristics which allow the differentiation of the genera and species that the family includes.

It is not easy to describe the mind of crowds with exactness, because its organisation varies not only according to race and composition, but also according to the nature and intensity of the exciting causes to which crowds are subjected. The same difficulty, however, presents itself in the psychological study of an individual. It is only in novels that individuals are found to traverse their whole life with an unvarying character. It is only the uniformity of the environment that creates the apparent uniformity of characters. I have shown elsewhere that all mental constitutions contain possibilities of character which may be manifested in consequence of a sudden change of environment. This explains how it was that among the most savage members of the French Convention were to be found inoffensive citizens who, under ordinary circumstances, would have been peaceable notaries or virtuous magistrates. The storm past, they resumed their normal character of quiet, law-abiding citizens. Napoleon found amongst them his most docile servants.

It being impossible to study here all the successive degrees of organisation of crowds, we shall concern ourselves more especially with such crowds as have attained to the phase of complete organisation. In this way we shall see what crowds may become, but not what they invariably are. It is only in this advanced phase of organisation that certain new and special characteristics are superposed on the unvarying and dominant character of the race; then takes place that turning already alluded to of all the feelings and thoughts of the collectivity in an identical direction. It is only under such circumstances, too, that what I have called above the *psychological law of the mental unity of crowds* comes into play.

Among the psychological characteristics of crowds there are some that they may present in common with isolated individuals, and others, on the contrary, which are absolutely peculiar to them and are only to be met with in collectivities. It is these special characteristics that we shall study, first of all, in order to show their importance.

The most striking peculiarity presented by a psychological crowd is the following: Whoever be the individuals that compose it, however like or unlike be their mode of life, their occupations, their character, or their intelligence, the fact that they have been transformed into a crowd puts them in possession of a sort of collective mind which makes them feel, think, and act in a manner quite different from that in which each individual of them would feel, think, and act were he in a state of isolation. There are certain ideas and feelings which do not come into being, or do not transform themselves into acts except in the case of individuals forming a crowd. The psychological crowd is a provisional being formed of heterogeneous elements, which for a moment are combined, exactly as the cells which constitute a living body form by their reunion a new being which displays characteristics very different from those possessed by each of the cells singly.

Contrary to an opinion which one is astonished to find coming from the pen of so acute a philosopher as Herbert Spencer, in the aggregate which constitutes a crowd there is in no sort a summing-up of or an average struck between its elements. What really takes place is a combination followed by the creation of new characteristics, just as in chemistry certain elements, when brought into contact—bases and acids, for example—combine to form a new body possessing properties quite different from those of the bodies that have served to form it.

It is easy to prove how much the individual forming part of a crowd differs from the isolated individual, but it is less easy to discover the causes of this difference.

To obtain at any rate a glimpse of them it is necessary in the first place to call to mind the truth established by modern psychology, that unconscious phenomena play an altogether preponderating part not only in organic life, but also in the operations of the intelligence. The conscious life of the mind is of small importance in comparison with its unconscious life. The most subtle analyst, the most acute observer, is scarcely successful in discovering more than a very small number of the unconscious motives that determine his conduct. Our conscious acts are the outcome of an unconscious substratum created in the mind in the main by hereditary influences. This substratum consists of the innumerable common characteristics handed down from generation to generation, which constitute the genius of a race. Behind the avowed causes of our acts there undoubtedly lie secret causes that we do not avow, but behind these secret causes there are many others more secret still which we ourselves ignore. The greater part of our daily actions are the result of hidden motives which escape our observation.

It is more especially with respect to those unconscious elements which constitute the genius of a race that all the individuals belonging to it resemble each other, while it is principally in respect to the conscious elements of their character—the fruit of education, and yet more of exceptional hereditary conditions—that they differ from each other. Men the most unlike in the matter of their intelligence possess instincts, passions, and feelings that are very similar. In the case of everything that belongs to the realm of sentiment—religion, politics, morality, the affections and antipathies, etc.— the most eminent men seldom surpass the standard of the most ordinary individuals. From the intellectual point of view an abyss may exist between a great mathematician and his bootmaker, but from the point of view of character the difference is most often slight or non-existent.

It is precisely these general qualities of character, governed by forces of which we are unconscious, and possessed by the majority of the normal individuals of a race in much the same degree—it is precisely these qualities, I say, that in crowds become common property. In the collective mind the intellectual aptitudes of the individuals, and in con-

sequence their individuality, are weakened. The heterogeneous is swamped by the homogeneous, and the unconscious qualities obtain the upper hand.

This very fact that crowds possess in common ordinary qualities explains why they can never accomplish acts demanding a high degree of intelligence. The decisions affecting matters of general interest come to by an assembly of men of distinction, but specialists in different walks of life, are not sensibly superior to the decisions that would be adopted by a gathering of imbeciles. The truth is, they can only bring to bear in common on the work in hand those mediocre qualities which are the birthright of every average individual. In crowds it is stupidity and not mother-wit that is accumulated. It is not all the world, as is so often repeated, that has more wit than Voltaire, but assuredly Voltaire that has more wit than all the world, if by "all the world" crowds are to be understood.

If the individuals of a crowd confined themselves to putting in common the ordinary qualities of which each of them has his share, there would merely result the striking of an average, and not, as we have said is actually the case, the creation of new characteristics. How is it that these new characteristics are created? This is what we are now to investigate.

Different causes determine the appearance of these characteristics peculiar to crowds, and not possessed by isolated individuals. The first is that the individual forming part of a crowd acquires, solely from numerical considerations, a sentiment of invincible power which allows him to yield to instincts which, had he been alone, he would perforce have kept under restraint. He will be the less disposed to check himself from the consideration that, a crowd being anonymous, and in consequence irresponsible, the sentiment of responsibility which always controls individuals disappears entirely.

The second cause, which is contagion, also intervenes to determine the manifestation in crowds of their special characteristics, and at the same time the trend they are to take. Contagion is a phenomenon of which it is easy to establish the presence, but that it is not easy to explain. It must be classed among those phenomena of a hypnotic order, which we shall shortly study. In a crowd every sentiment and act is contagious, and contagious to such a degree that an individual readily sacrifices his personal interest to the collective interest. This is an aptitude very contrary to his nature, and of which a man is scarcely capable, except when he makes part of a crowd.

A third cause, and by far the most important, determines in the individuals of a crowd special characteristics which are quite contrary at times to those presented by the isolated individual. I allude to that suggestibility of which, moreover, the contagion mentioned above is neither more nor less than an effect.

To understand this phenomenon it is necessary to bear in mind certain recent physiological discoveries. We know today that by various processes an individual may be brought into such a condition that, having entirely lost his conscious personality, he obeys all the suggestions of the operator who has deprived him of it, and commits acts in utter contradiction with his character and habits. The most careful observations seem to prove that an individual immerged for some length of time in a crowd in action soon finds himself—either in consequence of the magnetic influence given out by the crowd, or from some other cause of which we are ignorant—in a special state, which much resembles the state of fascination in which the hypnotised individual finds himself in the hands of the hypnotiser. The activity of the brain being paralysed in the case of the hypnotised subject, the latter becomes the slave of all the unconscious activities of his spinal cord, which the hypnotiser directs at will. The conscious personality has entirely vanished; will and discernment are lost. All feelings and thoughts are bent in the direction determined by the hypnotiser.

Such also is approximately the state of the individual forming part of a psychological crowd. He is no longer conscious of his acts. In his case, as in the case of the hypnotised subject, at the same time that certain faculties are destroyed, others may be brought to a high degree of exaltation. Under the influence of a suggestion, he will undertake the accomplishment of certain acts with irresistible impetuosity. This impetuosity is the more irresistible in the case of crowds than in that of the hypnotised subject, from the fact that, the suggestion being the same for all the individuals of the crowd, it gains in strength by reciprocity. The individualities in the crowd who might possess a personality sufficiently strong to resist the suggestion are too few in number to struggle against the current. At the utmost, they may be able to attempt a diversion by means of different suggestions. It is in this way, for instance, that a happy expression, an image opportunely evoked, have occasionally deterred crowds from the most blood-thirsty acts.

We see, then, that the disappearance of the conscious personality, the predominance of the unconscious personality, the turning by means of suggestion and contagion of feelings and ideas in an identical direction, the tendency to immediately transform the suggested ideas into acts; these, we see, are the principal characteristics of the individual forming part of a crowd. He is no longer himself, but has become an automaton who has ceased to be guided by his will.

Moreover, by the mere fact that he forms part of an organised crowd, a man descends several rungs in the ladder of civilisation. Isolated, he may be a cultivated individual; in a crowd, he is a barbarian—that is, a creature acting by instinct. He possesses the spontaneity, the violence, the ferocity, and also the enthusiasm and heroism of primitive beings, whom he further tends to resemble by the facility with which he allows himself to be impressed by words and images—which would be entirely without action on each of the isolated individuals composing the crowd—and to be induced to commit acts contrary to his most obvious interests and his best-known habits. An individual in a crowd is a grain of sand amid other grains of sand, which the wind stirs up at will.

It is for these reasons that juries are seen to deliver verdicts of which each individual juror would disapprove, that parliamentary assemblies adopt laws and measures of which each of their members would disapprove in his own person. Taken separately, the men of the Convention were enlightened citizens of peaceful habits. United in a crowd, they did not hesitate to give their adhesion to the most savage proposals, to guillotine individuals most clearly innocent, and, contrary to their interests, to renounce their inviolability and to decimate themselves.

It is not only by his acts that the individual in a crowd differs essentially from himself. Even before he has entirely lost his independence, his ideas and feelings have undergone a transformation, and the transformation is so profound as to change the miser into a spendthrift, the sceptic into a believer, the honest man into a criminal, and the coward into a hero. The renunciation of all its privileges which the nobility voted in a moment of enthusiasm during the celebrated night of August 4, 1789, would certainly never have been consented to by any of its members taken singly.

The conclusion to be drawn from what precedes is, that the crowd is always intellectually inferior to the isolated individual, but that, from the point of view of feelings and of the acts these feelings provoke, the crowd may, according to circumstances, be better or worse than the individual. All depends on the nature of the suggestion to which the crowd is exposed. This is the point that has been completely misunderstood by writers who have only studied crowds from the criminal point of view. Doubtless a crowd is often criminal, but also it is often heroic. It is crowds rather than isolated individuals that may be induced to run the risk of death to secure the triumph of a creed or an idea, that may be fired with enthusiasm for glory and honour, that are led on—almost without bread and without arms, as in the age of the Crusades—to deliver the tomb of Christ from the infidel, or, as in '93, to defend the fatherland. Such heroism is without doubt somewhat unconscious, but it is of such heroism that history is made. Were peoples only to be credited with the great actions performed in cold blood, the annals of the world would register but few of them.

The Ideas, Reasoning Power, and Imagination of Crowds

Gustav LeBon

The ideas of crowds. Fundamental and accessory ideas—How contradictory ideas may exist simultaneously—The transformation that must be undergone by lofty ideas before they are accessible to crowds—The social influence of ideas is independent of the degree of truth they may contain. § 2. *The reasoning power of crowds.* Crowds are not to be influenced by reasoning—The reasoning of crowds is always of a very inferior order—There is only the appearance of analogy or succession in the ideas they associate. § 3. *The imagination of crowds.* Strength of the imagination of crowds—Crowds think in images, and these images succeed each other without any connecting link—Crowds are especially impressed by the marvellous—Legends and the marvellous are the real pillars of civilisation—The popular imagination has always been the basis of the power of statesmen—The manner in which facts capable of striking the imagination of crowds present themselves for observation.

§1. The Ideas of Crowds

When studying in a preceding work the part played by ideas in the evolution of nations, we showed that every civilisation is the outcome of a small number of fundamental ideas that are very rarely renewed. We showed how these ideas are implanted in the minds of crowds, with what difficulty the process is effected, and the power possessed by the ideas in question when once it has been accomplished. Finally we saw that great historical perturbations are the result, as a rule, of changes in these fundamental ideas.

Having treated this subject at sufficient length, I shall not return to it now, but shall confine myself to saying a few words on the subject of such ideas as are accessible to crowds, and of the forms under which they conceive them.

They may be divided into two classes. In one we shall place accidental and passing ideas created by the influences of the moment; infatuation for an individual or a doctrine, for instance. In the other will be classed the fundamental ideas, to which the environment, the laws of heredity and public opinion give a very great stability; such ideas are the religious beliefs of the past and the social and democratic ideas of today.

These fundamental ideas resemble the volume of the water of a stream slowly pursuing its course; the transitory ideas are like the small waves, for ever changing, which agitate its surface, and are more visible than the progress of the stream itself although without real importance.

At the present day the great fundamental ideas which were the mainstay of our fathers are tottering more and more. They have lost all solidity, and at the same time the institutions resting upon them are severely shaken. Every day there are formed a great many of those transitory minor ideas of which I have just been speaking; but very few of them to all appearance seem endowed with vitality and destined to acquire a preponderating influence.

Whatever be the ideas suggested to crowds they can only exercise effective influence on condition that they assume a very absolute, uncompromising, and simple shape. They present themselves then in the guise of images, and are only accessible to the masses under this form. These imagelike ideas are not connected by any logical bond of analogy or succession, and may take each other's place like the slides of a magic-lantern which the operator withdraws from the groove in which they were placed one above the other. This explains how it is that the most contradictory ideas may be seen to be simultaneously current in crowds. According to the chances of the moment, a crowd will come under the influence of one of the various ideas stored up in its understanding, and is capable, in consequence, of committing the most dissimilar acts. Its complete lack of the critical spirit does not allow of its perceiving these contradictions.

This phenomenon is not peculiar to crowds. It is to be observed in many isolated individuals, not only among primitive beings, but in the case of all those—the fervent sectaries of a religious faith, for instance—who by one side or another of their intelligence are akin to primitive beings. I have observed its presence to a curious extent in the case of educated Hindoos brought up at our European universities and having taken their degree. A number of Western ideas had been superposed on their unchangeable and fundamental hereditary or social ideas. According to the chances of the moment, the one or the other set of ideas showed themselves each with their special accompaniment of acts or utterances, the same individual presenting in this way the most flagrant contradictions. These contradictions are more apparent than real, for it is only hereditary ideas that have sufficient influence over the isolated individual to become motives of conduct. It is only when, as the result of the intermingling of different races, a man is placed between different hereditary tendencies that his acts from one moment to another may be really entirely contradictory. It would be useless to insist here on these phenomena, although their psychological importance is capital. I am of opinion that at least ten years of travel and observation would be necessary to arrive at a comprehension of them.

Ideas being only accessible to crowds after having assumed a very simple shape must often undergo the most thoroughgoing transformations to become popular. It is especially when we are dealing with somewhat lofty philosophic or scientific ideas that we see how far-reaching are the modifications they require in order to lower them to the level of the intelligence of crowds. These modifications are dependent on the nature of the crowds, or of the race to which the crowds belong, but their tendency is always belittling and in the direction of simplification. This explains the fact that, from the social point of view, there is in reality scarcely any such thing as a hierarchy of ideas—that is to say, as ideas of greater or less elevation. However great or true an idea may have been to begin with, it is deprived of almost all that which constituted its elevation and its greatness by the mere fact that it has come within the intellectual range of crowds and exerts an influence upon them.

Moreover, from the social point of view the hierarchical value of an idea, its intrinsic worth, is without importance. The necessary point to consider is the effects it produces. The Christian ideas of the Middle Ages, the democratic ideas of the last century, or the social ideas of today are assuredly not very elevated. Philosophically considered, they can only be regarded as somewhat sorry errors, and yet their power has been and will be immense, and they will count for a long time to come among the most essential factors that determine the conduct of States.

Even when an idea has undergone the transformations which render it accessible to crowds, it only exerts influence when, by various processes which we shall examine elsewhere, it has entered the domain of the unconscious, when indeed it has become a sentiment, for which much time is required.

For it must not be supposed that merely because the justness of an idea has been proved it can be productive of effective action even on cultivated minds. This fact may be quickly appreciated by noting how slight is the influence of the clearest demonstration on the majority of men. Evidence, if it be very plain, may be accepted by an educated person, but the convert will be quickly brought back by his unconscious self to his original conceptions. See him again after the lapse of a few days and he will put forward afresh his old arguments in exactly the same terms. He is in reality under the influence of anterior ideas, that have become sentiments, and it is such ideas alone that influence the more recondite motives of our acts and utterances. It cannot be otherwise in the case of crowds.

When by various processes an idea has ended by penetrating into the minds of crowds, it possesses an irresistible power, and brings about a series of effects, opposition to which is bootless. The philosophical ideas which resulted in the French Revolution took nearly a century to implant themselves in the mind of the crowd. Their irresistible force, when once they had taken root, is known. The striving of an entire nation towards the conquest of social equality, and the realisation of abstract rights and ideal liberties, caused the tottering of all thrones and profoundly disturbed the Western world. During twenty years the nations were engaged in internecine conflict, and Europe witnessed hecatombs that would have terrified Ghengis Khan and Tamerlane. The world had never seen on such a scale what may result from the promulgation of an idea.

A long time is necessary for ideas to establish themselves in the minds of crowds, but just as long a time is needed for them to be eradicated. For this reason crowds, as far as ideas are concerned, are always several generations behind learned men and philosophers. All statesmen are well aware today of the admixture of error contained in the fundamental ideas I referred to a short while back, but as the influence of these ideas is still very powerful they are obliged to govern in accordance with principles in the truth of which they have ceased to believe.

§2. The Reasoning Power of Crowds

It cannot absolutely be said that crowds do not reason and are not to be influenced by reasoning.

However, the arguments they employ and those which are capable of influencing them are, from a logical point of view, of such an inferior kind that it is only by way of analogy that they can be described as reasoning.

The inferior reasoning of crowds is based, just as is reasoning of a high order, on the association of ideas, but between the ideas associated by crowds there are only apparent bonds of analogy or succession. The mode of reasoning of crowds resembles that of the Esquimaux who, knowing from experience that ice, a transparent body, melts in the mouth, concludes that glass, also a transparent body, should also melt in the mouth; or that of the savage who imagines that by eating the heart of a courageous foe he acquires his bravery; or of the workman who, having been exploited by one employer of labour,

immediately concludes that all employers exploit their men.

The characteristics of the reasoning of crowds are the association of dissimilar things possessing a merely apparent connection between each other, and the immediate generalisation of particular cases. It is arguments of this kind that are always presented to crowds by those who know how to manage them. They are the only arguments by which crowds are to be influenced. A chain of logical argumentation is totally incomprehensible to crowds, and for this reason it is permissible to say that they do not reason or that they reason falsely and are not to be influenced by reasoning. Astonishment is felt at times on reading certain speeches at their weakness, and yet they had an enormous influence on the crowds which listened to them, but it is forgotten that they were intended to persuade collectivities and not to be read by philosophers. An orator in intimate communication with a crowd can evoke images by which it will be seduced. If he is successful his object has been attained, and twenty volumes of harangues—always the outcome of reflection—are not worth the few phrases which appealed to the brains it was required to convince.

It would be superfluous to add that the powerlessness of crowds to reason aright prevents them displaying any trace of the critical spirit, prevents them, that is, from being capable of discerning truth from error, or of forming a precise judgment on any matter. Judgments accepted by crowds are merely judgments forced upon them and never judgments adopted after discussion. In regard to this matter the individuals who do not rise above the level of a crowd are numerous. The ease with which certain opinions obtain general acceptance results more especially from the impossibility experienced by the majority of men of forming an opinion peculiar to themselves and based on reasoning of their own.

§3. The Imagination of Crowds

Just as is the case with respect to persons in whom the reasoning power is absent, the figurative imagination of crowds is very powerful, very active and very susceptible of being keenly impressed. The images evoked in their mind by a personage, an event, an accident, are almost as lifelike as the reality. Crowds are to some extent in the position of the sleeper whose reason, suspended for the time being, allows the arousing in his mind of images of extreme intensity which would quickly be dissipated could they be submitted to the action of reflection. Crowds, being incapable both of reflection and of reasoning, are devoid of the notion of improbability; and it is to be noted that in a general way it is the most improbable things that are the most striking.

This is why it happens that it is always the marvelous and legendary side of events that more specially strike crowds. When a civilisation is analysed it is seen that, in reality, it is the marvellous and the legendary that are its true supports. Appearances have always played a much more important part than reality in history, where the unreal is always of greater moment than the real.

Crowds being only capable of thinking in images are only to be impressed by images. It is only images that terrify or attract them and become motives of action.

For this reason theatrical representations, in which the image is shown in its most clearly visible shape, always have an enormous influence on crowds. Bread and spectacular shows constituted for the plebeians of ancient Rome the ideal of happiness, and they asked for nothing more. Throughout the successive ages this ideal has scarcely varied. Nothing has a greater effect on the imagination of crowds of every category than theatrical representations. The entire audience experiences at the same time the same emotions, and if these emotions are not at once transformed into acts, it is because the most unconscious spectator cannot ignore that he is the victim of illusions, and that he has laughed or wept over imaginary adventures. Sometimes, however, the sentiments suggested by the images are so strong that they tend, like habitual suggestions, to transform themselves into acts. The story has often been told of the manager of a popular theatre who, in consequence of his only playing sombre dramas, was obliged to have the actor who took the part of the traitor protected on his leaving the theatre, to defend him against the violence of the spectators, indignant at the crimes, imaginary though they were, which the traitor had committed. We have here, in my opinion, one of the most remarkable indications of the mental state of crowds, and especially of the facility with which they are suggestioned. The unreal has almost as much influence on them as the real. They have an evident tendency not to distinguish between the two.

The power of conquerors and the strength of States is based on the popular imagination. It is more particularly by working upon this imagination that crowds are led. All great historical facts, the rise of Buddhism, of Christianity, of Islamism, the Reformation, the French Revolution, and, in our own time, the threatening invasion of Socialism are the direct or indirect consequences of strong impressions produced on the imagination of the crowd.

Moreover, all the great statesmen of every age and every country, including the most absolute despots, have regarded the popular imagination as the basis of their power, and they have never attempted to govern in opposition to it. "It was by becoming a Catholic," said Napoleon to the Council of State, "that I terminated the Vendéen war. By becoming a Mussulman that I obtained a footing in Egypt. By becoming an Ultramontane that I won over the Italian priests, and had I to govern a nation of Jews I would rebuild Solomon's temple." Never perhaps since Alexander and Ceasar has any great man better understood how the imagination of the crowd should be impressed. His constant preoccupation was to strike it. He bore it in mind in his victories, in his harangues, in his speeches, in all his acts. On his deathbed it was still in his thoughts.

How is the imagination of crowds to be impressed? We shall soon see. Let us confine ourselves for the moment to saying that the feat is never to be achieved by attempting to work upon the intelligence or reasoning faculty, that is to say, by way of demonstration. It was not by means of cunning rhetoric that Antony succeeded in making the populace rise against the murderers of Caesar; it was by reading his will to the multitude and pointing to his corpse.

Whatever strikes the imagination of crowds presents itself under the shape of a startling and very clear image, freed from all accessory explanation, or merely having as accompaniment a few marvellous or mysterious facts; examples in point are a great victory, a great miracle, a great crime, or a great hope. Things must be laid before the crowd as a whole, and their genesis must never be indicated. A hundred petty crimes or petty accidents will not strike the imagination of crowds in the least, whereas a single great crime or a single great accident will profoundly impress them, even though the results be infinitely less disastrous than those of the hundred small accidents put together. The epidemic of influenza, which caused the death but a few years ago of five thousand persons in Paris alone, made very little impression on the popular imagination. The reason was that this veritable hecatomb was not embodied in any visible image, but was only learnt from statistical information furnished weekly. An accident which should have caused the death of only five hundred instead of five thousand persons, but on the same day and in public, as the outcome of an accident appealing strongly to the eye, by the fall, for instance, of the Eiffel Tower, would have produced, on the contrary, an immense impression on the imagination of the crowd. The probable loss of a transatlantic steamer that was supposed, in the absence of news, to have gone down in mid-ocean profoundly impressed the imagination of the crowd for a whole week. Yet official statistics show that 850 sailing vessels and 203 steamers were lost in the year 1894 alone. The crowd, however, was never for a moment concerned by these successive losses, much more important though they were as far as regards the destruction of life and property, than the loss of the Atlantic liner in question could possibly have been.

It is not, then, the facts in themselves that strike the popular imagination, but the way in which they take place and are brought under notice. It is necessary that by their condensation, if I may thus express myself, they should produce a startling image which fills and besets the mind. To know the art of impressing the imagination of crowds is to know at the same time the art of governing them.

Technology and the Circumpolar Village
Networking, Broadcasting, and Accessing the Future

V. Alia

We now find ourselves in the middle of the age of communication . . . the millennium is upon us and it seems at times we're more isolated than ever before. TV and computers are taking us further and further away from human contact. Yet, we yearn for human interaction . . .

Seventy-five years ago, we were all we had except for Saturday night radio. A hundred and fifty years ago, we were all we had. We must have been a hell of a lot more fascinating. We had to have been great storytellers. We certainly had a lot more time for each other . . . No TV to keep us amused, or e-mail love to find a relationship. Yet, the amount of information we have at our finger tips is astounding. Access such as we have never had before . . .

I wonder about our existence in the future and what communication skills will be required to survive . . . Can we live off our creativity and our ability to communicate?

Gary Farmer "Time in a Computer Chip"

Farmer's words of caution and inspiration infuse every aspect of *Aboriginal Voices,* the publication he founded and one that, despite his reservations, has a thriving Web page (see Appendix E). His concerns are heard widely in Aboriginal communities around the globe. But few people advocate avoiding the Internet or ignoring its potential power, especially in northern and remote communities. Instead, the trend is toward using that power to communicate the messages and languages of the senders clearly and carefully from community to community and from Aboriginal communities to the Outside. By the time this book is published, I suspect there will be as many new Web pages, e-mail addresses, and Web sites as are included in Appendix E.

While Gary Farmer struggles to find the proper balance between human and electronic contact from his informationally advantaged, urban home-base in Toronto, the founders of Nunavut are embracing new telecommunications technologies without hesitation. In 1996 the Nunavut Implementation Commission released a report about the role it hoped telecommunications would play in the new territory. "The road to Nunavut is along the information highway," they wrote (Bell 1996a, 16-7). In late 1999 Telesat Canada will launch the first in its new Nimiq satellite series, featuring a technology capable of bringing televisions signals into every Canadian home and paving

From *Uncovering the North*, pp. 97–113.

the way for the proposed Canada-wide Aboriginal television network. The Nimiq satellites will be companions to the Anik series, which continues with Telesat's announcement that it will launch the sixth generation of Anik satellites in 2000. The digital telecommunications network will create jobs for Nunavut citizens (a technician for each community as well as regional technologists and systems engineers), develop and link libraries and databases, and establish a sophisticated video-conferencing system that will amount to an arm of government.

The unique conditions of northern life are ideally suited to such experimentation. While teleconferences cannot replace direct human contact, they can certainly replace a good deal of the very difficult travel that stalls government processes and absorbs northern budgets. In Nunavut, futuristic communications systems will help maintain the Inuit way of governing, with power broadly distributed and structures decentralized. The wide-scattered, remote communities will be able to stay in touch without the dangers and delays experienced in the past. The system will allow members of the Legislative Assembly to attend meetings in their home communities without having to leave Iqaluit, or to attend caucus meetings in Iqaluit without having to leave their home communities.

Given sufficient funding and facilities, Nunavut's citizens will have greater access to each other and to government. And its well-developed videoconferencing system will reduce the enormous travel budget (in 1992-3, politicians in the government of the NWT spent $70 million on travel, about half of which was for Nunavut). As we have observed, northern travel not only absorbs funds but requires enormous expenditures of time because of the frequent delays caused by vagaries of weather and aging aircraft.

It is perhaps not surprising that the people of Nunavut are so comfortable travelling the information highway. They have long been well disposed to new technologies, having learned that new technologies could link with old ways and support an array of Inuit-run cultural literacy and communications projects. Indeed, they were among the first Canadians (and the first Aboriginal Canadians) to take television and radio into their own hands and to adapt television to their own needs.

As we have seen, representation on film has been replaced by a world in which film and television are partners. Before that could happen, broadcast programming and technology had to develop and reach a certain level of maturity. The following pages introduce some of the major milestones, challenges, and dilemmas facing northern Aboriginal people as they ease, and sometimes leap, into the technological future. After first considering the development of satellite television delivery and Aboriginal broadcasting, starting in the late 1960s, we look at the next stage — Television Northern Canada (TVNC) — which I and many others consider the most important achievement in Aboriginal communications in the world. TVNC is viewed in its international context, and a sketch is provided of kindred and sometimes connected projects such as Sámi broadcasting in Norway and Kalaallit broadcasting in Greenland.

The chapter also describes radio and telecommunications policy and addresses the impact of advertising on previously ad-free Aboriginal radio. It looks at radio and television as extensions of pre-broadcasting communications in "the circumpolar village," and considers two examples of the misuse of technology in promoting Aboriginal communications.

The Development of Northern Television

While most major northern television developments began in the early 1970s, there were important breakthroughs in the 1950s and '60s. CBC Northern Service, also known as CBC North, was established, as we have seen, in 1958. The service was originally from a group of ten former military and community radio stations, plus a shortwave service based in Montreal. CBC Northern Service operates from the following regional headquarters: CBC Yukon in Whitehorse; CBC Mackenzie in Yellowknife; CBC Eastern Arctic (Nunavut) in Iqaluit; CBC Western Arctic in Inuvik; CBC Kivalliq in Rankin Inlet; CBC Kuujjuaq Bureau in Kuujjuaq; and CBC Northern Service Quebec in Montreal.

After getting its Northern Service radio broadcasts fully under way in 1960, the CBC Northern Service proceeded to develop its television service. As in the case of radio, early northern television was produced primarily by and for non-Aboriginal people. The "Frontier Package," composed of four-hour packages of television programs as well as radio, was carried to seventeen communities starting in 1967. Its main claim to northernness was its availability in one northern region. The programs were taped from CBC's southern service and rebroadcast in the North. It eventually extended to the eastern Arctic, starting in Frobisher Bay in 1972, but the Frontier Package continued to be a relay service bringing programming by and about southern Canadians to the North.

The 1970s were a time of rapid change in society and in communications. During this decade, CBC's objective was to provide radio and television transmitters for every community with a population of 500 or more. Additional coverage was furnished by the territorial governments and a number of other agencies and organizations, which provided relay transmitters for most of the smaller communities, so that CBC broadcasts now reached almost all of the Canadian North.

The arrival of satellite-transmitted television marked an international breakthrough: Canada became the first country to develop a domestic telecommunications satellite system. In 1969 the Telesat Canada Bill established the Anik satellite system, which made it possible to distribute radio and television signals live. Telesat sent the first satellite-transmitted broadcast to Canadians over the Hermes Anik A satellite in 1972, and in 1973 CBC used the satellite to transmit the first live television newscast to the North (Television Northern Canada 1987, 15). In 1975 the Nunatsiakmiut Community Television Society began broadcasting over the satellite from Frobisher Bay (now Iqaluit – the name was changed in 1987) with support from the National Film Board. CBC's stations in Whitehorse, Yellowknife, Inuvik, and Iqaluit were able to serve a network of transmitters within the region surrounding each of the host-station communities.

In response to extensive lobbying by Inuit organizations in the late 1970s and early 1980s, the federal Department of Communications developed the Anik B trial-access program – a series of interactive audio and video experiments. In 1976 the satellite carried an experimental interactive audio project across northern Quebec. Titled Naaklavik I, the project linked eight radio stations. It was run by the Aboriginal communications society Taqramiut Nipingat Incorporated (TNI), which at the time was affiliated with the land claims lobby group the Northern Quebec Inuit Association (Roth and Valaskakis 1989, 225).

In 1978 the Anik B satellite carried the launch of the programs initiated by Project Inukshuk, named for the human-form stone sculptures that Inuit use to mark important places on the land. The federally funded project heralded the start of Inuit-produced television broadcasts. It was sponsored and organized by Inuit Tapirisat of Canada (ITC), with video production facilities in Frobisher Bay and Baker Lake. The Inukshuk project had several goals: "to train Inuit film and video producers, to establish Inuit production centres in the North, and to conduct interactive audio/video experiments utilizing the 12/14 GHz capability of the satellite to link six Arctic settlements" (Roth and Valaskakis 1989, 225). When Inukshuk first went to air in 1980, it sent sixteen and a half hours a week of television programming and teleconferencing to the six communities. A parallel project, Naaklavik II, was organized for northern Quebec, and was run by TNI. Based in Salluit, it served five communities.

From the start, it was known that these two projects were short-term and would receive only seed money. There were strong lobbying efforts by ITC and TNI to establish a permanent Inuit broadcasting service. In 1979 CBC opened a new northern service production centre in Rankin Inlet to serve the Keewatin region. Montreal remained the base for satellite-delivered radio service to the James Bay region. In 1980 the CRTC struck a committee to consider proposals to develop satellite television services for northern and remote communities. The nine-member committee, headed by Francois Thérrien, included John Amagoalik, who would become the first Aboriginal person to help set national communications policy in Canada. The committee emphasized the role of broadcasting in preserving and maintaining Aboriginal languages and cultures (CRTC 1986b, 515). The committee identified "a new broadcasting universe" and wrote, "Our first unanimous conclusion is that immediate action must be taken to meet the needs of the many Canadians who believe that, as regards broadcasting, they are being treated as second-class citizens . . . We cannot stress too strongly the immediacy of the problem: alternative television programming must be provided from Canadian satellites with no further delay" (CRTC 1980, 1).

In recognition of the CRTC's goal to ensure the distribution of more alternative programming to underserved areas, in 1981 Ottawa provided broadcast funding to both TNI and ITC. TNI used the funds to develop Inuktitut programming for northern Quebec, while ITC developed the Inuit Broadcasting Corporation (IBC), which produced radio and television, sharing a channel with CBC Northern Service on the Anik B satellite. Also in 1981, the CRTC licensed Canadian Satellite Communications Incorporated (CANCOM), a private satellite distribution service, with the stipulation that it make a significant commitment to providing Aboriginal programming. There were now two television distributors serving the North, CBC Northern Service and CANCOM (Roth 1996). In 1982 the Nunatsiakmiut Film Society, which was based in Frobisher Bay where it helped develop Inuit film and television, merged with IBC. Among the founders of the new amalgam was Joanasie Salamonie, one of the leaders who in 1971 had helped to establish the Inuit Tapirisat of Canada (ITC).[8]

Following the birth of the Northern Native Broadcast Access Program (NNBAP), there were complaints from the North that Inuit and other northerners had received short shrift from both satellite services, which gave priority to national and regional English network programming and often relegated IBC programming to late-night time slots or preempted it entirely (IBC 1985, 22). Ottawa's response was to strike a task force on broadcasting policy, which issued what became known as the Caplan-Sauvageau Report. It recommended CBC-produced Aboriginal-language broadcasts and a separate satellite system for the distribution of Aboriginal language programming (Canada 1986, 520-2).

The Aboriginal leadership criticized the report for using weak and ambiguous language, and in 1987 organized a meeting of all the northern Aboriginal communications societies to discuss the development of a dedicated satellite television channel (IBC 1985; TVNC 1987). They sought support from the federal government, the governments of Yukon and the Northwest Territories, and CBC Northern Service, which continued to share satellite space with the Aboriginal broadcast outlets. The communications societies issued a proposal for a non-profit corporation that would distribute, and eventually produce, programming by and for Aboriginal northerners. This proposal was to be realized with the creation of Television Northern Canada.

TVNC Enters — and Alters — the Picture

> At exactly 8:30 p.m., an Inuktitut voice signals the start of the world's largest aboriginal television network. Elder Akeeshoo Joamie of Iqaluit asks Jesus to guide TVNC to success. An English translation rolls slowly across the screen . . .
>
> The vision of TVNC became a reality with a montage of Inuit, Dene, Métis, Gwich'in, Kaska, Tuchone, Tlingit and non-aboriginal faces beamed to 22,000 households from Northern Labrador to the Yukon-Alaska border . . .
>
> TVNC is a non-profit consortium which aims to use television for social change.
>
> Lorraine Thomas, "Communicating across the Arctic"

When Television Northern Canada (TVNC) — a $10 million, federally funded dedicated satellite transponder service — began broadcasting via the Anik satellite system, it became the primary First Nations broadcasting distribution service in the North. TVNC now delivers programming in indigenous languages and English, sponsored by the governments of Yukon, NWT, and Nunavut, and by Arctic College and Yukon College, to over ninety-four communities from the Alaska-Yukon border to the Labrador coast, an area of 4.3 million square kilometres.

TVNC was incorporated 18 June 1990 as a non-profit corporation and licensed by the CRTC on 28 October 1991 to serve the Canadian North by "broadcasting cultural, social, political and educational programming to Canada's Native people," as its promotional literature says. The new network was heralded in both the northern and southern press. The *Ottawa Citizen* splashed the news, with three photographs, across most of a page, with the headline "Canada's Third National Network? TV Northern Canada is television by the North, about the North — and for the North" (Atherton 1991). The *Globe and Mail* gave the story more modest play in its National News section with the rather quiet headline "North Channels Its Resources." The reporter was more enthusiastic than the headline writers: "The network is the realization of a dream of many northerners to have a northern-produced alternative to the largely southern TV programming now coming into their homes" (Platiel 1992, A5). Three days after the *Globe and Mail* published the story by Native affairs reporter Rudy Platiel, the *Winnipeg Free Press* ran an almost identical story credited to Canadian Press, with a Toronto dateline. The *Winnipeg Free Press* gave it a more enthusiastic headline: "Nation's First Northern TV Network Launched Today" (Canadian Press 1992, C29) but buried it near the bottom of the major stories on one of its arts pages. The northern presses gave the story more prominence, usually on the front page. "TVNC Hits the Air," said the Yellowknife-based weekly *News/ North* (Saunders 1991).

TVNC was funded by the federal Department of Communications and is distributed via the Anik El satellite, with television uplink facilities in Iqaluit, Yellowknife, and Whitehorse. Its membership includes the Inuit Broadcasting Corporation; Inuvialuit Communications Society; Northern Native Broadcasting Yukon; Okalakatiget Society; Taqramiut Nipingat Incorporated; Native Communications Society of the NWT; Government of the Northwest Territories; Yukon College; and the National Aboriginal Communications Society. There are also associate members: CBC Northern Service; Kativik School Board; Labrador Community College; Northern Native Broad-casting Terrace; Wawatay Native Communications Society; and Telesat Canada.

TVNC serves approximately 100,000 people, roughly equally divided between Aboriginal and non-Aboriginal ancestry. The region's Aboriginal languages served by TVNC programming are Inuktitut, Inuvialuktun, Chipewyan, Dogrib, North and South Slavey, Cree, Gwich'in, Han, Kaska, Tagish, Northern and Southern Tutchone, and Tlingit. The vision of TVNC founders included a fully pan-Arctic and Canada-wide network that promises to greatly enhance the opportunities for north-south communication. In 1998 TVNC petitioned the CRTC to become a national Aboriginal television service, and in 1999 received permission to become the Aboriginal Peoples Television Network (APTN). The new service will be part of all the basic cable packages.

In a recently published decision renewing CANCOM's license for its national satellite relay distribution undertaking (SRDU), the CRTC reaffirmed its dedication to serving remote communities: "The Commission notes the concerns expressed in interventions regarding the reception quality of SRDU signals, particularly in Canada's High Arctic. The commission expects the licensee to ensure, as resources permit, that its signals are available for reception in all communities in Canada" (CRTC 1998, 2). The CRTC also underscored CANCOM's commitment to continue funding four northern Aboriginal radio network services at $250,000 annually; $85,000 for Wawatay's transmission facilities at Moose Factory, Ontario; and $150,000 to TVNC for satellite uplink facilities at Whitehorse, Yukon. CANCOM also agreed to continue to provide marketing assistance, and "to provide TVNC with five free hours per week of video uplink time for the delivery of southern based Aboriginal programming" (CRTC 1998, 3).

Given the scarcity of journalism education for northern Aboriginal people, especially after the failure of the Arctic College program noted in Chapter 2, IBC and TVNC have both become involved in training new journalists and offering programs to upgrade the skills of working journalists. As we noted in the previous chapter, since 1996, IBC has conducted training sessions at its New Media Centre in Iqaluit. In 1998 TVNC started a new service to help find appropriate programs for prospective journalism students as well as working professionals who want to improve their skills. As of 1998, TVNC has a Web page featuring internships and training programs for filmmakers. At the time of writing, the latest listing included the following programs, grants, and awards: the Canada Council for the Arts' Project Grants to Production Organizations for Media Arts Development; the Canadian Film and Television Production Association's National Training Programme as well as their International Intern Programme for Canadian Youth; a CTV Fellowship to attend the Banff Television Festival; the Manitoba Indian Cultural Education Centre's Aboriginal Broadcast Training Initiative; the National Film Board of Canada's Aboriginal Filmmaking Program; Ross Charles Awards to Aboriginal people specializing in telecommunications and broadcasting; and the Women's Technical

Internship from WTN (Women's Television Network) Foundation.

TVNC Programming

TVNC airs a broad spectrum of programming. In the early days of TVNC Lorraine Thomas summarized a typical Wednesday evening of TVNC fare: an English-language CBC Northern Service current affairs program from Yellowknife is followed by an Inuktitut production by IBC in Iqaluit, aimed at Inuit teens in the eastern Arctic; then, a distance learning course from Arctic College, a teen show produced in English by the NWT government's Culture and Communications Department, a show about traditions and current issues produced in Inuvialuktun by the Inuvialuit Communications Society for Inuvialuit in the western Arctic. "After a visit to the Inuvik region, TVNC swings over to Yukon leaders discussing current issues, produced by Northern Native Broadcast [sic] Yukon. An international documentary about aboriginal peoples . . . [then] an Inuktitut program . . . by CBC North [Northern Service]. National aboriginal issues are then covered . . . and the broadcast evening wraps up with the Government of the NWT's Question Period" (Thomas 1992, 20).

In 1995 TVNC, which was continuing to develop its programming, launched northern Canada's first daily newscast. *Nunatsiaq News* topped its front page with the story in Inuktitut syllabics, followed by the energetic English version headlined "TVNC Leaps into Daily Newscast": "It's only two minutes a day and it's produced by volunteers in Yellowknife, but it's northern Canada's first daily newscast and Television Northern Canada is hoping it will grow into something much bigger" (Bell 1995, 1, 2). The newscast originates in Yellowknife in the studios of the Native Communications Society of the NWT. Gerry Giberson, TVNC's director of operations, said the early effort is "more like a headline news service . . . than a full-fledged news report" and features a pan-Arctic review that points viewers to stories they can follow in more depth in other media. Giberson said "We're the only region in Canada, perhaps in North America that does not receive a daily regional television newscast. What we're trying to do is fill that gap" (Bell 1995, 1, 2).

One of the TVNC's first major stars was the children's superhero Super Shamou, an Inuk in cape and leotards played by Peter Tapatai. Super Shamou was created by Barney Pattunguyak and Peter Tapatai for IBC and was aired by IBC on the CBC Northern Service Network (Melanie Legault, personal communication, 18 November 1998). With humour, energy, and intelligence, the character addresses all of the most serious issues confronting northern children and adults. A Super Shamou comic book addresses everything from solvent abuse to community cooperation. The premier (and only) issue, which was published in both English-Inuktitut and French-Inuktitut versions, contains the story of the origin of the superhero, born a "mild-mannered Inuk" named Peter Tapatai and transformed by spells and charms into the hero who will "right wrongs and combat evil" and is told, "Peter, you have been chosen. The people of the Arctic must have peace and justice." *Super Shamou* gave birth to another popular TVNC-broadcast, IBC-produced children's program, *The Takuginai Family,* which teaches "respect for elders, traditional Inuit culture, and the Inuktitut language" (David 1998, 37). *Takuginai* means "look here" in Inuktitut (Burns 1992).

Still another Inuit children's show premiered in October 1998. Produced by the Kativik School Board for KSB-TV in Nunavik (Inuit northern Quebec) and broadcast over TVNC, *Allai* airs twice a week during the school year and features a puppet family who explore a range of issues on Inuktitut language, Inuit culture, and Nunavik geography (George 1998, 33).

Programs Produced by TVNC Members

The Government of the Northwest Territories (GNWT) produces seven hours of original programming each week for TVNC. *GNWT Presents* includes a variety of programming. *Live and Well* is an interactive discussion program. It broadcasts live with phone-in lines encouraging viewers to participate in discussing themes related to health and well being.

The Inuit Broadcasting Corporation produces five hours of original Inuktitut programming weekly. *Kippinguijautiit* (Things to pass time by) is a half-hour entertainment show with what IBC calls "funny and interesting stories on traditional and contemporary Inuit ways of life." It includes music, sports, and special events coverage. A 1992 audience survey named it the most popular Inuktitut-language program. *Qanuq Isumavit?* (What do you think?), IBC's only live production, runs two and a half hours and invites the audience to discuss current issues and events in detail, via phone-in links. *Qaggiq* (Drum dance gathering) is a half-hour journal of news and current affairs. *Takuginai* (Look here) is a half-hour program targeted at five to seven year olds but watched by people of all ages. Its young hosts are joined by Johnny the lemming and other locally made puppets. *Qaujisaut* (To see, to find out) is a half-hour program directed to Inuit youth "facing hard choices – caught between two cultures." *Qimaivvik* (Pass on knowledge) is a half-hour cultural program.

Two half-hour programs in the lnuvialuktun language are produced by the Inuvialuit Communications Society (ICS). *Tamapta* is a cultural and information program. *Suangaan* covers current events in the Beaufort region.

The Native Communications Society of the NWT (NCS) produces two half-hour programs a week called *Dene Weekly Perspective,* broadcast in four Dene languages – Dogrib, Chipewyan, North Slavey, and South Slavey.

Northern Native Broadcasting Yukon (NNBY) produces two programs for TVNC, one in English and one in Gwich'in. *NEDAA* (Your eye) is NNBY's flagship program, an award-winning hour-long magazine show. *Haa Shagoon* is a Gwich'in cultural program.

Each week the Okalakatiget Society produces a half-hour program: *Labradorimiut* (People of Labrador) is a magazine with current affairs, information, and entertainment. The program alternates between English and Inuktitut.

Taqramiut Nipingat Incorporated (TNI) produces four original programs totalling two hours a week: *Nunavimiut, Ungavamiut, Taqramiut,* and *TNI Presents.*

Although it does not produce its own programming, Yukon College presents a variety of educational programming acquired from other sources. In 1997-8 the featured program *Dotto's Data Cafe* dealt with the Internet.

Programs Produced by Associate Members

CBC Northern Service produces two half-hour daily news programs. *Igalaaq* (Window) is a daily news program in Inuktitut, hosted by Rassi Nashalik from Yellowknife. CBC *Northbeat is* a half-hour

program in English, hosted by Paul Andrew and Patricia Russell. It features news, profiles, and northern documentaries. Documentaries shown in lnuktitut on *Igalaaq* are repeated on *Northbeat* with English subtitles later the same night. CBC Northern Service also has a Real Audio service at its Web site, from which to download these programs.

Four hours of educational programming are provided by the Kativik School Board. *KSB Presents* offers a broad spectrum of programs, including work by other producers and original Inuktitut programs on business, economics, and history. *Education in Nunavik,* a monthly magazine included in the *KSB Presents* time slot, covers Kativik School Board activities.

Wawatay Native Communications Society produces a half-hour program in the Cree language. *Wawatay Presents* is a magazine that includes a range of issues, cultural affairs, documentaries, and entertainment.

The Pan-Arctic Vision

The intention of TVNC's founders was not only to have southern distribution, but to develop a broadcasting service that would eventually reach the entire circumpolar North. That objective, and the very existence of TVNC as a disseminating agent of Aboriginal languages, strongly suggests the need to modify Nelson Graburn's cultural-genocide vision formulated in the early 1980s. Like many Aboriginal and non-Aboriginal people, Graburn had argued that "television in the Arctic not only reinforces the use of English as a first language, but also it has become an instrument for slow assimilation and hence for cultural ethnocide" (1982, 7). In the 1970s the Anik satellite system had brought high-quality telephone service to the 25,000 Inuit living in fifty-seven communities and transmitted sixteen hours a day of English-language television programming over CBC (Valaskakis 1982, 20). Yet even in the early 1980s, when Graburn was writing, Kalaallit-Nunaata Radioa was producing regular Greenlandic television and radio programming, Taqramiut Nipingat was broadcasting Inuktitut radio in northern Quebec, and TVNC was already a gleam in the eyes of the pioneers on the Inukshuk project, who had been watching the evolution of satellite technology since 1970 (Graburn 1982, 16; Valaskakis 1982, 19).

Like Graburn, Valaskakis expressed concern about the relationship of television to the cultural marginalization of northern Aboriginal people. However, she foresaw more Native-language programming than ethnocide in Canada's northern future, and the rich programming outlined above seems to support her optimism.

Clearly the prominence of indigenous-language programming is key to allaying concerns about cultural marginalization of Aboriginal peoples. Canada is not the only northern nation where Aboriginal-language broadcasts are a priority. There are parallel developments throughout the circumpolar North. Nordic nations are cooperatively producing two Sámi language courses, *Davvin,* for people whose first language is not Sámi, and *Samas,* for primary Sámi speakers. A variety of media are in use, with textbooks linked to broadcasts on the national radio networks of Norway, Sweden, and Finland.

Sámi broadcasting is evolving slowly. As of 1994 there were only four to seven hours a year of Sámi-language programming in Sweden, and Norway had established a permanent Sámi television department that was producing ten to fifteen hours a year. Finland had no production units of its own, but was broadcasting four to six hours a year of programs from the Swedish and Norwegian networks (Minority Rights Group 1994, 162). Radio was more highly developed. Finland was the first country to establish a radio channel entirely in Sámi control (ibid., 163). The station produces all-day Sámi programming in northern Enare and Skolt Sámi dialects as well as Finnish, with about five hours a day of Sámi-language programming. Sámi Radio in Norway produces three broadcasts a day from Karasjok in the northern Sámi dialect and a small program from Trondheim in the southern Sámi dialect. Sweden produced a half-hour weekly national Swedish-language program on Sámi issues, three and a half hours a week of national programming in the Northern dialect, and a half-hour weekly program in the southern dialect. To broaden the scope and availability of Sámi programming, Salmi Radio departments in all three countries organized a cooperative news team that oversees transmission of news and public affairs programming throughout the region (ibid., 163).

In Alaska, the radio/telecommunications future is evolving differently, but with technologies that will eventually be closely tied to those in the rest of the North. In the Yup'ik village of Toksook Bay, in western Alaska (400 miles from the Russian border), the new Alaska Wireless company has installed boxes that bring in satellite-beamed transmissions and provide Internet access about "three times faster than the current standard at American corporations and 10 times faster than in most American homes" without the need for telephones, modems, or Internet user fees (Fine 1998, C1). Like Canada's Anik satellites, which have brought both telephone and TVNC services, the satellite link has the potential to bring, and transmit, not only the Internet but also indigenous programming to and from Alaska.

Success, Failure ... Recovery?

It would seem that the impressive roster of programs assembled within the first few years of TVNC's history would inspire increased support. Instead, in 1997, the Canadian government announced a 30 percent funding cut to TVNC to be spread over the 1997 and 1998 seasons. In response, the TVNC board of directors decided to work to turn TVNC from a northern to a national Aboriginal television network. The new network, formed in 1999, the Aboriginal Peoples Television Network, replaces TVNC (Miller 1998, 26-9). It will have an Aboriginal CEO and twenty-one Aboriginal board members from different regions. APTN is licensed to broadcast 120 hours of programming a week in English, French, and up to fifteen Aboriginal languages.

The TVNC cuts can be seen as the next step in a long line of withdrawals of government support from Aboriginal media. Since 1990 cuts have reflected the government's policy of increasingly encouraging the privatization of news media (for example, by allowing commercials on public radio and by diminishing or cancelling the funding of print media). The implication is that media institutions are meant to be profit making or at least self-sustaining. The reality is that many are forced into volunteerism — yet no one would suggest that Toronto's City-TV should switch to volunteer labour if it could not afford to continue broadcasting. There is an underlying double standard that assumes that although no self-respecting "mainstream" journalist would consider such an option, Aboriginal journalists should be willing to work for free to keep their media alive (literally at all cost). Canada has long supported the notion of allowing its citizens' many voices to be heard. These days the trend is toward corporate "wisdom" (not unlike that heard in the United States), which dictates the "new" funding policy: if you can't turn a profit, you don't deserve a voice.

The reactions to the 1990 round of funding cuts were many, and strong. A non-Native journalist wrote, "What a botched job! The way in which Secretary of State Gerry Weiner slashed funding for native newspapers and broadcasters is a classic case of political arbitrariness . . . It's a tale of failure to justify action by policy . . . a tale of shameless abandonment of what capable government administrations are supposed to do . . . There are ways of achieving federal savings without imperilling the existence of native media that have made a substantial contribution to education, civic consciousness and skills training in the last 20 years" (White 1990, A4).

Phil Fontaine, then head of the Assembly of Manitoba Chiefs, attributed the cuts in part to ignorance, but said "they also rise out of a deliberate strategy to silence those who have been vocal. This government doesn't appreciate dissent, in fact it won't tolerate it . . . The cause of aboriginal people is seen simply as an irritant" (Russell 1990, 12).

The early 1990s saw repeated federal cuts to the Northern Native Broadcast Access Program and the Aboriginal language programs. The axe continues to fall. A 1996 headline in *Nunatsiaq News* reads, "IBC Gets Nasty Surprise in Latest Budget." The story, which was not covered in the southern media, identifies a 14.7 percent budget cut "that will strip $250,000 from IBC's incoming revenue in 1996-97, nearly twice the shortfall that IBC officials had been expecting . . . Added to that is question after question about whether IBC will even survive in the future" (Bell 1996b, 14). IBC executive director Debbie Brisebois said the uncertainty is "really wearing people down, year after year." She said Inuit broadcasters were led to believe the cuts would be smaller. The duplicity and the unexpected loss "means another blow to the morale of IBC's underpaid and overworked staff" (ibid., 14).

Cuts to television broadcasting have been echoed in underfunding of radio. Given severe cutbacks, broken commitments, and insecurity about the future, northern community radio has had to struggle against the temptation to rely on whatever funding happens to come its way. Like the print media (although with more consistent success), community radio has come to depend on low wages, minimal staffing, volunteer personnel to supplement paid staff (where it exists at all), and other forms of assistance from within the community. Along with the formally CRTC-approved stations, "pirate" and "trail" or "moccasin telegraph" stations continue to thrive.

New CRTC policy, which was set in September 1990, offset some of the losses from the 1990 cutbacks and fostered greater independence, by permitting Native radio stations to earn advertising revenues. Stations without competitors were allowed almost unrestricted advertising, up to 250 minutes of sales spots per day (Langford 1990). However, not everyone considers the advent of advertising a positive development.

I was in Whitehorse, tuned in to CHON-FM, the radio station of Northern Native Broadcasting Yukon (NNBY) the day it shifted from a no-advertising policy to a broadcast day filled with ads. The effect was jarring, to say the least. At the time many people expressed concern about the intrusiveness of advertising in the broadcast day, but most NNBY staff members expressed relief that the station would survive the funding cuts and continue to serve its listeners (Alia 1991a). In a letter to me dated 6 December 1995, Helen Fallding, who was working at CHON-FM at the time it adopted the ads, reflected on the situation:

> I have lots of concerns about the move to commercial aboriginal radio. I have no Idea how it's all playing itself out at this point at CHON-FM, but while I was there, there was more and more white business "expertise" at the management and advertising sales level, aimed at increasing the station's commercial visability. The people hired had no clue about aboriginal culture or values and didn't seem interested in learning anything. The result [included] some terrible decisions. One top administrator saw the station as essentially a country-and-western station whose target audience should be C & W listeners, not aboriginal people. An ad salesperson designed ads for a strip show at a local tavern, which were aired. Perhaps these were growing pains and the board has taken back control.

The jury is still out as to the continuing extent of the "growing pains." In purely economic terms, CHON-FM is a stunning success. In 1998 the Yukon-wide service kept its seventeen community stations occupied with programming supported by $250,000 in advertising revenues (Curley 1993).

There have been other responses to cutbacks. One precedent-setting move came in Saskatchewan. When the CBC Saskatoon station was forced to shut down, employees obtained a grant from the Saskatchewan government and in December 1990 formed a corporation from which to manage a restructured employee-run station.

The Circumpolar Village: Strengths and Weaknesses

> Inuit are nomads— There is nothing that frustrates Inuit more than being made to remain in one spot . . . It is no wonder that Inuit treasure the Internet, for if they cannot bodily leave their communities, at least their minds can wander at will . . . [They] rejoice in the ability to compare opinions abroad, as they did when traveling at will.
>
> For the hamlet is the new iglu, and the Internet is the new Land.
>
> Rachel Qitsualik

The North's "small town" qualities, which were discussed in the introduction to this book, persist in the computer age. In fact, in many ways the Internet and satellite technology have picked up where town meetings left off. In some cases, they have *become* the town meetings. Satellites carry community-to-community meetings, enabling people to convene in weather that would prohibit travel and to bridge distances beyond the capabilities of budgets. The Internet carries interpersonal, intergroup, interregional, and international dialogue. It helps bring Aboriginal people and Aboriginal media to each other, and to non-Aboriginal people. It helps to "mainstream" marginalized media — a mixed blessing because "alternative" and "minority" media have in the past both lost and gained from privacy and smallness.

Most of the negative effects of technology are due not to the technology itself, but to the ways people use it. Often, there is such a romance with the possibilities, we fail to consider the relationship between the machinery and the actual human needs

and uses for its services. In the following sections I discuss two examples of what I consider shameful failures — failures all the more disappointing because each project should have had considerable success. The people in charge failed to consider the fact that the finest media productions and the availability of state-of-the-art technology are valuable only if they are distributed to people who can use them. In both cases, the agency in question lost funds, good will, and the opportunity to reach a global audience with the very works it was designed to promote.

Wasting Opportunities

Throughout the North, Aboriginal filmmakers and broadcasters are taking control of their own productions, and the presence of Outside filmmakers is diminishing. When Outsiders do come North, they are supervised, advised, and sometimes monitored by official and unofficial territorial, regional, or community authorities. More indigenous actors are being hired than in the past, and not always as extras. The Aboriginal broadcasters are tackling an increasing number of extended documentary projects: series, made-for-TV movies, and documentary films to be shown on their own networks and marketed elsewhere as well.

In 1998 the National Film Board sent out an Internet advertisement for its Aboriginal Directors Series. It was a wonderful way to promote Canadian Aboriginal filmmakers worldwide. However, would-be purchasers from outside Canada were then told the films could be purchased only from the New York distributor (at prices several hundred percent higher than those in Canada), or, in many cases, could not be purchased, rented, or shown outside Canada at all. To an extent, this is symptomatic of the NFB's poorly coordinated promotion and distribution programs in general. However, the effect on Aboriginal filmmakers is particularly problematic, given the NFB's special commitment to their work.

In the late 1990s I found myself in an ironic situation. As the first recipient of Western Washington University's Professorship in Canadian Culture (a position whose endowment came partly from the Canadian government), I was charged with the task of bringing Canadian culture to a wider audience in the United States. Because one of Canada's major cultural contributions is its wealth of films — particularly documentaries — and the National Film Board itself, it should come as no surprise that one of the first things I planned was a program of NFB films. Imagine my dismay upon learning there was no way to show them! Some could be purchased at wildly inflated prices from the American distributor (in 1998, a film costing Cdn$29.95 cost US$400.00). Some could not be shown at all. In a surreal conversation with an NFB official, I argued to no avail. It made no difference that I am both a Canadian and an American citizen, that I had come to Washington State directly from Canada for the sole purpose of teaching and demonstrating Canada's cultural riches. I was told that even the videos I had purchased for use in my Canadian university classes could not legally be shown to students in the United States. The situation never was resolved, and the people in Washington never did have access to most of the films I'd hoped to show. How silly it seems, to endow a culture chair and keep the culture locked away in private closets! It's time for someone to think more clearly, and for the various departments and programs to learn how to communicate more effectively with each other.

The second example involves CBC Northern Service recordings. Since the 1970s the CBC Northern Service has been creating a miniature recording industry of its own, an enterprise that has fed its programming day and encouraged a number of northern Aboriginal musicians. For several reasons, the project's only success has been its production — and airplay — of a number of fine recordings, using (in most cases) the finest technology, equipment, and personnel available.

At the same time that Greenland has sent a stunning array of recordings across its own country and to Denmark, Nunavut, and other parts of the world via well-developed public and private outlets, most of Canada's northern artists have remained narrowly distributed and little known. Only the occasional northern artist reaches a wider audience. It takes the Nashville machine or another American marketing outlet to push a Susan Aglukark or a Jerry Alfred beyond the Nunavut or the Yukon border.

CBC Northern Service launched its recording operation in 1973 with a two-record 45 rpm set of the Inuit singer Charlie Panigoniak. Two years later another two-record set was released, featuring the Sugluk Group from Sugluk (now Salluit) in northern Quebec. More funds were allocated in the late 1970s

and about 120 records were produced. Thanks largely to non-CBC recordings, some of the artists are quite well known today — for example, songwriter/singer and CBC broadcaster William Tagoona and singer/songwriter and prominent filmmaker Alanis Obomsawin. In the early 1980s the production unit was moved from Montreal to Ottawa and the recordings were released as twelve-inch stereo LPs (Linttell 1988, 292-3).

Unfortunately, CBC never made a major commitment to marketing or promoting the recordings. As with many other fine projects the corporation undertakes, this was apparently intended primarily to produce materials to air on CBC radio — an admirable but inadequate objective. In 1988 the communication officer for CBC Northern Service, Perry Linttell, described the more recent recordings as "commercially available," but such a designation requires a large imaginative stretch — they never have been easy to obtain.

The follow-up of marketing in the 1990s has been poor to nil, and the whole recording program remains one of CBC's best-kept secrets. I have had a hard time obtaining so-called "current" recordings, even from CBC. On a couple of occasions I was able to purchase albums in the lobby of the CBC studio in Whitehorse. Usually, when I ask about them in one of the northern broadcast outlets (in Whitehorse, Yellowknife, and Iqaluit) or in the national distribution office in Toronto, the response is a blank look.

CBC's shortsightedness about its recording artists is a shame — a major loss to the artists and to Canada's knowledge of its own artists, not to mention their promotion to the rest of the world. There has never been a consistent policy or consistent funding or promotion effort. Few people know the recordings even exist. With CBC's marketing office at its new Toronto headquarters, there is a perfect opportunity to re-issue the old albums on CD or cassette and to release some of the many other recordings done inhouse and given limited air-play. The CBC recording program remains one of the weakest links in the Canadian communications picture, and one that is especially damaging to northern artists for whom access is so costly and difficult.

As broadcast and electronic media expand, more information and culture are brought to more people, with less and less control from Ottawa. Questions of distribution and broadcast rights will still have to be negotiated nationally and internationally, but the opportunities for wider distribution will continue to increase and will eventually push some of the boundaries and bureaucratic tangles aside. Aboriginal northerners are learning to use the Internet to facilitate this process.

The North on the Net

When I began the research for this book in early 1990, the Internet was the province of a few "techies." Today, it is rapidly becoming the primary medium of expression for the voices of many individuals and groups. Of the earlier communication media, only radio continues to relay grassroots information frequently, freely, and rapidly throughout the North. In terms of North-South communication, the Internet is far more effective than radio. Thus, what may have begun as carefree local expressions are becoming increasingly carefully chosen and constructed messages. The same concerns Aboriginal journalists are expressing about who controls their newspapers, in discussions between editors and Aboriginal councils and politicians, affect Internet communications, which are often linked directly to the newspapers and therefore are subject to the same struggles for power, expression, and control. The one unarguable truth is that these sites are expanding and increasing and are likely to continue to do so in the foreseeable future.

By 1998 all fifty-eight of the communities in the Northwest Territories (including the portion that in 1999 became the Territory of Nunavut) were connected to the World Wide Web. The connections were the result of a two-year project undertaken by Ardicom, a consortium of predominantly Aboriginal-owned northern businesses (Zellen 1998, 50). Using cable services provided by the Arctic Co-op and NorthwesTel's telephone network, Ardicom's two-way, high-speed digital communications network will gradually expand to support a range of information services, including videoconferencing, telemedicine, distance education, and the Internet (Wilkin 1997, 10).

There is a variety of opinion among Aboriginal journalists and leaders on the benefits and dangers of the Internet. Several observers contrast the new medium with television, which has been viewed as the most assimilationist of the media. James Hmyshyn, a copy editor for Northern News Services

in Yellowknife, thinks the Internet is a less inherently assimilationist medium than television, because it strengthens the virtual community. At the same time, he acknowledges that communicators on the Net lose some of their cultural distinctness because of the worldwide connection. The Net paradoxically both dilutes and strengthens the culture of origin (Zellen 1998, 51-2).

Jim Bell, editor of *Nunatsiaq News,* also draws a contrast between television and the Net. In his view, the Internet provides an antidote to the cultural demolition that has occurred in non-Aboriginal television. Another observer contrasts the new technology's culture-preserving potential with the negative effects of television described in the famous speech of Inuit leader Rosemarie Kuptana: "We might liken the onslaught of southern television and the absence of native television to the neutron bomb ... Neutron bomb television ... destroys the soul of a people but leaves the shell of a people walking around" (Brisebois 1983, 107).

One way of countering this soul-destroying onslaught is through the preservation and dissemination of Aboriginal culture. Jim Bell sees great potential for Aboriginal communities in CD-ROM, digital video discs, and other multimedia technologies, which can provide storage for important audio and visual material (Zellen 1998, 52). These technologies offer an effective way to store and transmit oral histories, materials from community and regional archives, music, and visual art. Bell thinks the Internet offers a way of "fighting back" — a chance for Aboriginal people to "send the information the other way" (Zellen 1998, 52).

Fred Lepine, a Métis writer, musician, and philosopher from Hay River, NWT, loves the Internet but is less optimistic about its capacity for preserving cultural integrity. He sees the same lure of the "'outside world" that worried Inuit leaders who held out against the proliferation of non-northern, non-indigenous television in the Canadian North (Zellen 1998, 52).

To avoid being overwhelmed by the lure of the Outside, northern and Aboriginal groups must be able to put their own information on the Net. The Northwest Territories Community Access Program (CAP) was established to aid communities in developing their own Web sites and to teach uses of the Internet to people in the territories' communities.

There are now many rich sources on the Internet for and about northern indigenous peoples. Appendix E provides a list of such Internet resources current to February 1999. For a Canada-wide overview of information on first peoples, Miles Morrisseau recommends *The First Perspective On-Line,* which he calls "the best on-line publication for . . . news, information and current events in Native Canada . . . Unlike most publication sites, it doesn't just . . . try to suck you into buying the hard copy. It actually provides the best of the newspaper online" (Morrisseau 1997, 53). The beautiful, information-packed arts and culture magazine, *Aboriginal Voices,* has a Web page and an e-mail address (abvoices@inforamp.net). Aboriginal entrepreneurs are represented by *Native Cyber Trade,* with pages on arts and crafts, nations, Indian gaming, and resources (links). *Spirit of Aboriginal Enterprise* is a site created by First Nations Communications (FNC). It includes an on-line magazine, profiles of Aboriginal entrepreneurs, and an FNC page with movies — such as a tour of the Canadian Museum of Civilization — that can be downloaded in Quicktime format (Morrisseau 1997, 53).

The usefulness of the Net for northern peoples is not, of course, limited to Canada. In the Sámi world, 1996 marked the turning-point in the information explosion. Before 1996 there were Sámi Web sites in Finland and Sweden, and "a few pages on university servers in Norway" (Forsgren 1998, 34). In 1996 Sámi youth organizations created a Web site offering daily updates of the Fourth World Indigenous Youth Conference, an experimental beginning that spurred other projects. In 1997 the journal *Samefolket* (The Sámi people) and the North Sámi *Min Aigit* (Our time) created Web sites. While most communication is likely to continue to be in Swedish, Norwegian, and Finnish, the North Sámi are also able to use and promote their own language, with fonts developed by Apple. Apple also developed an Inuktitut program for use by Canadian Inuit in and around Nunavut and Nunavik and Dene fonts are now available for downloading for Windows and Macintosh in Dogrib, Chipewyan, North Slavey, and South Slavey.

In a recent development in the United States, the American Indian Radio on Satellite network distribution system (AIROS) began a twenty-four-hour-a-day distribution system, using the Internet and public radio. Run by Native American Public Telecommunications, it has partial funding from the Corporation for Public Broadcasting and headquar-

ters in Lincoln, Nebraska, with a Web site and e-mail address (see Appendix E). It also has a video distribution service, VMV, with an archive of Native American videos and public television programs available to tribal communities.

Phone, Fax, Frustration: Companions to the Networked North

It is clear from the rapid development of northern Web sites and distance education programs in Nunavut, NWT, Yukon, and elsewhere that northerners are often more familiar with high-tech communications than are southerners. Sophisticated computers have been commonplace in eastern Arctic adult education and other centres for years. Satellite dishes sit on ancient rocks in tiny settlements whose inhabitants still spend much of their lives on the land. The Inuit Circumpolar Conference 1989 General Assembly in Sisimiut, Greenland, presented a demonstration by representatives of the Inuit Cultural Institute of the program that translates English into Inuktitut syllabics.

In addition to these technologies, fax machines are a key communication tool in the North. Phone lines are the most reliable and least fallible means of reaching other communities and Outside, and they are used extensively. As Cairns has noted, "I think there is a fax machine in all but two communities in the western Arctic" (1990, 9). Northerners' enthusiasm for the fax machine mirrors their acceptance of other technologies. Notes Leona Meyer, "It's amazing . . . It has just sort of mushroomed and the smallest community has a fax machine to the point where some people seldom use the mails . . . any more. You sort of wonder how you existed without it" (1990, 25). Northerners use fax and e-mail as alternatives to costly air freight and slow postal service and are looking into other uses for the fax machine. Says Cairns, "I hope that new legislation would allow faxed documents to be accepted as if they were originals" (1990, 493-4). Others such as Lyle Walsh see possibilities for the fax machine on election day: "I am not a salesman for a fax machine, but you . . . look at the way you run elections and it is sort of 1932 technology" (1990). But every technology has its limitations, and facsimile is no exception. Some northern communities have only a single telephone, which means adding fax to already overused facilities. And like computer modems, fax machines can not be installed where there are only radio phones.

There is a huge gap between potential and actual availability of new technologies. In 1999 the CRTC is expected to provide for subsidies to improve telephone services in northern and remote regions. This will help bring the North more fully into the new communications universe. In 1997 Taqramiut Nipingat Inc., Nunavik's Inuit broadcasting service, tried to become an Internet service provider, with disastrous financial results. As of March 1999 only seven of Nunavik's fifteen communities had access to the Internet, and this was limited to public access sites maintained by freenet provider Nunavik.Net in six communities and a site at Kiluutaq School in Umiujaq (Appendix E). Calling for strong CRTC support, Jim Bell said. "Canada's thinly populated North is turning into a telecommunications slum ... [with] a few centres of relative privilege: Iqaluit, Yellowknife, and Whitehorse, for example" (Bell 1999, 9).

In summing up, it is well to bear in mind Gary Farmer's cautionary words about the limits to technology. The particular conditions in which northern communications are placed make every technological breakthrough a welcome event. Thoughtful northerners are aware of the pitfalls in assuming that technology will replace human-to-human contact.

Even in the Utopian vision of technology that the Nunavut founders have in mind, caution will have to be exercised.

Interactive computers provide a new medium for print, and are swiftly evolving into media that transmit visual and auditory material as well. Interactive radio carries voices across great and small distances. Interactive television goes a step further, allowing body language and facial expressions to be carried. Soon, virtual media will produce facsimiles of "real" experience, including tactile experience. None of these can replace the joys and stresses of communicating in person. But news media haven't been face-to-face since the days when troubadours and town criers roamed the streets. Their closest descendants are probably the storytellers who still inhabit longhouses, tents, and snowhouses, friendship centres, and public libraries. And, as Rachel Qitsualik has said, Aboriginal people continue both the nomadic and the communications traditions in today's communities, using today's technologies.

Leaving the new "iglu" and the new Internet "land" of Nunavut and heading west, the next chapter looks at the communications experiences of Yukoners, to see what can be learned from looking more deeply at communications in one northern region.

Cool Bodies: TV Ad Talk

M. Gillespie

It is now a common theoretical assumption among cultural theorists and anthropologists that social identities, differences and inequalities are shaped and legitimated through our material and cultural consumption (Appadurai, 1986; Douglas and Isherwood, 1979; McCracken, 1988; Miller, 1987). Bourdieu has given the now classic demonstration of the way in which distinctions of social class and status are expressed through distinctions in taste: 'taste classifies and it classifies the classifier' (1984: 6). This final chapter examines how ethnicity, as a form of cultural difference, shapes and in turn is shaped by material and symbolic consumption practices and aspirations. It investigates how young Punjabis identify and distinguish, critique and endorse particular hierarchies of taste and style in how they look, what they eat and drink, and in what they find beautiful or ugly, 'cool' or 'naff' (or 'pendu'). It demonstrates how, from a position of generally limited consumer potential, young people articulate their preferences, distinctions and aspirations as consumers through talk about the TV ads which they consume, both literally and metaphorically.

The need to be and look 'cool' and 'safe' was repeatedly stressed in the survey returns (see Appendix 11). Dress and other aspects of personal appearance and style had to be 'cool' above all, according to 66 per cent of boys. Girls gave it rather less priority; indeed among girls, only 47 per cent considered 'to look cool' as the prime consideration, and it was narrowly overtaken by 'to be respectable' (49 per cent) or 'to stay OK with my parents' (48 per cent) — matters to which boys claimed to attach rather less importance. This of course reflects both boys' greater freedom from parental constraint, and the wider range of public contexts in which they are likely to appear; and the paramount importance attached, in the parental culture of *izzat*, to female modesty and therefore girls' dress codes (cf. Yates, 1990: 78). Girls' pragmatism is reflected in their responses to the survey, but it is clear from fieldwork that they are highly inventive when it comes to subverting parental demands, as well as the norms of school uniform, in order to create a 'cool look' for themselves.

Ads which target young people address them as consumers in an international teenage market and aim simultaneously to construct and satisfy a range of consumer needs and problems, tastes and desires focussed around the body in a physical, social and aesthetic sense. Youth cultures are increasingly transnational cultures of consumption which apparently transcend ethnic and other divisions. However, the hierarchies of taste and style which are endorsed among the youth of Southall are marked not only by ethnic, gender and generational differences but also

From *Television, Ethnicity, and Cultural Change*, M. Gillespie, 1995, Routledge.

by material and other cultural differences. In their ad talk young people discuss these differences; they clarify distinctions between American, British and Indian consumer lifestyles and aspirations; and they talk in a manner that would otherwise appear utopian — unrealistic aspirations and desires and fantasies acquire varying degrees of plausibility and credibility in ad talk. The discourses of advertising are reproduced and recreated in everyday discussions of ads as they fantasise about how easy life would be if one used this product; or how successful, popular or beautiful one could be if one bought this product.

Consuming an ad for a product often involves buying into an image, an identity, a fantasy, a feeling and even, as we shall see in the case of the Coca Cola advertisements, a myth — a mythical construction of an American teenage lifestyle and of America itself. Arguably, America, as experienced through the media has itself become the prime object of consumption and a symbol of pleasure (Webster, 1988). The ad talk of Southall teenagers highlights the way in which ads sell products through promoting a set of associated values or qualities which are 'magically' transferred to, or conferred upon, the consumer in the act of their consumption (Williams, 1980). TV advertisements function as myths and metaphors, providing people with simple stories and explanations through which certain ideals and values are communicated and through which people organise their thoughts and experiences and come to make sense of the world in which they live.

This chapter focuses on three key areas of teenage consumer culture, all of which revolve around the body: fashion and style; body-care and beauty products; and food and drink. Young people's greater awareness of ads in these areas is apparent in their TV talk and is also evident from data obtained through a small-scale survey of seventy 16- and 17-year-olds (involving equal numbers of boys and girls). Selected results of this survey will be used to give an overview of local teenage consumer culture and perceptions of TV advertising. The second section explores the cultural significance of clothes for Southall youth, highlighting the particular appeal of black American 'street culture' and its incorporation into local style and fashion, and presenting a hierarchy of style types gleaned from ad talk. The section on body-care and beauty products investigates young people's preoccupation with matters of physical appearance, their criteria of physical attractive-ness, and their responses to the dominant ideology of beauty, purveyed by the mass media, which equates attractiveness with white skin colour. The fourth section addresses the reception of Coca Cola ads, and examines how young Punjabis' aspirations towards cultural change are articulated through talk about these ads, which are seen to represent a very desirable, though idealised, American teenage life-style. Finally, tastes in food, especially the appeal of fast foods from high-street outlets and preprepared microwavable foods, are examined in the context of local food culture and youth leisure activities.

Teenage Consumer Culture and TV Advertising

Consumer culture among the youth of Southall is marked by clear gender differences in spending power, most girls being at a material disadvantage as compared with boys when 'pocket money' is used as an index. According to survey data the majority of 16- and 17-year-old girls (56 per cent) receive between £1 and £5 pocket money per week, and 22 per cent do not receive pocket money on a regular basis at all. In contrast, just under 80 per cent of boys receive between £5 and £20 per week. Some boys (28 per cent) and fewer girls (18 per cent) are able to supplement the money that they receive from their parents through part-time employment. But such differences in material resources also derive from the greater participation of boys in public life and their higher status in most Punjabi families where they are treated preferentially when it comes to money and household duties.

It is customary that the eldest son in the family continues to live with his parents, brings his wife to live with them and provides for his ageing parents. Parents have a vested interest in treating their eldest son well, if not indulgently. By ensuring his material comfort while young they hope to secure their future comfort in old age. In contrast, daughters leave the family home — often at considerable expense, since a dowry is usually paid — and so are seen to represent a financial burden on families which is unlikely to produce a return. This is why the birth of a boy is usually celebrated while that of a girl is not. While some families do indeed adhere strictly to such traditional practices, especially the more religious families, many are re-inventing such traditions in the

British context and finding new ways of organising themselves so as to ensure that the family continues to look after elderly parents and other relatives. But it is still commonly accepted that in most families boys receive preferential treatment.

Young people may at times influence their parents' consumer decisions, especially those who mediate between 'British' and 'Indian' consumer preferences. Females appear to be more vulnerable to the persuasive powers of ads than boys, but it is likely that girls are simply more willing to admit to this. Sixty per cent of girls and 46 per cent of boys claim to have bought a product because they had seen an ad and wanted to try it. Just under 80 per cent of girls report having bought a body-care or beauty product because of an ad, as compared with only 28 per cent of boys. Sixty-eight per cent of girls report that they usually spend most of their money on food and drink, followed by magazines (42 per cent), music (20 per cent), clothes and beauty products (17 per cent). Many girls regularly buy Indian magazines such as *Cineblitz*, which covers new Hindi films, gossip about the stars and the latest Indian fashions. They also select from the range of British magazines for teenage girls such as *Just Seventeen* which covers romance, beauty and fashion. Boys spend most of their money on food and drink (45 per cent), followed by video games arcades (26 per cent). This is clearly a male-specific, public activity. In contrast girls neither play nor spend money on video games. Boys also spend more money than girls on videos, though spending on music cassettes is roughly similar.

One of the most tangible examples of the way that the discourses of TV and everyday life are intermeshed is when jingles, catch-phrases and humorous storylines of favourite ads are incorporated into everyday speech. Ads provide a set of shared cultural reference points, images and metaphors which spice local speech. There are countless examples of this in the data on TV talk but to mention just one: a common refrain which accompanies a spectacular feat, such as a goal, is the slogan, 'I bet *he* drinks Carling Black Label!' The exceptional subtlety and humour of some British ads no doubt encourages most young people (86 per cent) to think of TV ads as a form of entertainment rather than as a means of persuasion or information, although they are well aware of the persuasive functions of advertising. Girls especially appear to enjoy

discussing TV ads with their friends, perhaps as a recompense for their lack of consumer power. Yet just under half of all respondents claim that they find most ads boring and hardly ever discuss them, and just under 40 per cent claim that when the ads come on they usually go and get something to eat or drink — suggesting that they only pay attention to ads which they find entertaining. The majority of young people claim that they take most notice of ads with good music (78 per cent), a funny storyline (74 per cent) and attractive characters (58 per cent). Other criteria, identified by under 50 per cent of respondents, include: 'a good slogan', 'ads showing products I would like to have' and 'ads which show products which relate to my dreams'.

The most popular categories of ads among both boys and girls concern products which aim at satisfying the body in a physical, aesthetic or social sense. It is not surprising that ads for soft drinks and snack food feature prominently in their discussions of ads since these ads are specifically targeted at the youth market and most money is spent on these products. Thereafter, gender differences in preferences for ads appear. While boys go for humorous ads, girls tend to prefer ads which feature male characters whom they find attractive, appealing or, in local idiom, 'hunky'. At the time of the survey (Autumn 1990) beer ads were the most popular among boys (these are also the most heavily gender-stereotyped ads), followed by ads for the sale of Electricity Shares, British Satellite Broadcasting and Hamlet cigars, which all combine humorous stories and appealing jingles. The most popular ad among girls was for LA Gear trainers, which features Michael Jackson, followed by those for Gillette and Levi 501 jeans. According to girls, these all feature 'hunky' males.

Differences in educational and cultural competence also affect how ads are discussed. For example, low educational achievers tend to interpret TV ads more literally than their more academically orientated and successful counterparts. The latter prefer ads which challenge and flatter their intelligence by encouraging them to solve enigmas, to spot cultural references and to demonstrate their appreciation of more subtle and sophisticated forms of humour. They also pay much more attention to the formal and aesthetic features, as well as to the persuasive techniques, of an ad. The British advertising industry is in fact highly respectful of the visual literacy and critical sophistication of young consumers. Contrary to the widely held commonsense view that youth are particularly gullible and vulnerable to being persuaded to desire or buy useless items:

> No other group is considered as discriminating, cynical and resistant to the hard sell. Furthermore, no other group is as astute at decoding the complex messages, cross-references and visual jokes of current advertising (except perhaps the industry itself). These critical skills are untutored and seem to arise out of an unprecedented intimacy with the cultural form of the TV commercial. (Nava and Nava, 1992: 172)

Nava and Nava's industry-based research indicates that young people consume commercials independently of the products advertised. This is clearly often the case, though one should be wary of dismissing the economic effectiveness of advertising: ads do succeed in persuading. And, moreover, it is far from clear that young consumers' sophisticated literacy and critical scepticism regarding the artistic or cultural form of ads, which are more or less brazen about their persuasive intent, also extend to other forms.

The Hierarchy of Styles

Style is self-defining and culturally defining. Clothes are part of the social and symbolic construction of a self which can be seen, classified and judged. Stylistic change, innovation and re-invention are at the heart of the in-built obsolescence of the products of consumer culture, but they are also a tangible facet of the processes of cultural change. The cultural importance attached to clothes, and the social and symbolic meanings they articulate and express, raises important questions about social identity and the criteria of group membership. Clothes are markers of religious distinction: for example, Punjabi Hindu women tend to wear saris whereas Sikhs and Muslims wear *salwaar kameez* and *chunni* (baggy pyjama trousers, tunic and chiffon scarf). Sikh men are distinguished by their turban and Muslim men by a lace prayer-cap; and the size and shape of turbans distinguishes Sikhs of East African and Punjabi background, while other markers identify supporters of the Khalistan movement. However, some of these distinctions are tending to fade in Britain where, for example, many

Sikh men and boys cut their hair and do not wear turbans, and young people increasingly experiment with both 'western' and 'Indian' styles and fashion.

So clothes are an important manifestation, often a conscious public statement, of one's cultural affinities. While all young people wear 'western' clothes to school, 'Indian' clothes may be worn at home always, often or never, variously by desire or constraint. At family and religious celebrations — weddings, coming-of-age parties, at Diwali or Eid — 'Indian' clothes are always worn. Style may symbolise revolt. For example, on the Broadway, a miniskirt, tight T-shirt, high-heeled shoes and make-up would very speedily earn a girl the reputation of a 'slag' and would encourage all manner of harassment. On the other hand a girl who does not keep up with 'Indian' fashions is quickly labelled a *pendu* ('peasant'). The variety of styles and fashions open to young people and the kind of cultural distinctions, borrowings and cross-overs that characterise their lives is made explicit in the following interview exchange between two 16-year-old girls:

> HARJINDER: You see at home we're totally one thing, and at school we're totally a different thing, in our dress, our behaviour, language.
>
> KAMLESH: Not all of us, like, I'm the same at school as I am at home except in the way I dress. I'm not totally Indian at home cos my mum understands English, so it's easier to communicate in English, but when you come to school you have to sort of act the way other English people do, dress like them [. . .].
>
> HARJINDER: At school we're all mixed up, English, black, white, coloured, Sikhs, Muslims, Christians, Hindus, at home it's just one culture.
>
> KAMLESH: But you can't really say there's such a thing as British culture because within that you've got other people, you've got coloureds, English, Asians and blacks and sometimes you find each of these in a group [of friends] and they all mix their cultures together so you could pick up the way a Rasta person dresses or talks or white people who learn the Indian lingo [. . .].
>
> HARJINDER: And now Delhi is more westernised than Southall [. . .] they've got more variety there – more sari and suit [*salwaar kameez*] shops with brilliant and very modern styles. Lots of people in Southall are still living in the India they left behind them and they don't realise how fashions and other things have changed.

This paradox – the fact of greater conservatism in Southall than in modern India – is frequently commented upon (cf. Yates, 1990: 83f.). Compared with cosmopolitan, fashion-conscious, 'with-it' Bombay or other Indian cities which are open to change, Southall is seen by many as a *pendu* town dominated by village-bred, tradition-hound farmers. Certainly those with a rural background are slower to adopt new styles in 'Indian' clothing than those whose background is urban, whether Punjabi or East African.

The dynamism of cross-cultural interactions, cross-overs and borrowings among Southall youth is particularly apparent in the selective appropriation of black youth styles. Black American 'street culture' is a major force in popular youth cultures throughout Britain today, in terms of rap music and dance crazes as well as street fashion and style. Sportswear (trainers, shell suits and track suits) has become the popular 'street uniform' of local youngsters, and designer labels are of paramount importance. A new pair of trainers can cost some £80. Three months later they will be worn out, and this inbuilt obsolescence places considerable financial pressures on households, in some of which £80 may constitute the larger part of the family's weekly income. Cheaper labels are then often purchased and are frowned upon by those who can afford the more up-market products. The wrong label or shabby, dirty trainers can lead to mocking and bullying or to insults about a person's family being too poor to afford the 'right' label. Here the conspicuous consumerism and status competition between friends and rivals, endemic amongst 'western' youth, can become implicated in the more culturally specific patterns of status competition among families tied up with the notion of *izzat*. Cross-media advertising plays a crucial role in shaping teenage consumer culture and in making material values important. Opportunistic advertising, which extends across the worlds of sports, music and fashion, shapes consumer preferences and choices, exerting considerable financial pressure on parents and young people. Sportswear, jeans and leather or suede jackets are part of every fashion-conscious young person's wardrobe. 'Labels' are high-status consumer items. A 'puffy' Chipie jacket, for instance, can cost up to £300 in the UK (but many youths who can afford them have become reluctant to wear their jackets for fear of having them stolen).

Afro-Caribbeans have very high status among young Punjabis in Southall because, collectively, they are trend-setters in fashion, music and dance styles (cf. Gilroy, 1993b: 82). They are seen to be subject to less parental control and to enjoy greater mobility, enabling them to socialise 'outside' and 'bring fashion back into Southall'. They are considered to be 'honorary Americans': 'cool', 'streetwise, city kids', 'not easily put down', 'proud' and 'fit'. They are seen to have a tough, rebellious, assertive personal style which many Southall boys admire. Many Punjabi boys incorporate and appropriate elements of 'black culture' not only in their speech patterns, idioms and slang but also in their behaviour, dress and musical tastes. The sucking of teeth to express displeasure, and expressions such as 'yo man!', 'safe', 'bad' (meaning good), 'skank' (betray), 'vex' and 'y' know what I mean' are but a few examples of idioms appropriated from local black youth and popular black media and sports stars. Music is also a powerful focus of culturally convergent tastes, as evidenced in the example of ragga bhangra discussed earlier.

Sarita, a 15-year-old Hindu girl, claims she is drawn to 'black culture' but that this is discouraged by her parents. Attitudes to black people in the parental culture are often highly prejudiced. Most Punjabi parents do not wish their children to associate with black youth, citing a variety of reasons: their perceived rebelliousness, associations with crime and the police, and above all their 'otherness'. The pressures of endogamy are one of the most powerful forces affecting cross-cultural relations in Southall:

> I listen to reggae and soul music but my mum hates it if we start enthusing about black singers on *Top of the Pops*, you know saying he's gorgeous and that, so we play our feelings down, we don't show her how much we like the black guys cos she worries we'll get mixed up with them [. . .]. The parents think that to marry a black person is worse than marrying a *gore* [white person] and you know some Asians want to be white, I don't know why, but if I had the choice I'd be black.

The film *Mississippi Masala*, which centres on a romance between an Asian girl and a black boy, was, according to some informants, greeted with horror by parents, while young people enjoyed it greatly.

Black youth collectively set dress trends in Southall and are much admired for their 'personal style' as individuals. They are regarded as being fashionable 'outside' Southall, and this is one of the key criteria of style success among local youth. Such success is very much dependent upon where you shop, the labels you wear and your overall image. Departing from a discussion of the ads for Levi 501 jeans and LA Gear trainers, a group of 16- and 17-year-olds, one Friday afternoon in the sixth-form common room, drew up their own hierarchy of style types, identifying six categories of local style. They positioned themselves at the top among the 'classies' and their least stylish peers at the bottom with the *pendus*. Though the vagaries of fashion dictate that, by now, the content of this hierarchy will have changed, it is worth presenting in some detail because its structure tellingly reveals the key oppositions which underlie perceptions of style difference and which change less quickly. Being 'cool', it emerges, is a matter of detachment from specifically local, territorially-based styles. Thus the 'cool body' is 'cosmopolitan', in Hannerz's sense of a certain 'orientation' which he describes as:

> a willingness to engage with others [. . .], an intellectual and aesthetic stance of openness toward divergent cultural experience, a search for contrasts rather than uniformity [. . .], a matter of competence [. . . and] skill in manoeuvering more or less expertly within a particular system of meanings [. . .] (1990: 239)

By contrast, *pendus*, at the bottom of the hierarchy, are caricaturally depicted as locked into a closed local style, one which is doubly bound to a certain symbolic space: that of Southall; and beyond Southall, that of the Punjabi village. In between these extremes come categories on an ascending scale of boundedness and uniformity, closely correlating with perceived expensiveness or cheapness, but signifying far more than the level of disposable income. And the sixth category denotes an alternative style to the *pendu*, more 'image-conscious' but yet more strongly, though in a different way, bound to a particular symbolic territory.

Classy

To be 'cool' is to be 'classy': it is to head the style hierarchy. For classy dressers, 'authentic' labels matter: labels conspicuously connote affluence, and their cachet obtains both within and outside Southall.

But it is not one label or article of clothing that matters but the 'overall look'. Classies are into 'personal style': they flee uniformity and seek to distinguish themselves as individuals. They always shop in central London and buy expensive labels — such as 501 jeans and LA Gear trainers — but: 'Some people think that just by wearing LA Gear they look cool but they don't cos it's everything, their whole image that counts'. Classies always look 'cool' and 'safe'. They do not need to follow the latest fashion slavishly: 'If you go to the right shops it doesn't really matter what your idea of fashion is, you'll get the right gear, you don't have to follow the fashion in every detail'. Girls shop at the more up-market retail outlets such as Next, Miss Selfridge, Snob, River Island and Principles, and buy their shoes in Ravel, Dolcis and Lilley and Skinner. Boys shop at designer label shops like Pie Squared, Whack and Oaklands. The clothes they buy are always expensive and well-cut, and it is important to be 'trendy', but individual style is 'crucial': 'If someone else has got what you're wearing you don't want to wear it any more'. 'Classies' read fashion magazines: girls read *Just Seventeen* and *More*, boys read the very up-market glossies *GQ* and *Arena*. They get their ideas for fashionable ways of assembling a 'look' from watching what other people wear and from magazines, rather than from TV. There are accepted limits to their cosmopolitanism: most stick to styles which are within the bounds of locally acceptable clothing: 'I really like those Lycra hot pants and ski pants, but you could never wear those kinds of clingy clothes around Southall because you'd get leers and cut eyes [. . .] anyway they make my legs look too skinny'.

The 'classies' have individual style because they know how to mix and match their clothes. They are concerned to look original and wear their clothes well, and are very conscious of context. One example of a 'classy' combination would be: 'White massive jeans, BK Boots and a cropped jumper for everyday wear, or for a disco at the Hippodrome, a tight black velvet dress'. Although bhangra discos at the Hippodrome are for 'Asian' youth, 'Indian' clothes would not be worn to them by 'classies'. At one stage *patiala* or very baggy *salwar* (trousers), tight round the lower knee and ankle, were worn by classies on such occasions, but now they generally only wear *salwar kameez* at family occasions, where 'Indian' clothes would be 'in place'.

Style categories can never be rigid or exhaustive, but the 'classy' style category was felt to need particular differentiation. For example, classy clothes may be 'posh-smart' or 'casual-sporty':

> ABJINDER (17): I'd say I'm a casual-sporty type [. . .] that's all I can take cos I'm a bit overweight but look what I'm wearing — Levi's 501s, they cost around £30 and an Adidas top — the actual track-suit costs £90 — and my trainers are Condors, an American make, they're worth £60 [. . .]. I'm not dressed up cheaply but I don't really call that 'classy' fashion.

Hair-style — to which we will also return later in the context of body-care ads — is very important as part of the overall 'look' or 'image', as well as being a key 'ethnic signifier' (Mercer, 1987). Hair is an important symbol of Sikhism, a religion which prohibits the cutting of hair. Keeping long hair and wearing a turban may be read as sign of conformity to religious and cultural traditions. The turban may also be worn with pride and used to create a specifically Sikh youth style. Today, however, many young people are cutting their hair and discarding their turbans and long plaits. The pressures within the peer group to conform to the latest, shorter hair-styles are immense and a family crisis can ensue if a boy or girl cuts their hair. In some families cutting one's hair is seen as a major symbolic act of rebellion. But other parents accept that short hair is easier to manage and do not necessarily interpret it as an act of defiance. Many boys shave their hair along the sides above their ears in line with black street style. Girls wear their hair long and permed or in well-cut 'bobs', although the group agreed that 'perms are on their way out now.'

Hip-hop

Hip-hop is seen as a 'black/American' style, and its high position in the hierarchy reflects the high status of black and American youth cultures. Again, 'showing the label' is a way of creating a 'cool', fashionable, trendy and affluent image. These people wear 'smart', 'trendy' clothes with expensive labels: LA Gear or Fila trainers in suede, costing £60-£100, puffy Chipie jackets, Levi 501s or baggy jeans. They buy their clothes 'up London' or at expensive 'classified' shops (those which sell expensive labels). Most importantly, they look good outside

Southall. They are distinguished from 'classies' in that they are following fashion rather than creating 'their own look'.

Acid House

Acid House is seen as a 'white/English' style. It involves wearing colourful, hooded tops, baggy track-suit bottoms (tight at the ankle with buttons for girls) and massive, bulging trainers with the tongues hanging out. These people look fairly 'trendy' in Southall but not at all outside. They buy their clothes in markets and cheap shops in adjacent Ealing and Hounslow: 'Acid is just baggy clothes, it's not really caring what you look like, just feeling comfortable, it's sloppy, casual wear'. At the time of fieldwork this fashion was on the wane and those who continued to present themselves in this style were ridiculed by the classies as being 'behind' current trends:

> Like acid and hip-hop are two dance crazes so if they're dance crazes people wanna dance, be comfortable and look good at the same time, but in Southall people are into hip-hop more than acid, acid's like for kids, it's not that cool, you see a lot of little white kids running round acid-style but the cool dudes go for hip-hop.

Southallis

Southallis 'try to keep up with fashions' but they wear cheaper versions of the current styles, or what is referred to as 'normal fashion'. They buy clothes in cheap shops in Southall or adjacent towns: blouses with lie lacy collars and double-breasted fronts and cheap 'imitation' baggy trousers for girls, and for boys, cheap versions of expensive clothes — 'but you can tell the difference' — from the 'down-market' department stores such as C & A. The girls have 'masses of penned or hennaed hair'. The Southallis — as some call them, using a rarely heard term with derogatory overtones — try to appear 'westernised' but display a lack of fashion awareness and consumer power which bind them to the culture of the local territory.

Pendus

The same is true for the *pendus*, but more so. *Pendu* derives from the Punjabi word *pind*, or village, and young people use it (both as noun and as adjective) to encompass a range of derisory connotations from 'peasant', 'backward', 'thick' and 'uncouth' to 'traditional', 'uncool' and 'lacking style'. *Pendus* are 'out of place' among young people and belong in the parental culture. Often child and teenage migrants are denigrated as *pendus*. The caricature of a male *pendu* is someone who has just stepped off the plane from the Punjab, wearing flairs, huge shirt collars hanging out over a shrunken acrylic jumper and platform boots. His female counterpart wears ankle bracelets above white stilettos and a shiny satin-look, frilly blouse *outside* a pencil-thin skirt.

The term is applied to young people who do not try or cannot afford to follow youth fashions. They are viewed disdainfully as 'modern versions' of their parents or as 'playing safe just to please parents': 'They wear what they can get away with in the eyes of parents without completely selling out to them, they try their best not to look out of it, they wear cheap jeans and lacy jumpers in horrible colours'. *Pendus* shop for cheap clothes in 'Indian' shops on the Southall Broadway, and wear track suits from cheap local markets; or stone-washed, bleached jeans and jackets, checked shirts and trainers from Woolworths; or cheap, straight Farah jeans (a local label). Girls wear *jutiya* (Indian sandals) from local shoe shops and boys wear trainers with trousers rather than jeans: 'Ugh! No one else would dream of doing that!' They wear 'nasty jumpers with patterns or shiny beads on them', bought from stalls on the Broadway or in the local market:

> GURINDER: The girls wear *goti* [cardigans] which are either really long or like the one in the ad that comes on Hindi films, you know where there's this fat woman waddling through Southall Park and there's this man chasing her and she's scared cos she thinks he's after her so she runs faster and hides behind a tree and eventually he catches up with her and says 'I love your *goti* where did you buy it?' and she takes him to the shop on the Broadway and it's the most disgusting cardigan, pink with beads and pearls on it everywhere.

The *pendu* wears strong, uncoordinated colours and inappropriate combinations of elements of traditional 'Indian' dress with a version of 'western' style which is itself associated with poorer 'Asians' attempting — and failing — to look 'westernised'. The hateful details of *pendu* style were elaborated

with as much animation as were those of 'classy' style, in order to bring out the contrasts as fully as possible. *Pendus* are the antithesis of 'classies' in their alleged total ignorance of current fashion as well as lack of spending power — and as young people, in their more or less slavish adherence to the dress codes of the parental generation. Their clothes were referred to once as 'unclassy imports', implying cheap 'western'-style clothes manufactured abroad. This reference jars with the evidence in several of the above quotations that *pendus*, and to a lesser extent 'Southallis', are more likely than any other category to be wearing garments not only sold but manufactured in Southall itself. It is rather the wearers of these clothes who appear as 'imports'; they might be in rural Punjab. Their style is seen as an emblem of Southall's much-bemoaned status as an enclosed territory with few links to wider British society, whose inhabitants' links with India, furthermore, are not with the cosmopolitan, modern India of the big cities, but with 'poor and backward' villages.

Hard

The last style category is exclusively for boys who wish to present a 'hard' image, associated with membership of one of the local gangs. They appropriate the symbols of Sikhism to represent a special type of machismo:

> MANJIT (17): We associate certain people with particular types of habits and particular styles, for example [. . .] you'll see guys with black leather jackets, several large gold earrings, tight Lois black jeans, Adidas 'Gazelle' trainers — and an attitude problem [. . .]. They are influenced by western culture but 'they're more strong in their Indian background cos they've got big *karas* [steel bracelets worn on the right wrist by Sikhs [. . .]. Some still wear turbans [. . .]. They wear a lot of gold, Indian gold [. . .]. Often you'll see a large *khalsa* pendant around their necks [. . .]. They like to drive round in red Ford Capris or Cortinas [. . .]. They trade on their image as 'pure' in the Jat sense, tough and macho [. . .] but you'll rarely see one alone [. . .] they go round in groups of five or six and act tough but if you see them when they're alone they're like chickens some of them.

This style-type assembles different styles and symbols — combining Sikh emblems with 'western' garments connoting machismo — in order to convey locally specific meanings. This might be compared with what Hebdige refers to as 'bricolage' in subcultural styles, whereby a range of commodities are brought together in an ensemble which erases or subverts their 'straight' meanings (1988: 104). The 'transformation' of meaning involved here is in a sense more limited. For those unfamiliar with the Sikh religion and with the specific position of Jats in Southall, it would be difficult to read the signs. As explained earlier in my discussion of the 'Holy Smokes', this gang-member style was often associated with proclaimed support for the Khalistan movement. Again, the style is doubly linked with a territory but, in contrast to the *pendu* style, which merely signifies an unreflected connection with place in the form of a lack of any economic and cultural alternative, the 'hard' style announces a claim to territorial power both on the streets of Southall and in the Punjab.

The elaboration of this hierarchy of local styles began spontaneously, though it was completed with some prompting from me. Many informants subsequently confirmed it as an accurate depiction. It developed out of a discussion of the very popular TV ads for two highly sought-after labels. Clearly, TV advertising plays an important role in shaping youth fashions, notably in focusing desire on particular products and linking the wearing of 'cool' labels with certain desirable qualities of personal and group identity. But TV is only one channel among many and, in examining the impact of fashion advertisements, one should consider the power of the cross-media and intertextual circulation of images, music and narratives in ads targeted at the teenage consumer. But equally, as this data shows, it is essential to examine how the products of the global fashion industry, as well as other, national and local garment industries, are incorporated into local cultures in specific ways.

Body Beauty

Ads for body-care and beauty products often figure in young people's conversations. Both hair and skin are important 'ethnic signifiers', each representing 'a highly sensitive surface on which competing definitions of "the beautiful" are played out in a racial struggle' (Mercer, 1987: 32):

> Classical ideologies of race established a classificatory symbolic system of colour with 'black' and 'white' as signifiers of a fundamental polarisation of human worth in terms of 'superiority/inferiority'. Distinctions of aesthetic value, in terms of 'beautiful/ugly', have always been central to the way racism divides the world into binary oppositions in its adjudications of human worth. (Mercer, 1987: 35)

Thus the politics of 'racial' appearance is inevitably implicated in Southall teenagers' talk about these topics, though there is seldom explicit reference to the dominant assumption, purveyed by the media, that 'whiteness' is the measure of 'true beauty', or to the ideological status ascription of 'races' according to a 'scale of whiteness' (Hall, 1977).

Many features of young people's talk about these ads are no doubt common to all teenagers who are exposed to them. Girls show a much greater awareness of ads for beauty products than do boys, an awareness which is not solely confined to ads targeted at females. One of the most popular series of ads among girls, at the time of the survey, was for Gillette's 'new' line of shaving products, which were enjoyed because of the 'hunky' male character. Boys claim not to be influenced by the ads but clearly, certain brands of products are seen to confer 'classiness'. Labels matter here too:

> ABDUL (17): Which of the guys says I use Gillette to shave? They're not saying 'I use Gillette cos I like the ad' [. . .], they're just saying 'Oh God! Turn it over on the other side', whereas girls would think, 'Oh! he's all right' [. . .]. I use Gillette, it's nothing to do with the ad [. . .], I just picked up the gel quickly at the chemist [. . .]. I suppose I do go for the big name things [. . .]. At the end of the day, Gillette sounds much better [. . .]. See what I mean it gets to you, you have to have a named product, it's a bit of class rubbed in as well, I suppose it rubs off on you as well cos people like to be seen using classy products.

There is no evidence in this domain that ad consumption and product consumption are independent, as suggested by the argument of Nava and Nava (1992), cited earlier. The products are easily within the spending reach of the great majority of young people and the TV ads influence their buying greatly.

Interview data suggests that boys are just as pre-occupied with their physical appearance as girls. A key concern is body odour:

NIRMAL (18): Yeah of course I buy my own deodorant, I have done for a while [. . .]. You need strong soaps and deodorants at this age cos your hormones are working overtime [. . .], you tend to sweat a hell of a lot [. . .], bloody hell you sweat! and then you get spots and you try to control them [. . .]. We all used to buy products like Biactol, Clearasil, oh yeah, and Oxy 10.

Ads for spot creams and lotions are seen to play upon the insecurities of teenagers regarding body odours, acne and personal appearance more generally, and though they display critical distance to such ads, this does not mean that the ads have no effect:

DILIP (17): They're kind of psychological [. . .] cos they're showing a girl with a bucket over her head and how you feel when you go to a party with a face full of spots, and like when you use Oxy 10 they imply you won't need the bucket [. . .] and that girls will fall at your feet – that would be nice!

Such advertisements strike a raw or sensitive nerve in some teenagers, often defused in discussions (as the advertisers no doubt intend) by laughter. The ad for Clearasil works on the 'before–after' principle, suggesting that a young person's life can be transformed by using the product. Typically, it is claimed that it is not the speaker, but *other people*, who are affected by these ads:

BALBIR (16): Have you seen the Clearasil ad? The girl's really spotty and she's a heavy-metal fan dancing to music, her hair is all over the place, her room's a mess and she holds a mirror to her face and it cracks. Her sister who's really pretty gives her Clearasil. The next scene is where her sister goes to her bedroom and she's transformed into this beauty and her room's tidy and she's playing soft, romantic Marvin Gaye music and she's dancing with her boyfriend and the camera focuses on her as she admires her face [. . .]. Some girls are likely to go out and buy Clearasil after seeing this [. . .], this is something a lot of girls think is real.

But the pressures upon teenagers in Southall to conform to conventional standards of beauty propa-gated by the media of 'western' culture can pose particular problems for those who are sensitive about their skin colour. It is, after all, skin colour which is the focus of much racist abuse. Furthermore, an important criterion of beauty in the parental and peer culture alike is 'fairness' of skin, which is considered to be a sign of beauty. Often a description of a person will begin with a reference to the shade of their skin – to whether they are 'fair' or 'dark'. Dark-skinned people are considered unattractive and, to compound the matter even further, dark skin is associated with low caste. Dark facial hair is also viewed as unattractive and bleaching products are often used, mainly by girls, to lighten the skin and to disguise dark hair on the upper lip or on the side of the face. Similarly, facial scrubs are used in the hope of obtaining a blemish-free, 'fair' complexion. Indian ads for beauty products play upon such prejudices by promoting bleach products. Such advertisements commonly interrupt Hindi videos and discussions of face products often highlight the importance, to girls, of being fair-skinned (as well as their low opinion of Indian advertisements):

JASBINDER: I hate those ones for moisturising cream, 'Fair and Lovely' and they say it makes you whiter and whiter and then I think how stupid I don't want to get like that.

GURINDER: Yeah it's true these Indian ads are always going on about how to be white and everything white skin, white teeth.

AMRITA: And there's this ad for Vico Ayureval, it stinks, my mum has got that but it doesn't work [. . .], it's meant to make your skin smooth and fair.

GURINDER: You know my sister bought that and you know what it is? it's bleach! Because she tried it on her face, she came out in a rash.

The use of such products does not imply a desire to 'become white', or to engage in what Mercer (1987) calls a 'deracialising sell-out'. But dominant western ideology and the beauty criteria of Indian culture both set standards which devalue darkness, even though the positive ideals are not identical.

Hair, as we saw earlier, is an important factor for 'coolness'. This concerns both styling and hair quality. Ads for hair products – shampoos and gels – are commonly referred to and are recognised as having a very direct impact on consumer purchases. More people freely admit to being more influenced to buy hair products because of ads than is the case with any other product, apart from chocolate. The appeal of the hair ads is usually related to the desired aims of achieving the qualities of shine and thickness:

> DALVINDER: I like the Timotei and Silkience ads, it's the hair it's so lovely and soft and shiny [. . .]. I did buy Timotei after seeing the ad but now I like it.
>
> TEJINDER: I bought it cos of the ads too but I don't like it so I stopped using it.

Many girls were wearing their hair permed into curls in imitation of Michael Jackson, a 'cool' look which entailed using lots of moisturising products. It contrasted strongly with the 'traditional' and 'uncool' look of girls who wear their uncut hair in long plaits.

Teenagers' preoccupation with all these elements of personal appearance make them an easy target for the advertisers of beauty products. Girls and boys compete to attain recognition and status as an attractive person. In the peer culture, attractive girls and boys acquire very high status and are admired, desired and envied. The message of advertising for young people is that to be happy, popular and liked you have to be, above all, attractive, especially to the opposite sex. By consuming beauty products, young people hope to improve their image and attractiveness, and the ideologically loaded criteria of beauty propagated by the British media can sometimes cause problems of self-esteem. Exposure to popular Indian and Pakistani media provides young people in Southall with alternative models and standards of beauty, and some identify positively with, and emulate, images of beauty from the realm of Bombay fashion. But the widespread denigration of popular Indian culture more often leads young people to reject such models and to seek alternative role models in British, or most commonly in American culture. Indeed it is in relation to an idealised American teenage culture, represented in its most compelling form in Coca Cola ads, that young people express their aspirations towards cultural change.

You Can't Beat the Feeling: Coca Cola and Utopia

Coca Cola ads have sustained an unparalleled popularity among the youth of Southall over the last decade or so. Over the years, the ads and their accompanying jingles and songs — which have repeatedly been major chart hits — have entered every young person's repertoire of media knowledge. Coca Cola songs and slogans are familiar to all, and few would be unable to recite them upon request. They are seen to convey a 'feeling' which is captured in the slogan:

> DALVINDER: I love the Coca Cola ads, I don't know why, there's just something about them, they're just good, more lively, teenagers jumping around and having a laugh [. . .], I don't know [laughs] you just can't beat the feeling.

This slogan is a catch-phrase among local youth. Its very ambiguity (the reference to 'feeling' as both an emotional state and a physical experience), is the source of many a *double entendre*, especially in exchanges between boys and girls. The tensions inherent in that ambiguity seem to capture something of the nature of the emotional and sensual experience of adolescence.

Discussions of Coca Cola ads also refer to the 'feeling' that they convey in terms of the representation of a teenage world and lifestyle to which many young people aspire. It is an imagined or projected feeling of participating, albeit vicariously, in an idealised lifestyle where young people sing, dance, have fun, socialise, fall in love, and easily gain friends, status and popularity. The following exchange took place during a taped discussion between two 16-year-old vocational students about why they like their favourite advertisements. It captures the ads' utopian quality:

> SAMEERA: My favourite ads are the Coca Cola ads, they're American ads, I prefer American ads, I don't know why but I could watch them over and over again without getting bored [. . .]. I like them cos I just love drinking Coca Cola [. . .]. I enjoy listening to the music [. . .]. I think the characters are fantastic. Every time I see the ad I always feel tempted to go out and buy it, even when I go out shopping, I always buy Coke cos, well, I love the ad [. . .].
>
> SUKHI: Yeah, they're really happy and active cos they mix pop songs with kids in America, you know, the sun's always shining and everyone is smiling and it gives the impression of being free. The music and song puts more energy into it and like each line of the song is backed up with dancing, sports and fun [. . .]. 'You just can't beat the feeling!'
>
> SAMEERA: Yeah, and all races seem to get on well, their roles aren't changed around because of the colour

of their skin. There are no signs of people being angry [. . .].

SUKHI: They have a very tempting way of selling Coke [. . .], you know the one where the guy is sweating, he's thirsty as anything but he drinks it very slowly, taking his time as if it's something precious.

SAMEERA: Yeah, it's like after a hard day's work he's rewarded with a refreshing Coke. The little droplets of water on the bottle glisten and sort of add to the temptation. After watching the ad you think, 'Oh yeah, next time I need a cool drink, I'll have a Coke'.

SAMEERA: [. . .] then there's a boy and girl about to kiss but then, just as their lips are about to meet another shot comes [. . .].

The preference for American advertisements is stated without any explicit reasons being offered, but the chain of associations in the exchange implies that it is based on the attractiveness of the American teenage lifestyle portrayed. The feelings ascribed to the young people are conflated with the advertisement and the product. Coke-drinkers are seen to be 'happy', 'active' 'kids in America' where 'the sun is always shining', everyone is 'happy' and 'free', 'all races get on' and there are 'no signs of anger'.

'TV ad talk' is clearly influenced by the discourse of advertising itself which relates products to myths and dreams, fantasies and emotions, rewards and promises in order to sell products. Advertisements are the most condensed of all TV narratives and viewers have to make symbolic associations in order to read them. These associations become evident in ad talk, which can take on some of the persuasive rhetoric of the ads themselves. The repeated use of the word 'temptation' in several different contexts highlights an awareness of the persuasive techniques used. Sameera claims that when she sees the ad she is tempted to go out and buy a Coke both because she loves the ad and because she loves drinking Coke. Sukhi adds that the way 'they' sell Coke is tempting. The glistening droplets on the bottle in the ad 'add to the temptation'. Then Sameera introduces the idea of being rewarded with a Coke after a hard day's work, making the connection with Coke-drinking and leisure. Finally, the temptation of a kiss appears, only to disappear at the very end of the advertisement. In this account, thirst and desire are connected: thirst is satisfied by a Coke

but desire, as represented by the promise of a kiss, is left to the imaginative fulfilment. By placing the product within an idealised world of teenagers, free from parental and other constraints, a utopian vision of a teenage lifestyle is represented. The plausibility of the idyllic lifestyle and utopian relationships depicted by the ad is not questioned.

The following exchange between two 16-year-old vocational students further highlights the way in which the Coke ads lead some young people to engage in talk that would otherwise appear foolish or utopian:

GURVINDER: It makes you think that if you drink Coke that you will be popular and loved by people you didn't even know existed.

GITA: Innit, it's like everyone cares about each other, their relationships are simple, they all get on, life is peaceful and full of fun so enjoy it while you can.

GURVINDER: They all socialise together, boys and girls, everyone loves each other and if you buy Coke it makes you feel that you could be happy and free like them.

GITA: But I don't think the ads influence us to buy it, most of us buy it anyway.

GURVINDER: And old people won't be influenced because they think that soft drinks are bad for you anyway.

GITA: But I think you are supposed to value the feeling that you get after drinking it, you know [sings] 'you can't beat the feeling', and for such a small cost.

GURVINDER: The music is great as well and goes with the feeling.

Thus the consumption of Coke promises happiness, love, friendship, freedom and popularity. In the world promised by the ads, relationships are uncomplicated (unlike in real life); young people simply care for each other, everyone loves one another and socialises together (unlike in the peer culture where group boundaries are strong); life is fun and free (a teenage dream). If they do not feel themselves to be influenced by the ads, it is evidently only because they already have been: the girls buy Coke in any case. Finally, teenage tastes are distinguished from those of older people who think Coke is unhealthy.

Discussions of Coke ads invariably lead to a consideration of what it is like to be a teenager in America, articulated in contrast to what it is to be a teenager in Southall. The word most consistently used to describe American teenagers is 'free'. They are seen to have much greater freedom to do what they want, to participate in 'fun' activities; freedom from parental constraint; and especially, freedom to have boyfriends and girlfriends. The emphasis on freedom appears to be exaggerated, but when considered against the background of social constraints under which girls especially live, it becomes easier to appreciate.

Perceptions of American 'kids' obviously derive from a variety of media sources, but the Coke ads have undoubtedly played a formative influence in shaping perceptions of an idealised teenage lifestyle. The following exchange again highlights the rosy image of American 'kids' which is presented in the ads, as well as in the popular American 'college films' and 'vacation films' (such as *Dirty Dancing*), and TV series such as *Beverly Hills 90210* which revolves around the recreational pursuits of high-school teenagers:

GURINDER: American kids . . . they're ideal . . .

BALJIT: . . . they're really good-looking . . .

PERMINDER: . . . they all drink Coke and drive fast cars, like in *Beverley Hills 90210*, the girls are so pretty . . .

AMRITA: . . . Brandon is so cute . . .

GURINDER: . . . so's Dylan he's r-e-a-l-ly nice . . .

BALJIT: . . . they're free

PERMINDER: . . . all rich, they've got massive huge houses and they all dress smart and they've got wicked cars . . .

GURINDER: . . . they've got more things to do as well . . .

AMRITA: . . . they're all sunbaked aren't they . . .

BALJIT: . . . they're always going to pool parties . . .

PERMINDER: . . . they're all healthy . . .

BALJIT: . . . like the Coke ads make you think they're free and have lots of fun and they have . . .

GURINDER: . . . boyfriends! [All laugh]

The idealisation of American youth in the Coke ads is recognised by Baljit to be a constructed image, but the others talk about the representation as if it were 'the real thing' (another Coke slogan). This representation of American kids as rich and above all free (to have boyfriends) contrasts sharply with the lives of these girls who consider themselves neither rich nor free to have boyfriends. Thus the Coke ads and other media sources encourage girls to fantasize about what life might feel like as an attractive teenager in Beverly Hills.

Whilst the ideal of teenage freedom is a recurrent theme when Coke ads are discussed, some young people are also aware of the darker side of the 'American way of life':

KARIM (19): American kids have more freedom [. . .], freedom to rebel AND WIN, you know, like in films like *Dirty Dancing* [. . .] they rebel AND the family stays together but, over here, you rebel against your family, you're out on your own, parents won't tolerate certain things [. . .]. They have more freedom, they also have more of a drug problem, more violence and there's more of a colour problem there as well [. . .], the Hispanics and blacks are stuck in ghettos slums [. . .], even though they're American they're not integrated.

The impression of 'racial harmony' produced by the Coke to be contradicted by other available images, of 'ghetto' life and 'racial conflict'. Nevertheless, Coke — and Pepsi — are favourite drinks racial young people locally, strongly associated with a 'cool', 'safe', drinks among of the local Punjabi cafés, 'Rita's' in old Southall — a 'hang-out' for local youth in the lunch-hour — red cans of Coke stand on almost every table. Often, that is all there is on the table, because eating 'out' is expensive (compared to school dinners or home lunches) and most youngsters can only afford a kebab roll or a samosa and a can of Coke.

No other drink has quite the 'cool image' of Coke. The Pepsi ads are considered to be very attractive because they use famous stars like Michael Jackson, Tina Turner and Madonna, but most prefer the Este of Coke and claim to find Pepsi sweeter. 'I think they spend more money on the Pepsi ads but Coke ads are more for the common people and cos they're young people, you can sort of relate to them'. This idea that Coke is for the 'common people' relates to a perception of Coke being a drink consumed by young people in all parts of the world; it is testimony to the success of Coke's 'multi-focal' global marketing strategy (Webster, 1989; Robins, 1989). The 'cool' image of Coke evidently 'rubs off' on its consumers; and this creates problems for other drinks manufacturers.

For example, a company called Rubicon, producing 'exotic', 'tropical' canned drinks, based on flavours such as mango juice or passion-fruit, organised a vigorous TV advertising campaign specifically target ethnic-minority consumers, broadcasting on Channel 4 over several months during the period of fieldwork. In discussions of this campaign the consensus seemed to be that the major problem was that the can lacked style: 'I've tried it and I like the taste of the mango juice but the can is so awful you wouldn't be seen dead with it, it's so badly designed [. . .]. I hate it, it's so uncool.' And not only is the can 'uncool,' but the ad itself is seen by many to portray 'Asian' families as 'stupid':

> GURINDER: I hate that Rubicon ad, you know the one where there's this Indian family, the mum, dad and the two kids—the kids are so cute! I think they're *gore* [whites]—and they're all in the kitchen watching a Hindi film and the husband goes to his wife, 'Have you got any mango juice dear?' and they're all really engrossed in the film so they ignore him. Then he goes dancing round the kitchen to the fridge and gets out the mango juice and starts singing [. . .]. They're watching the bit in the film where Rajesh Kanna takes her to a hut [. . .] and the tune to the ad is the same as in the actual film, you know, it goes 'Rubicon must have some' [all laugh and sing it]. They're so stupid though, I hate the way they do that, it makes Indian people look really stupid.

However good it tastes, if a drink does not have the right kind of 'cool' image, the terms of which are pre-established by the dominant advertising media, many will not buy it. And such attempts to construct an 'ethnic' image are particularly unlikely to buy it. And such attempts to construct an 'ethnic' image are particularly unlikely to find favour among Southall youth. No 'Indian' ads were mentioned in the survey, but they were brought up in every group discussion and interview and critically or humorously juxtaposed to 'more sophisticated' British or American ads. The consistent denigration of 'Indian' ads — including both those for 'Indian' products appearing in 'Indian' media, and those targeting 'British Asians' in 'western' media — stands in sharp contrast to the high regard for 'western' ads targeted at teenagers.

In their ad talk about soft drinks young people establish hierarchies of consumer taste and style in sharp contrast to those which exist in the parental culture. The stylistic qualities and persuasive techniques of ads targeted at the parental generation are seen to be 'unsophisticated'. The representation of the 'Asian' family in the above example is considered to be demeaning. The father, dancing and

singing around the kitchen, is perceived as 'stupid'. Many young people who discussed this ad showed concern that it would just reinforce negative stereotypes of 'Asians'. They argue that, because there are so few representations of 'Asian' families on British TV, those that do appear have greater representational power. Yet implicit in this ad talk are a series of unanswered questions: How should an Indian father behave and act? What should an 'Asian' family look like? Why are the children found to be cute because *gore* ('white')? Gurinder's detailed and accurate recall of an ad she hates—including recognition of the intertextual reference to a Hindi movie—may be likened to the detail in which *pendu* style was elaborated, as a means of underlining the contrast between 'classy', 'cool' style and its antithesis.

In juxtaposing Rubicon and Coke in discussions about soft drinks advertisements young people are drawing connections between texts which are incomparable in certain crucial ways; they seem to be unaware that the Rubicon advertisements are targeted at 'British Asian' families, and mother as shoppers, whereas those for Coca Cola are aimed specifically at teenagers. However, they feel themselves to be implicated in these ads as young 'British Asians', and are highly critical of the way adult 'Asians' are invariably portrayed as having Indian accents. As young people born and brought up in Britain, without Indian accents for the most part, they often express aspirations toward a greater participation in mainstream British society, from which they feel cut off by Southall's 'island' status. Representations which emphasize the 'foriegnness' of 'Asians' are seen to further alienate them from society. Such concerns override the fact that the depiction of a family watching a popular Hindi movie and the playful behavior of the father are features of the ad which make it attractive to many local adults. For young people, it is a further unwelcome marker of their difference.

Their comments reveal a sense of the excessive 'burden of representation' which affects those few images of 'Asians' which appear in mainstream media, especially on British TV. As Williamson points out, this is a question of collective cultural power: 'the more power any group has to create and wield representations, the less [any one image] is required to be representative' (1993: 116). Young people are faced with what they believe are inappropriate representations of 'Asians' in the very few British TV ads in which they are portrayed. Ads in 'Indian' media fare no better, but are treated as objects of ridicule in the peer group. In criticizing both so vociferously, they are demarcating distinctions in taste and style between the parental and peer cultures, and also, at least implicitly and sometimes explicitly, expressing a desire for alternative images. Again, the politics of ethnicity are involved: Who represents us? Who speaks for us, or to us? Since the spaces available for public representation of what they see as their generational culture are so limited, and since neither British nor Indian media offer representations which they view as acceptable or appropriate, it is perhaps no wonder that they turn to a third, alternative space of fantasy identification: they draw on utopian images of America to construct a position of 'world teenagers' which transcends those available in Brisih or Indian cultures.

Fast Food and Fasting: Eating, Autonomy and the Big Mac

A similar process can be observed in talk about food ads. Food is not only a basic human requirement but a fundamental aspect of material culture. Taste in food is the archetype of all tastes (Bourdieu, 1984: 79). It is also one of the most significant markers of ethnicity in plural societies. One of the legacies of British imperialism is the presence of 'Asian' restaurants and take-aways in virtually every high street: 'Indian' (and other 'ethnic') settlers have redefined 'white' British food culture over the past decades. Southall is the major 'Indian' wholesale and retail centre in Britain. The majority of local retail outlets are owned and managed by 'Indians' who sell 'Indian' food products. There is also a plethora of cafés and restaurants which service the local population. However, at the time of fieldwork, there were no national supermarket chains or franchised fast-food outlets in Southall, and the availability of certain types of 'English' food products was very limited. Pizzas and beefburgers were very popular foods among young people, but only available in adjacent towns and suburbs. It was a frequent source of complaint that one could 'only' eat 'Indian' food in Southall: an index that living in Southall means not 'really' living in Britain. But on the other hand this also meant opportunities for 'escape' from Southall to the 'outside': going to the cinema in Ealing or Hounslow and having a pizza or a McDonald's was very much a feature of the teenage leisure scene, an occasion to participate in peer-group activities away from the surveillance of parents and elders.

The public and private consumption of 'English' or 'American' food is perceived not simply as feature of the teenage scene but also as a way of feeling or appearing part of the wider society and culture. Above all perhaps, it is a means of distinguishing oneself from those who are seen to eat 'only' Indian food. TV ads are the main source of information about 'new' food products on the market, which are often not locally available. Through their discussions of food ads, young people provide an account of their tastes and preferences in food and consider a range of factors affecting their food consumption: parental control over their diet; religious restrictions on foods; health and beauty concerns; financial constraints; and the impact of domestic technologies, such as the microwave oven and the fridge freezer, on their food consumption, and the way in which these have stimulated the purchase of pre-packaged foods.

The majority of the young people in this study eat Indian food in their homes on a daily basis. Local schools are required to provide food for Hindu, Sikh and Muslim pupils, in line with religious prohibitions on beef and pork. Ironically, it is the teachers who avidly consume this food, much to the amusement of the young people who consider it to be tasteless by comparison with home cooking and with the food available in local restaurants. Students who eat in the canteen prefer 'English' fast foods such as chips and beans, pizzas, sausages or fritters. Some go to the local shops and buy a can of Coke and a packet of crisps, some go to one of the local Punjabi cafés, and others get fish and chips, whilst a small number of boys spend their dinner money in the games arcades. Approximately £1–£2 is spent per day on lunch by those who do not receive free school meals or return home for lunch. The arrangements made for lunch not only act as a means of organising peer-group relations during the lunch-hour but also provide an indication of one's consumer power or lack of it, as well as being a way of distinguishing cultural tastes in food. The idea of 'English' food (other than the school canteen variety) is found to be very appealing, though the experience may not live up to the anticipation:

> NIRMAL: When I was younger it was like a delicacy having English food, you just never had it and you didn't really know what it was and you felt you were missing out on something [. . .]. Then I went on a school trip [. . .]. I was glad to get home for some home cooking.

But 'English', in this kind of context, usually means 'fast', 'convenience', 'frozen' or 'junk food'.

There is a tendency in the peer context for young people to express a dislike of 'Indian' food. This may be a way of appearing 'westernised', a way of expressing resistance to parental attempts to control their diet, or a way of complaining about the lack of variety in their day-to-day food consumption, rather than a genuine distaste for 'Indian' food *per se*. In the following exchange, a group of 16-year-old girls discuss the special appeal of McDonald's ads and express resentment at their parents' attempts to control their diet:

> AMRITA: The thing is Mum and Dad only cook Indian food.
> DALVINDER: I don't like Indian food very much . . .
> TEJINDER: . . . especially not 365 days a year . . . .
> DALVINDER: . . . then it gets disgusting, it's like we have to have Indian food, we have it every lunchtime and again in the evening, but we have to have it in the family.
> TEJINDER: With your mum and dad you have to sit down and eat chapatis, you have to, if you don't you get into trouble and they start giving you a lecture, 'Oh! you're turning English, you're not Indian' and stuff like that.
> DALVINDER: And if you don't eat your *dal* [lentils] they give you a lecture on the poor, starving people in Ethiopia [. . .] but you can parcel my food to them, give me a McDonald's any day, I don't know cos 'it makes your day', it's just a feeling you get, 'it makes your day'.
> TEJINDER: It makes your mouth water.

Clearly the appeal of McDonald's and Coca Cola ads and slogans succeeds on a very similar level; and burgers connote freedom because they represent a food which you don't *have to have*.

The negotiation of what one eats is but another facet of the way young people negotiate their relationship to the parental culture, and parental attempts to control their behaviour more generally. The desire to consume 'English' food regularly is seen by parents as one further index of 'westernisation', and most parents try to retain some control over how far their children become 'westernised'. 'Indian' food is an important and distinctive aspect of Punjabi culture, and to show a dislike or distaste for Indian food is perceived to be a rebellion against 'the culture'.

The solution to the 'problem' of eating Indian food every day is, for some, provided by fast foods such as burgers. When asked why McDonald's beefburgers are so appealing, the response was formulated in terms of the slogan, 'Well, it makes your day', and 'it's just a feeling you get'. The nature of the 'feeling' becomes apparent when notions of 'freedom', 'choice' and financial independence are related to the ability to eat what you want. But the 'feeling' is also associated with a trip to McDonald's capturing a moment of 'freedom' outside Southall: freedom from the watchful eye of the parental culture and freedom to participate on the 'teenage scene'. McDonald's and Pizza Hut are considered to be both the cheapest and the 'best' of fast foods. The McDonald's outlets in the Hounslow and Ealing are places where boys and girls can safely meet and where courting rituals are conducted discretely. In a market survey of 240 'Asian' school students in west London (40 per cent of whom were from Southall), conducted in 1991 by an 'Asian' advertising company, Channel A, 'burger bars' (46 per cent) were the most regularly frequented of places after the cinema (69 per cent). On several occasions I accompanied informants to McDonald's only to find that large groups of Southall 'escapees' had occupied the entire upstairs section:

> DALVINDER: It's good to get out of Southall, go down Hounslow with me mates and sit in McDonald's, get a Big Mac and a Coke . . .
> AMRITA: . . . yeah, and have a good gossip . . .
> DALVINDER: . . . and check out the guys [giggling] . . .
> AMRITA: . . . and get checked out by the guys.

The apparent rejection of Indian food by many young people in the peer culture can be seen as a gesture expressing the desire to establish some degree of independence from the family culture and at the same time to exert some control over one's own body. Teenagers experience their bodies as, in many respects, beyond their control. Rapid and often sudden physical and hormonal changes can be quite difficult to deal with and some young people respond by trying to gain more control over what they eat. Unlike hair and skin colour, 'ethnic signifiers' which are more or less completely beyond personal control, body-shape can, to some extent, be controlled by means of dieting. Body-shape ideals are strongly influenced by the media, and may also have a 'racial', ideological dimension. 'Indian' food is regarded as being fattening, due to the amount of *ghee* (purified butter) added to curries. It may be referred to as 'village' or *pendu* food, and its 'filling' and 'fattening' qualities, when it is contrasted with 'healthy' 'western' food, mark it as low status, in a hierarchy similar to that described by Bourdieu, who found that French working-class or rural peasant food, similarly, was seen as 'fattening' (1984: 190). Girls in particular, but by no means exclusively, are under considerable peer and media pressure to look slim and 'fit' in accordance with 'western' norms. Many girls diet and cases of anorexia nervosa are not uncommon in this age group. Punjabi culture provides legitimating opportunities for extreme dieting practices: fasting for religious reasons is common among women and girls, who may fast up to two days a week, especially when they are 'petitioning God' for a special request. But 'fasting' is sometimes the excuse girls give to parents for dieting in pursuit of a slim body.

It is not difficult to see the appeal of certain low-fat, 'fast' foods among girls, and in some cases also among their mothers:

> INDERJEET: I tell my mum not to put so much *ghee* in the food but my dad likes it like that [. . .]. My mum's been influenced by some of, the fast food ads and so have I — like the one for Bird's Eye Healthy Options, it's low-calorie food, when you see that you just wanna run round to your local shop to buy it — you can just stuff it in the microwave when you can't be bothered to cook.

Parents try to discourage their children from eating 'English' food — that is 'fast', 'convenience', 'frozen' or 'junk' food — as it is considered to be unhealthy and unwholesome. They too have their hierarchy of values attached to different foods, which they try to foster in, or impose upon, their children:

> BALJIT: My mum goes [Indian accent], 'It's good for you, *dal*, go on eat up,' and when you go to the doctor he says, 'Eat *dal*, *saag* [spinach], *subji* [veg-

etable curry] and *roti* [unleavened wheat bread] like a good girl' [. . .]. My mum's always on about *saag* and how good it is for you, they think if you don't eat Indian food that you'll fall into bad health.

There are even more compelling, financial reasons why some parents encourage their children to eat Indian food:

> PERMINDER: Indian food works out much cheaper, you just buy a big bag of *dal*, some vegetables [. . .]. We only have meat at the weekends [. . .]. You can't have English food, like pizzas and frozen foods every day cos that works out too expensive compared to Indian food.

Financial constraints will obviously affect the diet that young people have and this acts as a marker of social difference. In low-income households it is not unusual for *dal*, *subji* and *rod* to be the staple daily diet. Thus, many households are vegetarian less for religious reasons (vegetarianism is associated with religiosity and spiritual purity among Sikhs and Hindus) and more because meat is simply too expensive and considered to be a luxury for special occasions. Low-income households are extremely unlikely to buy 'convenience' foods. But, where income will permit, young vegetarians are easily persuaded to buy frozen vegetarian foods by TV food ads.

Religious prohibitions on pork for Muslims and beef for Hindus and Sikhs means that neither of these meats can be bought locally. Yet many youngsters transgress religious taboos in consuming 'fast' foods, Hindus by eating beefburgers and Muslims by selecting the 'Spicy Sausage' pizza at Pizza Hut (spicy and 'hot' foods are well-liked by most young people). Thus participation in a 'fast-food teenage scene', in some cases, threatens parental religious rules. Young people sometimes breach these taboos in an act of defiance against their parents. Moreover, peer pressures may be exerted in order to encourage transgression, which poses a serious moral dilemma for some; while conversely, some young people's refusal to consume these foods becomes a strong statement of allegiance to their religious and cultural identity.

Take-away pizzas, fish and chips and Kentucky Fried Chicken are enjoyed as a 'treat' by some families to accompany a video at the weekend. Many interviewees reported that they had some form of take-away 'English' food at least once a week at home to 'break with habit': 'Yeah, we like to do that too at the weekend, you know, get fish and chips or something and watch a video'. However, probably the most significant changes in eating habits, routines and arrangements have occurred as a result of the widespread take-up of the microwave oven and deep-freeze among Southall families. Microwave ovens are very popular and became common in high-income households in Southall in the early 1980s. For those households which have a deep-freeze and a microwave oven and can afford fast food, the ads for convenience foods have a great attraction: 'You don't have to have Indian food [. . .], your freezer's full with whatever you want'.

These technologies open up further possibilities, which young people find very appealing, for exercising a degree of control not only over what one eats but also, in some cases, over when and with whom one eats in the home. It can mean the opportunity to avoid parents at meal-times and establish independent eating habits. There is also some evidence to suggest that it encourages boys to cater for themselves:

PERMINDER: I'm going to try Napolena, you can make your own pizza, it's just a pizza base and then you add your own topping.

NIRMAL: [. . .] I don't eat with my parents any more, I eat later, especially now that I'm studying for exams, like sometimes I'll sit with them, but I eat when I like now.

PARAMJIT: Yeah, I think the microwave is a real advantage, you don't have to spend much time cooking, you can eat when you want [. . .] and best of all it means that my lazy brother even manages to throw something in and sort his own food out and that's saying something.

The changes in family food rituals enabled by these technologies are likely to have far-reaching implications, given the symbolic and material centrality of food and eating arrangements in the transmission of cultural traditions.

Frozen 'Indian' foods however are not generally appreciated, partly because the standards of home cooking are so much better. 'Have you seen the one for English-made Indian food, we've tried the dal but there's a weird taste to it, I think it could be the preservatives'. These products usually meet with particular resistance on the part of mothers, who consider home cooking to be of better quality and

taste and more healthy: 'When these ads come on my mum always goes "I can make it better anyway" [. . .]. Mum's answer to everything: "Home-made's best!"' Moreover, as with 'ethnic' canned drinks, there is also a high degree of sensitivity towards the stereotypical portrayal of 'Indian' people in ads for 'Indian' fast foods. These have become more prevalent on British TV, and are widely perceived as an attempt by the advertisers to sell 'frozen Indian culture'. But such sensitivity is not shared or recognised by all, as is evident in the following discussion between two 16-year-old boys:

NIRMAL: Have you seen the Indian couple doing a British ad you know, these fast foods.

RANJIT: Oh, you mean English-made Indian food.

NIRMAL: Yeah.

RANJIT: But they're really westernised, they're not like traditional Indians.

NIRMAL: They are, I think it's quite patronising in fact, they, like sell a different culture and say, 'Ah . . . it's so sweet!', it's like frozen Indian culture.

RANJIT: [laughs] What do you mean patronising?

NIRMAL: The ad is patronising cos they only use Indian people for these types of product.

RANJIT: But in one way they're just trying to get their point across that, hey! this is Indian food.

NIRMAL: But they stereotype them [. . .] they all have accents.

RANJIT: But most of them do speak with accents.

NIRMAL: Not all of them, you don't speak with an accent do you? But you were born here.

RANJIT: Yeah but what about the Findus punch-line? [laughing].

NIRMAL: Oh yeah.

RANJIT: When the wife brings the pudding to her husband and he goes, [Indian accent] 'What's that dear?' and she says, [Indian accent] 'Oh! it's spotted Dick' [laughs].

NIRMAL: But it's taking the piss, it shows that Indians don't know the English language or their food!

Thus quite different readings can be made of the same ad. Ranjit finds the couple both 'westernised' and amusing and is little concerned about stereotypical portrayals. He quite readily accepts that many 'Indian' people speak with ('Indian') accents and it does not bother him that they should be represented as such. Nirmal on the other hand shows concern about the 'burden of representation' (Mercer, 1988) carried by such TV ads. 'Indians' only appear on

British TV to advertise the stereotypical 'Indian-ness' of ('western') products, and are portrayed as stereotypically ignorant of the English language and English foods. As with the Rubicon ads, such representations are seen as an indication of 'foreign' status: 'They make us out to be more foreign than we actually are — as if we are not part of their culture, but we are!'

There is a marked lack of images on British TV, but also on on 'Asian' or 'Indian' TV and video, which young people in Southall feel able to identify with or which confirm a recognition of their identity by others. McDonald's in the sphere of food, and Coca Cola in the sphere of drink, are seen to represent an alternative. These brands connote, both through the suggestions conveyed by the imagery, songs and slogans of their ads, and through the particular place assumed by their consumption in local life, an ideal 'freedom' which transcends boundaries. Not only the numerous boundaries which divide Southall internally — boundaries of religion and caste, gender and generation — and those which divide Southall from the wider British society 'out-side'; but also the global boundaries of ethnicity and nationality are portrayed in the Coke ads as transcended through a sense of easy participation in a global youth culture modelled on an American teenage dream. This idealised global youth culture is shaped by consumption practices: it expresses the utopian desire for a world in which everybody is equally 'cool', 'safe', affluent and free to consume at will. Yet even though the expression of this desire is to a great extent constrained by the logic and imagery of consumerism, the talk about Coke ads consistently highlights the style of open, expansive sociability which they represent; and this suggests that the desire at stake here may be understood as the desire for full integration into a pluralistic society where the social implications of cultural differences are minimal. Thus in talking of Coke ads — and elsewhere in their ad talk — young people in Southall articulate, negatively and positively, aspirations for cultural change which deserve to be taken seriously as the potential matrix of a future, genuinely pluralist culture.

Printed Matter

Canadian Newspapers

Christopher Dornan

With the obvious exceptions of those that carry themselves as "national" titles in their respective linguistic communities—the *Globe and Mail,* the *National Post* and *Le Devoir*—Canadian newspapers are typically parochial undertakings, serving an urban or local constituency. This is as true of a circulation giant such as the *Toronto Star* as it is of the *Hill Times,* a weekly tabloid catering to a readership of politicians and staffers on Ottawa's Parliament Hill. A century ago, this meant that newspapers serving different markets were independently owned by proprietors who themselves resided in those markets.

Over the course of the twentieth century, however, economic imperatives in the newspaper industry all but eradicated the independent and locally owned title, as proprietors recognized that profits are increased by sharing the costs of news-gathering and production among a number of papers, and that financial stability comes with owning multiple holdings in a variety of markets. Hence, what became the Southam newspaper chain began with one title, the *Hamilton Spectator,* but as early as 1923 the company also owned the *Ottawa Citizen,* the *Calgary Herald,* the *Edmonton Journal,* the *Winnipeg Tribune* and the *Vancouver Province.* Over the rest of the century, the trend moved inexorably toward chain ownership; corporate control; proprietorship by companies with cross-media holdings; market rationalization in which newspapers no longer competed head-to-head for the same readers, but carved up urban markets between them; and a concentration of ownership in which fewer and fewer companies came to acquire more and more of the nation's outlets of print journalism.

It is this feature of the newspaper industry—in which local titles with near-monopolies in local demographic communities are the properties of national corporate entities—that has most commonly excited concern among critics. Bluntly, the fear is that when members of a local demographic market have no alternative but to depend on a single title as a source of social intelligence, and when a small number of corporations owns these agencies of public address, corporate owners may be in a position to use their holdings to promote a particular view of political and economic affairs at the expense of alternative perspectives. The worry is that proprietors might restrict the range of debate within newspapers and skew news coverage so as to favour select interests, thus propagandizing the population. Were this to happen, it would be anathema to democracy, which requires that citizens be fully and fairly informed on the issues of the day so as to be able to come to sound decisions on how they wish to be governed. Partisan control over public expression would amount to control over public opinion, and therefore to control over the political process itself.

The Changing Face of Canadian Newspapers

Canadian newspaper publishing has long been accompanied by anxiety over the extent of corporate concentration of ownership. Typically, these worries have waxed and waned in light of developments in the industry, spiking with each new consolidation of corporate control and receding in moments of expansion or quiescence. Concentration of newspaper ownership was a principal concern of the Special Senate Committee on Mass Media (the Davey Committee) in 1970. The simultaneous closings of the *Winnipeg Tribune* and the *Ottawa Journal* in 1980—which left the Thomson corporation's *Free Press* with a monopoly in Winnipeg and Southam's *Citizen* with a monopoly in Ottawa—prompted an official inquiry into the state of the industry, the 1981 Royal Commission on Newspapers (the Kent Commission). From the early 1980s until the mid-1990s, however, the issue of press concentration abated as a matter of policy concern. In part, this was because the period was marked by relative stability in the industry, and indeed expansion, as the *Sun* chain of tabloids entered various Southam-dominated markets, the *Globe and Mail* launched a satellite-printed national edition, one by one the urban broadsheets began to publish on Sundays, and the *Financial Post* turned from a weekly into a daily in direct competition with the *Globe and Mail's* Report on Business (Dornan 2000, 54). In the latter half of the 1990s, however, concern over consolidated control of the Canadian newspaper industry was rekindled as a consequence of the actions of a single company: Conrad Black's Hollinger Inc., which emerged as the dominant newspaper proprietor in the country. With the departure of Black from the Canadian newspaper scene in 2001, debate over concentration and control in the newspaper industry became if anything more inflamed, as all but a few of the major titles are now in the hands of companies that also own broadcast networks, Internet portals, and cable and telecommunication distribution systems.

On November 1, 2001, in the wake of the events of September 11 and in the midst of the U.S. bombing campaign in Afghanistan, the front-page photograph in the *Globe and Mail* was notable. For days, the front pages of the nation's newspapers had shown F-18 fighters roaring off the decks of American aircraft carriers, Northern Alliance soldiers pointing shoulder-launched rockets at distant Taliban positions, street demonstrations in Pakistan, and violent confrontations between Palestinians and Israeli Defence Forces. This day, the *Globe* chose to feature above the fold a full-colour portrait of Conrad Black, resplendent in his red ermine robes, on the occasion of his investiture in the British House of Lords as Lord Black of Crossharbour. By devoting such prominent attention to the man and the occasion, the *Globe* was acknowledging the influence its great rival had wielded in the country in the previous five years through his actions in the newspaper industry, while simultaneously marking the end of that influence and hence the end of a tumultuous chapter in Canadian newspaper publishing. The period ahead for the industry promises to be no less turbulent, but the year 2001 likely marks a fault line between two moments in its history.

In 1996, Black took control of the Southam chain of broadsheets in urban markets from Montreal to Vancouver, and ignited a remarkable interlude of activity in a media industry that had long been unremarkable in its stolid performance (see Table 1). Once dismissed as yesterday's medium—an obsolescent cultural form catering to an aging and dwindling readership, and slowly but surely losing its prominence in the social and economic life of the nation—the newspaper was suddenly a hot property. There was the birth of a new national daily in Anglophone Canada, a full-blown newspaper war in the largest city in the country, and a flurry of changes in ownership as the country's largest communication corporations sought either to acquire or divest themselves of newspaper properties according to their respective strategies of how best to position themselves for the multimedia future. In the space of four years, for example, the *Guelph Mercury* changed proprietorship five times. Originally owned by the Thomson corporation, it was purchased by Conrad Black's Hollinger Inc. in 1995 when Thomson sold a raft of its smaller Canadian papers so as to concentrate on electronic publishing ventures. In 1998, Hollinger included it in a package acquired by Sun Media in exchange for the *Financial Post*, an acquisition essential to Hollinger's plans to launch a national political- and business-oriented daily. Sun

Table 1 **Timeline of Ownership Changes in the Canadian Media Industry**

1994

Conrad Black's Hollinger Inc. purchases the Regina *Leader-Post* and the Saskatoon *Star-Phoenix* from Saskatchewan's Armadale Co.

1995

Hollinger purchases a raft of papers from Thomson corp.

1996

Hollinger acquires control of Southam corp.

1997

The London Free Press is purchased by Sun Media from the Blackburn family.

1998

Hollinger acquires the Financial Post from Sun Media in exchange for the Hamilton Spectator, the Kitchener-Waterloo Record, the Guelph Mercury, and the Cambridge Reporter.

October 27, 1998

Hollinger/Southam launches the National Post.

December 1998

The Toronto Star acquires the Hamilton Spectator, the Kitchener-Waterloo Record, the Guelph Mercury, and the Cambridge Reporter from Sun Media; Quebecor purchases Sun Media.

April 2000

Hollinger announces its Canadian newspapers are for sale, excluding its major urban dailies.

July 2000

In a transaction worth some $3.5 billion, CanWest Global agrees to purchase most of Hollinger's daily and weekly newspapers, including thirteen of Southam's major urban dailies and a 50 per cent interest in the National Post.

September 2000

BCE Inc. buys majority control of the Globe and Mail. Its subsidiary, Bell Globemedia, comes to include CTV, Bell Sympatico, ExpressVu, and the Globe and Mail.

November 2000

A sudden downturn in the bond market restructures the CanWest Global/Hollinger deal, shaving some titles from the package. The deal proceeds, valued at $3.2 billion.

2000

Thomson sells the Lethbridge Herald and the Medicine Hat News to Horizon Operations Ltd. of B.C. Osprey Media Group, headed by Michael Sifton, whose family had owned Armadale in 1994, purchases sixteen smaller Ontario dailies from Hollinger.

August 2001

Conrad Black sells his remaining interest in the National Post to CanWest Global.

November 2001

Thomson sells its last remaining daily newspapers, the Winnipeg Free Press and the Brandon Sun, to Canadian Newspapers Company, a company formed by Ron Stern and Bob Silver, partners in the Winnipeg-based textile manufacturer Western Glove Works. Hollinger sells its last two Ontario dailies, the Chatham Daily News and the Sarnia Observer, to Osprey Media.

Media was then bought by Quebecor, which in turn sold the *Mercury* in 1999 to the Toronto *Star*.

The result is that, by 2002, with only a handful of exceptions, every major Canadian daily newspaper was the property of a parent owner with interests that extend far beyond newspaper publishing. The *Sun* chain of tabloids is owned by Quebecor, which also owns, in addition to its Quebec newspaper titles,

Quebecor World printing, the Videotron cable company, and the TVA network. The Southam dailies, including the *National Post*, are owned by CanWest Global Communications Corp., a broadcasting company. And the *Globe and Mail* is a property of Bell Globemedia, which also owns the CTV network and the Bell Sympatico Internet service provider, which in turn is owned by Bell Canada Enterprises (BCE),

Table 2   **Canadian Daily Newspaper Circulation 1990–2001**

YEAR	# of Dailies	Copies Mon-Fri Average	Copies/ Saturday	Copies/ Sunday	Total Copies/ Weekly	Average Sold Per Publishing Day
1990	108	5,638,729	5,894,245	3,227,134	37,315,025	5,814,510
1991	108	5,474,027	5,733,488	3,184,431	36,288,055	5,228,124
1992	108	5,357,172	5,735,296	3,192,564	35,713,721	5,553,409
1993	108	5,340,462	5,742,539	3,271,337	35,716,186	5,517,913
1994	108	5,285,338	5,748,793	3,242,760	35,418,224	5,491,150
1995	104	5,068,068	5,813,309	3,137,573	34,291,222	5,309,600
1996	106	4,978,201	5,706,756	3,096,107	33,593,868	5,191,677
1997	105	4,780,217	5,568,377	2,986,865	32,456,325	5,108,709
1998	105	4,768,951	5,591,107	3,010,498	32,446,631	5,004,913
1999	106	4,986,095	5,711,058	3,108,606	33,750,142	5,177,072
2000	104	4,970,102	5,682,906	3,093,650	33,627,066	5,166,255
2001	104				33,710,216	5,184,571

Source: Canadian Newspaper Association, Newspaper Facts, Dec. 2001.

the telecommunications giant—all of which invites the question of what these corporations intend for the newspaper properties they now control, what this portends for the practice of journalism in Canada, and what it may mean for the publics these newspapers serve.

Make no mistake: even in an expanding media environment marked by the advent of entirely new concourses of communication, newspapers remain vital to social, political and economic affairs, from the local to the national. In a nation of some thirty million, Canadian Newspaper Association (CNA) data show that in 2001, Canada's 104 daily papers sold an average combined total of 5,184,571 copies per day, and these are purchased across all social classes—though readership increases with income, education and job responsibility (see Table 2).

(In November 2001, the Saint John *Times Globe* was absorbed by the New Brunswick *Telegraph Journal*, both owned by the Irving family's Brunswick News Inc.; the *Telegraph Journal* became a two-edition paper, one serving the local market of Saint John and the other a provincial daily serving all of New Brunswick. As well, in February 2002, the Cambridge *Reporter* moved from daily to twice-weekly publication. Consequently, by early 2002 there were 102 daily newspapers published in Canada, as opposed to 143 in 1911 (see Table 3).

Despite the recent newspaper war, with its aggressive circulation drives, total average circula-

tion of all Canadian dailies is down from a peak of 5,824,736 in 1989—a drop of 640,000 copies per day over the past twelve years, even as the population of the country has grown. Nonetheless, it remains a substantial number. And although readership is demographically uneven—older people are more attentive to newspapers than younger—nonetheless, 57 per cent of Canadians over the age of eighteen report reading a paper on an average weekday, 64 per cent read a newspaper on the weekend, and 83 per cent report having read a newspaper in the past week (Canadian Newspaper Association 2001). As has been pointed out elsewhere, this means that more people read newspapers regularly than view Canadian films, read Canadian books, patronize the Canadian arts, purchase Canadian recordings or watch Canadian television drama and light entertainment. As a fact of this country's cultural life, newspapers are rivalled only by domestic sport and by news and current affairs programming on radio and television (Dornan 1996, 60).

As an advertising vehicle, they are no less important to affairs of commerce. They are, in fact, the single largest advertising medium in the country. In 2000, according to CNA data, newspaper advertising revenue reached a historical high of just over $2.58 billion. This accounts for a quarter of the total national advertising expenditure in 2000 of some $10 billion. The private television broadcasting networks, by comparison, accounted for $1.76 billion

Table 3 2001 Canadian Daily Newspaper Circulation by Ownership*

Owner	# of Papers	Weekly Circulation	Average Issue Circulation
Southern Publications	27	11,437,605	1,792,906
Quebecor Inc.	15	6,968,043	1,019,809
Torstar	5	4,621,724	686,851
Power Corp. of Canada	7	3,049,424	458,115
Bell/Globemedia	1	2,185,663	364,277
Osprey Media	18	1,536,963	247,021
Canadian Newspapers Co.	2	1,039,837	148,548
Halifax-Herald Ltd.	2	713,870	104,731
Brunswick News Inc.	3	675,278	116,472
Horizon	5	630,319	93,232
Hollinger Cdn. N.L.P.	10	326,277	59,361
Independents	5	314,700	57,078
Black Press	1	114,388	19,065
Annex Publ. & Printing	2	94,125	17,125

* Based on 2001 ABC Fas-Fax ended March 31, 2001 or other Publisher's Statements collected by the Canadian Newspaper Association. *Note: Hollinger Cdn. N.L.P. denotes Hollinger Canadian Newspapers, Limited Partnership.*

in advertising revenue; the entire radio industry reaped just over $1 billion; the specialty TV channels $381 million; consumer magazines $434 million; outdoor ads $293 million, and so on. Internet advertising—to which we will return—amounted to only $109 million, or a mere 4 per cent of the money spent on newspaper advertising (see Table 4).

Perhaps more important, in a country in which news and journalism in their various forms are the pre-eminent domestic communication genre, newspapers are the bedrock of an information culture. It is true that Canada can point with some pride to its domestic feature film industry, its recording industry and its independent television production industry— sectors that barely existed some thirty years ago— but for the most part these entertainment enterprises remain overshadowed by the cultural exports of the juggernaut to our south. Journalism is relatively cheap to produce when compared to the per-hour production costs of programs such as *Da Vinci's Inquest*. News is also inherently parochial. It is largely (although not exclusively) preoccupied with local, regional or national concerns. Even its attention to the world beyond our national borders is inflected with an interest in how events *there* affect us *here*, if only by touching our emotions. That is as good a definition of news as any: it is a running

chronicle of what is meant to matter to us in the here and now; a means by which an agenda of concern is established. Because news is therefore unavoidably parochial, it cannot easily be provided by foreign undertakings. Hence, the distinctive Canadian communication genre is journalism. And though news and current affairs programming is a prominent feature of the television schedules, while political talk looms large on private and public sector radio, newspapers remain essential to the enterprise of Canadian journalism. In every city, the newsrooms of the local daily newspapers dwarf the staffs of the local broadcast news teams; the sheer amount and variety of information contained in the daily paper far outstrips what can be contained in a local newscast; and the morning newspaper remains for the most part the daily briefing book for the broadcast operations, cueing them as to what stories to follow. Even at the national level, the editorial staffs of the *Globe and Mail* and the *National Post* vastly outnumber the complement of personnel in the national newsrooms of the CBC, CTV or Global.

Newspapers are therefore not merely profitable ventures of manifest utility. They are essential to Canadian civic life. And yet they are constitutionally saddled with a tension—one might say an absurdity—that reveals itself most starkly just at

Table 4 **Advertising Revenue by Medium**

Net Advertising Revenue—Millions of Dollars

	1995	1996	1997	1998	1999	2000
Daily newspapers	1,900	1,960	2,303	2,379	2,429	2,580
Television—Total	1,850	1,982	2,100	2,312	2,378	2,456
Public and non-commercial TV					n/a	*265
Specialty TV					304	381
Private TV (including infomercials)					1,759	1,763
Direct mail	991	1,110	1,168	1,251	1,190	1,200
Yellow Pages	864	892	899	935	975	1,000
Radio	758	792	849	921	954	1,002
Community newspapers	579	597	634	765	788	820
General magazines	316	318	347	381	389	434
Trade magazines	229	233	252	277	283	295
Outdoor	167	200	220	250	270	293
Other print	47	48	48	49	49	50
Internet	—	—	10	25	56	109
Total	7,700	8,132	8,829	9,543	9,759	*10,190

* estimated.

Source: Canadian Newspaper Association, *Newspaper Facts* December 2001.

those moments when the service newspapers provide is most valued and most required.

The tension resides in the following: Newspapers are the antennae of the economy. Because their advertising revenue derives from the full range of commercial announcements, a softening of newspaper advertising can be the first foreshadowing of an economic downturn. Broadly, newspapers carry three different types of advertising.

First, and the largest of the three categories, are retail ads purchased by businesses exactly like the local city newspaper itself—businesses whose trade is city-wide, but whose customers peter out just beyond the municipal boundaries: furniture outlets, electronics stores, supermarkets, franchises and auto dealerships. These account for almost 47 per cent of newspapers' advertising income. (Mom-and-Pop pizza delivery joints, for example, do not bother to advertise in the local urban daily, since they service pockets of limited circumference while the paper casts its net over the entire city. Who could find or remember an ad for a local pizza delivery business in the pages of the Toronto *Star?*)

Second are classified ads—a form of advertising almost exclusive to newspapers, since they cannot readily be accommodated by radio, television or magazines. Classifieds chart a panoply of any city's daily commerce, from help wanted to apartments for rent; from companions sought to puppies on offer; from items for sale to the birth and death announcements. Together, these account for some 34 per cent of newspaper advertising revenue.

Finally, national ads for companies such as auto manufacturers and phone companies account for the remaining 20 per cent. This is the smallest of the three categories in terms of total revenue, although companies in this category are newspapers' largest advertising clients (see Table 5).

Because newspapers therefore map the entire spectrum of legitimate trade, from the marketing efforts of the automotive giants to one's neighbour unloading a used sofa, no industry is more sensitive to fluctuations in advertising expenditure. At the same time, few industries are less able to adapt to fluctuations in advertising income.

The reason for this is twofold. First, newspapers subsist on advertising income. They do charge their readers for the purchase of their product, but only a pittance. The price of a newspaper has always been less than the price of a cup of coffee. More than

Table 5 2000 Top 10 Advertisers in Canadian Media

Advertiser	Total spending in all media	Total spending in dailies	% change vs 1999
General Motors Car Dealerships	$84,004,600	$76,641,300	+12.3%
Chrysler Car Dealerships	$72,932,900	$68,754,700	+21.3%
Chrysler Dodge Jeep Dealers	$82,610,800	$63,653,900	+20.8%
Weshild Holdings Ltd.	$78,315,300	$59,458,800	+39.2%
Chevrolet Oldsmobile Dealers Association	$62,856,900	$56,315,400	+3.7%
Pontiac Buick Cadillac Dealers Association	$63,501,300	$56,315,400	+4.5%
Ford Consolidated Local Car Dealerships	$60,769,900	$55,439,300	+18.6%
Ford Dealers Association	$65,299,300	$48,314,600	+391.0%
Sears CanadaInc.	$75,156,400	$47,464,700	−7.2%
Rogers Communications Inc.	$85,879,600	$41,725,500	+15.5%

Source: Canadian Newspaper Association, Newspaper Facts December 2001/A.C. Neilsen.

80 per cent of a typical Canadian daily newspaper's income derives from advertising. Second, the costs of producing, manufacturing and distributing a newspaper are relatively fixed. The editorial content has to be generated. The physical artifact of the paper has to roll off the presses. Copies of the paper must be delivered via fleets of trucks to carriers who then distribute them to households, offices, hotels, newsagents and vending boxes. In times of economic doldrums, other industries—the automotive manufacturers, for example—can reduce expenditures by scaling back production. If there should be less demand for their product, they can downscale production, putting less of their product on the market. They can shut down assembly lines and lay off employees. Newspapers enjoy no such latitude.

Newspapers, recall, are in two different businesses simultaneously, each utterly dependent on the other and yet catering to two different classes of customer. First, newspapers sell a cheap and instantly disposable *product*—a package of paper and ink—to a clientele of almost everyone in quantities that dwarf other businesses. Apart from industries that trade in products that are physically ingested—hamburgers, beer, cups of coffee, cigarettes—few other Canadian industries sell more than five million units of their product per day. Not the razor blade industry, not the toilet paper industry, not the toothpaste manufacturers. Second, and concurrently, newspapers sell a more expensive *service* to a customer base of companies

and individuals who wish to catch the attention of as many people as possible. As agencies of public address, newspapers rent themselves out as promotional vehicles for other businesses. As the adage goes, they sell eyeballs to advertisers.

There is therefore a dislocation between the major source of the newspaper industry's revenue and the point-of-purchase demand for its product. The fact that advertising budgets may be tight does not mean there is any less street-level demand for the physical product of the morning newspaper.

Even in periods of economic slowdown, therefore, newspapers cannot cut back on distribution costs without reducing their circulations, when size of circulation is the index by which advertising rates are set. They cannot reduce their outlay on newsprint without reducing the physical dimensions of the paper, making their very pages narrower (something Canadian broadsheets did during the recession of the early 1990s and more and more U.S. dailies resorted to in 2000–2001), printing fewer copies or whittling away the newshole—the editorial contents of the paper, the very reason customers buy the product in the first place. They cannot markedly downsize the editorial staff without compromising the editorial contents. Nor, in moments of reduced consumer confidence and disposable income, can they increase subscription and vending prices without running the risk of losing customers. Nonetheless, when advertising revenue dries up, they may attempt to do all these things in order to cut costs, balance the books, maintain the profit margin, service the corporate debt and satisfy the shareholders.

The essential tension at the heart of the newspaper industry, therefore, is that in times of economic hardship the public naturally becomes more anxious, and an anxious public is all the more hungry for information. Yet those very circumstances may undermine the newspaper's capacity to provide to the best of its capabilities the very product its customers seek.

This tension balloons into an absurdity at a moment, not simply of cyclical economic slowdown, but of perceived crisis—a moment such as that experienced in the last quarter of 2001 in the wake of September 11. Just when there was an unprecedented appetite and a manifest need for comprehensive news coverage at home and abroad, not to mention the full range of public debate that a mature democracy demands in uncertain and volatile times, newspapers found their operational budgets strained. They were well aware of their civic obligations, but they were equally confronted by financial realities.

The signs of an economic slowdown, at least as measured by newspaper revenue, were a year old by the time of September 11. Although advertising revenue in 2000 had been the highest in the industry's history, in the last quarter of 2000 it had declined by 1.1 per cent over the previous quarter. Similarly, newspaper circulation revenues—the 20 per cent source of income newspapers receive from their purchase by readers—had been running ahead of 1999 figures until the fourth quarter of 2000, when they dropped by 7.4 per cent against the last quarter of 1999. In fact, circulation revenues at the end of 2000 were the lowest they had ever been since the Canadian Newspaper Association began collecting such data in 1995. Meanwhile, in the first half of 2001, total run-of-press advertising lineage (that is, advertisements printed on the pages of newspapers, as opposed to insert advertising—flyers or brochures piggy-backing on the newspaper's city-wide distribution system) dropped by 4.6 per cent. In May 2001, Quebecor cut 302 positions at Sun Media, or 5 per cent of the workforce.

At the same time, newsprint prices dropped from US$605 a tonne in June 2001 to US$535 a tonne in October. Although this may seem to play to newspapers' advantage—lower newsprint prices presumably mean lower production costs—in fact it is an indication of diminishing demand for newsprint in light of falling advertising lineage. Normally, newspapers start building up their inventories of newsprint in September in order to prepare for larger papers bulked with advertising during the Christmas retail season. In September 2001, that did not seem to be happening. The antennae of the economy appeared to be anticipating a precipitous economic downturn. In October, almost a month after 9/11, Quebecor World, the largest commercial printer on the planet, announced that it was closing six plants and laying off 2,400 employees, or 6 per cent of its workforce.

So, just when newspapers were being compelled to boost their expenditures on news coverage by sending correspondents to Afghanistan, Pakistan and elsewhere in the Middle East with no idea how long the conflict might continue, just when circulation was soaring, and just when there was a clear demand for as much news as possible, centripetal financial pressures were insisting that newspapers reduce expenditures and cut back on production costs.

Hence, on September 17, less than a week after September 11, and in an effort to stem financial losses that had amounted to some $200 million in the three years of the paper's existence, the new outright owners of the *National Post*, CanWest Global, laid off 130 employees, including fifty journalists, and eliminated whole precincts of the paper. Gone were Sports, the Arts and Life section, local Toronto coverage, the experimental double-page Avenue spread, the Weekend Post and the Review sections. Company officials estimated this would save some $45 million a year. The idea was to concentrate on what were seen as the core strengths and selling points of the *Post*—its national news and political affairs coverage, and its business section—and to jettison supposedly peripheral content, but the move did not seem to have been thought through. Advertisers and readers reacted badly—it develops that those who follow the stock markets also follow professional sports—and within weeks, limited sports and arts coverage had returned to the *Post*. Quebecor, meanwhile, laid off senior Sun Media reporter Matthew Fisher while he was in northern Afghanistan, delivering the bad news via the very satellite phone he used to file his stories. And readers who purchased a copy of the *National Post* on October 8, Thanksgiving, received a paper that had two sections, both labeled A, and both devoted entirely to the air assault in Afghanistan, but with no *Financial Post*, no sports news, no entertainment coverage and no classifieds. The reason for the peculiar edition was that management, in a bid to save money on newsprint and employee overtime, had decided not to publish that holiday Monday. But on Sunday the U.S. air strikes against the Taliban began. After a series of frantic telephone calls, the decision not to publish was overturned and a skeleton staff rushed into the newsroom to produce a paper.

In a sense, the newspaper industry was lucky. Though appalling and unsettling, the events of September 11 and their aftermath—from the anthrax scare to the prospect of a protracted war in Afghanistan and a Pakistan aflame and ungovernable—fuelled a widespread appetite for news and made newspapers all the more relevant to readers. At the same time, the surprisingly speedy rout of the Taliban regime meant that the expensive proposition of full-bore coverage of events in a distant and inhospitable part of the world did not have to be sustained indefinitely. Finally, the economic downturn that many feared would simply worsen in the wake of September 11 did not, in the end, materialize. By March 2002, economic indicators appeared to suggest that in Canada recession had been weathered. Nonetheless, the fourth quarter of 2001 illustrated certain incongruities in a profit-driven news industry dependent on advertising revenue; it made evident the tension between what is required of the newspaper industry as an agency of public intelligence and the commercial realities that can mitigate against what is required.

When public anxiety over the al-Qaeda assault on the United States and the response of the Western nations was at its height, little attention was paid to what, by comparison, seemed trifling matters, such as the concentration of ownership in the domestic Canadian media. Even the dismissal of 130 *National Post* employees on September 17, though ruefully noted, caused little stir, perhaps also because it was widely recognized that the financial losses being incurred by the *Post* simply could not be sustained. By the end of 2001 and the early months of 2002, however, concern over the state and conduct of ownership in the newspaper industry had reawakened.

The Politics of Newspaper Concentration

In December 2001, CanWest Global unveiled a new corporate policy by which its urban Southam dailies would carry "national" editorials written or commissioned from within the chain by head office in Winnipeg. Initially, these would appear only once a week, rising later to a frequency of three per week. As innocuous as such an initiative may sound to non-journalists, it was greeted with alarm and dismay by many within the Southam newsrooms. Certainly, it signaled a departure from the traditional Southam practice, in which local editorial boards were generally run independently from corporate head office and were free to take editorial stands as they chose. Some saw the move as the first sign of the application of a broadcasting model to the newspaper industry, in which regional titles would be seen as mere local affiliates in a nationwide network of newspapers that would carry more and more centrally produced content.

Since no deviation from the new, nationally dispensed opinions was allowed in the editorials of the local papers, the *prima facie* worry was that the national editorials would straitjacket the local dailies, forever embalming them in agreement on issue after issue via the sedimentary deposit of company policy. The local editorial boards were invited to elaborate on the national editorials using local examples and evidence, but the sheer operational difficulties were readily apparent. Over time, a mass of editorial judgments from the executive suites would accumulate, which the local boards would be expected to keep track of and to which they would henceforth have to hew. They would be placed in the position of having to second-guess their own regional opinions in light of the views handed down from Winnipeg. More worrying to some was the prospect that the national editorials would not simply make the company's positions on national issues known to the public, but more insidiously they would serve as a vehicle whereby upper management let employees across the chain know where the papers' priorities and emphases in news coverage should lie.

Southam journalists had already seen the new proprietors, the Asper family, express exasperation with the journalistic conduct of the newsrooms under their control. In March 2001, David Asper, chair of the Southam publications committee, had written an opinion piece that ran in all the Southam dailies in which he chastised the national media, including his own papers, for unfairly hounding Jean Chrétien about financial improprieties in his home riding of Shawinigan. Mr. Asper, a lawyer, hinted that the incessant questioning of the Prime Minister's dealings amounted to a form of "public mischief," a criminal act, and argued that "our national political affairs have been hijacked by mischevious unfair scandal mongering." At the time, CanWest Global owned only 50 per cent of the *National Post*, the paper that had done more than any other to bring the allegations of impropriety to light. The *Post* ran Mr. Asper's broadside, but a day later than the other Southam papers and accompanied by vigorous rebuttals. Nonetheless, the incident suggested that the Aspers and their senior management took an interest, not merely in editorial opinion, but in the course of news coverage as well.

In an April 2001 speech to the Calgary Chamber of Commerce, David Asper made his views plain on what he thought was wrong with Canadian journalism and what issues CanWest intended to place on the national agenda through its newspapers. He complained of being "sick and tired" of the depiction of "redneck" Alberta in the national media, and of "our legitimate constitutional and national concerns being always subordinate to the interests of Ontario, and especially Quebec. We believe that the prism of how our country has been presented, in virtually all so-called 'national media,' has been viewed through Toronto and Ottawa."

He said the family was clear on the issues that should be brought before the public, including: a Triple-E Senate; parliamentary reform; one Supreme Court justice from each province; removal of the constitution's "notwithstanding" clause and constitutional vetoes; enshrinement of property rights in the constitution; the right of the electorate to recall MPs; public scrutiny of judges and other senior government officials; an end to deficits and debt-financing; lower capital-gains taxes; and a taxpayers' Bill of Rights (Haggett 2001).

The speech had the merit of being an unequivocal admission of where the family's political convictions lay. Journalists, however, worried that they were to be the instruments whereby this agenda of

reform would be promoted in the public forum. They were mindful, too, of the June 2001 dismissal from the Southam chain of high-profile political columnist Lawrence Martin, who had been in the forefront of those posing questions discomfiting to the Prime Minister about financial dealings in his riding. Southam management insisted that Mr. Martin's dismissal had nothing to do with his performance and was merely a cost-saving measure to reduce duplication of material within the chain. Indeed, speaking on August 24, 2001, on taking outright control of the *National Post*, CanWest Global CEO and president Leonard Asper directly addressed the issue of Mr. Martin's removal: "No journalist in our organization," he said, "has anything to fear about what they write. Nobody will be let go because they criticized Jean Chretien or any other alleged reason that our usually nefarious and treacherous and certainly ill-intending competitors like to ascribe to us" (Lindgren 2001).

Unpersuaded, some Southam journalists believed the owners were using a heavy hand to micromanage the contents of the papers so as to suit a party line. They noted that Michael Goldbloom, the publisher of the *Montreal Gazette*, resigned shortly after CanWest Global took control of the paper, apparently unwilling to work with the Aspers. David Beers, a feature writer with the *Vancouver Sun*, was dismissed from his job—ostensibly for budgetary reasons—after he wrote a column defending left-wing feminist Sunera Thobani's views on the events of September 11. It was argued that columns had been altered or killed when they took issue with company policy or deviated from a pro-Israeli position on the Middle East. Stephen Kimber, the director of the School of Journalism at the University of King's College, Halifax, who had been a freelance columnist for twenty years for the Southam-owned *Halifax Daily News*, resigned his column when the paper refused to run a contribution in which he questioned the national editorial policy.

The imposition of the national editorials was therefore merely a flash point for the larger concern that the contents of the papers were being regimented according to a particular set of political convictions. At the *Montreal Gazette*, almost every non-management member of the newsroom eventually signed their names to an open letter of protest that ran in competing news outlets and on a website set up by the dissenters, and for two days reporters withheld bylines on their stories as a gesture of defiance. They were then ordered by management to return their bylines and to cease public criticism of the company on pain of disciplinary action.

The reaction of David Asper to the protest by the *Gazette* staffers was vehement. "They have launched a childish protest," he said in a speech to Oakville business leaders, "with all of the usual self-righteousness . . . part of the ongoing pathetic politics of the Canadian left . . . why don't they just quit and have the courage of their convictions?" By January 2002, CanWest's actions had been denounced in the Quebec legislature and by the Newspaper Guild, the Quebec Federation of Professional Journalists and the Canadian Association of Journalists, which called for a government inquiry into the consequences of concentration of ownership in the Canadian media. On January 30, the day of CanWest Global's annual shareholder meeting, the Southam papers carried a lengthy op-ed article by Murdoch Davis, editor-in-chief of Southam News, responding to the criticisms of the company in an infuriated tone consistent with that adopted by Mr. Asper. According to Mr. Davis, there was not a shred of truth to changes that content was being controlled by head office or by editors at the dailies so as to conform to a preferred perspective. Allegations to this effect, he insisted, were baseless conspiracy theories being spun by uninformed malcontents eager to believe the worst. He admitted that there had been isolated incidents of columns being withheld, but only because these had been factually inaccurate. "It isn't censorship to decline a column that has incorrect facts and other flaws."

Nonetheless, the controversy refused to die. In March, a reporter with the Southam-owned *Regina Leader-Post* covered a speech at the University of Regina's School of Journalism by Haroon Siddiqui, editorial page emeritus of the *Toronto Star*, in which he accused CanWest management of creeping censorship in refusing to run opinion pieces that disagreed with the company's editorial policy. The reporter's account of the speech was altered to remove any mention of censorship—thus, in one of those ironies beloved by journalists, inviting charges that management had censored the word "censorship"—and she withdrew her byline, prompting a one-day byline

strike by nine of her fellow *Leader-Post* journalists in support. Other media outlets took notice and called the paper for comment. Four of the *Leader-Post's* reporters went on record with their misgivings. Within days, all ten who had removed their bylines had received letters of censure from management, and the four who expressed their concerns to other media outlets were suspended for five days.

Then, on June 16, the day after he had been awarded an honorary doctorate from Carleton University in recognition of his thirty-one-year career in Ottawa journalism and his service to the local community, Russell Mills, publisher of the Southam-owned *Ottawa Citizen*, was dismissed by David Asper. According to Mills, he was offered a financial settlement to remain mute about the circumstances of his firing while the outside world would be told that he was merely retiring. He refused, saying "I hadn't spent a career in journalism in search of the truth to leave on a lie" (Harris-Adler 2002, 50).

The real reason for his dismissal, according to Mills, was that he, as publisher, had approved a lengthy *Citizen* article that detailed the collected "untruths" of Prime Minister Jean Chrétien, as well as an editorial arguing that the time had come for the Prime Minister to step down. If so, the clear suggestion was that the Asper family intended to orchestrate the news coverage of the Southam papers in a partisan manner beholden to a Prime Minister locked in an intra-party power struggle with a powerful rival whom the Prime Minister had himself dismissed from cabinet. Journalists across the country read the Mills firing as an unequivocal signal from CanWest/Southam's Winnipeg head office. Within the journalistic community, Russell Mills was seen as a careful company soldier, a man who had spent sixteen years as publisher of the *Ottawa Citizen* under a succession of corporate owners. If Mills could be dismissed, then presumably no one was safe. The action appeared to put the lie to Leonard Asper's earlier insistence that "No journalist in our organization has anything to fear about what they write."

The Mills incident was headline news across the country. CanWest management waited five days before responding to the furor. Eventually, Leonard Asper appeared before the media to contest Mills' version of events, arguing that Mills was dismissed because of insubordination and a lack of "diversity of sources of all opinions" in the *Citizen* under Mills' stewardship. That is, in a neat rhetorical turn, Mills was fired not in violation of journalistic principles, but because he himself had violated those principles, passing off conjecture about the Prime Minister as fact and presiding over a paper that favored a particular political perspective at the expense of competing views. Mills, in response, launched a libel action.

The controversy generated by the Mills incident appeared to cool the more aggressive, or at least high-profile, aspects of CanWest's management of Southam editorial content. Quietly, the national editorials—once intended to run at a frequency of three per week—all but disappeared from the pages of the Southam papers. Management retained the right to issue must-run national opinion pieces to the member papers, but suddenly seemed to feel the compulsion to do so only infrequently. The sabre-rattling speeches and op-ed attacks on the company's critics dried up.

What is at issue in all this? Few, surely, would dispute the right of a newspaper proprietor to set the editorial policies of his or her holdings, even if one disagrees with these policies. Merely stating an editorial view, after all, does not amount to mind control of the masses. Far from it: those who regularly turn to the editorials (one of the least-read sections of any newspaper) tend to be contentious sorts, eager to take issue with the considered opinions of the newspaper.

However, it is one thing to set an editorial policy whose expression is confined to the editorial columns. It would be quite another were that policy extended to the opinion and op-ed sections such that demurring voices were expunged, belittled or marginalized. And it would be another matter entirely were it to be shown that news coverage was being manipulated so as to conform to an overtly ideological preference. The professional routines of "objective" journalism are in place precisely, in part, to shield journalists from the blandishments and pressures of unscrupulous publishers who would skew accounts of current events to suit their own interests. The promise made by newspapers to their readers is that the reportage offers reliable accounts rendered (to the best of reporters' abilities) with fidelity to what actually occurred.

For its part, CanWest has argued repeatedly that the mere fact of a national editorial policy does not mean that dissent and debate are to be extinguished in the pages of the Southam dailies. The *National Post* presumably spoke for CanWest's head office when it wrote in an editorial on the issue: "Editors, editorial writers and others can express differing views in signed pieces; many already have. Other views are welcome, even invited. Counter-arguments and contrary views have been published, just as with all editorials, and will continue to be. Many contrary letters are printed" (January 29, 2002). As well, in a March television interview on I-channel with the *National Post's* Matthew Fraser, Israel Asper insisted that the new editorial policy was simply a means for the company to put forward a national viewpoint on national issues, nothing more, and that it certainly did not mean the company would brook no disagreement in the pages of its papers. "Does that mean we will hold off on dissent?" he asked. "Absolutely not. Does that mean our own writers can't say 'You're crazy' in print? Absolutely, yes they can."

If the proprietor is true to his word, then he understands that the civic value of a newspaper (not to mention its commercial viability) lies in it being a compendium not only of reportage, but of competing interpretation—a daily almanac of argument, contention and debate. Then what does it matter whether there is a centrally endorsed editorial policy? Newspapers would remain intact as a forum for the national conversation on which democracy depends.

Critics both within and outside the Southam chain, however, doubt that the upper echelons of the CanWest management will indeed be true to their word—not that they are dishonest, but that what they will recognize as legitimate dissent will be strictly circumscribed. Genuinely dissenting views, ones that take issue with the very premises of any given editorial policy, may run the risk of being dismissed as factually inaccurate and therefore unworthy of publication. As Murdoch Davis direly warned in his op-ed article of January 30, 2002: "It is a basic tenet of journalism and Canadian law that to be fair, comment must be based on the facts." Indeed, in the case of the *Regina Leader-Post*, the rationale for deleting any reference to "censorship" appeared to be the conviction that, since no censorship had actually taken place, Mr. Siddiqui's charges were factually false. In the case of Russell Mills, according to Leonard Asper, the former employee's crime had been to present as "fact" an investigation into the conduct of the Prime Minister that was merely "conjecture."

But even if it were true that the Southam owners and their agents had been covertly manipulating the contents of the papers—and as outrageous a transgression as this might seem on its face—one must recognize that all newspapers adopt a posture toward the world that is reflected in their news coverage: the choice of which stories to pursue and how these are played. As a consequence, different newspapers see the "facts" in different lights; there is no natural, obvious or neutral version of events, despite the insistence of every newspaper that its accounts are straightforwardly true. Thus, the *Toronto Star* has long carried itself as a paper with a social conscience (as opposed to the business-oriented dailies of Bay Street), which means that in practice it is a small-l liberal paper traditionally affiliated with the large-L Liberal party. The *Toronto Sun*, meanwhile, is patently coloured by a populist conservatism. The *Globe and Mail*, for its part, is a conservative journal of a different hue, capable of embracing social reforms that might ally it with elements of the left (rights for gays and lesbians, decriminalization of soft drugs). And it is no secret that the *National Post* was created by Conrad Black in large part to champion a stripe of conservatism that Mr. Black found lamentably lacking in Canadian political discourse. None of these dailies wilfully falsifies its news coverage to suit an ideological predisposition, but they do come to see events and social affairs through the lens of their respective identities (see Dornan and Pyman 2001 for an illustration of this).

In the case of the Southam papers, the controversy stems from the fact that some journalists believe they are being pressured to render accounts, not as they honestly perceive things, but in accord with how their superiors in a distant head office would prefer things to be: that a perspective not shared by newsworkers themselves is being imposed on the product they produce. This is all the more fractious given the traditional character—or lack thereof—of many of the Southam titles. In a market such as Toronto, with four paid-circulation dailies competing for different types of readers, it is no accident that each paper comes to acquire a vivid and distinctive personality. The Southam dailies, by contrast, long enjoyed near-monopoly status in their respective markets. They therefore strove for universal circulation, and in doing so they could not risk alienating potential readers. As a consequence, they avoided any overt political point-of-view in their news content. The typical blandness of most Canadian broadsheets, then, was the result of market economics. The "politicization" or "Asperation" of the Southam chain—if that is indeed what is occurring—is not, therefore a corruption of Canadian journalistic practice as much as it is an extension (albeit a ham-fisted one) of existing practice from the largest urban centres to the regions. Ironically, for all their fulminations about Toronto-centrism in the Canadian media, CanWest management may be reforming the Southam papers according to a Toronto model.

If one believes that this is a lamentable, even a dangerous development, the culprit is presumably not so much the Asper family as the fact of concentration of ownership in the newspaper industry, which provides proprietors with the opportunity to impose their views on a large number of titles simultaneously. But a variety of studies have shown that whether newspapers value their civic responsibilities, and how they understand these responsibilities, has little to do with whether they are independently owned or part of a chain. Some corporately owned papers perform very well according to received standards of journalistic quality, just as some independent papers perform very poorly. It all depends on the owners. As has been pointed out elsewhere,

> This begs certain questions for those who would regulate the press in order to correct market dysfunction or corporate rapacity. . . . [I]f the performance of newspapers is ultimately a consequence of the decisions and priorities of those who own and manage them, what mechanisms might be put in place to ensure that either the "right" people occupy these decision-making positions, or, if the "wrong" people cannot be prevented from owning and operating newspapers, to constrain them to act in a way at odds with their own inclinations? Beyond that, assuming such mechanisms could be put in place, what would guarantee that they would be compatible with the imperatives of a free society? (Dornan 2000, 57–58)

Finally, one should ask what prompted the acquisition of newspaper properties by the broadcasting and telecommunications interests in the first place, and whether these new alignments of corporate ownership are stable. At the time of the merger, the *Globe and Mail* seemed on secure ground in its affiliation with CTV and its new proprietor BCE. The *Globe* is a single property with national reach and a valuable brand image, not an archipelago of local titles, and BCE is a company awash in profits, not debts. Quebecor, by comparison, spent a fortune to acquire Videotron and so far does not appear to be either comfortable or confident in its ownership of Sun Media. CanWest Global, similarly, spent $3.2 billion to acquire the Southam papers and is carrying $4 billion in debt. Nor is it clear that any great cost efficiencies are about to be realized simply because a broadcasting network, whose profits largely derive from airing popular U.S. programming, now owns a string of local newspapers and a money-losing national title with a reputation for ideological idiosyncrasy. In the case of the Bell Globemedia venture, BCE, a telecom giant whose interest are in the infrastructure of communication, wanted profitable content that might flow through that infrastructure. The *Globe and Mail* and CTV presumably were to provide that, with the paper feeding additional national content to its new broadcasting partner, while CTV and Bell Sympatico would offer a broadcasting and computer-mediated display window for the print operation. However, even this convergence strategy was thrown into doubt by the abrupt departure of BCE chief Jean Monty, the architect of the strategy, in April 2002, and the consequent immediate speculation that the new BCE management might sell off the "content provider" acquisitions. And if true corporate "synergies"—to use the industry's faddish phrase—are elusive in the case of Bell Globemedia, it is doubtful they will be realized in the case of CanWest Global or Quebecor. So what motivated the other players' aggressive newspaper-purchasing spree?

Part of the answer is to be found in the most recent trends in advertising placement and revenue (see Table 4 above). Even with a downturn in the last quarter, advertising revenue in almost all of the traditional media was up appreciably in 2000 over 1999. Newspaper ad revenue increased by 6 per cent, radio by 4.7 per cent, and outdoor advertising by 7.8 per cent. In traditional private-sector network television, by comparison, ad revenue increased by only 0.23 per cent. Meanwhile, Internet advertising increased by almost 100 per cent over the previous year. In fact, Web advertising in Canada went from $10 million in 1997 to $25 million in 1998, and from $56 million in 1999 to $109 million in 2000—essentially doubling from one year to the next. The non-newspaper companies, then, have been buying up the newspaper companies because they are convinced that the advertising profits of the future lie in purveying Web content; because in Canada one of the few forms of homegrown content with an assured market is news; and because the major proven, available and robust sources of news are the newspapers.

As well, newspapers come with a stranglehold on a lucrative form of advertising that is simply incompatible with broadcasting: the classifieds. It accounts, though, for 34 per cent of newspapers' advertising income of $2.58 billion, or some $877 million. But while classified advertising may be impossible to accommodate via traditional broadcasting, it is perfectly suited for the Web. Imagine hunting for a new home in a city to which one is about to be transferred. Via the Web, one can search for properties with specific features and in particular price ranges. One can see pictures of the properties, even presumably take virtual tours of the premises. Not only that, but classifieds as a form of media content are ridiculously cheap to produce, since the content is generated by the very people who are paying to place the ads. For all these reasons, the media companies are convinced that spectacular profits lie in store for the enterprise that can harness Web content and computerized classifieds. And since the newspapers are not only a source of content but hold title to the classified market, they are essential to any cyberspace strategy. Yesterday's medium is the key to the future.

Nonetheless, it is not at all clear that news or journalism will be a profitable source of Web content. The Web is splendid as a delivery vehicle for what one might call tickertape journalism: the blunt announcement of breaking developments. But the Web's real forte is interactivity. As a computer-mediated matrix of interconnected participants, the strength of the Web is the traditional weakness of media such as television or newspapers. What is E-bay if not the sum total of all the contributions of all the visitors to the site, buyers and sellers? E-bay is nothing but perpetual exchange: pure interactivity. Journalism, by comparison, is by definition unidirectional. It is about a single, centralized source speaking with authority and credibility to a dispersed audience. It may be that journalism, as a genre of content, is as ill-suited to cyberspace as it was to cinema, and that it will be as vestigial to the Internet as newsreels were to the movies. In that case, the billion dollar investments of the broadcasters in the paper-and-ink newsrooms will simply have been a means to capture the classified market.

With all that in mind, the most interesting newspaper in Canada in 2002—by circumstance rather than by deed—was the Winnipeg *Free Press*. It is not only the last remaining truly independent urban title, unaffiliated with any broadcaster, cable company, telecommunication giant or Internet provider—and therefore a throwback in the era of convergence—but it is the leading newspaper of the city in which CanWest Global's corporate headquarters reside, and therefore the paper best situated to provide close, non-partisan scrutiny of CanWest's corporate dealings. An old-fashioned newspaper is positioned to be the best source of intelligence on a new, multimedia conglomerate.

In the end, all news is local.

Bibliography

Canadian Newspaper Association. 2001. "Newspaper Facts." December.

Dorman, Christopher. 1996. "Newspaper Publishing." In *The Cultural Industries in Canada: Problems, Policies and Prospects,* ed. Michael Dorlans. Toronto: James Lorimer.

——. 2000. "Newspaper Economics and Concentration: Select Problems and Complications." In *La Concentration de la Press Ecrite: Un « Vieux » Problème Non Résolu. Les Cahiers-Médias.* Numéro 11.

Dornan, Christopher, and Heather Pyman. 2001. "Facts and Arguments: Newspaper Coverage of the Campaign." In *The Canadian General Election of 2000,* ed. Jon Pammett and Christopher Dornan, Toronto: The Dundurn Group.

Haggett, Scott. 2001. *Calgary Herald*, April 21, A4.

Hartos-Adler, Rosa. 2002. "The roar of the paper tiger." *Ottawa City,* August/Sept., 50–53.

Lindgren, April, 2001. *Ottawa Citizen,* August 25, D3.

Paywalls

————◆————

David M. Estok

Key Words

Paywalls
Newspaper industry
Future of Newspapers

Abstract

This commentary explores the ramifications of declining newspaper revenues due to a growing percentage of readers who use the internet to access news content. The author explores the ramifications of the *New York Times, San Francisco Chronicle, Newsday* and *Popular Science* adopting a paywall. He also discusses *The Daily*, a newspaper which exists exclusively on the iPad. Another model discussed is that of Apple's iTunes and its potential for newspaper content distribution. Paywalls are put forward as a possible means of redress for this problem.

"The meeting" is being held in newspaper executive offices across Canada. In an industry that has been devastated by declining revenue, increased competition for advertising dollars, high costs, falling paid circulation and the steady, continuing erosion of single copy sales, can paying for access to Canadian newspaper websites be that far off?

"Paywalls" or "pay sponges" are an attempt by publishers to ensure any content that they produce generates some revenue for them. They are not new. Publications such as the *Wall Street Journal* erected paywalls years ago to ensure some of their expensive and costly content would not be on the internet for free. Most media properties did the exact opposite. As the internet took hold, they "shoveled" content — in most cases all of their publications' content — into websites and essentially gave away for free what they were asking people to pay for on other platforms such as magazines and newspapers.

Now the *New York Times*, the grandfather of all media companies and one of the most influential and important newspapers in the world, has announced it will no longer give out content for free. They introduced "digital subscriptions" which *Times* publisher Arthur Sulzberger Jr., in an open letter to readers, called a "significant transition" for the media giant. The plan, which is first being tested in Canada, means that if you are a regular subscriber to the newspaper you still have "full and free access to our

Email: david.estok@sympatico.ca, Twitter: @DavidEstok

news, information, opinion and the rest of our rich offerings on your computer, smartphone and tablet," Sulzberger wrote (2011, para. 3). If not, you are limited to reading 20 articles a month from the website. If you want any more, you have to pay.

Newspapers in Canada are reviewing the *Times* approach and so are other U.S. publications. The *San Francisco Chronicle* has confirmed it is considering a paywall but not the "metered approach" of the *Times*. The *Chronicle* will charge a flat fee of $9.95 a month versus the *Times'* charge of $15 to $35 a month depending on the type of subscription. The *Chronicle* is also working on an iPad app. Rupert Murdoch's News Corp, has already introduced an iPad app through which it charges users for access to content in the *The Daily*, an internet-only newspaper, exclusive to the iPad.

The big question in Canadian newspaper executive offices is: Will it work here? Last year, the American publication *Newsday* introduced a paywall and readership plummeted. Without "eyeballs" won't advertisers be right behind in terms of abandoning the publication? How long does it take for computer hackers to find their way over the wall? In the case of the *Times*, it took less than twelve hours and four lines of code to crack the wall, putting a two year project with a reported cost of $40 million in danger less than one day after the project was launched. "Unfortunately, the long-awaited service is destined for failure," noted Leslie Horn, a writer for *PC Magazine* (2011, para. 1).

It is not so much the ease of getting around the technology that will make the project fail but rather the weak approach the news organization has taken, since the *Times* paywall does not apply to social media sites like Facebook and Twitter. "The relaxed nature of the paywall is the very reason that it won't work," Horn notes. "It boils down to the old adage: You can't have your cake and eat it, too. In this case, the *Times* seems to want both the traffic and the advertising dollars from casual browsers as well as the subscription-driven revenue from more serious readers" (2011, para. 5).

One thing remains clear: media companies, and Canadian newspapers in particular, cannot continue to give away content for free. While most organizations have recovered from terrible earnings after the great crash, in almost all cases they have kept their profits high not by growing the business, but rather through cost containment. This is not a sustainable strategy. Unless newspapers can find a sustainable way to charge for online content, or discover methods to produce revenue from digitized content, they will have no other choice but to continue cutting staff, newspaper size, and other expenses to reduce costs. These cuts will ultimately have an impact on quality.

Is this where Apple comes in? The company that people either love or hate saved the music industry with its iTunes model of content management. The iTunes subscription model starts with a subscriber giving the company a credit card, which is kept on record. After that, any application or piece of music available through iTunes, much of which is actually free, is purchased from Apple. No need to sign up for additional free apps. Simple. Now the company is trying to do the same thing for newspapers and magazines. "Apple envisions a world in which people don't consume any kind of digital media without its help," Forrester Research analyst James McQuivey told *BBC News* (BBC, 2011). A decision to offer *Popular Science* through the Apple store for $14.95 a month through iTunes reportedly resulted in 8,000 new subscribers in three weeks.

Is a platform shift to a new product like the iPad the solution? Newspaper companies have been reluctant to buy into the Apple model. First, there's the revenue split. Apple wants 30 per cent of the revenues from every new subscriber. Imagine turning over the subscription base it took you years to build and giving another company 30 per cent of your revenues? Then there is the worry that your customers all of a sudden are no longer *your* customers, rather they belong to Apple. With the sales of tablets expected to hit 300 million by 2014 and most of them being iPads, the results are hundreds of millions of dollars for Apple.

"While some newsrooms are trying Apple's app subscription model, many others are waiting on the sidelines," John Sturm of the Newspaper Association of America told reporters. "Information has become so important for the way publishers market to their customers, get renewals and target advertising based on peoples' behaviour and interests. But once a subscriber signs on through the iTunes store, it becomes a sort of closed system." (May, 2011).

There is little doubt that media companies in Canada want to charge for content if they think they can get away with it. Which model they adopt will be determined by the successes and failures of the early distribution models being proposed by newspapers and integrated consumer electronics companies like Apple. Whether or how media companies choose to do it using paywalls just might depend on what happens with the *New York Times*' experiment.

References

Horn, L. (2011, March 24). The New York Times paywall is destined for failure. *PC Mag*. Retrieved from http://www.pcmag.com/article2/0,2817,238 2579,00.asp

May, P. (2011, April 13). Apple angles for position of power in publishing world. *McClatchy-Tribune News Service*. Retrieved from http://www.canada .com/technology/Apple+angles+position+power+ publishing+world/4608167/story.html

Pressure mounts over Apple's 30% subscription charge. (2011, February 24). *BBC News*. Retrieved from http://www.bbc.co.uk

Sulzberger, A. (2011, March 17). A letter to our readers about digital subscriptions. *New York Times*. Retrieved from http://www.nytimes.com/

Book Publishers Scramble to Rewrite Their Future

Evan Hughes

While working in a bookstore in Boone, North Carolina, back in 2011, a 36-year-old college dropout named Hugh Howey started writing a series of sci-fi novellas called *Wool*. His stories were set in a postapocalyptic world where all human survivors live in an underground silo, a microsociety where resources are so scarce that one person has to die before another can be born. Howey had already published a book with a small press, but he wanted to retain creative control, and he didn't want to go through the arduous process of finding an agent. So he decided to put out the new books himself, selling digital downloads and print editions through Amazon. In the first six months he sold 14,000 copies. Each new installment met with immediate enthusiasm. Within hours he'd receive emails from readers hungry for more.

By January of last year, agents were calling Howey, looking to publish the books through more established channels, but he was reluctant. At that point, the *Wool* series was already making him close to $12,000 a month. Nelson Literary Agency founder Kristin Nelson won Howey over when she admitted that she wasn't sure traditional publishing could offer him anything better than what he was doing on his own. (When she recounted this remark at a recent industry conference, the publishing professionals in the audience shifted uncomfortably in their chairs.) By May, *Wool* was bringing in $130,000 a month, and Howey and Nelson had sold the film option to 20th Century Fox and Ridley Scott. A couple of publishers made seven-figure offers for the rights to sell the book in hardcover, paperback, and ebook, but Howey and Nelson turned them down. He'd make that much in a year of digital sales alone.

Then Simon & Schuster's president sent Nelson an email that opened the door to a six-figure deal for print rights only. It was an extraordinary concession—the publisher would agree to put its full marketing muscle behind *Wool* despite having to forgo the ebook revenue stream that has generated the bulk of the series's earnings. It's often said in publishing that with a blockbuster book, everybody wins. But with *Wool*, it's Hugh Howey who has won biggest.

After centuries in which books and the process of publishing them barely changed, the digital revolution has thrown the entire business up for grabs. It's a transformation that began with the rise of Amazon as an online bookseller and accelerated with the resulting decline of the physical bookstore. But with the shift to ebooks—which now represent upwards of 20 percent of big publishers' revenue, up from 1 percent in 2008—every aspect of the existing framework is now open to debate: how much books will cost, how long they'll be, whether they'll be edited, who will publish them, and whether authors will continue to be paid in advance to write them. It's a future that Amazon doesn't control and one where traditional publishers might eventually thrive, not just survive. The only certainty is that the venerable book business, a settled landscape for so long, is now open territory for anyone to claim.

Of all the worries in the publishing world these days, the king of them is cultural irrelevance. "The fact is that people don't read anymore," Steve Jobs told a reporter in 2008, blurting out the secret fear of bookish people everywhere. But consider this: In one week, people who don't read anymore bought about half a million copies of a really long book called *Steve Jobs*. In the past year, Vintage has sold one book from the *Fifty Shades of Grey* trilogy for every six American adults. The Big Six publishers—Random House, Penguin, Hachette, Macmillan, Simon & Schuster, and HarperCollins—all make money, and at profit margins that are likely better than they were 50 years ago.

Meanwhile, readers have an unprecedented array of options. E-readers have gotten consistently cheaper and better since the first Kindle shipped in 2007, giving customers instant access to millions of titles. For a couple of dollars you can buy a self-published sensation or a Kindle Single rather than a full-length book. Add it all together and you have a more vibrant market for literary material than ever before, with nearly 3 billion copies sold every year. Amazon likes to point out that new Kindle buyers go on to purchase almost five times as many books from Amazon, print and digital, in the ensuing year as they did in the prior one. "I believe we'll look back in five years," says Russ Grandinetti, VP of Kindle content for Amazon, "and realize that digital was one of the great expansions of the publishing business."

For all the digital optimism, not even Amazon is ready to declare the traditional model dead. In May 2011 the company announced that it was going head-to-head with the Big Six by launching a general-interest imprint in Manhattan, headed by respected industry veteran Larry Kirshbaum. It

signed up celebrity authors, paying a reported $850,000 for a memoir by *Laverne & Shirley* star Penny Marshall and winning over best-selling self-help author Timothy Ferriss. Tired of being undersold by Amazon and wary of its encroachment into their business, many brick-and-mortar booksellers refused to stock the titles. The boycott has worked so far: Marshall's book flopped, and Ferriss' undersold his previous offering. Ferriss says he doesn't regret his experiment with Amazon Publishing, but he allows, "I could have made more money—certainly up to this point—by staying with Random House."

Still, it's not clear that traditional publishers are well positioned to own the digital future. They are saddled with the costs of getting dead trees to customers—paper, printing, binding, warehousing, and shipping—and they cannot simply jettison those costs, because that system accounts for roughly 80 percent of their business. Ebooks continue to gain ground, but the healthiness of the profit margins is unclear. J. K. Rowling's latest book helps illustrate this bind. At a rumored advance of $7 million, Little, Brown essentially backed up an armored car to Rowling's house to pay her before seeing a nickel in revenue. The publisher then paid highly trained people to improve the novel and well-connected people to publicize and market it until it was inescapable. Little, Brown's landlord in Manhattan occasionally asks for rent too. If a reader can buy the Kindle edition for $8.99, the public might eventually find it absurd to pay $19.99 for a printed version, let alone the $35 that Little, Brown wants for the hardcover.

What's more, awarding huge contracts for books that may not even be written yet creates tremendous risk. The industry is plagued by what indie-publishing entrepreneur Richard Nash has called the "pathology of unearned advances." An author who gets a book deal is paid an advance against royalties, and if the royalties end up exceeding the advance, the author starts getting more checks. But that doesn't usually happen.

The uncertainty about a book's potential value cuts both ways. Daniel Menaker, former executive editor in chief of Random House, told me what happened when a fellow editor there presented a case to his colleagues for making an offer on Laura Hillenbrand's *Seabiscuit*: "People just laughed, and someone said, 'Talk about beating a dead horse.'" Good one! The editor, Jonathan Karp, luckily won the argument, and Random House bought the rights for only five figures. More than 2 million copies were in print even before the movie came out. Unfortunately, the more common scenario is that a publisher opens the vault for a book that tanks. Bantam paid a reported $2 million in 2005 for two novels from a sci-fi writer named Gordon Dahlquist. If the title *The Glass Books of the Dream Eaters* doesn't sound familiar, you're not alone.

The disappearance of the physical bookstore would endanger the entire book business—even Amazon.

The publishing houses stay afloat only because the megahits pay for the flops, and there's generally enough left over for profit. Predicting the success or failure of any given book is impossible. Menaker recalls Jason Epstein, who led Random House for four decades, telling him, "Make no mistake—this is gambling." Which is why the pricing pressure on ebooks is so scary to publishers: If they are the gambler at the slot machines, placing scores of bets and relying on the winnings to trump the losses, Amazon represents a casino that offers smaller and smaller payouts.

Beyond the immediate concern over prices, publishers also worry that the disappearance of the physical bookstore could endanger the entire book business, even (ironically) Amazon. Research has shown that readers don't tend to use online bookstores to discover books; they use them to purchase titles they find out about elsewhere—frequently at physical stores. (If you want to see a bookstore owner get angry, mention Amazon's Price Check app, which allows customers to scan an item in a physical store and buy it for less from Amazon then and there.) With no stores to browse in, publishers fear, book sales everywhere could take a significant hit.

This is one reason that, in 2010, five of the Big Six publishers worked with Apple to institute a new model to keep other retailers competitive with Amazon. In an attempt to win customers, Amazon had been routinely selling ebooks at a loss, paying, say, $12 to $15 wholesale for a popular ebook and then selling it for $9.99. Under the new so-called agency model, the publisher would have the power to set the price everywhere—between $12.99 and $14.99 for most best sellers—but the retailer would take 30 percent. That is, the publishers agreed to a scheme in which Amazon would make significantly more per book and they would make less. They were playing the long game, trying to protect physical stores and print sales and chip away at Amazon's overwhelming ebook market share.

After fighting the plan, Amazon caved. But the Department of Justice sued the five publishers and Apple for collusion, and Amazon described one of the resulting settlements as "a big win for Kindle owners." The recently announced merger of the two biggest of the Big Six, Random House and Penguin, is widely seen as a move to build an entity that can stand up to Amazon's market power.

In the long term, what publishers have to fear the most may not be Amazon but an idea it has helped engender—that the only truly necessary players in the game are the author and the reader. "I was at a meeting God knows how many years ago at MIT," former Random House chief Epstein says, "and someone used the word *disintermediation*. When I deconstructed that, I said, 'Oh my God, that's the end of the publishing business.'" At a time when a writer can post a novel online and watch the revenue pour in by direct deposit, the publishing industry's skill at making books, selling them by hand to bookstores, and managing the distribution of the product threatens to become irrelevant. In Epstein's vision, the writer may need a freelance editor, a publicist, and an agent who functions as a kind of business manager, but authors will keep a bigger share of the proceeds with no lumbering media corporation standing in the way.

So far this phenomenon has largely been limited to previously unknown writers like Hugh Howey. Amanda Hocking, a 26-year-old Minnesotan who worked days at an assisted-living facility, grossed about $2 million on ebooks in a little over a year with her paranormal romances and zombie novels for young adults. John Locke, a self-published crime writer, had already beaten Hocking to the 1-million-ebook mark on Amazon. And then, of course, there is E. L. James' *Fifty Shades of Grey*, which began as self-published *Twilight* fan fiction but wound up making 2012 so bountiful for Random House that it gave a $5,000 bonus to each employee.

But these are the exceptions. In general, new writers gain much more than they lose by signing with a major house. Most self-published authors have trouble selling a copy outside of their immediate family. Even if they have talent, they lack professional help or the imprimatur of quality that a publisher can bring. Indeed, *Fifty Shades*, which some have taken to be the definitive evidence in favor of self-publishing, is more accurately a demonstration of the opposite: The book became a massive commercial success only after Random House got involved, placing giant stacks of paperbacks in bookstores everywhere and buying huge ads in the London Underground.

The real danger to publishers is that big-ticket authors, who relied on the old system to build their careers, will abandon them now that they have established an audience. As Howey says, "When that happens, all bets are off." The John Grishams of the world already manage to extract excellent deals in the traditional way because of their huge and reliable sales, and few writers relish the work of being their own publisher. But as that work grows easier—as complex print distribution loses ground to low-cost digital delivery—the big names are starting to get tempted. Stephen King has been experimenting with bypassing his publisher, releasing his latest essay as a Kindle Single directly (albeit with some editing and promotion) through the Amazon store. The popular suspense writer Barry Eisler turned down a $500,000 book contract with the intention to self-publish—but before he could do so, Amazon Publishing offered him a sweetheart deal.

Pretty soon one of these famous writers will step up to the cliff and actually jump. Maybe it will be Tim Ferriss. His less-than-stellar results with Amazon might push him back to a traditional publisher—or in another direction entirely. A great deal of money hinges on what he and his fellow best-selling authors decide to do next. "I wouldn't be surprised if I self-published in the next few years," Ferriss says. "Wouldn't remotely surprise me."

Are You Smarter Than a Television Pundit?

Nate Silver

For many people, political prediction is synonymous with the television program *The McLaughlin Group,* a political roundtable that has been broadcast continually each Sunday since 1982 and parodied by *Saturday Night Live* for nearly as long. The show, hosted by John McLaughlin, a cantankerous octogenarian who ran a failed bid for the United States Senate in 1970, treats political punditry as sport, cycling through four or five subjects in the half hour, with McLaughlin barking at his panelists for answers on subjects from Australian politics to the prospects for extraterrestrial intelligence.

At the end of each edition of *The McLaughlin Group,* the program has a final segment called "Predictions," in which the panelists are given a few seconds to weigh in on some matter of the day. Sometimes, the panelists are permitted to pick a topic and make a prediction about anything even vaguely related to politics. At other times, McLaughlin calls for a "forced prediction," a sort of pop quiz that asks them their take on a specific issue.

Some of McLaughlin's questions—say, to name the next Supreme Court nominee from among several plausible candidates—are difficult to answer. But others are softballs. On the weekend before the 2008 presidential election, for instance, McLaughlin asked his panelists whether John McCain or Barack Obama was going to win.

That one ought not to have required very much thought. Barack Obama had led John McCain in almost every national poll since September 15, 2008, when the collapse of Lehman Brothers had ushered in the worst economic slump since the Great Depression. Obama also led in almost every poll of almost every swing state: in Ohio and Florida and Pennsylvania and New Hampshire—and even in a few states that Democrats don't normally win, like Colorado and Virginia. Statistical models like the one I developed for FiveThirtyEight suggested that Obama had in excess of a 95 percent chance of winning the election. Betting markets were slightly more equivocal, but still had him as a 7 to 1 favorite.

But McLaughlin's first panelist, Pat Buchanan, dodged the question. "The undecideds will decide this weekend," he remarked, drawing guffaws from the rest of the panel. Another guest, the *Chicago Tribune's* Clarence Page, said the election was "too close to call." Fox News' Monica Crowley was bolder, predicting a McCain win by "half a point." Only *Newsweek's* Eleanor Clift stated the obvious, predicting a win for the Obama-Biden ticket.

The following Tuesday, Obama became the president-elect with 365 electoral votes to John McCain's 173—almost exactly as polls and statistical models had anticipated. While not a landslide of historic proportions, it certainly hadn't been "too close to call": Obama had beaten John McCain by nearly ten million votes. Anyone who had rendered a prediction to the contrary had some explaining to do.

There would be none of that on *The McLaughlin Group* when the same four panelists gathered again the following week. The panel discussed the statistical minutiae of Obama's win, his selection of Rahm Emanuel as his chief of staff, and his relations with Russian president Dmitry Medvedev. There was no mention of the failed prediction—made on national television in contradiction to essentially all available evidence. In fact, the panelists made it sound as though the outcome had been inevitable all along; Crowley explained that it had been a "change election year" and that McCain had run a terrible campaign—neglecting to mention that she had been willing to bet on that campaign just a week earlier.

Rarely should a forecaster be judged on the basis of a single prediction—but this case may warrant an exception. By the weekend before the election, perhaps the only plausible hypothesis to explain why McCain could still win was if there was massive racial animus against Obama that had gone undetected in the polls. None of the panelists offered this hypothesis, however. Instead they seemed to be operating in an alternate universe in which the polls didn't exist, the economy hadn't collapsed, and President Bush was still reasonably popular rather than dragging down McCain.

Nevertheless, I decided to check to see whether this was some sort of anomaly. Do the panelists on *The McLaughlin Group*—who are paid to talk about politics for a living—have any real skill at forecasting?

I evaluated nearly 1,000 predictions that were made on the final segment of the show by McLaughlin and the rest of the panelists. About a quarter of the predictions were too vague to be analyzed or concerned events in the far future. But I scored the others on a five-point scale ranging from completely false to completely true.

The panel may as well have been flipping coins. I determined 338 of their predictions to be either mostly or completely false. The exact same number—338—were either mostly or completely true.

Nor were any of the panelists—including Clift, who at least got the 2008 election right—much better than the others. For each panelist, I calculated a percentage score, essentially reflecting the number of predictions they got right. Clift and the three other most frequent panelists—Buchanan, the late Tony Blankley, and McLaughlin himself—each received almost identical scores ranging from 49 percent to 52 percent, meaning that they were about as likely to get a prediction right as wrong. They displayed about as much political acumen as a barbershop quartet.

The McLaughlin Group, of course, is more or less explicitly intended as slapstick entertainment for political junkies. It is a holdover from the shouting match era of programs, such as CNN's *Crossfire,* that featured liberals and conservatives endlessly bickering with one another. Our current echo chamber era isn't much different from the shouting match era, except that the liberals and conservatives are confined to their own channels, separated in your cable lineup by a demilitarized zone demarcated by the Food Network or the Golf Channel.* This arrangement seems to produce higher ratings if not necessarily more reliable analysis.

But what about those who are paid for the accuracy and thoroughness of their scholarship—rather

***Figure 1* McLaughlin Group Predictions Analysis**

Completely true	285	39%
Mostly true	53	7%
Partly true, partly false	57	8%
Mostly false	70	10%
Completely false	268	37%
Total predictions evaluated	733	100%
Predictions not evaluated	249	

* Most major cable providers keep Fox News and MSNBC at least a couple of channels apart in their lineups.

than the volume of their opinions? Are political scientists, or analysts at Washington think tanks, any better at making predictions?

Are Political Scientists Better than Pundits?

The disintegration of the Soviet Union and other countries of the Eastern bloc occurred at a remarkably fast pace—and all things considered, in a remarkably orderly way.†

On June 12, 1987, Ronald Reagan stood at the Brandenburg Gate and implored Mikhail Gorbachev to tear down the Berlin Wall—an applause line that seemed as audacious as John F. Kennedy's pledge to send a man to the moon. Reagan was prescient; less than two years later, the wall had fallen.

On November 16, 1988, the parliament of the Republic of Estonia, a nation about the size of the state of Maine, declared its independence from the mighty USSR. Less than three years later, Gorbachev parried a coup attempt from hard-liners in Moscow and the Soviet flag was lowered for the last time before the Kremlin; Estonia and the other Soviet Republics would soon become independent nations.

If the fall of the Soviet empire seemed predictable after the fact, however, almost no mainstream political scientist had seen it coming. The few exceptions were often the subject of ridicule. If political scientists couldn't predict the downfall of the Soviet Union—perhaps the most important event in the latter half of the twentieth century—then what exactly were they good for?

Philip Tetlock, a professor of psychology and political science, then at the University of California at Berkeley, was asking some of the same questions. As it happened, he had undertaken an ambitious and unprecedented experiment at the time of the USSR's collapse. Beginning in 1987, Tetlock started collecting predictions from a broad

array of experts in academia and government on a variety of topics in domestic politics, economics, and international relations.

Political experts had difficulty anticipating the USSR's collapse, Tetlock found, because a prediction that not only forecast the regime's demise but also understood the reasons for it required different strands of argument to be woven together. There was nothing inherently contradictory about these ideas, but they tended to emanate from people on different sides of the political spectrum, and scholars firmly entrenched in one ideological camp were unlikely to have embraced them both.

On the one hand, Gorbachev was clearly a major part of the story—his desire for reform had been sincere. Had Gorbachev chosen to become an accountant or a poet instead of entering politics, the Soviet Union might have survived at least a few years longer. Liberals were more likely to hold this sympathetic view of Gorbachev. Conservatives were less trusting of him, and some regarded his talk of glasnost as little more than posturing.

Conservatives, on the other hand, were more instinctually critical of communism. They were quicker to understand that the USSR's economy was failing and that life was becoming increasingly difficult for the average citizen. As late as 1990, the CIA estimated—quite wrongly—that the Soviet Union's GDP was about half that of the United States (on a per capita basis, tantamount to where stable democracies like South Korea and Portugal are today). In fact, more recent evidence has found that the Soviet economy—weakened by its long war with Afghanistan and the central government's inattention to a variety of social problems—was roughly $1 trillion poorer than the CIA had thought and was shrinking by as much as 5 percent annually, with inflation well into the double digits.

Take these two factors together, and the Soviet Union's collapse is fairly easy to envision. By opening the country's media and its markets and giving his citizens greater democratic authority, Gorbachev had provided his people with the mechanism to catalyze a regime change. And because of the dilapidated state of the country's economy, they were happy to take him up on his offer. The center

---

† Of the series of revolutions in the Eastern bloc in 1989, only the one in Romania entailed substantial bloodshed.

was too weak to hold: not only were Estonians sick of Russians, but Russians were nearly as sick of Estonians, since the satellite republics contributed less to the Soviet economy than they received in subsidies from Moscow. Once the dominoes began falling in Eastern Europe—Czechoslovakia, Poland, Romania, Bulgaria, Hungary, and East Germany were all in the midst of revolution by the end of 1989—there was little Gorbachev or anyone else could do to prevent them from caving the country in. A lot of Soviet scholars understood parts of the problem, but few experts had put all the puzzle pieces together, and almost no one had forecast the USSR's sudden collapse.

Tetlock, inspired by the example of the Soviet Union, began to take surveys of expert opinion in other areas—asking the experts to make predictions about the Gulf War, the Japanese real-estate bubble, the potential secession of Quebec from Canada, and almost every other major event of the 1980s and 1990s. Was the failure to predict the collapse of the Soviet Union an anomaly, or does "expert" political analysis rarely live up to its billing? His studies, which spanned more than fifteen years, were eventually published in the 2005 book *Expert Political Judgment.*

Tetlock's conclusion was damning. The experts in his survey—regardless of their occupation, experience, or subfield—had done barely any better than random chance, and they had done worse than even rudimentary statistical methods at predicting future political events. They were grossly overconfident and terrible at calculating probabilities: about 15 percent of events that they claimed had *no chance* of occurring in fact happened, while about 25 percent of those that they said were *absolutely sure things* in fact failed to occur. It didn't matter whether the experts were making predictions about economics, domestic politics, or international affairs; their judgment was equally bad across the board.

The Right Attitude for Making Better Predictions: Be Foxy

While the experts' performance was poor in the aggregate, however, Tetlock found that some had done better than others. On the losing side were

those experts whose predictions were cited most frequently in the media. The more interviews that an expert had done with the press, Tetlock found, the *worse* his predictions tended to be.

Another subgroup of experts had done relatively well, however. Tetlock, with his training as a psychologist, had been interested in the experts' cognitive styles—how they thought about the world. So he administered some questions lifted from personality tests to all the experts.

On the basis of their responses to these questions, Tetlock was able to classify his experts along a spectrum between what he called *hedgehogs* and *foxes*. The reference to hedgehogs and foxes comes from the title of an Isaiah Berlin essay on the Russian novelist Leo Tolstoy—*The Hedgehog and the Fox.* Berlin had in turn borrowed his title from a passage attributed to the Greek poet Archilochus: "The fox knows many little things, but the hedgehog knows one big thing."

Unless you are a fan of Tolstoy—or of flowery prose—you'll have no particular reason to read Berlin's essay. But the basic idea is that writers and thinkers can be divided into two broad categories:

- **Hedgehogs** are type A personalities who believe in Big Ideas—in governing principles about the world that behave as though they were physical laws and undergird virtually every interaction in society. Think Karl Marx and class struggle, or Sigmund Freud and the unconscious. Or Malcolm Gladwell and the "tipping point."
- **Foxes,** on the other hand, are scrappy creatures who believe in a plethora of little ideas and in taking a multitude of approaches toward a problem. They tend to be more tolerant of nuance, uncertainty, complexity, and dissenting opinion. If hedgehogs are hunters, always looking out for the big kill, then foxes are gatherers.

Foxes, Tetlock found, are considerably better at forecasting than hedgehogs. They had come closer to the mark on the Soviet Union, for instance. Rather than seeing the USSR in highly ideological terms—as an intrinsically "evil empire," or as a relatively successful (and perhaps even admirable) example of a Marxist economic system—they instead saw it for

Figure 2   **Attitudes of Foxes and Hedgehogs**

How Foxes Think

Multidisciplinary: Incorporate ideas from different disciplines and regardless of their origin on the political spectrum.

Adaptable: Find a new approach—or pursue multiple approaches at the same time—if they aren't sure the original one is working.

Self-critical: Sometimes willing (if rarely happy) to acknowledge mistakes in their predictions and accept the blame for them.

Tolerant of complexity: See the universe as complicated, perhaps to the point of many fundamental problems being irresolvable or inherently unpredictable.

Cautious: Express their predictions in probabilistic terms and qualify their opinions.

Empirical: Rely more on observation than theory.

Foxes are better forecasters.

How Hedgehogs Think

Specialized: Often have spent the bulk of their careers on one or two great problems. May view the opinions of "outsiders" skeptically.

Stalwart: Stick to the same "all-in" approach—new data is used to refine the original model.

Stubborn: Mistakes are blamed on bad luck or on idiosyncratic circumstances—a good model had a bad day.

Order-seeking: Expect that the world will be found to abide by relatively simple governing relationships once the signal is identified through the noise.

Confident: Rarely hedge their predictions and are reluctant to change them.

Ideological: Expect that solutions to many day-to-day problems are manifestations of some grander theory or struggle.

Hedgehogs are weaker forecasters.

---

what it was: an increasingly dysfunctional nation that was in danger of coming apart at the seams. Whereas the hedgehogs' forecasts were barely any better than random chance, the foxes' demonstrated predictive skill.

Why Hedgehogs Make Better Television Guests

I met Tetlock for lunch one winter afternoon at the Hotel Durant, a stately and sunlit property just off the Berkeley campus. Naturally enough, Tetlock revealed himself to be a fox: soft-spoken and studious, with a habit of pausing for twenty or thirty seconds before answering my questions (lest he provide me with too incautiously considered a response).

"What are the incentives for a public intellectual?" Tetlock asked me. "There are some academics who are quite content to be relatively anonymous. But there are other people who aspire to be public intellectuals, to be pretty bold and to attach nonnegligible probabilities to fairly dramatic change. That's much more likely to bring you attention."

Big, bold, hedgehog-like predictions, in other words, are more likely to get you on television. Consider the case of Dick Morris, a former adviser to Bill Clinton who now serves as a commentator for Fox News. Morris is a classic hedgehog, and his strategy seems to be to make as dramatic a prediction as possible when given the chance. In 2005, Morris proclaimed that George W. Bush's handling of Hurricane Katrina would help Bush to regain his standing with the public. On the eve of the 2008 elections, he predicted that Barack Obama would win Tennessee and Arkansas. In 2010, Morris predicted that the Republicans could easily win one hundred seats in the U.S. House of Representatives. In 2011, he said that Donald Trump would run for the Republican nomination—and had a "damn good" chance of winning it.

All those predictions turned out to be horribly wrong. Katrina was the beginning of the end for Bush—not the start of a rebound. Obama lost Tennessee and Arkansas badly—in fact, they were among the only states in which he performed worse than John Kerry had four years earlier. Republicans had a good night in November 2010, but they gained sixty-three seats, not one hundred. Trump officially declined to run for president just two weeks after Morris insisted he would do so.

But Morris is quick on his feet, entertaining, and successful at marketing himself—he remains in the regular rotation at Fox News and has sold his books to hundreds of thousands of people.

Foxes sometimes have more trouble fitting into type A cultures like television, business, and politics. Their belief that many problems are hard to forecast—and that we should be explicit about accounting for these uncertainties—may be mistaken for a lack of self-confidence. Their pluralistic approach may be mistaken for a lack of conviction; Harry Truman famously demanded a "one-handed economist," frustrated that the foxes in his administration couldn't give him an unqualified answer.

But foxes happen to make much better predictions. They are quicker to recognize how noisy the data can be, and they are less inclined to chase false signals. They know more about what they don't know.

If you're looking for a doctor to predict the course of a medical condition or an investment adviser to maximize the return on your retirement savings, you may want to entrust a fox. She might make more modest claims about what she is able to achieve—but she is much more likely to actually realize them.

Why Political Predictions Tend to Fail

Fox-like attitudes may be especially important when it comes to making predictions about politics. There are some particular traps that can make suckers of hedgehogs in the arena of political prediction and which foxes are more careful to avoid.

One of these is simply partisan ideology. Morris, despite having advised Bill Clinton, identifies as a Republican and raises funds for their candidates—and his conservative views fit in with those of his network, Fox News. But liberals are not immune from the propensity to be hedgehogs. In my study of the accuracy of predictions made by *McLaughlin Group* members, Eleanor Clift—who is usually the most liberal member of the panel—almost never issued a prediction that would imply a more favorable outcome for Republicans than the consensus of the group. That may have served her well in predicting the outcome of the 2008 election, but she

was no more accurate than her conservative counterparts over the long run.

Academic experts like the ones that Tetlock studied can suffer from the same problem. In fact, a little knowledge may be a dangerous thing in the hands of a hedgehog with a Ph.D. One of Tetlock's more remarkable findings is that, while foxes tend to get better at forecasting with experience, the opposite is true of hedgehogs: their performance tends to *worsen* as they pick up additional credentials. Tetlock believes the more facts hedgehogs have at their command, the more opportunities they have to permute and manipulate them in ways that confirm their biases. The situation is analogous to what might happen if you put a hypochondriac in a dark room with an Internet connection. The more time that you give him, the more information he has at his disposal, the more ridiculous the self-diagnosis he'll come up with; before long he'll be mistaking a common cold for the bubonic plague.

But while Tetlock found that left-wing and right-wing hedgehogs made especially poor predictions, he also found that foxes of all political persuasions were more immune from these effects. Foxes may have emphatic convictions about the way the world *ought* to be. But they can usually separate that from their analysis of the way that the world actually is and how it is likely to be in the near future.

Hedgehogs, by contrast, have more trouble distinguishing their rooting interest from their analysis. Instead, in Tetlock's words, they create "a blurry fusion between facts and values all lumped together." They take a prejudicial view toward the evidence, seeing what they want to see and not what is really there.

You can apply Tetlock's test to diagnose whether you are a hedgehog: Do your predictions improve when you have access to more information? In theory, more information should give your predictions a wind at their back—you can always ignore the information if it doesn't seem to be helpful. But hedgehogs often trap themselves in the briar patch.

Consider the case of the *National Journal* Political Insiders' Poll, a survey of roughly 180 politicians, political consultants, pollsters, and pundits. The survey is divided between Democratic and Republican partisans, but both groups are asked the same questions. Regardless of their political persuasions, this group leans hedgehog: political operatives are proud of their battle scars, and see themselves as locked in a perpetual struggle against the other side of the cocktail party.

A few days ahead of the 2010 midterm elections, *National Journal* asked its panelists whether Democrats were likely to retain control of both the House and the Senate. There was near-universal agreement on these questions: Democrats would keep the Senate but Republicans would take control of the House (the panel was right on both accounts). Both the Democratic and Republican insiders were also almost agreed on the overall magnitude of Republican gains in the House; the Democratic experts called for them to pick up 47 seats, while Republicans predicted a 53-seat gain—a trivial difference considering that there are 435 House seats.

National Journal, however, also asked its panelists to predict the outcome of eleven individual elections, a mix of Senate, House, and gubernatorial races. Here, the differences were much greater. The panel split on the winners they expected in the Senate races in Nevada, Illinois, and Pennsylvania, the governor's race in Florida, and a key House race in Iowa. Overall, Republican panelists expected Democrats to win just one of the eleven races, while Democratic panelists expected them to win 6 of the 11. (The actual outcome, predictably enough, was somewhere in the middle—Democrats won three of the eleven races that *National Journal* had asked about.)

Obviously, partisanship plays some role here: Democrats and Republicans were each rooting for the home team. That does not suffice to explain, however, the unusual divide in the way that the panel answered the different types of questions. When asked in *general* terms about how well Republicans were likely to do, there was almost no difference between the panelists. They differed profoundly, however, when asked about specific cases—these brought the partisan differences to the surface.

Too much information can be a bad thing in the hands of a hedgehog. The question of how many seats Republicans were likely to gain on Democrats overall is an abstract one: unless you'd studied all 435 races, there was little additional detail that could help you to resolve it. By contrast, when asked about any one particular race—say, the Senate race in Nevada—the panelists had all kinds of information at their disposal: not just the polls there, but also news accounts they'd read about the race, gossip they'd heard from their friends, or what they thought about the candidates when they saw them on televi-

sion. They might even know the candidates or the people who work for them personally.

Hedgehogs who have lots of information construct stories—stories that are neater and tidier than the real world, with protagonists and villains, winners and losers, climaxes and denouements—and, usually, a happy ending for the home team. The candidate who is down ten points in the polls is going to win, goddamnit, because I know the candidate and I know the voters in her state, and maybe I heard something from her press secretary about how the polls are tightening—and have you seen her latest commercial?

When we construct these stories, we can lose the ability to think about the evidence critically. Elections typically present compelling narratives. Whatever you thought about the politics of Barack Obama or Sarah Palin or John McCain or Hillary Clinton in 2008, they had persuasive life stories: reported books on the campaign, like *Game Change,* read like tightly bestselling novels. The candidates who ran in 2012 were a less appealing lot but still more than sufficed to provide for the usual ensemble of dramatic clichés from tragedy (Herman Cain?) to farce (Rick Perry).

You can get lost in the narrative. Politics may be especially susceptible to poor predictions precisely because of its human elements: a good election engages our dramatic sensibilities. This does not mean that you must feel totally dispassionate about a political event in order to make a good prediction about it. But it does mean that a fox's aloof attitude can pay dividends.

A Fox-Like Approach to Forecasting

I had the idea for FiveThirtyEight* while waiting out a delayed flight at Louis Armstrong New Orleans International Airport in February 2008. For some reason—possibly the Cajun martinis had stirred something up—it suddenly seemed obvious that someone needed to build a Web site that predicted how well Hillary Clinton and Barack Obama, then still in heated contention for the Democratic nomination, would fare against John McCain.

---

* FiveThirtyEight's name refers to the number of votes in the Electoral College (538).

My interest in electoral politics had begun slightly earlier, however—and had been mostly the result of frustration rather than any affection for the political process. I had carefully monitored the Congress's attempt to ban Internet poker in 2006, which was then one of my main sources of income. I found political coverage wanting even as compared with something like sports, where the "Moneyball revolution" had significantly improved analysis.

During the run-up to the primary I found myself watching more and more political TV, mostly MSNBC and CNN and Fox News. A lot of the coverage was vapid. Despite the election being many months away, commentary focused on the inevitability of Clinton's nomination, ignoring the uncertainty intrinsic to such early polls. There seemed to be too much focus on Clinton's gender and Obama's race. There was an obsession with determining which candidate had "won the day" by making some clever quip at a press conference or getting some no-name senator to endorse them— things that 99 percent of voters did not care about.

Political news, and especially the important news that really affects the campaign, proceeds at an irregular pace. But news coverage is produced every day. Most of it is filler, packaged in the form of stories that are designed to obscure its unimportance.* Not only does political coverage often lose the signal— it frequently accentuates the noise. If there are a number of polls in a state that show the Republican ahead, it won't make news when another one says the same thing. But if a new poll comes out showing the Democrat with the lead, it will grab headlines— even though the poll is probably an outlier and won't predict the outcome accurately.

The bar set by the competition, in other words, was invitingly low. Someone could look like a genius simply by doing some fairly basic research into what really has predictive power in a political campaign. So I began blogging at the Web site Daily Kos, posting detailed and data-driven analyses on issues like polls and fundraising numbers. I studied which polling firms had been most accurate in the past, and how much winning one state—Iowa, for

instance—tended to shift the numbers in another. The articles quickly gained a following, even though the commentary at sites like Daily Kos is usually more qualitative (and partisan) than quantitative. In March 2008, I spun my analysis out to my own Web site, FiveThirtyEight, which sought to make Predictions about the general election.

The FiveThirtyEight forecasting model started out pretty simple— basically, it took an average of polls but weighted them according to their past accuracy—then gradually became more intricate. But it abided by three broad principles, all of which are very fox-like.

Principle I: Think Probabilistically

Almost all the forecasts that I publish, in politics and other fields, are probabilistic. Instead of spitting out just one number and claiming to know exactly what will happen, I instead articulate a range of possible outcomes. On November 2, 2010, for instance, my forecast for how many seats Republicans might gain in the U.S. House looks like what you see in Figure 3.

The most likely range of outcomes—enough to cover about half of all possible cases—was a Republican gain of between 45 and 65 seats (their actual gain was 63 seats). But there was also the possibility that Republicans might win 70 or 80 seats— if almost certainly not the 100 that Dick Morris had predicted. Conversely, there was also the chance that Democrats would hold just enough seats to keep the House.

The wide distribution of outcomes represented the most honest expression of the uncertainty in the real world. The forecast was built from forecasts of each of the 435 House seats individually—and an exceptionally large number of those races looked to be extremely close. As it happened, a remarkable 77 seats were decided by a single-digit margin. Had the Democrats beaten their forecasts by just a couple of points in most of the competitive districts, they could easily have retained the House. Had the Republicans done the opposite, they could have run their gains into truly astonishing numbers. A small change in the political tides could have produced a dramatically different result; it would have been foolish to pin things down to an exact number.

---

* The classic form of media bias is "rooting for the story"— hoping for a more dramatic outcome that might increase newspaper sales.

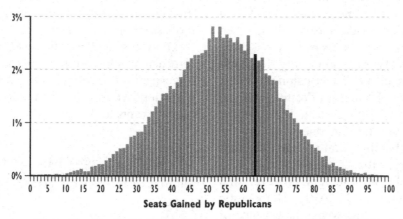

Figure 3 FiveThirtyEight House Forecast, November 2, 2010

This probabilistic principle also holds when I am forecasting the outcome in an individual race. How likely is a candidate to win, for instance, if he's ahead by five points in the polls? This is the sort of question that FiveThirtyEight's models are trying to address.

The answer depends significantly on the type of race that he's involved in. The further down the ballot you go, the more volatile the polls tend to be: polls of House races are less accurate than polls of Senate races, which are in turn less accurate than polls of presidential races. Polls of primaries, also, are considerably less accurate than general election polls. During the 2008 Democratic primaries, the average poll missed by about eight points, far more than implied by its margin of error. The problems in polls of the Republican primaries of 2012 may have been even worse. In many of the major states, in fact—including Iowa, South Carolina, Florida, Michigan, Washington, Colorado, Ohio, Alabama, and Mississippi—the candidate ahead in the polls a week before the election *lost*.

But polls do become more accurate the closer you get to Election Day. Figure 4 presents some results from a simplified version of the FiveThirtyEight Senate forecasting model, which uses data from 1998 through 2008 to infer the probability that a candidate will win on the basis of the size of his lead in the polling average. A Senate candidate with a five-point lead on the day before the election, for instance, has historically won his race about 95 percent of the time—almost a sure thing, even though

news accounts are sure to describe the race as "too close to call." By contrast, a five-point lead a year before the election translates to just a 59 percent chance of winning—barely better than a coin flip.

The FiveThirtyEight models provide much of their value in this way. It's very easy to look at an election, see that one candidate is ahead in all or most of the polls, and determine that he's the favorite to win. (With some exceptions, this assumption will be correct.) What becomes much trickier is determining exactly how much of a favorite he is. Our brains, wired to detect patterns, are always looking for a signal, when instead we should appreciate how noisy the data is.

I've grown accustomed to this type of thinking because my background consists of experience in two disciplines, sports and poker, in which you'll see pretty much everything at least once. Play

Figure 4 **Probability of Senate Candidate Winning, Based on Size of Lead in Polling Average**

	SIZE OF LEAD			
Time Until Election	1 Point	5 Points	10 Points	20 Points
One day	64%	95%	99.7%	99.999%
One week	60%	89%	98%	99.97%
One month	57%	81%	95%	99.7%
Three months	55%	72%	87%	98%
Six months	53%	66%	79%	93%
One year	52%	59%	67%	81%

enough poker hands, and you'll make your share of royal flushes. Play a few more, and you'll find that your opponent has made a royal flush when you have a full house. Sports, especially baseball, also provide for plenty of opportunity for low-probability events to occur. The Boston Red Sox failed to make the playoffs in 2011 despite having a 99.7 percent chance of doing so at one point—although I wouldn't question anyone who says the normal laws of probability don't apply when it comes to the Red Sox or the Chicago Cubs.

Politicians and political observers, however, find this lack of clarity upsetting. In 2010, a Democratic congressman called me a few weeks in advance of the election. He represented a safely Democratic district on the West Coast. But given how well Republicans were doing that year, he was nevertheless concerned about losing his seat. What he wanted to know was exactly how much uncertainty there was in our forecast. Our numbers gave him, to the nearest approximation, a 100 percent chance of winning. But did 100 percent really mean 99 percent, or 99.99 percent, or 99.9999 percent? If the latter—a 1 in 100,000 chance of losing—he was prepared to donate his campaign funds to other candidates in more vulnerable districts. But he wasn't willing to take a 1 in 100 risk.

Political partisans, meanwhile, may misinterpret the role of uncertainty in a forecast; they will think of it as hedging your bets and building in an excuse for yourself in case you get the prediction wrong. That is not really the idea. If you forecast that a particular incumbent congressman will win his race 90 percent of the time, you're also forecasting that he should lose it 10 percent of the time. The signature of a good forecast is that each of these probabilities turns out to be about right over the long run.

Tetlock's hedgehogs were especially bad at understanding these probabilities. When you say that an event has a 90 percent chance of happening, that has a *very* specific and objective meaning. But our brains translate it into something more subjective. Evidence from the psychologists Daniel Kahneman and Amos Tversky suggests that these subjective estimates don't always match up with the reality. We have trouble distinguishing a 90 percent chance that the plane will land safely from a 99 percent chance or a 99.9999 percent chance, even though these imply vastly different things about whether we ought to book our ticket.

With practice, our estimates can get better. What distinguished Tetlock's hedgehogs is that they were too stubborn to learn from their mistakes. Acknowledging the real-world uncertainty in their forecasts would require them to acknowledge to the imperfections in their theories about how the world was supposed to behave—the last thing that an ideologue wants to do.

Principle 2: Today's Forecast Is the First Forecast of the Rest of Your Life

Another misconception is that a good prediction shouldn't change. Certainly, if there are wild gyrations in your forecast from day to day, that may be a bad sign—either of a badly designed model, or that the phenomenon you are attempting to predict isn't very predictable at all. In 2012, when I published forecasts of the Republican primaries in advance of each state, solely according to the polls there, the probabilities often shifted substantially just as the polls did.

When the outcome is more predictable—as a general election is in the late stages of the race—the forecasts will normally be more stable. The comment that I heard most frequently from Democrats after the 2008 election was that they turned to FiveThirtyEight to help keep them calm.* By the end of a presidential race, as many as thirty or forty polls might be released every day from different states, and some of these results will inevitably fall outside the margin of error. Candidates, strategists, and television commentators—who have some vested interest in making the race seem closer than it really is—might focus on these outlier polls, but the FiveThirtyEight model found that they usually didn't make much difference.

Ultimately, the right attitude is that you should make the best forecast possible *today*—regardless of what you said last week, last month, or last year. Making a new forecast does not mean that the old forecast just disappears. (Ideally, you should keep a record of it and let people evaluate how well you did

---

* Not surprisingly, no Democrats told me this after the 2010 campaign—when our models consistently showed them losing badly.

over the whole course of predicting an event.) But if you have reason to think that yesterday's forecast was wrong, there is no glory in sticking to it. "When the facts change, I change my mind," the economist John Maynard Keynes famously said, "What do you do, sir?"

Some people don't like this type of course-correcting analysis and mistake it for a sign of weakness. It seems like cheating to change your mind—the equivalent of sticking your finger out and seeing which way the wind is blowing. The critiques usually rely, implicitly or explicitly, on the notion that politics is analogous to something like physics or biology, abiding by fundamental laws that are intrinsically knowable and predicable. (One of my most frequent critics is a professor of neuroscience at Princeton.) Under those circumstances, new information doesn't matter very much; elections should follow a predictable orbit, like a comet hurtling toward Earth.

Instead of physics or biology, however, electoral forecasting resembles something like poker: we can observe our opponent's behavior and pick up a few clues, but we can't see his cards. Making the most of that limited information requires a willingness to update one's forecast as newer and better information becomes available. It is the alternative—failing to change our forecast because we risk embarrassment by doing so—that reveals a lack of courage.

Principle 3: Look for Consensus

Every hedgehog fantasizes that they will make a daring, audacious, outside-the-box prediction—one that differs radically from the consensus view on a subject. Their colleagues ostracize them; even their golden retrievers start to look at them a bit funny. But then the prediction turns out to be exactly, profoundly, indubitably right. Two days later, they are on the front page of the *Wall Street Journal* and sitting on Jay Leno's couch, singled out as a bold and brave pioneer.

Every now and then, it might be correct to make a forecast like this. The expert consensus can be wrong—someone who had forecasted the collapse of the Soviet Union would have deserved most of the kudos that came to him. But the fantasy scenario is hugely unlikely. Even though foxes, myself included, aren't really a conformist lot, we get wor-

ried anytime our forecasts differ radically from those being produced by our competitors.

Quite a lot of evidence suggests that aggregate or group forecasts are more accurate than individual ones, often somewhere between 15 and 20 percent more accurate depending on the discipline. That doesn't necessarily mean the group forecasts are *good*. (We'll explore this subject in more depth later in the book.) But it does mean that you can benefit from applying multiple perspectives toward a problem.

"Foxes often manage to do inside their heads what you'd do with a whole group of hedgehogs," Tetlock told me. What he means is that foxes have developed an ability to emulate this consensus process. Instead of asking questions of a whole group of experts, they are constantly asking questions of themselves. Often this implies that they will aggregate different types of information together—as a group of people with different ideas about the world naturally would—instead of treating any one piece of evidence as though it is the Holy Grail. (FiveThirtyEight's forecasts, for instance, typically combine polling data with information about the economy, the demographics of a state, and so forth.) Forecasters who have failed to heed Tetlock's guidance have often paid the price for it.

Beware Magic-Bullet Forecasts

In advance of the 2000 election, the economist Douglas Hibbs published a forecasting model that claimed to produce remarkably accurate predictions about how presidential elections would turn out, based on just two variables, one related to economic growth and the other to the number of military casualties. Hibbs made some very audacious and hedgehogish claims. He said accounting for a president's approval rating (historically a very reliable indicator of his likelihood to be reelected) would not improve his forecasts at all. Nor did the inflation rate or the unemployment rate matter. And the identity of the candidates made no difference: a party may as well nominate a highly ideological senator like George McGovern as a centrist and war hero like Dwight D. Eisenhower. The key instead, Hibbs asserted, was a relatively obscure economic variable called real disposable income per capita.

So how did the model do? It forecasted a landslide victory for Al Gore, predicting him to win the election by 9 percentage points. But George W. Bush won instead after the recount in Florida. Gore did win the nationwide popular vote, but the model had implied that the election would be nowhere near close, attributing only about a 1 in 80 chance to such a tight finish.

There were several other models that took a similar approach, claiming they had boiled down something as complex as a presidential election to a two-variable formula. (Strangely, none of them used the *same* two variables.) Some of them, in fact, have a far worse track record than Hibbs's method. In 2000, one of these models projected a nineteen-point victory for Gore and would have given billions-to-one odds against the actual outcome.

These models had come into vogue after the 1988 election, in which the fundamentals seemed to favor George H. W. Bush—the economy was good and Bush's Republican predecessor Reagan was popular—but the polls had favored Michael Dukakis until late in the race. Bush wound up winning easily.

Since these models came to be more widely published, however, their track record has been quite poor. On average, in the five presidential elections since 1992, the typical "fundamentals-based" model—one that ignored the polls and claimed to discern exactly how voters would behave without them—has missed the final margin between the major candidates by almost 7 percentage points. Models that take a more fox-like approach, combining economic data with polling data and other types of information, have produced more reliable results.

Weighing Qualitative Information

The failure of these magic-bullet forecasting models came even though they were quantitative, relying on published economic statistics. In fact, some of the very worst forecasts that I document in this book are quantitative. The ratings agencies, for instance, had models that came to precise, "data-driven" estimates of how likely different types of mortgages were to default. These models were dangerously wrong because they relied on a self-serving assumption—that the default risk for different mortgages had little to do with one another—that made no sense in the midst of a housing and credit bubble. To be certain, I have a strong preference for more

quantitative approaches in my own forecasts. But hedgehogs can take any type of information and have it reinforce their biases, while foxes who have practice in weighing different types of information together can sometimes benefit from accounting for qualitative along with quantitative factors.

Few political analysts have a longer track record of success than the tight-knit team that runs the Cook Political Report. The group, founded in 1984 by a genial, round-faced Louisianan named Charlie Cook, is relatively little known outside the Beltway. But political junkies have relied on Cook's forecasts for years and have rarely had reason to be disappointed with their results.

Cook and his team have one specific mission: to predict the outcome of U.S. elections, particularly to the Congress. This means issuing forecasts for all 435 races for the U.S. House, as well as the 35 or so races for the U.S. Senate that take place every other year.

Predicting the outcome of Senate or gubernatorial races is relatively easy. The candidates are generally well known to voters, and the most important races attract widespread attention and are polled routinely by reputable firms. Under these circumstances, it is hard to improve on a good method for aggregating polls, like the one I use at FiveThirtyEight.

House races are another matter, however. The candidates often rise from relative obscurity—city councilmen or small-business owners who decide to take their shot at national politics—and in some cases are barely known to voters until just days before the election. Congressional districts, meanwhile, are spread throughout literally every corner of the country, giving rise to any number of demographic idiosyncrasies. The polling in House districts tends to be erratic at best when it is available at all, which it often isn't.

But this does not mean there is no information available to analysts like Cook. Indeed, there is an abundance of it: in addition to polls, there is data on the demographics of the district and on how it has voted in past elections. There is data on overall partisan trends throughout the country, such as approval ratings for the incumbent president. There is data on fund-raising, which must be scrupulously reported to the Federal Elections Commission.

Other types of information are more qualitative, but are nonetheless potentially useful. Is the candidate a good public speaker? How in tune is her platform with the peculiarities of the district? What type of ads is she running? A political campaign is essentially a small business: How well does she manage people?

Of course, all of that information could just get you into trouble if you were a hedgehog who wasn't weighing it carefully. But Cook Political has a lot of experience in making forecasts, and they have an impressive track record of accuracy.

Cook Political classifies races along a seven-point scale ranging from Solid Republican—a race that the Republican candidate is almost certain to win—to Solid Democrat (just the opposite). Between 1998 and 2010, the races that Cook described as Solid Republican were in fact won by the Republican candidate on 1,205 out of 1,207 occasions—well over 99 percent of the time. Likewise, races that they described as Solid Democrat were won by the Democrat in 1,226 out of 1,229 instances.

Many of the races that Cook places into the Solid Democrat or Solid Republican categories occur in districts where the same party wins every year by landslide margins—these are not that hard to call. But Cook Political has done just about as well in races that require considerably more skill to forecast. Elections they've classified as merely "leaning" toward the Republican candidate, for instance, have in fact been won by the Republican about 95 percent of the time. Likewise, races they've characterized as leaning to the Democrat have been won by the Democrat 92 percent of the time. Furthermore, the Cook forecasts have a good track record even when they disagree with quantitative indicators like polls.

I visited the Cook Political team in Washington one day in September 2010, about five weeks ahead of that November's elections, and spent the afternoon with David Wasserman, a curly-haired thirtysomething who manages their House forecasts.

The most unique feature of Cook's process is their candidate interviews. At election time, the entryway to the fifth floor of the Watergate complex, where the Cook offices are located, becomes a literal revolving door, with candidates dropping by for hourlong chats in between fund-raising and strategy sessions. Wasserman had three interviews scheduled on the day that I visited. He offered to let me sit in on one of them with a Republican candidate named

Dan Kapanke. Kapanke was hoping to unseat the incumbent Democrat Ron Kind in Wisconsin's Third Congressional District, which encompasses a number of small communities in the southwestern corner of the state. Cook Political had the race rated as Likely Democrat, which means they assigned Kapanke only a small chance of victory, but they were considering moving it into a more favorable category, Lean Democrat.

Kapanke, a state senator who ran a farm supply business, had the gruff demeanor of a high-school gym teacher. He also had a thick Wisconsin accent: when he spoke about the La Crosse Loggers, the minor-league baseball team that he owns, I wasn't certain whether he was referring to "logger" (as in timber cutter), or "lager" (as in beer)—either one of which would have been an apropos nickname for a ball club from Wisconsin. At the same time, his plainspokenness helped to overcome what he might have lacked in charm—and he had consistently won his State Senate seat in a district that ordinarily voted Democratic.

Wasserman, however, takes something of a poker player's approach to his interviews. He is stone-faced and unfailingly professional, but he is subtly seeking to put the candidate under some stress so that that they might reveal more information to him.

"My basic technique," he told me, "is to try to establish a comfortable and friendly rapport with a candidate early on in an interview, mostly by getting them to talk about the fuzzy details of where they are from. Then I try to ask more pointed questions. *Name an issue where you disagree with your party's leadership.* The goal isn't so much to get them to unravel as it is to get a feel for their style and approach."

His interview with Kapanke followed this template. Wasserman's knowledge of the nooks and crannies of political geography can make him seem like a local, and Kapanke was happy to talk shop about the intricacies of his district—just how many voters he needed to win in La Crosse to make up for the ones he'd lose in Eau Claire. But he stumbled over a series of questions on allegations that he had used contributions from lobbyists to buy a new set of lights for the Loggers' ballpark.

It was small-bore stuff; it wasn't like Kapanke had been accused of cheating on his wife or his taxes. But it was enough to dissuade Wasserman from changing the rating. Indeed, Kapanke lost his election that November by about 9,500 votes, even though Republicans won their races throughout most of the similar districts in the Midwest.

This is, in fact, the more common occurrence; Wasserman will usually maintain the same rating after the interview. As hard as he works to glean new information from the candidates, it is often not important enough to override his prior take on the race.

Wasserman's approach works because he is capable of evaluating this information without becoming dazzled by the candidate sitting in front of him. A lot of less-capable analysts would open themselves to being charmed, lied to, spun, or would otherwise get hopelessly lost in the narrative of the campaign. Or they would fall in love with their *own* spin about the candidate's interview skills, neglecting all the other information that was pertinent to the race.

Wasserman instead considers everything in the broader political context. A terrific Democratic candidate who aces her interview might not stand a chance in a district that the Republican normally wins by twenty points.

So why bother with the candidate interviews at all? Mostly, Wasserman is looking for red flags—like the time when the Democratic congressman Eric Massa (who would later abruptly resign from Congress after accusations that he sexually harassed a male staffer) kept asking Wasserman how old he was. The psychologist Paul Meehl called these "broken leg" cases—situations where there is something so glaring that it would be foolish not to account for it.

Catching a few of these each year helps Wasserman to call a few extra races right. He is able to weigh the information from his interviews without *over-weighing* it, which might actually make his forecasts worse. Whether information comes in a quantitative or qualitative flavor is not as important as how you use it.

It Isn't Easy to Be Objective

In this book, I use the terms *objective* and *subjective* carefully. The word *objective* is sometimes taken to be synonymous with *quantitative,* but it isn't. Instead it means seeing beyond our personal biases and prejudices and toward the truth of a problem.

Pure objectivity is desirable but unattainable in this world. When we make a forecast, we have a choice from among many different methods. Some of these might rely solely on quantitative variables like polls, while approaches like Wasserman's may consider qualitative factors as well. All of them, however, introduce decisions and assumptions that have to be made by the forecaster. Wherever there is human judgment there is the potential for bias. The way to become more objective is to recognize the influence that our assumptions play in our forecasts and to question ourselves about them. In politics, between our ideological predispositions and our propensity to weave tidy narratives from noisy data, this can be especially difficult.

So you will need to adopt some different habits from the pundits you see on TV. You will need to learn how to express—and quantify—the uncertainty in your predictions. You will need to update your forecast as facts and circumstances change. You will need to recognize that there is wisdom in seeing the world from a different viewpoint. The more you are willing to do these things, the more capable you will be of evaluating a wide variety of information without abusing it.

In short, you will need to learn how to think like a fox. The foxy forecaster recognizes the limitations that human judgment imposes in predicting the world's course. Knowing those limits can help her to get a few more predictions right.

The Revolt of the Elites

Christopher Lasch

Once it was the "revolt of the masses" that was held to threaten social order and the civilizing traditions of Western culture. In our time, however, the chief threat seems to come from those at the top of the social hierarchy, not the masses. This remarkable turn of events confounds our expectations about the course of history and calls long-established assumptions into question.

When Jose Ortega y Gasset published *The Revolt of the Masses*, first translated into English in 1932, he could not have foreseen a time when it would be more appropriate to speak of a revolt of elites. Writing in the era of the Bolshevik Revolution and the rise of fascism, in the aftermath of a cataclysmic war that had torn Europe apart, Ortega attributed the crisis of Western culture to the "political domination of the masses." Today it is the elites, however—those who control the international flow of money and information, preside over philanthropic foundations and institutions of higher learning, manage the instruments of cultural production and thus set the terms of public debate—that have lost faith in the values, or what remains of them, of the West. For many people the very term "Western civilization" now calls to mind an organized system of domination designed to enforce conformity to bourgeois values and to keep the victims of patriarchal oppression—women, children, homo-

sexuals, people of color—in a permanent state of subjection.

From Ortega's point of view, one that was widely shared at the time, the value of cultural elites lay in their willingness to assume responsibility for the exacting standards without which civilization is impossible. They lived in the service of demanding ideals. "Nobility is defined by the demands it makes on us—by obligations, not by rights." The mass man, on the other hand, had no use for obligations and no understanding of what they implied, "no feeling for [the] great historical duties." Instead he asserted the "rights of the commonplace." At once resentful and self-satisfied, he rejected "everything that is excellent, individual, qualified, and select." He was "incapable of submitting to direction of any kind." Lacking any comprehension of the fragility of civilization or the tragic character of history, he lived unthinkingly in the "assurance that tomorrow [the world] will be still richer, ampler, more perfect, as if it enjoyed a spontaneous, inexhaustible power of increase." He was concerned only with his own well-being and looked forward to a future of "limitless possibilities" and "complete freedom." His many failings included a "lack of romance in his dealings with women." Erotic love, a demanding ideal in its own right, had no attraction for him. His attitude toward the body was severely practical: He made a cult of physical fitness and submitted to hygienic regimens that promised to keep it in good repair and to extend its longevity. It was, above all, however, the "deadly hatred of all that is not itself" that characterized the mass mind, as Ortega described it. Incapable of wonder or respect, the mass man was the "spoiled child of human history."

All these habits of mind, I submit, are now more characteristic of the upper levels of society than of the lower or middle levels. It can hardly be said that ordinary people today look forward to a world of "limitless possibility." Any sense that the masses are riding the wave of history has long since departed. The radical movements that disturbed the peace of the twentieth century have failed one by one, and no successors have appeared on the horizon. The industrial working class, once the mainstay of the socialist movement, has become a pitiful remnant of itself. The hope that "new social movements" would take its place in the struggle against capitalism, which briefly sustained the left in the late seventies and early eighties, has come to nothing. Not only do the new social movements—feminism, gay rights, welfare rights, agitation against racial discrimination—have nothing in common, but their only coherent demand aims at inclusion in the dominant structures rather than at a revolutionary transformation of social relations.

It is not just that the masses have lost interest in revolution; their political instincts are demonstrably more conservative than those of their self-appointed spokesmen and would-be liberators. It is the working and lower middle classes, after all, that favor limits on abortion, cling to the two-parent family as a source of stability in a turbulent world, resist experiments with "alternative lifestyles," and harbor deep reservations about affirmative action and other ventures in large-scale social engineering. More to Ortega's point, they have a more highly developed sense of limits than their betters. They understand, as their betters do not, that there are inherent limits on human control over the course of social development, over nature and the body, over the tragic elements in human life and history. While young professionals subject themselves to an arduous schedule of physical exercise and dietary controls designed to keep death at bay—to maintain themselves in a state of permanent youthfulness, eternally attractive and remarriageable—ordinary people, on the other hand, accept the body's decay as something against which it is more or less useless to struggle.

Upper-middle-class liberals, with their inability to grasp the importance of class differences in shaping attitudes toward life, fail to reckon with the class dimension of their obsession with health and moral uplift. They find it hard to understand why their hygienic conception of life fails to command universal enthusiasm. They have mounted a crusade to sanitize American society: to create a "smoke-free environment," to censor everything from pornography to "hate speech," and at the same time, incongruously, to extend the range of personal choice in matters where most people feel the need of solid moral guidelines. When confronted with resistance to these initiatives, they betray the venomous hatred that lies not far beneath the smiling face of upper-middle-class benevolence. Opposition makes humanitarians forget the liberal virtues they claim to uphold. They become petulant, self-righteous, intolerant. In the heat of political controversy, they find it impossible to conceal their contempt for those who stubbornly refuse to see the light—those who "just don't get it," in the self-satisfied jargon of political rectitude.

Simultaneously arrogant and insecure, the new elites, the professional classes in particular, regard the masses with mingled scorn and apprehension. In the United States, "Middle America"—a term that has both geographical and social implications—has come to symbolize everything that stands in the way of progress: "family values," mindless patriotism, religious fundamentalism, racism, homophobia, retrograde views of women. Middle Americans, as they appear to the makers of educated opinion, are hopelessly shabby, unfashionable, and provincial, ill informed about changes in taste or intellectual trends, addicted to trashy novels of romance and adventure, and stupefied by prolonged exposure to television. They are at once absurd and vaguely menacing—not because they wish to overthrow the old order but precisely because their defense of it appears so deeply irrational that it expresses itself, at the higher reaches of its intensity, in fanatical religiosity, in a repressive sexuality that occasionally erupts into violence against women and gays, and in a patriotism that supports imperialist wars and a national ethic of aggressive masculinity.

The general course of recent history no longer favors the leveling of social distinctions but runs more and more in the direction of a two-class society in which the favored few monopolize the advantages of money, education, and power. It is undeniable, of course, that the comforts of modern life are still distributed far more widely than they were before the Industrial Revolution. It was this democratization of comfort that Ortega had in mind when he spoke of the "rise of the historical level." Like many others, Ortega was struck by the unheard-of abundance generated by the modern division of labor, by the transformation of luxuries into necessities, and by the popularization of standards of comfort and convenience formerly confined to the rich. These facts—the material fruits of modernization—are not in question. In our time, however, the democratization of abundance—the expectation that each generation would enjoy a standard of living beyond the reach of its predecessors—has given way to a reversal in which age-old inequalities are beginning to reestablish themselves, sometimes at a frightening rate, sometimes so gradually as to escape notice.

The global disparity between wealth and poverty, the most obvious example of this historic reversal, has become so glaring that it is hardly necessary to review the evidence of growing inequality. In Latin America, Africa, and large parts of Asia, the sheer growth in numbers, together with the displacement of rural populations by the commercialization of agriculture, has subjected civic life to unprecedented strains. Vast urban agglomerations—they can scarcely be called cities—have taken shape, overflowing with poverty, wretchedness, disease, and despair. Paul Kennedy projects twenty of these "megacities" by 2025, each with a population of eleven million or more. Mexico City will already have more than twenty-four million inhabitants by the year 2000, São Paulo more than twenty-three million, Calcutta sixteen million, Bombay fifteen-and-a-half million. The resulting strain on housing, sanitation, transportation, and other civic facilities can easily be foreseen, but the hellish conditions likely to follow defy the most doom-ridden imagination. Even now the devastation is so great that the only available response to the sensational scenes of squalor and starvation with which people are daily regaled by the media is one less of indignation than of helpless indifference.

As the collapse of civic life in these swollen cities continues, not only the poor but the middle classes will experience conditions unimaginable a few years ago. Middle-class standards of living can be expected to decline throughout what is all too hopefully referred to as the developing world. In a country like Peru, once a prosperous nation with reasonable prospects of evolving parliamentary institutions, the middle class for all practical purposes has ceased to exist. A middle class, as Walter Russell Mead reminds us in his study of the declining American empire *Mortal Splendor*, "does not appear out of thin air." Its power and numbers "depend on the overall wealth of the domestic economy," and in countries, accordingly, where "wealth is concentrated in the hands of a tiny oligarchy and the rest of the population is desperately poor, the middle class can grow to only a limited extent. . . . [It] never escapes its primary role as a servant class to the oligarchy." Unfortunately this description now applies to a growing list of nations that have prematurely reached the limits of economic development, countries in which a rising "share of their own national product goes to foreign investors or creditors." Such a fate may well await unlucky nations, including the United States, even in the industrial world.

It is the crisis of the middle class, and not simply the growing chasm between wealth and poverty, that needs to be emphasized in a sober analysis of our prospects. Even in Japan, the very model of successful industrialization in the last two or three decades, public opinion polls conducted in 1987 revealed a growing belief that the country could no longer be described as middle-class, ordinary people having failed to share in the vast fortunes accumulated in real estate, finance, and manufacturing.

The changing class structure of the United States presents us, sometimes in exaggerated form, with changes that are taking place all over the industrial world. People in the upper 20 percent of the income structure now control half the country's wealth. In the last twenty years they alone have experienced a net gain in family income. In the brief years of the Reagan administration alone, their share of the national income rose from 41.6 percent to 44 percent. The middle class, generously defined as those with incomes ranging from fifteen to fifty thousand dollars a year, declined from 65 percent of the population in 1970 to 58 percent in 1985. These figures convey only a partial, imperfect impression of momentous changes that have taken place in a remarkably short period of time. The steady growth of unemployment, now expanded to include white-collar workers, is more revealing. So is the growth of the "contingent labor force." The number of part-time jobs has doubled since 1980 and now amounts to a quarter of available jobs. No doubt this massive growth of part-time employment helps to explain why the number of workers covered by retirement plans, which rose from 22 percent to 45 percent between 1950 and 1980, slipped back to 42.6 percent by 1986. It also helps to explain the decline of union membership and the steady erosion of union influence. All these developments, in turn, reflect the loss of manufacturing jobs and the shift to an economy increasingly based on information and services.

In 1973 a high school graduate would have earned an average income (in 1987 dollars) of $32,000. By 1987 high school graduates, if they were lucky enough to find steady employment at all, could expect to make less than $28,000—a decline of 12 percent. High school dropouts could still make almost $20,000 a year in 1973, on the average; by 1987 this figure had fallen by 15 percent to a new low of $16,000. Even a college education in itself no longer assures affluence: in the same period the average earnings of college graduates increased only from $49,500 to $50,000.

Affluence these days—or for many Americans mere survival, for that matter—requires the additional income provided by women's participation in the labor force. The prosperity enjoyed by the professional and managerial classes, which make up most of the upper 20 percent of the income structure, derives in large part from the emerging marital pattern inelegantly known as assortative mating—the tendency of men to marry women who can be relied on to bring in income more or less equivalent to their own. Doctors used to marry nurses, lawyers and executives their secretaries. Now upper-middle-class men tend to marry women of their own class, business or professional associates with lucrative careers of their own. "What if the $60,000 lawyer marries another $60,000 lawyer," Mickey Kaus asks in his book *The End of Equality*, "and the $20,000 clerk marries a $20,000 clerk? Then the difference between their incomes suddenly becomes the difference between $120,000 and $40,000," and "although the trend is still masked in the income statistics by the low average wages of women," Kaus adds, "it's obvious to practically everyone, even the experts, that something like this is in fact hap-

pening." It is unnecessary, incidentally, to seek much further for an explanation of feminism's appeal to the professional and managerial class. Female careerism provides the indispensable basis of their prosperous, glamorous, gaudy, sometimes indecently lavish way of life.

The upper middle class, the heart of the new professional and managerial elites, is defined, apart from its rapidly rising income, not so much by its ideology as by a way of life that distinguishes it, more and more unmistakably, from the rest of the population. Even its feminism—that is, its commitment to the two-career family—is a matter more of practical necessity than of political conviction. Efforts to define a "new class" composed of public administrators and policy makers, relentlessly pushing a program of liberal reforms, ignore the range of political opinions among the professional and managerial elites. These groups constitute a new class only in the sense that their livelihoods rest not so much on the ownership of property as on the manipulation of information and professional expertise. Their investment in education and information, as opposed to property, distinguishes them from the rich bourgeoisie, the ascendancy of which characterized an earlier stage of capitalism, and from the old proprietary class—the middle class in the strict sense of the term—that once made up the bulk of the population.

Since they embrace a wide variety of occupations—brokers, bankers, real estate promoters and developers, engineers, consultants of all kinds, systems analysts, scientists, doctors, publicists, publishers, editors, advertising executives, art directors, moviemakers, entertainers, journalists, television producers and directors, artists, writers, university professors—and since they lack a common political outlook, it is also inappropriate to characterize managerial and professional elites as a new ruling class. Alvin Gouldner, in one of the most convincing attempts to anatomize the "new class," found the unifying element in their "culture of critical discourse," but even though this formulation captures an essential feature of the secular, analytical attitude that now prevails in the higher circles, it exaggerates the intellectual component in the culture of the new elites and their interest in the rationalization of life, just as it minimizes their continuing fascination with the capitalist market and their frenzied search for profits.

A more salient fact is that the market in which the new elites operate is now international in scope. Their fortunes are tied to enterprises that operate across national boundaries. They are more concerned with the smooth functioning of the system as a whole than with any of its parts. Their loyalties— if the term is not itself anachronistic in this context are international rather than regional, national, or local. They have more in common with their counterparts in Brussels or Hong Kong than with the masses of Americans not yet plugged into the network of global communications.

Robert Reich's category of "symbolic analysts" serves, apart from its syntactical incoherence, as a useful, empirical, and rather unpretentious description of the new class. These are people, as Reich describes them, who live in a world of abstract concepts and symbols, ranging from stock market quotations to the visual images produced by Hollywood and Madison Avenue, and who specialize in the interpretation and deployment of symbolic information. Reich contrasts them with the two other principal categories of labor: "routine production workers," who perform repetitive tasks and exercise little control over the design of production, and "in-person servers," whose work also consists of routine, for the most part, but "must be provided person-to-person" and therefore cannot be "sold worldwide." If we allow for the highly schematic and necessarily imprecise character of these categories, they correspond closely enough to everyday observation to give us a fairly accurate impression not only of the occupational structure but of the class structure of American society, since the "symbolic analysts" are clearly rising while the other categories, which make up 80 percent of the population, are declining in wealth and status.

A more serious objection than imprecision is Reich's extravagantly flattering portrait of the "symbolic analysts." In his eyes, they represent the best and brightest in American life. Educated at "elite private schools" and "high-quality suburban schools," where they are tracked through advanced courses," they enjoy every advantage their doting parents can provide.

Their teachers and professors are attentive to their academic needs. They have access to state-of-the-art scientific laboratories, interactive computers and video systems in the classroom, language laboratories, and high-tech school libraries. Their classes are relatively small; their peers are intellectually stimulating. Their parents take them to museums and cultural events, expose them to foreign travel, and give them music lessons. At home are educational books, educational toys, educational videotapes, microscopes, telescopes, and personal computers replete with the latest educational software.

These privileged young people acquire advanced degrees at the "best [universities] in the world," the superiority of which is proved by their ability to attract foreign students in great numbers. In this cosmopolitan atmosphere they overcome the provincial folkways that impede creative thought, according to Reich. "Skeptical, curious, creative," they become problem solvers par excellence, equal to any challenge. Unlike those who engage in mind-numbing routines, they love their work, which engages them in lifelong learning and endless experimentation.

Unlike old-fashioned intellectuals, who tend to work by themselves and to be jealous and possessive about their ideas, the new brain workers—producers of high-quality "insights" in a variety of fields ranging from marketing and finance to art and entertainment—operate best in teams. Their "capacity to collaborate" promotes "system thinking"—the ability to see problems in their totality, to absorb the fruits of collective experimentation, and to "discern larger causes, consequences, and relationships." Since their work depends so heavily on "networking," they settle in "specialized geographical pockets" populated by people like them. These privileged communities Cambridge, the Silicon Valley, Hollywood—become "wondrously resilient" centers of artistic, technical, and promotional enterprise. They represent the epitome of intellectual achievement, in Reich's admiring view, and of the good life conceived as the exchange of "insights," "information," and professional gossip. The geographical concentration of knowledge producers, once it reaches a critical mass, incidentally provides a market for the growing class of "in-person servers" who cater to their needs.

It is no accident that Hollywood is home to a conspicuously large number of voice coaches, fencing trainers, dancing instructors, performers' agents, and suppliers of photographic, acoustic and lighting equipment. Also found in close proximity are restaurants with precisely the right ambience favored by producers wooing directors and directors wooing screenwriters, and everyone in Hollywood wooing everyone else.

Universal admission to the class of "creative" people would best meet Reich's ideal of a democratic society, but since this goal is clearly unattainable, the next best thing, presumably, is a society composed of "symbolic analysts" and their hangers-on. The latter are themselves consumed with dreams of stardom but are content, in the meantime, to live in the shadow of the stars waiting to be discovered and are symbiotically united with their betters in a continuous search for marketable talent that can be compared, as Reich's imagery makes clear, only with the rites of courtship. One might add the more jaundiced observation that the circles of power—finance, government, art, entertainment—overlap and become increasingly interchangeable. It is significant that Reich turns to Hollywood for a particularly compelling example of the "wondrously resilient" communities that spring up wherever there is a concentration of "creative" people. Washington becomes a parody of Tinseltown; executives take to the airwaves, creating overnight the semblance of political movements; movie stars become political pundits, even presidents; reality and the simulation of reality become more and more difficult to distinguish. Ross Perot launches his presidential campaign from the "Larry King Show." Hollywood stars take a prominent part in the Clinton campaign and flock to Clinton's inaugural, investing it with the glamour of a Hollywood opening. TV anchors and interviewers become celebrities; celebrities in the world of entertainment take on the role of social critics. The boxer Mike Tyson issues a three-page open letter from the Indiana prison where he is serving a six-year term for rape, condemning the president's "crucifixion" of assistant attorney general for civil rights nominee Lani Guinier. The starstruck Rhodes Scholar Robert Reich, prophet of the new world of "abstraction, system thinking, experimentation, and collaboration," joins the Clinton administration in the incongruous capacity of secretary of labor, administrator, in other words, of the one category of employment ("routine production") that has no future at all (according to his own account) in a society composed of "symbolic analysts" and "in-person servers."

Only in a world in which words and images bear less and less resemblance to the things they appear to describe would it be possible for a man like Reich to refer to himself, without irony, as secretary of labor or to write so glowingly of a society governed by the best and brightest. The last time the "best and brightest" got control of the country, they dragged it into a protracted, demoralizing war in Southeast Asia, from which the country has still not fully recovered. Yet Reich seems to believe that a new generation of Whiz Kids can do for the faltering American economy what Robert McNamara's generation failed to do for American diplomacy: to restore, through sheer brainpower, the world leadership briefly enjoyed by the United States after World War II and subsequently lost not, of course, through stupidity so much as through the very arrogance—the "arrogance of power," as Senator William Fulbright used to call it—to which the "best and brightest" are congenitally addicted.

This arrogance should not be confused with the pride characteristic of aristocratic classes, which rests on the inheritance of an ancient lineage and on the obligation to defend its honor. Neither valor and chivalry nor the code of courtly, romantic love, with which these values are closely associated, has any place in the world view of the best and brightest. A meritocracy has no more use for chivalry and valor than a hereditary aristocracy has for brains. Although hereditary advantages play an important part in the attainment of professional or managerial status, the new class has to maintain the fiction that its power rests on intelligence alone. Hence it has little sense of ancestral gratitude or of an obligation to live up to responsibilities inherited from the past. It thinks of itself as a self-made elite owing its privileges exclusively to its own efforts. Even the concept of a republic of letters, which might be expected to appeal to elites with such a large stake in higher education, is almost entirely absent from their frame of reference. Meritocratic elites find it difficult to imagine a community, even a community of the intellect, that reaches into both the past and the future and is constituted by an awareness of intergenerational obligation. The "zones" and "networks" admired by Reich bear little resemblance to communities in any traditional sense of the term. Populated by transients, they lack the continuity that derives from a sense of place and from standards of conduct self-consciously cultivated and handed down from generation to generation. The "community" of the best and brightest is a community of contemporaries, in the double sense that its members think of themselves as agelessly youthful and that the mark of this youthfulness is precisely their ability to stay on top of the latest trends.

Ortega and other critics described mass culture as a combination of "radical ingratitude" with an unquestioned belief in limitless possibility. The mass man, according to Ortega, took for granted the benefits conferred by civilization and demanded them "peremptorily, as if they were natural rights." Heir of all the ages, he was blissfully unconscious of his debt to the past. Though he enjoyed advantages brought about by the general "rise in the historic level," he felt no obligation either to his progenitors or to his progeny. He recognized no authority outside himself, conducting himself as if he were "lord of his own existence." His "incredible ignorance of history" made it possible for him to think of the present moment as far superior to the civilizations of the past and to forget, moreover, that contemporary civilization was itself the product of centuries of historical development, not the unique achievement of an age that had discovered the secret of progress by turning its back on the past.

These habits of mind, it would seem, are more accurately associated with the rise of meritocracy than with the "revolt of the masses." Ortega himself admitted that the "prototype of the mass man" was the "man of science"—the "technician," the specialist, the "learned ignoramus" whose mastery of "his own tiny corner of the universe" was matched only by his ignorance of the rest. But the process in question does not derive simply from the replacement of the old-fashioned man of letters by the specialist, as Ortega's analysis implies; it derives from the intrinsic structure of meritocracy itself. Meritocracy is a parody of democracy. It offers opportunities for advancement, in theory at least, to anyone with the talent to seize them, but "opportunities to rise," as R. H. Tawney points out in *Equality*, "are no substitute for a general diffusion of the means of civilization," of the "dignity and culture" that are needed by all "whether they rise or not." Social mobility does not undermine the influence of elites; if anything, it helps to solidify their influence by supporting the illusion that it rests solely on merit. It merely strengthens the likelihood that elites will exercise power irresponsibly, precisely because they recognize so few obligations to their predecessors or to the communities they profess to lead. Their lack of gratitude disqualifies mer-

itocratic elites from the burden of leadership, and in any case, they are less interested in leadership than in escaping from the common lot—the very definition of meritocratic success.

The inner logic of meritocracy has seldom been more rigorously exposed than in Michael Young's dystopic vision in his *The Rise of the Meritocracy, 1870-2033,* a work written in the tradition of Tawney, G. D. H. Cole, George Orwell, E. P. Thompson, and Raymond Williams. Young's narrator, a historian writing in the fourth decade of the twenty-first century, approvingly chronicles the "fundamental change" of the century and a half beginning around 1870: the redistribution of intelligence "between the classes." "By imperceptible degrees an aristocracy of birth has turned into an aristocracy of talent." Thanks to industry's adoption of intelligence testing, the abandonment of the principle of seniority, and the growing influence of the school at the expense of the family, "the talented have been given the opportunity to rise to the level which accords with their capacities, and the lower classes consequently reserved for those who are also lower in ability." These changes coincided with a growing recognition that economic expansion was the "overriding purpose" of social organization and that people ought to be judged by the single test of how much they increase production. Meritocracy, in Young's description, rests on a mobilized economy driven by the compulsion to produce.

The recognition that meritocracy is more efficient than heredity was not enough, in itself, to inspire or justify a "psychological change on the vast scale that the economy required." Indeed, "The hereditary principle would never have been overthrown," continues Young's narrator, ". . . without the aid of a new religion—and that religion was socialism." Socialists, "mid-wives of progress," contributed to the eventual triumph of meritocracy by encouraging large-scale production, by criticizing the family as the nursery of acquisitive individualism, and, above all, by ridiculing hereditary privilege and the "current criterion of success." ("It's not what you know but who you are that counts.") "The main body of socialists were far more critical of the inequality due to unearned than to earned income—the stereotype was of the rich man who had inherited a fortune from his father." In Young's world, only a handful of sentimental egalitarians condemned inequality as such and "quaintly spoke of the 'dignity of labour' as though manual and mental work were of equal worth." These same sentimentalists clung to the delusion that a system of common schools, because it promoted a "common culture," was an essential component of a democratic society. Fortunately their "over-optimistic belief in the educability of the majority" did not survive the test of experience, as Sir Hartley Shawcross noted in 1956: "I do not know a single member of the Labour Party, who can afford to do so, who does not send his children to a public school [i.e., to what would be called a private school in the United States]." A doctrinaire belief in equality collapsed in the face of the practical advantages of an educational system that "no longer required the clever to mingle with the stupid."

Young's imaginative projection of postwar trends in Great Britain sheds a great deal of light on similar trends in the United States, where a seemingly democratic system of elite recruitment leads to results that are far from democratic: segregation of social classes; contempt for manual labor; collapse of the common schools; loss of a common culture. As Young describes it, meritocracy has the effect of making elites more secure than ever in their privileges (which can now be seen as the appropriate reward of diligence and brainpower) while nullifying working-class opposition. "The best way to defeat opposition," Young's historian observes, "is [by] appropriating and educating the best children of the lower classes while they are still young." The educational reforms of the twentieth century "enabled the clever child to leave the lower class . . . and to enter into a higher class into which he was fitted to climb." Those who were left behind, knowing that "they have had every chance," cannot legitimately complain about their lot. "For the first time in human history the inferior man has no ready buttress for his self-regard."

It should not surprise us, then, that meritocracy also generates an obsessive concern with "self-esteem." The new, therapies (sometimes known collectively as the recovery movement) seek to counter the oppressive sense of failure in those who fail to climb the educational ladder, while leaving the existing structure of elite recruitment—acquisition of educational credentials—intact. Since the sense of failure no longer appears to have any rational basis, it presumably requires therapeutic attention. Without much conviction, therapists send the message that the failure of academic misfits, the home-

less, the unemployed, and other losers is no fault of their own: that the cards are stacked against them, that tests measuring academic achievement are culturally biased, and that academic achievement has become hereditary, in effect, since the upper middle classes pass on to their children the accumulated advantages that virtually guarantee advancement. As Young observes, people on the left (like their opponents on the right) are happiest when attacking hereditary privilege. They ignore the real objection to meritocracy—that it drains talent away from the lower classes and thus deprives them of effective leadership—and content themselves with dubious arguments to the effect that education does not live up to its promise of fostering social mobility. If it did, they seem to imply, no one would presumably have any reason to complain.

An aristocracy of talent—superficially an attractive ideal, which appears to distinguish democracies from societies based on hereditary privilege—turns out to be a contradiction in terms: The talented retain many of the vices of aristocracy without its virtues. Their snobbery lacks any acknowledgment of reciprocal obligations between the favored few and the multitude. Although they are full of "compassion" for the poor, they cannot be said to subscribe to a theory of noblesse oblige, which would imply a willingness to make a direct and personal contribution to the public good. Obligation, like everything else, has been depersonalized; exercised through the agency of the state, the burden of supporting it falls not on the professional and managerial class but, disproportionately, on the lower-middle and working classes. The policies advanced by new-class liberals on behalf of the downtrodden and oppressed—racial integration of the public schools, for example—require sacrifices from the ethnic minorities who share the inner cities with the poor, seldom from the suburban liberals who design and support those policies.

To an alarming extent the privileged classes—by an expansive definition, the top 20 percent—have made themselves independent not only of crumbling industrial cities but of public services in general. They send their children to private schools, insure themselves against medical emergencies by enrolling in company-supported plans, and hire private security guards to protect themselves against the mounting violence against them. In effect, they have removed themselves from the common life. It is not just that they see no point in paying for public services they no longer use. Many of them have ceased to think of themselves as Americans in any important sense, implicated in America's destiny for better or worse. Their ties to an international culture of work and leisure—of business, entertainment, information, and "information retrieval"—make many of them deeply indifferent to the prospect of American national decline. In Los Angeles the business and professional classes now see their city as the "gateway" to the Pacific Rim. Even if the rest of the country is on the verge of collapse, they say, the West Coast "just can't stop growing no matter what," in the words of Tom Lieser, an economist at Security Pacific. "This is fantasy land and nothing will be able to put a stop to that." Joel Kotkin, a business writer who moved to Los Angeles in the mid-seventies and immediately became one of the city's leading boosters, agrees that the coastal economy is exempt from the "great angst of the Atlantic world." Recent hard times in California have not notably diminished this optimism.

In the borderless global economy, money has lost its links to nationality. David Rieff, who spent several months in Los Angeles collecting material for his book *Los Angeles: Capital of the Third World*, reports that "at least two or three times a week, . . . I could depend on hearing someone say that the future 'belonged' to the Pacific Rim." The movement of money and population across national borders has transformed the "whole idea of place," according to Rieff. The privileged classes in Los Angeles feel more kinship with their counterparts in Japan, Singapore, and Korea than with most of their own countrymen.

The same tendencies are at work all over the world. In Europe referenda on unification have revealed a deep and widening gap between the political classes and the more humble members of society, who fear that the European Economic Community will be dominated by bureaucrats and technicians devoid of any feelings of national identity or allegiance. A Europe governed from Brussels, in their view, will be less and less amenable to popular control. The international language of money will speak more loudly than local dialects. Such fears underlie the reassertion of ethnic particularism in Europe, while the decline of the nation-state weakens the only authority capable of holding ethnic rivalries in check. The revival of tribalism, in turn, reinforces a reactive cosmopolitanism among elites.

Curiously enough, it is Robert Reich, notwithstanding his admiration for the new class of "symbolic analysts," who provides one of the most penetrating accounts of the "darker side of cosmopolitanism." Without national attachments, he reminds us, people have little inclination to make sacrifices or to accept responsibility for their actions. "We learn to feel responsible for others because we share with them a common history, . . . a common culture, . . . a common fate." The denationalization of business enterprise tends to produce a class of cosmopolitans who see themselves as "world citizens, but without accepting . . . any of the obligations that citizenship in a polity normally implies." But the cosmopolitanism of the favored few, because it is uninformed by the practice of citizenship, turns out to be a higher form of parochialism. Instead of supporting public services, the new elites put their money into the improvement of their own self-enclosed enclaves. They gladly pay for private and suburban schools, private police, and private systems of garbage collection; but they have managed to relieve themselves, to a remarkable extent, of the obligation to contribute to the national treasury. Their acknowledgment of civic obligations does not extend beyond their own immediate neighborhoods. The "secession of the symbolic analysts," as Reich calls it, provides us with a particularly striking instance of the revolt of elites against the constraints of time and place.

The world of the late twentieth century presents a curious spectacle. On the one hand, it is now united, through the agency of the market, as it never was before. Capital and labor flow freely across political boundaries that seem increasingly artificial and unenforceable. Popular culture follows in their wake. On the other hand, tribal loyalties have seldom been so aggressively promoted. Religious and ethnic warfare breaks out in one country after another: in India and Sri Lanka; in large parts of Africa; in the former Soviet Union and the former Yugoslavia.

It is the weakening of the nation-state that underlies both these developments—the movement toward unification and the seemingly contradictory movement toward fragmentation. The state can no longer contain ethnic conflicts, nor, on the other hand, can it contain the forces leading to globalization. Ideologically nationalism comes under attack from both sides: from advocates of ethnic and racial particularism but also from those who argue that the only hope of peace lies in the internationalization of everything from weights and measures to the artistic imagination.

The decline of nations is closely linked, in turn, to the global decline of the middle class. Ever since the sixteenth and seventeenth centuries, the fortunes of the nation-state have been bound up with those of the trading and manufacturing classes. The founders of modern nations, whether they were exponents of royal privilege like Louis XIV or republicans like Washington and Lafayette, turned to this class for support in their struggle against the feudal nobility. A large part of the appeal of nationalism lay in the state's ability to establish a common market within its boundaries, to enforce a uniform system of justice, and to extend citizenship both to petty proprietors and to rich merchants, alike excluded from power under the old regime. The middle class understandably became the most patriotic, not to say jingoistic and militaristic, element in society. But the unattractive features of middle-class nationalism should not obscure its positive contributions in the form of a highly developed sense of place and a respect for historical continuity—hallmarks of the middle-class sensibility that can be appreciated more fully now that middle-class culture is everywhere in retreat. Whatever its faults, middle-class nationalism provided a common ground, common standards, a common frame of reference without which society dissolves into nothing more than contending factions, as the Founding Fathers of America understood so well—a war of all against all.

The Lost Art of Argument

Christopher Lasch

For many years now we have been regaled with the promise of the information age. The social effects of the communications revolution, we are told, will include an insatiable demand for trained personnel, an upgrading of the skills required for employment, and an enlightened public capable of following the issues of the day and of making informed judgments about civic affairs. Instead we find college graduates working at jobs for which they are vastly overqualified. The demand for menial labor outstrips the demand for skilled specialists. The postindustrial economy, it appears, promotes an interchangeability of personnel, a rapid movement from one type of work to another, and a growing concentration of the labor force in technically backward, labor-intensive, nonunion sectors of the economy. Recent experience does not bear out the expectation that technological innovations, improvements in communications in particular, will create an abundance of skilled jobs, eliminate disagreeable jobs, and make life easy for everyone. Their most important effect, on the contrary, is to widen the gap between the knowledge class and the rest of the population, between those who find themselves at home in the new global economy and who "relish the thought that the information flows to them can become bigger" all the time (in the words of Arno Penzias of AT&T Bell Laboratories) and those who, having little use for cellular phones, fax machines, or on-line information services, still live in what Penzias contemptuously refers to as the Age of Paper Work.

As for the claim that the information revolution would raise the level of public intelligence, it is no secret that the public knows less about public affairs than it used to know. Millions of Americans cannot begin to tell you what is in the Bill of Rights, what Congress does, what the Constitution says about the powers of the presidency, how the party system emerged or how it operates. A sizable majority, according to a recent survey, believe that Israel is an Arab nation. Instead of blaming the schools for this disheartening ignorance of public affairs, as is the custom, we should look elsewhere for a fuller explanation, bearing in mind that people readily acquire such knowledge as they can put to good use. Since the public no longer participates in debates on national issues, it has no reason to inform itself about civic affairs. It is the decay of public debate, not the school system (bad as it is), that makes the public ill informed, notwithstanding the wonders of the age of information. When debate becomes a lost art, information, even though it may be readily available, makes no impression.

What democracy requires is vigorous public debate, not information. Of course, it needs information too, but the kind of information it needs can be generated only by debate. We do not know what we need to know until we ask the right questions, and we can identify the right questions only by subjecting our own ideas about the world to the test of public controversy. Information, usually seen as the precondition of debate, is better understood as its by-product. When we get into arguments that focus and fully engage our attention, we become avid seekers of relevant information. Otherwise we take in information passively— if we take it in at all.

Political debate began to decline around the turn of the century, curiously enough at a time when the press was becoming more "responsible," more professional, more conscious of its civic obligations. In the early nineteenth century the press was fiercely partisan. Until the middle of the century papers were often financed by political parties. Even when they became more independent of parties, they did not embrace the ideal of objectivity or neutrality. In 1841 Horace Greeley launched his *New York Tribune* with the announcement that it would be a "journal removed alike from servile partisanship on the one hand and from gagged, mincing neutrality on the other." Strong-minded editors like Greeley, James Gordon Bennett, E. L. Godkin, and Samuel Bowles objected to the way in which the demands of party loyalty infringed upon editorial independence, making the editor merely a mouthpiece for a party or faction, but they did not attempt to conceal their own views or to impose a strict separation of news and editorial content. Their papers were journals of opinion in which the reader expected to find a definite point of view, together with unrelenting criticism of opposing points of view.

It is no accident that journalism of this kind flourished during the period from 1830 to 1900, when popular participation in politics was at its height. Of the eligible voters, 80 percent typically went to the polls in presidential elections. After 1900 the percentage declined sharply (to 65 percent in 1904 and 59 percent in 1912), and it has continued to decline more or less steadily throughout the twentieth century. Torchlight parades, mass rallies, and gladiatorial contents of oratory made nineteenth-century politics an object of consuming popular interest, in which journalism served as an extension of the town meeting. The nineteenth-century press created a public forum in which issues were hotly debated. Newspapers not only reported political controversies but participated in them, drawing in their readers as well. Print culture rested on the remnants of an oral tradition. Print was not yet the exclusive medium of communication, nor had it severed its connection with spoken language. The printed language was still shaped by the rhythms and requirements of the spoken word, in particular by the conventions of verbal argumentation. Print served to create a larger forum for the spoken word, not yet to displace or reshape it.

The Lincoln-Douglas debates exemplified the oral tradition at its best. By current standards, Lincoln and Douglas broke every rule of political discourse. They subjected their audiences (which were as large as fifteen thousand on one occasion) to a painstaking analysis of complex issues. They spoke with considerably more candor, in a pungent, colloquial, sometimes racy style, than politicians think prudent today. They took clear positions from which it was difficult to retreat. They conducted themselves as if political leadership carried with it an obligation to clarify issues instead of merely getting elected.

The contrast between these justly famous debates and present-day presidential debates, in which the media define the issues and draw up the ground rules, is unmistakable and highly unflattering to ourselves. Journalistic interrogation of political candidates—which is what debate has come to— tends to magnify the importance of journalists and to diminish that of the candidates. Journalists ask questions—prosaic, predictable questions for the most part—and press the candidates for prompt, specific answers, reserving the right to interrupt and to cut the candidates short whenever they appear to stray from the prescribed topic. To prepare for this ordeal, candidates rely on their advisers to stuff them full of facts and figures, quotable slogans, and anything else that will convey the impression of wide-ranging, unflappable competence. Faced not only with a battery of journalists ready to pounce on the slightest misstep but with the cold, relentless scrutiny of the camera, politicians know that everything depends on the management of visual impressions. They must radiate confidence and decisiveness and never appear to be at a loss for words. The nature of the occasion requires them to exaggerate the reach and effectiveness of public policy, to give the impression that the right programs and the right leadership can meet every challenge.

The format requires all candidates to look the same: confident, untroubled, and therefore unreal. But it also imposes on them the obligation to explain what makes them different from the others. Once the question has to be asked, it answers itself. Indeed, the question is inherently belittling and degrading, a good example of TV's effect of lowering the object of estimation, of looking through every disguise, deflating every pretension. Bluntly stated with the necessary undertone of all-pervasive skepticism that is inescapably part of the language of TV, the question turns out to be highly rhetorical. What makes *you* so special? Nothing.

This is the quintessential question raised by TV, because it is in the medium's nature to teach us, with relentless insistence, that no one is special, contrary claims notwithstanding. At this point in our history the best qualification for high office may well be a refusal to cooperate with the media's program of self-aggrandizement. A candidate with the courage to abstain from "debates" organized by the media would automatically distinguish himself from the others and command a good deal of public respect. Candidates should insist on directly debating each other instead of responding to questions put to them by commentators and pundits. Their passivity and subservience lower them in the eyes of the voters. They need to recover their self-respect by challenging the media's status as arbiters of public discussion. A refusal to play by the media's rules would make people aware of the vast, illegitimate influence the mass media have come to exercise in American politics. It would also provide the one index of character that voters could recognize and applaud.

What happened to the tradition exemplified by the Lincoln-Douglas debates? The scandals of the Gilded Age gave party politics a bad name. They confirmed the misgivings entertained by the "best men" ever since the rise of Jacksonian democracy. By the 1870s and 1880s a bad opinion of politics had come to be widely shared by the educated classes. Genteel reformers—"mugwumps" to their enemies—demanded a professionalization of politics, designed to free the civil service from party control and to replace political appointees with trained experts. Even those who rejected the invitation to

declare their independence from the party system, like Theodore Roosevelt (whose refusal to desert the Republican party infuriated the "independents"), shared the enthusiasm for civil service reform. The "best men" ought to challenge the spoilsmen on their own turf, according to Roosevelt, instead of retreating to the sidelines of political life.

The drive to clean up politics gained momentum in the progressive era. Under the leadership of Roosevelt, Woodrow Wilson, Robert La Follette, and William Jennings Bryan, the progressives preached "efficiency," "good government," "bipartisanship," and the "scientific management" of public affairs and declared war on "bossism." They attacked the seniority system in Congress, limited the powers of the Speaker of the House, replaced mayors with city managers, and delegated important governmental functions to appointive commissions staffed with trained administrators. Recognizing that political machines were welfare agencies of a rudimentary type, which dispensed jobs and other benefits to their constituents and thereby won their loyalty, the progressives set out to create a welfare state as a way of competing with the machines. They launched comprehensive investigations of crime, vice, poverty, and other "social problems." They took the position that government was a science, not an art. They forged links between government and the university so as to assure a steady supply of experts and expert knowledge. But they had little use for public debate. Most political questions were too complex, in their view, to be submitted to popular judgment. They liked to contrast the scientific expert with the orator, the latter a useless windbag whose rantings only confused the public mind.

Professionalism in politics meant professionalism in journalism. The connection between them was spelled out by Walter Lippmann in a notable series of books: *Liberty and the News* (1920), *Public Opinion* (1922), and *The Phantom Public* (1925). These provided a founding charter for modern journalism, the most elaborate rationale for a journalism guided by the new ideal of professional objectivity. Lippmann held up standards by which the press is still judged—usually with the result that it is found wanting.

What concerns us here, however, is not whether the press has lived up to Lippmann's standards but how he arrived at those standards in the first place. In 1920 Lippmann and Charles Merz published a long essay in the *New Republic* examining press coverage of the Russian Revolution. This study, now forgotten, showed that American papers gave their readers an account of the Revolution distorted by anti-Bolshevik prejudices, wishful thinking, and sheer ignorance. *Liberty and the News* was also prompted by the collapse of journalistic objectivity during the war, when the newspapers had appointed themselves "defenders of the faith." The result, according to Lippmann, was a "break-down of the means of public knowledge." The difficulty went beyond war or revolution, the "supreme destroyers of realistic thinking." The traffic in sex, violence, and "human interest"—staples of modern mass journalism—raised grave questions about the future of democracy. "All that the sharpest critics of democracy have alleged is true if there is no steady supply of trustworthy and relevant news."

In *Public Opinion* and *The Phantom Public*, Lippmann answered the critics, in effect, by redefining democracy. Democracy did not require that the people literally govern themselves. The public's stake in government was strictly procedural. The public interest did not extend to the substance of decision making: "The public is interested in law, not in the laws; in the method of law, not in the substance." Questions of substance should be decided by knowledgeable administrators whose access to reliable information immunized them against the emotional "symbols" and "stereotypes" that dominated public debate. The public was incompetent to govern itself and did not even care to do so, in Lippmann's view. But as long as rules of fair play were enforced, the public would be content to leave government to experts—provided, of course, that the experts delivered the goods, the ever-increasing abundance of comforts and conveniences so closely identified with the American way of life.

Lippmann acknowledged the conflict between his recommendations and the received theory of democracy, according to which citizens ought to participate in discussions of public policy and to have a hand, if only indirectly, in decision making. Democratic theory, he argued, had roots in social conditions that no longer obtained. It presupposed an "omnicompetent citizen," a "jack of all trades" who could be found only in a "simple self-contained community." In the "wide and unpredictable environment" of the modern world, the old ideal of citizenship was obsolete. A complex industrial society required a government carried on by officials who would necessarily be guided—since any form of direct democracy was now impossible—either by public opinion or by expert knowledge. Public opinion was unreliable because it could be united only by an appeal to slogans and "symbolic pictures." Lippmann's distrust of public opinion rested on the epistemological distinction between truth and mere opinion. Truth, as he conceived it, grew out of disinterested scientific inquiry; everything else was ideology. The scope of public debate accordingly had to be severely restricted. At best public debate was a disagreeable necessity—not the very essence of democracy but its "primary defect," which arose only because "exact knowledge," unfortunately, was in limited supply. Ideally public debate would not take place at all; decisions would be based on scientific "standards of measurement" alone. Science cut through "entangling stereotypes and slogans," the "threads of memory and emotion" that kept the "responsible administrator" tied up in knots.

The role of the press, as Lippmann saw it, was to circulate information, not to encourage argument. The relationship between information and argument was antagonistic, not complementary. He did not take the position that reliable information was a necessary precondition of argument; on the contrary, his point was that information precluded argument, made argument unnecessary. Arguments were what took place in the absence of reliable information. Lippmann had forgotten what he learned (or should have learned) from William James and John Dewey: that our search for reliable information is itself guided by the questions that arise during arguments about a given course of action. It is only by subjecting our preferences and projects to the test of debate that we come to understand what we know and what we still need to learn. Until we have to defend our opinions in public, they remain opinions in Lippmann's pejorative sense—half-formed convictions based on random impressions and unexamined assumptions. It is the act of articulating and defending our views that lifts them out of the category of "opinions," gives them shape and definition, and makes it possible for others to recognize them as a description of their own experience as well. In short, we come to know our own minds only by explaining ourselves to others.

The attempt to bring others around to our own point of view carries the risk, of course, that we may adopt their point of view instead. We have to enter imaginatively into our opponents' arguments, if only for the purpose of refuting them, and we may end up being persuaded by those we sought to persuade. Argument is risky and unpredictable, therefore educational. Most of us tend to think of it (as Lippmann thought of it) as a clash of rival dogmas, a shouting match in which neither side gives any ground. But arguments are not won by shouting down opponents. They are won by changing opponents' minds—something that can happen only if we give opposing arguments a respectful hearing and still persuade their advocates that there is something wrong with those arguments. In the course of this activity we may well decide that there is something wrong with our own.

If we insist on argument as the essence of education, we will defend democracy not as the most efficient but as the most educational form of government, one that extends the circle of debate as widely as possible and thus forces all citizens to articulate their views, to put their views at risk, and to cultivate the virtues of eloquence, clarity of thought and expression, and sound judgment. As Lippmann noted, small communities are the classic locus of democracy—not because they are "self-contained," however, but simply because they allow everyone to take part in public debates. Instead of dismissing direct democracy as irrelevant to modern conditions, we need to re-create it on a large scale. From this point of view the press serves as the equivalent of the town meeting.

This is what Dewey argued, in effect—though not, unfortunately, very clearly—in *The Public and Its Problems* (1927), a book written in reply to Lippmann's disparaging studies of public opinion. Lippmann's distinction between truth and information rested on a "spectator theory of knowledge," as James W. Carey explains in his *Communication as Culture*. As Lippmann understood these matters, knowledge is what we get when an observer, preferably a scientifically trained observer, provides us with a copy of reality that we can all recognize. Dewey, on the other hand, knew that even scientists argue among themselves. "Systematic inquiry," he contended, was only the beginning of knowledge, not its final form. The knowledge needed by any community—whether it was a community of scientific inquirers or a political community—emerged only from "dialogue" and "direct give and take."

It is significant, as Carey points out, that Dewey's analysis of communication stressed the ear rather than the eye. "Conversation," Dewey wrote, "has a vital import lacking in the fixed and frozen words of written speech. . . . The connections of the ear with vital and outgoing thought and emotion are immensely closer and more varied than those of the eye. Vision is a spectator; hearing is a participator."

The press extends the scope of debate by supplementing the spoken word with the written word. If the press needs to apologize for anything, it is not that the written word is a poor substitute for the pure language of mathematics. What matters, in this connection, is that the written word is a poor substitute for the spoken word. It is an acceptable substitute, however, as long as written speech takes spoken speech and not mathematics as its model. According to Lippmann, the press was unreliable because it could never give us accurate representations of reality, only "symbolic pictures" and stereotypes. Dewey's analysis implied a more penetrating line of criticism. As Carey puts it, "The press, by seeing its role as that of informing the public, abandons its role as an agency for carrying on the conversation of our culture." Having embraced Lippmann's ideal of objectivity, the press no longer serves to cultivate "certain vital habits" in the community: "the ability to follow an argument, grasp the point of view of another, expand the boundaries of understanding, debate the alternative purposes that might be pursued."

The rise of the advertising and public relations industries, side by side, helps to explain why the press abdicated its most important function—enlarging the public forum—at the same time that it became more "responsible." A responsible press, as opposed to a partisan or opinionated one, attracted the kind of readers advertisers were eager to reach: well-heeled readers, most of whom probably thought of themselves as independent voters. These readers wanted to be assured that they were reading all the news that was fit to print, not an editor's idiosyncratic and no doubt biased view of things. Responsibility came to be equated with the avoidance of controversy because advertisers were willing to pay for it. Some advertisers were also willing to pay for sensationalism, though on the whole they preferred a respectable readership to sheer numbers. What they clearly did not prefer was "opinion"—not because they were impressed with Lippmann's philosophical arguments but because opinionated reporting did not guarantee the right audience. No doubt they also hoped that an aura of objectivity, the hallmark of responsible journalism, would also rub off on the advertisements that surrounded increasingly slender columns of print.

In a curious historical twist, advertising, publicity, and other forms of commercial persuasion themselves came to be disguised as information. Advertising and publicity substituted for open debate. "Hidden persuaders" (as Vance Packard called them) replaced the old-time editors, essayists, and orators who made no secret of their partisanship. Information and publicity became increasingly indistinguishable. Most of the "news" in our newspapers—40 percent, according to the conservative estimate of Professor Scott Cutlip of the University of Georgia—consists of items churned out by press agencies and public relations bureaus and then regurgitated intact by the "objective" organs of journalism. We have grown accustomed to the idea that most of the space in newspapers, so called, is devoted to advertising—at least two-thirds in most newspapers. But if we consider public relations as another form of advertising, which is hardly farfetched since private, commercially inspired enterprises fuel both, we now have to get used to the idea that much of the "news" consists of advertising too.

The decline of the partisan press and the rise of a new type of journalism professing rigorous standards of objectivity do not assure a steady supply of usable information. Unless information is generated by sustained public debate, most of it will be irrelevant at best, misleading and manipulative at worst. Increasingly information is generated by those who wish to promote something or someone—a product, a cause, a political candidate or officeholder—without arguing their case on its merits or explicitly advertising it as self-interested material either. Much of the press, in its eagerness to inform the public, has become a conduit for the equivalent of junk mail. Like the post office—another institution that once served to extend the sphere of face-to-face discussion and to create "committees of correspondence"—it now delivers an abundance of useless, indigestible information that nobody wants, most of which ends up as unread waste. The most important effect of this obsession with information, aside from the destruction of trees for paper and the mounting burden of "waste management," is to undermine the authority of the word. When words are used merely as instruments of publicity or propaganda, they lose their power to persuade. Soon they cease to mean anything at all. People lose the capacity to use language precisely and expressively or even to distinguish one word from another. The spoken word models itself on the written word instead of the other way around, and ordinary speech begins to sound like the clotted jargon we see in print. Ordinary speech begins to sound like "information"—a disaster from which the English language may never recover.

The Downside of the Digital Age

———— •◆• ————

Joseph Distel

Keywords

Digital Revolution
Cyberbullying
Memory
Dystopia
Social Media
Smartphones
Digital Culture

Abstract

This commentary discusses how the digital revolution has advanced human society in undeniably profound ways. But not all the changes have been improvements. The collateral damage acknowledged as consequences of the Digital Age includes the emboldened threat of invasion of privacy, the development and proliferation of online deception, and the tragedies of cyberbullying and perpetual harassment, among others. And while sexting converts hormonal teenagers into self-pornographers, the world wide web's permanent memory banks rob young and old users of the chance to erase the scarlet letters of their digital pasts. As for human memory, it has eroded as its technological supplements have become its substitutes.

Introduction: The Two-Sided Legacy of Steve Jobs

In the days, hours and minutes following the death of Steve Jobs on October 5, 2011, scores of online articles marked the passing of Apple's co-founder and former CEO with effusive praise and ample laudatory references and remarks. Hailed as a visionary genius (Moses, 2011), a trailblazer (Greenburg, 2011), a "philosopher-king" (Foley, 2011), a "world-changer" (Anthony, 2011), "a modern-day Leonardo da Vinci" (Knickerbocker, 2011), and "kind of like this generation's John Lennon" (Parker, 2011), Jobs exited this world exceptionally admired for his extraordinary contributions and achievements.

U.S. President Barack Obama remarked that Jobs was "among the greatest of American innovators— brave enough to think differently, bold enough to believe he could change the world and talented enough to do it" (Effron, 2011). Bob Iger, president of the Walt Disney Company, described Jobs as "such an original, with a thoroughly creative, imaginative mind that defined an era" (Effron, 2011). And, in a one-sentence tribute, Howard Stringer, president and CEO of Sony Corp., said, "The digital age has lost its leading light, but Steve's innovations and creativity will inspire dreamers and thinkers for generations" ("Sony CEO Stringer," 2011).

With Jobs having passed away so recently, the following concept may be perceived as callous, perhaps even bordering on sacrilege, but if Steve Jobs, the "mastermind behind Apple's iPhone, iPad, iPod, iMac and iTunes" (Potter & Curry, 2011) is to be so unreservedly credited for so many of the advances of the digital age, should he not be assigned at least some blame for the problems that continue to emerge as a direct consequence of our increasingly hi-tech world?

Cyberbullying, Online Deception, and the End of Personal Privacy

"JAMIE [sic] IS STUPID, GAY, FAT ANND [sic] UGLY. HE MUST DIE!" spewed one of the messages posted anonymously on 14-year-old Jamey Rodemeyer's profile page on Formspring, a social networking website. The Buffalo, N.Y. high school student had indicated on several social websites that he was struggling with his sexuality, and that he had become the target of bullies. "I always say how bullied I am, but no one listens," he posted on his Facebook page in early September 2011. "What do I have to do so people will listen to me?" (James, 2011).

Another offensive post on Rodemeyer's Formspring page read, "I wouldn't care if you died. No one would. So just do it:) It would make everyone WAY more happier!" (James, 2011). Rodemeyer, described by his parents as "a smiley, happy boy who loved to play his cello" (James, 2011), committed suicide in mid-September 2011.

About four months earlier, Rodemeyer posted a YouTube video in support of the "It Gets Better" project, an online initiative intended to reassure troubled and potentially suicidal lesbian, gay and bisexual youth that, despite the taunting, bullying and physical abuse they face as teenagers, life improves after high school. "Love yourself and you're set," he told viewers after chronicling his torment in school. "I promise you, it will get better" (Tan, 2011).

In the case of 17-year-old Alexis Pilkington of West Islip, Long Island, N.Y., the mean-spirited posts persisted after her March 2010 suicide. A memorial site created on Facebook by her friends quickly became littered with personal insults, sexually suggestive comments, even images of nooses and people with their heads blown off. Similar content appeared on Formspring (Kotz, 2010).

Numerous other stories are just as repulsively tragic. On October 17, 2006, three weeks shy of her 14th birthday, Megan Meier of Daddenne Prairie, Mo., hanged herself in her bedroom closet after she received messages on MySpace—supposedly from a 16-year-old boy named Josh Evans (Maag, 2007). Meier, who had a history of depression, became inconsolable when, after more than a month of cyber chatting (but never meeting or actually speaking) with Josh, she received this message from him on October 15: "I don't like the way you treat your friends, and I don't know if I want to be friends with you" (Maag, 2007). Meier also discovered that electronic bulletins were being posted about her, with such comments as "Megan Meier is a slut. Megan Meier is fat" ("Parents: Cyber Bullying," 2007).

Six weeks after their daughter's suicide, Tina and Ron Meier were informed by a neighbor that Megan had been the victim of a cruel hoax. The character of Josh Evans had been invented by another teen-aged girl (Brady, 2008), and she and the mother of another girl had used it to gain Megan's trust and learn what she was saying about the woman's daughter ("Parents: Cyber Bullying," 2007). Megan Meier died never knowing the terrible truth about her fatal online relationship.

A different kind of deception was perpetrated by William Melchert-Dinkel, but with similar irreversible results. Posing as a depressed woman in her 20s, Melchert-Dinkel, a male nurse living in Minnesota, connected with 18-year-old Nadia Kajouji, a student at Carleton University in Ottawa, Ontario, in 2008, and 32-year-old Mark Drybrough of Coventry, England, approximately three years earlier (Ambroz, 2010). Melchert-Dinkel allegedly used Yahoo and Google chats to instruct his two despondent contacts on how to tie and hang a noose. He also allegedly encouraged them to use a webcam so he could witness the suicides ("Minnesota nurse charged," 2010). In a message to Kajouji, who drowned in March 2008 after throwing herself into Ottawa's Rideau River, Melchert-Dinkel, using the name "Cami," wrote, "if you wanted to do hanging we could have done it together on line so it would not have been so scary for you" (Williams, 2010).

Tyler Clementi, an 18-year-old gay student at Rutgers University in New Jersey, jumped to his death from the George Washington Bridge, which spans the Hudson River, on September 22, 2010 (Gendar, Sandoval & McShane, 2010). As reported in the *New York Daily News,* Clementi killed himself after his "dorm-room rendezvous [with another male] was surreptitiously streamed on the Web via his [roommate's] hidden camera" (Gendar, Sandoval & McShane, 2010).

Three nights before Clementi's death, his roommate Dharun Ravi, also 18, wrote on Twitter, "Roommate asked for the room till midnight. I went into Molly's room and turned on my webcam. I saw him making out with a dude. Yay" (Gendar, Sandoval & McShane, 2010). The "Molly" Ravi refers to is 18-year-old Molly Wei, a fellow Rutgers student who resided on the same floor as Clementi and Ravi (Pilkington, 2010). Using Skype and Wei's computer, Ravi allegedly accessed the webcam on his own computer, which was located in the dorm room he shared with Clementi (Pilkington, 2010). It is claimed that Ravi broadcast the details of his voyeuristic escapade to the 150 followers of his Twitter feed. Two nights later, Ravi tweeted, "Anyone with iChat, I dare you to video chat me between the hours of 9:30 and 12. Yes it's happening again" (Pilkington, 2010).

As Adam Hanft (2010), founder and CEO of Hanft Projects and an occasional writer for *The Daily Beast, The Huffington Post* and *Politics Daily,* sees it, social media killed Tyler Clementi. Hanft (2010) writes:

> [Clementi's death is] a story of what happens when two ordinary, probably decent people get swept up in the notion that the world exists for our manipulation and delectation—to be proliferated through whatever channels we have available—while we stay safely and remotely removed from harm. Facebook, Twitter, Tumblr, Flickr, YouTube—they are all unmediated platforms for whatever runs into our brains, or whatever our brains run into [...] Today's social media world prides itself on an ethic of sharing. It runs on amped-up immediacy that races ahead of our ability to reflect, judge and consider. We post, we comment, we exchange in what is increasingly a new kind of reflex behavior. In terms of brain biology, what happens is that our ability to calmly consider is pushed down by a deeper instinct. And the "automatic" part of our brain—which is the most ancient system—jumps

ahead of the "reflective" part [...] Distance provides emotional safety. The same buffer that technology offered Clementi's videographers is a criticism often leveled against the drone attacks on Pakistan. There's no doubt that remote killing is easy and sanitized; you can be sure that if someone had to stand in the corner of the bedroom and film the sex scene, Tyler Clementi would be alive today. Instead a drone camera was installed and the video automated. Remote killing is what happened in Rutgers.

As reflected in the above stories and comments, social networking sites, webcams and e-mail have made bullying, intimidation, deception and emotional manipulation much easier and more tempting for the perpetrators because they now can be invasive and abusive with merely a few clicks and keystrokes, much more frequently, and seemingly from a place of comfort and seclusion. Their simple actions can now also cause greater, more lasting damage. As Gorman and McLean (2009) note:

> While bullying is not new, the online environment can embolden persecutors (not coming face-to-face with their victim, feeling protected by anonymity), provide access to previously private activities (photographs taken on mobile phones in a school sports change room can quickly be uploaded to a website and distributed widely), and exacerbate the effects of bullying (victims are unable to escape—cyberbullying knows no boundaries and transcends the schoolyard—and demeaning or humiliating information can be spread to a global audience in a short time). (p. 247)

Among the questions the author of this paper posed to his interview subjects was: "What do you believe is the most realistic, proactive protection against cyberbullying, given the widespread acceptance of chatrooms, video sharing, instant messaging, and so on?" Jim G. (note: all names of interview subjects for this paper have been changed), a 43-year-old gay man from Stoney Creek, Ontario, who estimates he spends 18 hours per week online, responded:

> There has always been bullying, and, there will, sadly, always be bullying. People have just found new and more sophisticated ways of doing it [...] The Internet is based on hate, and it's easier for people to post things anonymously. We have created a place where anyone can now be a bully because even weak people can hide behind their

computers now. We need to be able to find these haters and punish them. ("Jim G.," personal communication, October 5, 2011)

The sentiments expressed by Jim G. complement those of Christopher Wolf, former chair of the International Network Against Cyber-Hate (INACH), who, in an address to INACH in November 2007, stated:

> In the Internet era, it appears there are more people interested in spewing hate than in countering it. On the social networking sites and on YouTube, inflammatory, hate-filled content overwhelms the limited efforts to promote tolerance and to teach diversity. And, as we have seen, hate speech inspires violence. (Wolf, 2007)

Hanft's (2010) reference to an "amped-up immediacy that races ahead of our ability to reflect, judge and consider" pertains to countless uses and abuses of today's digital technology. When immediacy meets impulsiveness, the consequences, as in the cases involving Tyler Clementi and Jamey Rodemeyer, can be deadly. In other cases, the results may be far less severe but life-altering in their own way.

Sex, Tech and Regrets

Consider the story of the three female high school students, aged 14 and 15, from Pennsylvania who were charged in 2008 with manufacturing, disseminating or possessing child pornography after they allegedly took nude or semi-nude photographs of themselves and shared the photos with male classmates via their cell phones. Two male students, aged 16 and 17, were also charged with possessing child pornography (Brunker, 2009). While some critics called this reaction extreme, the local police captain hoped the charges laid against the teenagers would send a strong message to other minors familiar with and/or interested in the practice of so-called "sexting" (Brunker, 2009).

"It's very dangerous," said Police Capt. George Seranko. "Once it's on a cell phone, that cell phone can be put on the Internet where everyone in the world can get access to that juvenile picture. You don't realize what you are doing until it's already done" (Brunker, 2009).

In late 2008, the National Campaign to Prevent Teen and Unplanned Pregnancy and its research partners released a study called "Sex and Tech" that examined technology's role in the sex lives of teens and young adults. Of the teens aged 13 to 19 that had participated in the study, **19 percent** stated they had sent a sexually suggestive picture or video of themselves to someone via e-mail, cell phone or by another mode, and 31 percent had received a nude or semi-nude picture from someone else (Lenhart, 2009).

A March 2009 study conducted by Cox Communications in partnership with the National Center for Missing and Exploited Children and Harris Interactive reported that **9 percent** of teens aged 13–18 had sent a sexually suggestive text message or e-mail with nude or nearly-nude photos, **3 percent** had forwarded one, and **17 percent** had received one (Lenhart, 2009).

Sexting can be a high-tech way to flirt with someone, or it can be a means to harass other people. Intentions aside, it's a practice that can quickly and easily complicate many lives. As Clark-Flory (2009) notes:

> These digital offerings bring the potential for humiliation and blackmail if the photos or video get into the wrong hands—and, let's face it, they often do. Acting as your girlfriend's personal porno star is one thing; ending up a pedophile's favorite child pinup is quite another [...] [so] there's good reason to be concerned about teens being self-pornographers. (paras. 13–14)

Reimer (2009) echoes a point worth emphasizing:

> The problem is that, unlike love letters that can be tossed in the fireplace when the relationship is over, nothing in cyberspace ever really gets deleted. A relationship goes south, and an aggrieved party can use those indiscreet photos and messages to hurt and humiliate. There are even websites just for the purpose of burning your ex." (paras. 13–14)

Permanent Records Open to a Global Public

Of course, not everyone needs to worry about X-rated photographs or racy videos following them into their future; for some people, the source of anxiety might be a candid photo from a frat-house party, a disparaging Facebook post about an overbearing boss, an online notation of an ill-considered political donation, or simply an irresponsible, perhaps alcohol-induced, blog entry or consumer comment that threatens to resurface at the most inopportune time.

Indeed, every moment we, someone we know, or someone we don't know posts online a photo, video, comment or other content that represents us and/or reflects back on us in some small or large way, it becomes yet another piece of our permanent digital record. And, as soon as that information gets online (if not before), we lose control of it, and it essentially belongs to the masses who then may be able to twist, turn or repackage it however and as often as they like. In an article in *The New York Times Magazine* entitled "The Web Means the End of Forgetting," Rosen (2010) writes:

> With Web sites like LOL Facebook Moments, which collects and shares embarrassing personal revelations from Facebook users, ill-advised photos and online chatter are coming back to haunt people months or years after the fact. Examples are proliferating daily: there was the 16-year-old British girl who was fired from her office job for complaining on Facebook, "I'm so totally bored!!"; there was the 66-year-old Canadian psychotherapist who tried to enter the United States but was turned away at the border—and barred permanently from visiting the country—after a border guard's Internet search found that the therapist had written an article in a philosophy journal describing his experiments 30 years ago with L.S.D. (para. 2)

In a recent survey by Microsoft, 75 percent of U.S. recruiters and human resources professionals reported that their companies require them to conduct online research on their candidates, and many of them look to search engines, social networking sites, photo- and video-sharing sites, online gaming sites, and personal websites and blogs for their information (Rosen, 2010, para. 3).

Rosen (2010) goes on to write:

> It's often said that we live in a permissive era, one with infinite second chances. But the truth is that for a great many people, the permanent memory banks of the Web increasingly means there are *no* second chances—no opportunities to escape a scarlet letter in your digital past. Now the worst thing you've done is often the first thing everyone knows about you. (para. 8)

Rosen's (2010) reference to Nathaniel Hawthorne's 1850 novel *The Scarlet Letter* is apropos. Hawthorne's celebrated work follows Hester Prynne, a woman forced by her colonial New England village to wear the scarlet letter *A* to represent her sin of adultery. As Solove (2007) observes in his book "The Future of Reputation: Gossip, Rumor, and Privacy on the Internet," "the Internet is bringing back the scarlet letter in digital form—an indelible record of people's past deeds" (p. 11).

The author of this paper posed the following question to his interview subjects: "When you or your child(ren) engage in online activity, how conscious are you of the online content's indelibility as it's being posted or shared, and how comfortable are you with the prospect of the information casually posted or shared today re-emerging and influencing other people's judgements of you or your child(ren) in the future?"

Sharon D., a 43-year-old receptionist and crisis responder from Kitchener, Ontario, who estimates she spends about three hours per week using Facebook and e-mail nonprofessionally, offered the following as part of her answer:

> My mother told me something I've never let go of. She said, "Never put anything in writing that you can't take back." I live by those words to this day. I shy away from posting relationship status [and other] personal information [like] what I ate for breakfast because it's my business and mine alone. ("Sharon D.," personal communication, October 7, 2011)

With her response, Jill P., a 40-something interior decorator and professional fundraiser, also residing in Kitchener, Ontario, kept her four children, ages 17 to 23, squarely in mind:

> I constantly caution my children to be extremely careful [of] what they share [online], as prospective employers can always Google or Facebook them. I think it's difficult for teenagers to really see long-term impacts of their social networking, as most live in the moment and do not understand how the adult mind works and how adults hold people to different standards than their peers do. ("Jill P.," personal communication, October 6, 2011)

Jim G.'s answer suggests mixed feelings about his self-censorship:

> I quite honestly think about everything I write on the Internet. I try to be myself, but [I] make sure

I phrase things in ways not to make me look too bad or opinionated. I do not talk about particular stuff like where I work, religion, or intimate details of my relationship too often. I don't think too much about [my information] never being able to be erased, but [I] try not to ever put anything out there that people will judge too harshly [...] Early in my life I was afraid to speak my mind and [I] tried to make everyone happy. I need to speak more openly and honest now, and I would never go back to the days where I didn't speak at all. ("Jim G.," personal communication, October 5, 2011)

Imagine that you could never escape your past and that you could never be allowed to redefine yourself in the eyes of others. Imagine that you and other people, both strangers and friends, could witness various episodes and artifacts from your life pre-sobriety, pre-therapy, pre-personal epiphany or pre-normal adult maturation over and over again. That awkward fielding error that cost your high school ball team the regional championship. That embarrassing karaoke performance from a long-ago New Year's Eve. That regrettable Halloween costume. That immature act of vengeance against your ex. That mawkish love letter. That incriminating photo. That "between-friends" video clip. That off-the-cuff remark. That racial slur. That lie.

Thanks to the astounding archiving ability of the Internet, not all memories fade away as easily as they used to. As Mayer-Schonberger (2009) articulates it:

Memory impedes change. That is true for all memory. In analog times, however, memory remained expensive—and comprehensive, timely, and affordable access to it was largely elusive. We used external memory deliberately, not casually, and not all the time. Employed sparingly and judiciously, memory is a valuable treasure, it seasons our decision-making like a delicate spice. Digital remembering, on the other hand, today is so omnipresent, costless, and seemingly "valuable"— due to accessibility, durability, and comprehensiveness—that we are tempted to employ it constantly. Utilized in such indiscriminating fashion, digital memory not only dulls the judgment of the ones who remember but also denies those who are remembered the temporal space to evolve. (p. 126)

Mayer-Schonberger (2009) adds:

As humans we do not travel ignorantly through time. With our capacity to remember, we are able to compare, to learn, and to experience time as change. Equally important is our ability to forget, to unburden ourselves from the shackles of our past, and to live in the present. For millennia, the relationship between remembering and forgetting remained clear. Remembering was hard and costly, and humans had to choose deliberately what to remember. The default was to forget. In the digital age, in what is perhaps the most fundamental change for humans since our humble beginnings, that balance of remembering and forgetting has become inverted. Committing information to digital memory has become the default, and forgetting the exception. (p. 196)

Draining Our Brains for Questionable Gains

It could be argued that the modem technology of our digital age is actually doing each of us a favor by archiving our lives and providing us such easy access to our past, for who needs to actively remember information when it's just a few mouse-clicks away? However, those of us who use technology such as the Internet on a frequent basis are each receiving that favor at a price, and the asset of ours that is dwindling is, ironically enough, our memory.

Carr (2010), author of "The Shallows: What the Internet Is Doing to Our Brains," writes that:

The more we use the Web, the more we train our brain to be distracted—to process information very quickly and very efficiently but without sustained attention. That helps to explain why many of us find it hard to concentrate even when we're away from our computers. Our brains become adept at forgetting, inept at remembering. Our growing dependence on the Web's information stores may in fact be the product of a self-perpetuating, self-amplifying loop. As our use of the Web makes it harder for us to lock information into our biological memory, we're forced to rely more and more on the Net's capacious and easily searchable artificial memory, even if it makes us shallower thinkers. (p. 194)

To this point, among others, interview subjects for this paper were asked, "Based on your own experiences and/or your observations of others, what is your opinion of the suggestion that people's increasing use of digital technology is adversely affecting their memory, deep or critical thinking skills, ability to concentrate and ignore distractions, and resistance to developing impulsive and/or addictive behaviors?"

Twenty-five-year-old Wendy C., a resident of Kitchener, Ontario, has no children and spends an estimated 20 hours per week participating in social media and other associated activities. She said that when she surfs the Internet, she does so mostly for news and celebrity gossip. In her response to the above question, she admitted relying on digital technology to help her remember certain responsibilities:

> For example, if I am by a computer and I want to remind myself to pick something up, to do something later on during the day, or to pay my bills online, I will e-mail myself [...] I am not certain if I have a bad memory, or if the convenience of a computer or my phone is making me lazy and not wanting to remember certain things. ("Wendy C.," personal communication, October 8, 2011)

Brandy K., a 45-year-old painter and freelance fact-checker who lives in Paris, Ontario, estimated she spends between 25 and 30 hours per week on social media sites. Having recently ended a long-term lesbian relationship with "Fran," she soon after re-established contact with a former partner who now lives in Minnesota. Regarding any related issues with her memory, Brandy said:

> Because of the short bursts of interaction with many people, without face-to-face time, I sometimes lose track of who I've told what to. For instance, through all the crap with Fran, I would have many friends texting, messaging me, etc., and I would update as succinctly as I could, but I would lose track of who I had updated what to. Skype is a little different, because when you have an actual conversation with someone, it's a natural back-and-forth, [and] it's not like minutes or hours pass between responses, plus you get that face-time with the person [...] I also find when you know that you have things "on your phone," you know you have a record of it. So when I make plans with someone, I don't feel a strong need to commit the details to memory since I know I can just look back to my phone. In the old days, I would repeat the time a few times to myself and mark it down on my calendar as soon as I got home. ("Brandy K.," personal communication, October 9, 2011)

Brandy and Wendy (and so many others with similar dependence) might want to ponder these words from Carr (2010):

> The Web provides a convenient and compelling supplement to personal memory, but when we start using the Web as a substitute for personal memory, bypassing the inner processes of consolidation, we risk emptying our minds of their riches. (p. 192)

Interestingly, as Brandy explained when she addressed the concept of digital technology exacerbating impulsive or addictive behavior, her relationship with "Fran" began on an online dating website, and several online dating sites also contributed to the relationship's eventual breakdown.

> I think Fran already had an impulsive disorder, [and] the Internet absolutely ramped that up [...] I think her being on dating sites [during our relationship] was definitely an impulse issue. She needed that immediate gratification. She put ads on, and within hours she was fielding responses. The more ads she put up, the more attention she was getting. But I feel pretty strongly that the Internet doesn't cause these problems, but it certainly makes them evident and often brings out bad behavior in people. ("Brandy K.," personal communication, October 9, 2011)

As for digital technology adversely affecting a person's ability to concentrate and ignore distractions, research points to some distressing news there as well. As Carr (2010) summarizes:

> Our use of the Internet involves many paradoxes, but the one that promises to have the greatest long-term influence over how we think is this one: the Net seizes our attention only to scatter it. We focus intensively on the medium itself, on the flickering screen, but we're distracted by the medium's rapid-fire delivery of competing messages and stimuli. Whenever and wherever we log on, the Net presents us with an incredibly seductive blur [...] The Net's cacophony of stimuli short-circuits both conscious and unconscious thought, preventing our minds from thinking either deeply or creatively. Our brains turn into simple, signal-processing units, quickly shepherding information into consciousness and then back out again. (pp. 118–119)

Mona F., a 39-year-old resident of central Pennsylvania who describes herself as disabled, has a 10-year-old daughter with special needs. She believes wholeheartedly that digital technology can present formidable challenges to people with addictive and impulsive tendencies:

> If someone has an addictive personality, the risks are that much greater because digital technology is no different for that individual than a slot machine, smoking, drinking, etc., due to the instant gratification factor [...] Moreover, I know from experience with my own child that digital technology can be very harmful for children who already have difficulty with impulsive behavior due to mental health diagnoses such as ADHD (attention deficit hyperactivity disorder), Asperger's Disorder, and ODD (oppositional defiant disorder). The extreme movement on the digital screens over stimulate the brains of people with these diagnoses, contributing to difficulties like loss of sleep and an overall inability to slow down their brain activity. ("Mona F.," personal communication, October 10, 2011)

Compromising Our Abilities to Think Big, Get Close, Break Free, and Go Far

Other interview subjects commented almost nostalgically about the sacrifices they believe have been forced by the digital revolution, deep thinking and an appreciation of knowledge being among them. Consider the response from Edward J., a 45-year Canadian Forces chaplain with the rank of captain, currently stationed in Kabul, Afghanistan, to the following set of questions: "How do you think the digital age has influenced how people under 30 view themselves, their relationships, and their responsibilities to the future? What, if anything, has it done to their work ethic and personal productivity? How has your own use of digital technology shaped your sense of self, your work ethic and productivity?"

> I have a sense that, due to the influence of the instant availability of material on the Web and the ubiquity of information, that knowledge—its value—has been downgraded. I can look up anything on Wikipedia and find out all about it in a couple of minutes. It's a great resource. However, I didn't have to work [much to get the information]; I didn't have to troll through a library, read exten-

sively, collate that information, and ruminate on it. I simply typed a query and received a response almost instantly. All knowledge is now data, and data is not held in as high esteem as knowledge. [Knowledge] is gained through labor—experience, thoughtfulness, reflection, interaction with others—[data] is simply obtained. This also speaks to the place of wisdom in society today. It was once said that having knowledge is not the same as having wisdom; wisdom is the application of knowledge and its intersection with life and experience. If anything, the digital age has exacerbated this. ("Edward J.," personal communication, October 6, 2011)

Although Edward's response misses much of the thrust of the posed questions, it is nonetheless insightful and certainly relevant to the topic of this paper. But for an opinion from someone under 30, attention must turn back to Wendy, who shares part of Edward's view but goes on to comment on digital tools' impact on human relationships:

> I think that some people may rely too much on technology and that will make them less motivated in their responsibilities to either themselves or to their future [...] People under 30 are [so] used to having things in an instant and information at their fingertips that they have forgotten about the conventional ways of researching information, i.e., the public library. I also think that because people under 30 have had so much exposure to the constant technological innovations they are forgetting about personal relationships. The digital age has, in some instances, diminished an intimate conversation between two people. Before the digital age, a conversation either over the phone or in person was the norm. Now, instant messaging and Facebook are used as the main communications tools for relationships. ("Wendy C.," personal communication, October 8, 2011)

A quick check of the dictionary points to a key distinction between personal communications and digital communications. The word "personal" pertains "to the self," while the word "digital" pertains "to the fingers." As Jill implied, when communication starts to favor the fingers so blatantly and discount the participation of the whole human body, it reduces what has the potential to be a complex, nuanced exchange to little more than a sharing of language.

Of young people who converse primarily via digital technology, Jill noted:

> I think they are losing valuable communication skills—the whole concept of seeing what people *aren't* saying and interpreting gestures and facial expressions to understand the meaning of the words they are using. Eye contact and being able to read people and develop an emotional intelligence could be lost on many of these teenagers. ("Jill P.," personal communication, October 6, 2011)

Perhaps unconsciously alluding to cases like those of Megan Meier, Nadia Kajouji, and Mark Drybrough mentioned earlier, Mona drew a connection between digital relationships and the pretense of understanding, support and closeness from which some are borne:

> I believe that it is very difficult to develop a personal relationship [dependent mostly on digital technology] because online conversation is much different than face-to-face communication due to the depth of emotion that is missing in online communication. For this reason, much of the emotion is assumed and interpreted by the *"Sitz im Leben"* ("setting in life") of the reader. Moreover, I feel that one can be lured to have a false sense of security in the person on the other end of the communication, hence one or both individuals could find themselves in a dangerous situation leading to loss of money, family, and even life. ("Mona F.," personal communication, October 10, 2011)

That false sense of security that Mona mentioned has turned countless people, particularly young people, into victims of online frauds and digital deceptions, and too often the perpetrators have eluded reasonable reprimand. Bauerlein (2008), author of "The Dumbest Generation: How the Digital Age Stupefies Young Americans and Jeopardizes Our Future," argues that many of the under-30 digital tech users are allowing themselves to be duped each moment they immerse themselves in their favorite online activities:

> The Web universe licenses young Americans to indulge their youth, and the ubiquitous rhetoric of personalization and empowerment—MySpace, YouTube, etc.—disguises the problem and implants false expectations well into adulthood. They don't realize that success in popular online youthworlds breeds incompetence in school and in the workplace. With no guidance from above, with content purveyors aiming to attract audiences, not educate them, young users think that communications come easy. With fewer filters on people's input and output, young users think that their opinions count and their talents suffice. They don't realize what it really takes to do well. (p. 158)

And Gabler (2011), in an opinion column in *The New York Times Sunday Review* entitled "The Elusive Big Idea," writes of participating witnesses to the digital age both young and old when he points to yet another depressing development:

> We prefer knowing to thinking because knowing has more immediate value. It keeps us in the loop, keeps us connected to our friends and our cohort. Ideas are too airy, too impractical, too much work for too little reward. Few talk ideas. Everyone talks information, usually personal information. Where are you going? What are you doing? Whom are you seeing? These are today's big questions [...] We have become information narcissists, so uninterested in anything outside ourselves and our friendship circles or in any tidbit we cannot share with those friends that if a Marx or a Nietzsche were suddenly to appear, blasting his ideas, no one would pay the slightest attention [...] What the future portends is more and more information—Everests of it. There won't be anything we won't know. But there will be no one thinking about it.

If we are to believe what the above experts and authorities have so eloquently stated, we now exist in an age of information overload and trivial pursuits, inescapable pasts and constricted futures, sexting students and savvy seducers, nascent global narcissism and "(s)he who has the most Facebook friends wins," and reconfigured brain circuitry but mediocre minds.

We know how Eve's apple transformed Adam's world, and now we can understand better than ever the monumental ways in which Steve Jobs' Apple has helped to transform ours.

The evidence stands as a warning to every active participant of the Digital Age to recognize the risks, threats and temptations before them and to respond to them responsibly, both for their own individual welfare and for that of the global society of which they are a remarkably influential and powerful part.

Works Cited

Ambroz, J. (2010, April 24). Former Minnesota nurse charged in two suicides: Faribault, Minn. man made 10 suicide pacts online. Retrieved October 9, 2011, from http://www.myfox twin cities.com/dpp/ news/minnesota /william-melchert-dinkel-suicide-pacts-online-apr-23-2010

Anthony, T. (2011, October 6). The world-changer: Steve Jobs knew what we wanted. Retrieved October 8, 2011, from http://hosted.ap.org/dynamic/stories/U/US_JOBS_THE_WORLD_CHANGER?PSITE=AP&SECTION=HOME&TEMPLATE=DEFAULT&CTIME=2011-10-05-21-43-56

Bauerlein, M. (2008). *The dumbest generation: How the digital age stupefies young Americans and jeopardizes our future* (*Or, don't trust anyone under 30).* New York: Penguin Group (U.S.A.) Inc.

Brady, J. (2008, April 1). Exclusive: Teen talks about her role in Web hoax that led to suicide. Retrieved October 8, 2011, from http://abcnews.go.com/ GMA/ story?id=4560582&page=1

Brunker, M. (2009, January 15). Sexting surprise: Teens face child porn charges. Retrieved October 10, 2011, from http://www.msnbc.msn.com/id/28679588#.Tp0Hb71xjt8

Carr, N. (2010). The shallows: *What the Internet is doing to our brains.* New York: W. W. Norton & Co., Inc.

Clark-Flory, T. (2009, February 20). The new pornographers. Retrieved October 10, 2011, from http://www.salon.com/2009/02/20/sexting_teens/

Effron, L. (2011, October 5). President Obama, Mark Zuckerberg, others react to Steve Jobs' death. Retrieved October 8, 2011, from http://abcnews.go.com/Technology/reaction-steve-jobs-death/story?id=14678187

Foley, S. (2011, October 7). Steve Jobs: The man who suffered no fools will be an impossible act to follow. Retrieved October 9, 2011, from http://www.belfastelegraph.co.uk/lifestyle/technology-gadgets/steve-jobs-the-man-who-suffered-no-fools-will-be-an-impossible-act-to-follow-16060448.html

Gabler, N. (2011, August 13). The Elusive Big Idea [Electronic version]. *The New York Times Sunday Review.* Retrieved October 11, 2011, from http:www.nytimes.com/2011/08/14/opinion/ Sunday/the-elusive-big-idea.html

Gendar, A., Sandoval, E., & McShane, L. (2010, September 29). Rutgers freshman kills self after classmates use hidden camera to watch his sexual activity: sources [Electronic version]. *The New York Daily News.* Retrieved October 9, 2011, from http:articles.nydailynews.com/2010-09-29/news/27076776_1_roommate-twitter-criminal probe

Gorman, L., & McLean, D. (2009). *Media and society into the 21st century: A historical introduction.* West Sussex, U.K.: John Wiley & Sons, Ltd.

Greenburg, Z. O. (2011, October 6). Steve Jobs: The death of the most important man in music. Retrieved October 7, 2011, from http://www.forbes.com/sites/zackomalleygreenburg/2011/10/06/steve-jobs-the-death-of-the-most-important-man-in-music/

Hanft, A. (2010, October 1). Opinion: How social media killed Tyler Clementi. Retrieved October 9, 2011, from http://www.aolnews.com/2010/10/01/opinion-how-social-media-killed-tyler-clementi/

James, S. D. (2011, September, 22). Jamey Rodemeyer suicide: Police consider criminal Bullying charges. Retrieved October 8, 2011, from http://abcnews.go.com/Health/Jamey-rodemeyer-suicide-ny-police-open-criminal-investigation/ story?id=14580832

Kajouji's video diary shows path to suicide. (2009, October 9). Retrieved October 9, 2011, from http://www.cbc.ca/news/Canada/Ottawa/story/2009/10/09/ottawa-kajouji-fifth-estate-diary-suicide.html

Knickerbocker, B. (2011, October 6). Steve Jobs wanted to change the world, and he did (video) [Electronic version]. *The Christian Science Monitor.* Retrieved October 8, 2011, from http://www.csmonitor.com/USA/2011/1006/Steve-Jobs-wanted-to-change-the-world-and-he-did-video

Kotz, P. (2010, March 25). Alexis Pilkington, 17, commits suicide: Another victim of cyberbullying? Retrieved October 8, 2011, from http://www. truecrimereport.com/2010/03/alexis_pilkington_17_commits_s.php

Lenhart, A. (2009). Teens and sexting: How and why minor teens are sending sexually suggestive nude or nearly nude images via text messaging [Electronic version]. Pew Research Center. Retrieved October 10, 2011, from http://pewinternet.ogr/~/media//Files/Reports/20/09/PIP_Teens_and_Sexting.pdf

Maag, C. (2007, November 28). A hoax turned fatal draws anger but no charges [Electronic version]. *The New York Times.* Retrieved October 9, 2011, from http://www.nytimes.com/2007/ 11/28/us/28 hoax.html?_r=1&oref=slogin

Mayer-Schonberger, V. (2009). *Delete: The virtue of forgetting in the digital age.* Princeton: Princeton University Press.

Minnesota nurse charged with assisting in British and Canadian suicides. (2010, April 24). Retrieved October 8, 2011, from http://www. couriermail. com.au/news/breaking-news/ minnesota-nurse-charged-with-assisting- in-british-and-canadian-suicides/story-e6freonf- 1225857829324

Moses, A. (2011, October 13). Who is the next Steve Jobs? Retrieved October 17, 2011, from www.watoday.com.au/technology/technology- news/who-is-the-next-steve-jobs- 20111013llxo.html

Parents: Cyber bullying led to teen's suicide. (2007, November 19). Retrieved October 9, 2011, from http://abcnews.go.com/GMA/Story?id-3882520

Parker, R. (2011, October 7). iSad: Tears and trib- utes around the world as Apple's legions of fans mark the death of Steve Jobs. Retrieved October 9, 2011, from http://www.dailymail.com.uk/ news/ article-2045903/Steve-Jobs-dead-Tributes- Apples-legions-fans-mark-death-hero.html

Pilkington, E. (2010, September 30). Tyler Clementi, student outed as gay on Internet, jumps to his death. Retrieved October 9, 2011, from http:// www.guardian.co.uk/world/2010/sep/30/tyler- clementi-gay-student-suicide

Potter, N., & Curry, C. (2011, October 6). Steve Jobs dies: Apple chief created personal computer, iPad, iPod, iPhone. Retrieved October 8, 2011, from http://news.yahoo.com/steve-jobs-dies-apple- chief- created-personal-computer-ipad-ipod- iphone.html

Reimer, S. (2009, January 6). The middle ages: Young people, texting and sexting. Retrieved October 10, 2011, from http://tdn.com/lifestyles/ article_18c2 74f6-ead0-5eb1-a5f0-9b41e8fef 808.html

Rosen, J. (2010, July 21). The Web means the end of forgetting [Electronic version]. *The New York Times Magazine.* Retrieved October 11, 2011, from http://www.nytimes.com/2010.07/25 magazine/ 25privacy-t2.html

Solove, D. J. (2007). *The future of reputation: Gossip, rumor, and privacy on the Internet.* New Haven: Yale University Press.

Sony CEO Stringer expresses sadness over Jobs' passing [Electronic version]. (2011, October 5). *The Washington Post.* Retrieved October 9, 2011, from http://www.washingtonpost.com/ business/sony-ceo-stringer-expresses-sadness-over- jobs-passing/2011/10/05/gIQAf9hsOL_story.html

Tan, S. (2011, September 27). Teenager struggled with bullying before taking his life [Electronic version]. *The Buffalo News.* Retrieved October 8, 2011, from http://www.buffalonews.com/city/ schools/ article563538.ece

Williams, C. (2010, April 23). Minn. man charged with aiding suicides via the Web [Electronic ver- sion]. *The Seattle Times.* Retrieved October 9, 2011, from http://seattletimes.newsource.com/html/ nationworld/2011683761_apusencouragingsuicides .html

Wolf, C. (2007, November 8). Opening remarks to the International Network Against Cyber- Hate. Retrieved October 8, 2011, from www.social networking.procon.org/view.answers. php?questionID-001614#answer-id-010391

The Story Behind the Story

Mark Bowden

If you happened to be watching a television news channel on May 26, the day President Obama nominated U.S. Circuit Court Judge Sonia Sotomayor to the Supreme Court, you might have been struck, as I was, by what seemed like a nifty investigative report.

First came the happy announcement ceremony at the White House, with Sotomayor sweetly saluting her elderly mother, who as a single parent had raised the prospective justice and her brother in a Bronx housing project. Obama had chosen a woman whose life journey mirrored his own: an obscure, disadvantaged beginning followed by blazing academic excellence, an Ivy League law degree, and a swift rise to power. It was a moving TV moment, well-orchestrated and in perfect harmony with the central narrative of the new Obama presidency.

But then, just minutes later, journalism rose to perform its time-honored pie-throwing role. Having been placed by the president on a pedestal, Sotomayor was now a clear target. I happened to be watching Fox News. I was slated to appear that night on one of its programs, *Hannity,* to serve as a willing foil to the show's cheerfully pugnacious host, Sean Hannity, a man who can deliver a deeply held conservative conviction on any topic faster than the speed of thought. Since the host knew what the sub-

ject matter of that night's show would be and I did not, I'd thought it best to check in and see what Fox was preoccupied with that afternoon.

With Sotomayor, of course — and the network's producers seemed amazingly well prepared. They showed a clip from remarks she had made on an obscure panel at Duke University in 2005, and then, reaching back still farther, they showed snippets from a speech she had made at Berkeley Law School in 2001. Here was this purportedly moderate Latina judge, appointed to the federal bench by a Republican president and now tapped for the Supreme Court by a Democratic one, unmasked as a Race Woman with an agenda. In one clip she announced herself as someone who believed her identity as a "Latina woman" (a redundancy, but that's what she said) made her judgment superior to that of a "white male," and in the other she all but unmasked herself as a card-carrying member of the Left Wing Conspiracy to use America's courts not just to apply and interpret the law but, in her own words, to *make policy,* to perform an end run around the other two branches of government and impose liberal social policies by fiat on an unsuspecting American public.

In the Duke clip, she not only stated that appellate judges make policy, she did so in a disdainful mock disavowal before a chuckling audience of apparently like-minded conspirators. "I know this is on tape and I should never say that, because we don't make law, I know," she said before being interrupted by laughter. "Okay, I know. I'm not promoting it, I'm not advocating it, I'm … you know," flipping her hands dismissively. More laughter.

Holy cow! I'm an old reporter, and I know legwork when I see it. Those crack journalists at Fox, better known for coloring and commenting endlessly on the news than for actually breaking it, had unearthed not one but two explosive gems, and had been primed to expose Sotomayor's darker purpose *within minutes of her nomination*! Leaving aside for the moment any question about the context of these seemingly damaging remarks — none was offered — I was impressed. In my newspaper years, I prepared my share of advance profiles of public figures, and I know the scut work that goes into sifting through a decades-long career. In the old days it meant digging through packets of yellowed clippings in the morgue, interviewing widely, searching for those moments of controversy or surprise that revealed something interesting about the subject. How many rulings, opinions, articles, legal arguments, panel discussions, and speeches had there been in the judge's long years of service? What bloodhound producer at Fox News had waded into this haystack to find these two choice needles?

Then I flipped to MSNBC, and lo!… they had the exact same two clips. I flipped to CNN… same clips. CBS… same clips. ABC… same clips. Parsing Sotomayor's 30 years of public legal work, somehow every TV network had come up with precisely the same moments! None bothered to say who had dug them up; none offered a smidgen of context. They all just accepted the apparent import of the clips, the substance of which was sure to trouble any fair-minded viewer. By the end of the day just about every American with a TV set had heard the "make policy" and "Latina woman" comments. By the end of the nightly news summaries, millions who had never heard of Sonia Sotomayor knew her not only as Obama's pick, but as a judge who felt superior by reason of her gender and ethnicity, and as a liberal activist determined to "make policy" from the federal bench. And wasn't it an extraordinary coincidence that all these great news organizations, functioning independently — because this, after all, is the advantage of having multiple news-gathering sources in a democracy — had come up with exactly the same material in advance?

They hadn't, of course. The reporting we saw on TV and on the Internet that day was the work not of journalists, but of political hit men. The snippets about Sotomayor had been circulating on conservative Web sites and shown on some TV channels for weeks. They were new only to the vast majority of us who have better things to do than vet the record of every person on Obama's list. But this is precisely what activists and bloggers on both sides of the political spectrum do, and what a conservative organization like the Judicial Confirmation Network exists to promote. The JCN had gathered an attack dossier on each of the prospective Supreme Court nominees, and had fed them all to the networks in advance.

This process — political activists supplying material for TV news broadcasts — is not new, of course. It has largely replaced the work of on-the-scene reporters during political campaigns, which have become, in a sense, perpetual. The once-quadrennial clashes between parties over the White House are now simply the way our national business is conducted. In our exhausting 24/7 news cycle, demand for timely information and analysis is greater than ever. With journalists being laid off in droves, savvy political operatives have stepped eagerly into the breach. What's most troubling is not that TV-news producers mistake their work for journalism, which is bad enough, but that young people drawn to journalism increasingly see no distinction between disinterested reporting and hit-jobbery. The very smart and capable young men (more on them in a moment) who actually dug up and initially posted the Sotomayor clips both originally described themselves to me as part-time, or aspiring, journalists.

The attack that political operatives fashioned from their work was neither unusual nor particularly effective. It succeeded in shaping the national debate over her nomination for weeks, but more serious assessments of her record would demolish the caricature soon enough, and besides, the Democrats have a large majority in the Senate; her nomination was approved by a vote of 68–31. The incident does, however, illustrate one consequence of the collapse of professional journalism. Work formerly done by reporters and producers is now routinely performed by political operatives and amateur ideologues of one stripe or another, whose goal is not to educate the public but to *win*. This is a trend not likely to change.

Writing in 1960, the great press critic A. J. Liebling, noting the squeeze on his profession, fretted about the emergence of the one-newspaper town:

> The worst of it is that each newspaper disappearing below the horizon carries with it, if not a point of view, at least a potential emplacement for one. A city with one newspaper, or with a morning and an evening paper under one ownership, is like a man with one eye, and often the eye is glass.

Liebling, who died in 1963, was spared the looming prospect of the no-newspaper town. There is, of course, the Internet, which he could not have imagined. Its enthusiasts rightly point out that digital media are in nearly every way superior to paper and ink, and represent, in essence, an upgrade in technology. But those giant presses and barrels of ink and fleets of delivery trucks were never what made newspapers invaluable. What gave newspapers their value was the mission and promise of journalism — the hope that someone was getting paid to wade into the daily tide of manure, sort through its deliberate lies and cunning half-truths, and tell a story straight. There is a reason why newspaper reporters, despite polls that show consistently low public regard for journalists, are the heroes of so many films. The reporter of lore was not some blue blood or Ivy League egghead, beholden to society's powerful interests, be they corporate, financial, or political. We liked our newsmen to be Everymen — shoe-leather intellectuals, cynical, suspicious, and street-wise like Humphrey Bogart in *Deadline — U.S.A.* or Jimmy Stewart in *The Philadelphia Story* or Robert Redford and Dustin Hoffman in *All the President's Men.* The Internet is now replacing Everyman with *every man.* Anyone with a keyboard or cell phone can report, analyze, and pull a chair up to the national debate. If freedom of the press belongs to those who own one, today that is everyone. The city with one eye (glass or no) has been replaced by the city with a million eyes. This is wonderful on many levels, and is why the tyrants of the world are struggling, with only partial success, to control the new medium. But while the Internet may be the ultimate democratic tool, it is also demolishing the business model that long sustained newspapers and TV's net-

work-news organizations. Unless someone quickly finds a way to make disinterested reporting pay, to compensate the modern equivalent of the ink-stained wretch (the carpal-tunnel curmudgeon?), the Web may yet bury Liebling's cherished profession.

Who, after all, is willing to work for free?

Morgen Richmond, for one — the man who actually found the snippets used to attack Sotomayor. He is a partner in a computer-consulting business in Orange County, California, a father of two, and a native of Canada, who defines himself, in part, as a political conservative. He spends some of his time most nights in a second-floor bedroom/office in his home, after his children and wife have gone to bed, cruising the Internet looking for ideas and information for his blogging. "It's more of a hobby than anything else," he says. His primary outlet is a Web site called VerumSerum.com, which was co-founded by his friend John Sexton. Sexton is a Christian conservative who was working at the time for an organization called Reasons to Believe, which strives, in part, to reconcile scientific discovery and theory with the apparent whoppers told in the Bible. Sexton is, like Richmond, a young father, living in Huntington Beach. He is working toward a master's degree at Biola University (formerly the Bible Institute of Los Angeles), and is a man of opinion. He says that even as a youth, long before the Internet, he would corner his friends and make them listen to his most recent essay. For both Sexton and Richmond, Verum Serum is a labor of love, a chance for them to flex their desire to report and comment, to add their two cents to the national debate. Both see themselves as somewhat unheralded conservative thinkers in a world captive to misguided liberalism and prey to an overwhelmingly leftist mainstream media, or MSM, composed of journalists who, like myself, write for print publications or work for big broadcast networks and are actually paid for their work.

Richmond started researching Sotomayor after ABC News Washington correspondent George Stephanopoulos named her as the likely pick back on March 13. The work involved was far less than I'd imagined, in part because the Internet is such an amazing research tool, but mostly because Richmond's goal was substantially easier to achieve than a journalist's. For a newspaper reporter, the goal in researching any profile is to arrive at a deeper understanding of the subject. My own motivation, when I did it, was to present not just a smart and original picture of the person, but a fair picture. In the quaint protocols of my ancient newsroom career, the editors I worked for would have accepted nothing less; if they felt a story needed more detail or balance, they'd brusquely hand it back and demand more effort. Richmond's purpose was fundamentally different. He figured, rightly, that anyone Obama picked who had not publicly burned an American flag would likely be confirmed, and that she would be cheered all the way down this lubricated chute by the Obama-loving MSM. To his credit, Richmond is not what we in the old days called a "thumbsucker," a lazy columnist who rarely stirs from behind his desk, who for material just reacts to the items that cross it. (This defines the vast majority of bloggers.) Richmond is actually determined to add something new to the debate.

"The goal is to develop original stories that attract attention," he told me. "I was consciously looking for something that would resonate."

But not just anything resonant. Richmond's overarching purpose was to damage Sotomayor, or at least to raise questions about her that would trouble his readers, who are mostly other conservative bloggers. On most days, he says, his stuff on Verum Serum is read by only 20 to 30 people. If any of them like what they see, they link to it or post the video on their own, larger Web sites.

Richmond began his reporting by looking at university Web sites. He had learned that many harbor little-seen recordings and transcripts of speeches made by public figures, since schools regularly sponsor lectures and panel discussions with prominent citizens, such as federal judges. Many of the events are informal and unscripted, and can afford glimpses of public figures talking unguardedly about their ideas, their life, and their convictions. Many are recorded and archived. Using Google, Richmond quickly found a list of such appearances by Sotomayor, and the first one he clicked on was the video of the 2005 panel discussion at Duke University Law School. Sotomayor and two other judges, along with two Duke faculty members, sat behind a table before a classroom filled with stu-

dents interested in applying for judicial clerkships. The video is 51 minutes long and is far from riveting. About 40 minutes into it, Richmond says, he was only half listening, multitasking on his home computer, when laughter from the sound track caught his ear. He rolled back the video and heard Sotomayor utter the line about making policy, and then jokingly disavow the expression.

"What I found most offensive about it was the laughter," he says. "What was the joke? ... Here was a sitting appellate judge in a room full of law students, treating the idea that she was making policy or law from the bench as laughable." He recognized it as a telling in-joke that his readers would not find funny.

Richmond posted the video snippet on YouTube on May 2, and then put it up with a short commentary on Verum Serum the following day, questioning whether Sotomayor deserved to be considered moderate or bipartisan, as she had been characterized. "I'm not so sure this is going to fly," he wrote, and then invited readers to view the video. He concluded with sarcasm: "So she's a judicial activist ... I'm sure she is a moderate one though! Unbelievable. With a comment like this I only hope that conservatives have the last laugh if she gets the nomination."

A number of larger conservative Web sites, notably Volokh.com (the Volokh Conspiracy, published by UCLA law professor Eugene Volokh) and HotAir.com (published by conservative commentator Michelle Malkin), picked up the video, and on May 4 it was aired on television for the first time, by Sean Hannity.

On Malkin's Web site, Richmond had come across a short, critical reference to a speech Sotomayor had given at Berkeley Law School, in which, according to Malkin, the prospective Supreme Court nominee said "she believes it is appropriate for a judge to consider their 'experiences as women and people of color' in their decision making, which she believes should 'affect our decisions.'"

Malkin told me that her "conservative source" for the tidbit was privileged. She used the item without checking out the actual speech, which is what Richmond set out to find. He had some trouble because Malkin had placed the speech in 2002 instead of 2001, but he found it — the Honorable Mario G. Olmos Law & Cultural Diversity Memorial Lecture — in the Berkeley Law School's

La Raza Law Journal, bought it, and on May 5 posted the first detailed account of it on his blog. He ran large excerpts from it, and highlighted in bold the now infamous lines: "I would hope that a wise Latina woman with the richness of her experiences would more often than not reach a better conclusion than a white male who hasn't lived that life."

Richmond then commented:

> To be fair, I do want to note that the statement she made... is outrageous enough that it may have in fact been a joke. Although since it's published "as-is" in a law journal I'm not sure she is entitled to the benefit of the doubt on this. The text certainly does not indicate that it was said in jest. I have only a layperson's understanding of law and judicial history, but I suspect the judicial philosophy implied by these statements is probably pretty typical amongst liberal judges. Personally, I wish it seemed that she was actually really trying to meet the judicial ideal of impartiality, and her comments about making a difference are a concern as this does not seem to be an appropriate focus for a member of the judiciary. I look forward to hopefully seeing some additional dissection and analysis of these statements by others in the conservative legal community.

The crucial piece of Richmond's post, Sotomayor's "wise Latina woman" comment, was then picked up again by other sites, and was soon being packaged with the Duke video as Exhibits A and B in the case against Sonia Sotomayor. Richmond told me that he was shocked by the immediate, widespread attention given to his work, and a little startled by the levels of outrage it provoked. "I found her comments more annoying than outrageous, to be honest," he said.

In both instances, Richmond's political bias made him tone-deaf to the context and import of Sotomayor's remarks. Bear in mind that he was looking not simply to understand the judge, but to expose her supposed hidden agenda.

Take the Duke panel first: most of the video, for obvious reasons, held little interest for Richmond. My guess is that you could fit the number of people who have actually watched the whole thing into a Motel Six bathtub. Most of the talk concerned how to make your application for a highly competitive clerkship stand out. Late in the discussion, a student asked the panel to compare clerking at the district-court (or trial-court) level and clerking at the appellate level. Sotomayor replied that clerks serving trial judges are often asked to rapidly research legal questions that develop during a trial, and to assist the judge in applying the law to the facts of that particular case. The appellate courts, on the other hand, are in the business of making rulings that are "precedential," she said, in that rulings at the appellate level serve as examples, reasons, or justifications for future proceedings in lower courts. She went on to make the ostensibly controversial remark that students who planned careers in academia or public-interest law ought to seek a clerkship at the appellate level, because that's where "policy is made."

This is absolutely true, in the sense she intended: precedential decisions, by definition, make *judicial* policy. They provide the basic principles that guide future rulings. But both Sotomayor and her audience were acutely aware of how charged the word *policy* has become in matters concerning the judiciary—conservatives accuse liberal judges, not without truth, of trying to set *national* policy from the bench. This accusation has become a rallying cry for those who believe that the Supreme Court justices should adhere strictly to the actual language and original intent of the Constitution, instead of coloring the law with their own modish theories to produce such social experiments as school desegregation, *Miranda* warnings, abortions on demand, and so forth. The polite laughter that caught Richmond's ear was recognition by the law students that the judge had inadvertently stepped in a verbal cow pie. She immediately recognized what she had done, expressed mock horror at being caught doing so on tape, and then pronounced a jocular and exaggerated mea culpa, like a scoring runner in a baseball game tiptoeing back out onto the diamond to touch a base that he might have missed. Sotomayor went on to explain in very precise terms how and why decisions at the appellate level have broader intellectual implications than those at the lower level. It is where, she said, "the law is percolating."

Seen in their proper context, these comments would probably not strike anyone as noteworthy. If anything, they showed how sensitive Sotomayor and everyone else in the room had become to fears of an "activist court."

A look at the full "Latina woman" speech at Berkeley reveals another crucial misinterpretation.

To his credit, Richmond posted as much of the speech as copyright law allows, attempting to present the most important sentence in context. But he still missed the point. Sotomayor's argument was not that she sought to use her position to further minority interests, or that her gender and background made her superior to a white male. Her central argument was that the sexual, racial, and ethnic makeup of the legal profession has in fact historically informed the application of law, despite the efforts of individual lawyers and judges to rise above their personal stories—as Sotomayor noted she labors to do. Her comment about a "wise Latina woman" making a better judgment than a "white male who hasn't lived that life" referred specifically to cases involving racial and sexual discrimination. "Whether born from experience or inherent physiological or cultural differences... our gender and national origins may and will make a difference in our judging," she said. This is not a remarkable insight, nor is it even arguable. Consider, say, how an African-American Supreme Court justice might have viewed the *Dred Scott* case, or how a female judge—Sotomayor cited this in the speech—might have looked upon the argument, advanced to oppose women's suffrage, that females are "not capable of reasoning or thinking logically." The presence of blacks and women in the room inherently changes judicial deliberation. She said that although white male judges have been admirably able on occasion to rise above cultural prejudices, the progress of racial minorities and women in the legal profession has directly coincided with greater judicial recognition of their rights. Once again, her point was not that this progress was the result of deliberate judicial activism, but that it was a natural consequence of fuller minority and female participation.

One of her central points was that all judges are, to an extent, defined by their identity and experience, whether they like it or not.

"I can and do aspire to be greater than the sum total of my experiences," she said, "but I accept my limitations."

Richmond seems a bright and fair-minded fellow, but he makes no bones about his political convictions or the purpose of his research and blogging. He has some of the skills and instincts of a reporter but not the motivation or ethics. Any news organization that simply trusted and aired his editing of Sotomayor's remarks, as every one of them did, was abdicating its responsibility to do its own reporting. It was airing propaganda. There is nothing wrong with reporting propaganda, per se, so long as it is labeled as such. None of the TV reports I saw on May 26 cited VerumSerum.com as the source of the material, which disappointed but did not surprise Richmond and Sexton.

Both found the impact of their volunteer effort exciting. They experienced the heady feeling of every reporter who discovers that the number of people who actually seek out new information themselves, even people in the news profession, is vanishingly small. Show the world something it hasn't seen, surprise it with something new, and you fundamentally alter its understanding of things. I have experienced this throughout my career, in ways large and small. I remember the first time I did, very early on, when I wrote a magazine profile of a promising Baltimore County politician named Ted Venetoulis, who was preparing a run for governor of Maryland. I wrote a long story about the man, examining his record as county executive and offering a view of him that included both praise and criticism. I was 25 years old and had never written a word about Maryland politics. I was not especially knowledgeable about the state or the candidates, and the story was amateurish at best. Yet in the months of campaigning that followed, I found snippets from that article repeatedly quoted in the literature put out by Venetoulis and by his opponents. My story was used both to promote him and to attack him. To a large and slightly appalling extent, the points I made framed the public's perception of the candidate, who, as it happened, lost.

Several hours of Internet snooping by Richmond at his upstairs computer wound up shaping the public's perception of Sonia Sotomayor, at least for the first few weeks following her nomination. Conservative critics used the snippets to portray her as a racist and liberal activist, a picture even Richmond now admits is inaccurate. "She's really fairly moderate, compared to some of the other candidates on Obama's list," he says. "Given that conservatives are not going to like any Obama pick, she really wasn't all that bad." He felt many of the Web sites and TV commentators who used his work inflated its significance well beyond his own intent. But he was not displeased.

"I was amazed," he told me.

For his part, Sexton says: "It is a beautiful thing to live in this country. It's overwhelming and fantastic, really, that an ordinary citizen, with just a little bit of work, can help shape the national debate. Once you get a taste of it, it's hard to resist."

I would describe their approach as post-journalistic. It sees democracy, by definition, as perpetual political battle. The blogger's role is to help his side. Distortions and inaccuracies, lapses of judgment, the absence of context, all of these things matter only a little, because they are committed by both sides, and tend to come out a wash. Nobody is actually right about anything, no matter how certain they pretend to be. The truth is something that emerges from the cauldron of debate. No, not the truth: *victory,* because winning is way more important than being right. Power is the highest achievement. There is nothing new about this. But we never used to mistake it for journalism. Today it is rapidly replacing journalism, leading us toward a world where all information is spun, and where all "news" is unapologetically propaganda.

In this post-journalistic world, the model for all national debate becomes the trial, where adversaries face off, representing opposing points of view. We accept the harshness of this process because the consequences in a courtroom are so stark; trials are about assigning guilt or responsibility for harm. There is very little wiggle room in such a confrontation, very little room for compromise — only innocence or degrees of guilt or responsibility. But isn't this model unduly harsh for political debate? Isn't there, in fact, middle ground in most public disputes? Isn't the art of politics finding that middle ground, weighing the public good against factional priorities? Without journalism, the public good is viewed only through a partisan lens, and politics becomes blood sport.

Television loves this, because it is dramatic. Confrontation is all. And given the fragmentation of news on the Internet and on cable television, Americans increasingly choose to listen only to their own side of the argument, to bloggers and commentators who reinforce their convictions and paint the world only in acceptable, comfortable colors. Bloggers like Richmond and Sexton, and TV hosts like Hannity, preach only to the choir. Consumers of such "news" become all the more entrenched in their prejudices, and ever more hostile to those who disagree. The other side is no longer the honorable opposition, maybe partly right; but rather always wrong, stupid, criminal, even downright evil. Yet even in criminal courts, before assigning punishment, judges routinely order presentencing reports, which attempt to go beyond the clash of extremes in the courtroom to a more nuanced, disinterested assessment of a case. Usually someone who is neither prosecution nor defense is assigned to investigate. In a post-journalistic society, there is no disinterested voice. There are only the winning side and the losing side.

There's more here than just an old journalist's lament over his dying profession, or over the social cost of losing great newspapers and great TV-news operations. And there's more than an argument for the ethical superiority of honest, disinterested reporting over advocacy. Even an eager and ambitious political blogger like Richmond, because he is drawn to the work primarily out of political conviction, not curiosity, is less likely to experience the pleasure of finding something new, or of arriving at a completely original, unexpected insight, one that surprises even himself. He is missing out on the great fun of speaking wholly for himself, without fear or favor. This is what gives reporters the power to stir up trouble wherever they go. They can shake preconceptions and poke holes in presumption. They can celebrate the unnoticed and puncture the hyped. They can, as the old saying goes, afflict the comfortable and comfort the afflicted. A reporter who thinks and speaks for himself, whose preeminent goal is providing deeper understanding, aspires even in political argument to persuade, which requires at the very least being seen as fair-minded and trustworthy by those — and this is the key — who are inclined to *disagree* with him. The honest, disinterested voice of a true journalist carries an authority that no self-branded liberal or conservative can have. "For a country to have a great writer is like having another government," Alexander Solzhenitsyn wrote. Journalism, done right, is enormously powerful precisely because it does not seek power. It seeks truth. Those who forsake it to shill for a product or a candidate or a party or an ideology diminish their own power. They are missing the most joyful part of the job.

This is what H. L. Mencken was getting at when he famously described his early years as a *Baltimore Sun* reporter. He called it "the life of kings."

From the "Electronic Cottage" to the "Silicon Sweatshop"

Social Implications of Telemediated Work in Canada

Graham D. Longford and Barbara A. Crow

The work and workplaces of Canadians have undergone profound change over the last few decades, from the relative decline of jobs in manufacturing and primary industries and subsequent rise in service-sector employment, to the increasing use of contingent (part-time, temporary, and contract) workers and the entry of millions of women into the paid labour force. While such changes originate from a complex blend of global and domestic economic and social forces, the emergence of new information and communications technologies (ICTs) has also played an important part. In this essay we survey and evaluate the extent and effects of telemediated work in Canada, that is, work that depends upon or is carried out through the use of ICTs. Numerous and often conflicting studies on work and technology have appeared in the last decade, some controversial. Works by Rifkin (1995), Noble (1995), and Menzies (1996), for example, invoke near apocalyptic scenarios about the "end of work" and the formation of a mass cybertariat. Technology gurus like Don Tapscott, on the other hand, argue that work involving the production or use of ICTs constitutes the fastest growing source of employment in the new economy (Tapscott 1996, 188). Our task is rendered more difficult by the relative lack of empirical data in the area. Compared with recent studies of the impacts of organizational change, there is a lack of adequate study and analysis of the impact of telemediated work on such things as the availability of employment, skills and income, job security, and working conditions for many workers in the "knowledge-based economy." In an age when ICTs have been elevated to the status of a universal panacea, the need for better research and understanding is compelling.

Business and government leaders endorse the rapid proliferation and diffusion of new ICTs throughout the economy and workplace as key to Canada's future economic growth, prosperity, and competitiveness, and have portrayed them as enabling technologies capable of breaking down barriers to economic opportunity based on gender, race, disability, and geography (Boston Consulting Group [Canada] 2000; Information Highway Advisory Council 1997; National Broadband Task Force 2001). In our view, however, evidence for such widespread positive effects of ICTs is inconclusive at best. In fact, there is mounting evidence that the impact of ICTs on the nature, quantity, and quality of work in Canada is one of polarization, by reproducing and intensifying rather than overcoming historically recalcitrant barriers to economic opportunity and self-sufficiency. Without denying the benefits new ICTs have brought to many, their effects have been highly uneven.

For some, albeit a minority, the effect of ICTs on the nature of work and employment in the new economy has had many positive aspects: swelling their bank accounts, providing new opportunities for autonomy and creative collaboration with distant colleagues, and helping to accommodate family commitments, such as childcare or eldercare. At the other end of the spectrum lie hundreds of thousands of relatively unskilled, poorly paid teleservice agents working in conditions best described as "silicon sweatshops," where they are crowded into call centres, seated at workstations that will inevitably injure them, and subjected to continuous electronic monitoring. Somewhere in the middle lies a substantial majority of Canadians who share a simultaneous fascination with new technologies such as cell phones, pagers, and the Internet,[1] and an abiding suspicion that new technology poses a threat to their jobs and intrudes on their privacy and leisure time (Reid 1996, 127–44). Finally, even those who have succeeded in prospering in the new economy have paid a price, in the form of increased hours of work, increased stress, and a blurring of the distinction between work and home life.

In this essay, we follow the contours of the contemporary landscape of work in Canada, with particular attention paid to how it has been restructured and reshaped in recent years by the growing use of computer and telecommunications technology, and with a view to identifying emerging trends and issues with which employers, workers, policy-makers, and Canadian citizens in general must contend. With so much ink and air time in the popular media devoted to celebrating the benefits of these technologies, we have elected to focus on a number of more troublesome impacts. Among these emerging trends and issues are: increased polarization of the workforce between highly skilled, well-paid knowledge workers and a large pool of semi- and unskilled workers occupying poorly paid and increasingly precarious part-time, temporary, and contract positions; rising numbers of home-based teleworkers for whom coverage by employment standards and occupational health and safety legislation is uncertain; the persistence of a gendered and racialized division of labour in the new economy; geographic "clustering" of economic and employment opportunities in already economically privileged urban regions; declining working conditions and employment standards for all workers in the knowledge-based economy in terms of employment standards, job security, and stress; and the use of technology to electronically monitor the activities, performance,

whereabouts, and, increasingly, the private thoughts of growing numbers of workers. Current public policy, with its focus on promoting further technological innovation, has yet to acknowledge, let alone address, many of the issues raised below.

ICTs in the Canadian Workplace

Before examining the effects of ICTs on work and employment, let us first get an appreciation for the extent to which they have been incorporated into and are a part of the daily life of working Canadians. Two recent Statistics Canada surveys provide useful snapshots of the diffusion of ICTs in the paid workplace in Canada. Its 2001 *Electronic Commerce and Technology Use* survey reports that while e-commerce itself constitutes only a small part of economic activity, the use of ICTs such as the Internet, e-mail, electronic data interchange (EDI), and wireless communications in the workplace is significant. In 2000, 63 per cent of businesses used the Internet, 60 per cent used e-mail, 51 per cent used wireless communications, 26 per cent had websites, and 12 per cent used an intranet (Peterson 2001, 11–16). Public sector organizations report even higher use: 99 per cent use the Internet and e-mail; 73 per cent had websites; and 52 per cent used an intranet (Peterson 2001, 13, 16–17).

Another method used by Statistics Canada to measure the phenomenon has been to measure the prevalence of computer use by individual workers. As of 2000, computer use in private and public sector workplaces stood at 81 per cent and 100 per cent, respectively (Peterson 2001, 11). At the level of the individual worker, six out of ten employed Canadians use computers in their work, 80 per cent of these on a daily basis (Marshall 2001, 5–11). The latter figure represents roughly 6.5 million workers. These figures also represent a striking increase over the number using computers only a decade ago—a mere three in ten (Marshall 2001, 5).[2]

Not surprisingly, however, computer use at work varies across industrial sectors, occupational groups, and other demographic categories, including gender and education level. Public sector workers, firstly, were significantly more likely to work with computers (77 per cent) than private sector counterparts (56 per cent). Within the private sector, meanwhile, professional, scientific, and technical services firms report 95 per cent computer use, while only 66 per cent of firms in the accommodation and food services industry use them (Peterson 2001, 12). Incidence of use also varies according to occupation, education, income, and gender. Professionals and managers had among the highest rates of computer use, at 86 per cent and 78 per cent, respectively. In sales and service occupations, meanwhile, the figure stood at 39 per cent. Of workers with high school education or less, only 41 per cent report using computers, as compared to 85 per cent of those with university degrees. Computer use also correlates with income level; with a mere 36 per cent of those with incomes under $20,000 reporting computer use at work, while 80 per cent of those with incomes in excess of $60,000 use them (Marshall 2001, 6–7). Finally, women were more likely to use computers at work than men, by a margin of 60 per cent to 54 per cent. Much of this gap can be accounted for by the prevalence of women in clerical positions, however, who recorded 84 per cent computer use. Based on these figures, it is fair to say that computers and computer use have rapidly, albeit unevenly, become prevalent in the Canadian workplace.

Aside from computers, the proliferation of other new ICTs such as cell phones, pagers, and various other wireless devices has been significant. Cellular phone subscriptions in Canada rocketed from less than 100,000 to 9.9 million between 1987 and 2001 (Statistics Canada 1998b; 2001d). A substantial portion of these are used for business purposes. The growing importance of ICTs to the economy overall is also reflected in the magnitude of investment that has been poured into ICTs over the last decade. Private sector capital investment in ICTs grew by approximately 20 per cent per year in Canada throughout much of the 1990s, reaching $13.6 billion (CAN) by 1997 (Ertl 2001, 46; Rubin 2001), and overall expenditures on ICTs as a percentage of sales increased as well (Peterson 2001, 4). Public sector spending increases on ICTs have also risen dramatically in recent years. Federal government annual ICT expenditures, for example, increased from $3 billion to $5 billion between 1993 and 2000 (Longford 2001, 6).

With an appreciation for the rapid diffusion of new ICTs throughout the Canadian economy and paid workplace in recent decades, let us now turn to the question of what effects they have had on work, workers, and Canadian society as a whole.

Impact of ICTs on Work I: Demand, Security, Skills

The End of Work?

Competitive pressures, organizational changes, and human resource strategies—especially downsizing, delayering, outsourcing, and an increased reliance on part-time and temporary employment—have had a major impact on employment in the last two decades. There has been a significant shakeout in industries such as manufacturing and in occupations such as clerical work as a result of the introduction of new technologies over the last few decades. Thanks to robotics and computer-controlled just-in-time delivery, automotive manufacturers are able to produce cars at a much greater rate than even ten years ago, despite employing significantly fewer workers (McNally 2000, 268–70). Successive waves of automation have enabled Canada Post to handle a 45 per cent increase in mail volume since 1982, despite a 32 per cent drop in full-time employment (Bickerton and Louli 1995, 220). Overall employment in clerical positions in Canada decreased by 250,000 positions during the 1990s as a result of new technologies that increased productivity and enabled managers to assume responsibility themselves for clerical functions like word processing (Betcherman and McMullen 1998, 10). Similarly, airline ticket agents have suffered deskilling and job loss over the past decade and find those jobs remaining threatened by self-serve check-in kiosks currently being rolled out across the country (Shalla 1997, 76–96). Finally, in the mid-1990s, Human Resources Development Canada (HRDC) replaced 5,000 frontline staff with several thousand electronic self-serve kiosks, resulting in an annual personnel cost-savings of $200 million (Longford 2001, 12–13).

New ICTs have also facilitated the transfer of work out of Canada and into other countries. Between 1989 and 1992, 338,000 manufacturing jobs disappeared from Canada (Reid 1996). The loss of these jobs coincided with the Canada-U.S. Free Trade Agreement, which enabled employers to relocate operations south of the border. Many of Canada's high-tech corporate darlings of the 1990s, such as Nortel and JDS Uniphase, created more positions outside Canada than inside (Reid 1996,

292). Such transfers of work and the control and coordination of work in production facilities thousands of kilometres distant from head offices was also rendered possible by the introduction of new ICTs, including the fax machine, Electronic Data Interchange (EDI), cellular phones, and corporate intranets.

Still, for all the doomsday talk of the "end of work," it warrants pointing out that the employment rate in Canada has declined only marginally over the last couple of decades and hovers just over the 62 per cent mark (Statistics Canada 2001a).[3] Meanwhile, for all the hype about the knowledge-based economy, demand for many workers in occupations such as truck driving, cleaning, personal services, home care, and retail sales persists (Burke and Shields 2000, 103). Therefore, the fears of doomsayers appear at least somewhat exaggerated (Walters 2001, 78–83).

On the other hand, in spite of considerable hyperbole regarding the positive correlation between ICTs and economic and employment growth,[4] sober analysis has demonstrated that, while it hasn't been a "job killer," information technology has produced no employment bonanza either (Conference Board of Canada 1996). The average annual rate of employment growth ran at 2 per cent through the 1990s, the very same period during which, as we have seen, Canadian firms invested very heavily in ICTs. In fact, the experience of the information technology sector in Canada itself mirrors this phenomenon of near jobless growth in the wider economy. Between 1990 and 1997, the ICT sector's contribution to GDP in Canada grew at an annual rate of 6 per cent, eventually reaching 6.1 per cent of total output. Meanwhile, employment growth in the sector lagged at 2.8 per cent. In some sectors, such as telecommunications services and computer manufacturing, downsizing and restructuring led to net losses in employment (Denton and Pereboom 2000, 4–10). All told, the sector added perhaps 100,000 jobs to the economy of the 1990s, rising from 3.1 per cent to 3.5 per cent of all jobs in Canada (Ertl 2001, 18). While investment in the production and use of digital technologies clearly has the potential both to create as well as to destroy jobs, there is little evidence supporting the claim that ICTs create as many, if not more, jobs as they destroy.[5] What is clear is that new ICTs eliminate certain kinds of work and displace workers, mostly of a low to intermediate nature in skill level,

and thus create problems of adjustment in the near term at least (Betcherman and McMullen 1998, 12).

Just-in-Time Work

One of the most significant changes in the way Canadians work has been in the area of work arrangements, particularly the rise of "non-standard" employment such as part-time, temporary, and contract work, and own-account self-employment. As many as half of all Canadian workers, depending on one's definition of non-standard work, now find themselves working under such arrangements (Lowe 1999, 5). One and a half million, or 13 per cent, of employed Canadians are in temporary jobs (jobs with a specified end date), a 60 per cent increase since 1989 (Canadian Policy Research Networks 2002). Many of the firms taking advantage of new work arrangements are closely connected with either the use or production of new ICTs.[6] Numerous studies reveal a significant correlation between ICTs and the flexibilization of the workforce in terms of employment arrangements, such as increased use of part-time, temporary, outsourced, or contract workers (Benner and Dean 2000, 361–75; Betcherman and McMullen 1998, 1; Lowe, Schellenberg, and Davidman 1999, 43; Vosko 2000). Today, computerized systems offer employers an increasingly fine-grained view of workers' activities, productivity, and workload in real time. Such information can be used to optimize staffing levels according to demand and workload, to the point where employers can rely on "just-in-time" workers. At call centres, for example, phone systems compile data on such factors as average time on hold, number of calls in queue, average call length, and number of hang-ups. As one call centre software developer puts it: "Its whole purpose is to optimize the relationship between the number of people that they have on the phones versus the number of calls coming into their centre so that they can have just the right amount of people" (Guly 2000). The call centre industry in Canada employs half a million people, roughly 60 per cent of these on a part-time basis (Human Resources Development Canada 2002). Such technology is not confined to call centres by any means. Increasingly, it is being used to "optimize" work and staffing levels throughout all sectors of the private and public sector.

High-tech firms in the ICT sector itself, meanwhile, use such flexible staffing arrangements at an increasing rate, on the grounds that rapid technological change and pressure to reduce time-to-market for new products necessitates doing so. Firms in so-called high-tech "cluster" regions like Ottawa, or Silicon Valley and Seattle in the United States, have made liberal use of innovations like outsourcing, contract employment, and the use of temporary workers (Benner and Dean 2000, 361–66; Chun 2001, 127–54). Such regions serve as laboratories for incubating new employment practices and offer a window into the future landscape of work and employment in the new economy, where even the most skilled workers may find plenty of work in non-standard employment arrangements, but fewer jobs in the traditional sense. Silicon Valley in California has been singled out as the capital of non-standard work in the United States, where as much as 40 per cent of the region's workforce works under non-standard employment contracts (Benner and Dean 2000, 363–64). In Canada's software and computer services industry, meanwhile, fully 65,000 of 190,000 workers were reported to be self-employed in 1998, or almost 35 per cent. (Industry Canada 2000, 3, 8). In addition, Canada's high-tech sector is dependent upon a steady supply of skilled foreign workers coming on temporary work visas (Rao 2001). A project begun in 1997 to fast-track the processing of such visas for IT software development workers helped bring three thousand individuals into Canada by early 2000 (Citizenship and Immigration Canada 2000).

While such flexible work arrangements are clearly desired by many workers, an increasingly significant proportion find themselves in such arrangements involuntarily, indicating a considerable amount of under-employment (Jackson, Robinson, Baldwin, and Wiggins, 2000, 63). Furthermore, surveys consistently report that non-permanent, contingent workers are paid lower wages and salaries and enjoy little protection under labour laws and few if any benefits (United States General Accounting Office 2000, 18–30; Jackson, Robinson, Baldwin, and Wiggins 2000, 58–73; Vosko 2000, 200–29). Thus, even in the heart of the new economy, the bonanza of high paying jobs alleged to accompany the transition to a knowledge-based economy is part illusion.[7] As this population of contingent workers continues to grow, calls to close the gap in wages, security, employment standards, and working conditions between the perma-

nent and "flexible" workforces may grow louder. The struggle to improve working conditions and extend protection to such workers will be difficult, however, as employers and governments alike have worked to limit and roll back rather than extend protection to such workers.[8]

As more highly skilled and professional groups find themselves among the ranks of the temporary workforce, there are signs of renewed interest in union-organizing to defend and protect their interests. Witness the re-emergence of occupational unionism among temporary workers in Silicon Valley and Seattle under the banners of organizations like WashTech, FACEIntel, and Alliance@IBM (Alliance@IBM; Andresky Fraser 2001, 150–52; Washington Alliance of Technology Workers/CWA 2001). While this remains a largely American phenomenon, it may only be a matter of time before it emerges in Canada as well. What implications this might have for the broader labour movement, and for improvements in working conditions for contingent workers in general, remains to be seen.

Skills in the New Economy: Knowledge Workers or Cybertariat?

By some measures, workers in today's economy are more skilled and better educated than previous generations. Over half of Canada's workers possess a university or college degree, up from one-fifth twenty-five years ago. Jobs themselves have also been said to be more complex on the whole. The rising skill intensity of some forms of work and the increasingly qualified nature of the workforce have been portrayed as symptomatic of the growing importance of ICTs; hence mounting pressure to expose school children to computers as early as possible through programs such as the federal government's SchoolNet, and the mass production of diploma-wielding "IT" graduates from private and public business colleges. Evidence on the effect of ICTs on workplace skills is mixed, however. Betcherman and McMullen have found evidence of a modest up-skilling effect (McMullen 2001). According to their research, over half of job-types created as a result of introducing new computer technologies were of a professional nature, whereas only 11 per cent required intermediate levels of skill. Of the positions eliminated as a result of new computer-based technology, 60 per cent came from the lower skilled job-types, and only 7 per cent from the professional category. As well, workers in occupations with the most intensive use of computers—such as managers, administrators, and clerical workers—also report increases in the skill requirements, problem-solving, and autonomy involved in their jobs (Betcherman and McMullen 1998, 14).

On the other hand, a recent Statistics Canada survey reveals that uses of computers at work vary considerably and that not all involve a high degree of skill. The most common task reportedly performed on computers was word processing (83 per cent), followed by data entry (72 per cent), record keeping (69 per cent), spreadsheets (63 per cent), and Internet use (54 per cent). Other tasks requiring specialized skills and training were performed less frequently, and only 16 per cent engaged in any programming activities (Marshall 2001, 9). The evident increased use of computers in the workplace should not, therefore, automatically be equated with knowledge work. To what extent does it make sense to call a task like word processing a "skill" if already 83 per cent of computer users report proficiency at it? (Barney 2000, 153–55) Of course, many managers and other skilled workers use word processing and Web surfing to support highly cognate tasks such as report writing, but the mere fact that computer equipment is used in a given workplace is not an automatic indication of the deployment of highly skilled labour.

The varying degrees of skill involved in using computers are also indicated by where and how users report getting their training. Most employees report acquiring the ability to use computers in a relatively informal manner, as a result of trial-and-error or learning from family and co-workers (Statistics Canada 2001e). By way of contrast, the kind of "critical skills" deemed necessary for core occupations in knowledge-based industries like the ICT sector itself are obtainable only through pursuit of an advanced engineering or computer science degree at a limited number of elite institutions, followed by three to ten years of experience in a relevant technology area (Denton and Pereboom 2000, 13). Clearly, then, the prevalence of computers at work is not a reliable indicator of the growth of knowledge-intensive work. As we look, therefore, to assess and secure Canada's place in the emerging knowledge-based economy, we must be careful not to make a fetish of computers and other information technologies, the presence of which can be just as indicative of relatively simplified forms of work such as data entry or telemarketing as it is of high value-added knowledge work.

What the Betcherman and McMullen study also fails to shed light on is where and in what kinds of occupations those holding low to intermediate skill jobs that were eliminated wound up. Highly skilled occupations in knowledge-based sectors carry with them high costs of entry, in the form of specialized university education and professional training, which places them beyond the reach of a large portion of the population. With few new avenues of comparable employment open to them, many end up accepting jobs increasingly likely to involve less skill, pay and security than previous positions. Indeed, for all the discussion of Canada's transition to a knowledge-based economy, a list of the top ten jobs for men and women contains few associated with so-called "knowledge work," according to the 1996 Census. The leading job types included truck driver, janitor, retail sales, secretary, and cashier (Statistics Canada 1998a, 3–6). In other words, the up-skilling effect observed by Betcherman and McMullen is also a polarizing one, as it increases the widening skills, pay, and job security gap between skilled and unskilled workers.

The bifurcation of the labour force on the basis of skill also shows up in income distribution, where a growing trend toward an "hour-glass" economy is evident in Canada. Polarization between rich and poor and a general decline of middle- and working-class incomes are readily apparent (Jackson, Robinson, Baldwin, and Wiggins 2000, 113–38). While it is difficult to disentangle the distributional effects of ICTs from other factors, given what is known about its employment and labour market impacts, there can be little doubt that it plays some role in shaping distribution patterns in the Canadian political economy.[9] The two-tier system increasingly characteristic of occupational structures and income distribution in the information economy is reproduced in the quality of working life as well. Elite knowledge workers experience high degrees of autonomy and flexibility in their work, take advantage of high demand and highly portable skills, and operate on the basis of relations of cooperation, creative collaboration and partnering with peers (Symons 1997, 195–215). The information-worker "underclass," meanwhile, often engages in repetitive and stultifying tasks related to data entry, processing, and extraction, under working conditions in which hierarchy, subordination, and electronic surveillance figure prominently (Bryant 1995, 505–21; Symons 1997, 195–215; Whitaker 1999, 115–18).

Impact of ICTs on Work II: A Gendered and Racialized Division of Labour

The intensifying occupational and distributional hierarchies characteristic of the new economy are cross-cut by distinct gender and racial cleavages as well. New ICTs have been seen as having the potential to overcome systemic barriers to economic and educational opportunity based on gender, race, and disability. New forms of teleworking, for example, have been held out as particularly advantageous to women, racial minorities, and the disabled. For women, telework offers the possibility of combining work with family commitments and may provide an entry point into the workforce for less skilled or new immigrant women. The virtual workplace, others have argued, reduces the chances that a worker might be penalized or discriminated against based on their race, since the visual clues to racial difference are eliminated. Finally, telemediated work has also been portrayed as offering the potential to more fully integrate the disabled into the workforce by enabling such accommodations as telecommuting.[10] Unfortunately, aggregate trends in the place and status of women, racial minorities, and the disabled in the new information economy are not very encouraging.

Feminist analyses of digital technology have revealed the profoundly gendered nature of the division of labour within the new information economy. In addition to its contribution to the "feminization" of work in general, many new telemediated forms of non-standard employment, such as home-based call centre and clerical work, are doubly feminized insofar as women are disproportionately over-represented in them (Menzies 1997). The nature of computer use at work also varies by gender. Overall, while more women than men report using computers

(largely a reflection of the prevalence of women in clerical positions), men were more likely to perform a greater variety of tasks than women, particularly those associated with so-called knowledge work. Men were twice as likely to engage in programming tasks, and significantly more likely to use the Internet, produce graphics, or analyze data (Marshall 2001, 8). We are also witnessing a certain "technological masculinism" within high-tech employment itself (Sawchuck and Crow 1995). The effects of the gendered division of labour are manifested in the masculinization of scientific and computer technical expertise and hardware and software development (Brunet and Prioux 1989, 77–84; Stromber and Arnold 1987; Ullman 1995, 131–44).

In Canada, female employment in professional, technical, and managerial positions related to ICTs averages approximately 20 per cent in the private and public sectors (Avon 1996, 13; Treasury Board of Canada Secretariat 2000). Moreover, at the same time as the ICT sector has been experiencing impressive growth, there has been a worldwide decrease in the numbers of women in computer science (Wright 1997). Women tend to be concentrated in positions such as call centre agents, which are relatively low-paying (under $30,000) (Buchanan and Koch-Schulte 2001, 9–14), while being under-represented in the much more highly paid and secure positions in occupations like computer services and software development, where salaries regularly exceed $100,000. Such gender-based occupational and distributional hierarchies in the new economy are to some extent the reflection of gendered conceptions of the skills used by various workers (Buchanan and Koch-Schulte 2001, 9–14; Eyerman 2000; Putman and Fenety 2000; Shalla 1997). "Communication" skills highly regarded in the service industry, for example, and particularly in call centre work, are viewed as a "feminine" skill, as something that comes "naturally" to women, and hence is not highly valued and is not translatable into higher wages. Paradoxically, "communication" skills are highly valued in the managerial classes in telemediated work, but not in call centre work. All this suggests that the bifurcation of the labour force and polarization of incomes increasingly characteristic of the new economy will place a disproportionate share of the burden of poorly paid and insecure work upon the backs of women.

While there is little empirical research on the status of racialized peoples in terms of occupation and income in ICT-related forms of work, there is ample evidence pointing to the fact that they, too, tend to occupy the lower regions of occupational and income hierarchies in Canada. As Galabuzi argues, "adults in racialised groups are less likely than others to be employed in professional or managerial occupations. Instead, many are concentrated in lower-paying, clerical, service and manual jobs" (2001, 111).

Inequality and Social Cohesion in the New Economy

Increasingly, commentators from a variety of perspectives worry about the implications of such polarization and hierarchy for social cohesion. The mainstream consensus on dealing with the problem has focused on investments in "human capital" through education, training, and skills development (Courchene 2000, 6–14). Workers will best protect themselves from skills-obsolescence in the new economy, and the attendant decline in the demand and remuneration for their services, by engaging in continuous skills upgrading and "lifelong learning." There are some grounds for this view. University graduates in Canada, for example, benefited from a 47 per cent increase in employment during the 1990s, while non-graduates saw their total employment increase by a mere 2 per cent (Statistics Canada 2001e, 30). There is less consensus among governments, policy-makers, business, and educators however, regarding how best to support education and training. While governments and employers have paid lip service to their importance to society as a whole, the last decade has seen a contraction in opportunities for the most vulnerable workers and members of society in terms of education and training (Schmidt 2001). Government budget cuts and the deregulation of tuition fees in most provinces have led to shrinking budgets and rising costs to students and parents for education at all levels[11] Meanwhile, publicly funded training infrastructure in Canada has been cut back and increasingly privatized (McBride 2000, 167–71). Employer-sponsored training and skills development is significant, but is

increasingly focused on those who already possess high levels of education and skill, thereby entrenching existing inequalities of access to the kinds of education and training that would enable the less skilled to create opportunity for themselves.[12] Furthermore, the growth of non-standard work will lead to less employer-sponsored training, as part-time and temporary workers are much less likely to receive such training than those in traditional, full-time permanent positions (Statistics Canada 2001c).

Again, the patterns of gender and racial inequality in terms of employment in the new economy show up in terms of access to education and training opportunities as well (Galabuzi 2001, 111). The general thrust of current trends is toward the privatization of education, training, and skills development, and the placing of responsibility on individuals for their own employment outcomes, by inculcating the rhetoric and values of lifelong learning. Such a shifting of responsibility onto individuals, in our view, threatens to harden attitudes toward those deemed a "failure" in the new economy and to undermine societal cohesion as a result. As access to favourable employment opportunities and their associated social outcomes becomes increasingly dependent upon the possession of higher levels of skill and education, a commitment to equity requires a levelling of the playing field and a renewed dedication to creating universally accessible institutions for education and training.

Also cause for concern is a growing body of research suggesting that human-capital investment is only weakly correlated with favourable employment and economic outcomes. As a number of researchers have pointed out, the problem of accessing "good jobs" is more structural than the human-capital approach suggests. No matter how well educated we become, as one commentator notes, "we can't all be web designers," for the simple reason that the economy does not supply enough positions (Stanford 2001, 31). There are, for example, fifteen retail clerk positions in Canada for every job as a computer technician, and one-quarter of all university and college graduates are employed in clerical, sales, and menial jobs, suggesting significant levels of underemployment (Stanford 2001, 31).

Impact of ICTs on Work III: Locational Dynamics

The Eclipse of Geography and Distance? New Locational Dynamics of Work in Canada

In addition to their effects on the supply, quality, skill-intensity, and distributional patterns of work, new ICTs have been correlated with changes in the location of work, both within and between regions and countries. By detaching work from locale, a process dubbed "delocalization," ICTs have enabled the ready transfer of many kinds of work across regional and territorial boundaries, as well as the blurring of the boundary between the workplace and the home. The rise of networked computing, the Internet, and the growth of broadband infrastructure have encouraged the relocation of work along a number of vectors, reshaping the nature of work and employment in the process. In this section we examine the emergence and implications of four important shifts in the locational dynamics of work in Canada: the rising incidence of home-based telework; the growth of mobile telework; the increasing concentration of knowledge work in urban centres and surrounding regional high tech "clusters"; and the insertion of Canada into the emerging international division of telemediated labour. Popular views of these changes have been dominated by pastoral images of electronic cottaging offered up by Rheingold, among others, in which telecommuting professionals take advantage of ICTs to enjoy greater autonomy, contact with family, and freedom from the aggravation of daily commuting (Rheingold 1994). While some do enjoy these advantages, the shifting locational dynamics of work raise new concerns such as employment standards enforcement, work/home-life balance, traffic congestion, urban sprawl, and regional economic disparity. In several of these respects, what is perhaps most noteworthy is the *failure* of ICTs to produce positive effects.

Home-based Telework: Telecommuting or Cyberserfdom?

New ICTs like computers, fax machines, and modems have played a role in the recent resurgence of home-based work in Canada. The number of home-based workers, including employees and the self-employed, rose markedly between 1971 and 1995, from 613,000 to 2.8 million, increasing from 8 per cent to 17 per cent of the workforce (Akyeampong and Nadwodny 2001, 12–13). The percentage of employed Canadians performing some or all work from home increased from 3 per cent to 10 per cent between 1971 and 2000, according to Statistics Canada. Ekos Research, however, reported in 2001 that 11 per cent of employed Canadians work primarily from home, and that when periodic work at home (unpaid overtime, catching up on e-mail and paperwork, etc.) was included, the figure rose to 40 per cent (Ekos Research Associates 2001). By 1997, meanwhile, nearly 2.5 million Canadians were self-employed (twice as many as in the late 1970s), amounting to 16.2 per cent of the total labour force. During the 1990s, self-employment accounted for over three out of four new jobs added to the economy (Lin, Yates, and Picot 1999, 2). Such a dramatic rise was bound to have an impact on the incidence of home work, given that 50 per cent of the self-employed work at or from home. Upper estimates of the total number of such workers who could be classified as "teleworkers," that is, those whose home-based work is enabled by information and communications technologies, range from one million to 1.5 million (InnoVisions Canada/Canadian Telework Association 2001).

Since some of the largest annual increases in the number of self-employed homeworkers took place during the 1990s, a decade marked by significant corporate downsizing in white collar as well as blue collar occupations, many have argued that the rise in home-based self-employment reflects the existence of a large group of former employees unable to find traditional full-time work (Jackson, Robinson,

Baldwin, and Wiggins 2000, 49–61; Tal 2001). Other studies have suggested that the rise of home-based self-employment has more to do with the increasing availability and use of new ICTs, like PCs, mobile phones, fax machines, and the Internet, which have enabled individuals to work from home while remaining in close contact with clients and colleagues (Akyeampong and Nadwodny 2001). Whatever the reason for resorting to home-based work, ICTs play an undeniably important enabling role.

As with other impacts of ICTs, the implications and effects of increased home-based work, often called "telecommuting," are ambiguous and difficult to make generalizations about. Commentators like Mitchell, Negroponte, and Rheingold, for example, invoke bucolic scenes of "electronic cottagers" plying their electronic crafts in the comfort of their homes, while Gurstein and Menzies warn of the danger of homes being turned into silicon sweat-shops. In the new economy, however, workers in conditions approximating both of these stereotypes exist at once. In fact, home-based telework appears inherently polarizing in terms of the nature of the work involved and kinds of working conditions, security, and remuneration it entails.

Of the kinds of work that might take place outside conventional workplaces, repetitive low-skill data entry and clerical work, on the one hand, and highly cognate "symbolic analysis" such as report writing, on the other, appear to be the most sustainable. Home-based telework in Canada features plenty of both. In 1991, for example, the largest occupational category for female home-based workers was clerical work, which accounted for over 110,000 positions, followed closely by service and sales positions at 98,000 and 34,000, respectively (Menzies 1997, 113). Home-based clerical workers at the time earned a mean income of around $7,000, according to one of the few studies available (Menzies 1997, 113). At the other end of the spectrum, high-paying professional and semi-autonomous positions in managerial, social science, and educational occupations are also well-represented among home-based workers. For example, fully 25 per cent of employed and 44 per cent of self-employed individuals in managerial occupations work from home (Akyeampong and Nadwodny 2001, 15; Peruuse 1998).

The polarization of the home-based labour force around the figures of the "cyberserf" and the profes-sional "telecommuter" suggested by the above figures is reproduced at the level of working conditions. A semi-skilled single parent engaged in home-based teleservice work because she is unable to afford childcare is far more likely to be poorly paid, enjoy few benefits, and have little protection of the law. She is more likely to suffer job-related injury, will be cut off from vital social networks, training, advancement, and union-organizing opportunities available at conventional workplaces, and will experience the intrusion of surveillance and the blending of work and home-life as an imposition (Bernstein, Lippel, and Lamarche 2001; Felstead and Jewson 2000, 107–08; Gurstein 2002). The well-educated, self-employed, home-based consultant, meanwhile, often enjoys considerable flexibility and autonomy, oppor-tunities for creative collaboration with associates, and generous tax write-offs for business expenses, including a portion of his or her home (Symons 1997, 203–05). Having said that, the story for each of these figures is often more mixed. The home-based tele-service worker can save on transportation, food, and clothing costs associated with working outside the home, and, ironically, may be in a stronger position to lever employer compliance with labour standards as a result of electronic monitoring, the record of which can be valuable as proof of time worked, wages owed, and the all-important "employment relationship" (Bernstein, Lippel, and Lamarche 2001, 12). The average professional "telecommuter," meanwhile, also risks isolation and diminished access to social networks as a result of reduced face-to-face contact with clients and colleagues (Gillespie and Richardson 2000, 230–32). And while touted as enabling workers to balance better their work and family commitments, ICTs have failed to halt a steady increase in the number of workers experi-encing conflict and stress as a result of attempts to do so.[13] Indeed, new technologies are part of the problem, as they facilitate working at home after the regular work day and increase expectations of "24/7" availability (Duxbury and Higgins 2001, 8). In addi-tion, the anticipated reductions in traffic congestion and other environmental advantages of telecom-muting have not materialized. All of which is to say that it is impossible to generalize about the experi-ences of those workers whom new ICTs have enabled to return to the "electronic cottage."

Mobile Work

In addition to contributing to the resurgence of home-based work, new ICTs like cell phones, pagers, PDAs, and mobile e-mail devices have enticed or compelled many workers into mobile work, where the closest thing to a regular place of work is their cars, delivery van, or truck. Innovations in ICTs have spawned new patterns of travel associated with work, in which workers find themselves increasingly working in their cars, at the premises of associates or clients, and "hot-desking" for brief periods at a central office. Reliable figures on the number of such nomadic, mobile workers in Canada are difficult to come by. Place of Work statistics from the 1996 Census reveal that just over one million workers have no fixed workplace address, but its figures are too broad to accurately capture the extent of the phenomenon, as they do not distinguish mobile teleworkers from other mobile workers, such as tradespersons, whose work is less dependent upon enabling ICTs. Assuming a figure in the range of 5 per cent to 10 per cent of Canada's workforce, the number of nomadic, mobile teleworkers could exceed one million.

Mobile work has obvious advantages for employers. Having workers spend less time in the office and more time in the field can help salespersons "get closer to the customer," reduce office overhead and increase productivity. However, not all managers are comfortable with it since, as with telecommuting, it diminishes opportunities for managerial oversight and surveillance of work. Mobile employees pay a certain price as well. Reduced time in a regular office also means diminished opportunities for face-to-face interaction, socializing, and networking with colleagues, and reduced visibility of the sort that can lead to advancement and promotion within the company. Finally, while ICTs have been traditionally portrayed as suppressing the need for travel, the phenomenon of mobile telework appears to be part of a trend toward what the authors of one study refer to as "hypermobility," in which new ICTs change the locational dynamics of work in such a way as to increase rather than decrease the car-dependence of work by, for example, increasing the number of car trips made during the day (Gillespie and Richardson 2000, 228, 243; Miller 2000). According to U.S. studies, the increased incidence of home-based work has also produced little net reduction in vehicle miles travelled and has resulted in an increasing number of trips throughout the day within residential neighbourhoods, leading to greater noise, pollution, and congestion at off-peak periods (Gillespie and Richardson 2000, 228–45). One can see this reflected in the fact that some of the "smartest" cities in North America in terms of labour force skills and ICT infrastructure, such as San Francisco, Seattle, and Ottawa, have experienced worsened traffic congestion (Hill 2000; Laucious, 2000; Singer 2000). With fewer workers engaging in traditional commutes while many are increasing their daytime car use, ridership on public transportation has dropped as well, threatening the future quality and viability of such services (Gillespie and Richardson 2000, 236–38).

High-tech "Clusters": The Geography of Work in the New Economy

The decoupling of work and place enabled by ICTs is also affecting the location of work and employment on a regional and international basis. Within Canada, there are signs that the nature and location of work in the knowledge-based economy are having uneven effects on the development of regional, urban, and rural economies, and that the growth of the international teleservices market presents both opportunities and challenges for those aspiring to gain entry to or succeed within it.

One of the keenly anticipated benefits of new ICTs has been their potential to promote economic development in rural and remote locations throughout Canada, including aboriginal communities—areas traditionally dependent upon declining agricultural and primary industries. The vision, articulated most recently by the federal National Broadband Task Force, is of remote communities, connected by broadband digital networks, peopled by skilled knowledge workers able to overcome the barriers to employment and economic opportunity posed by distance. According to the Task Force:

> By reducing or even eliminating the economic costs traditionally associated with distance, broadband communications offer all Canadian communities the potential to capitalize on their natural and human endowments, and to compete effectively in

markets of whatever scale in their areas of comparative advantage. (National Broadband Task Force 2001, 24)

However, notwithstanding concerted attempts by both federal and provincial governments to lever ICTs to lessen the economic disparities among regions and between urban and rural communities, such as New Brunswick's attempt at refashioning itself as the call centre capital of Canada, there is mounting evidence that the knowledge-based economy, and the importance of ICTs to it, reinforces rather than reduces historic patterns of regional disparity.

Even as rural and remote communities promote themselves as increasingly "wired" and ready to participate in the new economy, a consensus has emerged around the increasing importance of "clustering" the development of high-tech, knowledge-based industries around largely existing urban centres in order to compete internationally. Cities have become more rather than less important in the new international division of labour, as nodal points for controlling the flow of goods and services and as hubs for R&D and specialized economic activity such as international financial services (Castells 2000, 424–40; Huws, Jagger and Bates, 2001; Sassen 1998). Business leaders and policy makers alike now argue that so-called high-tech "clusters" or "learning regions" such as Kitchener-Waterloo, Ottawa, Toronto, and Montreal, are key to competing in the global economy, because it is in such places that innovative, job-creating companies have access to so-called "untraded interdependencies," which are specific to locales, including: a critical mass of highly skilled labour; communications and transportation infrastructure; access to public and private R&D institutions and potential partners; large pools of venture capital; and the kind of quality of life that attracts workers (Courchene and Telmer 1998, 268–96; Nankivell 2001, 85–91; Wolfe 2000). The emphasis on clustering the development of knowledge-based industries around existing urban centres and surrounding suburban zones, however, flies in the face of expectations that ICTs will produce a more even spatial distribution of work across Canada, and threatens to exacerbate existing regional economic disparity and tension as governments focus investment and services on the economies of already privileged clusters.[14] Meanwhile, attempts to incubate and foster high-

tech clusters in historically "low tech" provinces have achieved limited success and have more often than not pitted jurisdictions against one another in intense "locational tournaments" involving competition for investment in low-wage industries such as call centre services, with each trying to outdo the other in offering tax holidays, regulatory concessions, and job subsidies to potential investors (Jang 2001; Joint Venture: Silicon Valley 1998; Savoie 2001, 102–5, 157–60; Tutton 2001).

High-tech cluster regions are noteworthy not only for their prosperity relative to rural areas, but for the heightened degree of economic and social polarization within, as local labour markets themselves become bifurcated between high-tech professionals and low-tech workers in janitorial services, electronics assembly, and personal services work. Castells refers to this as the phenomenon of the "dual city" increasingly characteristic of high-tech cluster regions (Castells 1999, 27–41). Silicon Valley and other high-tech clusters have increasingly taken on the form of what one commentator calls the "resort economy," in which a highly affluent minority enjoys fat salaries, lavish homes in gated communities, exclusive club memberships, and premium shopping and recreational opportunities insulated against the intrusions of the wider community, all supported and surrounded by the labour of a nearly invisible underclass of service and manual workers. While employees in the software industry, for example, routinely pull down salaries in excess of US$100,000, average salaries in the industry with the largest employment in Silicon Valley, local and visitor services, are under US$23,000 (Joint Venture: Silicon Valley 2000). Canadian communities such as Toronto and Ottawa-Hull are well down the path to social polarization laid down by high-tech meccas like Silicon Valley, as evidenced by overheated real estate markets, affordable-housing shortages, gentrification, and increased evictions and homelessness. (Hill 2000; Solnit and Schwartzenberg 2000; Layton 2000; Goodell 1999).

Finally, combined with the liberalization of trade, the growing international trade in informational goods and services is reshaping the international division of labour and Canada's place within it. Canada has achieved some noteworthy successes exporting computer and software services and tele-mediated customer services. However, the ease with which such work can be outsourced or transferred elsewhere is a constant threat. In computer and software services, for example, Canada's trade balance has been narrowing throughout the 1990s, steadily eroding a modest surplus, suggesting that the time when Canada becomes a net importer of such services may be near (Prabhu 1998, 8–9; Industry Canada 2000, 27). The low-wage call centre industry in the Atlantic provinces and elsewhere, meanwhile, faces increasing competition from tele-service outsourcing firms in India and the Caribbean, where generally well-educated English-speaking employees can be hired for less than half of what it costs to pay Canadian workers (McElroy 2001). Places like New Brunswick may find such work disappearing through the very same network from which it came. While the magnitude of the threat remains small for now, the trend toward outsourcing teleservices to offshore locations such as India is accelerating.[15]

Electronic Monitoring and Workplace Privacy

Part of the allure of applying ICTs to work is not only the labour cost savings achieved through process automation, but the ability to use these same technologies to monitor the production process. Such technologies enable firms not only to track sales, inventory, and production speeds, but to track the performance, whereabouts, and, increasingly, private thoughts and personal communications of employees. Today, the location and activities of millions of workers are more closely monitored than ever, thanks to innovations such as GPS locators, computer keystroke logs, and software designed to monitor employee e-mail and Internet use. Indeed, technology is now available to employers to review the Web-surfing habits and histories of prospective employees even before they are hired (Privacy Commissioner of Canada 1999). Aside from the anxiety and atmosphere of suspicion that such monitoring can foster among supervisors and employees, the intensification and spread of electronic monitoring poses a growing human rights challenge.

First, let us get a handle on the scope of the phenomenon. An initial indication of the spread of electronic monitoring and its effects on workers has been signaled by the rising frequency of media reports involving employee abuse of e-mail and Internet tools at work, uncovered by employer monitoring (CBC News Online Staff 2001; Canadian Press 2001). Firming up these anecdotal impressions of the increased use of electronic monitoring are recent statistics on employer uses of electronic monitoring. A recent survey of workplace monitoring and surveillance practices in the United States by the American Management Association (AMA) found that nearly 78 per cent of firms record and monitor employee communications and activities on the job, including their phone calls, e-mail, Internet site visits, and computer files (American Management Association 2001, 1). The U.S.-based Privacy Foundation, meanwhile, estimates that up to one-third of the online workforce, or roughly fourteen million U.S. employees, is under continuous surveillance for improper e-mail and Internet use (Privacy Foundation 2001). While no equivalent figures are available on the extent of the practice by Canadian employers, there is little doubt that it is widespread (Bryant 1995, 505–21).

Not only have the extent and intensity of surveillance changed with new technologies, but the targets as well. While the work of cashiers, data entry clerks, and call center agents has long been susceptible to electronic monitoring, new software tracking workflow, e-mail communication, and Internet use facilitates increased surveillance of professional, managerial, and technical personnel as well.

The main reasons cited by employers for adopting such technologies are the need to limit legal liability, conduct performance reviews, measure productivity, and ensure the security of proprietary information against disclosure (American Management Association 2001). The AMA study showed that limiting liability was the primary reason for introducing such technologies. The proliferation of computers, e-mail, and Internet access in the workplace has given rise to inappropriate uses of the technology, including visits to gambling and pornography sites, and the transmission of harassing e-mails of a sexual, racial, or religious nature. Arguably, such monitoring systems have helped enforce policies against racism and sexism in the workplace. However, the trend toward continuous monitoring, which effectively casts a pall of suspicion over all employees, invites the question of whether employees' privacy rights and some form of the presumption of innocence should be sacrificed at the altar of limiting corporate liability.

Privacy legislation in Canada currently provides little protection to employees, particularly in the private sector. Canada's *Privacy Act* (1982) covers government uses of citizens' personal information, while the more recent *Personal Information Protection and Electronic Documents Act* (2001) focuses on protecting consumers, in order to shore up confidence in the beleaguered e-commerce sector. The latter signals the ascendancy of an e-commerce conception of privacy and the displacement of a rights-based conception from the current debate within Canada (Steeves 2001, 49–56).[16] Privacy advocates, including Canada's Privacy Commissioner, increasingly worry that Canadians surrender their privacy rights, often unwittingly, immediately upon entering the workplace. Workers should be entitled to some expectation of privacy in the workplace in order to communicate with family members and interact with colleagues in a natural manner, which may include venting frustrations about employers and working conditions; freedom to do so without fear of surveillance or reprisal is an essential ingredient of a reasonable quality of working life. Such a right to privacy, as one advocate argues, "cannot be conjured away by means of an employment contract" (Privacy Commissioner of Canada 2000).

Conclusion

This article provides a cursory overview of the complex and far-reaching effects and implications of ICTs for paid work in Canada. As a counter-narrative to the boosterism of high-tech gurus and leaders in business and government, it maps areas of pressing concern seldom acknowledged as anything more than "potholes" on the information highway. In our view, however, the connections between ICTs and workplace and employment trends like labour force polarization, the growth of non-standard employment, the gendered division of labour, increased stress and hours of work, and the social and environmental costs of clustered development raise serious doubts about how benign the information economy and society of our near future will really be. We conclude with a series of recommen-

dations on ways to mitigate the more disturbing effects of ICTs on work and workers in Canada:

- Modernization of legislation in areas like employment insurance, occupational health and safety, pensions and benefits, and employment standards in order to prevent the growing numbers of contingent workers from being excluded from enjoying full rights of economic and workplace citizenship.
- Funding for empirical research aimed at better understanding the various populations of teleworkers and the challenges they confront.
- Rededication by governments to long-term labour adjustment and retraining policies and programs abandoned in the 1980s and 1990s, especially for workers displaced by new technology.
- Facilitation of opportunities for the formation of institutions and mechanisms of collective representation, including trade unions, for contingent and home-based workers.
- Investigation of the health and environmental impacts of ICTs and the forms and locational dynamics of work they support.
- Development and enactment of privacy legislation related to individuals as workers, in addition to protection already in place for citizens and consumers.
- Recommitment by government to regulating and planning the development of urban and suburban regions with a view to creating livable cities.
- Increased public investment in mass transportation.

Works Cited

Akyeampong, Ernest, and Richard Nadwodny. 2001. "Evolution of the Canadian Workplace: Work from Home." Perspectives on Labour and Income 2(9) (September). Ottawa: Statistics Canada.

Alliance@IBM. Available: http://www.allianceibm.org.

American Management Association. 2001. *AMA Survey: Workplace Monitoring & Surveillance, Summary of Key Findings*. New York: American Management Association.

Andresky Fraser, Jill. 2001. *White Collar Sweatshop: The Deterioration of Work and Its Rewards in Corporate America*. New York: W.W. Norton.

Association of Canadian Search, Employment and Staffing Services (ACSESS). 2001., "National Staffing Industry Association Commends Repeal of Employment Agencies Act," Press Release, May 4, 2001.

Avon, Emmanuelle. 1996. "Human Resources in Science and Technology in the Services Sector." Services, Science and Technology Division, Statistics Canada, Analytical Research Paper No. 8, July Ottawa: Minister of Industry, July.

Barney, Darin. 2000. *Prometheus Wired: The Hope for Democracy in the Age of Networked Technology*. Vancouver: University of British Columbia Press.

Benner, Chris, and Amy Dean. 2000. "Labour in the New Economy: Lessons from Labour Organizing in Silicon Valley." In *Nonstandard Work: The Nature and Challenges of Changing Employment Arrangements*, ed. Françoise Carré, Marianne A. Ferber, Lonnie Golden and Stephen A. Herzenberg, 361–75. Champaign, IL: Industrial Relations Research Association.

Bernstein, Stephanie, Katherine Lippel, and Lucie Lamarche. 2001. *Women and Homework: The Canadian Legislative Framework*. Ottawa: Status of Women Canada.

Betcherman, Gordon, and Kathryn McMullen., 1998. "Impact of Information and Communication Technologies on Work and Employment in Canada." CPRN Discussion Paper No. 10. Ottawa: Canadian Policy Research Networks, February.

Bickerton, Geoff, and Catherine Louli. 1995. "Decades of Change, Decades of Struggle: Postal Workers and Technological Change." In *Re-shaping Work: Union Responses to Technological Change*, ed. Christopher Schenk and John Anderson, 216–32. Don Mills, ON: Federation of Labour.

Boston Consulting Group [Canada]. 2000. "Fast Forward: Accelerating Canada's Leadership in the Information Economy." Report of the Canadian E-Business Opportunities Roundtable. Toronto: Boston Consulting Group [Canada].

Brunet, J., and S. Prioux. 1989. "Formal versus Grass-Roots Training: Women, Work and Computers." *Journal of Communication* 39(3): 77–84.

Bryant, S. 1995. "Electronic Surveillance in the Workplace." *Canadian Journal of Communication* 20(4): 505–21.

Buchanan, Ruth, and Sarah Koch-Schulte. 2001. "Gender on the Line: Technology, Restructuring and the Reorganization of Work in the Call Centre Industry." Ottawa: Status of Women Canada.

Burke, Mike, and John Shields. 2000. "Tracking Inequality in the New Canadian Labour Market." In *Restructuring and Resistance: Canadian Public Policy in an Age of Global Capitalism*, ed. Mike Burke, Colin Mooers, and John Shields, 98–123. Halifax: Fernwood.

CBC News Online Staff. 2001. "Navy Officer Disciplined for Accessing Internet Porn." June 19. Available: http://www.cbc.ca/cgi-bin/templates/view.cgi?category=Canada&story=/news/2001.06/18

Canadian Policy Research Networks. Available: http://www.cprn.org.

——. Job Quality.ca. Available: http://www.JobQuality.ca.

——. 2002. JobQuality.ca. Indicators. Available: http://www.jobquality.ca/indicator_e/sec001.stm. [January 23, 2002]

Canadian Press. 2001. "New Brunswick Cracks Down on Unauthorized Surfing." *globeandmail.com*, September 5.

Castells, Manuel. 1999. "The Informational City is a Dual City: Can it be Reversed?" In *High Technology and Low-Income Communities: Prospects for the Positive Use of Advanced Information Technology*, ed. Donald A. Schön, Bish Saynal and William J. Mitchell, 27–41. Cambridge, MA: MIT Press.

——. 2000. The Rise of the Network Society: The Information Age. vol. 1, 2d ed. London: Blackwell.

Chun, Jennifer Jihye. 2001. "Flexible Despotism: The Intensification of Insecurity and Uncertainty in the Lives of Silicon Valley's High-Tech Assembly Workers." In *The Critical Study of Work: Labour, Technology and Global Production*, ed. Rick Baldoz, Charles Koeber and Philip Kraft, 127–54. Philadelphia: Temple University Press.

Church, Elizabeth. 2001. "Workers' Priorities Changing after Sept. 11." *Globe and Mail*, October 15.

Citizenship and Immigration Canada. 2000. "Supporting Jobs in the High Tech Sector." News Release, January 21. Available: http://www.cic.gc.ca/english/press/00/0003-pre.html.

Conference Board of Canada. 1996. "Jobs in one Knowledge Based Economy: Information Technology and the Impact on Employment." Ottawa: Conference Board of Canada.

Courchene, Thomas. 2000. "A Mission Statement for Canada." *Policy Options* (July–August): 6–14.

——. 2001. "A State of Minds." Montreal: Institute for Research on Public Policy.

Courchene, Thomas, with Colin R. Telmer. 1998. *From Heartland to North American Region State: The Social, Fiscal and Federal Evolution of Ontario*. Toronto: University of Toronto Press.

Denton, Timothy, and Bert Pereboom. 2000. *Profile of the Information and Communications Technologies Sector*. Prepared for the Expert Panel on Skills, Advisory Council on Science and Technology. Ottawa: Industry Canada.

Duxbury, Linda, and Chris Higgins. 2001. "Work-Life Balance in the New Millennium: Where Are We? Where Do We Need to Go?" Discussion Paper No. W/12. Ottawa: Canadian Policy Research Networks, October.

Ekos Research Associates. 2001. "Canadians and Working From Home." May 18. Available: http://www.ivc.ca/part12.html.

Ertl, Heidi. 2001. "Beyond the Information Highway: Networked Canada." Ottawa: Statistics Canada.

Eyerman, Jane. 2000. *Women in the Office: Transitions in a Global Economy*. Toronto: Sumach Press.

Felstead, Alan, and Nick Jewson. 2000. *In Work, At Home: Towards an Understanding of Homeworking*. London: Routledge.

Forrester Research Inc. 2002. "3.3 Million US Service Jobs to Go Offshore." November 11. 2002, http://www.forrester.com/ER/Research/Brief/Excerpt/0,1317,15900,00.html [March 16, 2003].

Galabuzi, G. 2001. "Canada's Creeping Economic Apartheid: The Economic Segregation and Social Marginalisation of Racialised Groups." Toronto: CSJ Foundation for Research and Education, August.

Gillespie, Andrew, and Ronald Richardson. 2000. "Teleworking and the City: Myths of Workplace Transcendence and Travel Reduction." In *Cities in the Telecommunications Age: The Fracturing of Geographics*, ed. James O. Wheeler, Yuko Aoyama, and Barney Warf, 230–32. London: Routledge.

Goodell, Jeff. 1999. "Down and Out in Silicon Valley." *Rolling Stone*, December 9.

Guly, Christopher. 2000. "Cyber-Watchdog for Call Centres." *Ottawa Citizen*, July 4.

Gurstein, Penny. 2002. *Wired to the World, Chained to the Home: Telework in Daily Life*. Vancouver: University of British Columbia Press.

Hill, Bert. 2000. "Ottawa's Good-News Growth Comes at Bad-News Price: Author." *Ottawa Citizen*, September 26.

Hughes, Karen, and Graham Lowe. 2000. "Surveying the 'Post-Industrial' Landscape: Information Technologies and Labour Market Polarization in Canada." *Canadian Review of Sociology and Anthropology* 37(1): 29–53.

Huws, Ursula, Nick Jagger, and Siobhan O'Regan. 1999. "Teleworking and Globalization." Report Summary, Institute for Employment Studies Report 358. Available: http://www.employment-studies.co.uk/summary/358sum.html

Huws, Ursula, Nick Jagger and Peter Bates. 2001. "Where the Butterfly Alights: The Global Location of eWork." Report Summary, Institute for Employment Studies Report 378, April. Available: http://www.employment-studies.co.uk/summary/378sum.html

Industry Canada. 2000. *Information and Communications Technologies Statistical Review: 1990–1998*. Spectrum, Information Technologies and Telecommunications Sector. Ottawa: Industry Canada, July.

Information and Privacy Commissioner/Ontario. 1992. "Workplace Privacy: A Consultation Paper." June. Available: http://www/ipc.on.ca

Information Highway Advisory Council. 1997. "Preparing Canada for a Digital World: Final Report of the Information Highway Advisory Council." Ottawa: Industry Canada.

InnoVisions Canada/Canadian Telework Association, 2001. "Canadian Stats and Facts." Available: http://www.ivc.ca/part12.html [October 15, 2001].

Jackson, Andrew, David Robinson, Bob Baldwin, and Cindy Wiggins. 2000. "Falling Behind: The State of Working Canada 2000." Ottawa: Canadian Centre for Policy Alternatives.

Jang, Brent. 2001. "Its Share of Pain Belies Notion of Opulent Alberta." *Globe and Mail*, September 1.

Johnson, Karen, Donna Lero, and Jennifer Rooney. 2001. "Work-Life Compendium 2001: 150 Canadian Statistics on Work, Family & Well-Being." Guelph, ON: Centre for Families, Work and Well-Being, University of Guelph.

Joint Venture: Silicon Valley. 1998. "*1998 Index* Finds Silicon Valley Facing Challenges, But Community Starting to Respond." Press Release,

January 11. Available: http://www. jointventure.org. [January 23, 2002].

——. 2000. *2000 Index of Silicon Valley*. Available: http://www.jointventure.org. [January 23, 2002].

Laucious, Joanne. 2000. "High-Tech Boom Faces Roadblocks: Road System Needs Upgrades." *Ottawa Citizen*, August 3.

Layton, Jack. 2000. *Homelessness: The Making and Unmaking of a Crisis*. Toronto: Penguin/McGill Institute for the Study of Canada.

Lin, Zhengxi, Janice Yates, and Garnett Picot. 1999. "Rising Self-Employment in the Midst of High Unemployment: An Empirical Analysis of Recent Developments in Canada." Business and Labour Market Analysis, Analytical Studies Branch. Ottawa: Statistics Canada, March.

Longford, Graham. 2001. "Rethinking E-Government: Dilemmas of Public Service, Citizenship and Democracy in the Digital Age." Paper presented to the Canadian Political Science Association Annual General Meeting, Université Laval, Quebec City, Quebec, May 27–29.

Lowe, Graham, Grant Schellenberg, and Katie Davidman. 1999. "Rethinking Employment Relationships." CPRN Discussion Paper No. W/05, Changing Employment Relationships Series. Ottawa: Canadian Policy Research Networks.

Marshall, Katherine. 2001. "Working With Computers." *Perspectives on Labour and Income* 2(5). Ottawa: Statistics Canada.

McBride, Stephen. 2000. "Policy from What? Neoliberal and Human-Capital Theoretical Foundations of Recent Canadian Labour-Market Policy." In *Restructuring and Resistance: Canadian Public Policy in an Age of Global Capitalism*, ed. Mike Burke, Colin Mooers and John Shields, 159–77 Halifax: Fernwood.

McElroy, Damien. 2001. "Workers Know the Score." *National Post*, May 28.

McMullen, Kathryn. 2001. "Skill and Employment Effects of Computer Based Technologies." Canadian Policy Research Networks, Backgrounder.

McNally, David. 2000. "Globalization, Trade Pacts and Migrant Workers." In *Restructuring and Resistance: Canadian Public Policy in an Age of Global Capitalism*, ed. Mike Burke, Colin Mooers and John Shields, 268–70. Halifax: Fernwood.

Menzies, Heather. 1996. *Whose Brave New World? The Information Highway and the New Economy*. Toronto: Between the Lines.

——. 1997. "Telework, Shadow Work: The Privatization of Work in the New Digital Economy." *Studies in Political Economy* 53 (Summer): 103–23.

Miller, Eric J. 2000. "Transportation and Communication." In Trudi Bunting and Pierre Filion, *Canadian Cities in Transition: The Twenty-first Century*. 2d ed., 173–97. Toronto: Oxford.

Nankivell, Neville. 2001. "Why Canada's Capital Is a High-Tech Hotbed." *National Pos*, April 18.

National Broadband Task Force. 2001. "The New National Dream: Networking the Nation for Broadband Access." Report of the National Broadband Task Force. Ottawa: Industry Canada.

Noble, David. 1995. *Progress Without People: New Technology, Unemployment, and the Message of Resistance*. Toronto: Between the Lines.

Ontario Ministry of Labour. Your Guide to the Employment Standards Act. Available: http://www.gov.on.ca/LAB/english/es/guide/

Peruose, D. 1998. "Working at Home." *Perspectives on Labour and Income* 10(2) (Summer). Ottawa: Statistics Canada.

Peterson, Greg. 2001. "Electronic Commerce and Technology Use." Connectedness Series No. 5, Science, Innovation and Electronic Information Division, Statistics Canada. Ottawa: Minister of Industry.

Prabhu, Sirish. 1998. "The Software and Computer Services Industry: An Overview of Developments in the 1990s." Analytical Paper Series No. 17, Statistics Canada. Ottawa: Minister of Industry.

Privacy Commissioner of Canada. 1999. *Annual Report 1998–99*. Ottawa: Minister of Public Works and Government Services Canada.

——. 2000. *Annual Report 1999–2000*. Ottawa: Minister of Public Works and Government Services Canada.

Privacy Foundation. 2001. "One-Third of U.S. Online Workforce under Internet/E-Mail Surveillance." Privacy Watch, July 9. Available: http://www.privacyfoundation.org/privacywatch/report.asp?id=72&action=0

Putman, Carol, and Anne Fenety. 2000. "Who's on the Line?: Women in Call Centres Talk about their Work and its Impact on their Health and Well-Being." Halifax, NS: Dalhousie University, Maritime Centre of Excellence for Women's Health.

Rao, Badrinath. 2001. "Economic Migrants in a Global Labour Market: A Report on the Recruitment and Retention of Asian Computer Professionals by Canadian High Tech Firms." CPRN Discussion Paper No. W/13. Ottawa: Canadian Policy Research Networks.

Reid, Angus. 1996. *Shakedown: How the New Economy Is Changing Our Lives*. Toronto: Doubleday.

Rheingold, Howard. 1994. *The Virtual Community*, London: Secker and Warburg.

Rifkin, Jeremy. 1995. *The End of Work: The Decline of the Global Labor Force and the Dawn of the Post-Market Era*. New York: G.P. Putnam's Sons.

Rubin, Jeffrey. 2001. "How Long Will the Market Continue to Pay High Tech Multiples?" *Globe and Mail*, September 1.

Sassen, Saskia. 1998. *Globalization and Its Discontents: Essays on the New Mobility of People and Money*. New York: The New Press.

Savoie, Donald. 2001. *Pulling Against Gravity: Economic Development in New Brunswick During the McKenna Years*. Montreal: Institute for Research on Public Policy.

Sawchuck, Kim, and Barbara Crow. 1995. "Some Canadian Feminists Intervene in the Datasphere." Proceedings: Telecommunities '95 Equity on the Net, International Community Networking Conference. Victoria.

Schmidt, Lisa. 2001. "Canada Lagging Behind Many Countries in Adult Education finds Study." Canada.comNews, September 9. Available: http://www.canada.com

SchoolNet program. Available: http://www.schoolnet.ca/home/e/

Shalla, Vivian. 1997. "Technology and the Deskilling of Work: The Case of the Passenger Agents at Air Canada." In *Good Jobs, Bad Jobs, No Jobs: The Transformation of Work in the 21st Century*, ed. A. Duffy, D. Glenday, and N. Papo, 76–96. Toronto: Harcourt Brace and Co.

Singer, Zev. 2000. "West-End Land Crunch Hits Tech Sector." *Ottawa Citizen*, June 13.

Solnit, Rebecca, and Susan Schwartzenberg. 2000. *Hollow City: The Siege of San Francisco and the Crisis of American Urbanism*. London: Verso.

Stanford, Jim. 2001. "We Can't All Be Web Designers." *CCPA Monitor* 8(5) (October): 31.

Statistics Canada. 1998a. "1996 Census: Labour Force Activity, Occupation and Industry, Place of Work, Mode of Transportation to Work, Unpaid Work," *The Daily*, March 17, 3–6.

———. 1998b. "Cellular Telephone Service Industry: Historical Statistics." *The Daily*, April 1. Available: http://www.statcan.ca:80/Daily/English/980401/d980401.htm

———. 2001a. Labour Force Survey, August. Available: http://www.statcan.ca/english/Subjects/Labour/LFS/lfs-en.htm

———. 2001b. The Daily, August 27. Available: http://www.statcan.ca/Daily/English/010827/d010827b.htm

———. 2001c. "After the Layoff." The Daily, October 25. Available: http://www.statcan.ca:80/Daily/English/011025/d011025a.htm

———. 2001d. "Telecommunications Statistics: Third quarter 2001." *The Daily*, December 21.

———. 2001e. *Workplace and Employee Survey Compendium: 1999 Data*. Ottawa: Minister of Industry.

Steeves, Valerie. 2001. "Privacy Then and Now: Taking Stock Since IHAC." In *E-commerce vs. E-commons: Communications in the Public Interest*, ed. Marita Moll and Leslie Regan Shade, 49–56. Ottawa: Canadian Centre for Policy Alternatives.

Stromber, M. H., and C. Arnold. 1987. "Computer Chips and Paper Clips: Technology and Women's Employment, Vol. 2: Case Studies and Policy Perspectives, Panel on Technology and Women's Employment." Committee on Women's Employment and Related Social Issues. Washington, DC: National Research Council.

Symons, Frank. 1997. "Network Access, Skills and Equity in the Workplace: Polarization in Social Policy." *Canadian Journal of Communication* 22(2): 195–215.

Tal, Benjamin. 2001. "Trends in Small Business as of October 2001." Economics Division, Canadian Imperial Bank of Commerce. Available http://www.cibc.com/

Tapscott, Don. 1996. *The Digital Economy: Promise and Peril in the Age of Networked Intelligence*. Toronto: McGraw-Hill.

Treasury Board of Canada Secretariat. 2000. Employment Statistics for the Federal Public Service: April 1, 1999–March 31, 2000. Available: http://www.tbs-set.gc.ca/pubs_pol/hrpubs/pse-fpe/es-se99-00-1_e.html#_Toc501185760

Tutton, Michael. 2001. "N.S. Offering Record-Breaking Subsidies to Attract Call Centre Business." *Yahoo News Canada*, July 31.

Ullman, Ellen. 1995. "Out of Time: Reflections on the Programming Life." In *Resisting the Virtual Life: The Culture and Politics of Information*, ed. James Brook and Jain A. Boal, 131–44. San Francisco: City Lights.

United States General Accounting Office. 2000. "Contingent Workers: Incomes and Benefits Lag Behind those of the Rest of Workforce: Report to the Honorable Edward M. Kennedy and the Honorable Robert G. Torricelli," 18–30. U.S. Senate, Washington, DC.

Vosko, Leah. 2000. *Temporary Work: The Gendered Rise of a Precarious Employment Relationship.* Toronto: University of Toronto Press.

Walters, Gregory J. 2001. "Information Highway Policy, E-commerce and Work." In *E-commerce vs. E-commons: Communications in the Public Interest,* Marita Moll and Leslie Regan Shade, 78–83. Ottawa: Canadian Centre for Policy Alternatives.

Washington Alliance of Technology Workers/CWA. 2001. *Disparities Within the Digital World: Realities of the New Economy.* Prepared by The Worker Centre, King County Labor Council. Available: http://www.washtech.org

Whitaker, Reg. 1999. *The End of Privacy: How Total Surveillance Is Becoming a Reality.* New York: The New Press.

Wolfe, David. 2000. "Social Capital and Cluster Development in Learning Regions." Paper presented to the XVIII World Congress of the International Political Science Association, Quebec City, August 5.

Wright, R. 1997. "Women in Computing: A Cross-National Analysis." In *Women in Computing: Progression: From Where to What?,* ed. R. Lander and A. Adam, 72–82. Exeter, UK: Intellect Books.

Notes

1 Statistics Canada reports that by 1999 Internet and cell phone penetration of Canadian households reached 42 per cent and 32 per cent, respectively. See Ertl (2001, 38, 40). Elsewhere, Statistics Canada reports that there were 9.9 million cellular phone subscribers in Canada by 2001 (Statistics Canada 2001d).

2 Betcherman and McMullen (1998) report as little as 16 per cent of workers using new ICTs like computers as recently as 1985.

3 This is not to deny the emergence of some disturbing trends, such as growing underemployment and rising unemployment among certain groups, such as single mothers and young, unskilled males (Burke and Shields 2000, 98–123; Jackson, Robinson, Baldwin, and Wiggins 2000, 47–73).

4 The Liberal Party Red Book of 1993 stated, for example, that "it is the information and knowledge-based industries with their new products, new services, new markets for old and new products, and new processes for existing businesses that are providing the foundation for jobs and economic growth." Quoted in McBride (2000, 163).

5 Betcherman and McMullen (1998, 11) find little proof of a direct connection between ICT use and overall job growth. Their study reveals the strongest influence on job growth to be sales growth rather than ICT investment.

6 Traditionally associated with agricultural and construction work, the use of temporary workers is high in "knowledge sectors" like management and administrative services (24 per cent) educational services (19 per cent) and public administration (15 per cent) as well: CPRN, JobQuality.ca, Available: http://www.JobQuality.ca.

7 See, for example, a report on wages and working conditions in the IT sector in Seattle: Washington Alliance of Technology Workers/CWA (2001).

8 For example, amendments to Ontario's *Employment Standards Act* in 2000 repealed provisions regulating and licensing temporary employment agencies, and raised from 44 to 60 the maximum number of hours in the work week. The latter provision was eagerly sought by the ICT industry, which had sought exemptions under the previous Act on a routine basis. See Association of Canadian Search, Employment and Staffing Services (ACSESS) (2001), and Ontario Ministry of Labour, *Your Guide to the Employment Standards Act,* available at http://www.gov.on.ca/LAB/english/es/guide/.

9 For more detailed demonstrations of this link, see, for example: Betcherman and McMullen (1998, 15–17); and Hughes and Lowe (2000, 29–53).

10 Research results from the U.K., however, suggest little impact so far. The proportion of U.K. teleworkers with disabilities stands at 9 per cent, which is roughly the same proportion as in the traditional workforce (Huws, Jagger and O'Regan, 1999).

11 The most serious consequences for accessibility are to be found at the university level, where undergraduate tuition fees have increased 120 per cent, on average, in Canada since 1990 (Statistics Canada 2001b).

12 Almost 60 per cent of Canadian workers with only high school diplomas reported receiving no training during 1999, whereas only 30 per cent

of those with university degrees reported receiving no training (Statistics Canada 2001e, 30).

13 A 2000 survey found that 58 per cent of employees experience high levels of work-family role "overload," up from 47 per cent in 1990. Such stress is most acute among professional and managerial employees (Johnson et al. 2001, 53–54). Similar findings have been reported in Duxbury and Higgins (2001). See also Church (2001).

14 For the most part, decentralizing forces observed in the new economy have involved the movement of work and business away from central business districts to suburban nodes, rather than from metropolitan to rural or remote regions.

15 In November of 2002, the U.S.-based IT industry research firm Forrester Research Inc. issued a study predicting the loss of 3.3 million service jobs from the U.S. over the next 15 years due to off-shore outsourcing to countries such as India and China (Forrester Research Inc. 2002).

16 The clash between surveillance and basic legal rights in the workplace are discussed at length in Information and Privacy Commissioner/Ontario (1992).

Performance Studies
Interventions and Radical Research

Dwight Conquergood

According to Michel de Certeau, "what the map cuts up, the story cuts across" (1984:129). This pithy phrase evokes a postcolonial world criss-crossed by transnational narratives, diaspora affilia-tions, and, especially, the movement and multiple migrations of people, sometimes voluntary, but often economically propelled and politically coerced. In order to keep pace with such a world, we now think of "place" as a heavily trafficked inter-section, a port of call and exchange, instead of a cir-cumscribed territory. A boundary is more like a membrane than a wall. In current cultural theory, "location" is imagined as an itinerary instead of a fixed point. Our understanding of "local context" expands to encompass the historical, dynamic, often traumatic, movements of people, ideas, images, commodities, and capital. It is no longer easy to sort out the local from the global: transnational circula-tions of images get reworked on the ground and redeployed for local, tactical struggles. And global flows simultaneously are encumbered and energized by these local makeovers. We now are keenly aware that the "local" is a leaky, contingent construction, and that global forces are taken up, struggled over, and refracted for site-specific purposes. The best of the new cultural theory distinguishes itself from apolitical celebrations of mobility, flow, and easy border crossings by carefully tracking the transitive

circuits of power and the political economic pres-sure points that monitor the migrations of people, channel the circulations of meanings, and stratify access to resources (see Gilroy 1994; Appadurai 1996; Lavie and Swedenburg 1996; Clifford 1997; di Leonardo 1998; Joseph 1999; Ong 1999). We now ask: For whom is the border a friction-free zone of entitled access, a frontier of possibility? Who travels confidently across borders, and who gets ques-tioned, detained, interrogated, and strip-searched at the border (see Taylor 1999)?

But de Certeau's aphorism, "what the map cuts up, the story cuts across," also points to transgres-sive travel between two different domains of knowl-edge: one official, objective, and abstract—"the map"; the other one practical, embodied, and pop-ular—"the story." This promiscuous traffic between different ways of knowing carries the most radical promise of performance studies research. Per-formance studies struggles to open the space between analysis and action, and to pull the pin on the binary opposition between theory and practice. This embrace of different ways of knowing is radical because it cuts to the root of how knowledge is organized in the academy.

The dominant way of knowing in the academy is that of empirical observation and critical analysis from a distanced perspective: "knowing that," and

Dwight Conquergood, "Performance Studies: Interventions and Radical Research," TDR/The Drama Review, 46:2 (Summer 2002), pp. 145–156. © 2002 by New York University and the Massachusetts Institute of Technology.

"knowing about." This is a view from above the object of inquiry: knowledge that is anchored in paradigm and secured in print. This propositional knowledge is shadowed by another way of knowing that is grounded in active, intimate, hands-on participation and personal connection: "knowing how," and "knowing who." This is a view from ground level, in the thick of things. This is knowledge that is anchored in practice and circulated within a performance community, but is ephemeral. Donna Haraway locates this homely and vulnerable "view from a body" in contrast to the abstract and authoritative "view from above," universal knowledge that pretends to transcend location (1991:196).

Since the enlightenment project of modernity, the first way of knowing has been preeminent. Marching under the banner of science and reason, it has disqualified and repressed other ways of knowing that are rooted in embodied experience, orality, and local contingencies. Between objective knowledge that is consolidated in texts, and local know-how that circulates on the ground within a community of memory and practice, there is no contest. It is the choice between science and "old wives' tales" (note how the disqualified knowledge is gendered as feminine).

Michel Foucault coined the term "subjugated knowledges" to include all the local, regional, vernacular, naive knowledges at the bottom of the hierarchy—the low Other of science (1980:81-84). These are the nonserious ways of knowing that dominant culture neglects, excludes, represses, or simply fails to recognize. Subjugated knowledges have been erased because they are illegible; they exist, by and large, as active bodies of meaning, outside of books, eluding the forces of inscription that would make them legible, and thereby legitimate (see de Certeau 1998; Scott 1998).

What gets squeezed out by this epistemic violence is the whole realm of complex, finely nuanced meaning that is embodied, tacit, intoned, gestured, improvised, coexperienced, covert—and all the more deeply meaningful because of its refusal to be spelled out. Dominant epistemologies that link knowing with seeing are not attuned to meanings that are masked, camouflaged, indirect, embedded, or hidden in context. The visual/verbal bias of Western regimes of knowledge blinds researchers to meanings that are expressed forcefully through intonation, silence, body tension, arched eyebrows,

blank stares, and other protective arts of disguise and secrecy—what de Certeau called "the elocutionary experience of a fugitive communication" (2000:133; see Conquergood 2000). Subordinate people do not have the privilege of explicitness, the luxury of transparency, the presumptive norm of clear and direct communication, free and open debate on a level playing field that the privileged classes take for granted.

In his critique of the limitations of literacy, Kenneth Burke argued that print-based scholarship has built-in blind spots and a conditioned deafness:

> The [written] record is usually but a fragment of the expression (as the written word omits all telltale record of gesture and tonality; and not only may our "literacy" keep us from missing the omissions, it may blunt us to the appreciation of tone and gesture, so that even when we witness the full expression, we note only those aspects of it that can be written down). ([1950] 1969:185)

In even stronger terms, Raymond Williams challenged the class-based arrogance of scriptocentrism, pointing to the "error" and "delusion" of "highly educated" people who are "so driven in on their reading" that "they fail to notice that there are other forms of skilled, intelligent, creative activity" such as "theatre" and "active politics." This error "resembles that of the narrow reformer who supposes that farm labourers and village craftsmen were once uneducated, merely because they could not read." He argued that "the contempt" for performance and practical activity, "which is always latent in the highly literate, is a mark of the observer's limits, not those of the activities themselves" ([1958] 1983:309). Williams critiqued scholars for limiting their sources to written materials; I agree with Burke that scholarship is so skewed toward texts that even when researchers do attend to extralinguistic human action and embodied events they construe them as texts to be read. According to de Certeau, this scriptocentrism is a hallmark of Western imperialism. Posted above the gates of modernity, this sign: " 'Here only what is written is understood.' Such is the internal law of that which has constituted itself as 'Western' [and 'white']" (1984:161).

Only middle-class academics could blithely assume that all the world is a text because reading and writing are central to their everyday lives and occupational security. For many people throughout the world, however, particularly subaltern groups, texts are often inaccessible, or threatening, charged with the regulatory powers of the state. More often than not, subordinate people experience texts and the bureaucracy of literacy as instruments of control and displacement, e.g., green cards, passports, arrest warrants, deportation orders—what de Certeau calls "intextuation": "Every power, including the power of law, is written first of all on the backs of its subjects" (1984:140). Among the most oppressed people in the United States today are the "undocumented" immigrants, the so-called "illegal aliens," known in the vernacular as the people "sin papeles," the people without papers, *indocumentado/as*. They are illegal because they are not legible, they trouble "the writing machine of the law" (de Certeau 1984:141).

The hegemony of textualism needs to be exposed and undermined. Transcription is not a transparent or politically innocent model for conceptualizing or engaging the world. The root metaphor of the text underpins the supremacy of Western knowledge systems by erasing the vast realm of human knowledge and meaningful action that is unlettered, "a history of the tacit and the habitual" (Jackson 2000:29). In their multivolume historical ethnography of colonialism/ evangelism in South Africa, John and Jean Comaroff pay careful attention to the way Tswana people argued with their white interlocutors "*both* verbally and nonverbally" (1997:47; see also 1991). They excavate spaces of agency and struggle from everyday performance practices—clothing, gardening, healing, trading, worshipping, architecture, and homemaking—to reveal an impressive repertoire of conscious, creative, critical, contrapuntal responses to the imperialist project that exceeded the verbal. The Comaroffs intervene in an academically fashionable textual fundamentalism and fetish of the (verbal) archive where "text—a sad proxy for life—becomes all" (1992:26). "In this day and age," they ask, "do we still have to remind ourselves that many of the players on any historical stage cannot speak at all? Or, under greater or lesser duress, opt not to do so" (1997:48; see also Scott 1990)?

There are many ethnographic examples of how nonelite people recognize the opacity of the text and critique its dense occlusions and implications in historical processes of political economic privilege and systematic exclusion. In Belize, for example, Garifuna people, an African-descended minority

group, use the word *gapencillitin*, which means "people with pencil," to refer to middle- and upper-class members of the professional-managerial class, elites who approach life from an intellectual perspective. They use the word *mapencillitin*, literally "people without pencil," to refer to rural and working-class people, "real folks" who approach life from a practitioner's point of view.[2] What is interesting about the Garifuna example is that class stratification, related to differential knowledges, is articulated in terms of access to literacy. The pencil draws the line between the haves and the have-nots. For Garifuna people, the pencil is not a neutral instrument; it functions metonymically as the operative technology of a complex political economy of knowledge, power, and the exclusions upon which privilege is based.

In his study of the oppositional politics of black musical performance, Paul Gilroy argues that critical scholars need to move beyond this "idea and ideology of the text and of textuality as a mode of communicative practice which provides a model for all other forms of cognitive exchange and social interaction" (1994:77). Oppressed people everywhere must watch their backs, cover their tracks, suck up their feelings, and veil their meanings. The state of emergency under which many people live demands that we pay attention to messages that are coded and encrypted; to indirect, nonverbal, and extralinguistic modes of communication where subversive meanings and utopian yearnings can be sheltered and shielded from surveillance.

Gilroy's point is illustrated vividly by Frederick Douglass in a remarkable passage from his life narrative in which he discussed the improvisatory performance politics expressed in the singing of enslaved people. It is worth quoting at length:[3]

> But, on allowance day, those who visited the great house farm were peculiarly excited and noisy. While on their way, they would make the dense old woods, for miles around, reverberate with their wild notes. These were not always merry because they were wild. On the contrary, they were mostly of a plaintive cast, and told a tale of grief and sorrow. In the most boisterous outbursts of rapturous sentiment, there was ever a tinge of deep melancholy [...]. I have sometimes thought that the mere hearing of those songs would do more to impress truly spiritual-minded men and women with the soul-crushing and

death-dealing character of slavery, than the reading of whole volumes [...]. Every tone was a testimony against slavery [...]. The hearing of those wild notes always [...] filled my heart with ineffable sadness [...]. To those songs I trace my first glimmering conceptions of the dehumanizing character of slavery [...]. Those songs still follow me, to deepen my hatred of slavery, and quicken my sympathies for my brethren in bonds. ([1855] 1969:97–99)

Enslaved people were forbidden by law in 19th-century America to acquire literacy. No wonder, then, that Douglass, a former enslaved person, still acknowledged the deeply felt insights and revelatory power that come through the embodied experience of listening to communal singing, the tones, cadence, vocal nuances, all the sensuous specificities of performance that overflow verbal content: "they were tones loud, long, and deep" (99).

In order to know the deep meaning of slavery, Douglass recommended an experiential, participatory epistemology as superior to the armchair "reading of whole volumes." Douglass advised meeting enslaved people on the ground of their experience by exposing oneself to their expressive performances. In this way, Douglass anticipated and extended Johannes Fabian's call for a turn "from informative to performative ethnography" (1990:3), an ethnography of the ears and heart that reimagines participant-observation as coperformative witnessing:

> If any one wishes to be impressed with a sense of the soul-killing power of slavery, let him go to Colonel Lloyd's plantation, and, on allowance day, place himself in the deep pine woods, and there let him, in silence, thoughtfully analyze the sounds that shall pass through the chambers of his soul, and if he is not thus impressed, it will only be because "there is no flesh in his obdurate heart." (Douglass [1855] 1969:99)

Instead of reading textual accounts of slavery, Douglass recommended a riskier hermeneutics of experience, relocation, copresence, humility, and vulnerability: *listening to and being touched* by the protest performances of enslaved people. He understood that knowledge is *located*, not transcendent ("let him go" and "place himself in the deep pine woods, and there [...]"); that it must be *engaged*, not abstracted ("let him [...] analyze the sounds that shall pass through the chambers of his soul"); and that it is forged from *solidarity with*, not separation

from, the people ("quicken my sympathies for my brethren in bonds"). In this way, Douglass's epistemology prefigured Antonio Gramsci's call for engaged knowledge: "The intellectual's error consists in believing that one can know without understanding and even more without feeling and being impassioned [...] that is, without feeling the elementary passions of the people" (1971:418). Proximity, not objectivity, becomes an epistemological point of departure and return.

Douglass recommended placing oneself quietly, respectfully, humbly, in the space of others so that one could be surrounded and "impressed" by the expressive meanings of their music. It is subtle but significant that he instructed the outsider to listen "in silence." I interpret this admonition as an acknowledgment and subversion of the soundscapes of power within which the ruling classes typically are listened to while the subordinate classes listen in silence. Anyone who had the liberty to travel freely would be, of course, on the privileged side of domination and silencing that these songs evoked and contested. In effect, Douglass encouraged a participatory understanding of these performances, but one that muffled white privilege. Further, because overseers often commanded enslaved people to sing in the fields as a way of auditing their labor, and plantation rulers even appropriated after-work performances for their own amusement, Douglass was keenly sensitive to *how* one approached and entered subjugated spaces of performance.

The mise-en-scène of feeling-understanding-knowing for Douglass is radically different from the interpretive scene set forth by Clifford Geertz in what is now a foundational and frequently cited quotation for the world-as-text model in ethnography and cultural studies: "The culture of a people is an ensemble of texts, themselves ensembles, which the anthropologist strains to read over the shoulders of those to whom they properly belong" (1973:452). Whereas Douglass featured cultural performances that register and radiate dynamic "structures of feeling" and pull us into alternative ways of knowing that exceed cognitive control (Williams 1977), Geertz figures culture as a stiff, awkward reading room. The ethnocentrism of this textualist metaphor is thrown into stark relief when applied to the countercultures of enslaved and other dispossessed people. Forcibly excluded from acquiring literacy, enslaved people nonetheless created a culture of resistance. Instead of an "ensemble of texts," however, a repertoire of performance practices became the backbone of this counterculture where politics was "played, danced, and acted, as well as sung and sung about, because words [...] will never be enough to communicate its unsayable claims to truth" (Gilroy 1994:37).

In addition to the ethnocentrism of the culture-is-text metaphor, Geertz's theory needs to be critiqued for its particular fieldwork-as-reading model: "Doing ethnography is like trying to read [...] a manuscript" (10). Instead of listening, absorbing, and standing in solidarity with the protest performances of the people, as Douglass recommended, the ethnographer, in Geertz's scene, stands above and behind the people and, uninvited, peers over their shoulders to read their texts, like an overseer or a spy. There is more than a hint of the improper in this scene: the asymmetrical power relations secure both the anthropologist's privilege to intrude and the people's silent acquiescence (although one can imagine what they would say about the anthropologist's manners and motives when they are outside his reading gaze). The strain and tension of this scene are not mediated by talk or interaction; both the researcher and the researched face the page as silent readers instead of turning to face one another and, perhaps, open a conversation.

Geertz's now classic depiction of the turn toward texts in ethnography and cultural studies needs to be juxtaposed with Zora Neal Hurston's much earlier and more complex rendering of a researcher reading the texts of subordinate others:

> The theory behind our tactics: "The white man is always trying to know into somebody else's business. All right, I'll set something outside the door of my mind for him to play with and handle. He can read my writing but he sho' can't read my mind. I'll put this play toy in his hand, and he will seize it and go away. Then I'll say my say and sing my song."
> ([1935] 1990:3)

Hurston foregrounds the terrain of struggle, the field of power relations on which texts are written, exchanged, and read. Whereas Geertz does not problematize the ethnographer's will-to-know or access to the texts of others, Hurston is sensitive to the reluctance of the subordinate classes "to reveal that which the soul lives by" (2) because they understand

from experience the ocular politics that links the powers to see, to search, and to seize. Aware of the white man's drive to objectify, control, and grasp as a way of knowing, subordinate people cunningly set a text, a decoy, outside the door to lure him away from "homeplace" where subjugated but empowering truths and survival secrets are sheltered (hooks 1990). In Hurston's brilliant example, vulnerable people actually redeploy the written text as a tactic of evasion and camouflage, performatively turning and tripping the textual fetish against the white person's will-to-know. "So driven in on his reading," as Williams would say, he is blinded by the texts he compulsively seizes: "knowing so little about us, he doesn't know what he is missing" (Hurston [1935] 1990:2). Once provided with something that he can "handle," "seize," in a word, *apprehend,* he will go away and then space can be cleared for performed truths that remain beyond his reach: "then I'll say my say and sing my song." By mimicking the reifying textualism of dominant knowledge regimes, subordinate people can deflect its invasive power. This mimicry of textualism is a complex example of "mimetic excess" in which the susceptibility of dominant images, forms, and technologies of power to subversive doublings holds the potential for undermining the power of that which is mimed (Taussig 1993:254-55).

Note that in Hurston's account, subordinate people read and write, as well as perform. With her beautiful example of how a text can perform subversive work, she disrupts any simplistic dichotomy that would align texts with domination and performance with liberation. In Hurston's example, the white man researcher is a fool not because he values literacy, but because he valorized it to the exclusion of other media, other modes of knowing. I want to be very clear about this point: textocentrism—not texts—is the problem.

From her ethnographic fieldwork in the coal camps and "hollers" of West Virginia, Kathleen Stewart documents an especially vivid example of text-performance entanglements: how official signs and local performances play off and with each other in surprising and delightful ways. After a dog bit a neighbor's child, there was much talk and worry throughout the camp about liability and lawsuits:

> Finally Lacy Forest announced that he had heard that "by law" if you had a NO TRESPASSING sign on

your porch you couldn't be sued. So everyone went to the store in Beckley to get the official kind of sign. Neighbors brought back multiple copies and put them up for those too old or sick or poor to get out and get their own. Then everyone called everyone else to explain that the sign did not mean them. In the end, every porch and fence (except for those of the isolated shameless who don't care) had a bright NO TRESPASSING, KEEP OFF sign, and people visited together, sitting underneath the NO TRESPASSING signs, looking out. (1996:141; see also Conquergood 1997)[4]

Through the power of reframing, social performances reclaim, short-circuit, and resignify the citational force of the signed imperatives. Moreover, Ngũgĩ wa Thiong'o's concept of "orature" complicates any easy separation between speech and writing, performance and print, and reminds us how these channels of communication constantly overlap, penetrate, and mutually produce one another (1998).

The performance studies project makes its most radical intervention, I believe, by embracing *both* written scholarship *and* creative work, papers and performances. We challenge the hegemony of the text best by reconfiguring texts and performances in horizontal, metonymic tension, not by replacing one hierarchy with another, the romance of performance for the authority of the text. The "liminal-norm" that Jon McKenzie identifies as the calling card of performance studies (2001:41) manifests itself most powerfully in the struggle to live betwixt and between theory and theatricality, paradigms and practices, critical reflection and creative accomplishment. Performance studies brings this rare hybridity into the academy, a commingling of analytical and artistic ways of knowing that unsettles the institutional organization of knowledge and disciplines. The constitutive liminality of performance studies lies in its capacity to bridge segregated and differently valued knowledges, drawing together legitimated as well as subjugated modes of inquiry.

There is an emergent genre of performance studies scholarship that epitomizes this text-performance hybridity. A number of performance studies–allied scholars create performances as a supplement to, not substitute for, their written research. These performance pieces stand alongside and in metonymic tension with published research. The creative works are developed for multiple professional reasons: they deepen experiential and participatory engagement with materials both for the researcher and her audience; they provide a dynamic and rhetorically compelling alternative to conference papers; they offer a more accessible and engaging format for sharing research and reaching communities outside academia; they are a strategy for staging interventions. To borrow Amanda Kemp's apt phrase, they use "performance both as a way of knowing and as a way of showing" (1998:116). To add another layer to the enfolding convolutions of text and performance, several of these performance pieces have now been written up and published in scholarly journals and books (see Conquergood 1988; Becker, McCall, and Morris 1989; McCall and Becker 1990; Paget 1990; Pollock 1990; Jackson 1993, 1998; Allen and Garner 1995; Laughlin 1995; Wellin 1996; Jones 1997; Kemp 1998).

Performance studies is uniquely suited for the challenge of braiding together disparate and stratified ways of knowing. We can think through performance along three crisscrossing lines of activity and analysis. We can think of performance (1) as a work of *imagination,* as an object of study; (2) as a pragmatics of *inquiry* (both as model and method), as an optic and operator of research; (3) as a tactics of *intervention*, an alternative space of struggle. Speaking from my home department at Northwestern, we often refer to the three a's of performance studies: artistry, analysis, activism. Or to change the alliteration, a commitment to the three c's of performance studies: creativity, critique, citizenship (civic struggles for social justice). We struggle to forge a unique and unifying mission around the triangulations of these three pivot points:

1. *Accomplishment*—the making of art and remaking of culture; creativity; embodiment; artistic process and form; knowledge that comes from doing, participatory understanding, practical consciousness, performing as a way of knowing.

2. *Analysis*—the interpretation of art and culture; critical reflection; thinking about, through, and with performance; performance as a lens that illuminates the constructed creative, contingent, collaborative dimensions of human communication; knowledge that comes from contemplation and comparison; concentrated attention and contextualization as a way of knowing.

3. *Articulation*—activism, outreach, connection to community; applications and interventions; action research; projects that reach outside the academy and are rooted in an ethic of reciprocity and exchange; knowledge that is tested by practice within a community; social commitment, collaboration, and contribution/ intervention as a way of knowing: praxis.

Notwithstanding the many calls for embracing theory and practice, universities typically institutionalize a hierarchical division of labor between scholars/researchers and artists/practitioners. For example, the creative artists in the Department of Fine Arts are separated from the "serious" scholars in the Department of Art History. Even when scholars and practitioners are housed within the same department, there often is internal differentiation and tracking, e.g., the literary theorists and critics are marked off from those who teach creative and expository writing. This configuration mirrors an entrenched social hierarchy of value based on the fundamental division between intellectual labor and manual labor. In the academy, the position of the artist/practitioner is comparable to people in the larger society who work with their hands, who make things, and who are valued less than the scholars/theorists who work with their minds and are comparable to the more privileged professional-managerial class. Indeed, sometimes one of the reasons for forming schools of fine and performing arts is to protect artists/practitioners from tenure and promotion committees dominated by the more institutionally powerful scholar/researchers who do not know how to appraise a record of artistic accomplishment as commensurate with traditional criteria of scholarly research and publication. The segregation of faculty and students who make art and perform from those who think about and study art and performance is based on a false dichotomy that represses the critical-intellectual component of any artistic work, and the imaginative-creative dimension of scholarship that makes a difference. A spurious, counterproductive, and mutually denigrating opposition is put into play that pits so-called "mere technique, studio skills, know-how" against so-called "arid knowledge, abstract theory, sterile scholarship." This unfortunate schism is based on gross reductionism and ignorance of "how the other half lives." Students are cheated and disciplines diminished by this academic apartheid.

A performance studies agenda should collapse this divide and revitalize the connections between artistic accomplishment, analysis, and articulations with communities; between practical knowledge (knowing how), propositional knowledge (knowing that), and political savvy (knowing who, when, and where). This epistemological connection between creativity, critique, and civic engagement is mutually replenishing, and pedagogically powerful. Very bright, talented students are attracted to programs that combine intellectual rigor with artistic excellence that is critically engaged, where they do not have to banish their artistic spirit in order to become a critical thinker, or repress their intellectual self or political passion to explore their artistic side. Particularly at the PhD level, original scholarship in culture and the arts is enhanced, complemented, and complicated in deeply meaningful ways by the participatory understanding and community involvement of the researcher. This experiential and engaged model of inquiry is coextensive with the participant-observation methods of ethnographic research.

The ongoing challenge of performance studies is to refuse and supercede this deeply entrenched division of labor, apartheid of knowledges, that plays out inside the academy as the difference between thinking and doing, interpreting and making, conceptualizing and creating. The division of labor between theory and practice, abstraction and embodiment, is an arbitrary and rigged choice, and, like all binarisms, it is booby-trapped. It's a Faustian bargain. If we go the one-way street of abstraction, then we cut ourselves off from the nourishing ground of participatory experience. If we go the one-way street of practice, then we drive ourselves into an isolated cul-de-sac, a practitioner's workshop or artist's colony. Our radical move is to turn, and return, insistently, to the crossroads.

Notes

1. A shorter version of this paper was presented at the "Cultural Intersections" conference at Northwestern University, 9 October 1999. "Cultural Intersections" was the inaugural conference for Northwestern's Doctoral Studies in Culture: Performance, Theatre, Media, a new interdisciplinary PhD program.

2. I thank my Belizean colleague, Dr. Barbara Flores, for sharing this Garifuna material with me. I had the privilege of working with Dr. Flores when she was a graduate student at Northwestern.

3. An earlier version of the Frederick Douglass-Zora Neal Hurston discussion appeared in 1998 (Conquergood 1998).

4. Stewart's experimental ethnography is remarkably performance-sensitive and performance-saturated. Her text is replete with voices, sometimes explicitly quoted, but often evoked through literary techniques of indirect and double-voiced discourse so that the reader is simultaneously aware of the ethnographer's voice and the voices from the field, their interaction and gaps. The students in my critical ethnography seminar adapted and performed passages from the ethnography as a way of testing Stewart's stylistic innovations and textual evocations of performance.

References

Allen, Catherine J., and Nathan Garner
1995   "Condor Qatay: Anthropology in Performance." *American Anthropologist* 97, 1 (March):69–82.

Appadurai, Arjun
1996   *Modernity At Large: Cultural Dimensions of Globalization*. Minneapolis: University of Minnesota Press.

Becker, Howard S., Michal M. McCall, and Lori V. Morris
1989   "Theatres and Communities: Three Scenes." *Social Problems 36*, 2 (April):93–116.

Burke, Kenneth
1969 [1950]   *A Rhetoric of Motives*. Berkeley: University of California Press.

Certeau, Michel de
1984   *The Practice of Everyday Life*. Translated by Steven Rendall. Berkeley: University of California Press.

1998   *The Capture of Speech and Other Political Writings*. Edited by Luce Giard. Translated by Tom Conley. Minneapolis: University of Minnesota Press.
2000   *The Certeau Reader*. Edited by Graham Ward. Oxford: Blackwell.

Clifford, James
1997   *Routes: Travel and Translation in the Late Twentieth Century*. Cambridge: Harvard University Press.

Comaroff, Jean, and John Comaroff
1991   *Of Revelation and Revolution: Christianity, Colonialism, and Consciousness in South Africa*, Volume 1. Chicago: University of Chicago Press.
1992   *Ethnography and the Historical Imagination*. Boulder, CO: Westview.
1997   *Of Revelation and Revolution: The Dialectics of Modernity on a South African Frontier*, Volume 2. Chicago: University of Chicago Press.

Conquergood, Dwight
1988   "Health Theatre in a Hmong Refugee Camp: Performance, Communication, Culture." *TDR* 32, 3 (T119):174–208.
1997   "Street Literacy." In *Handbook of Research on Teaching Literacy through the Communicative and Visual Arts*, edited by James Flood, Shirley Brice Heath, and Diane Lapp, 354–75. New York: MacMillan.
1998   "Beyond the Text: Toward a Performative Cultural Politics." In *The Future of Performance Studies: Visions and Revisions*, edited by Sheron J. Dailey, 25–36. Washington, DC: National Communication Association.
2000   "Rethinking Elocution: The Trope of the Talking Book and Other Figures of Speech." *Text and Performance Quarterly* 20, 4 (October):325–41.

Douglass, Frederick
1969 [1855]   *My Bondage and My Freedom*. Introduction by Philip Foner. New York: Dover.

Fabian, Johannes
1990   *Pourer and Performance: Ethnographic Explorations through Proverbial Wisdom and Theater in Shaba, Zaire*. Madison: University of Wisconsin Press.

Foucault, Michel
1980 *Power/Knowledge*. Edited by Colin Gordon. Translated by Colin Gordon, Leo Marshall, John Mepham, and Kate Soper. New York: Pantheon.

Geertz, Clifford
1973 *The Interpretation of Cultures*. New York: Basic Books.

Gilroy, Paul
1994 *The Black Atlantic*. Cambridge: Harvard University Press.

Gramsci, Antonio
1971 *Selections from the Prison Notebooks*. Edited and translated by Quintin Hoare and Geoffrey Smith. New York: International.

Haraway, Donna
1991 *Simians, Cyborgs, and Women: The Reinvention of Nature*. New York: Routledge.

hooks, bell
1990 "Homeplace: A Site of Resistance." In *Yearning: Race, Gender, and Cultural Politics*, 41–49. Boston: South End Press.

Hurston, Zora Neal
1990 [1935] *Mules and Men*. New York: Harper.

Jackson, Shannon
1991 "Ethnography and the Audition: Performance As Ideological Critique." *Text and Performance Quarterly* 13, 1 (January):21–43.
1998 "White Noises: On Performing White, On Writing Performance." *TDR* 42, 1 (T157):49–64.
2000 *Lines of Activity: Performance, Historiography, Hull-House Domesticity*. Ann Arbor: University of Michigan Press.

Jones, Joni L.
1997 "sista docta: Performance as Critique of the Academy" *TDR* 41, 2 (T154):51–67.

Joseph, May
1999 *Nomadic Identities: The Performance of Citizenship*. Minneapolis: University of Minnesota Press.

Kemp, Amanda
1998 "This Black Body in Question." In *The Ends of Performance*, edited by Peggy Phelan and Jill Lane, 116–29. New York: New York University Press.

Laughlin, Robert
1995 "From All for All: A Tzotzil-Tzeital Tragicomedy." *American Anthropologist* 97, 3 (September):528–42.

Lavie, Smadar, and Ted Swedenburg, eds.
1996 *Displacement, Diaspora, and Geographies of Identity*. Durham: Duke University Press.

Leonardo, Micaela di
1998 *Exotics At Hume: Anthropologies, Others, American Modernity*. Chicago: University of Chicago Press.

McCall, Michal M., and Howard S. Becker
1990 "Performance Science." *Social Problems* 37, 1 (February): 117–32.

McKenzie, Jon
2001 *Perform or Else: From Discipline to Performance*. London: Routledge.

Ong, Aihwa
1999 *Flexible Citizenship: The Cultural Logics of Transnationality*. Durham: Duke University Press.

Paget, Marianne A.
1990 "Performing the Text." *Journal of Contemporary Ethnography* 19, 1 (April):136–55

Pollock, Della
1990 "Telling the Told: Performing *Like a Family*." *Oral History Review* 18, 2 (Fall): 1–36.

Scott, James C.
1990 *Domination and the Arts of Resistance*. New Haven: Yale University Press.
1998 *Seeing Like a State*. New Haven: Yale University Press.

Stewart, Kathleen
1996 *A Space on the Side of the Road: Cultural Poetics in an "Other" America*. Princeton, NJ: Princeton University Press.

Taussig, Michael
1993   *Mimesis and Alterity*. New York: Routledge.

Taylor, Diana
1999   "Dancing with Diana: A Study in Hauntology." *TDR* 43, 1 (T161):59–78.

Thiong'o, Ngũgĩ wa
1998   "Oral Power and Europhone Glory: Orature, Literature, and Stolen Legacies." In *Penpoints, Gunpoints, and Dreams: Towards a Critical Theory of the Arts and the State in Africa*. Oxford: Oxford University Press.

Wellin, Christopher
1996   "Life at Lake Home': An Ethnographic Performance in Six Voices; An Essay on Method, in Two." *Qualitative Sociology* 19, 4:497–516.

Williams, Raymond
1977   *Marxism and Literary Study*. Oxford: Oxford University Press.
1983 [1958]   *Culture and Society*. New York: Columbia University Press.

Playboy Interview

Marshall McLuhan

PLAYBOY: To borrow Henry Gibson's oft-repeated one-line poem on Rowan and Martin's *Laugh-In* — "Marshall McLuhan, what are you doin'?"

McLUHAN: Sometimes I wonder. I'm making explorations. I don't know where they're going to take me. My work is designed for the pragmatic purpose of trying to understand our technological environment and its psychic and social consequences. But my books constitute the *process* rather than the completed product of discovery; my purpose is to employ facts as tentative probes, as means of insight, of pattern recognition, rather than to use them in the traditional and sterile sense of classified data, categories, containers. I want to map new terrain rather than chart old landmarks.

But I've never presented such explorations as revealed truth. As an investigator, I have no fixed point of view, no commitment to any theory — my own or anyone else's. As a matter of fact, I'm completely ready to junk any statement I've ever made about any subject if events don't bear me out, or if I discover it isn't contributing to an understanding of the problem. The better part of my work on media is actually somewhat like a safe-cracker's. I don't know what's inside; maybe it's nothing. I just sit down and start to work. I grope, I listen, I test, I accept and discard; I try out different sequences — until the tumblers fall and the doors spring open.

PLAYBOY: Isn't such a methodology somewhat erratic and inconsistent — if not, as your critics would maintain, eccentric?

McLUHAN: Any approach to environmental problems must be sufficiently flexible and adaptable to encompass the entire environmental matrix, which is in constant flux. I consider myself a generalist, not a specialist who has staked out a tiny plot of study as his intellectual turf and is oblivious to everything else. Actually, my work is a depth operation, the accepted practice in most modern disciplines from psychiatry to metallurgy and structural analysis. Effective study of the media deals not only with the content of the media but with the media themselves and the total cultural environment within which the media function. Only by standing aside from any phenomenon and taking an overview can you discover its operative principles and lines of force. There's really nothing inherently startling or radical about this study — except that for some reason few have had the vision to undertake it. For the past 3500 years of the Western world, the effects of media — whether it's speech, writing, printing, photography, radio or television — have been systematically overlooked by social observers. Even in today's revolutionary electronic age, scholars evidence few signs of modifying this traditional stance of ostrichlike disregard.

PLAYBOY: Why?

McLUHAN: Because all media, from the phonetic alphabet to the computer, are extensions of man that cause deep and lasting changes in him and transform his environment. Such an extension is an intensification, an amplification of an organ, sense or function, and whenever it takes place, the central nervous system appears to institute a self-protective *numbing* of the affected area, insulating and anesthetizing it from conscious awareness of what's happening to it. It's a process rather like that which occurs to the body under shock or stress conditions, or to the mind in line with the Freudian concept of repression. I call this peculiar form of self-hypnosis Narcissus narcosis, a syndrome whereby man remains as unaware of the psychic and social effects of his new technology as a fish of the water it swims in. As a result, precisely at the point where a new media-induced environment becomes all-pervasive and transmogrifies our sensory balance, it also becomes invisible.

This problem is doubly acute today because man must, as a simple survival strategy, become aware of what is happening to him, despite the attendant pain of such comprehension. The fact that he has not done so in this age of electronics is what has made this also the age of anxiety, which in turn has been transformed into its *Doppelgänger* — the therapeutically reactive age of *anomie* and apathy. But despite our self-protective escape mechanisms, the total-field awareness engendered by electronic media is enabling us — indeed, compelling us — to grope toward a consciousness of the unconscious, toward a realization that technology is an extension of our own bodies. We live in the first age when change occurs sufficiently rapidly to make such pattern recognition possible for society at large. Until the present era, this awareness has always been reflected first by the artist, who has had the power — and courage — of the seer to read the language of the outer world and relate it to the inner world.

PLAYBOY: Why should it be the artist rather than the scientist who perceives these relationships and foresees these trends?

McLUHAN: Because inherent in the artist's creative inspiration is the process of subliminally sniffing out environmental change. It's always been the artist

who perceives the alterations in man caused by a new medium, who recognizes that the future is the present, and uses his work to prepare the ground for it. But most people, from truck drivers to the literary Brahmins, are still blissfully ignorant of what the media do to them; unaware that because of their pervasive effects on man, it is the medium itself that is the message, *not* the content, and unaware that the medium is also the *massage* — that, all puns aside, it literally works over and saturates and molds and transforms every sense ratio. The content or message of any particular medium has about as much importance as the stenciling on the casing of an atomic bomb. But the ability to perceive media-induced extensions of man, once the province of the artist, is now being expanded as the new environment of electric information makes possible a new degree of perception and critical awareness by nonartists.

PLAYBOY: Is the public, then, at last beginning to perceive the "invisible" contours of these new technological environments?

McLUHAN: People are beginning to understand the nature of their new technology, but not yet nearly enough of them — and not nearly well enough. Most people, as I indicated, still cling to what I call the rearview-mirror view of their world. By this I mean to say that because of the invisibility of any environment during the period of its innovation, man is only consciously aware of the environment that has *preceded* it; in other words, an environment becomes fully visible only when it has been superseded by a new environment; thus we are always one step behind in our view of the world. Because we are benumbed by any new technology — which in turn creates a totally new environment — we tend to make the old environment more visible; we do so by turning it into an art form and by attaching our-selves to the objects and atmosphere that characterized it, just as we've done with jazz, and as we're now doing with the garbage of the mechanical environment via pop art.

The present is always invisible because it's environmental and saturates the whole field of attention so overwhelmingly; thus everyone but the artist, the man of integral awareness, is alive in an earlier day. In the midst of the electronic age of software, of instant information movement, we still believe we're living in the mechanical age of hardware. At the height of the mechanical age, man turned back to earlier centuries in search of "pastoral" values. The

Renaissance and the Middle Ages were completely oriented toward Rome; Rome was oriented toward Greece, and the Greeks were oriented toward the pre-Homeric primitives. We reverse the old educational dictum of learning by proceeding from the familiar to the unfamiliar by going from the unfamiliar to the familiar, which is nothing more or less than the numbing mechanism that takes place whenever new media drastically extend our senses.

PLAYBOY: If this "numbing" effect performs a beneficial role by protecting man from the psychic pain caused by the extensions of his nervous system that you attribute to the media, why are you attempting to dispel it and alert man to the changes in his environment?

McLUHAN: In the past, the effects of media were experienced more gradually, allowing the individual and society to absorb and cushion their impact to some degree. Today, in the electronic age of instantaneous communication, I believe that our survival, and at the very least our comfort and happiness, is predicated on understanding the nature of our new environment because unlike previous environmental changes, the electric media constitute a total and near-instantaneous transformation of culture, values and attitudes. This upheaval generates great pain and identity loss, which can be ameliorated only through a conscious awareness of its dynamics. If we understand the revolutionary transformations caused by new media, we can anticipate and control them; but if we continue in our self-induced subliminal trance, we will be their slaves.

Because of today's terrific speed-up of information moving, we have a chance to apprehend, predict and influence the environmental forces shaping us — and thus win back control of our own destinies. The new extensions of man and the environment they generate are the central manifestations of the evolutionary process, and yet we still cannot free ourselves of the delusion that it is how a medium is used that counts, rather than what it does to us and with us. This is the zombie stance of the technological idiot. It's to escape this Narcissus trance that I've tried to trace and reveal the impact of media on man, from the beginning of recorded time to the present.

PLAYBOY: Will you trace that impact for us — in condensed form?

McLUHAN: It's difficult to condense into the format of an interview such as this, but I'll try to give you a brief rundown of the basic media breakthroughs. You've got to remember that my definition of media is broad: it includes any technology whatever that creates extensions of the human body and senses, from clothing to the computer. And a vital point I must stress again is that societies have always been shaped more by the nature of the media with which men communicate than by the content of the communication. All technology has the property of the Midas touch; whenever a society develops an extension of itself, all other functions of that society tend to be transmuted to accommodate that new form; once any new technology penetrates a society, it saturates every institution of that society. New technology is thus a revolutionizing agent. We see this today with the electric media and we saw it several thousand years ago with the invention of the phonetic alphabet, which was just as far-reaching an innovation — and had just as profound consequences for man.

PLAYBOY: What were they?

McLUHAN: Before the invention of the phonetic alphabet, man lived in a world where all the senses were balanced and simultaneous, a closed world of tribal depth and resonance, an oral culture structured by a dominant auditory sense of life. The ear, as opposed to the cool and neutral eye, is sensitive, hyperaesthetic and all-inclusive, and contributes to the seamless web of tribal kinship and interdependence in which all members of the group existed in harmony. The primary medium of communication was speech, and thus no man knew appreciably more or less than any other — which meant that there was little individualism and specialization, the hallmarks of "civilized" Western man. Tribal cultures even today simply cannot comprehend the concept of the individual or of the separate and independent citizen. Oral cultures act and react simultaneously, whereas the capacity to act without reacting, without involvement, is the special gift of "detached" literate man. Another basic characteristic distinguishing tribal man from his literate successors is that he lived in a world of *acoustic* space, which gave him a radically different concept of time-space relationships.

PLAYBOY: What do you mean by "acoustic space"?

McLUHAN: I mean space that has no center and no margin, unlike strictly visual space, which is an extension and intensification of the eye. Acoustic space is organic and integral, perceived through the simultaneous interplay of all the senses; whereas "rational" or pictorial space is uniform, sequential and continuous and creates a closed world with none of the rich resonance of the tribal echoland. Our own Western time-space concepts derive from the environment created by the discovery of phonetic writing, as does our entire concept of Western civilization. The man of the tribal world led a complex, kaleidoscopic life precisely because the ear, unlike the eye, cannot be focused and is synaesthetic rather than analytical and linear. Speech is an utterance, or more precisely, an *outering*, of all our senses at once; the auditory field is simultaneous, the visual successive. The modes of life of nonliterate people were implicit, simultaneous and discontinuous, and also far richer than those of literate man. By their dependence on the spoken word for information, people were drawn together into a tribal mesh; and since the spoken word is more emotionally laden than the written — conveying by intonation such rich emotions as anger, joy, sorrow, fear — tribal man was more spontaneous and passionately volatile. Audile-tactile tribal man partook of the collective unconscious, lived in a magical integral world patterned by myth and ritual, its values divine and unchallenged, whereas literate or visual man creates an environment that is strongly fragmented, individualistic, explicit, logical, specialized and detached.

PLAYBOY: Was it phonetic literacy alone that precipitated this profound shift of values from tribal involvement to "civilized" detachment?

McLUHAN: Yes, it was. Any culture is an order of sensory preferences, and in the tribal world, the senses of touch, taste, hearing and smell were developed, for very practical reasons, to a much higher level than the strictly visual. Into this world, the phonetic alphabet fell like a bombshell, installing sight at the head of the hierarchy of senses. Literacy propelled man from the tribe, gave him an eye for an ear and replaced his integral in-depth communal interplay with visual linear values and fragmented consciousness. As an intensification and amplification of the visual function, the phonetic alphabet diminished the role of the senses of hearing and touch and taste and smell, permeating the discontinuous culture of tribal man and translating its organic harmony and complex synaesthesia into the uniform, connected and visual mode that we still consider the norm of "rational" existence. The whole man became fragmented man; the alphabet shattered the charmed circle and resonating magic of the tribal world, exploding man into an agglomeration of specialized and psychically impoverished "individuals," or units, functioning in a world of linear time and Euclidean space.

PLAYBOY: But literate societies existed in the ancient world long before the phonetic alphabet. Why weren't *they* detribalized?

McLUHAN: The phonetic alphabet did not change or extend man so drastically just because it enabled him to read; as you point out, tribal culture had already coexisted with other written languages for thousands of years. But the phonetic alphabet was radically different from the older and richer hieroglyphic or ideogrammic cultures. The writings of Egyptian, Babylonian, Mayan and Chinese cultures were an extension of the senses in that they gave pictorial expression to reality, and they demanded many signs to cover the wide range of data in their societies — unlike phonetic writing, which uses semantically meaningless letters to correspond to semantically meaningless sounds and is able, with only a handful of letters, to encompass all meanings and all languages. This achievement demanded the separation of both sights and sounds from their semantic and dramatic meanings in order to render visible the actual sound of speech, thus placing a barrier between men and objects and creating a dualism between sight and sound. It divorced the visual function from the interplay with the other senses and thus led to the rejection from consciousness of vital areas of our sensory experience and to the resultant atrophy of the unconscious. The balance of the sensorium — or *Gestalt* interplay of all the senses — and the psychic and social harmony it engendered was disrupted, and the visual function was overdeveloped. This was true of no other writing system.

PLAYBOY: How can you be so sure that this all occurred solely because of phonetic literacy — or, in fact, if it occurred at all?

McLUHAN: You don't have to go back 3000 or 4000 years to see this process at work; in Africa today, a single generation of alphabetic literacy is enough to wrench the individual from the tribal web. When tribal man becomes phonetically literate, he may have an improved abstract intellectual grasp of the world, but most of the deeply emotional corporate family feeling is excised from his relationship with his social milieu. This division of sight and sound and meaning causes deep psychological effects, and he suffers a corresponding separation and impoverishment of his imaginative, emotional and sensory life. He begins reasoning in a sequential linear fashion; he begins categorizing and classifying data. As knowledge is extended in alphabetic form, it is localized and fragmented into specialties, creating division of function, of social classes, of nations and of knowledge — and in the process, the rich interplay of all the senses that characterized the tribal society is sacrificed.

PLAYBOY: But aren't there corresponding gains in insight, understanding and cultural diversity to compensate detribalized man for the loss of his communal values?

McLUHAN: Your question reflects all the institutionalized biases of literate man. Literacy, contrary to the popular view of the "civilizing" process you've just echoed, creates people who are much less complex and diverse than those who develop in the intricate web of oral-tribal societies. Tribal man, unlike homogenized Western man, was not differentiated by his specialist talents or his visible characteristics, but by his unique emotional blends. The internal world of the tribal man was a creative mix of complex emotions and feelings that literate men of the Western world have allowed to wither or have suppressed in the name of efficiency and practicality. The alphabet served to neutralize all these rich divergencies of tribal cultures by translating their complexities into simple visual forms; and the visual sense, remember, is the only one that allows us to *detach;* all other senses involve us, but the detachment bred by literacy disinvolves and detribalizes man. He separates from the tribe as a predominantly visual man who shares standardized attitudes, habits and rights with other civilized men. But he is also given a tremendous advantage over the nonliterate tribal man who, today as in ancient times, is hamstrung by cultural pluralism, uniqueness and discontinuity — values that make the African as easy prey for the European colonialist as the barbarian was for the Greeks and Romans. Only alphabetic cultures have ever succeeded in mastering connected linear sequences as a means of social and psychic organization; the separation of all kinds of experiences into uniform and continuous units in order to generate accelerated action and alteration of form — in other words, applied knowledge — has been the secret of Western man's ascendancy over other men as well as over his environment.

PLAYBOY: Isn't the thrust of your argument, then, that the introduction of the phonetic alphabet was not progress, as has generally been assumed, but a psychic and social disaster?

McLUHAN: It was both. I try to avoid value judgments in these areas, but there is much evidence to suggest that man may have paid too dear a price for his new environment of specialist technology and values. Schizophrenia and alienation may be the inevitable consequences of phonetic literacy. It's metaphorically significant, I suspect, that the old Greek myth has Cadmus, who brought the alphabet to man, sowing dragon's teeth that sprang up from the earth as armed men. Whenever the dragon's teeth of technological change are sown, we reap a whirlwind of violence. We saw this clearly in classical times, although it was somewhat moderated because phonetic literacy did not win an overnight victory over primitive values and institutions; rather, it permeated ancient society in a gradual, if inexorable, evolutionary process.

PLAYBOY: How long did the old tribal culture endure?

McLUHAN: In isolated pockets, it held on until the invention of printing in the 16th Century, which was a vastly important qualitative extension of phonetic literacy. If the phonetic alphabet fell like a bombshell on tribal man, the printing press hit him like a 100-megaton H-bomb. The printing press was the ultimate extension of phonetic literacy: Books could be reproduced in infinite numbers; universal literacy was at last fully possible, if gradually realized; and books became portable individual possessions. Type, the prototype of all machines, ensured the primacy of the visual bias and finally sealed the doom of tribal man. The new medium of linear, uniform, repeatable type reproduced information in unlimited quantities and at hitherto-impossible speeds, thus assuring the eye a position of total predominance in man's sensorium. As a drastic extension of man, it shaped and transformed his entire environment, psychic and social, and was directly responsible for the rise of such disparate phenomena as nationalism, the Reformation, the assembly line and its offspring, the Industrial Revolution, the whole concept of causality, Cartesian and Newtonian concepts of the universe, perspective in art, narrative chronology in literature and a psychological mode of introspection or inner direction that greatly intensified the tendencies toward individualism and specialization engendered 2000 years before by phonetic literacy. The schism between thought and action was institutionalized, and fragmented man, first sundered by the alphabet, was at last diced into bite-sized tidbits. From that point on, Western man was Gutenberg man.

PLAYBOY: Even accepting the principle that technological innovations generate far-reaching environmental changes, many of your readers find it difficult to understand how you can hold the development of printing responsible for such apparently unrelated phenomena as nationalism and industrialism.

McLUHAN: The key word is "apparently." Look a bit closer at both nationalism and industrialism and you'll see that both derived directly from the explosion of print technology in the 16th Century. Nationalism didn't exist in Europe until the Renaissance, when typography enabled every literate man to *see* his mother tongue analytically as a uniform entity. The printing press, by spreading mass-produced books and printed matter across Europe, turned the vernacular regional languages of the day into uniform closed systems of national languages — just another variant of what we call mass media — and gave birth to the entire concept of nationalism.

The individual newly homogenized by print saw the nation concept as an intense and beguiling image of group destiny and status. With print, the homogeneity of money, markets and transport also became possible for the first time, thus creating economic as well as political unity and triggering all the dynamic centralizing energies of contemporary nationalism. By creating a speed of information movement unthinkable before printing, the Gutenberg revolution thus produced a new type of visual centralized national entity that was gradually merged with commercial expansion until Europe was a network of states.

By fostering continuity and competition within homogeneous and contiguous territory, nationalism not only forged new nations but sealed the doom of the old corporate, noncompetitive and discontinuous medieval order of guilds and family-structured social organization; print demanded both personal fragmentation and social uniformity, the natural expression of which was the nation-state. Literate nationalism's tremendous speed-up of information movement accelerated the specialist function that was nurtured by phonetic literacy and nourished by Gutenberg, and rendered obsolete such generalist encyclopedic figures as Benvenuto Cellini, the goldsmith-*cum-condottiere-cum*-painter-*cum*-sculptor-*cum*-writer; it was the Renaissance that destroyed Renaissance Man.

PLAYBOY: Why do you feel that Gutenberg also laid the groundwork for the Industrial Revolution?

McLUHAN: The two go hand in hand. Printing, remember, was the first mechanization of a complex handicraft; by creating an analytic sequence of step-by-step processes, it became the blueprint of all mechanization to follow. The most important quality of print is its repeatability; it is a visual statement that can be reproduced indefinitely, and repeatability is the root of the mechanical principle that has transformed the world since Gutenberg. Typography, by producing the first uniformly repeatable commodity, also created Henry Ford, the first assembly line and the first mass production. Movable type was archetype and prototype for all subsequent industrial development. Without phonetic literacy and the printing press, modern industrialism would be impossible. It is necessary to recognize literacy as typographic technology, shaping not only production and marketing procedures but all other areas of life, from education to city planning.

PLAYBOY: You seem to be contending that practically every aspect of modern life is a direct consequence of Gutenberg's invention of the printing press.

McLUHAN: Every aspect of Western *mechanical* culture was shaped by print technology, but the modern age is the age of the *electric* media, which forge environments and cultures antithetical to the mechanical consumer society derived from print. Print tore man out of his traditional cultural matrix while showing him how to pile individual upon individual into a massive agglomeration of national and industrial power, and the typographic trance of the West has endured until today, when the electronic media are at last demesmerizing us. The Gutenberg

Galaxy is being eclipsed by the constellation of Marconi.

PLAYBOY: You've discussed that constellation in general terms, but what precisely are the electric media that you contend have supplanted the old mechanical technology?

McLUHAN: The electric media are the telegraph, radio, films, telephone, computer and television, all of which have not only extended a single sense of function as the old mechanical media did — i.e., the wheel as an extension of the foot, clothing as an extension of the skin, the phonetic alphabet as an extension of the eye — but have enhanced and externalized our entire central nervous systems, thus transforming all aspects of our social and psychic existence. The use of the electronic media constitutes a break boundary between fragmented Gutenberg man and integral man, just as phonetic literacy was a break boundary between oral-tribal man and visual man.

In fact, today we can look back at 3000 years of differing degrees of visualization, atomization and mechanization and at last recognize the mechanical age as an interlude between two great organic eras of culture. The age of print, which held sway from approximately 1500 to 1900, had its obituary tapped out by the telegraph, the first of the new electric media, and further obsequies were registered by the perception of "curved space" and non-Euclidean mathematics in the early years of the century, which revived tribal man's discontinuous time-space concepts — and which even Spengler dimly perceived as the death-knell of Western literate values. The development of telephone, radio, film, television and the computer have driven further nails into the coffin. Today, television is the most significant of the electric media because it permeates nearly every home in the country, extending the central nervous system of every viewer as it works over and molds the entire sensorium with the ultimate message. It is television that is primarily responsible for ending the visual supremacy that characterized all mechanical technology, although each of the other electric media have played contributing roles.

PLAYBOY: But isn't television itself a primarily visual medium?

McLUHAN: No, it's quite the opposite, although the idea that TV is a visual extension is an under-standable mistake. Unlike film or photograph, television is primarily an extension of the sense of touch rather than of sight, and it is the tactile sense that demands the greatest interplay of all the senses. The secret of TV's tactile power is that the video image is one of low intensity or definition and thus, unlike either photograph or film, offers no detailed information about specific objects but instead involves the active participation of the viewer. The TV image is a mosaic mesh not only of horizontal lines but of millions of tiny dots, of which the viewer is physiologically able to pick up only 50 or 60 from which he shapes the image; thus he is constantly filling in vague and blurry images, bringing himself into in-depth involvement with the screen and acting out a constant creative dialog with the iconoscope. The contours of the resultant cartoonlike image are fleshed out within the imagination of the viewer, which necessitates great personal involvement and participation; the viewer, in fact, becomes the screen, whereas in film he becomes the camera. By requiring us to constantly fill in the spaces of the mosaic mesh, the iconoscope is tattooing its message directly on our skins. Each viewer is thus an unconscious pointillist painter like Seurat, limning new shapes and images as the iconoscope washes over his entire body. Since the point of focus for a TV set is the viewer, television is Orientalizing us by causing us all to begin to look within ourselves. The essence of TV viewing is, in short, intense participation and low definition — what I call a "cool" experience, as opposed to an essentially "hot," or high definition — low participation medium like radio.

PLAYBOY: A good deal of the perplexity surrounding your theories is related to this postulation of hot and cool media. Could you give us a brief definition of each?

McLUHAN: Basically, a hot medium *ex*cludes and a cool medium *in*cludes; hot media are low in participation, or completion, by the audience and cool media are high in participation. A hot medium is one that extends a single sense with high definition. High definition means a complete filling in of data by the medium without intense audience participation. A photograph, for example, is high definition or hot; whereas a cartoon is low definition or cool, because the rough outline drawing provides very little visual data and requires the viewer to fill in or complete the image himself. The telephone, which gives the ear relatively little data, is thus cool, as is speech; both demand considerable filling in by the listener. On the other hand, radio is a hot medium because it sharply and intensely provides great amounts of high-definition auditory information that leaves little or nothing to be filled in by the audience. A lecture, by the same token, is hot, but a seminar is cool; a book is hot, but a conversation or bull session is cool.

In a cool medium, the audience is an active constituent of the viewing or listening experience. A girl wearing open-mesh silk stockings or glasses is inherently cool and sensual because the eye acts as a surrogate hand in filling in the low-definition image thus engendered. Which is why boys seldom make passes at girls who wear glasses. In any case, the overwhelming majority of our technologies and entertainments since the introduction of print technology have been hot, fragmented and exclusive, but in the age of television we see a return to cool values and the inclusive in-depth involvement and participation they engender. This is, of course, just one more reason why the medium is the message, rather than the content; it is the participatory nature of the TV experience itself that is important, rather than the content of the particular TV image that is being invisibly and indelibly inscribed on our skins.

PLAYBOY: Even if, as you contend, the medium is the ultimate message, how can you entirely discount the importance of content? Didn't the content of Hitler's radio speeches, for example, have some effect on the Germans?

McLUHAN: By stressing that the medium is the message rather than the content, I'm not suggesting that content plays *no* role — merely that it plays a distinctly subordinate role. Even if Hitler had delivered botany lectures, some other demagog would have used the radio to retribalize the Germans and rekindle the dark atavistic side of the tribal nature that created European fascism in the Twenties and Thirties. By placing all the stress on content and practically none on the medium, we lose all chance of perceiving and influencing the impact of new technologies on man, and thus we are always dumfounded by — and unprepared for — the revolutionary environmental transformations induced by new media. Buffeted by environmental changes he cannot comprehend, man echoes the last plaintive cry of his tribal ancestor, Tarzan, as he plummeted to earth: "Who greased my vine?" The German Jew victimized by the Nazis

because his old tribalism clashed with their new tribalism could no more understand why his world was turned upside down than the American today can understand the reconfiguration of social and political institutions caused by the electric media in general and television in particular.

PLAYBOY: How is television reshaping our political institutions?

McLUHAN: TV is revolutionizing every political system in the Western world. For one thing, it's creating a totally new type of national leader, a man who is much more of a tribal chieftain than a politician. Castro is a good example of the new tribal chieftain who rules his country by a mass-participational TV dialog and feedback; he governs his country on camera, by giving the Cuban people the experience of being directly and intimately involved in the process of collective decision making. Castro's adroit blend of political education, propaganda and avuncular guidance is the pattern for tribal chieftains in other countries. The new political showman has to literally as well as figuratively put on his audience as he would a suit of clothes and become a corporate tribal image — like Mussolini, Hitler and F. D. R. in the days of radio, and Jack Kennedy in the television era. All these men were tribal emperors on a scale theretofore unknown in the world, because they all mastered their media.

PLAYBOY: How did Kennedy use TV in a manner different from his predecessors — or successors?

McLUHAN: Kennedy was the first TV President because he was the first prominent American politician to ever understand the dynamics and lines of force of the television iconoscope. As I've explained, TV is an inherently cool medium, and Kennedy had a compatible coolness and indifference to power, bred of personal wealth, which allowed him to adapt fully to TV. Any political candidate who doesn't have such cool, low-definition qualities, which allow the viewer to fill in the gaps with his own personal identification, simply electrocutes himself on television — as Richard Nixon did in his disastrous debates with Kennedy in the 1960 campaign. Nixon was essentially hot; he presented a high-definition, sharply-defined image and action on the TV screen that contributed to his reputation as a phony — the "Tricky Dicky" syndrome that has dogged his footsteps for years. "Would you buy a used car from this man?" the political cartoon asked — and the answer was "no," because he didn't project the cool aura of disinterest and objectivity that Kennedy emanated so effortlessly and engagingly.

PLAYBOY: Did Nixon take any lessons from you the last time around?

McLUHAN: He certainly took lessons from somebody, because in the recent election it was Nixon who was cool and Humphrey who was hot. I had noticed the change in Nixon as far back as 1963 when I saw him on *The Jack Paar Show.* No longer the slick, glib, aggressive Nixon of 1960, he had been toned down, polished, programmed and packaged into the new Nixon we saw in 1968: earnest, modest, quietly sincere — in a word, cool. I realized then that if Nixon maintained this mask, he could be elected President, and apparently the American electorate agreed last November.

PLAYBOY: How did Lyndon Johnson make use of television?

McLUHAN: He botched it the same way Nixon did in 1960. He was too intense, too obsessed with making his audience love and revere him as father and teacher, and too classifiable. Would people feel any safer buying a used car from L. B. J. than from the old Nixon? The answer is, obviously, "no." Johnson became a stereotype — even a parody — of himself, and earned the same reputation as a phony that plagued Nixon for so long. The people wouldn't have cared if John Kennedy lied to them on TV, but they couldn't stomach L. B. J. even when he told the truth. The credibility gap was really a communications gap. The political candidate who understands TV — whatever his party, goals or beliefs — can gain power unknown in history. How he uses that power is, of course, quite another question. But the basic thing to remember about the electric media is that they inexorably transform every sense ratio and thus recondition and restructure all our values and institutions. The overhauling of our traditional political system is only one manifestation of the retribalizing process wrought by the electric media, which is turning the planet into a global village.

PLAYBOY: Would you describe this retribalizing process in more detail?

McLUHAN: The electronically induced technological extensions of our central nervous system, which

I spoke of earlier, are immersing us in a world-pool of information movement and are thus enabling man to incorporate within himself the whole of mankind. The aloof and dissociated role of the literate man of the Western world is succumbing to the new, intense depth participation engendered by the electronic media and bringing us back in touch with ourselves as well as with one another. But the instant nature of electric-information movement is decentralizing — rather than enlarging — the family of man into a new state of multitudinous tribal existences. Particularly in countries where literate values are deeply institutionalized, this is a highly traumatic process, since the clash of the old segmented visual culture and the new integral electronic culture creates a crisis of identity, a vacuum of the self, which generates tremendous violence — violence that is simply an identity quest, private or corporate, social or commercial.

PLAYBOY: Do you relate this identity crisis to the current social unrest and violence in the United States?

McLUHAN: Yes, and to the booming business psychiatrists are doing. All our alienation and atomization are reflected in the crumbling of such time-honored social values as the right of privacy and the sanctity of the individual; as they yield to the intensities of the new technology's electric circus, it seems to the average citizen that the sky is falling in. As man is tribally metamorphosed by the electric media, we all become Chicken Littles, scurrying around frantically in search of our former identities, and in the process unleash tremendous violence. As the preliterate confronts the literate in the postliterate arena, as new information patterns inundate and uproot the old, mental breakdowns of varying degrees — including the collective nervous breakdowns of whole societies unable to resolve their crises of identity — will become very common.

It is not an easy period in which to live, especially for the television-conditioned young who, unlike their literate elders, cannot take refuge in the zombie trance of Narcissus narcosis that numbs the state of psychic shock induced by the impact of the new media. From Tokyo to Paris to Columbia, youth mindlessly acts out its identity quest in the theater of the streets, searching not for goals but for roles, striving for an identity that eludes them.

PLAYBOY: Why do you think they aren't finding it within the educational system?

McLUHAN: Because education, which should be helping youth to understand and adapt to their revolutionary new environments, is instead being used merely as an instrument of cultural aggression, imposing upon retribalized youth the obsolescent visual values of the dying literate age. Our entire educational system is reactionary, oriented to past values and past technologies, and will likely continue so until the old generation relinquishes power. The generation gap is actually a chasm, separating not two age groups but two vastly divergent cultures. I can understand the ferment in our schools, because our educational system is totally rearview mirror. It's a dying and outdated system founded on literate values and fragmented and classified data totally unsuited to the needs of the first television generation.

PLAYBOY: How do you think the educational system can be adapted to accommodate the needs of this television generation?

McLUHAN: Well, before we can start doing things the right way, we've got to recognize that we've been doing them the wrong way — which most pedagogs and administrators and even most parents still refuse to accept. Today's child is growing up absurd because he is suspended between two worlds and two value systems, neither of which inclines him to maturity because he belongs wholly to neither but exists in a hybrid limbo of constantly conflicting values. The challenge of the new era is simply the total creative process of *growing up* — and mere teaching and repetition of facts are as irrelevant to this process as a dowser to a nuclear power plant. To expect a "turned on" child of the electric age to respond to the old education modes is rather like expecting an eagle to swim. It's simply not within his environment, and therefore incomprehensible.

The TV child finds it difficult if not impossible to adjust to the fragmented, visual goals of our education after having had all his senses involved by the electric media; he craves in-depth involvement, not linear detachment and uniform sequential patterns. But suddenly and without preparation, he is snatched from the cool, inclusive womb of television and exposed — within a vast bureaucratic structure of courses and credits — to the hot medium of print. His natural instinct, conditioned by the electric

media, is to bring all his senses to bear on the book he's instructed to read, and print resolutely rejects that approach, demanding an isolated visual attitude to learning rather than the *Gestalt* approach of the unified sensorium. The reading postures of children in elementary school are a pathetic testimonial to the effects of television: children of the TV generation separate book from eye by an average distance of four and a half inches, attempting psychomimetically to bring to the printed page the all-inclusive sensory experience of TV. They are becoming Cyclops, desperately seeking to wallow in the book as they do in the TV screen.

PLAYBOY: Might it be possible for the "TV child" to make the adjustment to his educational environment by synthesizing traditional literate-visual forms with the insights of his own electric culture — or must the medium of print be totally unassimilable for him?

McLUHAN: Such a synthesis is entirely possible, and could create a creative blend of the two cultures — if the educational establishment was aware that there *is* an electric culture. In the absence of such elementary awareness, I'm afraid that the television child has no future in our schools. You must remember that the TV child has been relentlessly exposed to all the "adult" news of the modern world — war, racial discrimination, rioting, crime, inflation, sexual revolution. The war in Vietnam has written its bloody message on his skin; he has witnessed the assassinations and funerals of the nation's leaders; he's been orbited through the TV screen into the astronaut's dance in space, been inundated by information transmitted via radio, telephone, films, recordings and other people. His parents plopped him down in front of a TV set at the age of two to tranquilize him, and by the time he enters kindergarten, he's clocked as much as 4000 hours of television. As an IBM executive told me, "My children had lived several lifetimes compared to their grandparents when they began grade one."

PLAYBOY: If you had children young enough to belong to the TV generation, how would you educate them?

McLUHAN: Certainly not in our current schools, which are intellectual penal institutions. In today's world, to paraphrase Jefferson, the least education is the best education, since very few young minds can survive the intellectual tortures of our educational system. The mosaic image of the TV screen generates a depth-involving *nowness* and simultaneity in the lives of children that makes them scorn the distant visualized goals of traditional education as unreal, irrelevant and puerile. Another basic problem is that in our schools there is simply too much to learn by the traditional analytic methods; this is an age of information overload. The only way to make the schools other than prisons without bars is to start fresh with new techniques and values.

PLAYBOY: A number of experimental projects are bringing both TV and computers directly into the classrooms. Do you consider this sort of electronic educational aid a step in the right direction?

McLUHAN: It's not really too important if there is ever a TV set in each classroom across the country, since the sensory and attitudinal revolution has already taken place at home before the child ever reaches school, altering his sensory existence and his mental processes in profound ways. Book learning is no longer sufficient in any subject; the children all say now, "Let's *talk* Spanish," or "Let the Bard be *heard*," reflecting their rejection of the old sterile system where education begins and ends in a book. What we need now is educational crash programing in depth to first understand and then meet the new challenges. Just putting the present classroom on TV, with its archaic values and methods, won't change anything; it would be just like running movies on television; the result would be a hybrid that is neither. We have to ask what TV can do, in the instruction of English or physics or any other subject, that the classroom cannot do as presently constituted. The answer is that TV can deeply involve youth in the process of learning, illustrating graphically the complex interplay of people and events, the development of forms, the multileveled interrelationships between and among such arbitrarily segregated subjects as biology, geography, mathematics, anthropology, history, literature and languages.

If education is to become relevant to the young of this electric age, we must also supplant the stifling, impersonal and dehumanizing multiversity with a multiplicity of autonomous colleges devoted to an in-depth approach to learning. This must be done immediately, for few adults really comprehend the intensity of youth's alienation from the frag-

mented mechanical world and its fossilized educational system, which is designed in their minds solely to fit them into classified slots in bureaucratic society. To them, both draft card and degree are passports to psychic, if not physical, oblivion, and they accept neither. A new generation is alienated from its own 3000-year heritage of literacy and visual culture, and the celebration of literate values in home and school only intensifies that alienation. If we don't adapt our educational system to their needs and values, we will see only more dropouts and more chaos.

PLAYBOY:. Do you think the surviving hippie subculture is a reflection of youth's rejection of the values of our mechanical society?

McLUHAN: Of course. These kids are fed up with jobs and goals, and are determined to forge their own roles and involvement in society. They want nothing to do with our fragmented and specialist consumer society. Living in the transitional identity vacuum between two great antithetical cultures, they are desperately trying to discover themselves and fashion a mode of existence attuned to their new values; thus the stress on developing an "alternate life style." We can see the results of this retribalization process whenever we look at *any* of our youth — not just at hippies. Take the field of fashion, for example, which now finds boys and girls dressing alike and wearing their hair alike, reflecting the unisexuality deriving from the shift from visual to tactile. The younger generation's whole orientation is toward a return to the native, as reflected by their costumes, their music, their long hair and their sociosexual behavior. Our teenage generation is already becoming part of a jungle clan. As youth enters this clan world and all their senses are electrically extended and intensified, there is a corresponding amplification of their sexual sensibilities. Nudity and unabashed sexuality are growing in the electric age because as TV tattoos its message directly on our skins, it renders clothing obsolescent and a barrier, and the new tactility makes it natural for kids to constantly touch one another — as reflected by the button sold in the psychedelic shops: IF IT MOVES, FONDLE IT. The electric media, by stimulating all the senses simultaneously, also give a new and richer sensual dimension to everyday sexuality that makes Henry Miller's style of randy rutting old-fashioned and obsolete. Once a society enters the all-involving tribal mode, it is inevitable that our attitudes toward sexuality change. We see, for example, the ease with which young people live guiltlessly with one another, or, as among the hippies, in communal ménages. This is completely tribal.

PLAYBOY: But aren't most tribal societies sexually restrictive rather than permissive?

McLUHAN: Actually, they're both. Virginity is not, with a few exceptions, the tribal style in most primitive societies; young people tend to have total sexual access to one another until marriage. But after marriage, the wife becomes a jealously guarded possession and adultery a paramount sin. It's paradoxical that in the transition to a retribalized society, there is inevitably a great explosion of sexual energy and freedom; but when that society is fully realized, moral values will be extremely tight. In an integrated tribal society, the young will have free rein to experiment, but marriage and the family will become inviolate institutions, and infidelity and divorce will constitute serious violations of the social bond, not a private deviation but a collective insult and loss of face to the entire tribe. Tribal societies, unlike detribalized, fragmented cultures with their stress on individualist values, are extremely austere morally, and do not hesitate to destroy or banish those who offend the tribal values. This is rather harsh, of course, but at the same time, sexuality can take on new and richer dimensions of depth involvement in a tribalized society.

Today, meanwhile, as the old values collapse and we see an exhilarating release of pent-up sexual frustrations, we are all inundated by a tidal wave of emphasis on sex. Far from liberating the libido, however, such onslaughts seem to have induced jaded attitudes and a kind of psychosexual *Weltschmerz*. No sensitivity of sensual response can survive such an assault, which stimulates the mechanical view of the body as capable of experiencing specific thrills, but not total sexual-emotional involvement and transcendence. It contributes to the schism between sexual enjoyment and reproduction that is so prevalent, and also strengthens the case for homosexuality. Projecting current trends, the love machine would appear a natural development in the near future — not just the current computerized datefinder, but a machine whereby ultimate orgasm is achieved by direct mechanical stimulation of the pleasure circuits of the brain.

PLAYBOY: Do we detect a note of disapproval in your analysis of the growing sexual freedom?

McLUHAN: No, I neither approve nor disapprove. I merely try to understand. Sexual freedom is as natural to newly tribalized youth as drugs.

PLAYBOY: What's natural about drugs?

McLUHAN: They're natural means of smoothing cultural transitions, and also a short cut into the electric vortex. The upsurge in drug taking is intimately related to the impact of the electric media. Look at the metaphor for getting high: turning on. One turns on his consciousness through drugs just as he opens up all his senses to a total depth involvement by turning on the TV dial. Drug taking is stimulated by today's pervasive environment of instant information, with its feedback mechanism of the inner trip. The inner trip is not the sole prerogative of the LSD traveler; it's the universal experience of TV watchers. LSD is a way of miming the invisible electronic world; it releases a person from acquired verbal and visual habits and reactions, and gives the potential of instant and total involvement, both all-at-onceness and all-at-oneness, which are the basic needs of people translated by electric extensions of their central nervous systems out of the old rational, sequential value system. The attraction to hallucinogenic drugs is a means of achieving empathy with our penetrating electric environment, an environment that in itself is a drugless inner trip.

Drug taking is also a means of expressing rejection of the obsolescent mechanical world and values. And drugs often stimulate a fresh interest in artistic expression, which is primarily of the audile-tactile world. The hallucinogenic drugs, as chemical simulations of our electric environment, thus revive senses long atrophied by the overwhelmingly visual orientation of the mechanical culture. LSD and related hallucinogenic drugs, furthermore, breed a highly tribal and communally oriented subculture, so it's understandable why the retribalized young take to drugs like a duck to water.

PLAYBOY: A Columbia coed was recently quoted in *Newsweek* as equating you and LSD. "LSD doesn't mean anything until you consume it," she said. "Likewise McLuhan." Do you see any similarities?

McLUHAN: I'm flattered to hear my work described as hallucinogenic, but I suspect that some of my academic critics find me a bad trip.

PLAYBOY: Have you ever taken LSD yourself?

McLUHAN: No, I never have. I'm an observer in these matters, not a participant. I had an operation last year to remove a tumor that was expanding my brain in a less pleasant manner, and during my prolonged convalescence I'm not allowed any stimulant stronger than coffee. Alas! A few months ago, however, I was almost "busted" on a drug charge. On a plane returning from Vancouver, where a university had awarded me an honorary degree, I ran into a colleague who asked me where I'd been. "To Vancouver to pick up my LL.D.," I told him. I noticed a fellow passenger looking at me with a strange expression, and when I got off the plane at Toronto Airport, two customs guards pulled me into a little room and started going over my luggage. "Do you know Timothy Leary?" one asked. I replied I did and that seemed to wrap it up for him. "All right," he said. "Where's the stuff? We know you told somebody you'd gone to Vancouver to pick up some LL.D." After a laborious dialog, I persuaded him that an LL.D. has nothing to do with consciousness expansion — just the opposite, in fact — and I was released. Of course, in light of the present educational crisis, I'm not sure there isn't something to be said for making possession of an LL.D. a felony.

PLAYBOY: Are you in favor of legalizing marijuana and hallucinogenic drugs?

McLUHAN: My personal point of view is irrelevant, since all such legal restrictions are futile and will inevitably wither away. You could as easily ban drugs in a retribalized society as outlaw clocks in a mechanical culture. The young will continue turning on no matter how many of them are turned off into prisons, and such legal restrictions only reflect the cultural aggression and revenge of a dying culture against its successor.

Speaking of dying cultures, it's no accident that drugs first were widely used in America by the Indians and then by the Negroes, both of whom have the great cultural advantage in this transitional age of remaining close to their tribal roots. The cultural aggression of white America against Negroes and Indians is not based on skin color and belief in radical superiority, whatever ideological clothing may be used to rationalize it, but on the white man's inchoate awareness that the Negro and Indian — as men with deep roots in the resonating echo chamber of the discontinuous, interrelated tribal world — are actually physically and socially superior to the fragmented, alienated and dissociated man of Western civilization. Such a recognition, which stabs at the heart of the white man's entire social value system, inevitably generates violence and genocide. It has been the sad fate of the Negro and the Indian to be tribal men in a fragmented culture — men born ahead of rather than behind their time.

PLAYBOY: How do you mean?

McLUHAN: I mean that at precisely the time when the white younger generation is retribalizing and generalizing, the Negro and the Indian are under tremendous social and economic pressure to go in the opposite direction: to detribalize and specialize, to tear out their tribal roots when the rest of society is rediscovering theirs. Long held in a totally subordinate socioeconomic position, they are now impelled to acquire literacy as a prerequisite to employment in the old mechanical service environment of hardware, rather than adapt themselves to the new tribal environment of software, or electric information, as the middle-class white young are doing. Needless to say, this generates great psychic pain, which in turn is translated into bitterness and violence. This can be seen in the microcosmic drug culture; psychological studies show that the Negro and the Indian who are turned on by marijuana, unlike the white, are frequently engulfed with rage; they have a low high. They are angry because they understand under the influence of the drug that the source of their psychic and social degradation lies in the mechanical technology that is now being repudiated by the very white overculture that developed it — a repudiation that the majority of Negroes and Indians cannot, literally, afford because of their inferior economic position.

This is both ironic and tragic, and lessens the chances for an across-the-board racial *détente* and reconciliation, because rather than diminishing and eventually closing the sociopsychic differences between the races, it widens them. The Negro and the Indian seem to always get a bad deal; they suffered first because they were tribal men in a mechanical world, and now as they try to detribalize and structure themselves within the values of the mechanical culture, they find the gulf between them and a suddenly retribalizing society widening rather than narrowing. The future, I fear, is not too bright for either — but particularly for the Negro.

PLAYBOY: What, specifically, do you think will happen to him?

McLUHAN: At best, he will have to make a painful adjustment to two conflicting cultures and technologies, the visual-mechanical and the electric world; at worst, he will be exterminated.

PLAYBOY: Exterminated?

McLUHAN: I seriously fear the possibility, though God knows I hope I'm proved wrong. As I've tried to point out, the one inexorable consequence of any identity quest generated by environmental upheaval is tremendous violence. This violence has traditionally been directed at the tribal man who challenged visual-mechanical culture, as with the genocide against the Indian and the institutionalized dehumanization of the Negro. Today, the process is reversed and the violence is being meted out, during this transitional period, to those who are nonassimilable into the new tribe. Not because of his skin color but because he is in a limbo between mechanical and electric cultures, the Negro is a threat, a rival tribe that cannot be digested by the new order. The fate of such tribes is often extermination.

PLAYBOY: What can we do to prevent this from happening to America's Negro population?

McLUHAN: I think a valuable first step would be to alert the Negro, as well as the rest of society, to the nature of the new electric technology and the reasons it is so inexorably transforming our social and psychic values. The Negro should understand that the aspects of himself he has been conditioned to think of as inferior or "backward" are actually *superior* attributes in the new environment. Western man is obsessed by the forward-motion folly of step-by-step "progress," and always views the discontinuous synaesthetic interrelationships of the tribe as primitive. If the Negro realizes the great advantages of his heritage, he will cease his lemming leap into the senescent mechanical world.

There are encouraging signs that the new black-power movement — with its emphasis on Negritude and a return to the tribal pride of African cultural and social roots — is recognizing this, but unfortunately a majority of Negro Americans are still determined to join the mechanical culture. But if they can be persuaded to follow the lead of those who wish to rekindle their sparks of tribal awareness, they will be strategically placed to make an easy transition to the new technology, using their own enduring tribal values as environmental survival aids. They should take pride in these tribal values, for they are rainbow-hued in comparison with the pallid literate culture of their traditional masters.

But as I said, the Negro arouses hostility in whites precisely because they subliminally recognize that he is closest to that tribal depth involvement and simultaneity and harmony that is the richest and most highly developed expression of human consciousness. This is why the white political and economic institutions mobilize to exclude and oppress Negroes, from semiliterate unions to semiliterate politicians, whose slim visual culture makes them hang on with unremitting fanaticism to their antiquated hardware and the specialized skills and classifications and compartmentalized neighborhoods and life styles deriving from it. The lowest intellectual stratum of whites view literacy and its hardware environment as a novelty, still fresh and still status symbols of achievement, and thus will be the last to retribalize and the first to initiate what could easily become a full-blown racial civil war. The United States as a nation is doomed, in any case, to break up into a series of regional and racial ministates, and such a civil war would merely accelerate that process.

PLAYBOY: On what do you base your prediction that the United States will disintegrate?

McLUHAN: Actually, in this case as in most of my work, I'm "predicting" what has already happened and merely extrapolating a current process to its logical conclusion. The Balkanization of the United States as a continental political structure has been going on for some years now, and racial chaos is merely one of several catalysts for change. This isn't a peculiarly American phenomenon; as I pointed out earlier, the electric media always produce psychically integrating and socially decentralizing effects, and this affects not only political institutions within the existing state but the national entities themselves.

All over the world, we can see how the electric media are stimulating the rise of ministates: in Great Britain, Welsh and Scottish nationalism are recrudescing powerfully; in Spain, the Basques are demanding autonomy; in Belgium, the Flemings insist on separation from the Walloons; in my own country, the *Quebecois* are in the first stages of a war of independence; and in Africa, we've witnessed the germination of several ministates and the collapse of several ambitiously unrealistic schemes for regional confederation. These ministates are just the opposite of the traditional centralizing nationalisms of the past that forged mass states that homogenized disparate ethnic and linguistic groups within one national boundary. The new ministates are decentralized tribal agglomerates of those same ethnic and linguistic groups. Though their creation may be accompanied by violence, they will not remain hostile or competitive armed camps but will eventually discover that their tribal bonds transcend their differences and will thereafter live in harmony and cultural cross-fertilization with one another.

This pattern of decentralized ministates will be repeated in the United States, although I realize that most Americans still find the thought of the Union's dissolution inconceivable. The U.S., which was the first nation in history to begin its national existence as a centralized and literate political entity, will now play the historical film backward, reeling into a multiplicity of decentralized Negro states, Indian states, regional states, linguistic and ethnic states, etc. Decentralism is today the burning issue in the 50 states, from the school crisis in New York City to the demands of the retribalized young that the oppressive multiversities be reduced to a human scale and the mass state be debureaucratized. The tribes and the bureaucracy are antithetical means of social organization and can never coexist peacefully; one must destroy and supplant the other, or neither will survive.

PLAYBOY: Accepting, for the moment, your contention that the United States will be "Balkanized" into an assortment of ethnic and linguistic ministates, isn't it likely that the results would be social chaos and internecine warfare?

McLUHAN: Not necessarily. Violence can be avoided if we comprehend the process of decentralism and retribalization, and accept its outcome while moving to control and modify the dynamics of change. In any case, the day of the super state is over; as men not only in the U.S. but throughout the world are united into a single tribe, they will forge a diversity of viable decentralized political and social institutions.

PLAYBOY: Along what lines?

McLUHAN: It will be a totally retribalized world of depth involvements. Through radio, TV and the computer, we are already entering a global theater in which the entire world is a Happening. Our whole cultural habitat, which we once viewed as a mere container of people, is being transformed by these media and by space satellites into a living organism, itself contained within a new macrocosm or connubium of a supraterrestrial nature. The day of the individualist, of privacy, of fragmented or "applied" knowledge, of "points of view" and specialist goals is being replaced by the over-all awareness of a mosaic world in which space and time are overcome by television, jets and computers — a simultaneous, "all-at-once" world in which everything resonates with everything else as in a total electrical field, a world in which energy is generated and perceived not by the traditional connections that create linear, causative thought processes, but by the intervals, or gaps, which Linus Pauling grasps as the languages of cells, and which create synaesthetic discontinuous integral consciousness.

The open society, the visual off-spring of phonetic literacy, is irrelevant to today's retribalized youth; and the closed society, the product of speech, drum and ear technologies, is thus being reborn. After centuries of dissociated sensibilities, modern awareness is once more becoming integral and inclusive, as the entire human family is sealed to a single universal membrane. The compressional, implosive nature of the new electric technology is retrogressing Western man back from the open plateaus of literate values and into the heart of tribal darkness, into what Joseph Conrad termed "the Africa within."

PLAYBOY: Many critics feel that your own "Africa within" promises to be a rigidly conformist hive world in which the individual is totally subordinate to the group and personal freedom is unknown.

McLUHAN: Individual talents and perspectives don't have to shrivel within a retribalized society; they merely interact within a group consciousness that has the potential for releasing far more creativity than the old atomized culture. Literate man is alienated, impoverished man; retribalized man can lead a far richer and more fulfilling life — not the life of a mindless drone but of the participant in a seamless web of interdependence and harmony. The implosion of electric technology is transmogrifying literate, fragmented man into a complex and depth-structured human being with a deep emotional awareness of his complete interdependence with all of humanity. The old "individualistic" print society was one where the individual was "free" only to be alienated and dissociated, a rootless outsider bereft of tribal dreams; our new electronic environment compels commitment and participation, and fulfills man's psychic and social needs at profound levels.

The tribe, you see, is not conformist just because it's inclusive; after all, there is far more diversity and less conformity within a family group than there is within an urban conglomerate housing thousands of families. It's in the village where eccentricity lingers, in the big city where uniformity and impersonality are the milieu. The global-village conditions being forged by the electric technology stimulate more discontinuity and diversity and division than the old mechanical, standardized society; in fact, the global village makes maximum disagreement and creative dialog inevitable. Uniformity and tranquillity are not hallmarks of the global village; far more likely are conflict and discord as well as love and harmony — the customary life mode of any tribal people.

PLAYBOY: Despite what you've said, haven't literate cultures been the only ones to value the concepts of individual freedom, and haven't tribal societies traditionally imposed rigid social taboos — as you suggested earlier in regard to sexual behavior — and ruthlessly punished all who do not conform to tribal values?

McLUHAN: We confront a basic paradox whenever we discuss personal freedom in literate and tribal cultures. Literate mechanical society separated the individual from the group in space, engendering privacy; in thought, engendering point of view; and in work, engendering specialism — thus forging all the values associated with individualism. But at the same time, print technology has homogenized man, creating mass militarism, mass mind and mass uniformity; print gave man private habits of individualism and a public role of absolute conformity. That is why the young today welcome their retribalization, however dimly they perceive it, as a

release from the uniformity, alienation and dehumanization of literate society. Print centralizes socially and fragments psychically, whereas the electric media bring man together in a tribal village that is a rich and creative mix, where there is actually *more* room for creative diversity than within the homogenized mass urban society of Western man.

PLAYBOY: Are you claiming, now, that there will be no taboos in the world tribal society you envision?

McLUHAN: No, I'm not saying that, and I'm not claiming that freedom will be absolute — merely that it will be less restricted than your question implies. The world tribe will be essentially conservative, it's true, like all iconic and inclusive societies; a mythic environment lives beyond time and space and thus generates little radical social change. All technology becomes part of a shared ritual that the tribe desperately strives to keep stabilized and permanent; by its very nature, an oral-tribal society — such as Pharaonic Egypt — is far more stable and enduring than any fragmented visual society. The oral and auditory tribal society is patterned by acoustic space, a total and simultaneous field of relations alien to the visual world, in which points of view and goals make social change an inevitable and constant byproduct. An electrically imploded tribal society discards the linear forward-motion of "progress." We can see in our own time how, as we begin to react in depth to the challenges of the global village, we all become reactionaries.

PLAYBOY: That can hardly be said of the young, whom you claim are leading the process of retribalization, and according to most estimates are also the most radical generation in our history.

McLUHAN: Ah, but you're talking about politics, about goals and issues, which are really quite irrelevant. I'm saying that the result, not the current process, of retribalization makes us reactionary in our basic attitudes and values. Once we are enmeshed in the magical resonance of the tribal echo chamber, the debunking of myths and legends is replaced by their religious study. Within the consensual framework of tribal values, there will be unending diversity — but there will be few if any rebels who challenge the tribe itself.

The instant involvement that accompanies instant technologies triggers a conservative, stabilizing, gyroscopic function in man, as reflected by the second-grader who, when requested by her teacher to compose a poem after the first Sputnik was launched into orbit, wrote: "The stars are so big / The earth is so small / Stay as you are." The little girl who wrote those lines is part of the new tribal society; she lives in a world infinitely more complex, vast and eternal than any scientist has instruments to measure or imagination to describe.

PLAYBOY: If personal freedom will still exist — although restricted by certain consensual taboos — in this new tribal world, what about the political system most closely associated with individual freedom: democracy? Will it, too, survive the transition to your global village?

McLUHAN: No, it will not. The day of political democracy as we know it today is finished. Let me stress again that individual freedom itself will not be submerged in the new tribal society, but it will certainly assume different and more complex dimensions. The ballot box, for example, is the product of literate Western culture — a hot box in a cool world — and thus obsolescent. The tribal will is consensually expressed through the simultaneous interplay of all members of a community that is deeply interrelated and involved, and would thus consider the casting of a "private" ballot in a shrouded polling booth a ludicrous anachronism. The TV networks' computers, by "projecting" a victor in a Presidential race while the polls are still open, have already rendered the traditional electoral process obsolescent.

In our software world of instant electric communications movement, politics is shifting from the old patterns of political representation by electoral delegation to a new form of spontaneous and instantaneous communal involvement in all areas of decision making. In a tribal all-at-once culture, the idea of the "public" as a differentiated agglomerate of fragmented individuals, all dissimilar but all capable of acting in basically the same way, like interchangeable mechanical cogs in a production line, is supplanted by a mass society in which personal diversity is encouraged while at the same time everybody reacts and interacts simultaneously to every stimulus. The election as we know it today will be meaningless in such a society.

PLAYBOY: How will the popular will be registered in the new tribal society if elections are passé?

McLUHAN: The electric media open up totally new means of registering popular opinion. The old concept of the plebiscite, for example, may take on new relevance; TV could conduct daily plebiscites by presenting facts to 200,000,000 people and providing a computerized feedback of the popular will. But voting, in the traditional sense, is through as we leave the age of political parties, political issues and political goals, and enter an age where the collective tribal image and the iconic image of the tribal chieftain is the overriding political reality. But that's only one of countless new realities we'll be confronted with in the tribal village. We must understand that a totally new society is coming into being, one that rejects *all* our old values, conditioned responses, attitudes and institutions. If you have difficulty envisioning something as trivial as the imminent end of elections, you'll be totally unprepared to cope with the prospect of the forthcoming demise of spoken language and its replacement by a global consciousness.

PLAYBOY: You're right.

McLUHAN: Let me help you. Tribal man is tightly sealed in an integral collective awareness that transcends conventional boundaries of time and space. As such, the new society will be one mythic integration, a resonating world akin to the old tribal echo chamber where magic will live again: a world of ESP. The current interest of youth in astrology, clairvoyance and the occult is no coincidence. Electric technology, you see, does not require words any more than a digital computer requires numbers. Electricity makes possible — and not in the distant future, either — an amplification of human consciousness on a world scale, without any verbalization at all.

PLAYBOY: Are you talking about global telepathy?

McLUHAN: Precisely. Already, computers offer the potential of instantaneous translation of any code or language into any other code or language. If a data feedback is possible through the computer, why not a feed-*forward* of thought whereby a world consciousness links into a world computer? Via the computer, we could logically proceed from translating languages to bypassing them entirely in favor of an integral cosmic unconsciousness somewhat similar to the collective unconscious envisioned by Bergson. The computer thus holds out the promise of a technologically engendered state of universal understanding and unity, a state of absorption in the logos that could knit mankind into one family and create a perpetuity of collective harmony and peace. This is the *real* use of the computer, not to expedite marketing or solve technical problems but to speed the process of discovery and orchestrate terrestrial — and eventually galactic — environments and energies. Psychic communal integration, made possible at last by the electronic media, could create the universality of consciousness foreseen by Dante when he predicted that men would continue as no more than broken fragments until they were unified into an inclusive consciousness. In a Christian sense, this is merely a new interpretation of the mystical body of Christ; and Christ, after all, is the ultimate extension of man.

PLAYBOY: Isn't this projection of an electronically induced world consciousness more mystical than technological?

McLUHAN: Yes — as mystical as the most advanced theories of modern nuclear physics. Mysticism is just tomorrow's science dreamed today.

PLAYBOY: You said a few minutes ago that *all* of contemporary man's traditional values, attitudes and institutions are going to be destroyed and replaced in and by the new electric age. That's a pretty sweeping generalization. Apart from the complex psychosocial metamorphoses you've mentioned, would you explain in more detail some of the specific changes you foresee?

McLUHAN: The transformations are taking place everywhere around us. As the old value systems crumble, so do all the institutional clothing and garbage they fashioned. The cities, corporate extensions of our physical organs, are withering and being translated along with all other such extensions into information systems, as television and the jet — by compressing time and space — make all the world one village and destroy the old city-country dichotomy. New York, Chicago, Los Angeles — all will disappear like the dinosaur. The automobile, too, will soon be as obsolete as the cities it is currently strangling, replaced by new antigravitational technology. The marketing systems and the stock market as we know them today will soon be dead as the dodo, and automation will end the traditional concept of the job, replacing it with a *role,* and giving men the breath of leisure. The electric media will create a world of dropouts from the old fragmented society, with its neatly compartmentalized analytic functions, and cause people to drop *in* to the new integrated global-village community.

All these convulsive changes, as I've already noted, carry with them attendant pain, violence and war — the normal stigmata of the identity quest — but the new society is springing so quickly from the ashes of the old that I believe it will be possible to avoid the transitional anarchy many predict. Automation and cybernation can play an essential role in smoothing the transition to the new society.

PLAYBOY: How?

McLUHAN: The computer can be used to direct a network of global thermostats to pattern life in ways that will optimize human awareness. Already, it's technologically feasible to employ the computer to program societies in beneficial ways.

PLAYBOY: How do you program an entire society — beneficially or otherwise?

McLUHAN: There's nothing at all difficult about putting computers in the position where they will be able to conduct carefully orchestrated programming of the sensory life of whole populations. I know it sounds rather science-fictional, but if you understood cybernetics you'd realize we could do it today. The computer could program the media to determine the given messages a people should hear in terms of their over-all needs, creating a total media experience absorbed and patterned by all the senses. We could program five hours less of TV in Italy to promote the reading of newspapers during an election, or lay on an additional 25 hours of TV in Venezuela to cool down the tribal temperature raised by radio the preceding month. By such orchestrated interplay of all media, whole cultures could now be programmed in order to improve and stabilize their emotional climate, just as we are beginning to learn how to maintain equilibrium among the world's competing economies.

PLAYBOY: How does such environmental programming, however enlightened in intent, differ from Pavlovian brainwashing?

McLUHAN: Your question reflects the usual panic of people confronted with unexplored technologies. I'm not saying such panic isn't justified, or that such environmental programing couldn't be brainwashing, or far worse — merely that such reactions are useless and distracting. Though I think the programming of societies could actually be conducted quite constructively and humanistically, I don't want to be in the position of a Hiroshima physicist extolling the potential of nuclear energy in the first days of August 1945. But an understanding of media's effects constitutes a civil defense against media fallout.

The alarm of so many people, however, at the prospect of corporate programming's creation of a complete service environment on this planet is rather like fearing that a municipal lighting system will deprive the individual of the right to adjust each light to his own favorite level of intensity. Computer technology can — and doubtless will — program entire environments to fulfill the social needs and sensory preferences of communities and nations. The *content* of that programming, however, depends on the nature of future societies — but that is in our own hands.

PLAYBOY: Is it really in our hands — or, by seeming to advocate the use of computers to manipulate the future of entire cultures, aren't you actually encouraging man to abdicate control over his destiny?

McLUHAN: First of all — and I'm sorry to have to repeat this disclaimer — I'm not advocating *anything;* I'm merely probing and predicting trends. Even if I opposed them or thought them disastrous, I couldn't stop them, so why waste my time lamenting? As Carlyle said of author Margaret Fuller after she remarked, "I accept the Universe": "She'd better." I see no possibility of a world-wide Luddite rebellion that will smash all machinery to bits, so we might as well sit back and see what is happening and what will happen to us in a cybernetic world. Resenting a new technology will not halt its progress.

The point to remember here is that whenever we use or perceive any technological extension of ourselves, we necessarily embrace it. Whenever we watch a TV screen or read a book, we are absorbing these extensions of ourselves into our individual system and experiencing an automatic "closure" or displacement of perception; we can't escape this perpetual embrace of our daily technology unless we escape the technology itself and flee to a hermit's cave. By consistently embracing all these technologies, we inevitably relate ourselves to them as servomechanisms. Thus, in order to make use of them at all, we must serve them as we do gods. The Eskimo is a servomechanism of his kayak, the cowboy of his horse, the businessman of his clock, the cyberneticist — and soon the entire world — of his computer. In other words, to the spoils belongs the victor.

This continuous modification of man by his own technology stimulates him to find continuous means of modifying it; man thus becomes the sex organs of the machine world just as the bee is of the plant world, permitting it to reproduce and constantly evolve to higher forms. The machine world reciprocates man's devotion by rewarding him with goods and services and bounty. Man's relationship with his machinery is thus inherently symbiotic. This has always been the case; it's only in the electric age that man has an opportunity to *recognize* this marriage to his own technology. Electric technology is a qualitative extension of this age-old man-machine relationship; 20th Century man's relationship to the computer is not by nature very different from prehistoric man's relationship to his boat or to his wheel — with the important difference that all previous technologies or extensions of man were partial and fragmentary, whereas the electric is total and inclusive. Now man is beginning to wear his brain outside his skull and his nerves outside his skin; new technology breeds new man. A recent cartoon portrayed a little boy telling his nonplused mother: "I'm going to be a computer when I grow up." Humor is often prophecy.

PLAYBOY: If man can't prevent this transformation of himself by technology — or *into* technology — how can he control and direct the process of change?

McLUHAN: The first and most vital step of all, as I said at the outset, is simply to understand media and their revolutionary effects on all psychic and social values and institutions. Understanding is half the battle. The central purpose of all my work is to convey this message, that by understanding media as they extend man, we gain a measure of control over them. And this is a vital task, because the immediate interface between audile-tactile and visual perception is taking place everywhere around us. No civilian can escape this environmental blitzkrieg, for there is, quite literally, no place to hide. But if we diagnose what is happening to us, we can reduce the ferocity of the winds of change and bring the best elements of the old visual culture, during this transitional period, into peaceful coexistence with the new retribalized society.

If we persist, however, in our conventional rearview-mirror approach to these cataclysmic developments, all of Western culture will be destroyed and swept into the dustbin of history. If literate Western man were really interested in preserving the most creative aspects of his civilization, he would not cower in his ivory tower bemoaning change but would plunge himself into the vortex of electric technology and, by understanding it, dictate his new environment — turn ivory tower into control tower. But I can understand his hostile attitude, because I once shared his visual bias.

PLAYBOY: What changed your mind?

McLUHAN: Experience. For many years, until I wrote my first book, *The Mechanical Bride,* I adopted an extremely moralistic approach to all environmental technology. I loathed machinery, I abominated cities, I equated the Industrial Revolution with original sin and mass media with the Fall. In short, I rejected almost every element of modern life in favor of a Rousseauvian utopianism. But gradually I perceived how sterile and useless this attitude was, and I began to realize that the greatest artists of the 20th Century — Yeats, Pound, Joyce, Eliot — had discovered a totally different approach, based on the identity of the processes of cognition and creation. I realized that artistic creation is the playback of ordinary experience — from trash to treasures. I ceased being a moralist and became a student.

As someone committed to literature and the traditions of literacy, I began to study the new environment that imperiled literary values, and I soon realized that they could not be dismissed by moral outrage or pious indignation. Study showed that a totally new approach was required, both to save what deserved saving in our Western heritage and to help man adopt a new survival strategy. I adapted some of this new approach in *The Mechanical Bride*

by attempting to immerse myself in the advertising media in order to apprehend their impact on man, but even there some of my old literate "point of view" bias crept in. The book, in any case, appeared just as television was making all its major points irrelevant.

I soon realized that recognizing the symptoms of change was not enough; one must understand the *cause* of change, for without comprehending causes, the social and psychic effects of new technology cannot be counteracted or modified. But I recognized also that one individual cannot accomplish these self-protective modifications; they must be the collective effort of society, because they affect all of society; the individual is helpless against the pervasiveness of environmental change: the new garbage — or mess-age — induced by new technologies. Only the social organism, united and recognizing the challenge, can move to meet it.

Unfortunately, no society in history has ever known enough about the forces that shape and transform it to take action to control and direct new technologies as they extend and transform man. But today, change proceeds so instantaneously through the new media that it may be possible to institute a global education program that will enable us to seize the reins of our destiny — but to do this we must first recognize the kind of therapy that's needed for the effects of the new media. In such an effort, indignation against those who perceive the nature of those effects is no substitute for awareness and insight.

PLAYBOY: Are you referring to the critical attacks to which you've been subjected for some of your theories and predictions?

McLUHAN: I am. But I don't want to sound uncharitable about my critics. Indeed, I appreciate their attention. After all, a man's detractors work for him tirelessly and for free. It's as good as being banned in Boston. But as I've said, I can understand their hostile attitude toward environmental change, having once shared it. Theirs is the customary human reaction when confronted with innovation: to flounder about attempting to adapt old responses to new situations or to simply condemn or ignore the harbingers of change — a practice refined by the Chinese emperors, who used to execute messengers bringing bad news. The new technological environments generate the most pain among those least prepared to alter their old value structures. The literati find the new electronic environment far more threatening than do those less committed to literacy as a way of life. When an individual or social group feels that its whole identity is jeopardized by social or psychic change, its natural reaction is to lash out in defensive fury. But for all their lamentations, the revolution has already taken place.

PLAYBOY: You've explained why you avoid approving or disapproving of this revolution in your work, but you must have a private opinion. What is it?

McLUHAN: I don't like to tell people what I think is good or bad about the social and psychic changes caused by new media, but if you insist on pinning me down about my own subjective reactions as I observe the reprimitivization of our culture, I would have to say that I view such upheavals with total personal dislike and dissatisfaction. I do see the prospect of a rich and creative retribalized society — free of the fragmentation and alienation of the mechanical age — emerging from this traumatic period of culture clash; but I have nothing but distaste for the *process* of change. As a man molded within the literate Western tradition, I do not personally cheer the dissolution of that tradition through the electric involvement of all the senses: I don't enjoy the destruction of neighborhoods by high-rises or revel in the pain of identity quest. No one could be less enthusiastic about these radical changes than myself. I am not, by temperament or conviction, a revolutionary; I would prefer a stable, changeless environment of modest services and human scale. TV and all the electric media are unraveling the entire fabric of our society, and as a man who is forced by circumstances to live within that society, I do not take delight in its disintegration.

You see, I am not a crusader; I imagine I would be most happy living in a secure preliterate environment; I would never attempt to change my world, for better or worse. Thus I derive no joy from observing the traumatic effects of media on man, although I do obtain satisfaction from grasping their modes of operation. Such comprehension is inherently cool, since it is simultaneously involvement and detachment. This posture is essential in studying media. One must begin by becoming extraenvironmental, putting oneself beyond the battle in order to study and understand the configuration of forces. It's vital to adopt a posture of arrogant superiority; instead of scurrying into a corner and wailing about what

media are doing to us, one should charge straight ahead and kick them in the electrodes. They respond beautifully to such resolute treatment and soon become servants rather than masters. But without this detached involvement, I could never objectively observe media; it would be like an octopus grappling with the Empire State Building. So I employ the greatest boon of literate culture: the power of man to act without reaction — the sort of specialization by dissociation that has been the driving motive force behind Western civilization.

The Western world is being revolutionized by the electric media as rapidly as the East is being Westernized, and although the society that eventually emerges may be superior to our own, the process of change is agonizing. I must move through this pain-wracked transitional era as a scientist would move through a world of disease; once a surgeon becomes personally involved and disturbed about the condition of his patient, he loses the power to help that patient. Clinical detachment is not some kind of haughty pose I affect — nor does it reflect any lack of compassion on my part; it's simply a survival strategy. The world we are living in is not one I would have created on my own drawing board, but it's the one in which I must live, and in which the students I teach must live. If nothing else, I owe it to them to avoid the luxury of moral indignation or the troglodytic security of the ivory tower and to get down into the junk yard of environmental change and steam-shovel my way through to a comprehension of its contents and its lines of force — in order to understand how and why it is metamorphosing man.

PLAYBOY: Despite your personal distaste for the upheavals induced by the new electric technology, you seem to feel that if we understand and influence its effects on us, a less alienated and fragmented society may emerge from it. Is it thus accurate to say that you are essentially optimistic about the future?

McLUHAN: There are grounds for both optimism and pessimism. The extensions of man's consciousness induced by the electric media could conceivably usher in the millennium, but it also holds the potential for realizing the Anti-Christ — Yeats' rough beast, its hour come round at last, slouching toward Bethlehem to be born. Cataclysmic environmental changes such as these are, in and of themselves, morally neutral; it is how we perceive them and react to them that will determine their ultimate psychic and social consequences. If we refuse to see them at all, we will become their servants. It's inevitable that the world-pool of electronic information movement will toss us all about like corks on a stormy sea, but if we keep our cool during the descent into the maelstrom, studying the process as it happens to us and what we can do about it, we can come through.

Personally, I have a great faith in the resiliency and adaptability of man, and I tend to look to our tomorrows with a surge of excitement and hope. I feel that we're standing on the threshold of a liberating and exhilarating world in which the human tribe can become truly one family and man's consciousness can be freed from the shackles of mechanical culture and enabled to roam the cosmos. I have a deep and abiding belief in man's potential to grow and learn, to plumb the depths of his own being and to learn the secret songs that orchestrate the universe. We live in a transitional era of profound pain and tragic identity quest, but the agony of our age is the labor pain of rebirth.

I expect to see the coming decades transform the planet into an art form; the new man, linked in a cosmic harmony that transcends time and space, will sensuously caress and mold and pattern every facet of the terrestrial artifact as if it were a work of art, and man himself will become an organic art form. There is a long road ahead, and the stars are only way stations, but we have begun the journey. To be born in this age is a precious gift, and I regret the prospect of my own death only because I will leave so many pages of man's destiny — if you will excuse the Gutenbergian image — tantalizingly unread. But perhaps, as I've tried to demonstrate in my examination of the postliterate culture the story begins only when the book closes.

The Shallows: The Vital Paths

Nicholas Carr

Friedrich Nietzsche was desperate. Sickly as a child, he had never fully recovered from injuries he suffered in his early twenties when he fell from a horse while serving in a mounted artillery unit in the Prussian army. In 1879, his health problems worsening, he'd been forced to resign his post as a professor of philology at the University of Basel. Just thirty-four years old, he began to wander through Europe, seeking relief from his many ailments. He would head south to the shores of the Mediterranean when the weather turned cool in the fall, then north again, to the Swiss Alps or his mother's home near Leipzig, in the spring. Late in 1881, he rented a garret apartment in the Italian port city of Genoa. His vision was failing, and keeping his eyes focused on a page had become exhausting and painful, often bringing on crushing headaches and fits of vomiting. He'd been forced to curtail his writing, and he feared he would soon have to give it up.

At wit's end, he ordered a typewriter—a Danish-made Malling-Hansen Writing Ball—and it was delivered to his lodgings during the first weeks of 1882. Invented a few years earlier by Hans Rasmus Johann Malling-Hansen, the principal of the Royal Institute for the Deaf-Mute in Copenhagen, the writing ball was an oddly beautiful instrument. It resembled an ornate golden pincushion. Fifty-two keys, for capital and lowercase letters as well as numerals and punctuation marks, protruded from the top of the ball in a concentric arrangement scientifically designed to enable the most efficient typing possible. Directly below the keys lay a curved plate that held a sheet of typing paper. Using an ingenious gearing system, the plate advanced like clockwork with each stroke of a key. Given enough practice, a person could type as many as eight hundred characters a minute with the machine, making it the fastest typewriter that had ever been built.

The writing ball rescued Nietzsche, at least for a time. Once he had learned touch typing, he was able to write with his eyes closed, using only the tips of his fingers. Words could again pass from his mind to the page. He was so taken with Mailing-Hansen's creation that he typed up a little ode to it:

> The writing ball is a thing like me: made of iron
> Yet easily twisted on journeys.
> Patience and tact are required in abundance,
> As well as fine fingers, to use us.

In March, a Berlin newspaper reported that Nietzsche "feels better than ever" and, thanks to his typewriter, "has resumed his writing activities."

But the device had a subtler effect on his work. One of Nietzsche's closest friends, the writer and composer Heinrich Köselitz, noticed a change in the style of his writing. Nietzsche's prose had become tighter, more telegraphic. There was a new forcefulness to it, too, as though the machine's power—its "iron"—was, through some mysterious metaphysical mechanism, being transferred into the words it pressed into the page. "Perhaps you will through this instrument even take to a new idiom," Köselitz wrote in a letter, noting that, in his own work, "my 'thoughts' in music and language often depend on the quality of pen and paper."

"You are right," Nietzsche replied. "Our writing equipment takes part in the forming of our thoughts."

While Nietzsche was learning to type on his writing ball in Genoa, five hundred miles to the northeast a young medical student named Sigmund Freud was working as a neurophysiology researcher in a Vienna laboratory. His specialty was dissecting the nervous systems of fish and crustaceans. Through his experiments, he came to surmise that the brain, like other bodily organs, is made up of many separate cells. He later extended his theory to suggest that the gaps between the cells—the "contact barriers," as he termed them—play an essential role in governing the functions of the mind, shaping our memories and our thoughts. At the time, Freud's conclusions lay outside the mainstream of scientific opinion. Most doctors and researchers believed that the brain was not cellular in construction but rather consisted of a single, continuous fabric of nerve fibers. And even among those who shared Freud's view that the brain was made of cells, few paid any attention to what might be going on in the spaces between those cells.

Engaged to be wed and in need of a more substantial income, Freud soon abandoned his career as a researcher and went into private practice as a psychoanalyst. But subsequent studies bore out his youthful speculations. Armed with ever more powerful microscopes, scientists confirmed the existence of discrete nerve cells. They also discovered that those cells—our neurons—are both like and unlike the other cells in our bodies. Neurons have central cores, or somas, which carry out the functions common to all cells, but they also have two kinds of tentacle-like appendages—axons and dendrites—that transmit and receive electric pulses. When a neuron is active, a pulse flows from the soma to the tip of the axon, where it triggers the release of chemicals called neurotransmitters. The

neurotransmitters flow across Freud's contact barrier—the synapse, we now call it—and attach themselves to a dendrite of a neighboring neuron, triggering (or suppressing) a new electric pulse in that cell. It's through the flow of neurotransmitters across synapses that neurons communicate with one another, directing the transmission of electrical signals along complex cellular pathways. Thoughts, memories, emotions—all emerge from the electrochemical interactions of neurons, mediated by synapses.

During the twentieth century, neuroscientists and psychologists also came to more fully appreciate the astounding complexity of the human brain. Inside our skulls, they discovered, are some 100 billion neurons, which take many different shapes and range in length from a few tenths of a millimeter to a few feet. A single neuron typically has many dendrites (though only one axon), and dendrites and axons can have a multitude of branches and synaptic terminals. The average neuron makes about a thousand synaptic connections, and some neurons can make a hundred times that number. The thousands of billions of synapses inside our skulls tie our neurons together into a dense mesh of circuits that, in ways that are still far from understood, give rise to what we think, how we feel, and who we are.

Even as our knowledge of the physical workings of the brain advanced during the last century, one old assumption remained firmly in place: most biologists and neurologists continued to believe, as they had for hundreds of years, that the structure of the adult brain never changed. Our neurons would connect into circuits during childhood, when our brains were malleable, and as we reached maturity the circuitry would become fixed. The brain, in the prevailing view, was something like a concrete structure. After being poured and shaped in our youth, it hardened quickly into its final form. Once we hit our twenties, no new neurons were created, no new circuits forged. We would, of course, continue to store new memories throughout our lives (and lose some old ones), but the only structural change the brain would go through in adulthood was a slow process of decay as the body aged and nerve cells died.

Although the belief in the adult brain's immutability was deeply and widely held, there were a few heretics. A handful of biologists and psychologists saw in the rapidly growing body of brain research indications that even the adult brain was malleable, or "plastic." New neural circuits could form throughout our lives, they suggested, and old ones might grow stronger or weaker or wither away entirely. The British biologist J. Z. Young, in a series of lectures broadcast by the BBC in 1950, argued that the structure of the brain might in fact be in a constant state of flux, adapting to whatever task it's called on to perform. "There is evidence that the cells of our brains literally develop and grow bigger with use, and atrophy or waste away with disuse," he said. "It may be therefore that every action leaves some permanent print upon the nervous tissue."

Young was not the first to propose such an idea. Seventy years earlier, the American psychologist William James had expressed a similar intuition about the brain's adaptability. The "nervous tissue," he wrote in his landmark *Principles of Psychology,* "seems endowed with a very extraordinary degree of plasticity." As with any other physical compound, "either outward forces or inward tensions can, from one hour to another, turn that structure into something different from what it was." James quoted, approvingly, an analogy that the French scientist Léon Dumont had drawn, in an earlier essay about the biological consequences of habit, between the actions of water on land and the effects of experience on the brain: "Flowing water hollows out a channel for itself which grows broader and deeper; and when it later flows again, it follows the path traced by itself before. Just so, the impressions of outer objects fashion for themselves more and more appropriate paths in the nervous system, and these vital paths recur under similar external stimulation, even if they have been interrupted for some time." Freud, too, ended up taking the contrarian position. In "Project for a Scientific Psychology," a manuscript he wrote in 1895 but never published, he argued that the brain, and in particular the contact barriers between neurons, could change in response to a person's experiences.

Such speculations were dismissed, often contemptuously, by most brain scientists and physicians. They remained convinced that the brain's plasticity ended with childhood, that the "vital paths," once laid, could not be widened or narrowed, much less rerouted. They stood with Santiago Ramón y Cajal, the eminent Spanish physician, neuroanatomist, and Nobel laureate, who in 1913 declared, with a tone that left little room for debate, "In the adult [brain] centres, the nerve paths are

something fixed, ended, immutable. Everything may die, nothing may be regenerated." In younger days, Ramón y Cajal had himself expressed doubts about the orthodox view—he had suggested, in 1894, that the "organ of thought is, within certain limits, malleable, and perfectible by well-directed mental exercise"—but in the end he embraced the conventional wisdom and became one of its most eloquent and authoritative defenders.

The conception of the adult brain as an unchanging physical apparatus grew out of, and was buttressed by, an Industrial Age metaphor that represented the brain as a mechanical contraption. Like a steam engine or an electric dynamo, the nervous system was made up of many parts, and each had a specific and set purpose that contributed in some essential way to the successful operation of the whole. The parts could not change, in shape or function, because that would lead, immediately and inexorably, to the breakdown of the machine. Different regions of the brain, and even individual circuits, played precisely defined roles in processing sensory inputs, directing the movements of muscles, and forming memories and thoughts; and those roles, established in childhood, were not susceptible to alteration. When it came to the brain, the child was indeed, as Wordsworth had written, the father to the man.

The mechanical conception of the brain both reflected and refuted the famous theory of dualism that René Descartes had laid out in his *Meditations* of 1641. Descartes claimed that the brain and the mind existed in two separate spheres: one material, one ethereal. The physical brain, like the rest of the body, was a purely mechanical instrument that, like a clock or a pump, acted according to the movements of its component parts. But the workings of the brain, argued Descartes, did not explain the workings of the conscious mind. As the essence of the self, the mind existed outside of space, beyond the laws of matter. Mind and brain could influence each other (through, as Descartes saw it, some mysterious action of the pineal gland), but they remained entirely separate substances. At a time of rapid scientific advance and social upheaval, Descartes' dualism came as a comfort. Reality had a material side, which was the realm of science, but it also had a spiritual side, which was the realm of theology—and never the twain shall meet.

As reason became the new religion of the Enlightenment, the notion of an immaterial mind lying outside the reach of observation and experiment seemed increasingly tenuous. Scientists rejected the "mind" half of Cartesian dualism even as they embraced Descartes' idea of the brain as a machine. Thought, memory, and emotion, rather than being the emanations of a spirit world, came to be seen as the logical and predetermined outputs of the physical operations of the brain. Consciousness was simply a by-product of those operations. "The word Mind is obsolete," one prominent neurophysiologist ultimately declared. The machine metaphor was extended, and further reinforced, by the arrival of the digital computer—a "thinking machine"—in the middle of the twentieth century. That's when scientists and philosophers began referring to our brain circuits, and even our behavior, as being "hardwired," just like the microscopic circuits etched into the silicon substrate of a computer chip.

As the idea of the unchangeable adult brain hardened into dogma, it turned into a kind of "neurological nihilism," according to the research psychiatrist Norman Doidge. Because it created "a sense that treatment for many brain problems was ineffective or unwarranted," Doidge explains, it left those with mental illnesses or brain injuries little hope of treatment, much less cure. And as the idea "spread through our culture," it ended up "stunting our overall view of human nature. Since the brain could not change, human nature, which emerges from it, seemed necessarily fixed and unalterable as well." There was no regeneration; there was only decay. We, too, were stuck in the frozen concrete of our brain cells—or at least in the frozen concrete of received wisdom.

It's 1968. I'm nine years old, a run-of-the-mill suburban kid playing in a patch of woods near my family's home. Marshall McLuhan and Norman Mailer are on prime-time TV, debating the intellectual and moral implications of what Mailer describes as "man's acceleration into a super-technological world." *2001* is having its first theatrical run, leaving moviegoers befuddled, bemused, or just plain annoyed. And in a quiet laboratory at the University of Wisconsin in Madison, Michael Merzenich is cutting a hole in a monkey's skull.

Twenty-six years old, Merzenich has just received a doctorate in physiology from Johns Hopkins, where he studied under Vernon Mountcastle, a pioneering neuroscientist. He has come to Wisconsin to do postdoctoral research in brain mapping. It's been known for years that every area of a person's body is represented by a corresponding area in the cerebral cortex, the brain's wrinkled outer layer. When certain nerve cells in the skin, are stimulated—by being touched or pinched, say—they send an electric pulse through the spinal cord to a particular cluster of neurons in the cortex, which translates the touch or the pinch into a conscious sensation. In the 1930s, the Canadian neurosurgeon Wilder Penfield had used electrical probes to draw the first sensory maps of people's brains. But Penfield's probes were crude instruments, and his maps, while groundbreaking in their time, lacked precision. Merzenich is using a new kind of probe, the hair-thin microelectrode, to create much finer maps that will, he hopes, provide new insight into the brain's structure.

Once he has removed a piece of the monkey's skull and exposed a small portion of its brain, he threads a microelectrode into the area of the cortex that registers sensations from one of the animal's hands. He begins tapping that hand in different places until the neuron beside the tip of the electrode fires. After methodically inserting and reinserting the electrode thousands of times over the course of a few days, he ends up with a "micromap" showing in minute detail, down to the individual nerve cell, how the monkey's brain processes what its hand feels. He repeats the painstaking exercise with five more monkeys.

Merzenich proceeds to the second stage of his experiment. Using a scalpel, he makes incisions in the hands of the animals, severing the sensory nerve. He wants to find out how the brain reacts when a peripheral nerve system is damaged and then allowed to heal. What he discovers astounds him. The nerves in the monkeys' hands grow back in a haphazard fashion, as expected, and their brains, also as expected, become confused. When, for example, Merzenich touches the lower joint of a finger on one monkey's hand, the monkey's brain tells the animal that the sensation is coming from the tip of the finger. The signals have been crossed, the brain map scrambled. But when Merzenich conducts the same sensory tests a few months later, he finds that the mental confusion has been cleared up. What the monkeys' brains tell them is happening to their hands now matches what's really happening. The brains, Merzenich realizes, have reorganized themselves. The animals' neural pathways have woven themselves into a new map that corresponds to the new arrangement of nerves in their hands.

At first, he can't believe what he's seen. Like every other neuroscientist, he's been taught that the structure of the adult brain is fixed. Yet in his lab he has just seen the brains of six monkeys undergo rapid and extensive restructuring at the cellular level. "I knew it was astounding reorganization, but I couldn't explain it," Merzenich will later recall. "Looking back on it, I realized that I had seen evidence of neuroplasticity. But I didn't know it at the time. I simply didn't know what I was seeing. And besides, in mainstream neuroscience, nobody would believe that plasticity was occurring on this scale."

Merzenich publishes the results of his experiment in an academic journal. Nobody pays much heed. But he knows he's onto something, and over the course of the next three decades he conducts many more tests on many more monkeys, all of which point to the existence of broad plasticity in the brains of mature primates. In a 1983 paper documenting one of the experiments, Merzenich declares flatly, "These results are completely contrary to a view of sensory systems as consisting of a series of hard-wired machines." At first dismissed, Merzenich's meticulous work finally begins to receive serious notice in the neurological community. It ends up setting off a wholesale reevaluation of accepted theories about how our brains work. Researchers uncover a trail of experiments, dating back to the days of William James and Sigmund Freud, that record examples of plasticity. Long ignored, the old research is now taken seriously.

As brain science continues to advance, the evidence for plasticity strengthens. Using sensitive new brain-scanning equipment, as well as microelectrodes and other probes, neuroscientists conduct more experiments, not only on lab animals but on people. All of them confirm Merzenich's discovery. They also reveal something more: The brain's plasticity is not limited to the somatosensory cortex, the area that governs our sense of touch. It's universal. Virtually all of our neural circuits—whether they're involved in feeling, seeing, hearing, moving, thinking, learning, perceiving, or remembering— are subject to change. The received wisdom is cast aside.

The adult brain, it turns out, is not just plastic but, as James Olds, a professor of neuroscience who directs the Krasnow Institute for Advanced Study at George Mason University, puts it, "very plastic." Or, as Merzenich himself says, "massively plastic." The plasticity diminishes as we get older—brains do get stuck in their ways—but it never goes away. Our neurons are always breaking old connections and forming new ones, and brand-new nerve cells are always being created. "The brain," observes Olds, "has the ability to reprogram itself on the fly, altering the way it functions."

We don't yet know all the details of how the brain reprograms itself, but it has become clear that, as Freud proposed, the secret lies mainly in the rich chemical broth of our synapses. What goes on in the microscopic spaces between our neurons is exceedingly complicated, but in simple terms it involves various chemical reactions that register and record experiences in neural pathways. Every time we perform a task or experience a sensation, whether physical or mental, a set of neurons in our brains is activated. If they're in proximity, these neurons join together through the exchange of synaptic neurotransmitters like the amino acid glutamate. As the same experience is repeated, the synaptic links between the neurons grow stronger and more plentiful through both physiological changes, such as the release of higher concentrations of neurotransmitters, and anatomical ones, such as the generation of new neurons or the growth of new synaptic terminals on existing axons and dendrites. Synaptic links can also weaken in response to experiences, again as a result of physiological and anatomical alterations. What we learn as we live is embedded in the ever-changing cellular connections inside our heads. The chains of linked neurons form our minds' true "vital paths." Today, scientists sum up the essential dynamic of neuroplasticity with a saying known as Hebb's rule: "Cells that fire together wire together."

One of the simplest yet most powerful demonstrations of how synaptic connections change came in a series of experiments that the biologist Eric Kandel performed in the early 1970s on a type of large sea slug called *Aplysia*. (Sea creatures make particularly good subjects for neurological tests because they tend to have simple nervous systems and large nerve cells.) Kandel, who would earn a Nobel Prize for his work, found that if you touch a slug's gill, even very lightly, the gill will immediately and reflexively recoil. But if you touch the gill repeatedly, without causing any harm to the animal, the recoiling instinct will steadily diminish. The slug will become habituated to the touch and learn to ignore it. By monitoring slugs' nervous systems, Kandel discovered that "this learned change in behavior was paralleled by a progressive weakening of the synaptic connections" between the sensory neurons that "feel" the touch and the motor neurons that tell the gill to retract. In a slug's ordinary state, about ninety percent of the sensory neurons in its gill have connections to motor neurons. But after its gill is touched just forty times, only ten percent of the sensory cells maintain links to the motor cells. The research "showed dramatically," Kandel wrote, that "synapses can undergo large and enduring changes in strength after only a relatively small amount of training."

The plasticity of our synapses brings into harmony two philosophies of the mind that have for centuries stood in conflict: empiricism and rationalism. In the view of empiricists, like John Locke, the mind we are born with is a blank slate, a "tabula rasa." What we know comes entirely through our experiences, through what we learn as we live. To put it into more familiar terms, we are products of nurture, not nature. In the view of rationalists, like Immanuel Kant, we are born with built-in mental "templates" that determine how we perceive and make sense of the world. All our experiences are filtered through these inborn templates. Nature predominates.

The *Aplysia* experiments revealed, as Kandel reports, "that both views had merit—in fact they complemented each other." Our genes "specify" many of "the connections among neurons—that is, which neurons form synaptic connections with which other neurons and when." Those genetically determined connections form Kant's innate templates, the basic architecture of the brain. But our experiences regulate the strength, or "long-term effectiveness," of the connections, allowing, as Locke had argued, the ongoing reshaping of the mind and "the expression of new patterns of behavior." The opposing philosophies of the empiricist and the rationalist find their common ground in the synapse. The New York University neuroscientist Joseph LeDoux explains in his book *Synaptic Self* that nature and nurture "actually speak the same language. They both ultimately achieve their mental and behavioral effects by shaping the synaptic organization of the brain."

The brain is not the machine we once thought it to be. Though different regions are associated with different mental functions, the cellular components do not form permanent structures or play rigid roles. They're flexible. They change with experience, circumstance, and need. Some of the most extensive and remarkable changes take place in response to damage to the nervous system. Experiments show, for instance, that if a person is struck blind, the part of the brain that had been dedicated to processing visual stimuli—the visual cortex—doesn't just go dark. It is quickly taken over by circuits used for audio processing. And if the person learns to read Braille, the visual cortex will be redeployed for processing information delivered through the sense of touch. "Neurons seem to 'want' to receive input," explains Nancy Kanwisher of MIT's McGovern Institute for Brain Research: "When their usual input disappears, they start responding to the next best thing." Thanks to the ready adaptability of neurons, the senses of hearing and touch can grow sharper to mitigate the effects of the loss of sight. Similar alterations happen in the brains of people who go deaf: their other senses strengthen to help make up for the loss of hearing. The area in the brain that processes peripheral vision, for example, grows larger, enabling them to see what they once would have heard.

Tests on people who have lost arms or legs in accidents also reveal how extensively the brain can reorganize itself. The areas in the victims' brains that had registered sensations in their lost limbs are quickly taken over by circuits that register sensations from other parts of their bodies. In studying a teenage boy who had lost his left arm in a car crash, the neurologist V. S. Ramachandran, who heads the Center for Brain and Cognition at the University of California at San Diego, discovered that when he had the young man close his eyes and then touched different parts of his face, the patient believed that it was his missing arm that was being touched. At one point, Ramachandran brushed a spot beneath the boy's nose and asked, "Where do you feel that?" The boy replied, "On my left pinky. It tingles." The boy's brain map was in the process of being reorganized, the neurons redeployed for new uses. As a result of such experiments, it's now believed that the sensations of a "phantom limb" felt by amputees are largely the result of neuroplastic changes in the brain.

Our expanding understanding of the brain's adaptability has led to the development of new therapies for conditions that used to be considered untreatable. Doidge, in his 2007 book *The Brain That Changes Itself,* tells the story of a man named Michael Bernstein who suffered a severe stroke when he was fifty-four, damaging an area in the right half of his brain that regulated movement in the left side of his body. Through a traditional program of physical therapy, he recovered some of his motor skills, but his left hand remained crippled and he had to use a cane to walk. Until recently, that would have been the end of the story. But Bernstein enrolled in a program of experimental therapy, run at the University of Alabama by a pioneering neuroplasticity researcher named Edward Taub. For as many as eight hours a day, six days a week, Bernstein used his left hand and his left leg to perform routine tasks over and over again. One day he might wash the pane of a window. The next day he might trace the letters of the alphabet. The repeated actions were a means of coaxing his neurons and synapses to form new circuits that would take over the functions once carried out by the circuits in the damaged area in his brain. In a matter of weeks, he regained nearly all of the movement in his hand and his leg, allowing him to return to his everyday routines and throw away his cane. Many of Taub's other patients have experienced similarly strong recoveries.

Much of the early evidence of neuroplasticity came through the study of the brain's reaction to injuries, whether the severing of the nerves in the hands of Merzenich's monkeys or the loss of sight, hearing, or a limb by human beings. That led some scientists to wonder whether the malleability of the adult brain might be limited to extreme situations. Perhaps, they theorized, plasticity is essentially a healing mechanism, triggered by trauma to the brain or the sensory organs. Further experiments have shown that that's not the case. Extensive, perpetual plasticity has been documented in healthy, normally functioning nervous systems, leading neuroscientists to conclude that our brains are always in flux, adapting to even small shifts in our circumstances and behavior. "We have learned that neuroplasticity is not only possible but that it is constantly in action," writes Mark Hallett, head of the Medical Neurology Branch of the National Institutes of Health. "That is the way we adapt to changing conditions, the way we learn new facts, and the way we develop new skills."

"Plasticity," says Alvaro Pascual-Leone, a top neurology researcher at Harvard Medical School, is "the normal ongoing state of the nervous system throughout the life span." Our brains are constantly changing in response to our experiences and our behavior, reworking their circuitry with "each sensory input, motor act, association, reward signal, action plan, or [shift of] awareness." Neuroplasticity, argues Pascual-Leone, is one of the most important products of evolution, a trait that enables the nervous system "to escape the restrictions of its own genome and thus adapt to environmental pressures, physiologic changes, and experiences." The genius of our brain's construction is not that it contains a lot of hardwiring but that it doesn't. Natural selection, writes the philosopher David Buller in *Adapting Minds,* his critique of evolutionary psychology, "has not designed a brain that consists of numerous prefabricated adaptations" but rather one that is able "to adapt to local environmental demands throughout the lifetime of an individual, and sometimes within a period of days, by forming specialized structures to deal with those demands." Evolution has given us a brain that can literally change its mind—over and over again.

Our ways of thinking, perceiving, and acting, we now know, are not entirely determined by our genes. Nor are they entirely determined by our childhood experiences. We change them through the way we live—and, as Nietzsche sensed, through the tools we use. Years before Edward Taub opened his rehabilitation clinic in Alabama, he conducted a famous experiment on a group of right-handed violinists. Using a machine that monitors neural activity, he measured the areas of their sensory cortex that processed signals from their left hands, the hands they used to finger the strings of their instruments. He also measured the same cortical areas in a group of right-handed volunteers who had never played a musical instrument. He found that the brain areas of the violinists were significantly larger than those of the nonmusicians. He then measured the size of the cortical areas that processed sensations from the subjects' right hands. Here, he found no differences between the musicians and the nonmusicians. Playing a violin, a musical tool, had resulted in substantial physical changes in the brain. That was true even for the musicians who had first taken up their instruments as adults.

When scientists have trained primates and other animals to use simple tools, they've discovered just how profoundly the brain can be influenced by technology. Monkeys, for instance, were taught how to use rakes and pliers to take hold of pieces of food that would otherwise have been out of reach. When researchers monitored the animals' neural activity throughout the course of the training, they found significant growth in the visual and motor areas involved in controlling the hands that held the tools. But they discovered something even more striking as well: the rakes and pliers actually came to be incorporated into the brain maps of the animals' hands. The tools, so far as the animals' brains were concerned, had become part of their bodies. As the researchers who conducted the experiment with the pliers reported, the monkeys' brains began to act "as if the pliers were now the hand fingers."

It's not just repeated physical actions that can rewire our brains. Purely mental activity can also alter our neural circuitry, sometimes in far-reaching ways. In the late 1990s, a group of British researchers scanned the brains of sixteen London cab drivers who had between two and forty-two years of experience behind the wheel. When they compared the scans with those of a control group, they found that the taxi drivers' posterior hippocampus, a part of the brain that plays a key role in storing and manipulating spatial representations of a person's surroundings, was much larger than normal. Moreover, the longer a cab driver had been on the job, the larger his posterior hippocampus tended to be. The researchers also discovered that a portion of the drivers' anterior hippocampus was smaller than average, apparently a result of the need to accommodate the enlargement of the posterior area. Further tests indicated that the shrinking of the anterior hippocampus might have reduced the cabbies' aptitude for certain other memorization tasks. The constant spatial processing required to navigate London's intricate road system, the researchers concluded, is "associated with a relative redistribution of gray matter in the hippocampus."

Another experiment, conducted by Pascual-Leone when he was a researcher at the National Institutes of Health, provides even more remarkable evidence of the way our patterns of thought affect the anatomy of our brains. Pascual-Leone recruited people who had no experience playing a piano, and he taught them how to play a simple melody consisting of a short series of notes. He then split the participants into two groups. He had the members of one group practice the melody on a keyboard for two hours a day over the next five days. He had the members of the other group sit in front of a keyboard for the same amount of time but only imagine playing the song—without ever touching the keys. Using a technique called transcranial magnetic stimulation, or TMS, Pascual-Leone mapped the brain activity of all the participants before, during, and after the test. He found that the people who had only imagined playing the notes exhibited precisely the same changes in their brains as those who had actually pressed the keys. Their brains had changed in response to actions that took place purely in their imagination—in response, that is, to their thoughts. Descartes may have been wrong about dualism, but he appears to have been correct in believing that our thoughts can exert a physical influence on, or at least cause a physical reaction in, our brains. We become, neurologically, what we think.

Michael Greenerg, in a 2008 essay in the *New York Review of Books,* found the poetry in neuroplasticity. He observed that our neurological system, "with its branches and transmitters and ingeniously spanned gaps, has an improvised quality that seems to mirror the unpredictability of thought itself." It's "an ephemeral place that changes as our experience changes." There are many reasons to be grateful that our mental hardware is able to adapt so readily to experience, that even old brains can be taught new tricks. The brain's adaptability hasn't just led to new treatments, and new hope, for those suffering from brain injury or illness. It provides all of us with a mental flexibility, an intellectual litheness, that allows us to adapt to new situations, learn new skills, and in general expand our horizons.

But the news is not all good. Although neuroplasticity provides an escape from genetic determinism, a loophole for free thought and free will, it also imposes its own form of determinism on our behavior. As particular circuits in our brain strengthen through the repetition of a physical or mental activity, they begin to transform that activity into a habit. The paradox of neuroplasticity, observes Doidge, is that, for all the mental flexibility it grants us, it can end up locking us into "rigid behaviors." The chemically triggered synapses that link our neurons program us, in effect, to want to keep exercising the circuits they've formed. Once we've wired new circuitry in our brain, Doidge writes, "we long to keep it activated." That's the way the brain fine-tunes its operations. Routine activities are carried out ever more quickly and efficiently, while unused circuits are pruned away.

Plastic does not mean elastic, in other words. Our neural loops don't snap back to their former state the way a rubber band does; they hold onto their changed state. And nothing says the new state has to be a desirable one. Bad habits can be ingrained in our neurons as easily as good ones. Pascual-Leone observes that "plastic changes may not necessarily represent a behavioral gain for a given subject." In addition to being "the mechanism for development and learning," plasticity can be "a cause of pathology."

It comes as no surprise that neuroplasticity has been linked to mental afflictions ranging from depression to obsessive-compulsive disorder to tinnitus. The more a sufferer concentrates on his symptoms, the deeper those symptoms are etched into his neural circuits. In the worst cases, the mind essentially trains itself to be sick. Many addictions, too, are reinforced by the strengthening of plastic pathways in the brain. Even very small doses of addictive drugs can dramatically alter the flow of neurotransmitters in a person's synapses, resulting in long-lasting alterations in brain circuitry and function. In some cases, the buildup of certain kinds of neurotransmitters, such as dopamine, a pleasure-producing cousin to adrenaline, seems to actually trigger the turning on or off of particular genes, bringing even stronger cravings for the drug. The vital paths turn deadly.

The potential for unwelcome neuroplastic adaptations also exists in the everyday, normal functioning of our minds. Experiments show that just as the brain can build new or stronger circuits through physical or mental practice, those circuits can weaken or dissolve with neglect. "If we stop exercising our mental skills," writes Doidge, "we do not just forget them: the brain map space for those skills is turned over to the skills we practice instead." Jeffrey Schwartz, a professor of psychiatry at UCLA's medical school, terms this process "survival of the busiest." The mental skills we sacrifice may be as valuable, or even more valuable, than the ones we gain. When it comes to the *quality* of our thought, our neurons and synapses are entirely indifferent. The possibility of intellectual decay is inherent in the malleability of our brains.

That doesn't mean that we can't, with concerted effort, once again redirect our neural signals and rebuild the skills we've lost. What it does mean is that the vital paths in our brains become, as Monsieur Dumont understood, the paths of least resistance. They are the paths that most of us will take most of the time, and the farther we proceed down them, the more difficult it becomes to turn back.

A Digression

on what the brain thinks about when it thinks about itself

The function of the brain, Aristotle believed, was to keep the body from overheating. A "compound of earth and water," brain matter "tempers the heat and seething of the heart," he wrote in *The Parts of Animals*, a treatise on anatomy and physiology. Blood rises from the "fiery" region of the chest until it reaches the head, where the brain reduces its temperature "to moderation." The cooled blood then flows back down through the rest of the body. The process, suggested Aristotle, was akin to that which "occurs in the production of showers. For when vapor steams up from the earth under the influence of heat and is carried into the upper regions, so soon as it reaches the cold air that is above the earth, it condenses again into water owing to the refrigeration, and falls back to the earth as rain." The reason man has "the largest brain in proportion to his size" is that "the region of the heart and of the lung is hotter and richer in blood in man than in any other animal." It seemed obvious to Aristotle that the brain could not possibly be "the organ of sensation," as Hippocrates and others had conjectured, since "when it is touched, no sensation is produced." In its insensibility, "it resembles," he wrote, "the blood of animals and their excrement."

It's easy, today, to chuckle at Aristotle's error. But it's also easy to understand how the great philosopher was led so far astray. The brain, packed neatly into the bone-crate of the skull, gives us no sensory signal of its existence. We feel our heart beat, our lungs expand, our stomach churn—but our brain, lacking motility and having no sensory nerve endings, remains imperceptible to us. The source of consciousness lies beyond the grasp of consciousness. Physicians and philosophers, from classical times through the Enlightenment, had to deduce the brain's function by examining and dissecting the clumps of grayish tissue they lifted from the skulls of corpses and other dead animals. What they saw usually reflected their assumptions about human nature or, more generally, the nature of the cosmos. They would, as Robert Martensen describes in *The Brain Takes Shape,* fit the visible structure of the brain into their preferred metaphysical metaphor, arranging the organ's physical parts "so as to portray likeness in their own terms."

Writing nearly two thousand years after Aristotle, Descartes conjured up another watery metaphor to explain the brain's function. To him, the brain was a component in an elaborate hydraulic "machine" whose workings resembled those of "fountains in the royal gardens." The heart would pump blood to the brain, where, in the pineal gland, it would be transformed, by means of pressure and heat, into "animal spirits," which then would travel through "the pipes" of the nerves. The brain's "cavities and pores" served as "apertures" regulting the flow of the animal spirits throughout the rest of the body. Descartes' explanation of the brain's role fit neatly into his mechanistic cosmology, in which, as

Martensen writes, "*all* bodies operated dynamically according to optical and geometric properties" within self-contained systems.

Our modern microscopes, scanners, and sensors have disabused us of most of the old fanciful notions about the brain's function. But the brain's strangely remote quality—the way it seems both part of us and apart from us—still influences our perceptions in subtle ways. We have a sense that our brain exists in a state of splendid isolation, that its fundamental nature is impervious to the vagaries of our day-to-day lives. While we know that our brain is an exquisitely sensitive monitor of experience, we want to believe that it lies beyond the influence of experience. We want to believe that the impressions our brain records as sensations and stores as memories leave no physical imprint on its own structure. To believe otherwise would, we feel, call into question the integrity of the self.

That was certainly how I felt when I began to worry that my use of the Internet might be changing the way my brain was processing information. I resisted the idea at first. It seemed ludicrous to think that fiddling with a computer, a mere tool, could alter in any deep or lasting way what was going on inside my head. But I was wrong. As neuroscientists have discovered, the brain—and the mind to which it gives rise—is forever a work in progress. That's true not just for each of us as individuals. It's true for all of us as a species.

Chatterboxes

Steven Pinker

By the 1920s it was thought that no corner of the earth fit for human habitation had remained unexplored. New Guinea, the world's second largest island, was no exception. The European missionaries, planters, and administrators clung to its coastal lowlands, convinced that no one could live in the treacherous mountain range that ran in a solid line down the middle of the island. But the mountains visible from each coast in fact belonged to two ranges, not one, and between them was a temperate plateau crossed by many fertile valleys. A million Stone Age people lived in those highlands, isolated from the rest of the world for forty thousand years. The veil would not be lifted until gold was discovered in a tributary of one of the main rivers. The ensuing gold rush attracted Michael Leahy, a footloose Australian prospector, who on May 26, 1930, set out to explore the mountains with a fellow prospector and a group of indigenous low-land people hired as carriers. After scaling the heights, Leahy was amazed to see grassy open country on the other side. By nightfall his amazement turned to alarm, because there were points of light in the distance, obvious signs that the valley was populated. After a sleepless night in which Leahy and his party loaded their weapons and assembled a crude bomb, they made their first contact with the highlanders. The astonishment was mutual. Leahy wrote in his diary:

> It was a relief when the [natives] came in sight, the men . . . in front, armed with bows and arrows, the women behind bringing stalks of sugarcane. When he saw the women, Ewunga told me at once that there would be no fight. We waved to them to come on, which they did cautiously, stopping every few yards to look us over. When a few of them finally got up courage to approach, we could see that they were utterly thunderstruck by our appearance. When I took off my hat, those nearest to me backed away in terror. One old chap came forward gingerly with open mouth, and touched me to see if I was real. Then he knelt down, and rubbed his hands over my bare legs, possibly to find if they were painted, and grabbed me around the knees and hugged them, rubbing his bushy head against me . . . . The women and children gradually got up courage to approach also, and presently the camp was swarming with the lot of them, all running about and jabbering at once, pointing to . . . everything that was new to them.

That "jabbering" was language—an unfamiliar language, one of eight hundred different ones that would be discovered among the isolated highlanders right up through the 1960s. Leahy's first contact

Excerpts from pp. 25–54 from *The Language Instinct by Steven Pinker.* Copyright © 1994 by Steven Pinker. Reprinted by permission of HarperCollins Publishers.

repeated a scene that must have taken place hundreds of times in human history, whenever one people first encountered another. All of them, as far as we know, already had language. Every Hottentot, every Eskimo, every Yanomamö. No mute tribe has ever been discovered, and there is no record that a region has served as a "cradle" of language from which it spread to previously languageless groups.

As in every other case, the language spoken by Leahy's hosts turned out to be no mere jabber but a medium that could express abstract concepts, invisible entities, and complex trains of reasoning. The highlanders conferred intensively, trying to agree upon the nature of the pallid apparitions. The leading conjecture was that they were reincarnated ancestors or other spirits in human form, perhaps ones that turned back into skeletons at night. They agreed upon an empirical test that would settle the matter. "One of the people hid," recalls the highlander Kirupano Eza'e, "and watched them going to excrete. He came back and said, 'Those men from heaven went to excrete over there.' Once they had left many men went to take a look. When they saw that it smelt bad, they said, 'Their skin might be different, but their shit smells bad like ours.' "

The universality of complex language is a discovery that fills linguists with awe, and is the first reason to suspect that language is not just any cultural invention but the product of a special human instinct. Cultural inventions vary widely in their sophistication from society to society; within a society, the inventions are generally at the same level of sophistication. Some groups count by carving notches on bones and cook on fires ignited by spinning sticks in logs; others use computers and microwave ovens. Language, however, ruins this correlation. There are Stone Age societies, but there is no such thing as a Stone Age language. Earlier in this century the anthropological linguist Edward Sapir wrote, "When it comes to linguistic form, Plato walks with the Macedonian swineherd, Confucius with the head-hunting savage of Assam."

To pick an example at random of a sophisticated linguistic form in a nonindustrialized people, the linguist Joan Bresnan recently wrote a technical article comparing a construction in Kivunjo, a Bantu language spoken in several villages on the slopes of Mount Kilimanjaro in Tanzania, with its counterpart construction in English, which she describes as "a

West Germanic language spoken in England and its former colonies." The English construction is called the dative and is found in sentences like *She baked me a brownie* and *He promised her Arpège,* where an indirect object like me or her is placed after the verb to indicate the beneficiary of an act. The corresponding Kivunjo construction is called the applicative, whose resemblance to the English dative, Bresnan notes, "can be likened to that of the game of chess to checkers." The Kivunjo construction fits entirely inside the verb, which has seven prefixes and suffixes, two moods, and fourteen tenses; the verb agrees with its subject, its object, and its benefactive nouns, each of which comes in sixteen genders. (In case you are wondering, these "genders" do not pertain to things like cross-dressers, transsexuals, hermaphrodites, androgynous people, and so on, as one reader of this chapter surmised. To a linguist, the term *gender* retains its original meaning of "kind," as in the related words *generic, genus,* and *genre.* The Bantu "genders" refer to kinds like humans, animals, extended objects, clusters of objects, and body parts. It just happens that in many European languages the genders correspond to the sexes, at least in pronouns. For this reason the linguistic term *gender* has been pressed into service by nonlinguists as a convenient label for sexual dimorphism; the more accurate term *sex* seems now to be reserved as the polite way to refer to copulation.) Among the other clever gadgets I have glimpsed in the grammars of so-called primitive groups, the complex Cherokee pronoun system seems especially handy. It distinguishes among "you and I," "another person and I," "several other people and I," and "you, one or more other persons, and I," which English crudely collapses into the all-purpose pronoun *we.*

Actually, the people whose linguistic abilities are most badly underestimated are right here in our society. Linguists repeatedly run up against the myth that working-class people and the less educated members of the middle class speak a simpler or coarser language. This is a pernicious illusion arising from the effortlessness of conversation. Ordinary speech, like color vision or walking, is a paradigm of engineering excellence—a technology that works so well that the user takes its outcome for granted, unaware of the complicated machinery hidden behind the panels. Behind such "simple" sentences as *Where did he go?* and or *The guy I met killed himself*, used automatically by any English speaker, are dozens of subroutines that arrange the words to express the meaning. Despite decades of effort, no artificially engineered language system comes close to duplicating the person in the street, HAL and C3PO notwithstanding.

But though the language engine is invisible to the human user, the trim packages and color schemes are attended to obsessively. Trifling differences between the dialect of the mainstream and the dialect of other groups, like *isn't any* versus *ain't no*, *those books* versus *them books*, and *dragged him away* versus *drug him away*, are dignified as badges of "proper grammar." But they have no more to do with grammatical sophistication than the fact that people in some regions of the United States refer to a certain insect as a *dragonfly* and people in other regions refer to it as a *darning needle*, or that English speakers call canines *dogs* whereas French speakers call them *chiens*. It is even a bit misleading to call Standard English a "language" and these variations "dialects," as if there were some meaningful difference between them. The best definition comes from the linguist Max Weinreich: a language is a dialect with an army and a navy.

The myth that nonstandard dialects of English are grammatically deficient is widespread. In the 1960s some well-meaning educational psychologists announced that American black children had been so culturally deprived that they lacked true language and were confined instead to a "non-logical mode of expressive behavior." The conclusions were based on the students' shy or sullen reactions to batteries of standardized tests. If the psychologists had listened to spontaneous conversations, they would have rediscovered the commonplace fact that American black culture is everywhere highly verbal; the subculture of street youths in particular is famous in the annals of anthropology for the value placed on linguistic virtuosity. Here is an example, from an interview conducted by the linguist William Labov on a stoop in Harlem. The interviewee is Larry, the roughest member of a teenage gang called the Jets. (Labov observes in his scholarly article that "for most readers of this paper, first contact with Larry would produce some fairly negative reactions on both sides.")

> You know, like some people say if you're good an' shit, your spirit goin' t'heaven . . . 'n' if you bad,

your spirit goin' to hell. Well, bullshit! Your spirit goin' to hell anyway, good or bad.

[Why?]

Why? I'll tell you why. 'Cause, you see, doesn' nobody really know that it's a God, y'know, 'cause I mean I have seen black gods, white gods, all color gods, and don't nobody know it's really a God. An' when they be sayin' if you good, you goin' t'heaven, tha's bullshit, 'cause you ain't goin' to no heaven, 'cause it ain't no heaven for you to go to.

[. . . jus' suppose that there is a God, would he be white or black?]

He'd be white, man.

[Why?]

Why? I'll tell you why. 'Cause the average whitey out here got everything, you dig? And the nigger ain't got shit, y'know? Y'understan'? So—um—for—in order for *that* to happen, you know it ain't no black God that's doin' that bullshit.

First contact with Larry's grammar may produce negative reactions as well, but to a linguist it punctiliously conforms to the rules of the dialect called Black English Vernacular (BEV). The most linguistically interesting thing about the dialect is how linguistically uninteresting it is: if Labov did not have to call attention to it to debunk the claim that ghetto children lack true linguistic competence, it would have been filed away as just another language. Where Standard American English (SAE) uses *there* as a meaningless dummy subject for the copula, BEV uses *it* as a meaningless dummy subject for the copula (compare SAE's *There's really a God* with Larry's *It's really a God*). Larry's negative concord (*You ain't goin' to no heaven*) is seen in many languages, such as French (*ne . . . pas*). Like speakers of SAE, Larry inverts subjects and auxiliaries in nondeclarative sentences, but the exact set of the sentence types allowing inversion differs slightly. Larry and other BEV speakers invert subjects and auxiliaries in negative main clauses like *Don't nobody know;* SAE speakers invert them only in questions like *Doesn't anybody know?* and a few other sentence types. BEV allows its speakers the option of deleting copulas (*If you bad*); this is not random laziness but a systematic rule that is virtually identical to the contraction rule in SAE that reduces *He is* to *He's, You are* to *You're*, and *I am* to *I'm*. In both dialects, *be* can erode only in certain kinds of sentences. No SAE speaker would try the following contractions:

Yes he is! → Yes he's!

I don't care what you are. → I don't care what you're.

Who is it? → Who's it?

For the same reasons, no BEV speaker would try the following deletions:

Yes he is! → Yes he!

I don't care what you are. → I don't care what you.

Who is it? → Who it?

Note, too, that BEV speakers are not just more prone to eroding words. BEV speakers use the full forms of certain auxiliaries (*I have seen*), whereas SAE speakers usually contract them (*I've seen*). And as we would expect from comparisons between languages, there are areas in which BEV is more precise than standard English. *He be working* means that he generally works, perhaps that he has a regular job; *He working* means only that he is working at the moment that the sentence is uttered. In SAE, *He is working* fails to make that distinction. Moreover, sentences like *In order for that to happen, you know it ain't no black God that's doin' that bullshit* show that Larry's speech uses the full inventory of grammatical paraphernalia that computer scientists struggle unsuccessfully to duplicate (relative clauses, complement structures, clause subordination, and so on), not to mention some fairly sophisticated theological argumentation.

Another project of Labov's involved tabulating the percentage of grammatical sentences in tape recordings of speech in a variety of social classes and social settings. "Grammatical," for these purposes, means "well-formed according to consistent rules in the dialect of the speakers." For example, if a speaker asked the question *Where are you going?*; the respondent would not be penalized for answering *To the store*, even though it is in some sense not a complete sentence. Such ellipses are obviously part of 'the grammar of conversational English; the alternative, *I am going to the store*, sounds stilted and is almost never used. "Ungrammatical" sentences, by this definition, include randomly broken-off sentence fragments, tongue-tied hemming and hawing, slips of the tongue, and other forms of word salad. The results of

Labov's tabulation are enlightening. The great majority of sentences were grammatical, especially in casual speech, with higher percentages of grammatical sentences in working-class speech than in middle-class speech. The highest percentage of ungrammatical sentences was found in the proceedings of learned academic conferences.

The ubiquity of complex language among human beings is a gripping discovery and, for many observers, compelling proof that language is innate. But to tough-minded skeptics like the philosopher Hilary Putnam, it is no proof at all. Not everything that is universal is innate. Just as travelers in previous decades never encountered a tribe without a language, nowadays anthropologists have trouble finding a people beyond the reach of VCR's, Coca-Cola, and Bart Simpson T-shirts. Language was universal before Coca-Cola was, but then, language is more useful than Coca-Cola. It is more like eating with one's hands rather than one's feet, which is also universal, but we need not invoke a special hand-to-mouth instinct to explain why. Language is invaluable for all the activities of daily living in a community of people: preparing food and shelter, loving, arguing, negotiating, teaching. Necessity being the mother of invention, language could have been invented by resourceful people a number of times long ago. (Perhaps, as Lily Tomlin said, man invented language to satisfy his deep need to complain.) Universal grammar would simply reflect the universal exigencies of human experience and the universal limitations on human information processing. All languages have words for "water" and "foot" because all people need to refer to water and feet; no language has a word a million syllables long because no person would have time to say it. Once invented, language would entrench itself within a culture as parents taught their children and children imitated their parents. From cultures that had language, it would spread like wildfire to other, quieter cultures. At the heart of this process is wondrously flexible human intelligence, with its general multipurpose learning strategies.

So the universality of language does not lead to an innate language instinct as night follows day. To convince you that there is a language instinct, I will have to fill in an argument that leads from the jabbering of modern peoples to the putative genes for grammar. The crucial intervening steps come from my own professional specialty, the study of language development in children. The crux of the argument is that complex language is universal because *children actually reinvent it,* generation after generation—not because they are taught, not because they are generally smart, not because it is useful to them, but because they just can't help it. Let me now take you down this trail of evidence.

The trail begins with the study of how the particular languages we find in the world today arose. Here, one would think, linguistics runs into the problem of any historical science: no one recorded the crucial events at the time they happened. Although historical linguists can trace modern complex languages back to earlier ones, this just pushes the problem back a step; we need to see how people create a complex language from scratch. Amazingly, we can.

The first cases were wrung from two of the more sorrowful episodes of world history, the Atlantic slave trade and indentured servitude in the South Pacific. Perhaps mindful of the Tower of Babel, some of the masters of tobacco, cotton, coffee, and sugar plantations deliberately mixed slaves and laborers from different language backgrounds; others preferred specific ethnicities but had to accept mixtures because that was all that was available. When speakers of different languages have to communicate to carry out practical tasks but do not have the opportunity to learn one another's languages, they develop a makeshift jargon called a pidgin. Pidgins are choppy strings of words borrowed from the language of the colonizers or plantation owners, highly variable in order and with little in the way of grammar. Sometimes a pidgin can become a lingua franca and gradually increase in complexity over decades, as in the "Pidgin English" of the modern South Pacific. (Prince Philip was delighted to learn on a visit to New Guinea that he is referred to in that language as *fella belong Mrs. Queen.*)

But the linguist Derek Bickerton has presented evidence that in many cases a pidgin can be transmuted into a full complex language in one fell swoop: all it takes is for a group of children to be exposed to the pidgin at the age when they acquire their mother tongue. That happened, Bickerton has argued, when children were isolated from their parents and were tended collectively by a worker who spoke to them in the pidgin. Not content to reproduce the fragmentary word strings, the children injected grammatical complexity where none existed before, resulting in a brand-new, richly expressive language. The language that results when children make a pidgin their native tongue is called a creole.

Bickerton's main evidence comes from a unique historical circumstance. Though the slave plantations that spawned most creoles are, fortunately, a thing of the remote past, one episode of creolization occurred recently enough for us to study its principal players. Just before the turn of the century there was a boom in Hawaiian sugar plantations, whose demands for labor quickly outstripped the native pool. Workers were brought in from China, Japan, Korea, Portugal, the Philippines, and Puerto Rico, and a pidgin quickly developed. Many of the immigrant laborers who first developed that pidgin were alive when Bickerton interviewed them in the 1970s. Here are some typical examples of their speech:

> Me capé buy, me check make.
> Building—high place—wall pat—time—nowtime—
>   an' den —a new tempecha eri time show you.
> Good, dis one. Kaukau any-kin' dis one. Pilipine
>   islan' no good. No mo money.

From the individual words and the context, it was possible for the listener to infer that the first speaker, a ninety-two-year-old Japanese immigrant talking about his earlier days as a coffee farmer, was trying to say "He bought my coffee; he made me out a check." But the utterance itself could just as easily have meant "I bought coffee; I made him out a check," which would have been appropriate if he had been referring to his current situation as a store owner. The second speaker, another elderly Japanese immigrant, had been introduced to the wonders of civilization in Los Angeles by one of his many children, and was saying that there was an electric sign high up on the wall of the building which displayed the time and temperature. The third speaker, a sixty-nine-year-old Filipino, was saying "It's better here than in the Philippines; here you can get all kinds of food, but over there there isn't any money to buy food with." (One of the kinds of food was "pfrawg," which he caught for himself in the marshes by the method of "kank da head.") In all these cases, the speaker's intentions had to be filled in by the listener. The pidgin did not offer the speakers the ordinary grammatical resources to convey these messages—no consistent word order, no prefixes or suffixes, no tense or other temporal and logical markers, no structure more complex than a simple clause, and no consistent way to indicate who did what to whom.

But the children who had grown up in Hawaii beginning in the 1890s and were exposed to the pidgin ended up speaking quite differently. Here are some sentences from the language they invented, Hawaiian Creole. The first two are from a Japanese papaya grower born in Maui; the next two, from a Japanese/Hawaiian ex-plantation laborer born on the big island; the last, from a Hawaiian motel manager, formerly a farmer, born in Kauai:

Da firs japani came ran away from japan come.
"The first Japanese who arrived ran away from Japan to here."

Some filipino wok o'he-ah dey wen' couple ye-ahs in filipin islan'.
"Some Filipinos who worked over here went back to the Philippines for a couple of years."

People no like t'come fo' go wok.
"People don't want to have him go to work [for them]."

One time when we go home inna night dis ting stay fly up.
"Once when we went home at night this thing was flying about."

One day had pleny of dis mountain fish come down.
"One day there were a lot of these fish from the mountains that came down [the river]."

Do not be misled by what look like crudely placed English verbs, such as *go, stay,* and *came,* or phrases like *one time.* They are not haphazard uses of English words but systematic uses of Hawaiian Creole grammar: the words have been converted by the creole speakers into auxiliaries, prepositions, case markers, and relative pronouns. In fact, this is probably how many of the grammatical prefixes and suffixes in established languages arose. For example, the English past-tense ending *-ed* may have evolved from the verb *do: He hammered* was originally something like *He hammer-did.* Indeed, creoles *are* bona fide languages, with standardized

word orders and grammatical markers that were lacking in the pidgin of the immigrants and, aside from the sounds of words, not taken from the language of the colonizers.

Bickerton notes that if the grammar of a creole is largely the product of the minds of children, unadulterated by complex language input from their parents, it should provide a particularly clear window on the innate grammatical machinery of the brain. He argues that creoles from unrelated language mixtures exhibit uncanny resemblances perhaps even the same basic grammar. This basic grammar also shows up, he suggests, in the errors children make when acquiring more established and embellished languages, like some underlying design bleeding through a veneer of whitewash. When English-speaking children say

Why he is leaving?
Nobody don't likes me.
I'm gonna full Angela's bucket.
Let Daddy hold it hit it,

they are unwittingly producing sentences that are grammatical in many of the world's creoles.

Bickerton's particular claims are controversial, depending as they do on his reconstruction of events that occurred decades or centuries in the past. But his basic idea has been stunningly corroborated by two recent natural experiments in which creolization by children can be observed in real time. These fascinating discoveries are among many that have come from the study of the sign languages of the deaf. Contrary to popular misconceptions, sign languages are not pantomimes and gestures, inventions of educators, or ciphers of the spoken language of the surrounding community. They are found wherever there is a community of deaf people, and each one is a distinct, full language, using the same kinds of grammatical machinery found worldwide in spoken languages. For example, American Sign Language, used by the deaf community in the United States, does not resemble English, or British Sign Language, but relies on agreement and gender systems in a way that is reminiscent of Navajo and Bantu.

Until recently there were no sign languages at all in Nicaragua, because its deaf people remained isolated from one another. When the Sandinista government took over in 1979 and reformed the educational system, the first schools for the deaf were created. The schools focused on drilling the children in lip reading and speech, and as in every case where that is tried, the results were dismal. But it did not matter. On the playgrounds and schoolbuses the children were inventing their own sign system, pooling the makeshift gestures that they used with their families at home. Before long the system congealed into what is now called the Lenguaje de Signos Nicaragüense (LSN). Today LSN is used, with varying degrees of fluency, by young deaf adults, aged seventeen to twenty-five, who developed it when they were ten or older. Basically, it is a pidgin. Everyone uses it differently, and the signers depend on suggestive, elaborate circumlocutions rather than on a consistent grammar.

But children like Mayela, who joined the school around the age of four, when LSN was already around, and all the pupils younger than her, are quite different. Their signing is more fluid and compact, and the gestures are more stylized and less like a pantomime. In fact, when their signing is examined close up, it is so different from LSN that it is referred to by a different name, Idioma de Signos Nicaragüense (ISN). LSN and ISN are currently being studied by the psycholinguists Judy Kegl, Miriam Hebe Lopez, and Annie Senghas. ISN appears to be a creole, created in one leap when the younger children were exposed to the pidgin signing of the older children—just as Bickerton would have predicted. ISN has spontaneously standardized itself; all the young children sign it in the same way. The children have introduced many grammatical devices that were absent in LSN, and hence they rely far less on circumlocutions. For example, an LSN (pidgin) signer might make the sign for "talk to" and then point from the position of the talker to the position of the hearer. But an ISN (creole) signer modifies the sign itself, sweeping it in one motion from a point representing the talker to a point representing the hearer. This is a common device in sign languages, formally identical to inflecting a verb for agreement in spoken languages. Thanks to such consistent grammar, ISN is very expressive. A child can watch a surrealistic cartoon and describe its plot to another child. The children use it in jokes, poems, narratives, and life histories, and it is coming to serve as the glue that holds the community together. A language has been born before our eyes.

But ISN was the collective product of many children communicating with one another. If we are to attribute the richness of language to the mind of the child, we really want to see a single child adding some increment of grammatical complexity to the input the child has received. Once again the study of the deaf grants our wish.

When deaf infants are raised by signing parents, they learn sign language in the same way that hearing infants learn spoken language. But deaf children who are not born to deaf parents—the majority of deaf children—often have no access to sign language users as they grow up, and indeed are sometimes deliberately kept from them by educators in the "oralist" tradition who want to force them to master lip reading and speech. (Most deaf people deplore these authoritarian measures.) When deaf children become adults, they tend to seek out deaf communities and begin to acquire the sign language that takes proper advantage of the communicative media available to them. But by then it is usually too late; they must then struggle with sign language as a difficult intellectual puzzle, much as a hearing adult does in foreign language classes. Their proficiency is notably below that of deaf people who acquired sign language as infants, just as adult immigrants are often permanently burdened with accents and conspicuous grammatical errors. Indeed, because the deaf are virtually the only neurologically normal people who make it to adulthood without having acquired a language, their difficulties offer particularly good evidence that successful language acquisition must take place during a critical window of opportunity in childhood.

The psycholinguists Jenny Singleton and Elissa Newport have studied a nine-year-old profoundly deaf boy, to whom they gave the pseudonym Simon, and his parents, who are also deaf. Simon's parents did not acquire sign language until the late ages of fifteen and sixteen, and as a result they acquired it badly. In ASL, as in many languages, one can move a phrase to the front of a sentence and mark it with a prefix or suffix (in ASL, raised eyebrows and a lifted chin) to indicate that it is the topic of the sentence. The English sentence *Elvis I really like* is a rough equivalent. But Simon's parents rarely used this construction and mangled it when they did. For example, Simon's father once tried to sign the thought *My friend, he thought my second child was deaf.* It came out as *My friend thought, my second child, he thought he was deaf*—a bit of sign salad that violates not only ASL grammar but, according to Chomsky's theory, the Universal Grammar that governs all naturally acquired human languages (later in this chapter we will see why). Simon's parents had also failed to grasp the verb inflection system of ASL. In ASL, the verb *to blow* is signed by opening a fist held horizontally in front of the mouth (like a puff of air). Any verb in ASL can be modified to indicate that the action is being done continuously: the signer superimposes an arclike motion on the sign and repeats it quickly. A verb can also be modified to indicate that the action is being done to more than one object (for example, several candles): the signer terminates the sign in one location in space, then repeats it but terminates it at another location. These inflections can be combined in either of two orders: *blow* toward the left and then toward the right and repeat, or *blow* toward the left twice and then *blow* toward the right twice. The first order means "to blow out the candles on one cake, then another cake, then the first cake again, then the second cake again"; the second means "to blow out the candles on one cake continuously, and then blow out the candles on another cake continuously." This elegant set of rules was lost on Simon's parents. They used the inflections inconsistently and never combined them onto a verb two at a time, though they would occasionally use the inflections separately, crudely linked with signs like *then*. In many ways Simon's parents were like pidgin speakers.

Astoundingly, though Simon saw no ASL but his parents' defective version, his own signing was far better ASL than theirs. He understood sentences with moved topic phrases without difficulty, and when he had to describe complex videotaped events, he used the ASL verb inflections almost perfectly, even in sentences requiring two of them in particular orders. Simon must somehow have shut out his parents' ungrammatical "noise." He must have latched on to the inflections that his parents used inconsistently, and reinterpreted them as mandatory. And he must have seen the logic that was implicit, though never realized, in his parents' use of two kinds of verb inflection, and reinvented the ASL system of superimposing both of them onto a single verb in a specific order. Simon's superiority to his parents is an example of creolization by a single living child.

Actually, Simon's achievements are remarkable only because he is the first one who showed them to a psycholinguist. There must be thousands of Simons: ninety to ninety-five percent of deaf children are born to hearing parents. Children fortunate enough to be exposed to ASL at all often get it from hearing parents who themselves learned it, incompletely, to communicate with their children. Indeed, as the transition from LSN to ISN shows, sign languages themselves are surely products of creolization. Educators at various points in history have tried to invent sign systems, sometimes based on the surrounding spoken language. But these crude codes are always unlearnable, and when deaf children learn from them at all, they do so by converting them into much richer natural languages.

Extraordinary acts of creation by children do not require the extraordinary circumstances of deafness or plantation Babels. The same kind of linguistic genius is involved every time a child learns his or her mother tongue.

First, let us do away with the folklore that parents teach their children language. No one supposes that parents provide explicit grammar lessons, of course, but many parents (and some child psychologists who should know better) think that mothers provide children with implicit lessons. These lessons take the form of a special speech variety called Motherese (or, as the French call it, Mamanaise): intensive sessions of conversational give-and-take, with repetitive drills and simplified grammar. ("Look at the *doggie*! See the *doggie*? There's a *doggie*!") In contemporary middle-class American culture, parenting is seen as an awesome responsibility, an unforgiving vigil to keep the helpless infant from falling behind in the great race of life. The belief that Motherese is essential to language development is part of the same mentality that sends yuppies to "learning centers" to buy little mittens with bull's-eyes to help their babies find their hands sooner.

One gets some perspective by examining the folk theories about parenting in other cultures. The !Kung San of the Kalahari Desert in southern Africa believe that children must be drilled to sit, stand, and walk. They carefully pile sand around their infants to prop them upright, and sure enough, every one of these infants soon sits up on its own. We find this amusing because we have observed the results of the experiment that the San are unwilling to chance: we don't teach our children to sit, stand, and walk, and they do it anyway, on their own schedule. But other groups enjoy the same condescension toward us. In many communities of the world, parents do not indulge their children in Motherese. In fact, they do not speak to their prelinguistic children at all, except for occasional demands and rebukes. This is not unreasonable. After all, young children plainly can't understand a word you say. So why waste your breath in soliloquies? Any sensible person would surely wait until a child has developed speech and more gratifying two-way conversations become possible. As Aunt Mae, a woman living in the South Carolina Piedmont, explained to the anthropologist Shirley Brice Heath: "Now just how crazy is dat? White folks uh hear dey kids say sump'n, dey say it back to 'em, dey aks 'em 'gain and 'gain 'bout things, like they 'posed to be born knowin'." Needless to say, the children in these communities, overhearing adults and other children, learn to talk, as we see in Aunt Mae's fully grammatical BEV.

Children deserve most of the credit for the language they acquire. In fact, we can show that they know things they could not have been taught. One of Chomsky's classic illustrations of the logic of language involves the process of moving words around to form questions. Consider how you might turn the declarative sentence *A unicorn is in the garden* into the corresponding question, *Is a unicorn in the garden?* You could scan the declarative sentence, take the auxiliary is, and move it to the front of the sentence:

a unicorn is in the garden. →
is a unicorn   in the garden?

Now take the sentence *A unicorn that is eating a flower is in the garden.* There are two is's. Which gets moved? Obviously, not the first one hit by the scan; that would give you a very odd sentence:

a unicorn that is eating a flower is in the garden. →
is a unicorn that   eating a flower is in the garden?

But why can't you move that *is*? Where did the simple procedure go wrong? The answer, Chomsky noted, comes from the basic design of language. Though sentences are strings of words, our mental algorithms for grammar do not pick out words by their linear positions, such as "first word," "second word," and so on. Rather, the algorithms group words into phrases, and phrases into even bigger phrases, and give each one a mental label, like "subject noun phrase" or "verb phrase." The real rule for

forming questions does not look for the first occurrence of the auxiliary word as one goes from left to right in the string; it looks for the auxiliary that comes after the phrase labeled as the subject. This phrase, containing the entire string of words *a unicorn that is eating a flower,* behaves as a single unit. The first *is* sits deeply buried in it, invisible to the question-forming rule. The second *is,* coming immediately after this subject noun phrase, is the one that is moved:

[a unicorn that is eating a flower] is in the garden. →
is [a unicorn that is eating a flower]   in the garden?

Chomsky reasoned that if the logic of language is wired into children, then the first time they are confronted with a sentence with two auxiliaries they should be capable of turning it into a question with the proper wording. This should be true even though the wrong rule, the one that scans the sentence as a linear string of words, is simpler and presumably easier to learn. And it should be true even though the sentences that would teach children that the linear rule is wrong and the structure-sensitive rule is right—questions with a second auxiliary embedded inside the subject phrase—are so rare as to be non-existent in Motherese. Surely not every child learning English has heard Mother say *Is the doggie that is eating the flower in the garden?* For Chomsky, this kind of reasoning, which he calls "the argument from the poverty of the input," is the primary justification for saying that the basic design of language is innate.

Chomsky's claim was tested in an experiment with three-, four-, and five-year-olds at a daycare center by the psycholinguists Stephen Crain and Mineharu Nakayama. One of the experimenters controlled a doll of Jabba the Hutt, of *Star Wars* fame. The other coaxed the child to ask a set of questions, by saying, for example, "Ask Jabba if the boy who is unhappy is watching Mickey Mouse." Jabba would inspect a picture and answer yes or no, but it was really the child who was being tested, not Jabba. The children cheerfully provided the appropriate questions, and, as Chomsky would have predicted, not a single one of them came up with an ungrammatical string like *Is the boy who unhappy is watching Mickey Mouse?,* which the simple linear rule would have produced.

Now, you may object that this does not show that children's brains register the subject of a sentence.

Perhaps the children were just going by the meanings of the words. *The man who is running* refers to a single actor playing a distinct role in the picture, and children could have been keeping track of which words are about particular actors, not which words belong to the subject noun phrase. But Crain and Nakayama anticipated the objection. Mixed into their list were commands like "Ask Jabba if it is raining in this picture." The *it* of the sentence, of course, does not refer to anything; it is a dummy element that is there only to satisfy the rules of syntax, which demand a subject. But the English question rule treats it just like any other subject: *Is it raining?* Now, how do children cope with this meaningless placeholder? Perhaps they are as literal-minded as the Duck in *Alice's Adventures in Wonderland:*

> "I proceed [said the Mouse]. 'Edwin and Morcar, the earls of Mercia and Northumbria, declared for him; and even Stigand, the patriotic archbishop of Canterbury, found it advisable—' "
>
> "Found *what*?" said the Duck.
>
> "Found *it*," the Mouse replied rather crossly: "of course you know what 'it' means."
>
> "I know what 'it' means well enough, when *I* find a thing," said the Duck: "it's generally a frog, or a worm. The question is, what did the archbishop find?"

But children are not ducks. Crain and Nakayama's children replied, *Is it raining in this picture?* Similarly, they had no trouble forming questions with other dummy subjects, as in "Ask Jabba if there is a snake in this picture," or with subjects that are not things, as in "Ask Jabba if running is fun" and "Ask Jabba if love is good or bad."

The universal constraints on grammatical rules also show that the basic form of language cannot be explained away as the inevitable outcome of a drive for usefulness. Many languages, widely scattered over the globe, have auxiliaries, and like English, many languages move the auxiliary to the front of the sentence to form questions and other constructions, always in a structure-dependent way. But this is not the only way one could design a question rule. One could just as effectively move the leftmost auxiliary in the string to the front, or flip the first and last words, or utter the entire sentence in mirror-reversed order (a trick that the human mind is capable of; some people learn to talk backwards to amuse themselves and amaze their friends). The particular ways that languages do form questions are arbitrary,

species-wide conventions; we don't find them in artificial systems like computer programming languages or the notation of mathematics. The universal plan underlying languages, with auxiliaries and inversion rules, nouns and verbs, subjects and objects, phrases and clauses, case and agreement, and so on, seems to suggest a commonality in the brains of speakers, because many other plans would have been just as useful. It is as if isolated inventors miraculously came up with identical standards for typewriter keyboards or Morse code or traffic signals.

Evidence corroborating the claim that the mind contains blueprints for grammatical rules comes, once again, out of the mouths of babes and sucklings. Take the English agreement suffix *-s* as in *He walks*. Agreement is an important process in many languages, but in modern English it is superfluous, a remnant of a richer system that flourished in Old English. If it were to disappear entirely, we would not miss it, any more than we miss the similar *-est* suffix in *Thou sayest*. But psychologically speaking, this frill does not come cheap. Any speaker committed to using it has to keep track of four details in every sentence uttered:

- whether the subject is in the third person or not: *He walks* versus *I walk*.
- whether the subject is singular or plural: *He walks* versus *They walk*.
- whether the action is present tense or not: *He walks* versus *He walked*.
- whether the action is habitual or going on at the moment of speaking (its "*aspect*"): *He walks to school* versus *He is walking to school*.

And all this work is needed just to use the suffix once one has learned it. To learn it in the first place, a child must (1) notice that verbs end in *-s* in some sentences but appear bare-ended in others, (2) begin a search for the grammatical causes of this variation (as opposed to just accepting it as part of the spice of life), and (3) not rest until those crucial factors— tense, aspect, and the number and person of the subject of the sentence—have been sifted out of the ocean of conceivable but irrelevant factors (like the number of syllables of the final word in the sentence, whether the object of a preposition is natural or manmade, and how warm it is when the sentence is uttered). Why would anyone bother?

But little children do bother. By the age of three and a half or earlier, they use the *-s* agreement suffix in more than ninety percent of the sentences that require it, and virtually never use it in the sentences that forbid it. This mastery is part of their grammar explosion, a period of several months in the third year of life during which children suddenly begin to speak in fluent sentences, respecting most of the fine points of their community's spoken language. For example, a preschooler with the pseudonym Sarah, whose parents had only a high school education, can be seen obeying the English agreement rule, useless though it is, in complex sentences like the following:

> When my mother *hangs* clothes, do you let 'em rinse out in rain?
> Donna *teases* all the time and Donna has false teeth.
> I know what a big chicken *looks* like.
> Anybody *knows* how to scribble.
> Hey, this part *goes* where this one is, stupid.
> What *comes* after "C"?
> It *looks* like a donkey face.
> The person *takes* care of the animals in the barn.
> After it *dries* off then you can make the bottom.
> Well, someone *hurts* hisself and everything.
> His tail *sticks* out like this.
> What *happens* if ya press on this hard?
> Do you have a real baby that *says* googoo gaga?

Just as interestingly, Sarah could not have been simply imitating her parents, memorizing verbs with the -*s*'s pre-attached. Sarah sometimes uttered word forms that she could not possibly have heard from her parents:

> When she *be's* in the kindergarten . . .
> He's a boy so he *gots* a scary one. [costume]
> She *do's* what her mother tells her.

She must, then, have created these forms herself, unconscious version of the English agreement rule. The very concept of imitation is suspect to begin with (if children are general imitators, why don't they imitate their parents' habit of sitting quietly in airplanes?), but sentences like these show clearly that language acquisition cannot be explained as a kind of imitation.

——— ·•· ———

One step remains to complete the argument that language is a specific instinct, not just the clever solution to a problem thought up by a generally brainy species. If language is an instinct, it should have an identifiable seat in the brain, and perhaps even a special set of genes that help wire it into place. Disrupt these genes or neurons, and language should suffer while the other parts of intelligence carry on; spare them in an otherwise damaged brain, and you should have a retarded individual with intact language, a linguistic idiot savant. If, on the other hand, language is just the exercise of human smarts, we might expect that injuries and impairments would make people stupider across the board, including their language. The only pattern we would expect is that the more brain tissue that is damaged, the duller and less articulate the person should be.

No one has yet located a language organ or a grammar gene, but the search is on. There are several kinds of neurological and genetic impairments that compromise language while sparing cognition and vice versa. One of them has been known for over a century, perhaps for millennia. When there is damage to certain circuits in the lower parts of the frontal lobe of the brain's left hemisphere—say, from a stroke or bullet wound—the person often suffers from a syndrome called Broca's aphasia. One of these victims, who eventually recovered his language ability, recalls the event, which he experienced with complete lucidity:

> When I woke up I had a bit of a headache and thought I must have been sleeping with my right arm under me because it felt all pins-and-needly and numb and I couldn't make it do what I wanted. I got out of bed but I couldn't stand; as a matter of fact I actually fell on the floor because my right leg was too weak to take my weight. I called out to my wife in the next room and no sound came—I couldn't speak. . . . I was astonished, horrified. I couldn't believe that this was happening to me and I began to feel bewildered and frightened and then I suddenly realized that I must have had a stroke. In a way this rationalization made me feel somewhat relieved but not for long because I had always thought that the effects of a stroke were permanent in every case. . . . I found I could speak a little but even to me the words seemed wrong and not what I meant to say.

As this writer noted, most stroke victims are not as lucky. Mr. Ford was a Coast Guard radio operator when he suffered a stroke at the age of thirty-nine. The neuropsychologist Howard Gardner interviewed him three months later. Gardner asked him about his work before he entered the hospital.

"I'm a sig . . . no . . . man . . . uh, well, . . . again." These words were emitted slowly, and with great effort. The sounds were not clearly articulated; each syllable was uttered harshly, explosively, in a throaty voice . . . .

"Let me help you," I interjected. "You were a signal . . . "

"A sig-nal man . . . right," Ford completed my phrase triumphantly.

"Were you in the Coast Guard?"

"No, er, yes, yes . . . ship . . . Massachu . . . chusetts . . . Coast-guard . . . years." He raised his hands twice, indicating the number "nineteen."

"Oh, you were in the Coast Guard for nineteen years."

"Oh . . . boy . . . right . . . right," he replied.

"Why are you in the hospital, Mr. Ford?"

Ford looked at me a bit strangely, as if to say, Isn't it patently obvious? He pointed to his paralyzed arm and said, "Arm no good," then to his mouth and said, "Speech . . . can't say . . . talk, you see."

"What happened to you to make you lose your speech?"

"Head, fall, Jesus Christ, me no good, str, str . . . oh Jesus . . . stroke."

"I see. Could you tell me, Mr. Ford, what you've been doing in the hospital?"

"Yes, sure. Me go, er, uh, P.T. nine o'cot, speech . . . two times . . . read . . . wr . . . ripe, er, rike, er, write . . . practice . . . get-ting better."

"And have you been going home on week-ends?"

"Why, yes . . . Thursday, er, er, er, no, er, Friday . . . Bar-ba-ra . . . wife . . . and, oh, car . . . drive . . . purnpike . . . you know .. . rest and . . . tee-vee."

"Are you able to understand everything on television?"

"Oh, yes, yes . . . well . . . al-most."

Obviously Mr. Ford had to struggle to get speech out, but his problems were not in controlling his vocal muscles. He could blow out a candle and clear his throat, and he was as linguistically hobbled when he wrote as when he spoke. Most of his handicaps centered around grammar itself. He omitted endings like *-ed* and *-s* and grammatical function words like *or, be,* and *the,* despite their high frequency in the language. When reading aloud, he skipped over the function words, though he successfully read content words like *bee* and *oar* that had the same sounds. He named objects and recognized their names extremely well. He understood questions when their gist could be deduced from their content words, such as "Does

a stone float on water?" or "Do you use a hammer for cutting?," but not ones that required grammatical analysis, like "The lion was killed by the tiger; which one is dead?"

Despite Mr. Ford's grammatical impairment, he was clearly in command of his other faculties. Gardner notes: "He was alert, attentive, and fully aware of where he was and why he was there. Intellectual functions not closely tied to language, such as knowledge of right and left, ability to draw with the left (unpracticed) hand, to calculate, read maps, set clocks, make constructions, or carry out commands, were all preserved. His Intelligence Quotient in nonverbal areas was in the high average range." Indeed, the dialogue shows that Mr. Ford, like many Broca's aphasics, showed an acute understanding of his handicap.

Injuries in adulthood are not the only ways that the circuitry underlying language can be compromised. A few otherwise healthy children just fail to develop language on schedule. When they do begin to talk, they have difficulty articulating words, and though their articulation improves with age, the victims persist in a variety of grammatical errors, often into adulthood. When obvious nonlinguistic causes are ruled out—cognitive disorders like retardation, perceptual disorders like deafness, and social disorders like autism—the children are given the accurate but not terribly helpful diagnostic label Specific Language Impairment (SLI).

Language therapists, who are often called upon to treat several members in a family, have long been under the impression that SLI is hereditary. Recent statistical studies show that the impression may be correct. SLI runs in families, and if one member of a set of identical twins has it, the odds are very high that the other will, too. Particularly dramatic evidence comes from one British family, the K's, recently studied by the linguist Myrna Gopnik and several geneticists. The grandmother of the family is language-impaired. She has five adult children. One daughter is linguistically normal, as are this daughter's children. The other four adults, like the grandmother, are impaired. Together these four had twenty-three children; of them, eleven were language-impaired, twelve were normal. The language-impaired children were randomly distributed among the families, the sexes, and the birth orders.

Of course, the mere fact that some behavioral pattern runs in families does not show that it is genetic. Recipes, accents, and lullabies run in families, but they have nothing to do with DNA. In this case, though, a genetic cause is plausible. If the cause were in the environment—poor nutrition, hearing the defective speech of an impaired parent or sibling, watching too much TV, lead contamination from old pipes, whatever—then why would the syndrome capriciously strike some family members while leaving their near age-mates (in one case, a fraternal twin) alone? In fact, the geneticists working with Gopnik noted that the pedigree suggests a trait controlled by a single dominant gene, just like pink flowers on Gregor Mendel's pea plants.

What does this hypothetical gene do? It does not seem to impair overall intelligence; most of the afflicted family members score in the normal range in the nonverbal parts of IQ tests. (Indeed, Gopnik studied one unrelated child with the syndrome who routinely received the best grade in his mainstream math class.) It is their language that is impaired, but they are not like Broca's aphasics; the impression is more of a tourist struggling in a foreign city. They speak somewhat slowly and deliberately, carefully planning what they will say and encouraging their interlocutors to come to their aid by completing sentences for them. They report that ordinary conversation is strenuous mental work and that when possible they avoid situations in which they must speak. Their speech contains frequent grammatical errors, such as misuse of pronouns and of suffixes like the plural and past tense:

> It's a flying finches, they are.
> She remembered when she hurts herself the other day.
> The neighbors phone the ambulance because the man fall off the tree.
> The boys eat four cookie.
> Carol is cry in the church.

In experimental tests they have difficulty with tasks that normal four-year-olds breeze through. A classic example is the *wug*-test, another demonstration that normal children do not learn language by imitating their parents. The testee is shown a line drawing of a birdlike creature and told that it is a *wug*. Then a picture of two of them is shown, and the child is told, "Now there are two of them; there are two _____." Your typical four-year-old will blurt out *wugs*, but the language-impaired adult is stymied. One of the adults Gopnik studied laughed nervously

and said, "Oh, dear, well carry on." When pressed, she responded, "Wug . . . wugness, isn't it? No. I see. You want to pair . . . pair it up. OK." For the next animal, *zat*, she said, "Za . . . ka . . . za . . . zackle." For the next, *sas*, she deduced that it must be "sasses." Flushed with success, she proceeded to generalize too literally, converting *zoop* to "zoop-es" and *tob* to "tob-ye-es," revealing that she hadn't really grasped the English rule. Apparently the defective gene in this family somehow affects the development of the rules that normal children use unconsciously. The adults do their best to compensate by consciously reasoning the rules out, with predictably clumsy results.

Broca's aphasia and SLI are cases where language is impaired and the rest of intelligence seems more or less intact. But this does not show that language is separate from intelligence. Perhaps language imposes greater demands on the brain than any other problem the mind has to solve. For the other problems, the brain can limp along at less than its full capacity; for language, all systems have to be one hundred percent. To clinch the case, we need to find the opposite dissociation, linguistic idiot savants—that is, people with good language and bad cognition.

Here is another interview, this one between a fourteen-year-old girl called Denyse and the late psycholinguist Richard Cromer; the interview was transcribed and analyzed by Cromer's colleague Sigrid Lipka.

> I like opening cards. I had a pile of post this morning and not one of them was a Christmas card. A bank statement I got this morning!
>
> [A bank statement? I hope it was good news.]
>
> No it wasn't good news.
>
> [Sounds like mine.]
>
> I hate . . . , My mum works over at the, over on the ward and she said "not another bank statement." I said "it's the second one in two days." And she said "Do you want me to go to the bank for you at lunchtime?" and I went "No, I'll go this time and explain it myself." I tell you what, my bank are awful. They've lost my bank book, you see, and I can't find it anywhere. I belong to the TSB Bank and I'm thinking of changing my bank 'cause they're so awful. They keep, they keep losing . . . [someone comes in to bring some tea] Oh, isn't that nice.
>
> [Uhm. Very good.]

They've got the habit of doing that. They lose, they've lost my bank book twice, in a month, and I think I'll scream. My mum went yesterday to the bank for me. She said "They've lost your bank book again." I went "Can I scream?" and I went, she went "Yes, go on." So I hollered. But it is annoying when they do things like that. TSB, Trustees aren't . . . uh the best ones to be with actually. They're hopeless.

I have seen Denyse on videotape, and she comes across as a loquacious, sophisticated conversationalist—all the more so, to American ears, because of her refined British accent. (*My bank are awful*, by the way, is grammatical in British, though not American, English.) It comes as a surprise to learn that the events she relates so earnestly are figments of her imagination. Denyse has no bank account, so she could not have received any statements in the mail, nor could her bank have lost her bankbook. Though she would talk about a joint bank account she shared with her boyfriend, she had no boyfriend, and obviously had only the most tenuous grasp of the concept "joint bank account" because she complained about the boyfriend taking money out of her side of the account. In other conversations Denyse would engage her listeners with lively tales about the wedding of her sister, her holiday in Scotland with a boy named Danny, and a happy airport reunion with a long-estranged father. But Denyse's sister is unmarried, Denyse has never been to Scotland, she does not know anyone named Danny, and her father has never been away for any length of time. In fact, Denyse is severely retarded. She never learned to read or write and cannot handle money or any of the other demands of everyday functioning.

Denyse was born with spina bifida ("split spine"), a malformation of the vertebrae that leaves the spinal cord unprotected. Spina bifida often results in hydrocephalus, an increase in pressure in the cerebrospinal fluid filling the ventricles (large cavities) of the brain, distending the brain from within. For reasons no one understands, hydrocephalic children occasionally end up like Denyse, significantly retarded but with unimpaired—indeed, overdeveloped—language skills. (Perhaps the ballooning ventricles crush much of the brain tissue necessary for everyday intelligence but leave intact some other portions that can develop language circuitry.) The various technical terms for the condition include "cocktail party conversation," "chatterbox syndrome," and "blathering."

Fluent grammatical language can in fact appear in many kinds of people with severe intellectual impairments, like schizophrenics, Alzheimer's patients, some autistic children, and some aphasics. One of the most fascinating syndromes recently came to light when the parents of a retarded girl with chatterbox syndrome in San Diego read an article about Chomsky's theories in a popular science magazine and called him at MIT, suggesting that their daughter might be of interest to him. Chomsky is a paper-and-pencil theoretician who wouldn't know Jabba the Hutt from the Cookie Monster, so he suggested that the parents bring their child to the laboratory of the psycholinguist Ursula Bellugi in La Jolla.

Bellugi, working with colleagues in molecular biology, neurology, and radiology, found that the child (whom they called Crystal), and a number of others they have subsequently tested, had a rare form of retardation called Williams syndrome. The syndrome seems to be associated with a defective gene on chromosome 11 involved in the regulation of calcium, and it acts in complex ways on the brain, skull, and internal organs during development, though no one knows why it has the effects it does. The children have an unusual appearance: they are short and slight, with narrow faces and broad foreheads, flat nasal bridges, sharp chins, star-shaped patterns in their irises, and full lips. They are sometimes called "elfin-faced" or "pixie people," but to me they look more like Mick Jagger. They are significantly retarded, with an IQ of about 50, and are incompetent at ordinary tasks like tying their shoes, finding their way, retrieving items from a cupboard, telling left from right, adding two numbers, drawing a bicycle, and suppressing their natural tendency to hug strangers. But like Denyse they are fluent, if somewhat prim, conversationalists. Here are two transcripts from Crystal when she was eighteen:

And what an elephant is, it is one of the animals. And what the elephant does, it lives in the jungle. It can also live in the zoo. And what it has, it has long, gray ears, fan ears, ears that can blow in the wind. It has a long trunk that can pick up grass or pick up hay . . . If they're in a bad mood, it can be terrible . . . If the elephant gets mad, it could stomp; it could charge. Sometimes elephants can charge, like a bull can charge. They have big, long, tusks. They can damage a car . . . It could be dangerous. When they're in a pinch, when they're in a bad mood, it can be terrible. You don't want an elephant as a pet. You want a cat or a dog or a bird.

This is a story about chocolates. Once upon a time, in Chocolate World there used to be a Chocolate Princess. She was such a yummy princess. She was on her chocolate throne and then some chocolate man came to see her. And the man bowed to her and he said these words to her. The man said to her, "Please, Princess Chocolate. I want you to see how I do my work. And it's hot outside in Chocolate World, and you might melt to the ground like melted butter. And if the sun changes to a different color, then the Chocolate World—and you—won't melt. You can be saved if the sun changes to a different color. And if it doesn't change to a different color, you and Chocolate World are doomed.

Laboratory tests confirm the impression of competence at grammar; the children understand complex sentences, and fix up ungrammatical sentences, at normal levels. And they have an especially charming quirk: they are fond of unusual words. Ask a normal child to name some animals, and you will get the standard inventory of pet store and barnyard: dog, cat, horse, cow, pig. Ask a Williams syndrome child, and you get a more interesting menagerie: uni-corn, pteranodon, yak, ibex, water buffalo, sea lion, saber-tooth tiger, vulture, koala, dragon, and one that should be especially interesting to paleontologists, "brontosaurus rex." One eleven-year-old poured a glass of milk into the sink and said, "I'll have to evacuate it"; another handed Bellugi a drawing and announced, "Here, Doc, this is in remembrance of you."

———————

People like Kirupano, Larry, the Hawaiian-born papaya grower, Mayela, Simon, Aunt Mae, Sarah, Mr. Ford, the K's, Denyse, and Crystal constitute a field guide to language users. They show that complex grammar is displayed across the full range of human habitats. You don't need to have left the Stone Age; you don't need to be middle class; you don't need to do well in school; you don't even need to be old enough for school. Your parents need not bathe you in language or even command a language. You don't need the intellectual wherewithal to function in society, the skills to keep house and home together, or a particularly firm grip on reality. Indeed, you can possess all these advantages and still not be a competent language user, if you lack just the right genes or just the right bits of brain.

Mentalese

Steven Pinker

The year 1984 has come and gone, and it is losing its connotation of the totalitarian nightmare of George Orwell's 1949 novel. But relief may be premature. In an appendix to *Nineteen Eighty-Four*, Orwell wrote of an even more ominous date. In 1984, the infidel Winston Smith had to be converted with imprisonment, degradation, drugs, and torture; by 2050, there would be no Winston Smiths. For in that year the ultimate technology for thought control would be in place: the language Newspeak.

> The purpose of Newspeak was not only to provide a medium of expression for the world-view and mental habits proper to the devotees of Ingsoc [English Socialism], but to make all other modes of thought impossible. It was intended that when Newspeak had been adopted once and for all and Oldspeak forgotten, a heretical thought—that is, a thought diverging from the principles of Ingsoc—should be literally unthinkable, at least so far as thought is dependent on words. Its vocabulary was so constructed as to give exact and often very subtle expression to every meaning that a Party member could properly wish to express, while excluding all other meanings and also the possibility of arriving at them by indirect methods. This was done partly by the invention of new words, but chiefly by eliminating undesirable words and by stripping such words as remained of unorthodox meanings, and so far as possible of all secondary meanings whatever.

> To give a single example. The word *free* still existed in Newspeak, but it could only be used in such statements as "This dog is free from lice" or "This field is free from weeds." It could not be used in its old sense of "politically free" or "intellectually free," since political and intellectual freedom no longer existed even as concepts, and were therefore of necessity nameless.

> . . . A person growing up with Newspeak as his sole language would no more know that equal had once had the secondary meaning of "politically *equal*," or that free had once meant "intellectually *free*," than, for instance, a person who had never heard of chess would be aware of the secondary meanings attaching to *queen* and *rook*. There would be many crimes and errors which it would be beyond his power to commit, simply because they were nameless and therefore unimaginable.

But there is a straw of hope for human freedom: Orwell's caveat "at least so far as thought is dependent on words." Note his equivocation: at the end of the first paragraph, a concept is unimaginable and therefore nameless; at the end of the second, a concept is nameless and therefore unimaginable. *Is* thought dependent on words? Do people literally think in English, Cherokee, Kivunjo, or, by 2050, Newspeak? Or are our thoughts couched in some silent medium of the brain—a language of thought, or "mentalese"—and merely clothed in words whenever we need to communicate them to a listener? No question could be more central to understanding the language instinct.

In much of our social and political discourse, people simply assume that words determine thoughts. Inspired by Orwell's essay "Politics and the English Language," pundits accuse governments of manipulating our minds with euphemisms like *pacification* (bombing), *revenue enhancement* (taxes), and *nonretention* (firing). Philosophers argue that since animals lack language, they must also lack consciousness — Wittgenstein wrote, "A dog could not have the thought 'perhaps it will rain tomorrow'" — and therefore they do not possess the rights of conscious beings. Some feminists blame sexist thinking on sexist language, like the use of *he* to refer to a generic person. Inevitably, reform movements have sprung up. Many replacements for he have been suggested over the years, including *E, hesh, po, tey, co, jhe, ve, xe, he'er, thon*, and *na*. The most extreme of these movements is General Semantics, begun in 1933 by the engineer Count Alfred Korzybski and popularized in long-time best-sellers by his disciples Stuart Chase and S. I. Hayakawa. (This is the same Hayakawa who later achieved notoriety as the protest-defying college president and snoozing U.S. senator.) General Semantics lays the blame for human folly on insidious "semantic damage" to thought perpetrated by the structure of language. Keeping a forty-year-old in prison for a theft he committed as a teenager assumes that the forty-year-old John and the eighteen-year-old John are "the same person," a cruel logical error that would be avoided if we referred to them not as *John* but as *John$_{1972}$* and *John$_{1994}$*, respectively. The verb to *be* is a particular source of illogic, because it identifies individuals with abstractions, as in *Mary is a woman*, and licenses evasions of responsibility, like Ronald Reagan's famous nonconfession *Mistakes were made*. One faction seeks to eradicate the verb altogether.

And supposedly there is a scientific basis for these assumptions: the famous Sapir-Whorf hypothesis of linguistic determinism, stating that people's thoughts are determined by the categories made available by their language, and its weaker version, linguistic relativity, stating that differences among languages cause differences in the thoughts of their speakers. People who remember little else from their college education can rattle off the factoids: the languages that carve the spectrum into color words at

different places, the fundamentally different Hopi concept of time, the dozens of Eskimo words for snow. The implication is heavy: the foundational categories of reality are not "in" the world but are imposed by one's culture (and hence can be challenged, perhaps accounting for the perennial appeal of the hypothesis to undergraduate sensibilities).

But it is wrong, all wrong. The idea that thought is the same thing as language is an example of what can be called a conventional absurdity: a statement that goes against all common sense but that everyone believes because they dimly recall having heard it somewhere and because it is so pregnant with implications. (The "fact" that we use only five percent of our brains, that lemmings commit mass suicide, that the *Boy Scout Manual* annually outsells all other books, and that we can be coerced into buying by subliminal messages are other examples.) Think about it. We have all had the experience of uttering or writing a sentence, then stopping and realizing that it wasn't exactly what we meant to say. To have that feeling, there has to be a "what we meant to say" that is different from what we said. Sometimes it is not easy to find *any* words that properly convey a thought. When we hear or read, we usually remember the gist, not the exact words, so there has to be such a thing as a gist that is not the same as a bunch of words. And if thoughts depended on words, how could a new word ever be coined? How could a child learn a word to begin with? How could translation from one language to another be possible?

The discussions that assume that language determines thought carry on only by a collective suspension of disbelief. A dog, Bertrand Russell noted, may not be able to tell you that its parents were honest though poor, but can anyone really conclude from this that the dog is *unconscious*? (Out cold? A zombie?) A graduate student once argued with me using the following deliciously backwards logic: language must affect thought, because if it didn't, we would have no reason to fight sexist usage (apparently, the fact that it is offensive is not reason enough). As for government euphemism, it is contemptible not because it is a form of mind control but because it is a form of lying. (Orwell was quite clear about this in his masterpiece essay.) For example, "revenue enhancement" has a much broader meaning than "taxes," and listeners naturally assume that if a politician had meant "taxes" he would have said "taxes." Once a euphemism is pointed out, people are not so brainwashed that they have trouble understanding the deception. The National Council of Teachers of English annually lampoons government doublespeak in a widely reproduced press release, and calling attention to euphemism is a popular form of humor, like the speech from the irate pet store customer in *Monty Python's Flying Circus*:

> This parrot is no more. It has ceased to be. It's expired and gone to meet its maker. This is a late parrot. It's a stiff. Bereft of life, it rests in peace. If you hadn't nailed it to the perch, it would be pushing up the daisies. It's rung down the curtain and joined the choir invisible. This is an ex-parrot.

As we shall see in this chapter, there is no scientific evidence that languages dramatically shape their speakers' ways of thinking. But I want to do more than review the unintentionally comical history of attempts to prove that they do. The idea that language shapes thinking seemed plausible when scientists were in the dark about how thinking works or even how to study it. Now that cognitive scientists know how to think about thinking, there is less of a temptation to equate it with language just because words are more palpable than thoughts. By understanding *why* linguistic determinism is wrong, we will be in a better position to understand how language itself works when we turn to it in the next chapters.

The linguistic determinism hypothesis is closely linked to the names Edward Sapir and Benjamin Lee Whorf. Sapir, a brilliant linguist, was a student of the anthropologist Franz Boas. Boas and his students (who also include Ruth Benedict and Margaret Mead) were important intellectual figures in this century, because they argued that nonindustrial peoples were not primitive savages but had systems of language, knowledge, and culture as complex and valid in their world view as our own. In his study of Native American languages Sapir noted that speakers of different languages have to pay attention to different aspects of reality simply to put words together into grammatical sentences. For example, when English speakers decide whether or not to put *-ed* onto the end of a verb, they must pay attention to

tense, the relative time of occurrence of the event they are referring to and the moment of speaking. Wintu speakers need not bother with tense, but when they decide which suffix to put on their verbs, they must pay attention to whether the knowledge they are conveying was learned through direct observation or by hearsay.

Sapir's interesting observation was soon taken much farther. Whorf was an inspector for the Hartford Fire Insurance Company and an amateur scholar of Native American languages, which led him to take courses from Sapir at Yale. In a much-quoted passage, he wrote:

> We dissect nature along lines laid down by our native languages. The categories and types that we isolate from the world of phenomena we do not find there because they stare every observer in the face; on the contrary, the world is presented in a kaleidoscopic flux of impressions which has to be organized by our minds—and this means largely by the linguistic systems in our minds. We cut nature up, organize it into concepts, and ascribe significances as we do, largely because we are parties to an agreement to organize it in this way—an agreement that holds throughout our speech community and is codified in the patterns of our language. The agreement is, of course, an implicit and unstated one, *but its terms are absolutely obligatory*; we cannot talk at all except by subscribing to the organization and classification of data which the agreement decrees.

What led Whorf to this radical position? He wrote that the idea first occurred to him in his work as a fire prevention engineer when he was struck by how language led workers to misconstrue dangerous situations. For example, one worker caused a serious explosion by tossing a cigarette into an "empty" drum that in fact was full of gasoline vapor. Another lit a blowtorch near a "pool of water" that was really a basin of decomposing tannery waste, which, far from being "watery," was releasing inflammable gases. Whorf's studies of American languages strengthened his conviction. For example, in Apache, *It is a dripping spring* must be expressed "As water, or springs, whiteness moves downward." "How utterly unlike our way of thinking!" he wrote.

But the more you examine Whorf's arguments, the less sense they make. Take the story about the worker and the "empty" drum. The seeds of disaster supposedly lay in the semantics of *empty*, which,

Whorf claimed, means both "without its usual contents" and "null and void, empty, inert." The hapless worker, his conception of reality molded by his linguistic categories, did not distinguish between the "drained" and "inert" senses, hence, flick . . . boom! But wait. Gasoline vapor is invisible. A drum with nothing but vapor in it looks just like a drum with nothing in it at all. Surely this walking catastrophe was fooled by his eyes, not by the English language.

The example of whiteness moving downward is supposed to show that the Apache mind does not cut tip events into distinct objects and actions. Whorf presented many such examples from Native American languages. The Apache equivalent of *The boat is grounded on the beach* is "It is on the beach pointwise as an event of canoe motion." *He invites people to a feast* becomes "He, or somebody, goes for eaters of cooked food." *He cleans a gun with a ramrod* is translated as "He directs a hollow moving dry spot by movement of tool." All this, to be sure, is utterly unlike our way of talking. But do we know that it is utterly unlike our way of thinking?

As soon as Whorl's articles appeared, the psycholinguists Eric Lenneberg and Roger Brown pointed out two non sequiturs in his argument. First, Whorf did not actually study any Apaches; it is not clear that he ever met one. His assertions about Apache psychology are based entirely on Apache grammar—making his argument circular. Apaches speak differently, so they must think differently. How do we know that they think differently? Just listen to the way they speak!

Second, Whorf rendered the sentences, as clumsy, word-for-word translations, designed to make the literal meanings seem as odd as possible. But looking at the actual glosses that Whorf provided, I could, with equal grammatical justification, render the first sentence as the mundane "Clear stuff—water—is falling." Turning the tables, I could take the English sentence "He walks" and render it "As solitary masculinity, leggedness proceeds." Brown illustrates how strange the German mind must be, according to Whorl's logic, by reproducing Mark Twain's own translation of a speech he delivered in flawless German to the Vienna Press Club:

I am indeed the truest friend of the German language—and not only now, but from long since—yes, before twenty years already . . . . I would only some changes effect. I would only the language method—the luxurious, elaborate construction compress, the eternal parenthesis suppress, do away with, annihilate; the introduction of more than thirteen subjects in one sentence forbid; the verb so far to the front pull that one it without a telescope discover can. With one word, my gentlemen, I would your beloved language simplify so that, my gentlemen, when you her for prayer need, One her yonder-up understands.

. . . I might gladly the separable verb also a little bit reform. I might none do let what Schiller did: he has the whole history of the Thirty Years' War between the two members of a separate verb in-pushed. That has even Germany itself aroused, and one has Schiller the permission refused the History of the Hundred Years' War to compose—God be it thanked! After all these reforms established be will, will the German language the noblest and the prettiest on the world be.

Among Whorf's "kaleidoscopic flux of impressions," color is surely the most eye-catching. He noted that we see objects in different hues, depending on the wavelengths of the light they reflect, but that physicists tell us that wavelength is a continuous dimension with nothing delineating red, yellow, green, blue, and so on. Languages differ in their inventory of color words: Latin lacks generic "gray" and "brown"; Navajo collapses blue and green into one word; Russian has distinct words for dark blue and sky blue; Shona speakers use one word for the yellower greens and the greener yellows, and a different one for the bluer greens and the nonpurplish blues. You can fill in the rest of the argument. It is language that puts the frets in the spectrum; Julius Caesar would not know shale from Shinola.

But although physicists see no basis for color boundaries, physiologists do. Eyes do not register wavelength the way a thermometer registers temperature. They contain three kinds of cones, each with a different pigment, and the cones are wired to neurons in a way that makes the neurons respond best to red patches against a green background or vice versa, blue against yellow, black against white. No matter how influential language might be, it would seem preposterous to a physiologist that it could reach down into the retina and rewire the ganglion cells.

Indeed, humans the world over (and babies and monkeys, for that matter) color their perceptual worlds using the same palette, and this constrains the vocabularies they develop. Although languages may disagree about the wrappers in the sixty-four crayon box—the burnt umbers, the turquoises, the fuchsias—they agree much more on the wrappers in the eight-crayon box—the fire-engine reds, grass greens, lemon yellows. Speakers of different languages unanimously pick these shades as the best examples of their color words, as long as the language has a color word in that general part of the spectrum. And where languages do differ in their color words, they differ predictably, not according to the idiosyncratic tastes of some word-coiner. Languages are organized a bit like the Crayola product line, the fancier ones adding colors to the more basic ones. If a language has only two color words, they are for black and white (usually encompassing dark and light, respectively). If it has three, they are for black, white, and red; if four, black, white, red, and either yellow or green. Five adds in both yellow and green; six, blue; seven, brown; more than seven, purple, pink, orange, or gray. But the clinching experiment was carried out in the New Guinea highlands with the Grand Valley Dani, a people speaking one of the black-and-white languages. The psychologist Eleanor Rosch found that the Dani were quicker at learning a new color category that was based on fire-engine red than a category based on an off-red. The way we see colors determines how we learn words for them, not vice versa.

The fundamentally different Hopi concept of time is one of the more startling claims about how minds can vary. Whorf wrote that the Hopi language contains "no words, grammatical forms, constructions, or expressions that refer directly to what we call 'time,' or to past, or future, or to enduring or lasting." He suggested, too, that the Hopi had "no general notion or intuition of TIME as a smooth flowing continuum in which everything in the universe proceeds at an equal rate, out of a future, through a present, into a past." According to Whorf, they did not conceptualize events as being like points, or lengths of time like days as countable things. Rather, they seemed to focus on change and process itself, and on psychological distinctions between presently known, mythical, and conjecturally distant. The Hopi also had little interest in "exact sequences, dating, calendars, chronology."

What, then, are we to make of the following sentence translated from Hopi?

Then indeed, the following day, quite early in the morning at the hour when people pray to the sun, around that time then he woke up the girl again.

Perhaps the Hopi are not as oblivious to time as Whorf made them out to be. In his extensive study of the Hopi, the anthropologist Ekkehart Malotki, who reported this sentence, also showed that Hopi speech contains tense, metaphors for time, units of time (including days, numbers of days, parts of the day, yesterday and tomorrow, days of the week, weeks, months, lunar phases, seasons, and the year), ways to quantify units of time, and words like "ancient," "quick," "long time," and "finished." Their culture keeps records with sophisticated methods of dating, including a horizon-based sun calendar, exact ceremonial day sequences, knotted calendar strings, notched calendar sticks, and several devices for timekeeping using the principle of the sundial. No one is really sure how Whorf came up with his outlandish claims, but his limited, badly analyzed sample of Hopi speech and his long-time leanings toward mysticism must have contributed.

Speaking of anthropological canards, no discussion of language and thought would be complete without the Great Eskimo Vocabulary Hoax. Contrary to popular belief, the Eskimos do not have more words for snow than do speakers of English. They do not have four hundred words for snow, as it has been claimed in print, or two hundred, or one hundred, or forty-eight, or even nine. One dictionary puts the figure at two. Counting generously, experts can come up with about a dozen, but by such standards English would not be far behind, with *snow, sleet, slush, blizzard, avalanche, hail, hardpack, powder, flurry, dusting*, and a coinage of Boston's WBZ-TV meteorologist Bruce Schwoegler, *snizzling*.

Where did the myth come from? Not from anyone who has actually studied the Yupik and Inuit-Inupiaq families of polysynthetic languages spoken from Siberia to Greenland. The anthropologist Laura Martin has documented how the story grew like an urban legend, exaggerated with each retelling. In 1911 Boas casually mentioned that Eskimos used four unrelated word roots for snow. Whorf embellished the count to seven and implied that there were more. His article was widely reprinted, then cited in textbooks and popular books on language, which led to successively inflated estimates in other textbooks, articles, and newspaper columns of Amazing Facts.

The linguist Geoffrey Pullum, who popularized Martin's article in his essay "The Great Eskimo Vocabulary Hoax," speculates about why the story got so out of control: "The alleged lexical extravagance of the Eskimos comports so well with the many other facets of their polysynthetic perversity: rubbing noses; lending their wives to strangers; eating raw seal blubber; throwing Grandma out to be eaten by polar bears." It is an ironic twist. Linguistic relativity came out of the Boas school, as part of a campaign to show that nonliterate cultures were as complex and sophisticated as European ones. But the supposedly mind-broadening anecdotes owe their appeal to a patronizing willingness to treat other cultures' psychologies as weird and exotic compared to our own. As Pullum notes,

> Among the many depressing things about this credulous transmission and elaboration of a false claim is that even if there *were* a large number of roots for different snow types in some Arctic language, this would *not*, objectively, be intellectually interesting; it would be a most mundane and unremarkable fact. Horsebreeders have various names for breeds, sizes, and ages of horses; botanists have names for leaf shapes; interior decorators have names for shades of mauve; printers have many different names for fonts (Carlson, Garamond, Helvetica, Times Roman, and so on), naturally enough. . . . Would anyone think of writing about printers the same kind of slop we find written about Eskimos in bad linguistics textbooks? Take [the following] random textbook . . ., with its earnest assertion "It is quite obvious that in the culture of the Eskimos . . . snow is of great enough importance to split up the conceptual sphere that corresponds to one word and one thought in English into several distinct classes . . ." Imagine reading: "It is quite obvious that in the culture of printers . . . fonts are of great enough importance to split up the conceptual sphere that corresponds to one word and one thought among non-printers into several distinct classes . . ." Utterly boring, even if true. Only the link to those legendary, promiscuous, blubber-gnawing hunters of the ice-packs could permit something this trite to be presented to us for contemplation.

If the anthropological anecdotes are bunk, what about controlled studies? The thirty-five years of research from the psychology laboratory is distinguished by how little it has shown. Most of the experiments have tested banal "weak" versions of the Whorfian hypothesis, namely that words can have some effect on memory or categorization. Some of these experiments have actually worked, but that is hardly surprising. In a typical experiment,

subjects have to commit paint chips to memory and are tested with a multiple-choice procedure. In some of these studies, the subjects show slightly better memory for colors that have readily available names in their language. But even colors without names are remembered fairly well, so the experiment does not show that the colors are remembered by verbal labels alone. All it shows is that subjects remembered the chips in two forms, a nonverbal visual image and a verbal label, presumably because two kinds of memory, each one fallible, are better than one. In another type of experiment subjects have to say which two out of three color chips go together; they often put the ones together that have the same name in their language. Again, no surprise. I can imagine the subjects thinking to themselves, "Now how on earth does this guy expect me to pick two chips to put together? He didn't give me any hints, and they're all pretty similar. Well, I'd probably call those two 'green' and that one 'blue,' and that seems as good a reason to put them together as any." In these experiments, language is, technically speaking, influencing a form of thought in some way, but so what? It is hardly an example of incommensurable world views, or of concepts that are nameless and therefore unimaginable, or of dissecting nature along lines laid down by our native languages according to terms that are absolutely obligatory.

The only really dramatic finding comes from the linguist and now Swarthmore College president Alfred Bloom in his book *The Linguistic Shaping of Thought*. English grammar, says Bloom, provides its speakers with the subjunctive construction: *If John were to go to the hospital, he would meet Mary*. The subjunctive is used to express "counterfactual" situations, events that are known to be false but entertained as hypotheticals. (Anyone familiar with Yiddish knows a better example, the ultimate riposte to someone reasoning from improbable premises: *Az di bobe volt gehat beytsim volt zi geven mayn zeyde*, "If my grandmother had balls, she'd be my grandfather.") Chinese, in contrast, lacks a subjunctive and any other simple grammatical construction that directly expresses a counterfactual. The thought must be expressed circuitously, something like "If John is going to the hospital . . . but he is not going to the hospital . . . but if he is going, he meets Mary."

Bloom wrote stories containing sequences of implications from a counterfactual premise and gave them to Chinese and American students. For example, one story said, in outline, "Bier was an eighteenth-century European philosopher. There was some contact between the West and China at that time, but very few works of Chinese philosophy had been translated. Bier could not read Chinese, but if he had been able to read Chinese, he would have discovered B; what would have most influenced him would have been C; once influenced by that Chinese perspective, Bier would then have done D," and so on. The subjects were then asked to check off whether B, C, and D actually occurred. The American students gave the correct answer, no, ninety-eight percent of the time; the Chinese students gave the correct answer only seven percent of the time! Bloom concluded that the Chinese language renders its speakers unable to entertain hypothetical false worlds without great mental effort. (As far as I know, no one has tested the converse prediction on speakers of Yiddish.)

The cognitive psychologists Terry Au, Yohtaro Takano, and Lisa Liu were not exactly enchanted by these tales of the concreteness of the Oriental mind. Each one identified serious flaws in Bloom's experiments. One problem was that his stories were written in stilted Chinese. Another was that some of the science stories turned out, upon careful rereading, to be genuinely ambiguous. Chinese college students tend to have more science training than American students, and thus they were *better* at detecting the ambiguities that Bloom himself missed. When these flaws were fixed, the differences vanished.

People can be forgiven for overrating language. Words make noise, or sit on a page, for all to hear and see. Thoughts are trapped inside the head of the thinker. To know what someone else is thinking, or to talk to each other about the nature of thinking, we have to use—what else, words! It is no wonder that many commentators have trouble even conceiving of thought without words—or is it that they just don't have the language to talk about it?

As a cognitive scientist I can afford to be smug about common sense being true (thought is different from language) and linguistic determinism being a conventional absurdity. For two sets of tools now make it easier to think clearly about the whole

problem. One is a body of experimental studies that break the word barrier and assess many kinds of nonverbal thought. The other is a theory of how thinking might work that formulates the questions in a satisfyingly precise way.

We have already seen an example of thinking without language: Mr. Ford, the fully intelligent aphasic discussed in Chapter 2. (One could, however, argue that his thinking abilities had been constructed before his stroke on the scaffolding of the language he then possessed.) We have also met deaf children who lack a language and soon invent one. Even more pertinent are the deaf adults occasionally discovered who lack any form of language whatsoever—no sign language, no writing, no lip reading, no speech. In her recent book *A Man Without Words*, Susan Schaller tells the story of Ildefonso, a twenty-seven-year-old illegal immigrant from a small Mexican village whom she met while working as a sign language interpreter in Los Angeles. Ildefonso's animated eyes conveyed an unmistakable intelligence and curiosity, and Schaller became his volunteer teacher and companion. He soon showed her that he had a full grasp of number: he learned to do addition on paper in three minutes and had little trouble understanding the base-ten logic behind two-digit numbers. In an epiphany reminiscent of the story of Helen Keller, Ildefonso grasped the principle of naming when Schaller tried to teach him the sign for "cat." A dam burst, and he demanded to be shown the signs for all the objects he was familiar with. Soon he was able to convey to Schaller parts of his life story: how as a child he had begged his desperately poor parents to send him to school, the kinds of crops he had picked in different states, his evasions of immigration authorities. He led Schaller to other languageless adults in forgotten corners of society. Despite their isolation from the verbal world, they displayed many abstract forms of thinking, like rebuilding broken locks, handling money, playing card games, and entertaining each other with long pantomimed narratives.

Our knowledge of the mental life of Ildefonso and other languageless adults must remain impressionistic for ethical reasons: when they surface, the first priority is to teach them language, not to study how they manage without it. But there are other languageless beings who have been studied experimentally, and volumes have been written about how they reason about space, time, objects, number, rate, causality, and categories. Let me recount three ingenious examples. One involves babies, who cannot think in words because they have not yet learned any. One involves monkeys, who cannot think in words because they are incapable of learning them. The third involves human adults, who, whether or not they think in words, claim their best thinking is done without them.

The developmental psychologist Karen Wynn has recently shown that five-month-old babies can do a simple form of mental arithmetic. She used a technique common in infant perception research. Show a baby a bunch of objects long enough, and the baby gets bored and looks away; change the scene, and if the baby notices the difference, he or she will regain interest. The methodology has shown that babies as young as five days old are sensitive to number. In one experiment, an experimenter bores a baby with an object, then occludes the object with an opaque screen. When the screen is removed, if the same object is present, the babies look for a little while, then get bored again. But if, through invisible subterfuge, two or three objects have ended up there, the surprised babies stare longer.

In Wynn's experiment, the babies were shown a rubber Mickey Mouse doll on a stage until their little eyes wandered. Then a screen came up, and a prancing hand visibly reached out from behind a curtain and placed a second Mickey Mouse behind the screen. When the screen was removed, if there were two Mickey Mouses visible (something the babies had never actually seen), the babies looked for only a few moments. But if there was only one doll, the babies were captivated—even though this was exactly the scene that had bored them before the screen was put in place. Wynn also tested a second group of babies, and this time, after the screen came up to obscure a *pair* of dolls, a hand visibly reached behind the screen and removed one of them. If the screen fell to reveal a single Mickey, the babies looked briefly; if it revealed the old scene with two, the babies had more trouble tearing themselves away. The babies must have been keeping track of how many dolls were behind the screen, updating their counts as dolls were added or subtracted. If the number inexplicably departed from what they expected, they scrutinized the scene, as if searching for some explanation.

Vervet monkeys live in stable groups of adult males and females and their offspring. The prima-tologists Dorothy Cheney and Robert Seyfarth have noticed that extended families form affiances like the Montagues and Capulets. In a typical interaction they observed in Kenya, one juvenile monkey wrestled another to the ground screaming. Twenty minutes later the victim's sister approached the perpetrator's sister and without provocation bit her on the tail. For the retaliator to have identified the proper target, she would have had to solve the following analogy problem: A (victim) is to B (myself) as C (perpetrator) is to X, using the correct relationship "sister of" (or perhaps merely "relative of"; there were not enough vervets in the park for Cheney and Seyfarth to tell).

But do monkeys really know how their group-mates are related to each other, and, more impressively, do they realize that different pairs of individuals like brothers and sisters can be related in the same way? Cheney and Seyfarth hid a loudspeaker behind a bush and played tapes of a two-year-old monkey screaming. The females in the area reacted by looking at the mother of the infant who had been recorded—showing that they not only recognized the infant by its scream but recalled who its mother was. Similar abilities have been shown in the long-tailed macaques that Verena Dasser coaxed into a laboratory adjoining a large outdoor enclosure. Three slides were projected: a mother at the center, one of her offspring on one side, and an unrelated juvenile of the same age and sex on the other. Each screen had a button under it. After the monkey had been trained to press a button under the offspring slide, it was tested on pictures of other mothers in the group, each one flanked by a picture of that mother's offspring and a picture of another juvenile. More than ninety percent of the time the monkey picked the offspring. In another test, the monkey was shown two slides, each showing a pair of monkeys, and was trained to press a button beneath the slide showing a particular mother and her juvenile daughter. When presented with slides of new monkeys in the group, the subject monkey always picked the mother-and-offspring pair, whether the offspring was male, female, infant, juvenile, or adult. Moreover, the monkeys appeared to be relying not only on physical resemblance between a given pair of monkeys, or on the sheer number of hours they had previously spent together, as the basis for recognizing they were kin, but on something more subtle in the history of their interaction. Cheney and

Seyfarth, who work hard at keeping track of who is related to whom in what way in the groups of animals they study, note that monkeys would make excellent primatologists.

Many creative people insist that in their most inspired moments they think not in words but in mental images. Samuel Taylor Coleridge wrote that visual images of scenes and words once appeared involuntarily before him in a dreamlike state (perhaps opium-induced). He managed to copy the first forty lines onto paper, resulting in the poem we know as "Kubla Khan," before a knock on the door shattered the images and obliterated forever what would have been the rest of the poem. Many contemporary novelists, like Joan Didion, report that their acts of creation begin not with any notion of a character or a plot but with vivid mental pictures that dictate their choice of words. The modern sculptor James Surls plans his projects lying on a couch listening to music; he manipulates the sculptures in his mind's eye, he says, putting an arm on, taking an arm off, watching the images roll and tumble.

Physical scientists are even more adamant that their thinking is geometrical, not verbal. Michael Faraday, the originator of our modern conception of electric and magnetic fields, had no training in mathematics but arrived at his insights by visualizing lines of force as narrow tubes curving through space. James Clerk Maxwell formalized the concepts of electromagnetic fields in a set of mathematical equations and is considered the prime example of an abstract theoretician, but he set down the equations only after mentally playing with elaborate imaginary models of sheets and fluids. Nikola Tesla's idea for the electrical motor and generator, Friedrich Kekulé's discovery of the benzene ring that kicked off modern organic chemistry, Ernest Lawrence's conception of the cyclotron, James Watson and Francis Crick's discovery of the DNA double helix—all came to them in images. The most famous self-described visual thinker is Albert Einstein, who arrived at some of his insights by imagining himself riding a beam of light and looking back at a clock, or dropping a coin while standing in a plummeting elevator. He wrote:

> The psychical entities which seem to serve as elements in thought are certain signs and more or less clear images which can be "voluntarily" reproduced and combined. . . . This combinatory play seems to be the essential feature in productive thought—

before there is any connection with logical construction in words or other kinds of signs which can be communicated to others. The above-mentioned elements are, in my case, of visual and some muscular type. Conventional words or other signs have to be sought for laboriously only in a secondary state, when the mentioned associative play is sufficiently established and can be reproduced at will.

Another creative scientist, the cognitive psychologist Roger Shepard, had his own moment of sudden visual inspiration, and it led to a classic laboratory demonstration of mental imagery in mere mortals. Early one morning, suspended between sleep and awakening in a state of lucid consciousness, Shepard experienced "a spontaneous kinetic image of three-dimensional structures majestically turning in space." Within moments and before fully awakening, Shepard had a clear idea for the design of an experiment. A simple variant of his idea was later carried out with his then-student Lynn Cooper. Cooper and Shepard flashed thousands of slides, each showing a single letter of the alphabet, to their long-suffering student volunteers. Sometimes the letter was upright, but sometimes it was tilted or mirror-reversed or both. As an example, here are the sixteen versions of the letter *F*:

0	+45	+90	+135	180	-135	-90	-45

The subjects were asked to press one button if the letter was normal (that is, like one of the letters in the top row of the diagram), another if it was a mirror image (like one of the letters in the bottom row). To do the task, the subjects had to compare the letter in the slide against some memory record of what the normal version of the letter looks like right-side up. Obviously, the right-side-up slide (0 degrees) is the quickest, because it matches the letter in memory exactly, but for the other orientations, some mental transformation to the upright is necessary first. Many subjects reported that they, like the famous sculptors and scientists, "mentally rotated" an image of the letter to the upright. By looking at the reaction times, Shepard and Cooper showed that this introspection was accurate. The upright letters were fastest, followed by the 45 degree letters, the 90 degree letters, and the 135 degree letters, with the 180 degree (upside-down) letters the slowest. In other words, the farther the subjects had to mentally rotate the letter, the longer they took. From the data, Cooper and Shepard estimated that letters revolve in the mind at a rate of 56 RPM.

Note that if the subjects had been manipulating something resembling *verbal descriptions* of the letters, such as "an upright spine with one horizontal segment that extends rightwards from the top and another horizontal segment that extends rightwards from the middle," the results would have been very different. Among all the topsy-turvy letters, the upside-down versions (180 degrees) should be fastest: one simply switches all the "top"s to "bottom"s and vice versa, and the "left"s to "right"s and vice versa, and one has a new description of the shape as it would appear right-side up, suitable for matching against memory. Sideways letters (90 degrees) should be slower, because "top" gets changed either to "right" or to "left," depending on whether it lies clockwise (+ 90 degrees) or counter-clockwise (–90 degrees) from the upright. Diagonal letters (45 and 135 degrees) should be slowest, because every word in the description has to be replaced: "top" has to be replaced with either "top right" or "top left," and so on. So the order of difficulty should be 0, 180, 90, 45, 135, not the majestic rotation of 0, 45, 90, 135, 180 that Cooper and Shepard saw in the data. Many other experiments have corroborated the idea that visual thinking uses not language but a mental graphics system, with operations that rotate, scan, zoom, pan, displace, and fill in patterns of contours.

———•———

What sense, then, can we make of the suggestion that images, numbers, kinship relations, or logic can be represented in the brain without being couched in words? In the first half of this century, philosophers had an answer: none. Reifying thoughts as things in the head was a logical error, they said. A picture or family tree or number in the head would require a little man, a homunculus, to look at it. And what would be inside *his* head—even smaller pictures, with an even smaller man looking at them? But the argument was unsound. It took Alan Turing, the brilliant British mathematician and philosopher, to make the idea of a mental representation scientifically respectable. Turing described a hypothetical machine that could be said to engage in reasoning. In fact this simple device, named a Turing Machine in his honor, is powerful enough to solve any problem that any computer, past, present, or future, can solve. And it clearly uses an internal symbolic representation—a kind of mentalese—without requiring a little man or any occult processes. By looking at how a Turing machine works, we can get a grasp of what it would mean for a human mind to think in mentalese as opposed to English.

In essence, to reason is to deduce new pieces of knowledge from old ones. A simple example is the old chestnut from introductory logic: if you know that Socrates is a man and that all men are mortal, you can figure out that Socrates is mortal. But how could a hunk of matter like a brain accomplish this feat? The first key idea is a *representation*: a physical object whose parts and arrangement correspond piece for piece to some set of ideas or facts. For example, the pattern of ink on this page

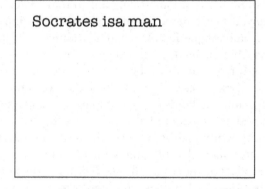

is a representation of the idea that Socrates is a man. The shape of one group of ink marks, Socrates, is a symbol that stands for the concept of Socrates. The shape of another set of ink marks, isa, stands for the concept of being an instance of, and the shape of the third, man, stands for the concept of man. Now, it is crucial to keep one thing in mind. I have put these ink marks in the shape of English words as a courtesy to you, the reader, so that you can keep them straight as we work through the example. But all that really matters is that they have different shapes, I could have used a star of David, a smiley face, and the Mercedes-Benz logo, as long as I used them consistently.

Similarly, the fact that the Socrates ink marks are to the left of the isa ink marks on the page, and the man ink marks are to the right, stands for the idea that Socrates is a man. If I change any part of the representation, like replacing isa with isasonofa, or flipping the positions of Socrates and man, we would have a representation of a different idea. Again, the left-to-right English order is just a mnemonic device for your convenience. I could have done it right-to-left or up-and-down, as long as I used that order consistently.

Keeping these conventions in mind, now imagine that the page has a second set of ink marks, representing the proposition that every man is mortal:

```
Socrates isa man
Every man ismortal




```

To get reasoning to happen, we now need a *processor*. A processor is not a little man (so one needn't worry about an infinite regress of homunculi inside homunculi) but something much stupider: a gadget with a fixed number of reflexes. A processor can react to different pieces of a representation and do something in response, including altering the representation or making new ones. For example, imagine a machine that can move around on a printed page. It has a cutout in the shape of the letter sequence isa, and a light sensor that can tell when the cutout is superimposed on a set of ink marks in the exact shape of the cutout. The sensor is hooked up to a little pocket copier, which can duplicate any set of ink marks, either by printing identical ink marks somewhere else on the page or by burning them into a new cutout.

Now imagine that this sensor-copier-creeper machine is wired up with four reflexes. First, it rolls down the page, and whenever it detects some isa ink marks, it moves to the left, and copies the ink marks

it finds there onto the bottom left corner of the page. Let loose on our page, it would create the following:

```
Socrates isa man
Every man ismortal



Socrates

```

Its second reflex, also in response to finding an isa, is to get itself to the right of that isa and copy any ink marks it finds there into the holes of a new cutout. In our case, this forces the processor to make a cutout in the shape of man. Its third reflex is to scan down the page checking for ink marks shaped like Every, and if it finds some, seeing if the ink marks to the right align with its new cutout. In our example, it finds one: the man in the middle of the second line. Its fourth reflex, upon finding such a match, is to move to the right and copy the ink marks it finds there onto the bottom center of the page. In our example, those are the ink marks ismortal. If you are following me, you'll see that our page now looks like this:

```
Socrates isa man
Every man ismortal



Socrates ismortal

```

A primitive kind of reasoning has taken place. Crucially, although the gadget and the page it sits on collectively display a kind of intelligence, there is nothing in either of them that is itself intelligent. Gadget and page are just a bunch of ink marks, cutouts, photocells, lasers, and wires. What makes the whole device smart is the exact *correspondence* between the logician's rule "If X is a Y and all Y's are Z, then X is Z" and the way the device scans, moves, and prints. Logically speaking, "X is a Y" means that what is true of Y is also true of X, and mechanically speaking, X isa Y causes what is printed next to the Y to be also printed next to the X. The machine, blindly following the laws of physics, just responds to the shape of the ink marks isa (without understanding what it means to us) and copies other ink marks in a way that ends up mimicking the operation of the logical rule. What makes it "intelligent" is that the sequence of sensing and moving and copying results in its printing a representation of a conclusion that is true if and only if the page contains representations of premises that are true. If one gives the device as much paper as it needs, Turing showed, the machine can do anything that any computer can do—and perhaps, he conjectured, anything that any physically embodied mind can do.

Now, this example uses ink marks on paper as its representation and a copying-creeping-sensing machine as its processor. But the representation can be in any physical medium at all, as long as the patterns are used consistently. In the brain, there might be three groups of neurons, one used to represent the individual that the proposition is about (Socrates, Aristotle, Rod Stewart, and so on), one to represent the logical relationship in the proposition (is a, is not, is like, and so on), and one to represent the class or type that the individual is being categorized as (men, dogs, chickens, and so on). Each concept would correspond to the firing of a particular neuron; for example, in the first group of neurons, the fifth neuron might fire to represent Socrates and the seventeenth might fire to represent Aristotle; in the third group, the eighth neuron might fire to represent men, the twelfth neuron might fire to represent dogs. The processor might be a network of other neurons feeding into these groups, connected together in such a way that it reproduces the firing pattern in one group of neurons in some other group (for example, if the eighth neuron is firing in group 3, the processor network would turn on the eighth neuron in some fourth group, elsewhere in the brain). Or the whole thing could be done in silicon chips. But in all three cases the principles are the same. The way the elements in the processor are wired up would cause them to sense and copy pieces of a representation, and to produce new representations, in a way that mimics the rules of reasoning. With many thousands of representations and a set of

somewhat more sophisticated processors (perhaps different kinds of representations and processors for different kinds of thinking), you might have a genuinely intelligent brain or computer. Add an eye that can detect certain contours in the world and turn on representations that symbolize them, and muscles that can act on the world whenever certain representations symbolizing goals are turned on, and you have a behaving organism (or add a TV camera and set of levers and wheels, and you have a robot).

This, in a nutshell, is the theory of thinking called "the physical symbol system hypothesis" or the "computational" or "representational" theory of mind. It is as fundamental to cognitive science as the cell doctrine is to biology and plate tectonics is to geology. Cognitive psychologists and neuroscientists are trying to figure out what kinds of representations and processors the brain has. But there are ground rules that must be followed at all times: no little men inside, and no peeking. The representations that one posits in the mind have to be arrangements of symbols, and the processor has to be a device with a fixed set of reflexes, period. The combination, acting all by itself, has to produce the intelligent conclusions. The theorist is forbidden to peer inside and "read" the symbols, "make sense" of them, and poke around to nudge the device in smart directions like some deus ex machina.

———————

Now we are in a position to pose the Whorfian question in a precise way. Remember that a representation does not have to look like English or any other language; it just has to use symbols to represent concepts, and arrangements of symbols to represent the logical relations among them, according to some consistent scheme. But though internal representations in an English speaker's mind don't *have* to look like English, they *could,* in principle, look like English—or like whatever language the person happens to speak. So here is the question: Do they in fact? For example, if we know that Socrates is a man, is it because we have neural patterns that correspond one-to-one to the English words *Socrates, is, a,* and *man,* and groups of neurons in the brain that correspond to the subject of an English sentence, the verb, and the object, laid out in that order? Or do we use some other code for representing concepts and their relations in our heads, a language of thought or mentalese that is not the same as any of the world's languages? We can answer this question by seeing whether English sentences embody the information that a processor would need to perform valid sequences of reasoning—without requiring any fully intelligent homunculus inside doing the "understanding."

The answer is a clear no. English (or any other language people speak) is hopelessly unsuited to serve as our internal medium of computation. Consider some of the problems.

The first is ambiguity. These headlines actually appeared in newspapers:

Child's Stool Great for Use in Garden
Stud Tires Out
Stiff Opposition Expected to Casketless Funeral
  Plan
Drunk Gets Nine Months in Violin Case
Iraqi Head Seeks Arms
Queen Mary Having Bottom Scraped
Columnist Gets Urologist in Trouble with His
  Peers

Each headline contains a word that is ambiguous. But surely the thought underlying the word is *not* ambiguous; the writers of the headlines surely knew which of the two senses of the words *stool*, *stud*, and *stiff* they themselves had in mind. And if there can be two thoughts corresponding to one word, thoughts can't be words.

The second problem with English is its lack of logical explicitness. Consider the following example, devised by the computer scientist Drew McDermott:

Ralph is an elephant.
Elephants live in Africa.
Elephants have tusks.

Our inference-making device, with some minor modifications to handle the English grammar of the sentences, would deduce "Ralph lives in Africa" and "Ralph has tusks." This sounds fine but isn't. Intelligent you, the reader, knows that the Africa that Ralph lives in is the same Africa that all the other elephants live in, but that Ralph's tusks are his own. But the symbol-copier-creeper-sensor that is supposed to be a model of you *doesn't* know that, because the distinction is nowhere to be found in any of the statements. If you object that this is just common sense, you would be right—but it's common sense that we're trying to account for, and

English sentences do not embody the information that a processor needs to carry out common sense.

A third problem is called "co-reference." Say you start talking about an individual by referring to him as *the tall blond man with one black shoe*. The second time you refer to him in the conversation you are likely to call him *the man*; the third time, just *him*. But the three expressions do not refer to three people or even to three ways of thinking about a single person; the second and third are just ways of saving breath. Something in the brain must treat them as the same thing; English isn't doing it.

A fourth, related problem comes from those aspects of language that can only be interpreted in the context of a conversation or text—what linguists call "deixis." Consider articles like *a* and *the*. What is the difference between *killed a policeman* and *killed the policeman*? Only that in the second sentence, it is assumed that some specific policeman was mentioned earlier or is salient in the context. Thus in isolation the two phrases are synonymous, but in the following contexts (the first from an actual newspaper article) their meanings are completely different:

A policeman's 14-year-old son, apparently
  enraged after being disciplined for a bad
  grade, opened fire from his house, *killing a
  policeman* and wounding three people before
  he was shot dead.
A policeman's 14-year-old son, apparently
  enraged after being disciplined for a bad
  grade, opened fire from his house, *killing the
  policeman* and wounding three people before
  he was shot dead.

Outside of a particular conversation or text, then, the words *a* and *the* are quite meaningless. They have no place in one's permanent mental database. Other conversation-specific words like *here*, *there*, *this*, *that*, *now*, *then*, *I*, *me*, *my*, *her*, *we*, and *you* pose the same problems, as the following old joke illustrates:

First guy: I didn't sleep with my wife before we
  were married, did you?
Second guy: I don't know. What was her maiden
  name?

A fifth problem is synonymy. The sentences

Sam sprayed paint onto the wall.
Sam sprayed the wall with paint.
Paint was sprayed onto the wall by Sam.
The wall was sprayed with paint by Sam.

refer to the same event and therefore license many of the same inferences. For example, in all four cases, one may conclude that the wall has paint on it. But they are four distinct arrangements of words. You know that they mean the same thing, but no simple processor, crawling over them as marks, would know that. Something else that is not one of those arrangements of words must be representing the single event that you know is common to all four. For example, the event might be represented as something like

(Sam spray paint$_i$) cause (paint$_i$ go to (on wall))

—which, assuming we don't take the English words seriously, is not too far from one of the leading proposals about what mentalese looks like.

These examples (and there are many more) illustrate a single important point. The representations underlying thinking, on the one hand, and the sentences in a language, on the other, are in many ways at cross-purposes. Any particular thought in our head embraces a vast amount of information. But when it comes to communicating a thought to someone else, attention spans are short and mouths are slow. To get information into a listener's head in a reasonable amount of time, a speaker can encode only a fraction of the message into words and must count on the listener to fill in the rest. But *inside a single head*, the demands are different. Air time is not a limited resource: different parts of the brain are connected to one another directly with thick cables that can transfer huge amounts of information quickly. Nothing can be left to the imagination, though, because the internal representations *are* the imagination.

We end up with the following picture. People do not think in English or Chinese or Apache; they think in a language of thought. This language of thought probably looks a bit like all these languages; presumably it has symbols for concepts, and arrangements of symbols that correspond to who did what to whom, as in the paint-spraying representation shown above. But compared with any given language, mentalese must be richer in some ways and simpler in others. It must be richer, for example, in

that several concept symbols must correspond to a given English word like *stool* or *stud*. There must be extra paraphernalia that differentiate logically distinct kinds of concepts, like Ralph's tusks versus tusks in general, and that link different symbols that refer to the same thing, like *the tall blond man with one black shoe* and *the man*. On the other hand, mentalese must be simpler than spoken languages; conversation-specific words and constructions (like *a* and *the*) are absent, and information about pronouncing words, or even ordering them, is unnecessary. Now, it could be that English speakers think in some kind of simplified and annotated quasi-English, with the design I have just described, and that Apache speakers think in a simplified and annotated quasi-Apache. But to get these languages of thought to subserve reasoning properly, they would have to look much more like each other than either one does to its spoken counterpart, and it is likely that they are the same: a universal mentalese.

Knowing a language, then, is knowing how to translate mentalese into strings of words and vice versa. People without a language would still have mentalese, and babies and many nonhuman animals presumably have simpler dialects. Indeed, if babies did not have a mentalese to translate to and from English, it is not clear how learning English could take place, or even what learning English would mean.

So where does all this leave Newspeak? Here are my predictions for the year 2050. First, since mental life goes on independently of particular languages, concepts of freedom and equality will be thinkable even if they are nameless. Second, since there are far more concepts than there are words, and listeners must always charitably fill in what the speaker leaves unsaid, existing words will quickly gain new senses, perhaps even regain their original senses. Third, since children are not content to reproduce any old input from adults but create a complex grammar that can go beyond it, they would creolize Newspeak into a natural language, possibly in a single generation. The twenty-first-century toddler may be Winston Smith's revenge.

The Media and the Campaign

Christopher Waddell and Christopher Dornan

Political parties invariably resent the coverage they receive from the media. They feel as though they are forced to fight election campaigns on two fronts, the first against their political opponents and the second against a press corps reflexively opposed to their ambitions for office. Now that the 2006 federal election is history, who has grounds to complain about how the media coverage played out?

Not the Conservative Party. For the most part, the press corps was impressed by the discipline of the Conservatives' campaign, so much so that three weeks into the contest many commentators wondered aloud why the superior Conservative effort had yet to gain traction with voters. Then the NDP released a letter it had received from the RCMP confirming a criminal investigation had been launched into leaks from the federal Department of Finance that may have been used for improper financial gain. The Conservatives had not been hammering the Liberals on the integrity issue — they judged that with the memory of the sponsorship scandal still fresh the Liberals' record on integrity would speak for itself — but the story could not help but play in their favour. That week, the first surges in Conservative support registered in the polls and the party went on to form the government.

The Conservative victory came neither because of the media coverage nor despite it. The Conservatives have no call to object to how the media covered their campaign.

The same is true of the Liberals. As infuriated as Liberal Party operatives may have been with the campaign coverage they received, it hardly mattered in the party's fortunes. Liberals complained that their party and its leader could not catch a break from the media. But the media did not make the Liberals' campaign hapless. They merely reported on its difficulties. There were simply too many missteps, and the Conservatives outmanoeuvred the Liberals at every turn. The seeds of the Martin defeat were sown long before the media started reporting an upturn in Conservative support right after the Christmas break. Media coverage was not a determining factor in how the Liberals fared.

The New Democrats were not happy with their media coverage either. They believed they were given short shrift in national media coverage, relegated to a sub-plot recognized only in passing. The NDP may well have been eclipsed in news coverage by the contest between the failing Liberals and the ascendant Conservatives, but the party remained a constant presence in the wings. If nothing else, the NDP put the prospect of strategic voting squarely on the agenda by appealing to skittish Liberal voters to "lend us your vote." And in the end, the New Democrats gained seats. Who is to say whether their media coverage helped them do so or blunted their chances of winning even more?

The Green Party, similarly, complained about being dismissed by the mainstream media. It was not accorded the same attention as the more established parties. Nonetheless, the media themselves made an issue of their own attention to the Greens. The party's exclusion from the leaders' debates, for example, triggered an automatic protest and an equally automatic news story about whether the Greens should be included. This provided an occasion for the media to point out how well the Greens had done in the previous election and that the Greens themselves were not without their internal party divisions. The Green Party, like the NDP, might protest its lack of prominence in the election news agenda, but its failure to win any seats was not a consequence of its treatment at the hands of the media.

Nor were the fortunes of the Bloc Québécois determined by the party's coverage. The Bloc won the lion's share of seats in Quebec. And yet the party was the author of its own misfortune. Overly confident too early in the contest — where could the threat to its candidates come from, given the implosion of Liberal support? — the BQ speculated about winning more than 50 percent of the Quebec vote in a federal election. Speculating on results is always a dangerous business for a political party, as it leaves it open to ridicule if the prediction doesn't come true.

It was an aspiration frustrated in part by the surprise victories of Conservative candidates in Quebec. At Christmas, no one expected the Conservatives to take a single seat in the province. And yet they took ten, and it was not the doing of the news media.

As a consequence, the only actors with cause to regret the media coverage of the 2006 election may be the news media themselves. At the time, they thought they were behaving responsibly in how they covered the campaign. In the aftermath, they may have their doubts.

The proper role of the news media in an election campaign is a delicate balancing act. On the one hand, they are obliged to provide a public platform whereby the political parties can put their respective policies before the electorate. It is not their place to hijack the contest by imposing their own agenda. At their best, they dutifully document the various parties' platforms and pronouncements, they cultivate interest in the course of the election on the part of the public, and

they moderate the debate with a view to informing the electorate as comprehensively as possible.

But this does not mean the news media should limit themselves to mere stenography. They may be the main conduits through which the politicians appeal to voters, but they should not be inert. Imperfectly, perhaps, the media are still the public's representatives during an election contest. It is within their mandate to pose questions to the politicians on the public's behalf — to raise issues of public interest and electoral consequence no matter that these might be discomfiting to the parties, each of which has a script to which it would prefer to hew and issues it would rather not address.

The Conservative strategy of releasing a policy announcement a day in the opening weeks of the election was not simply a device to methodically unveil the party's platform. It was a mechanism to seize control of the news agenda, to dominate the day-to-day coverage, and it was therefore a media management technique. Compelled by their own responsibilities to document each announcement as it came, the media as a result had few openings or opportunities to raise issues that were not on the Conservatives' playlist. The range of issues on which the party's social conservatism had in the past made many voters uneasy simply never arose with any prominence. Abortion, same-sex marriage, federal funding for the arts and culture, the future of the CBC, and so on — these were by and large absent concerns.

The Conservatives were aided in this regard by an incident on the first day of the campaign in which a reporter asked Stephen Harper "Do you love Canada?" Charitably, one might view the question as an awkward attempt to ask what version of Canada the Conservative leader imagined for the future, but it was seen at the time as the sort of ambush antagonism that gives journalism a bad name, implying as it did that Harper's policies amounted to an attack on all that the country holds dear. Even people who had no intention of voting for the Conservatives rolled their eyes in exasperation with the press. That put paid to any further impertinence on the part of the media, who henceforth merely reacted to campaign events rather than seize the lead in the electoral dance.

Ironically, then, what impressed the reporters covering the Conservative campaign — in particular the party's tight message discipline — was the very thing that neutralized the media, that made them bit players in the Conservatives' ultimately successful script for victory. In the main, the news media were even-handed and responsible in how they documented the course of the campaign. At the same time, they largely and inadvertently surrendered their role as autonomous agents.

The consequences of that became clear once the Conservatives assumed power. The new government's conduct toward the national press corps was an extension of its campaign strategy: the media were to be corralled, controlled, circumvented, and sidelined, just as the party's own members were to be strictly circumscribed in their dealings with the press. Some media access to ministers was restricted. The Prime Minister's handlers would determine who in the press corps could pose questions to the leader and under what conditions. Cabinet meetings would be held in secret. The press might not even be informed of visits by foreign heads of state.

All the elements of this approach have been tried by previous governments upon taking office to impose their own stamp on media relations, to avoid contradictions, and to keep everyone focused on the messages those in the Prime Minister's Office want delivered to Canadians. It sometimes works for a brief period of time but doesn't survive the ups and downs of a parliamentary session, the Commons question period, and the fact that government communications are too diverse to be controlled by any central organization. This attempt to keep the media subordinate is unlikely to work either. Politics is a turbulent business and managing the media is a mug's game. But for the Conservatives, at least, one of the lessons of the 2006 election was that the media *can* be played to electoral advantage.

Media complaints about this treatment left Canadians cold, as three months after the election opinion polls showed support for the new government at higher levels than the Conservatives received on election day. Nonetheless image is a crucial element of politics. While doing no immediate damage to Harper, if media relations becomes the first of many examples of centralization it could cumulatively threaten the credibility of the message Harper delivered during the campaign that he would run a different, less centrally controlled government than the Liberals.

The lack of public sympathy for media complaints may also reflect the degree to which some media predictions about the election were simply wrong. It had been a quarter of a century since Canadians last voted for a federal government in the middle of winter after a campaign that stretched over the Christmas–New Year's holiday. It had been almost as long since a campaign lasted fifty-six days. For the media as much as for the politicians, these were the initial challenges in the 2005–06 election campaign. No one could predict whether readers, listeners, and viewers would be interested in election news for that length of time or how much the weather might disrupt the campaign and the media's ability to cover it. There were fears that the weather and an uninterested electorate would conspire to keep voters at home, dropping turnout another step closer to only 50 percent of Canadians voting.

In the late November days leading up to the minority Liberal government's defeat in the House of Commons, the media predicted with seeming certainty that this would be the nastiest election campaign in Canadian history, full of personal attacks, and that the public would be very angry at having their holidays disrupted by electioneering. Politicians would pay the price. As it turned out, both predictions were wrong. Canadians were interested in the campaign from the start and even took heed of a key event that took place over the Christmas holidays that likely shaped the outcome: the NDP announcing that the RCMP would launch a criminal investigation into a possible leak from the office of Finance Minister Ralph Goodale of a government decision not to tax income trusts. Rather than being nasty, the 2005–06 election campaign was more about policy and less about personality than any campaign since the free trade election of 1988.

News Organizations and their Audiences

Throughout the campaign, Carleton University's School of Journalism and Communication and Decima Research Inc. conducted a series of Internet-based surveys, asking a sample of Canadians to complete a weekly emailed election questionnaire. In late November before the parliamentary defeat of the Liberals, Decima asked approximately twelve thousand members of the online eVox panel, which it uses for a range of email-based surveys, if they were planning to vote and wanted to be part of the election survey. The poll would track weekly changes in voters' attitudes over the course of the campaign about election issues, advertising, news coverage, and the performance of the media. Approximately nine thousand people agreed to participate. Between forty-five hundred and seven thousand responded to each weekly survey within seventy-two hours of receiving it.

The initial survey, between November 26 and December 1, established basic data about where Canadians get political news and what news organizations they would rely on during the campaign. Respondents could indicate as many different newspapers, networks, and channels as they wished. It was no surprise that television networks scored well, as that is how the majority of Canadians get their news. An almost equal number of people selected CTV and CBC television. Only the option of "your daily local newspaper" registered with more respondents, but this meant different papers according to where in Canada respondents lived. The importance of television as the dominant medium for campaign coverage is even more obvious when the responses naming CBC or CTV are combined with those mentioning cable news channels, CBC Newsworld, and CTV Newsnet.

Among francophones (largely but not exclusively in Quebec), television is even more important than in the rest of Canada as the primary election information source. One-third more people named one of the television networks than selected "your daily local newspaper."

More than one in three English Canadians (38 percent) outside Quebec said they would rely, but not exclusively, on CBC's main television newscast, *The National*, frequently or very frequently during the campaign. Albertans were the least likely to name *The National* (at 32 percent) and Atlantic Canadians the most (45 percent). Liberal (46 percent) and NDP voters (42 percent) were more likely than Conservative voters (33 percent) to say they would rely on *The National*. Along the same lines, 53 percent of those who say they are on the centre-left of the political spectrum were more likely to rely in part on *The National*. Its audience is slightly older and has higher incomes than the national average.

Similar numbers (38 percent) said they would rely on *CTV National News*. Slightly fewer British Columbia and Alberta residents than Central Canadians planned to rely on CTV, and CTV had a marginally larger audience in Ontario than CBC among survey respondents. Roughly equal percentages of Liberal and Conservative voters planned to rely on CTV, but fewer NDP voters were interested in CTV coverage. More people who described themselves in the centre and on the centre-right of the spectrum and more middle-income individuals planned to watch CTV than CBC.

The survey also found a significant share of the 26 percent who preferred *Global National* lived in B.C. and Alberta. Its newscast attracts a greater percentage of Conservative voters than supporters of either of the other parties. More Global viewers are female than male and they see themselves as more on the right and in the centre of the political spectrum.

The *Globe and Mail* was the leading newspaper, with 11 percent saying they would rely on it frequently or very frequently. The *Globe*'s audience for election coverage, more male than female and with higher incomes, spanned the political spectrum, but had slightly more readers who say they are left of centre than who say they are on the right. Almost half (46 percent) of those who named the *Globe* had at the campaign's start already decided how they would vote, with 47 percent choosing the Liberals, 25 percent Conservatives, and 13 percent NDP.

About half as many people (6 percent) planned to rely on the *National Post*. Its readers in the Carleton-Decima survey were more likely to be upper income and politically right of centre. More than half (55 percent) had already decided how they would vote, with 49 percent backing the Conservatives, 31 percent Liberals, and 13 percent NDP.

Almost one-quarter (22 percent) of those in the survey said they would rely in part on CBC Radio for campaign coverage. More of that group was male, upscale, and left of centre, and found in Atlantic Canada, Ontario, and B.C. The 13 percent of respondents who planned to rely on talk radio was predominantly male, older, and Conservative, and was composed of more decided than undecided voters.

The gap between television and newspapers was not as pronounced when people identified the single news organization they would rely on the most during the campaign.

CBC's *The National* and local dailies were tied at the top of the list with 13 percent each. *CTV National News* was cited as the single most relied upon news organization by 12 percent. CBC's program led CTV among men, Liberal and NDP voters, and in all regions except Ontario. CTV led very narrowly among women, in Ontario, and more clearly among Conservative voters. Internet news sites were next most frequently picked, selected by 10 percent. The *Global National* newscast and CBC Radio were each cited by 7 percent. In this survey, Global's audience is largest in B.C. and Alberta, and somewhat right of centre. Quebec residents were most likely to cite Radio-Canada's *Téléjournal* (23 percent), followed by local dailies at 15 percent, Internet news sites at 13 percent, and *La Presse* at 12 percent.

The choice of Internet news sites as the most important source for election coverage is remarkably high in this survey, almost equalling television. While there is no question that more and more people are getting their news from the Internet, the strong results for Internet news sites reflect the degree of Internet interest and sophistication among those responding to the survey.

Covering the Campaign

The length of the campaign was one factor influencing media coverage. Equally important for newspapers was the state of the long-running circulation war among the major dailies. The battle was at its height during the 2000 election, the *National Post*'s first federal campaign. Challenging the *Globe* for national newspaper supremacy, the *Post* matched its established rival almost story for story.

By the 2004 campaign the war was almost over, with the *Globe* proclaiming victory. The *Post* had been bought by CanWest and the new owners had cut staff and costs sharply to curtail losses. In 2004, the *Post* made no effort to match the range of the *Globe*'s coverage. That was still largely true in the 2005–06 campaign, even though the *Post* was in better shape than two years earlier. Its losses had stabilized and the paper was even hiring reporters, but it did not return to a head-to-head fight with the *Globe*. It was more selective in what it covered and how it went about doing so. It did not match the

number of features the *Globe* printed, the national scope of the *Globe*'s coverage, or the regular daily opinion polling that was a cornerstone of the *Globe*'s approach to this campaign.

The 2005–06 campaign lasted half as long again as the one in 2004. Predictably, the country's major newspapers all published many more stories this time around than in the thirty-six-day campaign in May–June 2004. The campaign also occurred during what is traditionally the slowest time of the year for news — December and January — which meant less competition from other news for space in papers or time on television.

The examination of newspaper coverage in this chapter builds on the studies done for *The Canadian General Election of 2000* (Dornan and Pyman) and *The Canadian Election of 2004* (Waddell). It is based on a database containing all campaign stories published in the *Globe and Mail* and the *Toronto Star* as they appeared in the Factiva electronic database from November 28, 2005, the day before the government fell, up to and including the published results of the election on January 24, 2006. The database also includes all election stories from the *National Post* in the FP Infomart electronic database between the same dates.

The *Globe* and *Post* both publish Monday to Saturday and the *Star* is a seven-days-a-week operation, but the *Globe* ran many more election stories than its competitors, just as in 2004.

Table 1 **Election stories**

	Globe	Post	Star
2000	764	710	522
2004	518	391	389
2006	978	796	779

Along with more stories came a shift in the type of stories carried by the three papers. For years, newspapers have struggled to respond to television as the primary source of news for Canadians. How can papers present fresh information in the morning, when their readers may have seen the same story on television the night before? That became an even larger problem with the rise of all-news cable channels in Canada that present news twenty-four hours a day. The all-news landscape changed in the summer of 2005, when the Canadian Radio-television and

Telecommunications Commission eased licence restrictions on CTV Newsnet. Whereas it had been restricted to providing only headline news, the new relaxed rules allowed it to compete directly with CBC Newsworld, which it did vigorously in this campaign. That not only put pressure on its TV competitor but also put more pressure on newspapers. Newspapers have responded to the immediacy of all-news television by shifting campaign coverage away from hard news. They have placed greater emphasis and prominence on columns and columnists that mix opinion and analysis, playing off the news and taking their readers beyond television's more immediate and terse hard news coverage. Newspaper editors and owners are betting that readers have already seen the facts on TV and are seeking context, depth, and analysis.

It has been easy for newspapers to make this shift, as the past several federal election campaigns have largely centred on personality rather than policy. Campaign strategy, advertising, media relations, and party war rooms that produce charges and counter-charges every campaign day — that kind of drama captivates reporters and columnists and makes for more colourful copy than policy differences between the competing parties.

This time, though, neither the media nor the other parties anticipated that from the outset the Conservatives would adopt a strategy that saw leader Stephen Harper announce a new policy every day and continue to do so well into January. His approach forced the media to cover this campaign differently. Newspaper and television reporters fight a daily battle for space and time for their stories with the pressure from editing desks always for shorter and tighter reports. When the campaign trail story became a new policy announcement every day, reporters had to devote time and space to details and background of the policy and its possible impact. They also needed to include a quotation or two from Harper and some specific policy reaction from other parties or interest groups. That frequently left no time or room for personality, strategy, or the mindless back and forth between leaders' tours that may have fascinated the media in the past but left the public cold.

Some of the announcements were unexpected, such as a commitment to cut the Goods and Services Tax (GST) by one percentage point, or a plan to pro-

vide tax relief for parents with children playing sports. The details of the Conservatives' proposal to provide $100 a month towards child care payments for all children under the age of six were likewise news. The Conservatives also made life easy for reporters on their leader's tour. Each announcement was simple and straightforward, with two or three central points that were easy to understand and readily explained to radio and television audiences and newspaper readers. The party restricted itself to a single announcement per day, and so that is what the media covered. By contrast, in the two weeks before the election the Liberals had flooded the country with spending announcements. That left them with nothing new to talk about once the campaign began. When the party began its policy announcements in January, they often came in flurries of two or three, which reduced their impact as reporters had trouble figuring out which was most important to highlight and found it equally tough to squeeze them all into their stories.

In response to the policy-driven Conservative campaign, newspapers adjusted their coverage balance to increase news and reduce columns and opinion. All three papers did so and devoted an almost identical share of coverage to news stories — one of many similarities in how they covered the campaign. The shift towards more news coverage also reflected the fact that newspapers have an advantage over television in a policy-driven campaign. Television cannot adequately present the details of policy announcements in a two-minute news report. It can just touch on the highlights. So anyone interested in the substance of policies had to read the papers or turn to Internet sources. The newspapers capitalized on the natural advantage of the print medium to flesh out and examine in detail the policies that surfaced in the campaign.

Table 2   **News stories (as a percentage of total number of stories)**

	Globe	Post	Star
2000	45	60	53
2004	47	40	55
2006	57	61	60

This change was least apparent in the *Toronto Star* because it had retained a stronger focus on news in past campaigns than the other two papers. News coverage jumped in the *Globe and Mail* but the most dramatic change was at the *National Post*. Job cuts there prior to 2004 meant fewer reporters, so the paper's columnists had been responsible for most of the coverage of that campaign. That also injected more opinion into the news pages of the paper, opinion that often reflected conservative viewpoints. By contrast, in the 2005–06 campaign, the *Post* followed the trend, devoting more space to news while columnists took a back seat. Of the three papers, the *Globe* remained the most heavily committed to columns and columnists.

Table 3 **Columns (as a percentage of total number of stories)**

	Globe	Post	Star
2000	32	21	28
2004	28	30	33
2006	25	22	20

All three papers printed more editorials about the campaign than they had in 2004. However, because all the papers had also increased the overall quantity of news, the proportion of coverage devoted to editorials actually decreased.

Table 4 **Editorials (as a percentage of total number of stories)**

	Globe	Post	Star
2000	5	7	9
2004	6	8	6
2006	5	5	5

None of the papers gave much space to the opinions of those not on their staff. Such a policy-intensive campaign would have been perfect for showcasing as wide a cross-section of views as possible on the policies proposed by the parties from such groups as business, social policy activists, the environmental movement, and foreign policy and defence advocates. As in 2004, the *Globe* gave the smallest share of its overall coverage to op-ed pieces, even though it publishes the most influential opinion page in the country.

Table 5 **Op-ed stories (as a percentage of total number of stories)**

	Globe	Post	Star
2000	7	8	1
2004	4	9	2
2006	4	6	6

Feature stories also played a less prominent role than they did in 2004 at both the *Globe* and the *Post*. Only the *Star* increased the share of coverage devoted to features from its 2004 levels.

Table 6 **Features (as a percentage of total number of stories)**

	Globe	Post	Star
2000	6	6	8
2004	15	13	4
2006	9	6	10

The most striking aspect of newspaper coverage is the degree to which all three papers made the same decisions about how to apportion their coverage between news, features, editorials, and columns. At a time when newspapers are losing readers to television and the Internet, none of the three was willing to take a chance in this campaign and do something dramatically different from its rivals. The lack of distinctiveness is obvious when comparing how the three papers allocated their coverage during this campaign.

Table 7 **Types of coverage (as a percentage of total coverage)**

	Globe	Post	Star
News	57.4	60.8	60.2
Editorial	4.7	5.4	4.6
Column	25.5	21.7	20.0
Op-ed	3.8	5.8	5.6
Feature	8.7	6.3	9.5

That uniformity even extended to the percentage of coverage devoted to each of the parties. All three papers paid greater attention to the Liberals than the Conservatives, even though in the second half of the campaign it was increasingly clear the Conservatives were going to form the next government. There were two minor anomalies: the Bloc received less coverage in the *Toronto Star*, as it wasn't running candidates where most *Star* readers lived, while the NDP did relatively better in the *Star*, in part reflecting the strength of the party in Toronto-area constituencies.

Table 8   **Party coverage (as a percentage of total coverage devoted to parties)**

	Globe	Post	Star
Liberal	42.8	43.8	44.6
Conservative	38.7	35.0	36.3
NDP	11.2	13.7	14.8
Bloc	5.5	5.4	2.9
Green	1.8	2.1	1.3

There were differences, though, in how the papers used their front pages. The *Globe* leaned towards the Liberals in the number of front-page stories it ran while the *Star* had slightly more Conservative stories than Liberal ones on its front page. There were an equal number of stories for each party on the *Post*'s front page. A good percentage of those stories at all three papers were negative rather than positive but at least the two parties appeared regularly on all three front pages. That's not true for the NDP, which complained with considerable justification that the media devoted much less time and space to its leader and its policies than to the other two parties.

Throughout the entire campaign, only two front-page headlines in the *Globe* mentioned the NDP. One on December 3 reported the decision of Canadian Auto Workers union president Buzz Hargrove to support Paul Martin and the Liberals instead of the New Democrats. The other, on December 12, stated "Liberals snatch NDP votes in Ontario; New Democrats' support level drops to single digits as Grits reach their highest mark since May." The NDP was furious about the headline, saying the story was flat out wrong. It took the *Globe* three days to admit the error. Even then it only ran a small and obtuse correction on page two that stated, "Figures for party support in Ontario were incorrect in a story published Monday. Poll respondents were asked which party had the most

momentum going into the Jan. 23 federal election as well as which party they would support. Those momentum numbers were wrongly cited as each party's level of support." The correction then noted the correct level of support for each party but did not state explicitly that there was no change in NDP support over the days in question. Angry with that delay in correcting the record, the NDP turned down an invitation to meet with the *Globe*'s editorial board in what became a campaign-long feud.

The New Democrats believed the *National Post*, the paper ideologically most distant from the NDP, actually gave it the most balanced coverage of the three papers. Front-page headlines support the NDP's view. The stories were not always favourable but at least the NDP appeared on the *Post*'s front page.

The *Globe*'s attention to the Bloc Québécois, even though very few of its readers could vote for the party, reflected both the paper's traditionally higher circulation in Quebec than either the *Post* or the *Star* and the fact that early in the campaign it appeared the Bloc might win the support of more than 50 percent of voters in Quebec, something no sovereigntist party had ever done.

Table 9   **Front-page stories (as a percentage of total election front-page stories)**

	Globe	Post	Star
Liberal	46.0	29.8	29.0
Conservative	36.8	29.8	33.9
NDP	0.0	5.3	1.6
Bloc	2.3	1.8	1.6
Green	0.0	1.8	0.0

The editorial pages of the three papers were more balanced in their treatment of the three national parties. The *Globe* paid more attention to the Conservatives than it did to the Liberals; and whereas in 2004 it had endorsed the Liberals, this time it called on its readers to support the Conservatives on the grounds that it was time for a change. Both the *National Post* and the *Toronto Star* stuck with their 2004 picks. The *Post* again backed the Conservatives while the *Star* as always called for another Liberal government.

Table 10 **Editorials (as a percentage of total editorials during the campaign)**

	Globe	Post	Star
Liberal	30.4	34.9	22.2
Conservative	37.0	27.9	19.4
NDP	4.3	7.0	8.3
Bloc	2.2	0.0	0.0
Green Party	0.0	0.0	0.0

There were some differences in the issues each paper chose to highlight and some things each chose to forego. For instance "reality checks" — a feature of past campaigns in which party statements and policies are tested against the facts of an issue — virtually disappeared from the three papers, although they remained a staple of television coverage.

The *Globe* and Mail

The *Globe* anchored its campaign coverage with a separate theme page each day of the week, usually on page five. On Monday it was campaign issues, Tuesday youth and media, Wednesday behind-the-scenes activities, Thursday belonged to candidates, Friday to strategy, and Saturday was the week in review. It was a smart innovation and effective as a daily focus for coverage. A diary of interesting election snippets or a campaign notebook usually filled out the page.

With many predicting a close result, the *Globe* also reported weekly on the views of individual undecided voters across the country, something it had not done in 2004. The other main focus for the *Globe* and the other papers was candidates. In an era of complaints about campaign coverage being too preoccupied with party leaders, the *Globe* devoted about 10 percent of its coverage to individual candidates and interesting races. As in 2004 the anchor for this was columnist Roy MacGregor, who travelled from coast to coast, profiling candidates and bringing a human dimension to elections and politics.

The largest chunk of the *Globe*'s news coverage was directed at party and campaign strategy. The other papers did the same thing. Each devoted almost one-fifth of their news coverage to strategy

issues. Ethics received more attention in the *Globe* than in either the *Post* or *Star*, as did federal-provincial relations and Quebec sovereignty. That was consistent with the *Globe* paying more attention to the Bloc Québécois than either the *Post* or the *Star*.

In the months after the 2004 election the *Globe* launched a separate British Columbia section only in papers distributed in that province. Reporters from the paper's Vancouver bureau filed forty-seven stories during the 2005–06 campaign that appeared only in that section, beyond the British Columbia stories that ran across the country in the paper's national edition. As a result, West Coast *Globe* readers received much more local coverage of issues such as the Chinese head tax and B.C. candidates and races than they had in the 2004 campaign.

The National Post

Almost 15 percent of the *Post*'s coverage centred on the leaders, compared to 11 percent at the *Star* and 10 percent at the *Globe*. Supplementing that, the *Post* injected some humour and coverage of off-beat issues with columns that almost daily asked the leaders questions that were often frivolous. An equally large chunk of the *Post*'s coverage was devoted to candidates, anchored by the paper's Ottawa columnist John Ivison, who played a similar role to Roy MacGregor's at the *Globe*, travelling the country, profiling candidates and close races. Consistent with the paper's conservative leanings, the *Post* had more than double the percentage of news stories on taxes, especially the Conservative pledge to cut the GST, than did the *Globe*. It also had a larger percentage of stories on federal budget issues than the *Globe*, but the *Globe* devoted a greater share of its space to Canada–U.S. matters than did the *Post*. None of the papers paid much attention to any other foreign policy issues, matching the way the parties ignored foreign policy during the campaign. The *Post* had a smaller share of social policy stories than either the *Globe* or the *Star*, while all three papers almost completely ignored the same-sex marriage issue.

The Toronto *Star*

The *Star* is always true to its Toronto roots, championing urban and social issues, and that was no different this time. The paper paid more attention than the others to candidates, although it concentrated almost exclusively on those running in the Greater Toronto Area. Of the three papers, the *Star* had the smallest percentage of stories on ethics issues and devoted only about two-thirds as much coverage as the *Post* did on the leaders. Campaign strategy was also slightly less prevalent in *Star* stories than in the other papers. More *Star* stories than *Globe* or *Post* stories dealt with youth and youth voting issues. The *Star* also paid more attention to voting rules and how to vote than the others. Not surprisingly, urban issues were a *Star* preoccupation, particularly crime, gun control, and handguns.

The core of the *Star*'s analytical coverage came from highly experienced columnists James Travers, Chantal Hebert, Graham Fraser, and Thomas Walkom, all of whom have been covering elections for at least twenty years. That experience showed in the sophistication of their analysis and commentary. The paper frequently used its Ottawa bureau chief Susan Delacourt as analyst and explainer of campaign developments under the tag line "Campaign Decoder." It was an effective variant of the now abandoned reality check concept.

Television

Just as the parties during an election campaign are locked into a contest with one another for voters' support, so too are news organizations locked into a contest with one another for readers, viewers, and listeners. It is in their interests, therefore, to engage the public in the election, particularly since covering elections in this vast country is an expensive proposition.

Noteworthy during this election were the campaign coverage innovations on the part of the networks to kindle viewer interest in the contest. In addition to the standard reportage from the campaign trail, the panels of commentators, the in-studio arguments between party operatives, and the town hall–style meetings with party leaders, all the networks resorted to unconventional features aimed at capturing eyeballs. CTV, for example, deployed six-

year-old Daniel Cook — star of his own television program aimed at the primary school set — as a campaign correspondent. The leader in campaign coverage theatrics, however, was CBC's *The National*, which introduced a range of features designed to make the election fun. These included:

- a segment in which candidates pitched their parties to undecided voters via "speed-dating" (also done by CTV);
- a regular "Taxi Chat" segment in which candidates got behind the wheel of a cab while a camera recorded their encounters with the members of the public they picked up as fares;
- the use of comedians — the Toronto comic Sean Cullen and a Winnipeg group called the Content Factory — to inject levity into the coverage;
- a regular segment called "Campaign Confidential" in which an anonymous former campaign insider (eventually revealed to be strategist Rick Anderson) offered his commentary on the contest as it unfolded;
- a regular "Road Trips" segment in which reporter Mark Kelly accompanied members of the electorate as they visited distant parts of the country: a voter from Montreal, for example, encountering the political culture of Alberta; and
- a feature in which the parties were given the opportunity and the airtime to produce their own news accounts of the campaign events of that day.

No doubt some viewers found these innovations frivolous, but in the main it was gratifying to see a little creativity being applied to the coverage. Elections are serious affairs, but that does not mean that the media should comport themselves at all times in deadly earnest.

Political Coverage — The Broader Context

Polls, Polls, Polls

Despite regular criticisms by academics and even some journalists that the media rely too much on public opinion poll results to shape how they cover campaigns, polls continued to play a central role. This was true for all media, even though the CBC proclaimed as it did in 2004 that it did not commission polls itself or report directly on other poll results. In truth that meant the CBC wouldn't report on polls unless they were interesting. When polls suggested public opinion was starting to shift towards the Conservatives just after the new year, the CBC reported and pursued that story just as aggressively as all the other news organizations.

There was a polling innovation in 2004, the daily tracking poll conducted by SES Research for the Canadian Public Affairs Channel (CPAC). The network and SES did it again just as successfully in this campaign. Each day at 2:00 p.m., CPAC placed the results of the previous day's polling of four hundred Canadians on its website and reporters logged on to get the latest update. It was the main topic of reporter conversation on the campaign trail once each day's numbers were released. Who was up and down on a daily basis framed how the media viewed and reported each party's campaign. CPAC's daily tracking poll merged the results of the previous three days' polling, dropping the oldest day as each new day was added. The media's faith in the accuracy of this poll was no doubt bolstered by the fact that the final SES results in 2004 were closest among all pollsters to the actual election results.

The *Globe and Mail* adopted a similar approach for this campaign, abandoning weekly polls for a daily tracking poll published in the paper. It was conducted by the Strategic Counsel, with former Progressive Conservative pollster and Strategic Counsel executive Allan Gregg as the spokesperson and analyst. With the Liberals leading and Conservatives showing no sign of movement before Christmas despite their daily policy announcements, the tracking poll wasn't featured prominently in the *Globe*'s coverage but it was there every day at the top of the rotating feature page. The tracking poll results moved into the spotlight in early January when they began to detect Conservative momentum, as the party moved past the Liberals both nationally and in Quebec. That was a major surprise, as Bloc Québécois voters were moving to the Conservatives, dashing the Bloc's dream of finally winning the support of 50 percent of Quebecers for a sovereigntist party in an election. In the final ten days, poll results not only drove *Globe* coverage, they were featured in front-page headlines and created controversy.

On January 16 the *Globe* announced in a front-page headline, "Tories enter home stretch just shy of majority, poll finds." The story stated that the Conservatives had the support of 40 percent of Canadians and had opened a thirteen-point lead over the Liberals. Two days later and just five days before voting, the paper reported the gap had widened to seventeen points — 41 percent to 24 percent. No other polling firm gave the Conservatives that much support or such a substantial lead over the Liberals. Even though differing methodologies used by individual companies makes it risky to compare results of polls done by separate firms, the *Globe*'s numbers seemed out of whack. Even corporate cousin CTV played down these results in its national nightly newscast, apparently fearing it was a rogue poll, the one in twenty that does not fall within the usual polling margin of error.

Then, as tracking poll results showed the Conservatives falling back to levels of support that other polling firms believed they had never exceeded, *Globe* coverage proclaimed the Liberals were narrowing the gap opened by the Conservatives. On January 20, the top of the paper's front page bluntly stated "Harper's lead takes a hit," noting that the gap was now 37 to 28 percent — much closer to the results other pollsters had shown all along. It was also a margin other polling companies believed had been relatively constant during the campaign's final week. The way the *Globe* treated the poll left a crucial question unanswered. Were the Liberals repeating the last weekend comeback that gave them a minority government in 2004, or did the *Globe* proclaim Harper's lead had taken a hit simply to avoid admitting its earlier headlines and polling results were wrong? Some viewed it even more cynically as either an attempt to scare people into voting Liberal to avoid a Conservative majority government or the result of having a Conservative pollster doing the polling. Neither was a credible complaint. The apparent surge in Conservative support seems more likely to have been an error in methodology under the pressure of conducting a large number of telephone interviews every night.

The last week's shenanigans highlighted how much the *Globe* built its coverage around poll results. Approximately 18 percent of the paper's front-page stories during the campaign dealt with polls or polling. That was significantly more than on the front pages of either the *National Post*, which used the *Globe*'s former polling partner Ipsos-Reid, or the *Toronto Star*, which used Ekos Research. Each devoted only about 11 percent of its front-page stories to polls and polling results. (See Chapter Ten.)

The *Star* followed the traditional once every week or ten days approach to polling through the first half of the campaign. But in the campaign's last two weeks, it matched the *Globe*'s daily tracking polls with its own. Ekos Research made up to five hundred calls a night, turning that night's numbers around for the next morning's paper. Every day reporters compared the *Globe* and *Star* results with those from SES/CPAC. The fluctuations in daily results revealed some of the methodological difficulties in turning around large tracking polls every night for morning newspapers. There is no time to call back people in the original sample selected at random who don't answer the phone, so others are added to make up the total, and that can skew the results. First edition deadlines and the three-hour time difference to British Columbia also meant the West Coast was probably underrepresented in most nights' results. Results also bounced up and down a great deal from night to night, making it hard to identify anomalies.

There had been concern about possible polling errors earlier in the campaign. On January 10, the *National Post* reported that Ekos, the *Star*, and *La Presse* had delayed publishing the results of a weekend poll that showed a surprising double-digit jump in support for the Conservatives because they were concerned about its accuracy. They added seven hundred calls to the original five hundred that had turned up a remarkable spike in Conservative support. The extra calls confirmed the initial sample's findings. The tide was turning towards the Conservatives and quickly.

While polls track changes in party support, it is much more difficult to figure out what impact poll results during a campaign may have on voting intentions. Voters know the polls exist, as 91 percent of those in the Decima-Carleton survey said they had noticed media coverage of opinion poll results. Almost half (49 percent) of the 4,972 people who returned email questionnaires between January 13 and 15 thought there was about the right amount of poll coverage in the media, while 41 percent said there was too much. Those who describe themselves on the left were more likely to think poll coverage

was excessive than those on the right. Many of those surveyed were also quick to discount any impact of poll coverage. Slightly more than half, 53 percent, of the survey's respondents said reading or hearing about poll results in the news has no impact on which party they will support.

However, opinion polls may contribute to some strategic voting. With the Conservatives leading in polls and an Ontario sample that was evenly split between Liberal and Conservative supporters, 19 percent of undecided voters said the poll results made them more likely to vote Liberal while only 11 percent said they were more likely to vote Conservative based on polls reported in the media.

Playing the Seat Projection Game

In the 2004 campaign, the major news organizations took their poll results and used them to project how many seats each party would win on election day. They were wrong: the results failed to match the predictions. The seat projection models in 2004 were based on the assumption that Progressive Conservative and Canadian Alliance voters from 2000 would all vote for the new Conservative Party in 2004. Having been burned once, the media were not keen to risk such predictions again.

Ironically the seat projection models would have worked much better in this election, as the same parties were running in 2006 as ran in 2004. But voter turnout was the potential spoiler this time around. The last winter election highlights the potential problem. In May 1979, 76 percent of Canadians voted, giving Joe Clark and the Conservatives a minority government. In the election the following February that returned a Liberal majority under Pierre Trudeau, winter weather meant that turnout fell to 69 percent. If the 2004 summer and 2006 winter election followed that pattern, turnout would drop to about 54 percent from the 61 percent of voters who went to the polls in 2004. The possibility of a seven percentage point drop in turnout when less than five percentage points separated first and second in more than fifty seats in 2004 made seat projections in this campaign an extremely risky business. News organizations did not want to be embarrassed two elections in a row. That was a smart call. As it developed, voter turnout would have undermined any seat projections but not the way many had anticipated. Turnout on January 23 was 65 percent, four percentage points higher than in 2004, and no model could have predicted which party those extra voters would support.

Matching its aggressive use of opinion poll results, the *Globe and Mail* was more adventurous on seat projections than its competitors. A two-line headline across the width of the front page on January 13 proclaimed "Pollster's seat projection puts Harper on the cusp of a majority." Almost all of the thirteen inches of the story on the front page highlighted the inexact nature of the seat projection game. It then continued without missing a beat in deciding that "with speculation focused on whether the Conservatives could form a majority government, the *Globe and Mail* has opted to publish the numbers based on the Strategic Counsel's polls." It was a questionable decision followed the next week by the prominent coverage given first to the poll that found the huge lead for the Conservatives and then to the Liberals apparently reducing that advantage. The final ten days of an election campaign is not the time to splash a story across a front page that could most charitably be described as only interesting if true.

Old Habits Die Slowly

Two other disturbing trends in recent political coverage also played a role in this campaign — the use of anonymous quotes and selective advance "leaks" of pending policy announcements, with the latter coming back to haunt the Liberals.

The reliance by political reporters on anonymous quotes has reached epidemic proportions in newspapers, and these dubious quotes appeared regularly in all three papers during the campaign. The use of unnamed sources and anonymous quotes has been blamed for a steady decline in media credibility in the United States, forcing leading news organizations such as the *New York Times*, the *Washington Post*, and the *Los Angeles Times* to introduce policies that limit the use of quotes from unnamed people. In Canada the media appear not to be concerned about the degree to which they encourage negative or derogatory attacks on politicians and others by protecting the identity of those who make unsubstantiated allegations.

In this campaign, the *Globe and Mail* ran a front-page story on January 10 by the paper's senior political reporter, Jane Taber, and reporter Bill Curry that was critical of the Liberal campaign. The story included direct and indirect quotes attributed variously to three different unnamed candidates, a veteran Liberal, a Martinite, some Liberal staffers, another Liberal staff member, some Ontario candidates, and a senior Liberal. Heritage Minister Liza Frulla, defending the campaign, appeared in paragraph twenty as the first named person in the story. While that was the most flagrant abuse, all three papers regularly included quotes from unnamed people in their stories. Readers had no idea who these people were, what axes they had to grind, or even whether they were fictions designed to allow reporters to inject their own comments into their stories. All the parties were victims of these media smears.

The Liberals also discovered they could no longer count on the media management strategy they had perfected during years in government. The Liberals took advantage of competition between news organizations to be first with news by providing advance information about upcoming policy announcements to selected television and newspaper reporters, allowing them to claim they had received "leaks" of government plans. Of course the leaks were carefully designed to highlight whatever aspects of any planned announcement the government wanted to emphasize. The media were too frequently willing accomplices in advancing the government's agenda.

The Liberals found themselves on the defensive early in this campaign, as they were unprepared for the daily Conservative policy announcements. They mistakenly believed that Canadians would start paying attention only after the holidays but realized they had to respond after more than a week of Conservatives grabbing the headlines. So they tried out one of their old media management tricks. On December 8 the newspapers all contained stories with selected details of a handgun ban Paul Martin would announce the next day in Toronto in response to a series of murders in the city. The "leak" worked just as it had when the Liberals were in government, giving the proposed ban two days of publicity. First came the pre-announcement story with officially approved highlights of what was going to be announced without any reaction, and then the second day's stories featured the actual announcement and reaction.

Things did not turn out as well when the party returned to the same media management strategy in early January. Resuming the campaign after New Year's, the Liberal campaign told reporters that Martin would deliver a major lunchtime speech in Winnipeg on January 3 to highlight Liberal values, co-ordinated with new television advertisements. It was all designed to kick off what Liberals believed was the real campaign. The speech was well received and initially reported, but later that day the campaign team heard rumours the Conservatives would announce the following morning a promise to repeal the $975 fee charged to immigrants. The Liberals responded by leaking that night their own hastily conceived plan to do the same thing. The Liberal immigration story made the front pages the next morning, reducing the coverage of the Conservative announcement that day but also obliterating coverage of Martin's speech and undermining the advertising strategy. They had been too smart by half and scooped themselves. It was not a good start to part two of the campaign.

Two days later Canadian Press ran what seemed to be a real leak, stating the Liberals would reveal the next day a plan to offer first- and final-year undergraduate university students free tuition. The story caught the Liberal communications team off guard, and they would only tell reporters on the Martin plane that the story was not entirely correct. That refusal to confirm the story and provide advance details of the next day's announcement led to heated confrontations with reporters on the tour. A bizarre series of stories followed in which reporters and columnists speculated on the possibility that a mole inside the Liberal campaign was leaking campaign announcements to the media and, improbably, to the Conservatives. No reporter ever presented any evidence to substantiate this assertion, but that did not stop media across the country speculating about the prospect for several days.

This all came as opinion polls picked up growing support for the Conservatives and that, combined with the troubles of the Liberal campaign, began to dominate media coverage. The campaign team had not helped its cause by delaying policy announcements until the second half of the campaign and then releasing them in clusters, rather than following the Conservatives' lead, perfected in December, of simple single daily announcements. The Liberal announcements were complicated and hard to distinguish from the flurry of spending announcements made in the two weeks before the campaign began. Reporters did not know what was new and what had been announced before so they decided to ignore much of it. Besides, with polls showing the Liberal support falling and Conservative support growing, particularly in Quebec, it was easier to ask questions about campaign strategy and fortunes. That was the way the last few campaigns had been covered by the media. Reporters and columnists were back on the ground many found more familiar, talking tactics, strategy, and personality — and demanding that politicians react to statements by another leader or anyone else for that matter. This kind of reporting required less research than trying to understand and explain complex policy proposals.

A perfect example was the day of the Liberal tuition announcement. Filing for *CTV National News* that night, Ottawa bureau chief Robert Fife, who had been in the midst of the leak fight on the plane the day before, ignored the details of the announcement completely in his story. Instead he focused on verbal stumbling in Martin's presentation, the small number of people in the room watching the Liberal leader speak, and criticism of the state of the Liberal campaign. The CBC television story that evening provided some of the details of the tuition policy, but in the days that followed CTV coverage of the Liberals, viewed through the same lens of the daily poll results it shared with the *Globe and Mail*, continued to ignore the substance of whatever Martin was saying on the campaign trail. Night after night CTV coverage of the Liberals focused on strategy and tactics, delivering a harshly negative impression of the state of the party's campaign and the effectiveness of its leader while ignoring its platform proposals. It was a theme other news organizations picked up in the campaign's final ten days. By then, much of the media had concluded that Martin was likely to lose the election, and whatever he was saying at this point was of minimal importance.

The Public Knows Best

Public reaction to the televised leaders' debates is an excellent demonstration of the gap that exists between how reporters view elections and what interests the public. In this campaign there were two sets of debates — the first pair in mid-December in Vancouver and the second in Montreal two weeks before voting day. The debate format in 2004 had quickly devolved into a two-hour, four-person, non-stop shouting match, interrupted by the occasional question. It was widely criticized. Those "debates" looked particularly bad when compared with the civilized and informative series of debates between George W. Bush and John Kerry in the U.S. presidential campaign in the fall of 2004. The television network organizers of the 2005–06 Canadian debates responded by introducing a much more rigid format. Each leader would answer specific questions directed to him, and then the others leaders could briefly comment, within the limits of a strict time schedule. While each leader was speaking, the others had to remain silent. There would be no verbal free-for-alls.

Most reporters and commentators instantly concluded as soon as the first two-hour session ended that the new format was a loser. They pushed the leaders in the post-debate scrums to agree that the event was boring. The leaders disagreed. In the process reporters revealed the degree to which they were out of touch with the opinions of Canadians. The Carleton-Decima survey discovered after the first set of debates on December 15–16 that almost half (45 percent) of those surveyed thought the new format was an improvement over the format of the 2004 debates while only 23 percent thought it was worse. That wasn't true in Quebec, where only one-quarter of those surveyed liked the new approach while 42 percent found it worse. Nationally, support for the new format was consistent across the ideological spectrum of voters while slightly more women than men preferred it.

Additional questions in the survey about which network Canadians chose to watch the debates backed up earlier findings about the ideological differences between each network's viewers. CBC debate viewers were more likely to be on the left of centre while a greater share of CTV and Global viewers leaned to the right. CTV and Global also had more female than male viewers. CBC had a larger male than female audience.

Ideological differences in audiences also emerged when decided voters for each party were asked which single news organization they relied on the most to help them reach conclusions about the debates. Liberals and New Democrats turned more

to CBC television and radio for debate analysis while Conservative voters were more likely to rely on CTV, local talk radio, and the Internet. Among newspapers, Liberals and New Democrats more often selected the *Globe and Mail* while Conservatives looked to the *National Post*. In Quebec, Radio-Canada/RDI was selected by 30 percent of Bloc Québécois voters and TVA/LCN was chosen by 28 percent of those who would vote for the Bloc.

Table 11 **Main media source for debate conclusions (percentage of each party's decided voters)**

	Liberal	Conservative	NDP	BQ
CBC TV/Newsworld	25	15	26	1
CTV/Newsnet	18	23	13	-
Global	7	7	8	-
Globe and Mail	4	2	3	-
National Post	1	3	-	-
CBC Radio	3	2	8	-
Local talk radio	0	6	2	-
Internet	4	7	2	-

The survey also found almost one-third of those responding did not consult the media at all in reaching their conclusions about the debate. Instead they relied on their own perceptions from watching the event.

Table 12 **Most influential factor in shaping debate conclusions (percentage)**

The debates themselves	31
Newspapers the day after	11
Immediate post-debate TV analysis	8
TV newscasts that night	8
All-news channels	4
Internet news sites	4
Internet blogs	1

Backing the Blackout

In 2006, election rules once again prevented news organizations from broadcasting or publishing any results until polls closed in the region of the country where the broadcast would be seen or heard. Internet news sites were prohibited from reporting results from anywhere in the country until the last polls closed in British Columbia at 10:00 p.m. EST, and satellite TV signals originating in Canada faced the same restrictions. Following the 2000 election, Paul Bryan, who ran a B.C.–based website, was charged by police with violating the Elections Act when he posted Eastern Canadian election results on his site before the polls had closed in B.C. He was acquitted prior to the 2004 election and that temporarily killed the blackout. An appeal court reversed the original acquittal, bringing the blackout back for 2006. That decision was appealed to the Supreme Court of Canada and a group of news organizations went to the Supreme Court asking for a quick hearing of the case prior to election day that might end the blackout. The Court, however, refused to juggle its hearing schedule to accommodate the media.

Almost one-third of those in a Decima-Carleton email survey in late December supported an end to the media blackout. In British Columbia almost half of those surveyed supported it. Across the country one-quarter of the 6,380 people questioned said they would take steps through websites, blogs, emails, and text and instant messaging systems to circumvent the blackout and get results before their polls closed. Those potential lawbreakers included 35 percent of B.C. respondents and 40 percent of those surveyed in the Vancouver area. One-third of those on the right but only one-quarter of those on the left said they would try to get around the blackout. That suggests the blackout is a bigger issue for small-*c* conservatives than small-*l* liberals.

Siding with the Winner

The Carleton-Decima survey also asked Canadians both early and later in the campaign whether they thought the coverage provided by various news organizations showed bias and which party they thought most journalists covering the campaign wanted to form the next government.

The questions were asked between December 7 and 9, before the first set of debates and with the Liberals holding a steady lead in published public opinion poll results. While a majority said either they could detect no leanings or they were unsure, 29 percent believed the *National Post* leaned towards the Conservative party, while 26 percent

believed CBC television leaned towards the Liberals and 22 percent believed CBC radio had the same tendencies. Only 4 percent thought CBC television leaned towards the Conservatives and 3 percent had that same view of CBC Radio.

In Quebec a similar majority were unsure or could not detect any leanings towards a specific party, but 29 percent believed Radio-Canada and *La Presse* both favoured the Liberals, while 26 percent thought TVA leaned towards the Bloc Québécois.

At the same time in early December, 40 percent of those surveyed believed that most journalists covering the campaign wanted the Liberals to form the next government, while only 15 percent believed most journalists wanted a Conservative victory. As the table indicates, those who describe themselves on the right of the political spectrum and Conservative voters were the most convinced that journalists were Liberal supporters.

The survey also asked whether respondents thought media coverage of each of the leaders had been too positive, too negative, or struck about the right balance. Opinion was most divided about Conservative Leader Stephen Harper and Liberal Leader Paul Martin.

The survey posed the same questions again between January 13 and 15. At this point in the campaign, the opinion polls showed a solid Conservative lead and the media were already speculating on the possibility of a Harper majority government. Opinion about media bias among the same group of people quizzed in December matched the change in opinion poll results. Now 40 percent said that most journalists wanted the Conservatives to win while only 19 percent thought most journalists wanted a Liberal victory. Those on the left were most likely to say most journalists wanted the Conservatives to win.

Perceptions about how the media treated the two main party leaders had also sharply changed. Now twice as many people (40 percent versus 19 percent in December) believed that media coverage of Paul Martin was overly negative. That view was strongest in British Columbia (47 percent) and weakest in Alberta (32 percent). Almost half as many (11 percent in mid-January versus 19 percent in December) now believed media coverage of the Liberal leader was overly positive. Views had also flipped on Stephen Harper. Almost twice as many as in December (27 percent versus 16 percent) now considered coverage of him as overly positive, but there was only a slight drop in the number who now viewed coverage of the Conservative leader as overly negative. On both occasions more than three-quarters (77 percent) of those surveyed believed coverage of New Democratic Party Leader Jack Layton struck about the right balance.

Conclusion

If audience satisfaction is the main determinant of success then the media did well in the 2006 election. In the campaign's second week, almost three-quarters of those responding to the Carleton-Decima survey said the media had done a good or excellent job covering the campaign. Those who planned to vote for the Conservatives were least likely to endorse the quality of media coverage, but 70 percent of even this group said coverage was good or excellent. Overall opinion had not changed among the entire group when they were asked the same questions as the campaign entered its final week. This time 75 percent viewed campaign coverage as good or excellent. However, the views of Conservatives had changed. With the party looking like a winner, 80 percent of Conservative supporters viewed the media's performance as good or excellent. It was a perfect example of the degree to which the media's performance in election campaigns is judged through partisan eyes.

There is a good explanation of public satisfaction with campaign coverage in 2005–06. The Liberal defeat in Parliament ended a minority government in which the antics of all the parties and the media coverage of those antics alienated many Canadians. Non-stop allegations of sleaze and scandal, name-calling, political manoeuvring, and backstabbing reduced parliamentary proceedings to the level of schoolyard bickering. That's what the media covered day after day. For many Canadians that's what political reporting and politics had become. It left them cold and they stopped listening, watching, and reading. Had the 2006 election been a nasty, aggressive slanging match it is unlikely that the campaign coverage would have received such positive reviews.

Instead the political players dropped the single-minded devotion to scandal they had demonstrated in Parliament over the previous eighteen months and talked policy day after day. This caught the Liberals completely off guard and forced the media to cover issues and policies. That change from concentrating on theatrics to focusing on substance captured the attention of Canadians in December. It also caught the Liberals and even the media by surprise. The predicted antagonism over a Christmastime election never materialized and the public turned out to be wide awake, not dozing off, during the campaign's first four weeks.

It was only in the campaign's final ten days that the pre-election media focus on personality and charges and counter-charges returned when the Conservatives ended their policy announcements. They had concluded, correctly, that they had said enough to get elected if they made no big mistakes in the final few days.

Even though the public was generally very satisfied with the 2005–06 election campaign coverage, there remain issues for the media to ponder. The use and misuse of public opinion data remains the largest concern. News organizations are continually searching for new gimmicks to promote the distinctiveness of their campaign coverage in a very competitive market where the Internet increasingly is crowding newspapers, radio, and television. That led directly to the seat projection debacle in 2004 and the controversies surrounding the accuracy of daily tracking polls in 2006. Both of these undermined rather than enhanced the media's credibility with the public. The parties shape their campaigns around their own polling, so the media needs to be polling as well to understand campaign decisions. However, poll results should be just one element of a news organization's campaign coverage strategy. Instead they have become the prism through which all campaign events are reported and analyzed, threatening public confidence in campaign coverage because polls are sometimes wrong.

Then there is the matter of sameness of coverage. The future of newspapers is being called into question by television and the Internet, which with their ability to deliver news instantly can steal readers. That should be a reason for each paper to be distinctive, to take different angles on stories, and to find different approaches designed to give the paper a clear identity that will build a loyal readership. Instead, the overwhelming impression of campaign coverage in the *Globe and Mail*, the *National Post*, and the *Toronto Star* is uniformity. All three papers covered the same issues the same way, leaving the impression that they are collectively interchangeable rather than individually essential. That's not a good strategy for survival.

This was also the first campaign in several in which newspapers increased their news coverage and reduced the amount of attention given to columns and opinion. Substance and issues, not superficiality and impressions, dominated newspaper, radio, and television reporting of the 2006 election and Canadians liked that. This was also the first election since 1988 — also an issues-based campaign about free trade with the United States — in which voter turnout did not drop. It rose by four percentage points over the turnout in 2004 to 64.9 percent of eligible voters. That is enough to argue that an election campaign where the media devoted more time and space to issues rather than personalities and concentrated on news rather than opinion may be the long-sought antidote to growing apathy about politics and public policy. It is an intriguing theory for the media and the parties to test when Canadians next go to the polls.

Among francophones (largely but not exclusively in Quebec), tele-vision is even more important than in the rest of Canada as the primary election information source. One-third more people named one of the television networks than selected "your daily local newspaper."

Epilogue: Reflections, Regrets, and Reconsiderations

Theodore C. Sorensen

"Do you ever tire of talking about John F. Kennedy?" I am sometimes asked. "No," I reply, "not as long as you do not tire of asking."

My eleven years with JFK were unquestionably the cornerstone of my professional life; and the cornerstone of our relationship was mutual trust. JFK brought me into his inner circle, confiding in me secrets that—had I discussed them with others—might have done serious harm to his political career, his public image, or perhaps his marriage. Noting my role and relationship with him, some have sought to replicate it. Decades after I left the White House, President Clinton's indefatigable press secretary Mike McCurry told me: "Everyone who comes to Washington wants to be you." I have heard such sentiments more than once. It is flattering, but what they really want is to work for John F. Kennedy.

Jackie once told a reporter that I was like "a little boy in so many ways . . . he hero worships Jack." She was right; he was my hero. My loyalty was often called single-minded, and the most frequently quoted quip in the press was "When Jack's injured, Ted bleeds." To a considerable extent I often judged others, including journalists and biographers, based not on what they said about me, but on whether they fully, favorably, and accurately reported JFK's role, his accomplishments, and his contributions.

I do not take seriously those scholars who cite me as an example of an over-powerful presidential aide who had unaccountable influence. I made no decisions and wielded no dangerous power of any kind, less probably than Harry Hopkins, Sherman, Adams, or Karl Rove. Moreover, my views were wholly compatible with those principles for which John F. Kennedy was elected and revered, especially peace around the world and justice here at home. To the extent that my suggestions, advice, and opinions influenced his decisions, I am proud as well as grateful. The world needs not only inspired leaders, but people to advise and assist them. I never confused which of us was the elected leader and which was the assistant. I understood the difference: advisors advise; assistants assist; counselors counsel; but ultimately, decisions are choices that only a president can and should make.

Some say that the age of giants is over, that the likes of Franklin Roosevelt and Winston Churchill and their peers are gone. It is true that Sarkozy is no de Gaulle, Mubarak is no Sadat, and George W. Bush is no John F. Kennedy. But knowing something of what it takes to reach the top, particularly in a democracy, I do not underestimate any man or woman who leads a nation, large or small.

In the decades since President Kennedy's death, some observers have said that my loyalty is excessive, still keeping his secrets, and still denying my full role. I do not think so. John F. Kennedy honed my political skills, judgment, and humor. The experience I gained by his side established my credentials for all of my post–White House endeavors. If he could see all that has happened since his death, I believe he would be pleased, but not surprised, by my continued dedication to his ideals.

In my early years with JFK, I learned not only loyalty but deference, reticence, becoming almost anonymous, never asserting, assuming, or bragging, for fear of antagonizing not only him, but also his father or his brother Robert, both of whom were fiercely protective of Jack's image and career. This reinforced traits of circumspection that had already been part of my upbringing, and they remain today central to my personal ethics, limiting what I assert or disclose even in this book—about JFK's personal life and mine.

Each of us helped shape the other's career to some extent. Over the years, noting his increasing leftward shift in the Senate and White House, many writers have speculated that I was the cause, reinforcing, perhaps even accelerating, his move to a more consistently idealistic liberalism. A *Washington Post* editorial, upon my departure from the White House, asserted, "Friends of Mr. Kennedy felt it no accident that the Senator moved steadily in a more liberal direction after the lean Nebraskan joined his staff." Perhaps.

At the time we met, he was wary of liberals, many of whom had been wary of him, his conservative father, and the family's friendship with Senator Joe McCarthy. "I'm not a liberal at all," JFK was quoted as saying shortly after I arrived. "I never joined the Americans for Democratic Action," an organization in which I had long participated. "I'm not comfortable with those people."

Yet even when it became apparent to him—as it must have early on—that I was a liberal who wanted far-reaching change, he became increasingly comfortable with me. Gradually, in the Senate, I crafted a more liberal perspective into some of his speeches, justifying liberal answers as best for the country and consistent with the principles of the national Democratic Party. Even then, his naturally cautious instincts kept him initially in a balanced, middle-of-the-road position that failed to satisfy many liberals, but did represent a change from his days in the House of Representatives.

In time, our views converged. When I first met his father in 1953, the Ambassador promptly said "You could never write for me—you're too liberal. But you're fine for Jack." Jack's own political philosophy expanded with his political growth. He started from his father's house as a conservative, whose exposure, through nationwide travel and politics, to new problems, perspectives, and people, including me, gradually revised his priorities and principles, accommodating the more liberal positions I was urging upon him. I started from my father's house as a liberal idealist, who learned from Kennedy—and from my exposure to practical politics in the Senate and national campaign—that philosophical purity can be so unrealistic as to deny the incremental success necessary to implement my ideals. The point at which our philosophies converged was pragmatic "idealism without illusion," the art of the possible, the ability to compromise on tactics without compromising principles.

I left Washington a long time ago. Not a single day has passed that I have not thought about JFK. For well over forty-five years, when I have referred in a conversation to "the president," I have meant only one person. Each November I am flooded with contrasting memories of Novembers gone by—his election in 1960, his peaceful resolution of the Cuban missile crisis in 1962, his murder in 1963.

Gillian has arranged in our home my cherished keepsakes from those special years: the engraved silver napkin ring that once sat on my table in the White House mess; the framed photograph that depicts the president and me departing the West Wing to a waiting limousine, a photograph that Jackie inscribed a few months after his death: "To Ted, who walked with the President so much of the way and who helped him climb to greatness." Most of all, I treasure the silver calendar of the month of October 1962, specially crafted for the president by Tiffany & Co. to highlight the thirteen days of the Cuban missile crisis, inscribed with both his initials and mine. He presented this same gift, individually inscribed with the recipient's initials, to each member of the ExComm.

Sometimes I am amused to imagine how he and Jackie would react to the absurdly large sums people pay at auctions for mementos from Kennedy lives. Mine are not for sale.

JFK's presidency was a time of high ideals; and those who remember it well still mourn its loss. After I saw Ethel at the Robert F. Kennedy Book Awards ceremony in 1991, she wrote me a lovely note: "Ted, I loved looking over at you and remembering your friendship with Jack and all the vitality, creativity and dreams of the New Frontier." More than one stranger has approached me on the streets of New York over the years, saying: "You bring back memories of wonderful times."

But sadly, in little more than forty years, the message from Washington has completely changed. It was all summed up in one of Garry Trudeau's *Doonesbury* cartoons. The strip's first panel showed the two lead characters joking in a bar, one saying, "Remember 'Ask not what your country can do for you, ask what you can do for your country.'" In the second panel, they laugh at this loudly, the whole box filled with "Ha Ha Ha." In the third, they have serious, downcast expressions, one asking, "What's so funny about that?" In the last panel, they both bury their faces and sob.

These days, I am weary of hearing commentators and would-be historians recite the cliché that JFK was all style, not substance. Overcoming the religious bigotry and other obstacles that seemed certain to make it impossible for him to be nominated, much less elected, required more than style. Peacefully obtaining the withdrawal of Soviet nuclear missiles from Cuba required more than style. Launching the Peace Corps, and the successful voyage of mankind to the moon, required more than style. Blazing the trail for equal rights after centuries of racial discrimination required more than style.

Less than fifty years later may be too early to say that John F. Kennedy was one of our greatest presidents. But I believe posterity will note that three of the most significant events in American history were the Cuban missile crisis, when he peacefully resolved the world's first nuclear confrontation, his reversal of this country's centuries-old subjugation of blacks, and his establishment of a robust space program enabling the human race to travel beyond the limits of Earth. That is the Kennedy legacy having an impact on all today.

What has happened to JFK's standards for dedication and innovation? The luster of public service has been tarnished by the increasing role of incompetent presidential cronies and corrupt lobbyists. Affirmative action has been reduced to patronizing photo opportunities for company brochures. His emphasis on the power of diplomacy and economic assistance has been replaced by a foreign policy increasingly reliant on the power of guns and threats.

A week after JFK's death, his widow wrote to Chairman Khrushchev:

> You and he were adversaries, but [were] allied in determination that the world not be blown up. . . . While big men know the need for restraint, little men will sometimes be moved more by fear and pride.

How sad that less than fifty years after Jackie wrote this, little men have mired this country in a mindless war.

Nor have JFK's standards of presidential oratory—and the standards of speech and English usage in the White House—been maintained. That's serious. The less often that Americans hear thoughtful public rhetoric, the more likely they are to be vulnerable to deceptive demagoguery. Kennedy's eloquence is deemed old-fashioned today. His style, say some, is too lofty in this hectic age of cynical sophistication.

Today presidential themes and drafts are edited by committee. Stirring phrases have been replaced by sound bites and applause lines. Majestic understatement has lost out to hyperbole. Presidents announce but do not inspire. Politicians are obsessed with making the nightly news instead of making history.

The trend away from Kennedy's core standards and ideals seems irreversible. But I still have faith in the ability of the American people to reverse those trends, just as JFK reversed a century of federal inattention to civil rights, reversed the increasing dangers of the nuclear arms race, reversed the long record of American failures in space exploration. Even his contest for the presidency in 1960 challenged what appeared to be irreversible prejudices against a Catholic in the White House. I still have faith in the American people to do the right thing.

It is because there are so few inspiring voices today that Kennedy's words continue to be quoted—and distorted. Immediately preceding the Iraq war, as the Bush neoconservatives sought historical precedents for their unprecedented invasion, President

Bush quoted a line from Kennedy's televised address to the nation on the Cuban missile crisis. Secretary of Defense Donald Rumsfeld asserted that Kennedy's conduct of that crisis was "certainly preventative and preemptive." It was nothing of the kind. Kennedy specifically rejected the option of launching a preemptive strike against Cuba, a step, he knew, that would lead to tragic escalation.

President Kennedy urged American citizens to ask what they could do for their country. Later presidents demeaned the public sector and exalted private interest. Kennedy wanted to explore outer space for peaceful uses; Reagan and Bush have sought to militarize it. Kennedy asked young Americans to serve in an independent Peace Corps, now compromised by the infiltration of representatives from the military.

John Kennedy's administration was a golden era. Nevertheless, like James Madison writing at age seventy about his "more full and matured view" of his decades-earlier participation at the Constitutional Convention, I see the past more clearly now. It was not Camelot. President Kennedy made errors, like the Bay of Pigs. He suffered setbacks, like his failure to obtain passage of such key legislation as Medicare. He dismissed too few mediocre officials, placed too much emphasis on civil defense in his first year and too little on civil rights, had a blind spot on Cuba and a deaf ear on China. In his first eighteen months, he gave Vietnam too many military advisors and too little of his attention. His determination to build a missile force so powerful that it would never be challenged or used may well have exceeded that standard, allocating to those obscenely expensive but idle weapons systems countless billions that could better have been used in rebuilding our schools, hospitals, and cities. In retrospect, his belief in a strong executive, and his invocation of America's obligation to world freedom, may have set a dangerous precedent for successors less able to lead with reason and restraint.

Near the end of his first year, he quickly corrected some personnel errors. But his biggest personnel error, which he never corrected or publicly regretted, was to continue in office the tyrannical director of the Federal Bureau of Investigation, J. Edgar Hoover. Arbitrary and undemocratic, Hoover became too powerful and difficult for either President Kennedy or Attorney General Robert Kennedy to manage fully. Reportedly JFK later justified his retention of Hoover with the statement: "You don't fire God." Mr. Hoover may have thought he was God, but I was never under that illusion.

Some years ago I obtained my FBI file under the Freedom of Information Act, indicating, among other things, that "in 1948 [I was 20 years old then] he was exempted from military service" and "had indicated he would take a non-combatant job" . . . "described as 'very liberal.'" It contained reports on my pre-White House position, including my years in JFK's Senate office, my prior government employment, and my "liberal" activities in college and law school and my good character. None was inaccurate or unverified, contradicting popular opinion that the FBI files are full of misinformation.

Clearly my post-government service life continued to be of interest to the FBI. Political activities within the Democratic Party were recounted, as was a private visit with my wife and children to leftist businessman Cyrus Eaton's summer home in Nova Scotia; my attendance at a China conference at a university in Montreal, characterizing a Chinese professor at the university as "an unofficial spokesman for Peking," adding that I had urged the conference to approve a resolution favoring "efforts to arrange private meetings between Mainland China and the United States." It was obvious that some mail from abroad addressed to me at my law office was intercepted and reviewed before it reached my desk.

My file also contained a letter from a private citizen to Hoover expressing, at great length, his concern that I might be "using the President and his dignity to destroy the grass-roots anti-Communist tide"—a useful reminder of the many different winds that blew across the country in those days.

SOMETIMES I PONDER THE "what ifs" in my story, of my repeated good luck. Like Benjamin Franklin, I often reflect on "the constant felicity of my life."

I have said from the start that my best luck was the genes with which I was endowed—the genes of Grandmother Sorensen who taught those neighbor women around a candlelit table in that little sod house on the prairie, the genes of Grandfather Chaikin who took off to India in search of his brothers and the world. Had my father not made his bold speech at Grand Island Baptist College and been invited by Walter Locke to come to Lincoln's

University of Nebraska and Unitarian Church, he might never have become a reform attorney general or produced a son interested in public service. Had my mother not been willing to "leave Main Street," marry my father, and accept a life of domesticity, I would not have inherited those wonderful Russian Jewish genes that mixed so well with my father's Danish heritage, and I would not have grown up with my four supportive, inspiring siblings. I am lucky now to have four wonderful children of my own, and to have shared almost four decades with my loving wife, Gillian.

Certainly the fact that as a much younger man from a distant plain, I had a chance to join John F. Kennedy during his tragically brief rise to fame, and share in that moment of history, can only be characterized as extraordinary good luck. I am lucky to have then pursued my law career in New York at Paul, Weiss. I am lucky to be an American. Yes, I am the luckiest man in the world.

But, like most Americans, I have also surmounted my share of sorrows—as a teenager, my mother's illness; the cruel loss of JFK, my mentor, best friend, and leader in 1963; and the loss, less than five years later, of his brother; and much later the loss of full use of my eyes in a stroke. All were hard blows. I persevere because I believe that the cause of a more peaceful and equitable world must be pursued, against all obstacles and setbacks. I am, I suppose, an inveterate optimist, holding fast to the belief that the good ultimately offsets the bad, and that success often follows failure. I have faith in the essential goodness of human beings, their willingness to use reason in negotiating with their enemies, and their ability to exercise wisdom in guiding a democracy.

Most of the events in my life that in hindsight appear to have been major turning points seemed natural at the time, some even routine. But what about those potential turning points that, in the words of historian A. J. P. Taylor, failed to turn? Had President Kennedy proceeded with his State Department reshuffle in the winter of 1962–1963, and made me his national security advisor, would I have succeeded or would I have been swallowed up by the recriminations over Vietnam? I like to think I would have succeeded had I been confirmed as President Carter's director of central intelligence; but perhaps I too would have been tarnished by that agency's continuing record of wrong predictions and wrongful conduct.

AS THE TWENTIETH CENTURY drew to its close at the end of calendar year 2000, I reflected on my blessings. Just five months earlier, at a celebration exquisitely planned and executed by Gillian, surrounded by our family and friends, our daughter, Juliet, took my arm, and I escorted her down our garden path to exchange her wedding vows with Ben Jones. It was a beautiful August day.

As the new century dawned, I was healthy at age seventy-two. My law practice was busy, fascinating, and making a positive contribution to the world. I lived in a safe, harmonious, and prosperous country that was respected abroad, governed by the wisest of constitutions and a bipartisan foreign policy emphasizing multilateral diplomacy, collective security, and international law. Within less than one year, all that changed. A stroke had impaired my eyesight and endurance, effectively ending my law practice, and a new president disregarded the Constitution, international law, and world opinion, promulgating a foreign policy based primarily on military might, not right. Islamic extremist terrorists successfully bombed the two cities in which I had spent most of my adult life, creating a new atmosphere of fear and suspicion. How suddenly my world and my life changed!

In September 2005, one month after Hurricane Katrina devastated one of the great cities of the American South, with minimal response from Washington, I received an eloquent letter from my son Phil:

> I can hear the depth of disappointment in your voice on the phone when you mention, however briefly, today's political landscape . . . How sad it must be for you to have played such a major role in what appeared to be a new direction—The New Frontier—with a mind that the ideas so engendered would bring forth expanded ideas and programs to build upon and never look back, only to see liars and cheats . . . slash and eliminate advances made by a formerly great society and . . . squander the goodwill and despoil the shining light of freedom for which our nation was known the world over.

Nevertheless, surveying my many decades, I realize how fortunate I was that the years in which I became politically aware and involved were a time of civility, decency, and integrity.

The shift in this country away from JFK's ideals is not a recent phenomenon. As early as the 1970s it was all summed up by an encounter with my old friend, Senator Pat Moynihan, on the streets of New York one evening. When I mildly suggested how he might modify some of his neoconservative positions, he responded, "Why, Ted, you sound just like a 1960s liberal!" I still am a 1960s liberal, and I am saddened to find my idealism—and Kennedy's idealism—considered by many to be a relic from some bygone, irretrievable past. More and more Americans seem to be losing hope for better government, growing more cynical with each new disappointment.

Those who governed America in the first half of the twentieth century left to their successors a country more respected and secure abroad, and less racially, religiously, and economically divided at home than the country they had inherited from their predecessors. The current generation of American decision makers is the first to break the tradition of leaving to its heirs a better society than it had inherited. It will be delivering to the next generation a country, once almost universally respected, that is now deeply resented and feared; a country weakened by a widening gap between rich and poor; a world of growing terrorist violence, proliferating weapons of mass destruction, and increasing environmental degradation. Our current executive branch is dominated by people who do not believe in government, too many of whom consequently show no competence at governing, except for granting privileges and patronage to their cronies. It truly is time to pass the torch to a new generation of leaders.

In May 2004 an antiwar commencement address I delivered in upstate New York met with unrestrained hostility, not from students or faculty, but from parents and townspeople in the audience determined to drown out my comparison of President Bush's disastrous response to terrorism with President Kennedy's measured response to the Cuban missile crisis. They booed, hissed, and stomped their feet, demanding that I leave the stage or shut up. I neither left the stage nor stopped speaking, but instead held the microphone closer and delivered more loudly the facts I thought each new graduate ought to hear. The important question that day was not what happened to me—but what had happened to our country?

Later that same month, asked by my friend and fellow Nebraskan Bob Kerrey to deliver the commencement address at the New School University, where he is president, I tried to answer that question.

"There is a time to laugh," the Bible tells us, "and a time to weep." Today I weep for the country I love, the country I proudly served, the country to which my four grandparents sailed over a century ago with hopes for a new land of peace and freedom. I cannot remain silent when that country is in the deepest trouble of my lifetime.

The damage done to this country by its own misconduct in the last few months and years, to its very heart and soul, is far greater and longer lasting than any damage that any terrorist could possibly inflict upon us.

Last week, a family friend of an accused American guard in Iraq recited the atrocities inflicted by our enemies on Americans, and asked: "Must we be held to a different standard?" My answer is yes.

Our greatest strength has long been not merely our military might but our moral authority. Our surest protection against assault from abroad has been not all our guards, gates and guns, or even our two oceans, but our essential goodness as a people. Our richest asset has been not our material wealth but our values. . . . A European host recently asked me to "Tell us about the good America, the America when Kennedy was in the White House." "It is still a good America," I replied. "The American people still believe in peace, human rights and justice; they are still a generous, fair minded, open-minded people."

I DO NOT WANT either my life or my story to conclude in the shadow of despair generated by our current national leadership; by our president's failures in leadership, competence, and integrity; by the failures of the courts and Congress to hold him constitutionally accountable and the failure of my own party in opposition to meet its obligations to oppose. But a one-man aberration, however disastrous, is not permanent. A democracy is by definition self-correcting. Here, the people are sovereign. Inept political leaders can be replaced. Foolish policies can be changed. *We the People* have learned from our mistakes and misfortunes. A new leader and a new era are on the way, and I will continue to fight, to write, and to hope.

Less than half a century ago, John F. Kennedy showed in fewer than a thousand days how quickly our country's role in the world can be changed for the better. Ultimately, I predict, the American people will grow sick of cynically corrupt political hypocrisy and turn on those who permit our security and international standing to erode, our environment to be despoiled, our fiscal problems to worsen, and our energy independence to wither. In time, they will return once again to the idealism of the New Frontier.

I'm still an optimist. I still believe that extraordinary leaders can be found and elected, that future dangers can be confronted and resolved, that people are essentially good and ultimately right in their judgments. I still believe that a world of law is waiting to emerge, enshrining peace and freedom throughout the world. I still believe that the mildest and most obscure of Americans can be rescued from oblivion by good luck, sudden changes in fortune, sudden encounters with heroes.

I believe it because I lived it.

Relationship with JFK

Theodore C. Sorensen

From January 1953, when I first reported for work in room 362 of the Old Senate Office Building, until the day late in November 1963 that I ran onto the south lawn of the White House to hand the president some papers as he walked toward the helicopter that would take him on the first leg of his trip to Dallas, I remember John F. Kennedy clearly. I remember him clearly despite the idolaters who have almost buried the memory of the real man under a Camelot myth too heroic to be human, despite the exaggerated attention and speculation, some malicious, some merely mindless, focused on allegations about his private life, and despite the revisionist detractors whose hindsight distortions of his life and record have not lessened his hold on America's affectionate memory.

I do not remember everything about him, because I never knew everything about him. No one did. Different parts of his life, work, and thoughts were seen by many people—but no one saw it all. He sometimes obscured his motives and almost always shielded his emotions. Too little of what he said privately was written down; all too little was written with his own hand or recorded in his own voice. Hindsight, grief, and wishful thinking no doubt make somewhat selective the recall of even those of us who knew him well. But what I do remember, I remember clearly—not as a professional historian or as a detached observer, but as a friend who misses him still.

John F. Kennedy was a natural leader. When he walked into a room, he became its center. When he spoke, people stopped and listened. When he grinned, even on television, viewers smiled back at him. He was much the same man in private as he was in public. It was no act—the secret of his magic appeal was that he had no magic at all. But he did have charisma. Historians still write about it. Charisma is often largely in the eye of the beholder, and that was particularly true in Kennedy's case. It had to be experienced to be believed. It wasn't only his looks or his words; it was a special lightness of manner, the irony, the teasing, the self-effacement, the patient "letting things be." Athough he could be steely and stern when frustrated, he never lost his temper. When times were bad, he knew they would get better—when they were good, he knew they could get worse.

JFK presented a strong, cool image, but was very human, capable of tears. He wept publicly when his and Jackie's son, Patrick, was born in August 1963 and lived only a short time. They had joyfully anticipated the arrival of their third child. Dr. Janet Travell related to me in a 1965 letter how the president and his wife had asked Dr. Travell to take over Jackie's care and keep her pregnancy private as long as possible. Dr. Travell and the attending physician were the only outsiders who knew, Dr. Travell wrote me, adding, "It was like a James Bond thriller how we managed until after Easter in Palm Beach," to keep it quiet.

Like my father, JFK was almost always calm. He once told me at length about a dramatic but comic episode, at a moment of deadly atmospheric quiet when the eye of an early 1950s hurricane passed over the family home on Cape Cod, and the chauffeur and butler—each suspecting the other of trifling with his wife—pursued each other with knives and golf clubs, upstairs, downstairs, all about the house, while JFK, otherwise alone in the house, sat calmly reading under a blanket on the front deck.

On my initial overnight stay in Hyannis Port I was most impressed by the fact that the Kennedys had a movie theater in their basement. Later opportunities to swim in family pools or off family ocean beaches in Palm Beach and Hyannis Port reinforced my awareness of our very different backgrounds.

During my first year in JFK's Senate office, when dropping me off after work to catch my bus home, he confessed that he had never ridden one in his life. Ah, the deprivations of the rich! Eight years later, when I donned my first ever white tie and tails for an elegant dinner at Versailles Palace, hosted in 1961 by Charles de Gaulle, as I came along the receiving line JFK whispered in my ear a mischievous question about what time I would need to return the outfit to the rental shop.

He never pretended that he was middle-class. I enjoyed the tale of his 1946 Boston appearance in his first campaign at a Democratic meeting in which many other local candidates were introduced ahead of him—each described by the chairman as "a young fellow who came up the hard way." Finally, when JFK was ushered to the podium, he began his speech by declaring: "I seem to be the only person here who did not come up the hard way."

Yet this millionaire Ivy Leaguer was not a snob. He loved sports, pop music, and movies; he had suffered injury and endured family tragedy; he had a wonderful sense of humor and a deep love of family. In the early Senate years, we occasionally walked over to Union Station for lunch. It was, he said, the only place in town serving genuine New England clam chowder and oyster stew. He possessed a real-

istic sense of himself, his limitations, and his shortcomings, and a rare quality among politicians—humility. Even as he welcomed his two younger brothers to Washington, he scoffed at the media notion that the Kennedy family would someday lend itself to so un-American a concept as a "Camelot dynasty," scoffing particularly at one writer's speculation that the three brothers might successively occupy the presidency through 1984, with the mantle then passing to their sons.

Was John F. Kennedy an intellectual? He read and wrote books, and was at home in discussions of American history, foreign policy, the presidency, and arcane issues of government and public policy. He enjoyed talking with intelligent women as much as intelligent men, including the brilliant author and Republican diplomat Clare Boothe Luce, of whom he later told me: "She's bitter because now all her power is derived from a man"—her husband, Henry. Compared to some of his predecessors and successors in the Oval Office, he was an intellectual giant. The poet Robert Frost, citing the new president's Irish and Harvard backgrounds, advised him "not to let the Harvard in you get too important." He didn't, but neither would he let it be suppressed. As a long-time political observer, I have noted that some highly educated politicians in Washington have thought that political success required them to conceal their intellects with coarse humor, slang, or bad grammar. Not JFK, who sprinkled erudite references in everyday conversation. Once, as senator, pulling his car up in front of a downtown Washington travel agency, he ignored the official "No Parking" sign, with a winking allusion to Shakespeare: "This is what Hamlet means by the 'insolence of office.'"

EARLY ON, TWO FACTS about his health were clear to me. First, like many middle-aged men, he suffered from a bad back. He was convinced that his World War II injuries in the Pacific had done further damage, and that the initial military hospital surgery on his back had increased the likelihood of pain without solving the problem. But it now seems more likely that his back problem was congenital, not due to either Harvard football or PT-109.

The other basic fact about John F. Kennedy's health was that he suffered from an adrenal insufficiency, the medical equivalent of Addison's disease. Early in his Senate days, he told me that he was vulnerable to high fevers and that he needed to go to bed when those fevers occurred. This occasionally meant the cancellation of speaking engagements, a telephone call I never enjoyed making, and even more occasionally my substituting for him—which I did enjoy.

Either malady—the bad back or the adrenal insufficiency—was a major problem by itself. The combination was worse. The operation to relieve his back pain in 1954 was dangerous, and twice delayed because of the additional risks posed both by the adrenal insufficiency and by the suppression of his immune system resulting from the steroids still used to treat that insufficiency. But he told me he was determined to have the operation to avoid spending the rest of his life on crutches. It was only a limited success.

Afterward he talked with me about the brighter side of hospital life—the cheering mail from friends and strangers, the constant attention from pretty nurses, the ample time to read, think, and write that would never have been available in his normal routine, and an increased empathy for those countless Americans of every age and class who are confined to their beds, whether at home or in a hospital.

In the late 1950s when we traveled the country together, I would ask each hotel to provide him with a hard mattress or bed board. When that failed, sometimes we moved his mattress onto the floor of his hotel room.

On the political circuit, I assumed that his practice of eating in his hotel room before a Democratic Party luncheon or dinner was intended to avoid the bad food and constant interruptions that characterized his time at the head table; but I now realize, after reading an analysis of his medical file, that his many stomach, intestinal, and digestive problems (of which I was largely unaware at that time) simply required a more selective diet.

In the White House, he continued to be treated by Dr. Janet Travell, whom—despite the doubts of the medical establishment—he trusted for her expertise and loyalty. It was Dr. Travell who recommended the rocking chair that became a Kennedy trademark. It helped his back. I was uncomfortable about a doctor of questionable reputation visiting the White House, Max Jacobson, known as "Dr. Feelgood" for his reportedly dubious prescriptions; but, upon inquiry, I was informed that he was treating Jackie, not the president.

In retrospect, it is amazing that, in all those years, he never complained about his ailments.

Occasionally he winced when his back was stiff or pained as he eased himself into or out of the bathtub, or picked up a heavy briefcase or one of his children. In 1961, after aggravating his back as president when planting a tree during a Canadian ceremony, he became far more careful. He even had his right shoulder checked before he threw out the first ball on opening day of Major League Baseball, and held a secret practice session behind the White House. The transcript of his vigorous participation in the 1961 Vienna summit meeting makes clear that neither his aching back—which flared up on that trip—nor any other health problems impaired his performance as president. The only complaint I remember, during the presidency, came when he worried that the steroids prescribed for his adrenal insufficiency, combined with the necessarily more sedentary existence in the White House following his long, physically rugged campaign, were increasing the fat in his face and belly.

At all times, he kept his sense of humor and perspective, and could joke about his medical problems, never becoming irritable with me or my colleagues. After one of the most exciting and exhausting days of his life—in West Berlin in June 1963—he told me about the medical theory of the body's "fight or flight syndrome" in response to the kind of stress produced by enormous danger or challenge. Since early times, he said, the body has responded to challenge by pumping more adrenaline, a very good thing for someone normally suffering an adrenal insufficiency, and in JFK's case, making him more high-spirited and healthy than ever.

EARLY IN OUR RELATIONSHIP, JFK and I discovered that we both saw plenty of humor in the world and hypocrisy in politics, and that we enjoyed kidding each other and laughing at ourselves. There was not a day in all the years that I worked with him that he did not relish witty exchanges and self-deprecating jibes. His sense of humor helped insulate him from excessive self-importance, helped him weather setbacks while in office, and helped him place both gains and losses in perspective. He was an outwardly humorous but inwardly serious man, in contrast with so many other American politicians who are essentially humorless, superficial, and frivolous in their thinking while going to great lengths to appear serious.

Humor was always part of his public speeches, but neither he nor I fully appreciated its value in speeches until the 1958 Gridiron Dinner, the annual Washington gathering in which journalists and politicians entertain one another with skits and gags, including an opportunity for one speaker from each major political party to show how funny he could be. After being afforded that opportunity in 1958, JFK agonized over it for weeks: "Why did I accept this? If the speech is a success, so what, I'm funny, that won't help a national campaign; but if I flop, it's all over town." With help from veteran Gridiron participants—attorney Clark Clifford and journalists Fletcher Knebel and Marquis Childs—we gathered to review and vote on more than one hundred suggestions I had compiled. JFK's father, who also had a good sense of humor, joined that jury, which sat for hours. JFK and I then worked and reworked a draft speech, until the big night arrived.

Having been tipped off that his speech would follow a skit portraying him as a free-spending candidate singing "Just Send the Bill to Daddy" to the tune of "My Heart Belongs to Daddy," JFK opened his remarks: "I just received the following message from my generous daddy: 'Dear Jack—Don't buy one vote more than is necessary—I'm damned if I'll pay for a landslide.'" The room exploded with laughter. Within a week, the remark was being quoted and praised all over Washington, and within a month all over the country. It defused the father's money issue that Eleanor Roosevelt and others had raised against him, and it proved that the senator could laugh at himself. Although Clark Clifford in his memoirs gave me credit for originating the joke, I stole it from Will Rogers.

Throughout his remarks that night, JFK gently needled everything and everyone, including his own political prospects, his religious problem ("my personal envoy to the Vatican will open negotiations for that trans-Atlantic tunnel immediately"), and his own party ("split right down the middle—more unity than we've had in 20 years"). And those are the funniest lines—maybe you had to be there.

It was a reassuring revelation to both JFK and me that he could make people laugh loudly, not merely listen with amusement. Thereafter he wanted jokes on current events and politics at practically every stop as we continued to crisscross the fifty states. Winning laughs became as enjoyable and almost as important as winning support. It helped politically too, with audiences skeptical of a young Harvard-educated intellectual; they liked him instantly and paid more attention.

Many of his best opening lines were repeated in town after town. As his demand expanded, I had to increase my supply, mining Will Rogers, Mark Twain, Finley Peter Dunne, and other old sources, as well as receiving contributions occasionally from comedian Mort Sahl and Kennedy brother-in-law Peter Lawford. In a letter to JFK while he was traveling abroad, I wrote from Washington: "I am refurbishing my supply of jokes for your use, but refuse to try them by letter or telephone where their true effect might be lost."

By the time of the 1960 presidential campaign, I had an enormous folder entitled "Humor File" that traveled around the country with my luggage. We avoided the tasteless, the cruel, and the obscure. We had one rule: If someone might be offended, cut it out. We learned this in his first year when he used a joke I had suggested as an opening line to a Washington hotel audience: "The cabdriver bringing me here did such a good job, I was going to give him a big tip and tell him to 'vote Democratic'—then I remembered the advice of Senator Green [reportedly a stingy millionaire] and gave the driver a small tip, and told him to 'vote Republican.'" Angry letters poured in from formerly supportive cabdrivers in Boston. Even his mother was not amused.

FEW COULD REALIZE, THEN or now, that beneath the glitter of his life and office, beneath the cool exterior of the ambitious politician, was a good and decent man with a conscience that told him what was right and a heart that cared about the well-being of those around him. During the early Senate years, when I was confined to bed with the flu, I was surprised when he drove up to our house, rang the bell, greeted my wife, and came upstairs to talk with me. On another occasion, when my lower back muscles went into spasm, he offered a long list of advice: Lift and carry nothing heavy; apply wet heat or hot pads; avoid soft mattresses and lengthy periods of standing. When I seemed not to be either improving or taking his advice, he demanded to know why. I assured him that I would follow his directions "as soon as a medical expert on bad backs gives me that advice"; he replied, "Let me tell you, on the basis of fourteen years' experience, that there is no such thing." But soon thereafter he arranged for me to visit Dr. Travell, in New York.

Perhaps because of the closeness of his own family, he was always kind to mine, inviting me and my wife, Camilla, to his wedding to Jackie on September 12, 1953, in Newport, Rhode Island. Unfortunately, the trip was too expensive for us, and we did not go. The following year he arranged for us to fly to New York, stay at his father's Park Avenue apartment, and see the hit Broadway musical *My Fair Lady*. When my father died in Nebraska in 1959, JFK made a donation to the University of Nebraska student loan fund that we had established in my father's name. He understood the importance to me of my three sons, my commitment to attend their Little League and football games, and their Saturday visits to the White House, where they would be remembered years later by the head usher for playing hide-and-seek in the West Wing lobby.

When I showed the president a note my son Eric had written to him on a Saturday visit ("Dear Mr. President: I like the White House. It is a neat place. You have nice people here. I would like to live in it someday"), the president wrote in the margin before returning it: "So do I. Sorry, Eric, you'll have to wait your turn." On January 19, 1961, the day before his inauguration, as he rested and prepared at the Georgetown home of his friend Bill Walton, the president-elect graciously welcomed me with my siblings, sons, and little nephews and nieces, who were listed on his official schedule right after the chairman of the Joint Chiefs of Staff and just before the new head of the Federal Aviation Agency.

On a few occasions we discussed my personal life. When I apologized to him because a story about my legal separation from Camilla appeared in the *Washington Star*, he smilingly replied that it was nothing compared to the foibles of other White House staff members he had discovered in reviewing their FBI files. When my years of work-related absences and consequent inattention to my family finally led to a formal, wrenching divorce, the president apologized to me, saying he felt responsible—I assumed he meant for the long hours his tasks required of me. But I told him the fault was wholly mine.

After my divorce, perhaps in an effort to improve my social life, he suggested I would look better wearing contact lenses instead of my old-fashioned horn-rimmed glasses. He was right, but I made

no change. In 1961, after he asked me to fly to Paris and sample French intellectual opinion in advance of his own arrival to see de Gaulle, he asked whether I would be taking a girlfriend with me. When I replied, with an astonished negative, he nodded with a grin: "No, you're right, that would be like taking a cow to cow country."

But he also respected my privacy. Late one night I slipped away from a boring social function at the White House to attend a private party, attended by my friend Gloria Steinem. I accidentally gashed my brow, and had to summon the assistant White House physician in the middle of the night. No doubt he reported his first aid mission to the president; but when I reported for work the next morning with my forehead bandaged and no explanation, JFK did not ask for one.

NEEDLESS TO SAY, JFK was a wonderful boss. We never argued, quarreled, shouted, or swore at each other. He never bawled me out. He never asked me to lie to anyone. He never misled or lied to me. In the early days, he did not treat me as the green kid that I was. He never asked me to write or do anything inconsistent with my principles, never asked me to write up or support any principle or proposal in which I did not believe—not surprising, inasmuch as we shared the same beliefs and values.

In both the Senate and the White House, his staff loved him. One happy demonstration of our affection was the surprise party we gave him for his forty-sixth birthday in May 1963, complete with a cake, toasts, and humorous fake telegrams and presents, including water wings supposedly sent from the World War II Japanese destroyer commander who had sunk his PT boat, and a pair of boxing gloves from his pugnacious political bête noire, Governor George C. Wallace of Alabama.

When mistakes occurred, whether in his campaign or in his presidency, he never blamed me or anyone else on his staff, or disavowed me or others when under political or journalistic pressure. To the contrary, he always defended and protected us. When a speech of his on which I had worked went well, or a political task I had undertaken for him succeeded, he often telephoned me the next day with profuse thanks.

There were occasions, of course, when he found fault with my work. One year, when he was on vacation from the Senate, I sent, in his name, a telegraphed message to a state Democratic Party dinner praising the local Democratic candidate for the U.S. Senate, thereby irritating the Republican incumbent, who complained to him on the Senate floor. He in turn complained to me. He did not like disparaging people, and particularly did not want me doing it to a colleague in his name.

Another lapse of judgment on my part incurred his understandable displeasure when I asked the pilot of the private plane we were chartering for a cross-country campaign trip to stop for me in New York, where I was on assignment, before picking him up in Cape Cod, thereby causing him to fall behind schedule.

On a more widely publicized occasion during his presidency, we were each vacationing with our respective families on Cape Cod on the weekend that the threat of a national rail strike caused him to cut short his visit. He had to wait for me at the Air Force One landing strip, long enough to permit the local newspaper to capture his impatient discomfort in a humorous series of photographs, showing him repeatedly checking his watch and walking restlessly outside the plane, until I finally arrived.

Unlike many in politics, he understood the importance of loyalty down as well as up. During my first year in the White House, 1961, I was invited to represent the president at ceremonies honoring the centennial of George Norris's birth in McCook, Nebraska, Norris's home base in the western part of the state. I took the opportunity to deplore statistics showing the continuing exodus of young families from the state, linking those statistics to the consequences of Nebraska's limited tax base for public school finance. My intention was to speak out in the blunt, provocative, and progressive tradition of Norris and my father. I warned Nebraskans that, without proper funding for public schools, the state could ultimately become "old [and] outmoded, a place to come from or a place to die."

Hundreds of letters poured into my White House office. Only a few were positive. One couple from Kearney expressed the hope that my "frank appraisal . . . will rock a few people out of their lethargy."

Another gratifying letter came from Senator Norris's son-in-law and longtime assistant, John P. Robertson: "You've said things that needed to be said . . ." But the state Republican national committeewoman reflected the tone of most of the letters when she demanded in a press statement that I apologize, adding, "If Ted Sorensen ever comes home again, even to die, it will be too soon."

Yet, when all this spilled into the national press, the president greeted me with the comment: "That's what happens when you permit a speechwriter to go out on his own!" When I apologized for any embarrassment I had caused him, he laughed it off: "I don't mind. They can criticize *you* all they want!"

Unlike most of his presidential successors, he was superb at handling criticism. When Nobel laureate Dr. Linus C. Pauling of Cal Tech, with his wife, joined a 1962 picket line outside the White House protesting the resumption of nuclear testing by Kennedy, the president responded by inviting the Paulings to a large dinner at the White House, where he and Jackie joked with Pauling about his giving the president such a hard time.

On another occasion, when thousands of students from across the country began a two-day demonstration for peace outside the White House on a bitterly cold day, the president sent two members of his kitchen staff out with hot coffee. The marching students dropped out of line in small groups to be served. Several demonstrators were even invited inside to meet with me and other aides. Another group tried to demonstrate in front of the Soviet embassy, but were turned away by the police.

His calm acceptance of criticism was rooted in a breezy confidence that he would succeed in every challenge. Jackie told me that when she had jokingly told his brother Teddy at a family dinner that, upon JFK's retirement, Teddy would need to yield his Massachusetts Senate seat back to him, Jack cautioned her afterward, "Don't tease Teddy about that. It makes him uncomfortable, and the Senate seat is very important to him. Don't worry about what I'll do after the White House. The future will take care of itself." His confidence reassured me of my own future, and I never worried about it, or imagined a future without him.

His only notable weakness as a boss was his reluctance—indeed, his inability—to fire anyone. Instead, he promoted them. During the Cuban missile crisis, the chief of naval operations inexcusably argued with both the secretary of defense and the president on how passive or aggressive the blockade should be. He became ambassador to Portugal. An early occupant of a sensitive defense post within the executive offices, though highly recommended by political sponsors to whom JFK felt indebted, proved to be a square peg in that round hole. The president appointed him to the federal bench.

I first discovered this Kennedy shortcoming back in the Senate when JFK told me that Evelyn Lincoln—the most loyal, devoted, hardworking, and totally trustworthy member of his team—did not have the intellectual capacity to handle his increasingly important telephone calls and correspondence, that he had tried firing her, but that she kept showing up at her desk every day anyway; and would I please try? I had no more success than he. JFK kept her on, took her to the White House, and continued to value her loyalty.

Throughout our years together, there was a dichotomy in our relationship. I was totally involved in the substantive side of his life, and totally uninvolved in the social and personal side. Except for a few formal banquets, we never dined together during the White House years. The times we were together socially over the eleven years we worked together were few enough that I can remember each one. In Boston, he took me along to two informal gatherings with friends, one addressed by his Senate colleague Leverett Saltonstall, and the other by the distinguished Boston author Edwin O'Connor. In Washington, he once took me along to a meeting of the Massachusetts Business Council, advising me to tell anyone who asked that I was from "West Hyannis Port, Massachusetts. No one at the dinner will be from there." I'm not sure there was any such place. On New Year's Eve during the 1960–1961 transition, when I was staying in a Palm Beach hotel with my three boys, he arranged for me to be invited to a glittering Palm Beach social bash, from which I slipped away early to be with my sons. Big, noisy parties were not my style.

There was another reason I was not part of his social circle: Coming from a different background, with few social skills, I never felt entirely comfortable with the cool crowd with whom he enjoyed partying, laughing, drinking, and gossiping. Nor did many of them conceal their lack of enthusiasm for a young, serious-minded, abstemious intellectual from the Midwest with a shy manner and horn-rimmed glasses. Their thinly veiled patronizing bothered me in the early days; but I never wanted to be JFK's drinking buddy; I wanted to be his trusted advisor. I felt lucky to have that role. Ultimately, only his brother Robert had more access and was consulted more often.

For eleven years I loved him, respected him, and believed in him, and I still do.